W9-BVD-818

Frommer's®

British Columbia

7th Edition

by Chloë Ernst & Chris McBeath

Published by:
JOHN WILEY & SONS, INC.
111 River St.
Hoboken, NJ 07030-5774

ISBN 978-1-118-11377-6 (paper); ISBN 978-1-118-11448-3 (ebk); ISBN 978-1-118-11447-6 (ebk);
ISBN 978-1-118-11446-9 (ebk)

Editor: Gene Shannon
Production Editor: Jana M. Stefanciosa
Cartographer: Andy Dolan
Photo Editor: Richard Fox
Production by Wiley Indianapolis Composition Services

Front Cover Photo: ©Richard Berry / Design Pics Inc. / Alamy Images
Description: Two canoes in a mountain lake, Lake O'Hara, British Columbia
Back Cover Photo: ©Chris Cheadle / Alamy Images
Description: Snowboarder takes air, British Columbia, Canada

For information on our other products and services or to obtain technical support, please contact our
Customer Care Department within the U.S. at 877/762-2974, outside the U.S. at 317/572-3993 or fax
317/572-4002.

Wiley also publishes its books in a variety of electronic formats. Some content that appears in print may
not be available in electronic formats.

Manufactured in the United States of America

5 4 3 2 1

CONTENTS

LIST OF MAPS

HOW TO CONTACT US

In researching this book, we discovered many wonderful places—hotels, restaurants, shops, and more. We're sure you'll find others. Please tell us about them, so we can share the information with your fellow travelers in upcoming editions. If you were disappointed with a recommendation, we'd love to know that, too. Please write to:

Frommer's British Columbia, 7th Edition
John Wiley & Sons, Inc. • 111 River St. • Hoboken, NJ 07030-5774

ADVISORY & DISCLAIMER

Travel information can change quickly and unexpectedly, and we strongly advise you to confirm important details locally before traveling, including information on visas, health and safety, traffic and transport, accommodations, shopping, and eating out. We also encourage you to stay alert while traveling and to remain aware of your surroundings. Avoid civil disturbances, and keep a close eye on cameras, purses, wallets, and other valuables.

While we have endeavored to ensure that the information contained within this guide is accurate and up-to-date at the time of publication, we make no representations or warranties with respect to the accuracy or completeness of the contents of this work and specifically disclaim all warranties, including without limitation warranties of fitness for a particular purpose. We accept no responsibility or liability for any inaccuracy or errors or omissions, or for any inconvenience, loss, damage, costs, or expenses of any nature whatsoever incurred or suffered by anyone as a result of any advice or information contained in this guide.

The inclusion of a company, organization, or website in this guide as a service provider and/or potential source of further information does not mean that we endorse them or the information they provide. Be aware that information provided through some websites may be unreliable and can change without notice. Neither the publisher nor author shall be liable for any damages arising herefrom.

ABOUT THE AUTHORS

As a west-coast travel writer, **Chloë Ernst** has skied on the slopes overlooking her Vancouver home, rafted rivers in Whistler, and caught waves on Pacific beaches. She also contributes to *Frommer's Vancouver & Victoria*, as well as various print and online publications. Read more about the travel writer's journeys at www.chloeernst.com.

With a lifetime of travel under her belt, **Chris McBeath** says she has yet to find a destination that beats the natural beauty and cosmopolitan nature of her home British Columbia. A seasoned travel writer with experience in many facets of the tourism industry, from chambermaid to management, aboard cruise ships and in top-ranked hotels, Chris brings to this book an insider's eye for what makes a great travel experience. In addition to bylines that include print, online, and i-app publications worldwide, Chris maintains her own travel website (www.greatest getaways.com), is the contributing editor of "The Art of a Getaway" for the Arts & Cultural Guide to British Columbia (www.art-bc.com), and is the author for *Frommer's Vancouver Island, the Gulf Islands & the San Juan Islands* and coauthor of *Frommer's Vancouver & Victoria*.

FROMMER'S STAR RATINGS, ICONS & ABBREVIATIONS

Every hotel, restaurant, and attraction listing in this guide has been ranked for quality, value, service, amenities, and special features using a **star-rating system.** In country, state, and regional guides, we also rate towns and regions to help you narrow down your choices and budget your time accordingly. Hotels and restaurants are rated on a scale of zero (recommended) to three stars (exceptional). Attractions, shopping, nightlife, towns, and regions are rated according to the following scale: zero stars (recommended), one star (highly recommended), two stars (very highly recommended), and three stars (must-see).

In addition to the star-rating system, we also use **seven feature icons** that point you to the great deals, in-the-know advice, and unique experiences that separate travelers from tourists. Throughout the book, look for:

special finds—those places only insiders know about

fun facts—details that make travelers more informed and their trips more fun

kids—best bets for kids and advice for the whole family

special moments—those experiences that memories are made of

overrated—places or experiences not worth your time or money

insider tips—great ways to save time and money

great values—where to get the best deals

The following abbreviations are used for credit cards:

AE	American Express	DISC	Discover	V	Visa
DC	Diners Club	MC	MasterCard		

TRAVEL RESOURCES AT FROMMERS.COM

Frommer's travel resources don't end with this guide. Frommer's website, **www.frommers. com**, has travel information on more than 4,000 destinations. We update features regularly, giving you access to the most current trip-planning information and the best airfare, lodging, and car-rental bargains. You can also listen to podcasts, connect with other Frommers.com members through our active-reader forums, share your travel photos, read blogs from guidebook editors and fellow travelers, and much more.

THE BEST OF BRITISH COLUMBIA

With the promise of extravagant wilderness scenery, dynamic Asian and First Nations culture, and cosmopolitan urban vitality, British Columbia is truly a many-faceted experience. Whether picnicking atop a Whistler glacier, taking a 4x4 safari through cowboy country, or sipping on an artisan cappuccino at Granville Island market, the vibe of West Coast hospitality is palpable.

Major Cities Although small-town British Columbia is very much an integral part of the province's history and particular lifestyle, Vancouver and Victoria are where the action is. Glam-seeking Vancouver pulsates with a sassy attitude that flaunts designer shopping, intoxicating restaurants, and a vibrant cultural ethnicity—all against drop-dead gorgeous scenery. Victoria, on Vancouver Island, is more laid-back, picturesque, and charmingly seductive. With innovative restaurants and amazing eco-adventures, it's a cool, capitol city with a gentler historical perspective.

The Countryside Almost two-thirds of British Columbia is pristine wilderness, so even for urbanites, the West Coast psyche is all about the outdoors. Here, the landscapes are as astounding as they are diverse: glacial mountains and desert canyons, mist-shrouded rainforest edging windswept beaches, and sun-filled valleys lush with award-winning wineries. Little wonder that such natural beauty inspired the beginnings of Greenpeace and is where the West Coast Wilderness Society holds sway.

Eating & Drinking As the original home of the 100-mile diet, British Columbia is a foodie's Nirvana. With some of the world's most fertile waters, farmlands, vineyards, and orchards, the strong "farm to fork" ethos means sublimely fresh regional cuisine. Dishes are often packed with fusion influences from the province's traditional First Nations food and varied Asian communities, the result of which is a whole new style of multi-ethnic, inventive flavors.

Arts & Culture The spirit of multicultural equanimity is a hallmark of Western Canada. Like elsewhere, immigration isn't without its problems, but the glorious mix of people and languages makes a rich contribution to the region, especially in its urban centers and cultural festivals. Totem poles and longhouses represent an earlier history but today, it is not anomalous to come across a Buddhist temple or mosque; to find hand-embroidered Indian saris in "Little India", or the exotic medicinal herbs of traditional Chinese medicine in many Chinese communities.

THE best TRAVEL EXPERIENCES

- **Wandering Vancouver's West End:** Vancouver is one of the most cosmopolitan cities in the world, and wandering the streets, people-watching, and sipping cappuccinos at street cafes can fill an entire weekend. Stroll up Robson Street with its busy boutique-shopping scene, turn down cafe-lined Denman Street, then stride into 400-hectare (988-acre) Stanley Park, a gem of green space with old-growth cedars, miles of walkways, and the city's excellent aquarium. See chapter 4.

- **Taking Tea in Victoria:** Yeah, it's a little corny, but it's also fun—and delicious. Tea, scones, clotted cream—who said the British don't know good food? The afternoon tea at the Empress is world-renowned, a little stuffy, and very expensive; if that doesn't sound quite like "your cup of tea", we'll show you other places where a good cuppa is more reasonably priced and a lot less formal. See chapter 5.

- **Ferrying through the Gulf Islands:** The Gulf Islands, a huddle of cliff-lined, forested islands between Vancouver Island and the British Columbia mainland, can be reached only via ferry. Hop from island to island, staying at excellent country inns and B&Bs; pedal the quiet farm roads on your bike, stopping to visit artists' studios or to quaff a pint in a cozy rural pub. The romantic getaway you've been dreaming of starts and ends right here on these idyllic islands. See chapter 6.

- **Traveling the Inside Passage:** The 15-hour Inside Passage ferry cruise aboard the MV *Northern Expedition* takes you from Vancouver Island's Port Hardy along an otherwise inaccessible coastline north to Prince Rupert, near the southern tip of the Alaska Panhandle. Orcas swim past the ferry, bald eagles soar overhead, and the dramatic scenery—a narrow channel of water between a series of mountain islands and the craggy mainland—is utterly spectacular. See chapter 10.

- **Wine Tasting in the Okanagan Valley:** The Okanagan Valley in central British Columbia has some of the most arid climatic conditions in Canada, but with irrigation, grape varietals like merlot, cabernet sauvignon, and pinot blanc flourish here. Vineyards line the edges of huge, glacier-dug lakes and clamber up the steep desert-valley walls. Taste delicious wines, go for a swim, play some golf, eat at excellent restaurants, and do it all again tomorrow. See chapter 12.

THE best ACTIVE VACATIONS

- **Hiking the West Coast Trail:** Hiking the entire length of the rugged 69km (43-mile) West Coast Trail, from Port Renfrew to Bamfield on Vancouver Island, takes 5 to 7 days, but it's truly the hike of a lifetime. This wilderness coastline, edged with old-growth forest and lined with cliffs, is utterly spectacular, and can be reached only on foot. This is not a trip for neophytes. If you're not up for it, consider an 11km (6¾-mile) day trip on the more easily accessible stretch just south of Bamfield. See p. 164.

- **Scuba Diving off Vancouver Island:** According to no less an authority than Jacques Cousteau, the waters off Vancouver Island offered some of the best diving in the world. And they still do. Nanaimo and Port Hardy are popular departure points, with outfitters ready to drop you into the briny world of the wolf eel, yellow-edged cadlina, and giant Pacific octopus. See chapters 7 and 8.

o **Kayaking Clayoquot Sound:** Paddle a kayak for 4 or 5 days through the waters of Clayoquot Sound on Vancouver Island's wilderness west coast, from the funky former fishing village of Tofino to a natural hot-springs bath near an ancient Native village. Along the way, you'll see thousand-year-old trees and glaciers, whales, and bald eagles. See p. 169.

o **Salmon Fishing from Campbell River:** Even though salmon fishing is not what it once was, Campbell River is still the "Salmon-Fishing Capital of the World." Join a day trip with an outfitter and fish the waters of Discovery Passage. Get ready to hook the big one! Even if your trophy salmon gets away (or you must release it), you'll see plenty of wildlife: bald eagles, seals, even orcas and porpoises. See p. 187.

o **Canoeing Bowron Lake Provincial Park:** Every summer, canoeists and kayakers set out to navigate a perfect 116km (72-mile) circle of six alpine lakes, with minimal portages in between. There are no roads or other signs of civilization beyond the launch point, except some well-placed cabins, campsites, and shelters. The full circuit is a 7-day trip, but the memories will last a lifetime. See p. 263.

o **Mountain Biking the Kettle Valley Rail Trail:** This rails-to-trails hiking and biking route travels from Okanagan Lake up and over Okanagan Mountain and Myra Canyon, crossing 17 trestles and traversing two tunnels on its 175km (109-mile) route. The entire circuit, which you can also do in sections, takes from 3 to 5 days, and provides lots of challenging grades and excellent scenery. See p. 279.

o **Heli-Skiing near Golden:** Helicopters lift adventurous skiers to the tops of the Selkirk and Purcell mountains that rise just west of Golden, accessing acres of virgin powder far from the lift lines and crowds of traditional ski resorts. **CMH Heli-Skiing** (© 800/661-0252) offers a variety of holidays, most based out of its private high-country lodges and reached only by helicopter. See p. 304.

THE best NATURE- & WILDLIFE-VIEWING

o **Tide Pools at Botanical Beach near Port Renfrew:** Waves have eroded potholes in the thrust of sandstone that juts into the Pacific at Botanical Beach, which remain water-filled when the waves ebb. Alive with starfish, sea anemones, hermit crabs, and hundreds of other sea creatures, these potholes are some of the best places on Vancouver Island to explore the rich intertidal zone. See p. 102.

o **Bald Eagles near Victoria:** Just a few miles north of Victoria is one of the world's best bald eagle–spotting sites: Goldstream Provincial Park. Recent counts put the number of eagles wintering here at around 4,000. (Dec and Jan are the best months for viewing, though there are eagles here year-round.) See p. 103.

o **Gray Whales at Pacific Rim National Park:** Few sights in nature match observing whales in the wild. March is the prime viewing time, as the whales migrate north from their winter home off Mexico. During March, both Tofino and Ucluelet celebrate the Pacific Rim Whale Festival; outfitters offer whale-watching trips out onto the Pacific. See chapter 7.

o **Orcas at Robson Bight:** From whale-watching boats out of Telegraph Cove or Port McNeill, watch orcas (killer whales) as they glide through the Johnstone

Strait in search of salmon, and rub their tummies on the pebbly beaches at Vancouver Island's Robson Bight, a protected whale-reserve. See p. 196.

o **Spawning Salmon at Adams River:** Every October, the Adams River fills with salmon, returning to their home water to spawn and die. While each autumn produces a large run of salmon, every fourth year (the next is 2014), an estimated 1.5 to 2 million sockeye salmon struggle upstream to spawn in the Adams River near Squilax. Roderick Haig-Brown Provincial Park has viewing platforms and interpretive programs. Some outfitters organize snorkeling tours. See p. 265 and p. 188.

o **Songbirds and Waterfowl at the Columbia River Wetlands:** Between Golden and Windermere, the Columbia River flows through a valley filled with fluvial lakes, marshes, and streams—perfect habitat for hundreds of species, including moose and coyotes. Protected as a wildlife refuge, the wetlands are on the migratory flyway that links Central America to the Arctic; in spring and fall, the waterways fill with thousands of birds—over 270 different species. Rafting outfitters in Golden operate float trips through the wetlands. See p. 305.

THE best FAMILY-VACATION EXPERIENCES

o **The Beaches near Parksville and Qualicum Beach:** The enormous sandy beaches near these towns warm in the summer sun, then heat the waters of Georgia Strait when the tides return. Some of the warmest (and safest) ocean waters in the Pacific Northwest are here, making for good swimming and family vacations. See chapter 7.

o **The MV _Frances Barkley_ (© 800/663-7192):** This packet steamer delivers mail and merchandise to isolated marine communities along the otherwise inaccessible Alberni Inlet, the longest fjord on Vancouver Island's rugged west coast. Along the way, you may spot eagles, bears, and porpoises. The MV _Frances Barkley_ is large enough to be stable, yet small enough to make this daylong journey from Port Alberni to Bamfield and back seem like a real adventure. See p. 161.

o **The Okanagan Lakes:** Sunny weather, sandy lake beaches, and miles of clean, clear water: If this sounds like the ideal family vacation, then head to the lake-filled Okanagan Valley. Penticton and Kelowna have dozens of family-friendly hotels, watersports rentals, and lakeside parks and beaches. Mom and Dad can enjoy the golf and wineries as well. See chapter 12.

o **Fort Steele Heritage Town (© 250/426-7352):** Once a 19th-century frontier boomtown turned ghost town, Fort Steele again bustles with life. Now a provincial heritage site, the town has been rebuilt, other historic structures have been moved in, and daily activities with living-history actors give this town a real feel of the Old West. See p. 309.

first nations CULTURE & HISTORY

o **Quw'utsun' Cultural Centre** (Duncan; © 877/746-8119): North of Victoria, this facility contains a theater, carving shed, ceremonial clan house, restaurant, and art gallery, all dedicated to preserving traditional Cowichan history and culture. Try to visit when the tribe is preparing a traditional salmon bake. See p. 138.

o **Nuyumbalees Cultural Centre** (formerly the Kwakiutl Museum and Cultural Center, Quadra Island; ✆ **250/285-3733**): To the Native peoples along the Northwest coast, the potlatch was one of the most important ceremonies, involving the reenactment of clan myths and ritual gift giving. When Canadian officials banned the potlatch in the 1920s, the centuries-old costumes, masks, and artifacts of the Kwagiulth tribe were confiscated and sent to museums in eastern Canada and England. When the items were repatriated in the early 1990s, the tribe built this handsome museum to showcase this incredible collection of Native art. See p. 190.

o **Alert Bay** (off Vancouver Island): One of the best-preserved and still vibrant Native villages in western Canada, Alert Bay is a short ferry ride from northern Vancouver Island. Totem poles face the waters, and cedar-pole longhouses are painted with traditional images and symbols. The **U'Mista Cultural Centre** (✆ **250/974-5403**) contains a collection of carved masks, baskets, and potlatch ceremonial objects. See p. 198.

o **Gwaii Haanas National Park Reserve and Haida Heritage Site** (Haida Gwaii; ✆ **877/559-8818**): A UNESCO World Heritage Site and a Canadian national reserve, this is the ancient homeland of the Haida people. Located on the storm-lashed islands formerly known as the Queen Charlottes, it isn't easy or cheap to get to: You'll need to kayak, boat, sail, or fly in on a floatplane. But once here, you'll get to visit the prehistoric village of **SGang Gwaay,** or **Ninstints,** on Anthony Island, abandoned hundreds of years ago and still shadowed by decaying totem poles. See p. 234.

o **'Ksan Historical Village** (Hazelton; ✆ **877/842-5518**): The Gitxsan people have lived for millennia at the confluence of the Skeena and Bulkley rivers, hunting and spearing salmon from the waters. On the site of an ancient village near present-day Hazelton, the Gitxsan have built a pre-Contact replica village, complete with longhouses and totem poles. No ordinary tourist gimmick, the village houses a 4-year carving school, Native-art gift shop, traditional-dance performance space, artists' studios, restaurant, and visitor center. See p. 242.

o **Squamish Lil'wat Cultural Centre** (Whistler; ✆ **866/441-7522**): An architectural showcase of soaring glass and stone celebrates the joint history and living cultures of the Squamish and Lil'wat First Nations. Besides displays of traditional artifacts, there's a traditional-food cafe, art gallery, and, outdoors, a Squamish longhouse and a replica Lil'wat "ístken" or "Pit House". See p. 215.

THE best MUSEUMS & HISTORIC SITES

o **Museum of Anthropology** (Vancouver; ✆ **604/822-5087**): Built to resemble a traditional longhouse, this splendid museum on the University of British Columbia campus contains one of the finest collections of Northwest Native art in the world. Step around back to visit two traditional longhouses. See p. 66.

o **Royal British Columbia Museum** (Victoria; ✆ **888/447-7977**): The human and natural history of coastal British Columbia is the focus of this excellent museum. Visit a frontier main street, view lifelike dioramas of coastal ecosystems, and gaze at ancient artifacts of the First Nations peoples. Outside, gaze upward at the impressive collection of totem poles. See p. 100.

o **The Museum at Campbell River** (Campbell River; © **250/287-3103**): The highlight of this regional museum is a multimedia presentation that retells a First Nations myth using carved ceremonial masks. Afterward, explore the extensive collection of contemporary aboriginal carving, then visit a fur trapper's cabin and see tools from a pioneer-era sawmill. See p. 187.

o **North Pacific Cannery National Historic Site** (Port Edward; © **250/628-3538**): Located on the waters of Inverness Passage, this isolated salmon cannery built an entire working community of 1,200 people—complete with homes, churches, and stores—on boardwalks and piers. Now a national historic site, the mothballed factory is open for tours, and you can even spend a night at the old hotel. See p. 228.

o **Barkerville** (83km/52 miles east of Quesnel; © **250/994-3332**): Reputedly once the largest city west of Chicago and north of San Francisco—about 100,000 people passed through during the 1860s—the gold-rush town of Barkerville is one of the best-preserved ghost towns in Canada. It comes to life in summer, when costumed "townspeople" go about their frontier way of life amid a completely restored late-Victorian pioneer town. See p. 263.

THE most SCENIC VIEWS

o **Vancouver from Cloud Nine** (© **604/687-0511**): Situated on the top floor of one of the tallest hotels in Vancouver, towering 42 floors above the city, the rotating restaurant/lounge Cloud Nine has 360-degree views that go on forever. See p. 82.

o **The Canadian Rockies from Eagle's Eye Restaurant** (© **250/344-8626**): The Kicking Horse Mountain Resort isn't just one of the newest skiing areas in the Canadian Rockies. This exciting development also boasts the highest-elevation restaurant in all of Canada. The Eagle's Eye sits at the top of the slopes, 2,410m (7,907 ft.) above sea level. Ascend the gondola to find eye-popping views of high-flying glaciered crags—and excellent cuisine. See p. 308.

o **Floral euphoria at Butchart Gardens** (Victoria; © **866/652-4422**): Spring and early summer deliver an absolutely stunning array of color from constantly changing (like a kaleidoscope) blossoming trees, plus perennial and annual flowers. It takes on a whole new personality when the famous fireworks take place on Saturday nights in the summertime. See p. 98.

o **Storm watching from Vancouver Island's west coast:** In winter, when the Pacific Ocean clashes up against the rugged coastline, the sky is alive with fury, and the trees bow horizontally in the wind; the sight is more surreal than a Turner painting. See p. 170.

THE most DRAMATIC DRIVES

o **The Sea-to-Sky Highway:** Officially Hwy. 99, this drive is a lesson in geology. Starting in West Vancouver, the amazing route begins at sea level at Howe Sound and the Squamish Cliffs—sheer rock faces rising hundreds of feet—then up a narrowing fjord, climbing up to Whistler, near the crest of the rugged, glacier-clad Coast Mountains. Continue over the mountains and drop onto Lillooet. Here, on the dry side of the mountains, is an arid plateau trenched by the rushing Fraser River. See p. 208.

The Sunshine Coast (The Coastal Circle): Hwy. 101 follows the mainland British Columbia coast from West Vancouver, crossing fjords and inlets twice on ferries on its way to Powell River. On the east side rise the soaring peaks of the Coast Mountains, and to the west lap the waters of the Georgia Strait, with the green bulk of Vancouver Island rising in the middle distance. From Powell River, you can cross over to Vancouver Island on the BC Ferries service to Comox. See chapter 7.

- **Williams Lake to Bella Coola:** Start at the ranching town of Williams Lake, and turn your car west toward the looming Coast Mountains. Hwy. 20 crosses the arid Chilcotin River plateau, famed for its traditional cattle ranches, until reaching the high country near Anaheim Lake. After edging through 1,494m (4,902-ft.) Heckman Pass, the route descends what the locals simply call "The Hill": a 32km (20-mile) stretch of road that drops from the pass to sea level with gradients of 18%. The road terminates at Bella Coola on the Pacific, where summer-only ferries depart for Port Hardy on northern Vancouver Island. See p. 259.

THE best WALKS & RAMBLES

- **Vancouver's Stanley Park Seawall:** Stroll, jog, run, blade, bike, skate, ride—whatever your favorite mode of transport is, use it, but by all means get out here and explore this wonderful park. See p. 72.

- **Victoria's Inner Harbour:** Watch the boats and aquatic wildlife come and go while walking along a pathway that winds past manicured gardens. The best stretch runs south from the Inner Harbour near the Parliament Buildings, past the Pacific Undersea Gardens, and on to Fisherman's Wharf. See chapter 5.

- **Strathcona Provincial Park:** Buttle Lake, which lies at the center of Strathcona Provincial Park, is the hub of several hiking trails that climb through old-growth forests to misty waterfalls and alpine meadows. Return to the trailhead, doff your hiking shorts, and skinny-dip in gem-blue Buttle Lake. See p. 192.

- **Osoyoos Deserts:** Whether at the Nk'Mip Desert Cultural Centre or the Osoyoos Desert Centre, wandering through the parched and landscaped trails reveal rare, wildlife treasures from Canada's only desert. Learning about the aboriginal cultures is all part of the deal. See p. 274.

- **The Wild Pacific Trail:** Boardwalks through Ucluelet's rainforest make this an ideal eco-adventure for 8- and 80-year-olds alike. The trail includes an easy walk along a dramatic coastline, as well as stairs that clamber down the cliffs to sandy coves. See p. 165.

- **Galloping Goose Trail:** Whether you walk, jog, cycle, or rollerblade, this rail-to-trail conversion starts in Victoria at the south end of the Selkirk Trestle, and weaves the back roads through urban, rural, and semi-wilderness landscapes. Different access points, many with parking areas, mean you can explore for an hour, a morning, or the entire day. See p. 103.

THE best LUXURY HOTELS & RESORTS

- **The Fairmont Hotel Vancouver** (Vancouver; ✆ **866/540-4452**): Built by the Canadian Pacific Railway on the site of two previous Hotel Vancouvers, this landmark opened in 1929. The château-style exterior, the lobby, and even the guest rooms—now thoroughly restored—are built in a style and on a scale reminiscent of the great European railway hotels. See p. 49.

- **The Fairmont Empress** (Victoria; ✆ **866/540-4429**: Architect Francis Rattenbury's masterpiece, the Empress has charmed princes (and their princesses), potentates, and movie moguls since 1908. If there's one hotel in Canada that represents a vision of bygone graciousness and class, this is it. See p. 90.

- **Hastings House Country House Hotel** (Salt Spring Island; ✆ **800/661-9255**): This farm matured into a country manor and was then converted into a luxury inn. The manor house is now an acclaimed restaurant; the barn and farmhouse have been remade into opulent suites. You'd feel like you've been transported to an idealized English estate, if it weren't for those wonderful views of the Pacific. See p. 123.

- **Poets Cove Resort and Spa** (South Pender Island; ✆ **888/512-7638**): Poets Cove may be on a remote bay on a rural island, but don't let the isolation fool you. The resort has beautifully furnished rooms, villas, and cottages, all overlooking a peaceful harbor. The spa, restaurant, and facilities are absolutely first class. A full menu of activities and eco-excursions will keep you (and the kids) busy throughout your stay. See p. 131.

- **The Wickaninnish Inn** (Tofino; ✆ **800/333-4604**): Standing stalwart in the forest above the sands of Chesterman Beach, this log, stone, and glass structure boasts incredible views over the Pacific and extremely comfortable luxury-level guest rooms. The dining room is equally superlative. See p. 173.

- **Four Seasons Resort Whistler** (Whistler; ✆ **888/935-2460**): This grand— even monumental—hotel is the classiest place to stay in Whistler, which is saying something. This is a hotel with many moods, from the Wagnerian scale of the stone-lined lobby to the precise gentility of the guest rooms to the faint and welcome silliness of the tiled and backlit stone fixtures of the restaurant. This is a hotel that's not afraid to make big statements. See p. 217.

- **Grand Okanagan Lakefront Resort** (Kelowna; ✆ **800/465-4651**): You can't get much closer to Okanagan Lake than this marina-fronted hotel, and you won't find more luxurious lodgings either, particularly the **Royal Private Villas.** In their own building, these sumptuous guest units are essentially luxury apartments, with access to a private rooftop infinity pool. See p. 288.

- **Sparkling Hill Resort** (Vernon; ✆ **877/275-1556**): As the first-of-its-kind in North America, this European-style wellness retreat is awe-inspiring as much for its amazing spa experiences as for its views, accommodations, and architectural design, including floor-to-ceiling windows and more than 3 million Swarovski crystals. See p. 292.

THE best B&Bs & COUNTRY INNS

○ **West End Guest House** (Vancouver; ✆ **604/681-2889**): This 1906 heritage home is filled with an impressive collection of Victorian antiques. Afternoon sherry precedes the evening turndown service, and the staff is very professional. See p. 53.

○ **Andersen House Bed & Breakfast** (Victoria; ✆ **250/388-4565**): Your hosts outfit their venerable 1891 Queen Anne home in only the latest decor, from raku sculptures to carved-wood African masks. Their taste is impeccable—the old place looks great. See p. 91.

○ **Guest House at Burrowing Owl Vineyards** (Oliver; ✆ **877/498-0620**): You would be forgiven if you felt you were in the vineyards of southern Italy. From the intimacy of your private deck, there's a sparkling swimming pool, flower-filled patios, and row upon row of vines. Everything here, from guest rooms to the restaurant to the wines themselves, are excellent.

○ **Old Farmhouse B&B** (Salt Spring Island; ✆ **250/537-4113**): The Old Farmhouse is an 1894 farmstead with a newly built guesthouse. The welcome you'll get here is as engaging and genuine as you'll ever receive, and the breakfasts are works of art. See p. 124.

○ **Galiano Oceanfront Inn & Spa** (Galiano Island; ✆ **877/530-3939**): Combine a magical island view, a wonderfully inventive restaurant, a full-service spa, plus luxury-level rooms, and you get this very handsome inn. Flanked by gardens and filled with major Northwest Native art, the Galiano Inn wears its high style very comfortably. See p. 127.

○ **Oceanwood Country Inn** (Mayne Island; ✆ **250/539-5074**): Overlooking Navy Channel, this inn offers top-notch lodgings and fine dining in one of the most extravagantly scenic locations on the West Coast. New owners have added contemporary charm to the English ambiance, while still maintaining a range of accommodations, from affordable and cozy garden-view rooms to luxury-level suites that open onto hot-tub decks and hundred-mile views. See p. 129.

○ **Fairburn Farm Culinary Retreat & Guesthouse** (Duncan; ✆ **250/746-4637**): This rambling farmhouse B&B sits amid some of the most bountiful farmland in Canada—so start cooking. This unusual operation is part culinary school, part country inn, and part pilgrimage site for Slow Food–movement devotees. Come here for the comfy guest rooms, and stay for the *terroir*. See p. 140.

○ **Mulvehill Creek Wilderness Inn and Bed & Breakfast** (Revelstoke; ✆ **877/837-8649**): Equidistant to a waterfall and Arrow Lake, this remote inn in the forest has everything going for it: nicely decorated rooms with locally made pine furniture, a beautiful lounge with fireplace, decks to observe the pool and garden, and gracious hosts who exemplify Swiss hospitality. Swimming, boating, fishing—it's all here, even a wedding chapel. See p. 299.

THE best RUSTIC ACCOMMODATIONS: LODGES, WILDERNESS RETREATS & LOG-CABIN RESORTS

○ **Tigh-Na-Mara Resort Hotel** (Parksville; ✆ 800/663-7373): Comfortably rustic log cabins in a forest at beach's edge: Tigh-Na-Mara has been welcoming families for decades, and the new luxury log suites are just right for romantic getaways. The spa is widely considered one of the best in Canada. See p. 159.

○ **Strathcona Park Lodge** (Strathcona Provincial Park; ✆ 250/286-3122): A wilderness summer camp for the whole family is what you'll find at Strathcona Park Lodge, with rustic lakeside cabins and guided activities that range from sea kayaking and fishing to rock climbing and mountaineering. See p. 194.

○ **Clayoquot Wilderness Resort** (Clayoquot Sound; ✆ 888/333-5405): These folks reinvented modern "glamping" (glamorous camping) on the West Coast. Accommodation tents are on platforms in the forest, and come beautifully furnished with all manner of antiques, en suite bathroom tents, and all the comforts of a luxurious hotel. All in the wilderness. See p. 171.

○ **Rockwater Secret Cove Resort** (Half Moon Bay; ✆ 877/296-4593): Staying with the glamping theme, these "platform tents" feel like a high-end hotel room since they come with flush toilets and a bathtub. Set amongst trees, high above the waters of the Strait of Georgia, and joined by a series of boardwalks, every unit has a fabulous view of the water. Love the resort's outdoor "spa without walls."

○ **Nakiska Ranch** (Wells Gray Park; ✆ 800/704-4841): Turn-of-the-20th-century log cabins, grazing cattle, and a backdrop of Wells Gray's majestic forests and mountains make Nakiska Ranch a stunning property. The six log, one-bedroom cabins each have a private patio and gas barbecue.

THE best NORTHWEST REGIONAL CUISINE

See "A Taste of British Columbia" in chapter 2 for more information on the style of cuisine unique to this region.

○ **West** (Vancouver; ✆ 604/738-8938): In a sleek, jewel-box dining room, fabulous West starts with classic techniques and the finest Pacific seafood, fish, and other regional ingredients to provide an up-to-the-second dining experience. Book the "chef's table" in the kitchen to watch the chefs at work. See p. 61.

○ **The Blue Crab Bar and Grill** (Victoria; ✆ 250/480-1999): You might think that the food would have a hard time competing with the view at this restaurant in the Coast Hotel, but you'd be wrong. The creative chef serves up the freshest seafood, the presentation is beautiful, and the dishes are outstanding. See p. 94.

○ **Sooke Harbour House** (Sooke; ✆ 250/642-3421): This small country inn has one of the most noted restaurants in all of Canada. Fresh regional cuisine is the specialty, with an emphasis on local seafood. Views over the Strait of Juan de Fuca to Washington's mighty Olympic Mountains are spectacular, nearly matching the wine list. See p. 135.

o **Locals Restaurant** (Comox Valley; ✆ **250/338-6493**): Everything about this cozy dining room is eco-aware, from its furnishings to its inventive food ethos. Local farmers make daily deliveries (that's why it has a shopping mall location), and pictures, stories, menu items, and wine selections all tell a regional story.

o **Masthead Restaurant** (Cowichan Bay; ✆ **250/748-3714**): Sitting above a busy marina, with islands and mountains rising in the distance, the Masthead's views are mesmerizing and its trappings—the century-old clapboard structure was built as a fine hotel—are charming. But the food here is absolutely up-to-date, an exploration of Vancouver Island's rich and diverse bounty. See p. 142.

o **Shelter** (Tofino; ✆ **250/725-3353**): Fine dining in Tofino has always been synonymous with the Pointe, the wonderful restaurant at the Wickaninnish Inn. But the tourist boom in Tofino created an explosion of fantastic new places in this remote corner of Vancouver Island. Check out Shelter for its youthful vigor and absolutely fresh and authentic flavors—everything is right off the boat or just off the land. See p. 174.

o **Araxi Restaurant & Bar** (Whistler; ✆ **604/932-4540**): A longtime Whistler favorite that just keeps on getting better. Chef James Walt is capable of gastronomic alchemy, producing dishes that are inventive yet tradition-based and full of flavor. Choose one of the tasting menus; then face the wondrous stupefaction by selecting something delicious from the 12,000-bottle wine inventory. See p. 221.

o **Bearfoot Bistro** (Whistler; ✆ **604/932-3433**): The food scene in Whistler is extremely dynamic, as you'd expect at North America's top ski resort and recent Olympic host. To get noticed amid Whistler's many restaurants requires something special—and Bearfoot Bistro's got it. With very inventive food served in three- or five-course meals, this is like having a cutting-edge Iron Chef in charge of your dinner. See p. 221.

o **All Seasons Café** (Nelson; ✆ **250/352-0101**): Innovative preparations and rich, hearty flavors are the hallmarks of the cuisine at this superlative restaurant in a downtown Nelson heritage home. Food this stylish and up-to-date would pass muster anywhere; to find it in Nelson is astonishing. See p. 315.

THE best FESTIVALS & SPECIAL EVENTS

o **Vancouver's Folk and Film Festivals:** The Folk Fest brings folk and world-beat music to a waterfront stage in Jericho Park. The setting is gorgeous, the music great, and the crowd something else. In October, the films of the world come to Vancouver. Serious film buffs buy a pass and see all 500 flicks (or as many as they can before their eyeballs fall out). See p. 25.

o **Celebration of Light** (Vancouver): This 3-night fireworks extravaganza takes place over English Bay in Vancouver. Three of the world's leading fireworks manufacturers are invited to represent their countries in competition against one another, setting their best displays to music. See p. 25.

- **Market in the Park** (Salt Spring Island): The little village of Ganges fills to bursting every Saturday morning, as local farmers, craftspeople, and flea marketers gather to talk, trade, and mill aimlessly. With all ages of hippies, sturdy housewives, fashion-conscious Eurotrash, and rich celebrities all mixed together, the event has the feel of a weird and benevolent ritual. See p. 122.
- **World Championship Bathtub Race** (Nanaimo): Imagine guiding a claw-foot tub across the 58km (36-mile) Georgia Strait from Nanaimo to Vancouver: That's how this hilarious and goofily competitive boat race began. Nowadays, dozens of tubbers attempt the crossing as part of July's weeklong Marine Festival, with a street fair, parade, and ritual boat burning and fireworks display. See p. 152.

BRITISH COLUMBIA IN DEPTH

The more you know about British Columbia, the more you're likely to enjoy and appreciate everything the region has to offer. The pages that follow include a brief history, a range of highly recommended books, a primer on the unique cuisine of the area, and more.

BRITISH COLUMBIA TODAY

Covering 948,600 sq. km (366,257 sq. miles), Canada's westernmost region has a lot to offer travelers, including dramatic landscapes, a vibrant arts culture, and unparalleled access to outdoor recreation. Separated from the rest of Canada by the Canadian Rockies, British Columbia beats to its own drummer. The weather is decidedly more temperate, the politics more maverick, and its cultural dynamic more closely aligned in spirit, at least, to the Pacific Northwest states of Washington and Oregon, than to, say, Ontario, Quebec, or Nova Scotia. Add the province's vibrant film industry, a visible and powerful gay and lesbian community, and a soft-focus New Age patina, and comparisons to California are common. And if you delve a little deeper, you may even come across the Cascadia movement of like-minded individuals who believe the entire region should become its own self-sufficient country.

In terms of cultural diversity and competing interests, there's a lot happening. The Asian influence is the most noticeable. It started with the import of Chinese laborers to work the TransCanada Railway in 1886 and grew from there, hitting a high point just before Hong Kong relinquished its status as a British colony in 1997, when many thousands of wealthy Chinese migrated to Canada, particularly Vancouver, to avoid an uncertain future in their homeland.

On the political front, British Columbia swings wildly from left to right, with barely a breather in between. It's a kind of renegade politics which sees more than its fair share of dissidents and highly politicized environmental issues. Anything that involves logging, agriculture, mining, fishing, and most recently, water, are especially contentious, often pitting urban and rural residents against each other.

It's easy to think of Canada as North America's Scandinavia—well ordered, stable, and culturally just a little sleepy. The truth is that during your own travels across British Columbia, you'll likely find this corner of Canada a fascinating amalgam of cultures, histories, and conflicting interests.

LOOKING BACK AT BRITISH COLUMBIA

NATIVE WESTERN CANADA   It is generally accepted that the Native peoples of North America arrived on this continent about 15,000 to 20,000 years ago from Asia, crossing a land bridge that spanned the Bering Strait. At the time, much of western Canada was covered with vast glaciers. Successive waves of these peoples moved south down either the coast or a glacier-free corridor that ran along the east face of the Rockies. As the climate warmed and the glaciers receded, the Native peoples moved north, following game animals like the woolly mammoth.

The ancestors of the tribes and bands that now live on the prairies of Alberta didn't make their year-round homes here in the pre-Contact era. The early Plains Indians wintered in the lake and forest country around present-day Manitoba, where they practiced basic agriculture. In summer and fall, hunting parties headed to the prairies of Alberta and Saskatchewan in search of buffalo. The move to a year-round homeland on the Great Plains was a comparatively recent event, caused by Native displacement as the eastern half of North America became increasingly dominated by European colonists. Thus, a number of linguistically and culturally unrelated tribes were forced onto the prairies at the same time, competing for food and shelter.

The Native peoples of the prairies relied on the buffalo for almost all their needs. The hide provided tepee coverings and leather for moccasins; the flesh was eaten fresh in season and preserved for later consumption; and the bones were used to create a number of tools. The Native peoples along the Northwest coast had a very different culture and lifestyle, and in all likelihood migrated to the continent much later than the Plains Indians. Living at the verge of the Pacific or along the region's mighty rivers, these early people settled in wooden longhouses in year-round villages, fished for salmon and shellfish, and used the canoe as their primary means of transport. The Pacific Northwest coast was one of the most heavily populated areas in pre-Contact America, and an extensive trading network developed. Because the temperate coastal climate and abundant wildlife made this a relatively hospitable place to live, the tribes were reasonably well-off, and the arts—carving and weaving in particular—flourished. Villages were organized according to clans, and elaborately carved totem poles portrayed ritual clan myths.

EUROPEAN EXPLORATION   The first known contact between Europeans and the Native peoples of western Canada came in the last half of the 18th century, as the Pacific Northwest coast became a prize in the colonial dreams of distant nations. Russia, Britain, Spain, and the United States each would assert a claim over parts of what would become British Columbia and Alberta.

In 1774, the Spanish explorer Juan Perez landed on the Queen Charlotte Islands (known today as Haida Gwaii), and then on the western shores of Vancouver Island, at Nootka Sound. England's James Cook made a pass along the Pacific Northwest coast, spending a couple weeks at Nootka Sound in 1778, where the crew traded trinkets for sea otter pelts. Later in the same journey, Cook visited China and discovered that the Chinese would pay a high price for otter furs.

Thus was born the Chinese trade triangle that would dominate British economic interests in the northern Pacific for 30 years. Ships entered the waters of the Pacific Northwest, their crews traded cloth and trinkets for pelts of sea otters, and then the ships set sail for China, where the skins were traded for tea and luxury items. After the ships returned to London, the Asian goods were sold.

Since the Spanish and the English had competing claims over the Pacific Northwest coast, these nations sent envoys to the region—the Spaniard Don Juan Francisco de la Bodega y Quadra and the British Captain George Vancouver—to further explore the territory and resolve who controlled it. The expeditions led by these explorers resulted in a complete mapping of the region and a competing mix of Spanish and English names for various land-points. Ownership of the territory wasn't resolved until 1793, when Spain renounced its claims.

Fur traders also explored the interior of British Columbia and the Alberta prairies. Two British fur-trading companies, the Hudson's Bay Company (HBC) and the North West Company, began to expand from their bases along the Great Lakes and Hudson's Bay, following mighty prairie rivers to the Rockies. Seeking to gain advantage over the Hudson's Bay Company, the upstart North West Company sent traders and explorers farther inland to open new trading posts and to find routes to the Pacific. Alexander Mackenzie became the first white man to cross the continent when he followed the Peace River across northern Alberta and British Columbia, crossing the Rockies and the Fraser River Plateau to reach Bella Coola, on the Pacific, in 1793.

Simon Fraser followed much of Mackenzie's route in 1808, before maneuvering the perilous rapids and canyons of the fast-moving Fraser River all the way to its mouth near present-day Vancouver. Another fur trader and explorer was David Thompson, who crossed the Rockies and established Kootenay House trading post on the upper Columbia River. In 1811, Thompson journeyed to the mouth of the Columbia, where he found Fort Astoria, an American fur-trading post, already in place. Competing American and British interests would dominate events in the Pacific Northwest for the next 2 decades. By the 1820s, seasonal fur-trading forts were established along the major rivers of the region. Cities like Edmonton, Kamloops, Prince George, and Hope all had their beginnings as trading posts. Each of the forts was given an assortment of trade goods to induce the local tribes to trap beaver, otter, fox, and wolf. Although the fur companies generally treated the Native populations with respect and fairness, there were tragic and unintentional consequences to the relationships that developed. While blankets, beads, and cloth were traded for furs, nothing was as popular or as effective as whiskey: Thousands of gallons of alcohol passed from the trading posts to local tribes, corrupting traditional culture and creating a cycle of dependence that enriched the traders while poisoning the Native peoples. The traders also unwittingly introduced European diseases to the local population, who had little or no resistance to such deadly scourges as smallpox and measles.

The Louisiana Purchase, which gave the U.S. control of all the territory along the Missouri River up to the 49th parallel and to the Continental Divide, and the Lewis and Clark Expedition from 1804 to 1806 gave the Americans a toe-hold in the Pacific Northwest. As part of the settlement of the War of 1812, the Pacific Northwest—which included all of today's Oregon, Washington, and much of British Columbia—was open to both British and American exploitation, though neither country was allowed to set up governmental institutions. In fact, Britain had effective control of this entire area through its proxies in the Hudson's Bay Company, which had quasi-governmental powers over its traders and over relations with the Native peoples, which included pretty much everyone who lived in the region.

B.C. CONSOLIDATES & JOINS CANADA From its headquarters at Fort Vancouver, on the north banks of the Columbia River near Portland, Oregon, the Hudson's Bay Company held sway over the river's huge drainage, which extended far into present-day Canada. However, with the advent of the Oregon Trail and settlement in what would become the state of Oregon, the HBC's control over this vast territory began to slip. In 1843, the Oregon settlers voted by a slim majority to form a government based on the American model. The HBC and Britain withdrew to the north of the Columbia River, which included most of Washington and B.C.

The U.S.-Canada boundary dispute became increasingly antagonistic. The popular slogan of the U.S. 1844 presidential campaign was "54/40 or fight," which urged the United States to occupy all of the Northwest up to the present Alaskan border. Finally, in 1846, the British and the Americans agreed to the present border along the 49th parallel. The HBC headquarters withdrew to Fort Victoria on Vancouver Island; many British citizens moved north as well. In order to better protect its interests and citizens, Vancouver Island became a crown colony in 1849—just in case the Americans grew more expansionist-minded. However, population in the Victoria area was small: In 1854, it counted only 250 white people.

Then, in 1858, gold-rush fever struck this remote area of the British Empire. The discovery of gold along the Fraser River, and in 1862 in the Cariboo Mountains, brought in a flood of people. The vast majority of the estimated 100,000 who streamed into the area were Americans coming up from the by-now-spent California gold fields. Fearing the United States' domination of mainland Canada, Britain named it a new colony, New Caledonia, in 1858. In 1866, the two colonies—Vancouver Island and the mainland—merged as the British colony of British Columbia.

As population and trade increased, the need for greater political organization grew. As a colony, British Columbia had little local control, and was largely governed by edict from London. In order for British Columbia to have greater freedom and self-determination, the choices were clear: join the prosperous United States to the south, with which it shared many historic and commercial ties, or join the new Dominion of Canada far to the east. It was a close call. Only after Ottawa promised to build a railroad to link eastern and western Canada, did B.C. delegates vote in 1871 to join Canada as the province of British Columbia.

THE RAILROADS LINK CANADA Meanwhile, as profits from trapping decreased, the rule of the HBC over the inland territory known as Ruperts Land relaxed, and in 1869, the Crown bought back the rights to the entire area. The border between the United States and Canada in the prairie regions was hazy at best, lawless at worst. Although selling whiskey to Native people was illegal, in the no-man's land between Montana and Canada, trade in alcohol was rife. Besides which, the Native population never recognized borders, and traveled nomadically as they had always done.

In response to uprisings and border incursions, the Canadian government created a new national police force, the Royal Canadian Mounted Police. In 1873, a contingent of Mounties began their journey across the Great Plains, establishing Fort Macleod (1874) in southern Alberta along with three other frontier forts, including Fort Calgary at the confluence of the Bow and Elbow rivers. The Mounties succeeded in stopping the illegal whiskey trade and creating conditions favorable for settlement. By 1875, there were 600 residents at Fort Calgary, lured by reports of vast and fertile grasslands.

However, for the prairies and the interior of Canada to support an agrarian economy, these remote areas needed to link to the rest of Canada. In 1879, the Canadian Pacific Railroad reached Winnipeg, and in 1883 arrived at Banff. Finding a route over the Rockies proved a major challenge: The grades were very steep, the construction season short, and much of the rail bed had to be hacked out of rock.

Canada's transcontinental railway also needed a mainland coastal terminus in British Columbia. As the new province's population center and capital, Victoria, was on an island, railroad engineers set their sites on the sheltered Burrard Inlet, then a sparse settlement of saloons, lumber mills, and farms. The first train arrived from Montreal in 1886, stopping at a thrown-together, brand-new town called Vancouver. A year later, the first ship docked from China, and Vancouver began its future as an integral trading center and transportation hub.

All along the railroad's transcontinental reach, towns, farms, ranches, and other industries sprang up. The railroads also brought foreign immigration. Entire communities of central and eastern European farmers appeared on the prairies overnight, the result of the railroads' extensive promotional campaign in places like the Ukraine. Other settlers came to western Canada seeking religious tolerance; many small towns started as utopian colonies for Hutterites, Mennonites, and Dukhobors.

All this development demanded lumber for construction, and in Canada, lumber—then as now—meant British Columbia. In return for building the transcontinental railroad, the CPR was granted vast tracts of land along its route. As the demand for lumber skyrocketed, these ancient forests met the saw. As the population, industry, logging, farming, and shipping all increased in western Canada, it was not just the local ecosystem that took a hit. Although European diseases wiped out enormous numbers of Native peoples, they had reasonably cooperative relations with the HBC trappers, who did little to overtly disturb their traditional life and culture.

That awaited the arrival of agriculture, town settlements, and Christian missionaries. After the HBC lost its long-standing role in Indian relations, authority was wielded by a federal agency in Ottawa. The Native peoples received no compensation for the land deeded over to the CPR, and increased contact with the whites who were flooding the region simply increased contact with alcohol, trade goods, and disease. The key social and religious ritual of the coastal Indians—the potlatch, a feast and gift-giving ceremony—was banned in 1884 by the provincial government under the influence of Episcopal missionaries. The massive buffalo herds of the open prairies were slaughtered to near-extinction in the 1870s and 1880s, leaving the once proud Plains Indians little choice but to accept confinement on reservations.

THE 20TH CENTURY The building of the Panama Canal, which was completed in 1914, meant easier access to markets in Europe and along North America's East Coast, bringing about a boom for the western Canadian economy. As big business grew, so did big unions. In Vancouver in the 1910s, workers organized into labor unions to protest working conditions and pay rates. A number of strikes hit key industries, and in several instances resulted in armed confrontations between union members and soldiers. However, one area where the unions, the government, and business could all agree was racism: The growing Chinese and Japanese populations were a problem they felt only punitive legislation and violence could solve. Large numbers of Chinese had moved to the province, first with the lure of gold, and then as workers in building the CPR; they were also important members of hard-rock mining communities and ran small businesses such as laundries. Japanese settlers came slightly later, establishing truck farms, orchards, and becoming the area's principal commercial fishermen. On several occasions, Vancouver's Chinatown and Little Tokyo were the scene of white mob violence, and in the 1920s, British Columbia passed legislation that effectively closed its borders to nonwhite immigration.

The period of the world wars was turbulent on many fronts. Settlers with British roots returned to Europe to fight the Germans in World War I, dying in great numbers and destabilizing the communities they left behind. Following the war, Canada experienced an economic downturn, which led to further industrial unrest and unemployment. After a brief recovery, the Wall Street crash of 1929 brought severe economic depression and hardship. Vancouver, with its comparatively mild climate, became a kind of magnet for young Canadian men—hungry, desperate, and out of work. The city, however, held no easy answers for these problems, and soon the streets were filled with demonstrations and riots. Vancouver was in the grip of widespread poverty. With the beginning of World War II, anti-German riots took hold of the city streets; and German-owned businesses were burned. In 1941, Japanese-Canadians were removed from their land and their fishing boats and interned by the government on farms and work camps in inland British Columbia, Alberta, and Saskatchewan.

Perversely, for other Canadians, social calm and prosperity returned as World War II progressed: the unemployed enlisting as foot soldiers against the Axis nations, and the shipbuilding and armaments-manufacturing industries bolstering the region's traditional farming, ranching, and lumbering.

After the war years, British Columbia prospered economically, especially under the leadership of the Social Credit Party, which was the party of business, free enterprise, and infrastructure. Father and son premiers, W. A. C. and Bill Bennett, effectively ruled the Social Credit Party and the province from 1952 until 1986. With close ties between government ministers and the resources they oversaw, business—mainly logging, mining, and manufacturing—certainly boomed, as did significant governmental scandals, opportunistic financial mischief, and major resource mismanagement. But none of these qualities are confined to right wing politics. The socialist New Democratic Party has had its fair share of shenanigans, too—all of which seem part and parcel of British Columbia's somewhat eccentric politics.

The 1990s saw a vast influx of Hong Kong Chinese to the Vancouver area, the result of fears accompanying the British handover of Hong Kong to the mainland Chinese in 1997. Unlike earlier migrations of Chinese to North America, these Hong Kong Chinese were middle- and upper-class merchants and business leaders. Real-estate prices shot through the roof, and entire neighborhoods became Chinese enclaves. Vancouver now has one of the world's largest Chinese populations outside of Asia.

Asians are not the only people bolstering western Canada's fast-growing population. Canada has relatively open immigration laws, resulting in a steady flow of newcomers from the Middle East, the Indian subcontinent, and Europe. Additionally, many young Canadians from the economically depressed eastern provinces see a brighter future in the west. With their strong economies and big-as-all-outdoors setting, British Columbia is a magnet for many seeking new lives and opportunities.

BRITISH COLUMBIA IN POPULAR CULTURE

Books

The following books on British Columbia provide background information, and can add immeasurably to your enjoyment of your trip. These suggestions contain books both in print and out of print—all are easily available in bookstores and Internet shopping sites.

CANADIAN HISTORY A basic primer on the country's complex history is *The Penguin History of Canada,* by Kenneth McNaught. *The Canadians,* by Andrew H. Malcolm, is an insightful and highly readable rumination on what it is to be Canadian, written by the former *New York Times* Canada bureau chief.

Peter C. Newman has produced an intriguing history of the Hudson's Bay Company, *Caesars of the Wilderness,* beginning with the early fur-trading days. *The Great Adventure,* by David Cruise and Alison Griffiths, tells the story of the Mounties and their role in the subduing of the Canadian west.

Pierre Berton is the preeminent popular historian of Canada. He has written nearly 50 books on Canada's rich past, all well researched and well written. His books cover many subjects, from the days of the Hudson's Bay Company and the fur trade to pondering on what it means to be Canadian in the 21st century.

For a specific history of British Columbia, try *British Columbia: An Illustrated History,* by Geoffrey Molyneux, or *The West Beyond the West: A History of British Columbia,* by Jean Borman. Review Vancouver's past with *Vancouver: A History in Photographs,* by Aynsley Wyse and Dana Wyse. The engaging *British Columbia History Along the Highway: A Traveler's Guide to the Fascinating Facts, Intriguing Incidents and Lively Legends in British Columbia's Remarkable Past,* by Ted Stone, is the book you'll want to take along in the car.

To learn about Canada's Native peoples, read *Native Peoples and Cultures of Canada,* by Alan D. McMillan, which includes both history and current issues. The classic book on Canada's indigenous peoples, *The Indians of Canada,* was written in 1932 by Diamond Jenness. The author's life is an amazing story in its own right, as he spent years living with various indigenous peoples across the country.

NATURAL HISTORY Two good general guides to the natural world in western Canada are the Audubon Society's *Pacific Coast,* by Evelyn McConnaghey, and *Western Forests,* by Stephen Whitney.

British Columbia: A Natural History, by Richard Cannings, is an in-depth guide to the province's plants, animals, and geography. *Plants and Animals of the Pacific Northwest: An Illustrated Guide to the Natural History of Western Oregon, Washington, and British Columbia,* by Eugene N. Kozloff, is another good general resource.

Bird-watchers might want to dig up a copy of *Familiar Birds of the Northwest,* by Harry B. Nehls.

Read about the natural history of extinct wildlife in *A Wonderful Life: The Burgess Shale and the Nature of History,* by Stephen Jay Gould, which details the discovery and scientific ramifications of the fossil beds found in Yoho National Park.

OUTDOOR PURSUITS Edward Weber's *Diving and Snorkeling Guide to the Pacific Northwest* is a good place to start if you're planning a diving holiday in the Northwest.

Mountain Bike Adventures in Southwest British Columbia, by Greg Maurer and Tomas Vrba, is just one of a cascade of books on off-road biking in western Canada.

A good hiking guide to western British Columbia is *Don't Waste Your Time in the B.C. Coast Mountains: An Opinionated Hiking Guide to Help you Get the Most from this Magnificent Wilderness,* by Kathy Copeland. *A Guide to Climbing and Hiking in Southwestern British Columbia,* by Bruce Fairley, also includes Vancouver Island. Frommer's also publishes *The Best Hiking Trips in British Columbia*, which covers day hikes throughout the province.

FICTION & MEMOIR Alice Munro's short fiction captures the soul of what it is to be Canadian in brief, though often wrenching, prose. Some of the stories in *The Love of a Good Woman* take place in Vancouver. Another good selection of short stories as well as poetry is *Fresh Tracks: Writing the Western Landscape,* a collection of writings by western Canadian authors.

Richard P. Hobson, Jr., writes of his experiences as a modern-day cowboy on the grasslands of central British Columbia in an acclaimed series of memoirs titled *Grass Beyond the Mountains: Discovering the Last Great Cattle Frontier on the North American Continent, The Rancher Takes a Wife,* and *Nothing Too Good for a Cowboy.*

Vancouver and southwestern British Columbia is and has been home to a number of noted international authors. Artist-writer Nick Bantock of *Griffin & Sabine* fame lives on the Gulf Islands. Mystery writer Laurali R. Wright lived in Vancouver, and her Karl Alberg mystery series usually took place in and around Vancouver. Jane Rule's *Desert of the Heart* was a breakthrough in lesbian fiction when it was published in 1964.

Generation X chronicler Douglas Coupland lives in Vancouver. Science-fiction writer William Gibson's dark vision of the cyber-future attracts a large young audience. W. P. Kinsella *(Shoeless Joe)* writes about baseball and First Nations issues from his home in the Lower Mainland.

Film & TV

British Columbia is one of the centers of film in Canada, and many Canadian features are set in Vancouver. Numerous Hollywood films have also been shot in the province: *Diary of a Wimpy Kid, Twilight, New Moon, Legends of the Fall, Little Women, Jumanji,* and *Rambo: First Blood* give an idea of the range of films done here. Television's groundbreaking series *The X-Files* was shot in and around the city for its first 4 years of production. (Vancouver doubles as many American cities, notably Washington, D.C.) *Superman, Sanctuary,* and *Stargate* have been long-time mainstays.

Music

Vancouver is a major trendsetter in Canadian music, particularly in the realms of folk and post-punk pop music. Diana Krall and Michael Buble are two of British Columbia's most famous, and current, exports.

Vancouver's leading role in Canadian rock doesn't mean that the city lacks a full array of classical music institutions, including the well-respected Vancouver Symphony Orchestra and Vancouver Opera Association. The city's love of music is also on display in its many music festivals, particularly the beloved Vancouver Folk Music

Festival, one of the largest and most laid-back folk festivals in North America. The Vancouver International Jazz Festival is another major musical event featuring a diverse line-up of musicians from around the world.

Vancouver is extremely ethnically diverse, providing a League-of-Nations-like multiplicity to its music scene, which moves beyond typical World Beat internationalism. You'll find Chinese, East Indian, and Russian punk bands, and lots of rock groups that blend central European and Eastern Mediterranean influences. Muslim punk, often referred to as "taqwacore" (a neologism formed from taqwa, Arabic for piety, and hardcore), is another genre popular in some Vancouver clubs. Secret Trial Five, an all-female punk band with its roots in Vancouver, has caused a sensation with its politically pointed, hard-edged sounds.

One of Vancouver's defining moments in folk-rock history is Joni Mitchell's "Big Yellow Taxi," which was a commentary on the city's rapid urbanization. Other early rock bands with Vancouver and B.C. roots were Bachman Turner Overdrive, Loverboy, and the Boomtown Rats.

Vancouver is currently a hotbed for indie rock and singer/songwriters that blend folk and rock. Notably recent bands with B.C. roots include The New Pornographers, with its side acts Destroyer and singer Neko Case; Ladyhawk; Said The Whale; and Left Spine Down.

EATING & DRINKING IN BRITISH COLUMBIA

Western Canada is home to excellent regional cuisine that relies on the area's natural abundance of produce, farm-raised game, grass-fed beef and lamb, and fresh-caught fish and shellfish. These high-quality ingredients are matched with inventive sauces and accompaniments, often based on native berries and wild mushrooms. In attempting to capture what the French call the *terroir,* or the native taste of the Northwest, local chefs are producing a delicious school of cooking with distinctive regional characteristics.

One of the hallmarks of Northwest cuisine is freshness. In places like Vancouver Island, chefs meet fishing boats to select the finest of the day's catch. The lower Fraser Valley and the interior of British Columbia are filled with small specialty farms and orchards. Visit Vancouver's Granville Island Market, Lonsdale Quay, or stop at a roadside farmer's stand to have a look at the incredible bounty of the land.

Cooks in western Canada are also very particular about where their food is sourced. Frequently, menus tell you exactly what farm grew your heirloom tomatoes, what ranch your beef was raised on, which orchard harvested your peaches, and what bay your oysters came from. To capture the distinct flavor of the Northwest—its *terroir*—means using only those products that swam in the waters or grew in or on the soil of the Northwest.

While many chefs marry the region's superior meat, fish, and produce to traditional French or Italian techniques, other cooks turn elsewhere for inspiration, especially across the Pacific to Asia. Pan-Pacific fusion cuisine is an ever-evolving style of cooking that matches the North American Pacific Coast's fare with flavors of Pacific Asia. There are no rules and the results can be subtle—the delicate taste of lemon grass or nori—or intense, with lashings of red curry or wasabi. Another style of Northwest cooking looks back to frontier times or to Native American techniques. There's no better way to experience salmon than at a traditional salmon bake at a Native village—most First Nations communities have an annual festival open to the general public—and many restaurants replicate this by baking salmon on a cedar plank. Several restaurants in the province specialize in full Northwest Native feasts.

FRUITS OF THE FIELD & FOREST   Although there's nothing exotic about the varieties of vegetables available in western Canada, what will seem remarkable to visitors from distant urban areas is the freshness and quality of the produce here. Many fine restaurants contract directly with small, often organic, farms for daily deliveries.

Fruit trees do particularly well in the hot central valleys of British Columbia, and apples, peaches, apricots, plums, and pears do more than grace the fruit basket. One hallmark of Northwest cuisine is mixing fruit with savory meat and chicken dishes. And as long as the chef is slicing apricots to go with sautéed chicken and thyme, she might as well chop up a few hazelnuts (filberts) to toss in: These nuts thrive in the Pacific Northwest. Berries of all kinds do well in the milder coastal regions. Cranberries grow in low-lying coastal plains—Richmond has one of the largest harvests in the world. The blueberry and its wild cousin, the huckleberry, are both used in all manner of cooking, from breads to savory chutneys. The astringent wild chokecherry, once used to make pemmican (a sort of Native American energy bar), is also finding its way into fine-dining restaurants.

Wild mushrooms grow throughout western Canada, and harvesting the chanterelles, morels, porcinis, and myriad other varieties is big business. Expect to find forest mushrooms in pasta, alongside a steak, in savory bread puddings, or braised with fish.

MEATS & SEAFOOD   Easily the most iconic of the Northwest's staples is the Pacific salmon. For thousands of years, the Native people have followed the cycles of the salmon, netting or spearing the fish, then smoking and preserving it for later use. The delicious and abundant salmon became the mainstay of settlers and early European residents as well. Although salmon fishing is now highly restricted and some salmon species are endangered, salmon is still very available. It is easily the most popular fish in the region, and is featured on practically every fine-dining menu in the Northwest.

However, there are other fish in the sea. The fisheries along Vancouver Island and the Pacific Coast are rich in bottom fish like sole, flounder, and halibut, which grow to enormous size here. Fresh-caught rock and black cod (also called sablefish) are equally delectable.

Although shellfish and seafood are abundant in the Pacific, it is only recently that many of the varieties have appeared on the dinner table. Oysters grow in a number of bays on Vancouver Island, and while wild mussels blanket the length of the coast, only a few sea farms grow mussels commercially. Fanny Bay, north of Qualicum Beach on Vancouver Island, is noted for both its oysters and its mussels. Another Northwest shellfish delicacy is the razor clam, a long, thin bivalve with a nutty and rich flavor. Shrimp of all sizes thrive off the coast of British Columbia, and one of the clichés of Northwest cooking is the unstinting use of local shrimp on nearly everything, from pizza to polenta. Local squid and octopus are gaining popularity, while sea urchin—abundant along the coast—is found in some high-end sushi restaurants, most is harvested for export to Japan.

Both British Columbia and Alberta have excellent ranch-raised beef and lamb. Steaks are a staple throughout the region, as is prime rib. Game meats are increasingly hip, especially in restaurants dedicated to Northwest cuisine. Buffalo and venison are offered frequently enough to no longer seem unusual, and farm-raised pheasant is easily available. It's harder to find meats like caribou or elk, however.

FRUITS OF THE VINEYARDS   British Columbia wines remain one of western Canada's greatest secrets. Scarcely anyone outside of the region has ever heard of these wines, yet many are delicious and, while not exactly cheap, still less expensive than comparable wines from California. There are wineries on Vancouver and Saturna islands and in the Fraser Valley, but the real center of British Columbia's winemaking is the Okanagan Valley. In this hot and arid climate, noble grapes like cabernet sauvignon, merlot, and chardonnay thrive when irrigated. You'll also find more unusual varietals, like Ehrenfelser and Marechal Foch. More than 100 wineries are currently producing wine in the Okanagan Valley; when combined with excellent restaurants in Kelowna and Penticton, this region becomes a great vacation choice for the serious gastronome.

RESTAURANTS   Canadians enjoy eating out, and you'll find excellent restaurants throughout British Columbia. Many of the establishments recommended in this guide serve Northwest regional cuisine, the qualities of which are outlined above.

However, there is a wealth of other kinds of restaurants available. If you're a meat eater, visit a traditional steakhouse in Vancouver or Victoria. In many smaller centers, Greek restaurants double as the local steakhouse so don't be surprised when you see a sign for, say, Zorba's Steakhouse; both steaks and souvlaki will probably be excellent.

Vancouver is one of the most ethnically diverse places on earth, and the selection of restaurants is mind-boggling. You'll find some of the best Chinese food this side of Hong Kong, as well as the cooking of Russia, Mongolia, Ghana, and Sri Lanka, along with every other country and ethnic group in between.

Several Canadian chain restaurants are handy to know about. White Spot restaurants serve basic but good-quality North American cooking. Often open 24 hours, these are great places for an eggs-and-hash-browns breakfast. Tim Horton's is the place to go for coffee and doughnuts, plus light snacks. Earl's serves a wide menu and frequently has a lively bar scene, as does Cactus Club. Both lean to grilled ribs and chicken, steaks, gourmet burgers, imaginative salads, and rice bowls. The Keg is another Canadian favorite, and a bit more sedate than Earl's, with more of a steakhouse atmosphere.

WHEN TO GO

When to go to B.C. depends on what you intend to do when you get there. Summer brings warm weather and mainly sunny skies, the most festivals and events, and consequently, hoards of visitors. However, even in the height of summer, there are places where crowds seem to evaporate; this guide offers suggestions for less-frequented parks and activities where you can experience the solitary pleasures of the Canadian wilderness.

By and large, winter means skiing, which is big business here. Vancouver and Whistler hosted the 2010 Winter Olympics, so facilities are top-draw. Recent years have also seen the opening of ever more upscale resorts, particularly in the mountains of southeast B.C., in the Okanagan, and on the western shores of Vancouver Island, where winter storm-watching is very chic.

Spring (Apr and May) and late fall (Oct through early Dec) are definitely off season, and in many ways can be the nicest times to visit. Hotel prices are often one-third to one-half of high-season rates, and you'll have dining rooms to yourselves. Come prepared for wet and changeable weather, but otherwise this can be a low-key, budget-pleasing time to visit.

The Weather

With the Pacific Ocean at its shores, Canada west of the Rocky Mountains has generally mild winters, with snow mostly at the higher elevations. Even though spring comes early—usually in March—gray clouds can linger through June. Dry summer weather is assured only after July 1, and can continue through October. Be aware that even in summer clouds and rain can be commonplace, so plan to spend several days here so that some sunny days will be a certainty. In winter, of course, the mountains fill with snow, but the weather may not be as cold as you'd expect. Chinook winds from the Alberta prairies can bring warm-air systems, boosting temperatures up to early spring levels. If you plan to travel across through any of British Columbia's mountainous regions in winter, make sure you have snow tires, chains, and a thermal blanket in case you get caught in a snowdrift.

Areas bordering the Rockies, such as Revelstoke and Golden, are prone to avalanches, so check with the local information center before setting out on your journey, let alone hitting the slopes. Remember to winterize your car through March, and that snow sometimes falls as late as May.

Evenings tend to be cool everywhere, particularly on or near water. In late spring and early summer, you'll need a supply of insect repellent if you're planning bush travel or camping.

Coastal B.C. can be very rainy in winter, and even in high summer (July and Aug) rain and fog are not uncommon. However, it's never very cold due to offshore currents.

For up-to-date weather conditions, check out www.weatheroffice.ec.gc.ca or www.theweathernetwork.com.

Daily Mean Temperature & Total Precipitation for Vancouver, B.C.

	JAN	FEB	MAR	APR	MAY	JUNE	JULY	AUG	SEPT	OCT	NOV	DEC
Temp (°F)	37	41	45	39	46	63	66	66	61	43	48	39
Temp (°C)	3	5	7	4	8	17	19	19	16	6	9	4
Precipitation (in.)	5.9	4.9	4.3	3.0	2.4	1.8	1.4	1.5	2.5	4.5	6.7	7.0

Daily Mean Temperature & Total Precipitation for Calgary, Alberta

	JAN	FEB	MAR	APR	MAY	JUNE	JULY	AUG	SEPT	OCT	NOV	DEC
Temp (°F)	25	32	37	52	61	70	73	73	63	55	37	28
Temp (°C)	–4	0	3	11	16	21	23	23	17	13	3	–2
Precipitation (in.)	.5	.4	.6	1	2.1	3	2.8	1.9	1.9	.6	.5	.5

Calendar of Events

PUBLIC HOLIDAYS

In British Columbia, there are nine official public holidays: New Year's Day (January 1); Good Friday; Victoria Day (the Monday on or preceding May 14); Canada Day (July 1); B.C. Day (first Monday in August); Labour Day (first Monday in September); Thanksgiving (second Monday in October); Remembrance Day (November 11); Christmas Day (December 25).

SEASONAL EVENTS

Canadians love a festival, and not even the chill of winter will keep them from celebrating. The Canadian events calendar is jammed with multicultural and historical activities, food and wine, the arts, rodeos, music and theater, even salmon and whales. Following are some seasonal highlights from British Columbia. Each community's special events are listed in the regional chapters that follow.

For an exhaustive list of events beyond those listed in this book, check http://events.frommers.com, where you'll find a searchable, up-to-the-minute roster of what's happening in cities all over the world.

WINTER

Chinese New Year, late January or early February, is wildly celebrated in Vancouver and Victoria with the Chinese community ringing it in with fire-crackers, dancing dragon parades, and other festivities.

Reino Keski-Salmi Loppet (www.skilarchhills.ca), January, held in Salmon Arm, is one of Canada's largest cross-country ski races.

TELUS Winter Classic (www.whistlerblackcomb.com), January, brings the world's top skiers and snowboarders, and lots of youthful energy, to Whistler.

SPRING

Pacific Rim Whale Festival (© 250/726-4641; www.pacificrimwhalefestival.com), March, celebrates the yearly return of up to 20,000 gray whales to the waters off Tofino and Ucluelet, Vancouver Island, B.C.

TD Vancouver International Jazz Festival (© 604/872-5200; www.vancouverjazz.com or www.coastaljazz.com), June, brings together almost 2,000 jazz musicians from around the world playing at some 40 venues. Over 150 concerts are free.

SUMMER

Bard on the Beach (© 604/737-0625 for information, 877/739-0559 for tickets; www.bardonthebeach.org), May–September, stages professional Shakespearean plays, beneath canvas tents at Vancouver's Vanier Park.

Vancouver Folk Festival (© 604/602-9798; www.thefestival.bc.ca), July, one of North America's top folk music events, Vancouver's festival brings Summer of Love musical stylings to a gorgeous bayside park.

Alcan International Dragon Boat Festival (www.dragonboat.ca), June, transforms Vancouver's False Creek (near Science World) into a colorful, and extremely competitive 3-day event of traditional dragonboat races. A smaller festival, but no less fun, takes place in Victoria's Inner Harbour.

Nanaimo Marine Festival (© 250/753-7223; www.bathtubbing.com), is a weeklong festival in late July. The highlight is the World Championship Bathtub Race, in which unusual watercraft (originally claw-foot bathtubs) motor from Nanaimo to Vancouver.

Celebration of Light (www.celebration-of-light.com), late July and early August, is a fireworks competition culminating with a huge pyrotechnical display accompanied by live music, all at Vancouver's English Bay Beach.

FALL

Okanagan Wine Festival (© 250/861-6654; www.thewinefestivals.com), the main event is still October, to coincide with the Okanagan's fall harvest, but additional festivals now take place in January, July, and May. All offer wine tastings, winery open houses, and dining events.

Vancouver International Film Festival (www.viff.org), early October, showcases an exhaustive, and often excellent, Canadian-made and avant-garde foreign films of many genres in movie theatres and studios all over the city.

Great Canadian Beer Festival (© 250/383-2332; www.gcbf.com), November, brings the country's top brewers to Victoria.

Cornucopia (© 800/435-5622; www.whistlercornucopia.com), mid-November, is Whistler's pre-ski season parade of sumptuous epicurean delights, foodie workshops, and winemaker dinners.

THE LAY OF THE LAND

With the Pacific Ocean on its west coast, and the Canadian Rockies to the east, Canada's westernmost province, British Columbia, is an incredibly diverse part of the country, with distinct regions that vary both in geography and culture.

Vancouver is one of the most beautiful and cosmopolitan cities in the world. While there are certainly good museums and tourist sights, what we love most are the incredible mosaic of people and languages, the bustle of the streets, the mountains reaching down into the sea, and the wonderful food. Kayaking and canoeing are just off your front step in False Creek and the Georgia Strait, and skiing just up the road at **Whistler/Blackcomb Mountain Resorts,** one of the continent's greatest ski areas—as was proven when Vancouver-Whistler hosted the 2010 Winter Olympic Games.

Vancouver Island is a world apart from busy urban Vancouver. **Victoria,** the British Columbia capitol, lies at the island's southern tip as a small, charming city with a magnificently scenic seaside location. It makes a lot of fuss about its Merry Olde Englishness, which can be frustrating amidst the crowds of summer visitors, but the city has a genteel welcome at other times of the year. The rest of the mountainous island ranges from rural to wild. It would be easy to spend an entire vacation just on Vancouver Island, especially if you take a few days for **sea kayaking** on the island's wilderness west coast near **Tofino,** or off the east coast in the beautiful **Gulf Islands.** Or you can learn to **scuba dive:** No less an authority than Jacques Cousteau has claimed that these waters are some of the best diving environments in the world. Vancouver Island is also home to dozens of First Nations Canadian bands. If you're shopping for **Native arts,** this is the best single destination in western Canada.

From the northern tip of Vancouver Island, you can take the 15-hour BC Ferries trip through the famed **Inside Passage** to Prince Rupert, a port town just shy of the Alaska Panhandle. Getting a glimpse of the dramatically scenic Inside Passage is what fuels the Alaska-to-Vancouver cruise-ship industry; by taking this route on BC Ferries, you'll save yourself thousands of dollars and catch the same views. From Prince Rupert, you can journey out to the mystical **Queen Charlotte Islands,** the ancient homeland of the Haida people, or turn inland and drive up the glacier-carved Skeena River valley to **Prince George,** on the Fraser River.

You can also reach the upper reaches of the Fraser River from Vancouver by following Hwy. 99 north past Whistler and Lillooet to the **Cariboo Country.** This secondary route follows the historic Cariboo Trail, a gold-rush stage-coach road blazed in the 1860s. Today, the road leads through cattle- and horse-covered grasslands, past 19th-century ranches, and by lakes thick with trout. The gold rush started at **Barkerville,** now one of North America's best-preserved ghost towns, which in summer comes alive with staged activity representing that era. In addition to this great family destination, the Cariboo Country offers the province's best **guest ranches** and rustic lakeside **fishing resorts.**

The Thompson River meets the Fraser River south of Lillooet. This mighty river's southern fork has its headwaters in the **Shuswap Lakes,** a series of interconnected lakes that are favorites of houseboaters. The north fork Thompson River rises in the mountains of **Wells Gray Provincial Park,** one of British Columbia's neglected gems. Hiking and camping are as compelling as in the nearby Canadian Rockies, but without the overwhelming crowds.

One of the best summer family destinations in western Canada is the **Okanagan Valley.** Stretching from Osoyoos at the U.S.-Canadian border nearly 200km (124 miles) north to Vernon, this arid canyon is filled with glacier-trenched lakes. In summer, they become the playground for all manner of watersports and the summer heat beats down on innumerable orchards and vineyards; the valley is the center for British Columbia's burgeoning wine industry, which for some wine enthusiasts rivals the vineyards of Napa Valley. Add to that a dozen golf courses and excellent lodging and dining in the cities of **Penticton** and **Kelowna,** and you've got the makings for an excellent vacation.

The **Canadian Rockies** are among the most dramatically scenic destinations in the world. Unfortunately, this is hardly a secret—the Alberta side of the Rockies positively drips with tourists in summer and early fall. That's why we suggest you head for the equally beautiful, but far less crowded, British Columbia side of the Rockies, which include **Glacier** and **Kootenay** national parks, plus **Mount Robson Provincial Park.**

RESPONSIBLE TRAVEL

In 2006, after years of protests and negotiations by First Nations tribes and environmentalists, Canada declared British Columbia's Great Bear Rainforest off-limits to loggers. This landmark decision preserves the largest remaining temperate coastal rainforest in the world, some 6 million hectares (15 million acres) that are home to rare white bears and support the highest concentration of grizzly bears in North America. It must also be noted that much of British Columbia's economy is based on "resource extraction" of one kind or another, logging being the most prevalent.

Vancouver and Victoria are meccas of ecotourism in all its many guises. From patronizing restaurants that use only locally harvested foods (the 100-mile diet was conceived in Vancouver) and non-endangered fish to enjoying natural, nonpolluting fun by paddling kayaks and hiking through beautiful rainforests, you can enjoy green holidays in both of these cities without sacrificing any fun or flavor. Many hotels in both cities take green practices so seriously that they've almost turned sustainability into a one-upmanship competition. Incidentally, if you're ordering fish, look for the "Ocean Wise" logo on the menu—it indicates what fresh, non-endangered fish has been sustainably harvested for the restaurant.

ESCORTED GENERAL-INTEREST TOURS

Travel by train lets you see the Rockies as you never would in a bus or behind the wheel of a car. The **Rocky Mountaineer Vacations,** 1150 Station St., First Floor, Vancouver, BC V6A 2X7 (✆ **877/460-3200;** www.rockymountaineer.com), bills its *Rocky Mountaineer* as "The Most Spectacular Train Trip in the World." During daylight hours between mid-April and mid-October, this sleek blue-and-white train winds past foaming waterfalls, ancient glaciers, snowcapped peaks, and roaring mountain streams. The *Rocky Mountaineer* gives you the options of traveling east from Vancouver; traveling west from Jasper, Calgary, or Banff; or taking round-trips.

John Steel Railtours (✆ **800/988-5778** [North America] or 800/7245-7245 [international]; www.johnsteel.com) offers both escorted and independent tour packages, many through the Rockies and the West and a few in other regions, which

GENERAL RESOURCES FOR responsible TRAVEL

Although one could make the case that any journey that includes travel in a car or airplane can't truly be "green," there are several ways that you can make your trip to western Canada more sustainable.

The **Hotel Association of Canada** (✆ **613/237-7149;** www.hotelassociation. ca) offers a voluntary program called the Green Key Program (www.greenkey global.com) that recognizes hotels and lodgings that are taking steps to reduce environmental impacts. Lodgings are rated from one to five Green Keys based on their performance in such areas as energy and water conservation, land use, and environmental management.

Green Travel Guide by Trail Canada (www.trailcanada.com/green) is another reference for green accommodations, activities, and restaurants in Canada.

In addition, B.C. offers eco-tourism opportunities that join adventure and recreation with sustainable travel practices.

Ecotour (www.ecotourdirectory.com) is a Web directory that provides listings for eco-tourism operators in Canada (and around the world).

Another valuable website is **www. greenlivingonline.com**, which offers extensive content on how to travel sustainably, including a travel and transport section and profiles of the best green shops and services in Vancouver.

Carbonfund (www.carbonfund.org), **TerraPass** (www.terrapass.org), and **Cool Climate** (http://coolclimate.berkeley.edu) provide info on "carbon offsetting," or offsetting the greenhouse gas emitted during flights. **Greenhotels** (www.green hotels.com) recommends green-rated member hotels around the world that fulfill the company's stringent environmental requirements.

Environmentally Friendly Hotels (www.environmentallyfriendlyhotels.com) offers more green accommodation ratings.

Volunteer **International** (www. volunteerinternational.org) has a list of questions to help you determine the intentions and the nature of a volunteer program. For general info on volunteer travel, visit **www.volunteerabroad.org** and **www.idealist.org**.

See www.frommers.com/planning for more tips on responsible travel.

combine train and other forms of travel. VIA Rail operates the train portions of John Steel tours. Packages run from 5 to 12 days, at all times of year, depending on the route, and combine stays in major cities and national parks.

For more information on escorted general-interest tours, including questions to ask before booking your trip, see www.frommers.com/planning.

ACTIVE VACATION PLANNER

See the individual destination chapters for specific details on how and where to enjoy the activities below.

BIKING Because many of British Columbia's highways are wide and well maintained, they are well suited for long-distance bicycle touring. Most resort areas offer rentals (it's a good idea to call ahead and reserve a bike).

While hiking trails tend to be off limits to mountain bikes, other trails are developed specifically for backcountry biking. Ask at national park and national forest information centers for a map of mountain-bike trails.

BOATING AND CRUISES   Water is a way of life in B.C.; boat charters and cruises are big business. Lesser known day and week-long trips with small working craft and/or packet freighters offer a more casual and offbeat way to see the nooks and crannies of fjords and bays that larger vessels cannot access. Most operate out of Campbell River, Gold River, and Port McNeill on Vancouver Island.

CANOEING & KAYAKING   Low-lying lakes and rivers form vast waterway systems across the land. Multiday canoeing trips make popular summer and early fall expeditions; you'll see lots of wildlife and keep as gentle a pace as you like. The Bowron Lakes in the Cariboo Country make an excellent weeklong paddle (with some portaging) through wilderness.

DIVING   An amazing array of marine life flourishes amid the 2,000 shipwrecks off the coast of British Columbia. Divers visit the area year-round to see the Pacific Northwest's unique underwater fauna and flora, and to swim among the ghostly remains of 19th-century whaling ships and 20th-century schooners.

The Pacific Rim National Park's Broken Group Islands are home to a multitude of sea life; the waters off the park's West Coast Trail are known as "the graveyard of the Pacific" for the hundreds of shipwrecks. Nanaimo and Campbell River, on Vancouver Island, are both centers for numerous dive outfitters.

FISHING   Angling is enjoyed across British Columbia. However, the famed halibut and salmon fisheries along the Pacific Coast face highly restricted catch limits in most areas, and outright bans on fishing in others. Not all salmon species are threatened, though, and rules governing fishing change quickly, so check locally with outfitters to find out if a season will open while you're visiting. Trout and bass are found throughout the region, some reaching great size in the lakes in the B.C. interior.

Fishing in Canada is regulated by local governments, and appropriate licenses are necessary. Angling for some fish is regulated by season; in some areas, catch-and-release fishing is enforced. Check with local authorities before casting your line.

If you're looking for a great fishing vacation with top-notch accommodations, contact **Oak Bay Marine Group,** 1327 Beach Dr., Victoria (© **800/663-7090** or 250/598-3366; www.obmg.com), which operates nine different resorts. Three are on Vancouver Island; the others are on remote islands and fjords along the north coast.

HIKING   Almost every national and provincial park in British Columbia is webbed with trails, ranging from easy nature hikes to long-distance backcountry trails. Late summer and early fall are good times to visit, since trails in the high country may be snowbound until July. For many people, the B.C. Canadian Rockies, with their abundance of parks and developed trail systems, provide the country's finest hiking. Before setting out, request trail information from the parks and buy a good map.

SEA KAYAKING   One of the best places to practice sea kayaking is in the sheltered bays, islands, and inlets along the coast of British Columbia; kayaks are especially good for wildlife-viewing. Most coastal towns have rentals, instruction, and guided trips. Handling a kayak isn't as easy as it looks, and you'll want to have plenty of experience in sheltered coves before heading out into the surf. Be sure to check the tide schedule and weather forecast before setting out, as well as what the coastal rock formations are. You'll need to be comfortable on the water and ready to get wet, as well as be a strong swimmer.

SKIING   Canada, a mountainous country with heavy snowfall, is one of the world's top ski destinations. Both downhill and cross-country skiing are open to all ages, though downhill skiing carries a higher price tag: A day on the slopes, with rental gear and lift ticket, can easily top C$150 per person.

For downhill skiing, the Okanagan's powder snow is perfect for family fun while northern B.C. has some pretty hot heli-skiing opportunities. All told, a top choice remains the 2010 Winter Olympics site, Whistler/Blackcomb near Vancouver. Readers of *Condé Nast Traveler* repeatedly name the latter with the title of Best Ski Resort in North America.

WHALE-WATCHING AND WILDLIFE VIEWING   Because so many whales pass the east coast of Vancouver Island on their migration to northerly feeding grounds, most tours are based on Vancouver Island. There are numerous operators in Victoria and they just get more plentiful the further up island you travel. Tours usually include other wildlife hot spots for eagles, sea lions, nesting bird colonies, and more—just in case the whales don't co-operate, which is rare.

WHITE-WATER RAFTING   Charging down a mountain river in a rubber raft is a popular thrill for visitors and locals alike. Trips range from daylong excursions, which demand little of a participant other than sitting tight, to long-distance trips through remote backcountry. Risk doesn't correspond to length of trip: Individual rapids and water conditions can make even a short trip a real adventure. You should be comfortable in water, and a good swimmer, if you're floating an adventurous river such as the Thompson or Fraser rivers, and the thrilling Kicking Horse River near Golden.

SUGGESTED ITINERARIES IN BRITISH COLUMBIA

C anada's westernmost province is not only large, but also packed with amazing must-see scenery and destinations. Whether traveling north–south, or heading across the province between the Canadian Rockies and Vancouver, the diverse landscapes are highly photogenic, and provide for a myriad of eco-adventures. These include wilderness treks for the adventurous, top-notch golf courses and ski-mountains, as well as award-winning wineries, most notably in B.C.'s interior. Our advice is to take your foot off the gas pedal, slow down, and savor the British Columbia experience. The following itineraries focus on the top areas covered by this book: Vancouver, Victoria, the Pacific coast, and the islands of British Columbia; and the route between these areas.

THE BACK ROADS OF INTERIOR B.C. IN 1 WEEK

Mountains are synonymous with British Columbia, and the Purcell and Selkirk mountain ranges are among the most dramatic. Not only are they less crowded than their more famous cousins to the east, they nudge up against the lush and anomalous desert landscapes of Okanagan wine country, and lead you across mountain plateaus and down through Whistler on your way to Vancouver.

Day 1: Exploring B.C.'s Mountain Parks

Savvy outdoor enthusiasts know that just west of crowded Banff and Jasper parks are two much less busy but equally stunning national parks, Glacier and Revelstoke. Located on Hwy. 1 west of the Continental Divide, **Glacier National Park** (p. 301) features hiking trails to the base of icefields, and Revelstoke boasts the **Meadows in the Sky Parkway** (p. 300), leading to flower-spangled alpine meadows. Spend the night in the charming mountain town of **Revelstoke** (p. 294).

The Back Roads of Interior B.C. in 1 Week

Days 2 & 3: The Okanagan Wine Country

Head west from Revelstoke, then drop south on Hwy. 97A at Sicamous. The
landscape quickly changes from lush forests to arid desert highlands. The
Okanagan Valley (chapter 12), filled with 128km-long (80-mile) Okanagan
Lake, is a fruit-growing paradise now famous for its burgeoning wine industry.
After arriving in **Kelowna** (p. 282), relax at the city's sandy lake beachfront and
check out the bustling restaurant scene. The following day, explore the valley's
more than 100 **wineries** (p. 273), many of them south of Kelowna toward
Penticton. The same irrigation that supports wine grapes sprinkles golf
courses—some of B.C.'s top courses overlook Okanagan Lake.

Day 4: West to Whistler

This is a road-trip day, starting on the so-called Peachland Connector (Hwy.
97C) that connects the Okanagan Valley to Merritt. From Merritt, leave the
freeway and follow secondary roads to **Lillooet** (p. 253). At this historic town
on the Fraser River begins one of the most dramatic mountain roads in British
Columbia, climbing up the Cayoosh Valley, cresting the Coastal Mountains, and
dropping into Whistler, one of the continent's top mountain resorts.

Days 5 & 6: Whistler

Whistler (see chapter 9) gained its fame as a ski destination—there's a reason that the 2010 Winter Olympics ski events were held at the exemplary **Whistler/ Blackcomb Resort** (p. 210)—but today Whistler is as busy in summer as winter. If you're a shopper, exploring the shops in **Whistler Village** (p. 210) can take most of a day, and with four championship golf courses nearby, duffers will find plenty of challenges. In summer, there's **glacier skiing** through August (p. 211), and hiking and biking trails start at the village edge. **Nightlife** in Whistler is very lively (p. 223), with a **dining** scene (p. 221) to rival Vancouver's.

Day 7: Drive to Vancouver

From Whistler, Hwy. 99 drops from mountain heights to sea level along the scenic **Sea-to-Sky Highway** (p. 252), before entering Vancouver from the north.

THE WILD & THE SOPHISTICATED ON VANCOUVER ISLAND IN 1 WEEK

Vancouver Island is home to rugged, nearly inaccessible rainforests and wilderness coastlines; the island also offers very sophisticated dining and lodging, often in the remote backcountry itself. This is the allure of exploring coastal British Columbia: After a challenging day sea-kayaking remote archipelagoes or hiking old-growth forest, you return to three-star lodging and dining. What follows is a full agenda; you may want to add 2 or 3 days to savor these suggestions more fully.

Day 1: The Gulf Islands

Begin your journey in Vancouver, driving to the ferry terminal at Tsawwassen to cross to the **Gulf Islands** (see chapter 6). BC Ferries links to five of these charmingly rural islands, and which island you choose will depend on your interests and inclinations. Of all the islands, Salt Spring Island has the broadest range of facilities as well as more frequent ferry routes.

Day 2: Duncan & the Cowichan Valley

Catch the morning **BC Ferries** (p. 113) run to Vancouver Island (from Salt Spring Island, take the Vesuvius/Crofton ferry) and travel north to **Duncan and the Cowichan Valley** (see chapter 6). This beautiful agricultural area is home to excellent wineries and organic farms and dairies. Just outside Duncan, the **Quw'utsun' Cultural Centre** (p. 138) preserves native Cowichan traditional ways of life, and downtown Duncan is studded with totem poles.

Days 3, 4 & 5: Tofino

From Duncan, drive north to Parksville and the junction with Hwy. 4. This road to Tofino and Vancouver Island's wild west coast is long and windy, so allow 3 hours to make the journey from Parksville. However, Tofino and the **Long Beach** portion of the Pacific Rim National Park (p. 162) are certainly worth the journey. Outfitters make it simple to get out onto calm and isolated bays on sea kayaks—a popular trip crosses a sound to visit a natural **hot springs** (p. 169). Rainforest **hikes,** deep-sea **fishing** trips, ocean **wildlife**-viewing tours, and lingering on the splendid sandy **beaches** are other options (p. 168).

Vancouver Island in 1 Week

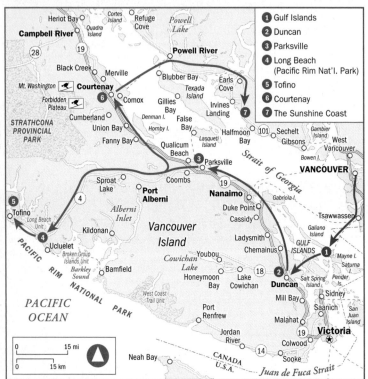

1 Gulf Islands
2 Duncan
3 Parksville
4 Long Beach (Pacific Rim Nat'l. Park)
5 Tofino
6 Courtenay
7 The Sunshine Coast

The B&Bs and lodges in Tofino, and less sophisticated Ucluelet, are first-rate. Many are nestled above remote beaches at the edge of the forest; others cling to rocky headlands. Some of Vancouver Island's most notable restaurants are here, and the local seafood is exquisite.

Day 6: Courtenay

Cross back to the east side of Vancouver Island from Tofino, but turn north at Parksville and drive up Hwy. 19 to the twin cities of **Courtenay** and **Comox** (see chapter 7). If you have kids in tow, consider signing them up for a fossil dig tour with the local museum; golfers might play a round on the excellent local course, while the eco-minded will relish a sunset kayak tour on the wildlife-rich Courtenay River estuary.

Day 7: Returning to Vancouver

The following day, cross from Comox via BC Ferries to the mainland and Powell River. Meander along the scenic **Sunshine Coast** (see chapter 9), before catching your final ferry across Howe Sound inlet to Horseshoe Bay, on Vancouver's north shore.

THE BEST OF VANCOUVER IN 1 DAY

This tour gives you an overview of what makes Vancouver so uniquely appealing. There are some places where you'll be exploring on foot, others where you'll drive to reach your destination. Nature, art, culture, and coffee are all part of today's itinerary. **Start:** Tourism Vancouver Visitor Centre, Burrard and Cordova streets.

1 Canada Place

Start your day outside, on the upper (deck) level of the city's giant **convention center** and **cruise-ship terminal** (p. 40), which juts out into Burrard Inlet across from the Tourism Vancouver Visitor Centre. From here you'll get a good sense of Vancouver's natural and urban topography, with the North Coast Mountains rising up before you; low-rise, historic Gastown to the east; Stanley Park to the west; and a forest of glass residential towers in between. Canada Place is busiest in summer, when up to four giant cruise ships may dock in 1 day.

2 Stanley Park ★★★

You can't really appreciate **Stanley Park** (p. 64) by driving through it in a car, so park your vehicle and head in on foot via Lagoon Drive. Surrounded by a famed pedestrian seawall, this giant peninsular park invites hours of exploration. A 1-hour carriage ride is the perfect way to see the highlights, including an amazing collection of totem poles, giant trees, and landscaped areas.

3 Vancouver Aquarium Marine Science Centre ★★

One of the best aquariums in North America is located right in Stanley Park. Have a look especially at the Arctic Canada exhibit with its beluga whales, and the Marine Mammal Deck, where you can see Pacific white-sided dolphins, sea otters, and other denizens of Pacific Northwest waters. See p. 65.

4 English Bay Beach ★★

If the weather is warm, take off your shoes and enjoy the grass, sand, and sunshine at English Bay Beach (p. 69), an all-season gathering spot on the south side of Stanley Park. You can pick up picnic eats or find takeout food on nearby Denman Street.

5 Robson Street & the West End

How you explore the West End is up to you. You can walk from English Bay Beach down Denman Street and then turn south on **Robson Street** (p. 75), taking in as much of the throbbing shopping and cafe scene as you want. It's also fun to explore the West End as a living neighborhood—the most densely populated in North America!

6 Caffè Artigiano ★★

For the best latte in town, as well as grilled Italian sandwiches and snacks, stop in at this busy cafe right across from the Vancouver Art Gallery. There's a perfect people-watching patio in front.

7 UBC Anthropology Museum ★★★

Hop in your car for the 20-minute drive to the outstanding **Museum of Anthropology at the University of British Columbia** (p. 66). Here, in one

The Best of Vancouver in 1 Day

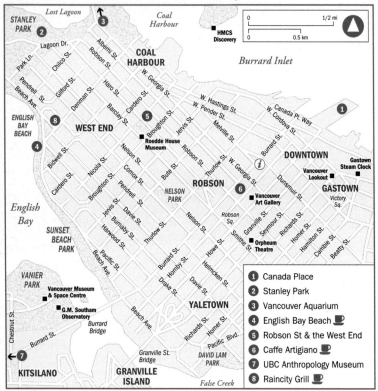

STANLEY PARK
Lost Lagoon
Coal Harbour
HMCS Discovery
Burrard Inlet

0   1/2 mi
0   0.5 km

Lagoon Dr.
Alberni St.
Robson St.
COAL HARBOUR
W. Georgia St.

Park Ln.
Chilco St.
Gilford St.
Denman St.
Haro St.
Cardero St.
Broughton St.
Jervis St.
W. Hastings St.
W. Pender St.
Melville St.
Canada Pl. Way
W. Cordova St.

Pendrell St.
Beach Ave.
ENGLISH BAY BEACH
WEST END
Barclay St.
Nelson St.
Roedde House Museum
Robson St.
Burrard St.

Bidwell St.
Cardero St.
Nicola St.
Broughton St.
Pendrell St.
Comox St.
Bute St.
Thurlow St.
W. Georgia St.
DOWNTOWN
Vancouver Lookout
Gastown Steam Clock

English Bay
Jervis St.
Davie St.
Thurlow St.
NELSON PARK
ROBSON
Nelson St.
Robson Sq.
Vancouver Art Gallery
GASTOWN
Victory Sq.
Dunsmuir St.

SUNSET BEACH PARK
Burnaby St.
Harwood St.
Beach Ave.
Pacific St.
Burrard St.
Hornby St.
Howe St.
Helmcken St.
Smithe St.
Granville St.
Seymour St.
Richards St.
Homer St.
Hamilton St.
Cambie St.
Beatty St.
Orpheum Theatre

VANIER PARK
Vancouver Museum & Space Centre
G.M. Southam Observatory
Burrard Bridge
Drake St.
Davie St.
Beach Ave.
YALETOWN
Richards St.
Homer St.

Chestnut St.
Burrard St.
Granville St. Bridge
DAVID LAM PARK
Pacific Blvd.

KITSILANO
GRANVILLE ISLAND
False Creek

1 Canada Place
2 Stanley Park
3 Vancouver Aquarium
4 English Bay Beach
5 Robson St & the West End
6 Caffe Artigiano
7 UBC Anthropology Museum
8 Raincity Grill

of North America's preeminent collections of First Nations Art, you'll encounter powerful totem poles, spirit masks, and totemic objects, all richly carved and profoundly mysterious.

8 Dinner

In the last decade, Vancouver has become one of the top dining cities in the world, filled with superb restaurants of all kinds. For a romantic dinner that will introduce you to the best of Vancouver's "eat local" food philosophy, reserve a table at **Raincity Grill,** where the windows overlook English Bay, and the regional cuisine is a perfect excuse to linger (p. 59).

THE BEST OF VICTORIA IN 1 DAY

Victoria is less than a quarter of the size of Vancouver, and you can easily hit the highlights in 1 day if you arrive on an early ferry. The scenic ferry ride—from Vancouver, Seattle, Anacortes, or Port Angeles—is part of the fun. Although Victoria's compact

The Best of Victoria in 1 Day

Map legend:
1. Inner Harbour
2. Royal B.C. Museum
3. Fairmont Empress
4. Butchart Gardens
5. Il Terrazzo Ristorante

Information ⓘ

core makes it easy to experience on foot, by bike, and via public transportation, having a car will help to maximize your sightseeing further afield.

1 Inner Harbour

Victoria's official facade, epitomized by a pair of landmark buildings designed by Francis Rattenbury, is reminiscent of an era that promoted the idea of a British Empire. A stroll along the Inner Harbour takes you past the **Provincial Legislature** , a massive stone edifice completed in 1898, and the famous Fairmont Empress Hotel, which dates from 1908 (p. 100 and p. 90, respectively). Along the busy waterfront you'll also find information on whale-watching excursions (p. 105), a popular Victoria pastime.

2 Royal British Columbia Museum ★★★

The highlight of this excellent museum (p. 100) is the First Peoples Gallery, an absorbing and thought-provoking showplace of First Nations art and culture. The Victorian-era streetscape feels very authentic, and the life-size wooly mammoth is a peek into the Ice Age. You can easily spend 3 hours here—more if you see an IMAX show.

3 The Fairmont Empress ★★

Tea at the Empress (p. 96) is a traditional affair that has remained a real treat despite its fame (and expense). Make it your main meal of the day (seatings at 12:30, 2, 2:30, and 5pm), and be sure to reserve in advance.

4 Butchart Gardens ★★★

This century-old garden (p. 98) is one of the gardening wonders of the world, meticulously planned and impeccably maintained. Though hordes of tourists can jam the paths in the summer months, time your visit for late afternoon and you'll have more room; plus you can stay for the fabulous summer fireworks display. This is also an excellent spot to have afternoon tea—less expensive than at the Empress, and sitting in their Dining Room is just lovely. The thing to do is head there upon arrival to claim a reservation time; then wander the gardens and turn up at your appointed time. Regular shuttles leave from Victoria, and include stops at the Butterfly Garden (p. 100).

5 Dinner

If there's time, have dinner at **Il Terrazzo Ristorante** (p. 95). Victoria's best Italian restaurant serves delicious, northern-Italian dishes and has a lovely patio for outdoor, summertime dining.

VANCOUVER

by Chloë Ernst

The setting is majestic and the city exciting, so it's no wonder that Vancouver lures visitors from around the globe. The rest of the world has taken notice of the blessed life people in these parts lead, and surveys often list Vancouver as one of the 10 best cities in the world to live in. It's also one of the 10 best to visit. In the *Condé Nast* Traveler Readers' Choice Awards, Vancouver has reigned often, including as the 2010 "Best City in the Americas."

In 2010, Vancouver hosted the 2010 Olympic and Paralympic Winter Games, showcasing its surrounding mountains and serene setting. Heady stuff for a spot that only about 25 years ago, before Expo '86—which added icons such as Canada Place, Science World, and the SkyTrain—was routinely derided as the world's biggest mill town.

ESSENTIALS
Getting There
BY PLANE
Daily direct flights between major U.S. cities and Vancouver are offered by **Air Canada** (© 888/247-2262; www.aircanada.com), **Alaska Airlines** (© 800/252-7522; www.alaskaair.com), **American Airlines** (© 800/433-7300; www.aa.com), **Continental** (© 800/231-0856; www.continental.com), **Frontier Airlines** (© 800/432-1359; www.frontierairlines.com), **Delta** (© 800/225-2525; www.delta.com), and **United Airlines** (© 800/538-2929; www.united.com).

GETTING INTO TOWN FROM THE AIRPORT   Vancouver International Airport (YVR; © **604/207-7077;** www.yvr.ca) is 14km (8⅔ miles) south of downtown.

Two Tourist Information Centres are located in the airport's arrivals areas: the information center on Level 2 of the Domestic terminal is open daily from 8:30am to 9:30pm, while the desk on Level 2 of the International terminal is open 24 hours. The easiest, fastest, and cheapest way to get into Vancouver from the airport is by the new Canada Line, which opened in late 2009 and is operated by Translink (© **604/953-3333;** www.translink.ca). The train zips into Vancouver in 26 minutes, stopping at stations in Yaletown, City Centre (downtown), and Waterfront (the SeaBus Terminal, near the Canada Place cruise-ship terminal). Prices for the Canada Line run from C$2.50 to C$3.75 (depending on time of day and the number of zones you travel). However, an additional C$5 surcharge will be tacked on to the single fare price when you travel from the airport to downtown Vancouver (this surcharge does not apply to return trips to the airport). A DayPass (C$9), which you can purchase from any authorized FareDealer location at the airport, might be a better alternative if you plan on doing any sightseeing the same day you fly in.

Aeroshuttle (℃ **877/921-9021** or 604/299-4444; www.aeroshuttleyvr.ca) provides **airport shuttle bus service** from both the Domestic and International terminals to downtown hotels on two loops: one through Yaletown and downtown, the other through downtown and the West End. Shuttles for each route leave the airport hourly from 8am to 8pm from May to September, 8am to 7pm October to April. Buses pick up passengers at downtown hotels from about 5am to 5pm from May to September, 6am to 5pm October to April. Check with your hotel or the shuttle website for an exact schedule. The trip takes 60–75 minutes, depending on the pick up location, and costs C$14 for adults and C$8.40 children 12 and over. Round-trip discounts available. Major credit cards and cash accepted, and you can purchase tickets from the driver.

The average **taxi** fare from the airport to a downtown Vancouver hotel is approximately C$30 plus tip, but the fare can run up to C$40 if the cab gets stuck in traffic. **Aerocar Service** (℃ **888/821-0021** or 604/298-1000; www.aerocar.ca) provides flat-rate sedan or stretch-limousine service from the airport, and fares are quoted based on destination. Sedan service runs C$43 per trip to downtown and C$52 to Canada Place, plus taxes and tip. Limousine service for up to six passengers costs C$50 to downtown and C$63 to Canada Place. Rates also available for groups of up to eight passengers. Look for Aerocars in front of the terminal; drivers accept cash or major credit cards.

Although no longer the official limousine provider at the airport, **LimoJet** (℃ **604-273-1331;** www.limojetgold.com) offers transport to downtown and other points. Meet-and-greet service at the arrivals area, plus transportation to downtown, costs C$75 per trip (not per person) to the airport from any downtown location, plus tax and tip, for up to three people (C$80 for up to six passengers).

Most major **car-rental firms** have airport counters and shuttles. Drivers heading into Vancouver from the airport should take the Arthur Laing Bridge, which leads directly to Granville Street, the most direct route to downtown.

BY SHIP & FERRY

Vancouver is the major embarkation point for cruises going up British Columbia's Inland Passage to Alaska. In the summer, up to four cruise ships a day berth at **Canada Place** cruise-ship terminal (℃ **604/665-9000;** www.portmetrovancouver.com). Public transit buses and taxis greet new arrivals, but you can also easily walk to many major hotels.

If you're arriving from Vancouver Island or Victoria, **BC Ferries** (℃ **888/223-3779** or 250/386-3431; www.bcferries.com) has three routes with daily sailings.

BY TRAIN & BUS

BY TRAIN   **VIA Rail Canada,** 1150 Station St., Vancouver (℃ **888/842-7245;** www.viarail.ca), has routes across the country. For travel within Canada, the **Canrailpass** offering 7 one-way trips within 21 days on any VIA routes (C$606 off-peak; C$969 peak) is available through www.viarail.com.

4

Essentials

VANCOUVER

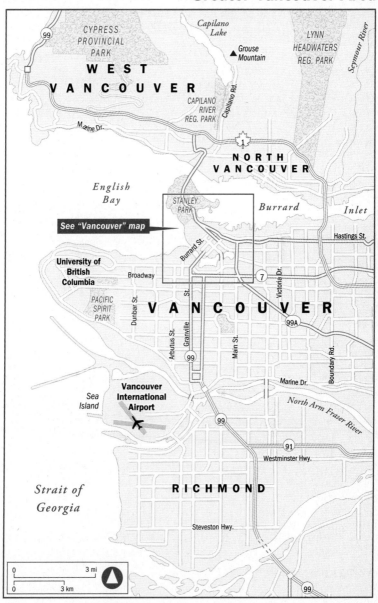

CYPRESS
PROVINCIAL
PARK

Capilano
Lake

LYNN
HEADWATERS
REG. PARK

Seymour River

**WEST
VANCOUVER**

▲ Grouse
Mountain

CAPILANO
RIVER
REG. PARK

Capilano Rd.

Marine Dr.

**NORTH
VANCOUVER**

English
Bay

STANLEY
PARK

Burrard

Inlet

See "Vancouver" map

Burrard St.

Hastings St.

**University of
British
Columbia**

Broadway

7

Victoria Dr.

PACIFIC
SPIRIT
PARK

VANCOUVER

Dunbar St.

99A

Arbutus St.

Granville St.

Main St.

Boundary Rd.

99

Sea
Island

**Vancouver
International
Airport**

Marine Dr.

North Arm Fraser River

99

91

Westminster Hwy.

Strait of
Georgia

RICHMOND

Steveston Hwy.

0   3 mi

0   3 km

99

Vancouver

HOTELS ■
Blue Horizon **17**
Buchan Hotel **10**
The Burrard **43**
The Fairmont Hotel Vancouver **21**
Fairmont Pacific Rim **25**
Four Seasons Hotel **27**
Georgian Court Hotel **30**
Granville Island Hotel **48**
Hostelling International Vancouver
  Downtown Hostel **44**
Hostelling International Vancouver
  Jericho Beach **57**
The Kingston Hotel **29**
The Listel Hotel **16**
Opus Hotel **38**
Pan Pacific Vancouver **26**
Rosewood Hotel Georgia **23**
St. Regis Hotel **28**
Sunset Inn & Suites **45**
The University of British Columbia
  Conference Centre **57**
West End Guest House **13**
Westin Bayshore Resort & Marina **9**
YWCA Hotel/Residence **31**

STANLEY PARK

Stanley Park Dr.

Lost Lagoon Dr.

Lost Lagoon

Coal
Harbour

Stanley Park Dr.

Devonian
Harbour
Park

Lost Lagoon Dr.

Park Ln.

Chilco St.

Georgia St.

Pender St.

Gilford St.

Denman St.

Haro St.

Robson St.

Alberni St.

English Bay
Beach Park

Barclay St.

Cardero St.

Nicola St.

Bute St.

Davie St.

Bidwell St.

Beach Ave.

Pendrell St.

Comox St.

Jervis St.

Nelson St.

Inukshuk

Broughton St.

Burnaby St.

WEST
END

Nelson
Park

Thurlow St.

Sunset
Beach Park

Harwood St.

Burrard St.

Hornby St.

Helmcken St.

Pacific St.

Howe St.

Beach Ave.

Drake St.

Hadden
Park

Ogden Ave.

Vanier
Park

McNicoll Ave.

Whyte Ave.

Chestnut St.

**Kits
Beach**

Creelman Ave.

Kitsilano
Beach
Park

Cornwall Ave.

Laburnum St.

Walnut St.

Granville St.

George
Wainborn
Park

York Ave.

Maple St.

GRANVILLE
ISLAND

Johnston St.

W 2nd Ave.

Burrard St.

Old Bridge St.

Cartwright St.

False

W 3rd Ave.

Fir St.

Sutcliffe Park

Arbutus St.

Cypress St.

Pine St.

W 4th Ave.

Lamey's Mill Rd.

KITSILANO

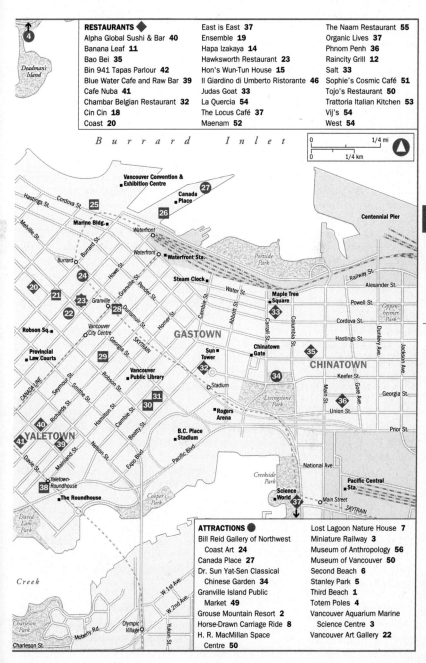

RESTAURANTS ◆
Alpha Global Sushi & Bar **40**
Banana Leaf **11**
Bao Bei **35**
Bin 941 Tapas Parlour **42**
Blue Water Cafe and Raw Bar **39**
Cafe Nuba **41**
Chambar Belgian Restaurant **32**
Cin Cin **18**
Coast **20**

East is East **37**
Ensemble **19**
Hapa Izakaya **14**
Hawksworth Restaurant **23**
Hon's Wun-Tun House **15**
Il Giardino di Umberto Ristorante **46**
Judas Goat **33**
La Quercia **54**
The Locus Café **37**
Maenam **52**

The Naam Restaurant **55**
Organic Lives **37**
Phnom Penh **36**
Raincity Grill **12**
Salt **33**
Sophie's Cosmic Café **51**
Tojo's Restaurant **50**
Trattoria Italian Kitchen **53**
Vij's **54**
West **54**

B u r r a r d   I n l e t

0 ——————— 1/4 mi
0 ——————— 1/4 km

ATTRACTIONS ●
Bill Reid Gallery of Northwest
    Coast Art **24**
Canada Place **27**
Dr. Sun Yat-Sen Classical
    Chinese Garden **34**
Granville Island Public
    Market **49**
Grouse Mountain Resort **2**
Horse-Drawn Carriage Ride **8**
H. R. MacMillan Space
    Centre **50**

Lost Lagoon Nature House **7**
Miniature Railway **3**
Museum of Anthropology **56**
Museum of Vancouver **50**
Second Beach **6**
Stanley Park **5**
Third Beach **1**
Totem Poles **4**
Vancouver Aquarium Marine
    Science Centre **3**
Vancouver Art Gallery **22**

Amtrak (© **800/872-7245;** www.amtrak.com) offers service from Seattle, with two trains daily (departing Seattle 7:40am and 6:50pm, arriving Vancouver 11:40am and 10:50pm); otherwise, the Seattle–Vancouver route is covered by an Amtrak bus.

BY BUS Greyhound Canada (© **800/231-2222** or 604/661-0328; www.greyhound.ca) offers daily bus service between Vancouver and all major Canadian cities, and between Vancouver and Seattle (at the border crossing, passengers disembark the bus and take their luggage through Customs). For information on Greyhound's cost-cutting Discovery Pass, which allows for unlimited travel in the U.S. and Canada, consult their website.

BY CAR

You'll probably be driving into Vancouver along one of two routes. **U.S. I-5** from Seattle becomes **Hwy. 99** when you cross the border at the Peace Arch. The 210km (130-mile) drive from Seattle takes about 2½ hours when there is no wait at the border. On the Canadian side of the 49th parallel, you'll drive through the cities of White Rock, Delta, and Richmond, pass under the Fraser River through the George Massey Tunnel, and cross the Oak Street Bridge. The highway ends there and becomes Oak Street, a busy urban thoroughfare heading toward downtown. Turn left at the first convenient major arterial (70th, 57th, 49th, 41st, 33rd, 16th, and 12th aves. will all serve) and proceed until you hit the next major street, which will be Granville Street. Turn right on Granville Street. This street heads directly into downtown Vancouver via the Granville Street Bridge.

Trans-Canada Hwy. 1 is a limited-access freeway that runs to Vancouver's eastern boundary, where it crosses the Second Narrows Bridge to North Vancouver. When traveling on Hwy. 1 from the east, exit at Cassiar Street and turn left at the first light onto Hastings Street (Hwy. 7A), which is adjacent to Exhibition Park. Follow Hastings Street 6.4km (4 miles) into downtown. When coming to Vancouver from parts north, take exit 13 (the sign says TAYLOR WAY, BRIDGE TO VANCOUVER) and cross the Lions Gate Bridge into Vancouver's West End.

Visitor Information

The **Tourism Vancouver Visitor Centre,** 200 Burrard St., Plaza Level (© **604/683-2000;** www.tourismvancouver.com), has an incredibly helpful and well-trained staff who are able to provide information, maps, and brochures, and can help you with all your travel needs, including hotel, cruise-ship, ferry, bus, and train reservations.

The free weekly tabloid the **Georgia Straight** (© 604/730-7000; www.straight.com), found in cafes, bookshops, and restaurants, provides up-to-date schedules of concerts, lectures, art exhibits, plays, recitals, and other happenings. Not free but equally good—and with more attitude—is the glossy city magazine **Vancouver** (© **604/877-7732;** www.vanmag.com), available on newsstands. The free guide called **Where Vancouver** (© 604/736-5586; www.where.ca) is available in many hotels and lists attractions, entertainment, upscale shopping, and fine dining. It also has good maps.

City Layout

With four different bodies of water lapping at its edges and miles of shoreline, Vancouver's geography can seem a bit complicated. **Downtown Vancouver** is on a peninsula: Think of it as an upraised thumb on the mitten-shaped Vancouver mainland. **Stanley Park,** the **West End, Yaletown,** and Vancouver's business and financial center (downtown) are located on this thumb of land bordered to the north by Burrard Inlet, the city's main deepwater harbor and port, to the west by English Bay, and to the south by False Creek. Farther west beyond English Bay is the Strait of Georgia, part of the Pacific Ocean. Just south across False Creek is **Granville Island,** famous for its public market, and the beach community of **Kitsilano.** This part of the city, called the **West Side,** covers the mainland, or the hand of the mitten. Its western shoreline looks out on the Strait of Georgia with the Pacific beyond, and the north arm of the Fraser River demarcates it to the south. Pacific Spirit Park and the University of British Columbia (UBC), a locus for visitors because of its outstanding Museum of Anthropology, take up most of the western tip of the West Side; the rest is mostly residential, with a sprinkling of businesses along main arterial streets. Both the mainland and peninsula are covered by a simple rectilinear street pattern. **North Vancouver** is the mountain-backed area across Burrard Inlet from downtown.

GETTING AROUND
By Public Transportation

Vancouver's public transportation system is the most extensive in Canada and includes service to all major tourist attractions, so it's not really necessary to have a car (especially if you're staying in the downtown area).

Translink (*©* **604/953-3333;** www.translink.ca) operates electric trolley buses, diesel buses, the SeaBus catamaran ferry, and the light-rail SkyTrain. It's an ecologically friendly, highly reliable, inexpensive system that allows you to get everywhere, including the beaches and ski slopes. Regular service runs from about 6am to 2am.

Schedules and routes are available online, at tourist information centers, at many major hotels, and on buses. Fares are based on the number of zones traveled, and are the same for buses, the SeaBus, and the SkyTrain. One ticket allows you to transfer from one mode of transport to another, in any direction, within 90 minutes. A one-way, one-zone fare (everything in central Vancouver) costs C$2.50. A two-zone fare—C$3.75—is required to travel to the airport or to nearby suburbs such as Richmond or North Vancouver, and a three-zone fare—C$5—is required for travel to the far-off city of Surrey. After 6:30pm on weekdays and all day on weekends and holidays, you can travel anywhere in all three zones for C$2.50. **DayPasses,** good on all public transit, cost C$9 for adults and C$7 for seniors, students, and children. They can be used for unlimited travel on weekdays or weekends and holidays.

Tip: Keep in mind that drivers do not make change, so you need the exact fare or a valid transit pass. Pay with cash or buy tickets and passes from ticket machines at stations, tourist information centers, both SeaBus terminals, and convenience stores, drugstores, and outlets displaying the FAREDEALER sign; most of these outlets also have transit maps showing all routes.

BY BUS Both diesel and electric-trolley buses service the city. Regular service on the busiest routes is about every 5-15 minutes from about 6am to 2am. Wheelchair-accessible buses and bus stops are identified by the international wheelchair symbol. Some key routes to keep in mind if you're touring the city by bus: **no. 5** (Robson St.), **no. 6** (Davie Street), **no. 10** (Granville Street), **no. 4** (UBC), **no. 2** (Kitsilano Beach to downtown), **no. 50** (Granville Island), **no. 19** (Stanley Park), **no. 240** (North Vancouver), and bus **no. 250** (West Vancouver–Horseshoe Bay).

BY SKYTRAIN   The SkyTrain is a fast, light-rail service between downtown Vancouver and the suburbs. The **Expo Line** trains operate from Waterfront to King George station, running along a scenic 27km (17-mile) route from downtown Vancouver east to Surrey through Burnaby and New Westminster in 39 minutes. There are 20 stations along this route; three downtown stations are underground and marked at street level. The **Millennium Line,** which opened in fall 2002, makes the same stops from Waterfront to Columbia, then branches to Sapperton, Braid, Lougheed town center, and loops back to Commercial Drive. All stations are wheelchair accessible; trains arrive every 2 to 5 minutes. **Canada Line,** the newest SkyTrain, began operating in October 2009, and links the Vancouver Airport to Yaletown, City Centre, and Waterfront Station (SeaBus terminal).

BY SEABUS   Catamaran ferries take passengers, cyclists, and wheelchair riders on a scenic 12-minute commute across Burrard Inlet between downtown's Waterfront Station and North Vancouver's Lonsdale Quay. On weekdays, a SeaBus leaves Waterfront Station every 15 minutes from 6:16am to 6:46pm, then every 30 minutes until 12:46am. SeaBuses depart Waterfront Station on Saturdays every half-hour from 6:16am to 10:16am, then every 15 minutes until 6:46pm, and then every half-hour until 12:46am. On Sundays and holidays, runs depart downtown every half-hour from 8:16am to 11:16am, every 15 minutes until 6:46pm, and finally every 30 minutes until 11:16pm. If catching the SeaBus from Lonsdale, all times are 14 minutes earlier than departure times from Waterfront Station. A lot to keep straight? Thankfully there's a countdown clock in each terminal that lets you know how long you'll wait until the next crossing. Note that the crossing is a two-zone fare on weekdays until 6:30pm.

By Taxi

Cab fares start at C$3.30 and increase at a rate of C$1.89 per kilometer. In the downtown area, you can expect to travel for less than C$12 plus tip. The typical fare for the 13km (8-mile) drive from downtown to the airport is C$30 to C$40.

Taxis are easy to find in front of major hotels, but flagging one down can be tricky. Call for a pickup from **Black Top** (© 604/731-1111), **Yellow Cab** (© 604/681-1111), or **MacLure's** (© 604/731-9211).

By Car

If you're just sightseeing around town, public transit and cabs will easily see you through. However, if you're planning to visit the North Shore Mountains or pursue other out-of-town activities, a car is necessary. Car insurance is compulsory in British Columbia. *Note:* The speed limit in Vancouver is 50kmph (31 mph); highway speed limits vary from 90 to 110kmph (56–68 mph).

All major downtown hotels have guest parking, either in-house or at nearby lots. Valet secure parking at most hotels costs about C$25 per day, plus taxes. Public parking is found at **Robson Square** (enter at Smithe and Howe sts.), **Pacific Centre** (Howe and Dunsmuir sts.), and **The Bay** department store (Seymour near Dunsmuir St.). You'll also find larger **parking lots** at the intersections of Thurlow and Georgia, Thurlow and Alberni, and Robson and Seymour streets.

Street meters accept C$2 and C$1 coins, as well as smaller change. Rules are posted and strictly enforced; generally, downtown and in the West End, metered parking is in effect 7 days a week from 9am to 10pm. (*Note:* Drivers are given about a 2-min. grace period before their cars are towed away when the 3pm no-parking rule goes into effect on many major thoroughfares.) Unmetered parking on side streets is often subject to neighborhood residency requirements: Check the signs. If you park in such an area without the appropriate sticker on your windshield, you'll get ticketed and towed. If your car is towed away or you need a towing service and aren't a CAA or an AAA member, call **Unitow** (© **604/251-1255**) or **Busters** (© **604/685-8181**). If you are parking on the street, remove all valuables from your car; break-ins are not uncommon.

By Bike

Vancouver is a biker's paradise. Along Robson and Denman streets near Stanley Park are plenty of places to rent bikes. (For specifics, see p. 70.) Paved paths crisscross through parks and along beaches. Helmets are mandatory, and riding on sidewalks is illegal except on designated bike paths. You can take your bike on the SeaBus anytime at no extra charge. Bikes are not allowed in the George Massey Tunnel, but a tunnel shuttle operates 10 times daily from May to mid-October and about 6 times daily the rest of the year to transport you across the Fraser River. All of the West Vancouver blue buses (including the bus to the Horseshoe Bay ferry terminal) can carry two bikes, first-come, first-served, free of charge.

By Miniferry

Crossing False Creek to Granville Island or beautiful Vanier Park on one of the zippy little miniferries is cheap and fun. These small, covered boats connect various points of interest; they are privately operated, so your public transit pass or ticket is not valid. It's well worth the extra money, though.

The **Aquabus** (© **604/689-5858;** www.theaquabus.com) docks at the south foot of Hornby Street, the Public Market on Granville Island, David Lam Park, Stamp's Landing, Yaletown at Davie Street, Plaza of Nations and Science World. Ferries operate daily from about 7am to 10:30pm (9:30pm in winter) and run every 3 to 15 minutes or so, but schedules change monthly. One-way fares are C$3.25 to C$6.50 for adults and C$1.75 to C$3.50 for seniors and children. A day pass is C$14 for adults and C$8 for seniors and children. You can take a 25-minute scenic boat ride (one complete circuit) for C$7 adults, C$4 seniors and children.

False Creek Ferries (© **604/684-7781;** www.granvilleislandferries.bc.ca) runs a similar route, stopping at the Maritime Museum, Aquatic Centre, Granville Island, David Lam Park, Yaletown, Stamp's Landing, Science World, and Plaza of Nations. Most routes run from about 9am to 8pm, depending on the leg and season. One-way fares are C$3to C$6 for adults and C$1.50 to C$2 for seniors and children.

[FastFACTS] VANCOUVER

Business Hours
Vancouver **banks** are open Monday through Thursday from 10am to 5pm and Friday from 10am to 6pm. Some banks, like TD Canada Trust, are also open on Saturday. **Stores** are generally open Monday through

Saturday from 10am to 6pm. Last call at most **restaurant bars** and **cocktail lounges** is between midnight and 2am.

Child Care If you need to rent cribs, car seats, playpens, or other baby accessories, **Wee Travel**

(© **604/222-4722;** www. weetravel.ca) delivers them right to your hotel or the airport.

Dentists Most major hotels have a dentist on call. **Vancouver Centre Dental Clinic,** Vancouver Centre Mall, 11-650

W. Georgia St. (☏ **604/682-1601**), is another option. You must make an appointment. The clinic is open Monday to Thursday 8:30am to 5pm (Wed until 6pm) and Friday 8:30am to 2pm.

Doctors Hotels usually have a doctor on call. **Ultima Medicentre,** Bentall Centre, 1055 Dunsmuir St. (☏ **604/683-8138**), is a drop-in clinic open Monday through Friday 8am to 5pm. Another drop-in medical center, **Care Point Medical Centre Walk-in Clinic,** 1175 Denman St. (☏ **604/681-5338**), is open Monday through Wednesday 8:30am to 9pm, Thursday to Saturday from 9am to 9pm, and Sunday 9am to 8pm. See also "Hotlines," below.

Hospitals **St. Paul's Hospital,** 1081 Burrard St. (☏ **604/682-2344**), is the closest facility to downtown and the West End. West Side Vancouver hospitals include **Vancouver General Hospital Health and Sciences Centre,** 855 W. 12th Ave. (☏ **604/875-4111**), and **BC Children's and Women's Hospital,** 4480 Oak St. (☏ **604/875-2345**). In North Vancouver, there's **Lions Gate Hospital,** 231 E. 15th St. (☏ **604/988-3131**).

Internet Access Free Internet access is available at the Vancouver **Public Library** Central Branch, 350 W. Georgia St. (☏ **604/331-3600**). **Internet Cafe** (616 Seymour St.; ☏ **604/681-1088**) charges C$2.50 for 30 minutes and is open until 10pm.

Laundry & Dry Cleaning **Westend Laundry,** 1061 Davie St. (☏ **604/682-2717**), offers self-service, drop-off service, and dry cleaning. **Swan Laundry** (1352 Burrard St.; ☏ **604/684-0323**; www.swan laundry.com) is unmissable with its bubblegum pink window and is open daily. Also, almost all hotels have laundry service.

Luggage Storage & Lockers Lockers are available at the main Vancouver railway station (which is also the main bus depot), **Pacific Central Station,** 1150 Station St., near Main Street and Terminal Avenue south of Chinatown (☏ **604/661-0328**).

Newspapers & Magazines The two local papers are the **Vancouver Sun** (www.vancouversun. com), published Monday through Saturday, and the **Province** (www.theprovince. com), published Sunday

through Friday mornings. The free weekly entertainment paper, the **Georgia Straight** (www.straight. com), comes out on Thursday, as does the **West Ender** (www. westender.com).

Pharmacies **Shopper's Drug Mart,** 1125 Davie St. (☏ **604/669-2424**), is open 24 hours. Several Safeway supermarket pharmacies are open late; the one on Robson and Denman is open until midnight.

Police For emergencies, dial ☏ **911.** This is a free call. Otherwise, the **Vancouver City Police** can be reached at ☏ **604/717-3535.**

Post Office The **main post office,** 349 W. Georgia St. at Homer Street (☏ **866/607-6301**), is open Monday through Friday from 9am to 5:30pm. You'll also find post office outlets in most Shopper's Drug Mart and some 7-Eleven stores with longer opening hours.

Weather Call ☏ **604/664-9010** for weather updates. Each local ski resort has its own snow report line: **Cypress Mountain** ☏ **604/419-7669; Whistler/Blackcomb** ☏ **604/687-7507.**

WHERE TO STAY

Most of Vancouver's hotels are in the downtown area or the West End. Central Vancouver is small and easily walkable, so in both of these neighborhoods you'll be close to major sights, services, and nightlife.

Quoted prices don't include the 12% **harmonized sales tax** and a 2% Vancouver **hotel room tax.** In spring 2013, British Columbia is expected to move back to its old tax system, which was formerly 5% goods and service tax, 8% provincial sales tax, and 2% hotel room tax. I list the rack rates, the rates you would receive if you walked in off the street and requested a room. By checking the hotel's website, you'll almost always find lower rates, including special "romance packages" and weekend-getaway specials. The highest listed price is for high season (mid-June to Sept).

Bus and/or public transportation information is given only for those hotels listed below that are outside of the Vancouver city center.

If you prefer to stay in a B&B, the **BC Bed & Breakfast Innkeepers Guild** (www.bcsbestbnbs.com) has listings of its members throughout the province. Online listings include a description, contact details, photos, and pricing.

Downtown & Yaletown
VERY EXPENSIVE
The Fairmont Hotel Vancouver ★★ ☺

A landmark in the city since Queen Elizabeth first opened the property in 1939, the Fairmont Hotel has been brought up to 21st-century standards but retains its traditional, old-fashioned elegance, like the trunk-sized closets. The rooms are spacious, quiet, and comfortable. The bathrooms (with tub/shower combinations) look a bit dated when compared with those at other downtown hotels in this price range, but that's part of the rich heritage charm. Courtyard suites feature a luxuriously furnished living room, separated from the bedroom by French doors. Guests can use the state-of-the-art gym with heated indoor pool. The hotel is family friendly and even has two resident dogs (former Seeing Eye dogs) that can be taken out for walks.

900 W. Georgia St., Vancouver, BC V6C 2W6. www.fairmont.com/hotelvancouver. © **866/540-4452** or 604/684-3131. Fax 604/662-1929. 556 units. C$180–C$410 double. Children 18 and under stay free in parent's room. AE, DC, DISC, MC, V. Parking C$43 (includes taxes). **Amenities:** 2 restaurants; bar; babysitting; concierge; executive-level rooms; health club; Jacuzzi; indoor pool; room service; sauna; rooms for those w/limited mobility; rooms for hearing-impaired guests. *In room:* A/C, TV w/pay movies, hair dryer, high-speed Internet (paid), minibar.

Fairmont Pacific Rim ★★★

Fairmont's newest Vancouver property is a real show-stopper. Located across from the new addition to the Canada Place Convention Centre, the Pacific Rim is luxurious and up-to-date, with all the amenities you could possibly want. The rooms—many of which have water views—are beautifully designed, especially the 18 suites with freestanding Japanese-style soaking tubs that look out over Burrard Inlet and the North Shore mountains. For families or sun lovers, book a Pool View room where the balcony opens up onto the rooftop pool deck. Dining options include Giovane, the hotel's Italian-inspired, local-focused cafe/bakery/deli, and Oru, a pan-Asian bistro. The signature Willow Stream Spa offers a complete menu or pampering treatments.

1038 Canada Place Way, Vancouver, BC V6C 0B9. www.fairmont.com/pacificrim. © **877/900-5350** or 604/695-5300. Fax 604/695-5301. 377 units. C$300–C$450 double; C$400–C$7,500 suite. Children 18 and under stay free in parent's room. AE, DC, DISC, MC, V. Valet or self-parking C$43 (incl. taxes). SkyTrain: Waterfront Station. **Amenities:** Restaurant; cafe/deli; bar; babysitting; concierge; executive-level rooms; health club; Jacuzzi; outdoor pool; room service; sauna; spa. *In room:* A/C, TV w/pay movies, DVD player, hair dryer, Internet (paid), minibar.

Opus Hotel ★★★

If you want to stay in a hip, happening, luxury hotel, try Opus—various reader polls have voted it one of the world's top hotels. It's the only hotel truly in Yaletown, the trendiest area for shopping and lounges. Each room is furnished according to one of five "personalities," with its own layout, color, and flavor—the luscious room colors are eye candy if you're tired of blah hotel interiors.

Heated-floor bathrooms are fitted with high-design sinks, soaker tubs, or roomy showers (or both). The cool Opus Bar serves an international tapas menu, and on weekends it becomes one of Yaletown's see-and-be-seen scenes. (Be forewarned: This area of Yaletown is "club central" and can be noisy until the wee hours; book a Courtyard Room if you don't want to be disturbed.)

322 Davie St., Vancouver, BC V6B 5Z6. www.opushotel.com. © **866/642-6787** or 604/642-6787. Fax 604/642-6780. 96 units. May–Oct C$360–C$550 double, C$815 and up suite; Nov–Apr C$230–C$430 double, C$740 and up suite. Children 17 and under stay free in parent's room. AE, DC, MC, V. Valet parking C$29. **Amenities:** Restaurant; bar; bikes; concierge; small exercise room; room service. *In room:* A/C, TV w/pay movies, hair dryer, minibar, Wi-Fi (paid).

Pan Pacific Vancouver ★★   This 23-story luxury hotel atop Canada Place is a key landmark on the Vancouver waterfront. Despite its size, the hotel excels in comfort and service, and it provides spectacular views of the North Shore Mountains, Burrard Inlet, and cruise ships arriving and departing from the terminal below. The rooms are spacious and comfortable, with contemporary furnishings and a soothing color palette. Bathrooms are large and luxurious. Guests have use of a heated outdoor pool and Jacuzzi overlooking the harbor. Spa Utopia offers a full array of pampering treatments.

300-999 Canada Place, Vancouver, BC V6C 3B5. www.panpacific.com/vancouver. © **800/937-1515** in the U.S., 800/663-1515 in Canada, or 604/662-8111. Fax 604/685-8690. www.panpacific. com. 504 units. May–Oct C$540–C$640 double; C$700–C$5,000 suite; Nov–Apr C$410–C$480 double, C$520 and up suite. AE, DC, DISC, MC, V. Valet parking C$30. **Amenities:** 2 restaurants; bar; babysitting; concierge; health club; Jacuzzi; outdoor heated pool; room service; sauna; spa. *In room:* A/C, TV w/pay movies, hair dryer, high-speed Internet (paid), minibar.

Rosewood Hotel Georgia ★★★   From its original layout to the renovated hotel that opened in mid-2011, the 1927 Hotel Georgia has halved its number of rooms and created roomier suites, multiple restaurants, and a saltwater pool. The design elements—tones of ivory, taupe, and chocolate brown—are unimposing, allowing the comforts of the space and the vast collection of Canadian art to stand-out. Bathrooms are exceptional, each with a separate tub and shower, heated floors, and double vanities. For the best views, request a southeast exposure to overlook the Vancouver Art Gallery. On-site you'll find a basement bar called **Prohibition,** buzzing lobby lounge **1927,** and inventive dining at street-level **Hawksworth Restaurant** (p. 56).

801 West Georgia St., Vancouver, BC, V6C 1P7. www.rosewoodhotelgeorgia.com. © **888/767-3966** or 604/682-5566. 155 units. July–Oct from $375 double; Nov–June from $295 double. AE, MC, V. Valet parking. **Amenities:** 3 restaurants; lounge; bar; babysitting; concierge; fitness center; indoor pool; room service; sauna; spa. *In room:* A/C, TV, DVD, hair dryer, minibar, MP3 docking station, Wi-Fi (free).

MODERATE

The Burrard ★   The Burrard has hinged its vibe of a 1956 motor inn into a hip hotel. Being right downtown makes it wonderfully convenient to clubs on Granville Street and dining in the West End. Besides replanting the spectacular inner courtyard that all the motel-like units face, a gutting renovation has brought a fun freshness to the inn. Gone are the pink tubs, instead replaced with white enamel and tiling, Moroccan ottomans, and triple-sheeting. Double-glazed windows have minimized traffic noise from busy Burrard Street, but it may still be best to request a room on the alley-side.

1100 Burrard St, Vancouver, BC, V6Z 1Y9. www.burrardinn.com. ✆ **800/663-0366** or 604/681-2331. 72 units. C$186–C$206 double. AE, MC, V. Parking C$20. **Amenities:** Bicycles; courtyard garden; access to nearby fitness club. *In-room:* A/C (portable units), TV w/movie channels, fridge, hair dryer, Internet (free), MP3 docking station.

Georgian Court Hotel ★ 🍴 This modern, 14-story brick hotel is extremely well located, just a block or two from B.C. Place Stadium, Rogers Arena, the Queen Elizabeth Theatre, the Playhouse, and the Vancouver Public Library. You can walk to Robson Square in about 10 minutes. The guest rooms are relatively large, nicely decorated, and have good-size bathrooms. And while the big-time celebs are usually whisked off to the glamorous top hotels, their entourages often stay at the Georgian Court, as it provides all the amenities and business-friendly extras such as two phones in every room, brightly lit desks, and complimentary high-speed Internet access—a service that other hotels almost always charge for.

773 Beatty St., Vancouver, BC V6B 2M4. www.georgiancourt.com. ✆ **800/663-1155** or 604/682-5555. Fax 604/682-8830. 180 units. C$200–C$250 double. AE, DC, MC, V. Parking C$16. **Amenities:** Restaurant; bar; babysitting; concierge; exercise room; Jacuzzi; room service; sauna; downtown shuttle (drop-off only). *In room:* A/C, TV, fridge, hair dryer, high-speed Internet (free).

St. Regis Hotel ★ 🛏 Many hotels in downtown Vancouver occupy newer buildings, so it's a pleasure to find one—and especially one as nice as the St. Regis—in a so-called "heritage building," dating from 1913. The owners have transformed it into a unique boutique hotel that's handsome inside and out, filled with contemporary art, and wired for up-to-the-minute Wi-Fi. The redesigned rooms and suites have a savvy, comfy, contemporary look to them. Plus, an impressive full breakfast is included in the room rate—it's the only downtown hotel to do so—and there's a great after-work crowd at the on-premises brewpub. The hotel is just 3 short blocks from the financial district, and close proximity to the shops at Pacific Centre. The new Canada Line SkyTrain from the airport stops a half block away at Granville and Dunsmuir.

602 Dunsmuir St., Vancouver, BC V6B 1Y6. www.stregishotel.com. ✆ **800/770-7929** or 604/681-1135. Fax 604/683-1126. 65 units. C$170 double; C$275–C$509 suite. Rates include breakfast. AE, MC, V. **Amenities:** Restaurant; bar/pub; Starbucks; concierge; executive-level rooms; access to nearby health club. *In room:* A/C, TV w/pay movies, hair dryer, minibar (in suites), MP3 docking station, Wi-Fi (free).

INEXPENSIVE

In addition to the establishments listed below, Downtown is home to the **Hostelling International Vancouver Downtown Hostel,** 1114 Burnaby St. (at Thurlow St.), Vancouver, BC V6E 1P1 (www.hihostels.ca; ✆ **888/203-4302** or 604/684-4565; fax 604/684-4540). High-season rates for nonmembers run from C$39 (dorm) to C$101 (double) and include a full breakfast. Another HI hostel, the **Vancouver Jericho Beach,** can be found on the West Side, 1515 Discovery St., Vancouver, BC V6R 4K5 (✆ **888/203-4303** or 604/224-3208).

The Kingston Hotel 🍴 An affordable downtown hotel is a rarity for Vancouver, but if you can do without the frills, the Kingston offers a clean, safe, inexpensive place to sleep and a complimentary continental breakfast to start your day. You won't find a better deal anywhere, and the premises have far more character than you'll find in a cookie-cutter motel. The Kingston is a Vancouver version of the kind of small budget B&B hotels found all over Europe. Just 13 of the 52 rooms have private bathrooms; the rest have hand basins and shared showers and toilets on each floor. The premises are well kept, and the location is central, so you can walk everywhere. The staff is friendly and helpful, and if you're just looking for a place to sleep and stow your bags, you'll be glad you found this place.

757 Richards St., Vancouver, BC V6B 3A6. www.kingstonhotelvancouver.com. © **888/713-3304** or 604/684-9024. Fax 604/684-9917. 52 units, 13 with private bathroom. C$85–C$95 double with shared bathroom; C$125–C$175 double with private bathroom. Additional person C$10. Senior discounts available. Rates include continental breakfast. AE, MC, V. Parking C$25 across the street. **Amenities:** Restaurant; bar; sauna. *In room:* TV (in units w/private bathrooms), Wi-Fi (free).

YWCA Hotel/Residence ★ 🐾 This attractive 12-story residence next door to the Georgian Court Hotel is an excellent choice for travelers on limited budgets. Bedrooms are simply furnished; most have TVs. Quite a few reasonably priced restaurants and a number of grocery stores are nearby. Three large and two small communal kitchens are available for guests' use, and all rooms have minifridges. The Y has three TV lounges and free access to the best gym in town, the nearby coed YWCA Fitness Centre. But perhaps best of all, the sales tax at this non-profit hotel is only 3.5% and all proceeds support the YWCA's projects.

733 Beatty St., Vancouver, BC V6B 2M4. www.ywcahotel.com. © **800/663-1424** or 604/895-5830. Fax 604/681-2550. 155 units, about ⅓ with private bathroom. C$71–C$87 double with shared bathroom; C$85–C$129 double with private bathroom. Weeklong discounts available. AE, MC, V. Parking C$12. **Amenities:** Access to YWCA facility. *In room:* A/C, TV, fridge, hair dryer, Wi-Fi (paid).

The West End

VERY EXPENSIVE

Westin Bayshore Resort & Marina ★★★ ☺ This is Vancouver's only resort hotel with its own marina, and the mountain and water views from all but a handful of its rooms are stunning. The Bayshore overlooks Coal Harbour and Stanley Park on one side, and Burrard Inlet and the city on the other. The hotel is in two buildings: the original low-rise from 1961 and a newer tower, with a giant pool, restaurant, and conference center between them. All the rooms, which received a makeover in 2009, are appointed with comfortable, contemporary West Coast decor and have floor-to-ceiling windows that open wide. In the newer tower, the rooms are a bit larger and have narrow balconies. The bathrooms in both buildings are nicely finished but fairly small. Children receive their own welcome package and will enjoy the indoor and outdoor pools.

1601 Bayshore Dr., Vancouver, BC V6G 2V4. www.westinbayshore.com. © **800/937-8461** or 604/682-3377. Fax 604/687-3102. 511 units. C$460 double; C$560 suite. Children 17 and under stay free in parent's room. AE, DC, MC, V. Self-parking C$36; valet parking C$41. **Amenities:** 2 restaurants; bar; Starbucks; babysitting; concierge; health club; Jacuzzi; 2 pools (1 indoor, 1 outdoor); room service; sauna; spa. *In room:* A/C, TV w/pay movies, hair dryer, minibar, Wi-Fi (paid).

EXPENSIVE

The Listel Hotel ★★ 🎁 What makes the Listel unique is its artwork. Hallways and suites on the top two Gallery floors are decorated with original pieces from the Buschlen Mowatt Gallery or, on the Museum floor, with First Nations artifacts from the UBC Museum of Anthropology (p. 66). Also unique is the fact that the Listel is the first Vancouver hotel to really go "green" with the use of solar power-generating panels. The hotel is luxurious without being flashy, and all the rooms and bathrooms feature top-quality bedding and handsome furnishings—though some bathrooms are larger than others, with separate soaker tub and shower. The roomy upper-floor suites facing Robson Street, with glimpses of the harbor and the mountains beyond, are the best bets. Rooms at the back are quieter but face the alley and nearby apartment buildings. In the evenings, you can hear live jazz at O'Doul's, the hotel's restaurant and bar. Downtown or Stanley Park is a 10-minute walk away.

1300 Robson St., Vancouver, BC V6E 1C5. www.thelistelhotel.com. ℰ 800/663-5491 or 604/684-8461. Fax 604/684-7092. 129 units. C$200–C$290 double; C$400–C$600 suite. AE, DC, DISC, MC, V. Parking C$26. Facility fee (3.5%) includes Internet and long-distance calling. **Amenities:** Restaurant; bar; concierge; executive-level rooms; exercise room; room service; Wi-Fi (incl. in facility fee). *In room:* A/C, TV w/pay movies, hair dryer, minibar.

MODERATE

Blue Horizon ⚓ This 31-story high-rise built in the 1960s has a great location on Robson Street, and underwent a top-to-bottom room renovation in 2011 that included new windows, fresh decor, and comfortable, modern furniture. Its rates remain a bargain almost year-round and upper floors have sweeping views; rooms feel a bit little like a high-rise motel but they are spacious and quiet. Most rooms are on a corner with wraparound windows and a balcony; superior rooms on floors 15 to 30 offer the best views. Book 05 and 07 rooms for a great vantage of the water and Stanley Park. Overall, the Blue Horizon is a good deal for this location. The hotel uses energy-efficient lighting, low-flow showerheads, and recycling bins.

1225 Robson St., Vancouver, BC V6E 1C3. www.bluehorizonhotel.com. ℰ 800/663-1333 or 604/688-1411. Fax 604/688-4461. 214 units. C$100–C$220 double; C$110–C$230 superior double; C$190–C$330 suite. Children 15 and under stay free in parent's room. AE, DC, MC, V. Parking C$15. **Amenities:** Restaurant; small exercise room; Jacuzzi; indoor pool; sauna. *In room:* A/C, TV w/pay movies, fridge, hair dryer, Internet (free).

Sunset Inn & Suites ★ ⚓ ☺ Just a couple of blocks from English Bay on the edge of the residential West End, the family-owned Sunset Inn offers roomy studios or one-bedroom apartments with balconies and fully equipped kitchens. Like many other hotels in this part of town, the Sunset Inn started life as an apartment building, meaning the rooms are larger than at your average hotel. Request an upper floor for better views; the executive rooms have been upgraded with touches like double vanities and rain showers. For those traveling with children, the one-bedroom suites have a separate bedroom and a pullout couch in the living room. All of the rooms were refurbished in 2008 with ongoing upgrades since. The beds are comfy, the staff is helpful and friendly, and the location is great for this price. Also, parking is free: a convenience that will run hefty charges at all downtown hotels.

1111 Burnaby St., Vancouver, BC V6E 1P4. www.sunsetinn.com. ℰ 800/786-1997 or 604/688-2474. Fax 604/669-3340. 50 units. Oct–May C$90–C$160 studio, C$110–C$210 1-bedroom; June–Sept C$160–C$230 studio, C$180–$475 1-bedroom. Additional adult C$10. Children 9 and under stay free in parent's room. Rates include continental breakfast. Weekly rates available. AE, DC, MC, V. Free parking. **Amenities:** Small exercise room. *In room:* A/C, TV, kitchen, MP3 docking station, Wi-Fi (free).

West End Guest House ★ 🏨 A heritage home built in 1906, the West End Guest House is a handsome example of what the neighborhood looked like before concrete towers and condos replaced the original Edwardian homes in the early 1950s. Decorated with early-20th-century antiques and a serious collection of vintage photographs of Vancouver taken by the original owners, this gay-friendly B&B is a calm, charming respite from the hustle and bustle of the West End. Six guest rooms feature feather mattresses and down duvets and the seventh is allergy-free with a silk duvet and foam mattress. The Grand Queen Suite, an attic-level bedroom with a brass bed, fireplace, sitting area, claw-foot bathtub, and skylights, is the best and most spacious room. Owner Evan Penner and his partner, Ron Cadarette, pamper their guests with a scrumptious breakfast and serve iced tea and sherry in the afternoon.

1362 Haro St., Vancouver, BC V6E 1G2. www.westendguesthouse.com. ✆ **888/546-3327** or 604/681-2889. Fax 604/688-8812. 7 units. Low season C$90–C$195 double; high season C$200–C$275 double. Rates include full breakfast. AE, DISC, MC, V. Free off-street parking. **Amenities:** Bikes. *In room:* TV/DVD, hair dryer, Wi-Fi (free).

INEXPENSIVE

Buchan Hotel 🍴 Built in 1926, this three-story building is tucked away on a quiet residential street in the West End, and it's a bargain for the location: just 2 blocks from Stanley Park and Denman Street. Like the Kingston (see above) downtown, this is a small European-style budget hotel that doesn't bother with frills or charming decor; unlike the Kingston, it isn't a B&B, so don't expect the second B. The standard rooms are quite plain; be prepared for close quarters and tiny bathrooms, half of which are shared. The best rooms are the executive rooms: four nicely furnished front-corner rooms with private bathrooms. The hotel also has in-house bike and ski storage, a patio restaurant, and a reading lounge.

1906 Haro St., Vancouver, BC V6G 1H7. www.buchanhotel.com. ✆ **800/668-6654** or 604/685-5354. Fax 604/685-5367. 60 units, 20 with private bathroom. C$60–C$86 double with shared bathroom; C$75–C$120 double with private bathroom; C$110–C$155 executive room. Children 12 and under stay free in parent's room. Weekly rates available. AE, DC, MC, V. Limited parking C$10. **Amenities:** Lounge. *In room:* TV, hair dryer, no phone, Wi-Fi (paid).

The West Side

EXPENSIVE

Granville Island Hotel ★ 🎁 One of Vancouver's best-kept secrets, this hotel is tucked away on the edge of Granville Island in a unique waterfront setting, a short stroll from theaters, galleries, and the fabulous Granville Island Public Market (p. 66). Rooms in the original wing are definitely fancier, so book these if you can, but the new wing is fine, too. Rooms are fairly spacious with traditional, unsurprising decor and large bathrooms with soaker tubs and rain showers; some units have balconies and great views over False Creek. If you don't have a car, the only potential drawback to a stay here is the location. During the daytime when the False Creek ferries are running, it's a quick ferry ride to Yaletown or the West End. After 10pm, however, you're looking at a C$15 to C$20 cab ride or an hour walk. The Island after dark is reasonably happening, and the hotel's waterside restaurant and brewpub are good-weather hangout spots with outdoor seating.

1253 Johnston St., Vancouver, BC V6H 3R9. www.granvilleislandhotel.com. ✆ **800/663-1840** or 604/683-7373. Fax 604/683-3061. 84 units. Oct–Apr starting at C$159 double, C$399 penthouse; May–Sept starting at C$259 double, C$499 penthouse. AE, DC, DISC, MC, V. Parking C$12. **Amenities:** Restaurant; brewpub; babysitting; small fitness room w/Jacuzzi and sauna; room service; access to nearby tennis courts. *In room:* A/C, TV w/pay movies, hair dryer, minibar, Wi-Fi (free).

INEXPENSIVE

The University of British Columbia Conference Centre ★ 🍴 The University of British Columbia Conference Centre is in a pretty, forested setting on the tip of Point Grey, convenient to Kitsilano and the University itself. If you don't have a car, it's a half-hour bus ride from downtown. Although the on-campus accommodations are actually student dorms most of the year, rooms are usually available. The rooms are nice, and many are being updated with a sleek, west coast decor. The 17-story Walter Gage Residence offers comfortable accommodations, many on

the upper floors with sweeping views of the city and ocean. One-bedroom suites come equipped with private bathrooms, kitchenettes, TVs, and phones. Each studio has a twin bed; each one-bedroom features a queen-size bed; a six-bed Towers room—a particularly good deal for families—features one double bed and five twin beds. The West Coast Suites, with a fresh Pacific style, are the most appealing, and have a very reasonable price. A buffet continental breakfast at the Student Union Building cafeteria is included with rooms.

5961 Student Union Blvd., Vancouver, BC V6T 2C9. www.ubcconferences.com. ℂ 888/822-1030 or 604/822-1000. Fax 604/822-1001. Approx. 1,500 units. Gage Towers units available approx. May 11–Aug 25; Pacific Spirit Hostel units available May 15–Aug 15; West Coast Suites and Marine Drive Residence units available year-round. Walter Gage Residences and Marine Drive Residences C$46–C$57 single w/shared bathroom, C$120–C$140 studio, C$150–C$180 suite; Pacific Spirit Hostel C$33–C$35 single, C$65–C$70 double; West Coast Suites C$160–C$200 suite. AE, MC, V. Parking C$7. Bus: 4, 14, 44, 84, or 99. **Amenities** (on campus): Restaurant; cafeteria, pub; weight room; access to campus Olympic-size swimming pool; sauna (C$5 per person); tennis courts. *In room:* A/C, TV, hair dryer, Wi-Fi (free).

WHERE TO EAT

For travelers who love to dine out and dine well, Vancouver is a delightful discovery. It's so good, in fact, that you could come here just to eat. And here's the capper: A fabulous meal at one of Vancouver's top restaurants costs about a third less than a similar meal would cost in New York, London, or San Francisco.

For restaurant meals in British Columbia, venues add the **12% harmonized sales tax (HST)** until spring 2013. Only **5% goods and services tax (GST)** will be added after that time as the province returns to its old tax system. Restaurant hours vary. Lunch is typically served from 11am to 2pm; Vancouverites begin dinner around 6:30pm, later in summer. Reservations are recommended at most restaurants and are essential at the city's top tables.

Downtown & Yaletown

VERY EXPENSIVE

Blue Water Cafe + Raw Bar ★★★ SEAFOOD   If you had to describe this busy, buzzy place in one word, it would be *fresh*, as only the best from sustainable and wild fisheries make it onto the menu. In fact, Blue Water won the top prize for "Best Seafood" and "Best Formal Restaurant" in the 2011 *Vancouver* magazine restaurant awards. If you love sushi and sashimi, the raw bar under the direction of Yoshiya Maruyama offers up some of the city's finest. On the other side of the room, Frank Pabst, the restaurant's executive chef, creates his dishes in a large open kitchen. For starters, try a medley of local oysters with various toppings, a sushi platter, or smoked sockeye salmon velouté. Main courses depend on whatever is in season: It might be spring salmon, halibut, Arctic char, tuna, white sturgeon, or BC sablefish.

1095 Hamilton St. (at Helmcken St.). ℂ **604/688-8078.** www.bluewatercafe.net. Reservations recommended. Main courses C$25–C$46. AE, DC, MC, V. Daily 5–11pm. Valet parking C$10.

EXPENSIVE

Chambar Belgian Restaurant ★★ 🍴 BELGIAN   One of Vancouver's favorite restaurants, Chambar occupies an intriguing space in a kind of no man's land on lower Beatty Street between Yaletown and Gastown. Michelin-trained chef Nico Schuermans and his wife, Karri, have worked hard to make the place a success, and plenty of plaudits have come their way. The menu features small and large plates.

Smaller choices typically include mussels cooked in white wine with bacon and cream (or with tomatoes and coconut cream), pistachio and chicken liver pate, or coquilles St. Jacques. Main dishes feature *tagine* of braised lamb shank with honey, and sesame halibut with a squid tagliatelle salad. For dessert, try the espresso cheese-cake with Belgian chocolate mousse or the lavender-milk chocolate pot de crème. Chambar specializes in Belgian beers, with some 40 varieties in bottles and on tap.

562 Beatty St. (C) **604/879-7119.** www.chambar.com. Reservations recommended. Small plates C$13–C$22; main courses C$29–C$33; 3-course set menu C$60. AE, MC, V. Daily 5pm–midnight. Bus: 5 or 17.

Coast ★★★ 🎁 SEAFOOD/INTERNATIONAL   The concept at Coast is to offer an extensive variety of fresh and non-endangered seafood from coasts around the world. The dining room is a handsomely designed affair with a central oyster bar and seating at various levels, including a second floor that allows you to look out over the busy scene below. Coast excels at just about everything it does, and the price for top-quality seafood is actually quite reasonable. The signature seafood platter, for example, comes with halibut, wild sea tiger prawns, sockeye salmon, Qualicum scallops, vegetables, and potato gnocchi, and costs only C$34 per person. Try the super sushi (the innovative sushi chef has come up with a delectable fish-and-chips hand roll), or any of the fresh fish or shellfish offerings. Service here is deft, friendly, and always on the mark.

1054 Alberni St. (C) **604/685-5010.** www.coastrestaurant.ca. Reservations recommended. Main courses C$18–C$46. AE, DC, MC, V. Mon–Thurs 11:30am–1am; Fri 11:30am–2am; Sat 4:30pm–2am; Sun 4:30pm–1am. Bus: 5 or 22.

Hawksworth Restaurant ★★★ PACIFIC NORTHWEST/SEAFOOD   On the street-level of the new Rosewood Hotel Georgia, Hawksworth Restaurant is the design of its namesake—Vancouver chef David Hawksworth. Three sections—a lounge, bright pearl room, and tranquil art room—create a vibe that is at once intimate and buzzy. Dishes are Canadian twists on familiar plates: Start with the charred octopus salad or 72-hour beef short ribs served with a black pepper jam, before moving on to Sooke River trout with brown butter, or grilled sturgeon crowned with a bacon consommé. Hawksworth presents dishes with a fabulously creative flair that assures the restaurant will be a new Vancouver favorite.

In the Rosewood Hotel Georgia (p. 50), 801 W. Georgia St. (C) **604/673-7000.** www.hawksworth restaurant.com. Reservations recommended. Main courses C$20–C$30. AE, MC, V. Mon–Fri 6:30–10am and 11:30am–2pm; Sat and Sun 7am–2:30pm; daily for dinner 5–11pm.

Il Giardino di Umberto Ristorante ★★ ITALIAN   Restaurant magnate Umberto Menghi started a small restaurant, tucked away in a yellow heritage house at the bottom of Hornby Street, nearly 4 decades ago. It still serves some of the best Italian fare, and has one of the prettiest garden patios in town. This larger restaurant now adjoins Umberto's in the original house. The bright, spacious dining room re-creates the ambience of an Italian villa and the menu leans toward Tuscany, with dishes that emphasize pasta and game. Entrees usually include classics such as *osso buco* with saffron risotto, and that Roman favorite, spaghetti carbonara. A daily list of specials makes the most of seasonal fresh ingredients, often offering outstanding seafood dishes. The wine list is comprehensive and well chosen.

1382 Hornby St. (btw. Pacific and Drake). (C) **604/669-2422.** www.umberto.com. Reservations recommended. Main courses C$20–C$44. AE, DC, MC, V. Mon–Fri 11:30am–3:30pm; Mon–Sat 5:30–11pm. Closed Sundays & holidays. Bus: 22.

MODERATE

Alpha Global Sushi & Bar ★ JAPANESE/TAPAS   On the periphery of both downtown and Yaletown, this lounge-like sushi bar attracts a pulsing crowd. The menu ranges from typical dishes, like spinach *goma-ae* and maki rolls, to slight twists, like a crab salad on avocado, a bacon and tofu salad, or salmon sashimi in a dill sauce. The portions are served in a tapas size, ideal for sharing over cocktails that the busy bartender shakes up. In fact the list of original cocktails is as equally inspired as the menu. Tables are intimate and all have window views for people-watching.

1099 Richards St. ✆ **604/633-0355.** www.plusalfa.com. Reservations recommended on weekends. Plates C$4–C$12. MC, V. Daily at 5pm.

Bin 941 Tapas Parlour ★ TAPAS/CASUAL   Still booming after more than a decade, Bin 941 remains the place for trendy tapas dining. True, the music's too loud and the room's too small, but the food that alights on the bar and eight tiny tables is delicious and fun, and the wine list is great. Look especially for local seafood such as scallops and tiger prawns, or the renowned chocolate fondue. In this sliver of a bistro sharing is unavoidable, so come prepared for socializing. The tables start to fill up at 6:30pm, and by 8pm, the hip and hungry have already formed a long and eager line.

941 Davie St. ✆ **604/683-1246.** www.bin941.com. Reservations not accepted. Plates C$8–C$18. MC, V. Daily 5pm–1:30am. Bus: 4, 6, 7 or 10.

Ensemble ★★ FRENCH/INTERNATIONAL/TAPAS   Run by young chef Dale MacKay, 2011 winner of the Food Network's Top Chef Canada, this restaurant hits a few things better-than right: it's affordable, slick, and lively. The menu refreshes with taster plates of tomato and watermelon salad or a crab-melon soup, but also comforts with black cod in a Thai broth or potato gnocchi in a tomato butter. The wine menu offers about a dozen by the glass, as well as a French-focused selection by the bottle. Although the room is often filled to capacity with a Robson Street crowd, it's also casual enough to drop in for a pint and a pulled pork sandwich.

850 Thurlow St. ✆ **604/569-1770.** www.ensemblerestaurant.com. Reservations recommended. Plates C$10–C$24. AE, MC, V. Tues–Sun 5–11pm.

INEXPENSIVE

Café Nuba ★ LEBANESE/VEGETARIAN   This sliver of a Seymour Street cafe is one of a growing number of Nuba Restaurants—a new favorite for quick, healthy, vegetarian and Lebanese eats. The secret-recipe falafel can make a cheap lunch in a pita (C$6) or as a platter with tabouleh, hummus, and rice or potatoes (C$10). A Gastown location (207 W. Hastings St.; ✆ **604/688-1655**) features a more formal dining room with longer hours.

1206 Seymour (at Davie St.). ✆ **778/371-3266.** www.nuba.ca. Main courses C$6–C$14. AE, MC, V. Mon–Sat 11:30am–9pm. Bus: 6.

Gastown & Chinatown

MODERATE

Bao Bei, A Chinese Brasserie ★★ CHINESE/TAPAS   Winning "Best New Restaurant" at the *Vancouver* Magazine 2011 Restaurant awards, Bao Bei often has an out-the-door line waiting to order from its innovate small-plates menu. The dining room is sleek, with a heritage Chinese charm that blends pale woods with floral textiles. Plates arrive as they are prepared, which promotes sharing but can mean a lag between dishes. The tofu duet serves up a marinated slice of soft soy bean curd

Making a major move beyond hotdogs and chestnuts, Vancouver's street food scene has expanded exponentially since 2010, when the first food truck vendors were awarded licenses. Most post hours, specials, and locations to their Twitter accounts. Here are the big dogs of the sidewalk-dining scene:

Japadog The old-school of Vancouver street food, this innovative Japanese hot dog stand still grills its Kurabata and Bratwurst, serving them topped with miso, nori, and edamame. On Burrard St. at Smithe St. Twitter: @japadog

The Kaboom Box This red truck's smoked salmon "salmwich" is already being called world-famous. Smoked on-site, the fish is Ocean Wise certified sustainable. On Granville St. at Robson St. Twitter: @thekaboombox

La Brasserie There's a single sandwich on offer: pulled chicken topped with French-fried onions, gravy, and mustard on a buttermilk bun—a total comfort food. On West Georgia St. at Granville St. Twitter: @La_Brasserie

The Re-Up BBQ Thanks to the tangy-spicy secret sauce, this pulled pork sandwich is entirely memorable. Outside the Vancouver Art Gallery, on West Georgia St. at Hornby St. Twitter: @reupbbq

Roaming Dragon Be it the Chinese pork belly sliders or Korean short rib tacos, the Roaming Dragon serves hugely popular Pan-Asian cuisine. The truck does change location for events, but often parks on Burrard St. at Robson St. Twitter: @roamingdragon

alongside crisp agadashi-style blocks. Potstickers are made fresh daily, and arrive crisp and not greasy. The restaurant only takes two reservations a night for large groups and none for smaller tables, so arrive early—even the tiny 12-seat bar and lounge is full by 6pm.

163 Keefer St. ☎ **604/688-0876.** www.bao-bei.ca. No reservations accepted (except large groups). Small plates C$8–C$18. AE, MC, V. Mon–Sat 5:30pm–midnight.

Judas Goat 🍴 TAPAS   This tiny (28-seat) tapas parlor is a cool addition to the Gastown dining scene. It's located in the scarily named but now-gentrified Blood Alley, a couple of doors down from Salt (see below). At Judas Goat, you check off what you want from a small list of tapas-style offerings that might include beef brisket meatballs, maple sugar sablefish, marinated mussels, or fennel salad. There's a small wine and beer list.

27 Blood Alley. ☎ **604/681-5090.** www.judasgoat.ca. Tapas C$4–C$26. AE, MC, V. Tues–Sat 5–11pm or midnight. Bus: 4, 7, 14, or 22.

Salt ★ CHARCUTERIE   The location of this dining spot in Gastown's Blood Alley might put some visitors off, and that's really a shame because Salt is unique, and it's a wonderful place to get a good, fairly inexpensive meal. The minimalistically modern room is set with communal spruce dining tables. Salt has no kitchen per se, as it serves only cured meats and artisan cheeses plus a daily soup, a couple of salads, and grilled meat and cheese sandwiches. For the tasting plate, you mix and match three of the meats and cheeses listed on the blackboard. To drink, choose from a selection of beers, and several good wines and whiskeys, or opt for a wine flight. As Blood Alley has no apparent street numbers, look for the upside-down salt shaker flag over the doorway. Try it for lunch if you're in Gastown.

45 Blood Alley, Gastown. ☎ **604/633-1912.** www.salttastingroom.com. Tasting plates C$15; lunch specials C$12. AE, MC, V. Daily noon–midnight. Bus: 4 or 7.

INEXPENSIVE

Phnom Penh Restaurant ★ VIETNAMESE   This family-run restaurant, serving Vietnamese and Cambodian cuisine, is a perennial contender for, and occasional recipient of, the *Vancouver* magazine award for the city's best Asian restaurant. Khmer dolls are suspended in glass cases, and the subdued lighting is a welcome departure from the harsh glare often found in inexpensive Chinatown restaurants. Try the hot-and-sour soup with prawns and lemon grass. The deep-fried garlic squid served with rice is a must-have, as is the tender, flame-kissed beef brochette. There's also the familiar (pho) and the foreign (frogs legs). For dessert, the fruit-and-rice pudding is an exotic treat. The service can be brusque—don't be shy to catch a server's eye, and you may have to share a table.

244 E. Georgia St. (near Main St.). ☎ **604/682-5777.** Main courses C$7–C$18. AE, MC, V. Mon–Thurs 10am–9pm; Fri–Sun 10am–10pm. Bus: 3 or 8.

The West End

EXPENSIVE

Cin Cin ★★★ MODERN ITALIAN   Vancouverites looking for great food and a romantic atmosphere frequent this award-winning, second-floor restaurant on Robson Street. The spacious dining room, done in a rustic Italian-villa style, surrounds an open kitchen built around a huge wood-fired oven and grill; the heated terrace is an equally pleasant dining and people-watching spot. The dishes, inspired by Italy but using locally sourced ingredients, change monthly, but your meal might begin with house-made Dungeness crab sausage with herb salad and lemon vinaigrette, followed by bison-filled gnocchi or biodynamic rice with scallops. Mouthwatering main courses include local fish and meat cooked in the wood-fired oven or on the wood grill, and a delicious pizza with sautéed wild mushrooms, peppercorn pecorino, and caramelized onions. The wine list is extensive, as is the selection of wines by the glass. The service is as exemplary as the food.

1154 Robson St. ☎ **604/688-7338.** www.cincin.net. Reservations recommended. Main courses C$25–C$40; fixed-price menu (5–6pm) C$45. AE, DC, MC, V. Daily 5pm–midnight. Bus: 5 or 22.

Raincity Grill ★★★ PACIFIC NORTHWEST   This top-starred restaurant on a busy, buzzy corner across from English Bay is a gem—painstaking in preparation, arty in presentation, and yet completely unfussy in atmosphere. Raincity Grill was one of the very first restaurants in Vancouver to embrace the "buy locally, eat seasonally" concept and pioneered the OceanWise sustainable seafood organization. The menu focuses on seafood, game, poultry, and organic vegetables from British Columbia and the Pacific Northwest. The room is long, low, and intimate. To sample a bit of everything, I recommend the seasonal "100 miles" tasting menu, a bargain at C$69, or C$103 with wine pairings. One recent tasting menu included beetroot salad, steamed mussels, beef carpaccio, roasted duck with gnocchi, a cheese selection with hazelnuts, and crème brûlée—all of it made with ingredients found within 161km (100 miles) of the restaurant. There's a takeout window on Denman Street, where you can get fish and chips to go for C$10.

1193 Denman St. ☎ **604/685-7337.** www.raincitygrill.com. Reservations recommended. Main courses C$12–C$19. AE, MC, V. Mon–Fri 11:30am–2:30pm and 5–10:30pm; Sat–Sun 10:30am–2:30pm (brunch) and 5–10:30pm. Bus: 5 or 6.

MODERATE

Hapa Izakaya ★ JAPANESE   Dinner comes at almost disco decibels in Robson Street's hottest Japanese "eat-drink place" (the literal meaning of Izakaya), where chefs call out orders, servers shout acknowledgments, and the maitre d' and owner keep up a running volley to staff about the (often sizable) wait at the door. The menu features sushi-style dishes such as agedashi tofu and *negitoro*—fresh tuna belly chopped with spring onions and served with bite-size bits of garlic bread. But look to the daily fresh sheets to select from inventive appetizers and meat dishes like a fish and chips roll or pork belly lettuce wrap. A scrumptious Korean hot pot and daily special vegetable goma-ae are also on the menu, for the non–raw fish eaters in your party. The service is fast and obliging, and the price per dish is reasonable. Other locations are in Kitsilano, at 1516 Yew St. (© **604/738-4272**), and Yaletown, at 1193 Hamilton St. (© **604/681-4272**).

1479 Robson St. © **604/689-4272.** www.hapaizakaya.com. Reservations recommended on weekends. Small plates C$6–C$24. AE, MC, V. Sun–Thurs 5:30pm–midnight; Fri and Sat 5:30pm–1am. Bus: 5.

INEXPENSIVE

Banana Leaf ★ MALAYSIAN   One of the city's best spots for Malaysian food, Banana Leaf is just a hop and a skip from English Bay. The menu includes inventive specials such as a spicy papaya and seafood soup, delicious South Asian mainstays such as *gado gado* (a salad with hot peanut sauce), *mee goreng* (fried egg noodles with vegetables, beef, egg, shrimp, and tofu), and occasional variations such as an Assam curry (seafood in a tamarind-curry sauce). Must-tries are sambal green beans and a signature chili crab. For dessert, don't pass up *pisang goreng*—fried banana with ice cream. The nine-course tasting menu (C$28) lets you sample a bit of everything. The small room is tastefully decorated in dark tropical woods; service is very friendly. Other locations are at 820 W. Broadway (© **604/731-6333**) and in Kitsilano at 3005 W. Broadway (© **604/734-3005**); same prices and hours apply.

1096 Denman St. © **604/683-3333.** www.bananaleaf-vancouver.com. Reservations not accepted. Main courses C$11–C$20. AE, MC, V. Sun–Thurs 11:30am–10pm; Fri–Sat 11:30am–11pm. Bus: 5.

Hon's Wun-Tun House CHINESE   Hon Kwong Ip opened a Chinatown restaurant 40 years ago, and this big, bright dining room on Robson Street is now one of four Vancouver locations. The Hong Kong tastes of wun-tun noodles and potstickers served here have been well received in Vancouver. The restaurant is also suited to family dining with a variety of barbequed meats and whole Peking ducks. The Chinatown location is at 268 Keefer St. (© **604/688-0871**).

1339 Robson St. © **604/685-0871.** www.hons.ca. Main courses C$10–C$24. MC, V. Daily 11am–11pm. Bus: 5.

The West Side

VERY EXPENSIVE

Tojo's Restaurant ★★★ JAPANESE   Tojo's is considered Vancouver's top Japanese restaurant, the place where celebs and food cognoscenti come to dine on the best sushi in town. It's expensive, but the food is absolutely fresh, inventive, and boy is it good. The dining room's main area wraps around Chef Tojo (who invented the California and BC rolls) and his sushi chefs with a giant curved maple sake bar and an adjoining sushi bar. Tojo's ever-changing menu offers such specialties as sea urchin on the half shell, herring roe, lobster claws, tuna, crab, and barbecue eel. Go for the

Chef's Arrangement—omakase—tell them how much you're willing to spend (per person), and let the good times roll.

1133 W. Broadway. Ⓒ **604/872-8050.** www.tojos.com. Reservations required. Main courses C$34–C$45; sushi/sashimi C$12–C$55; Chef's Arrangement C$70–C$200. AE, DC, MC, V. Mon–Sat 5–10pm. Closed Christmas week. Bus: 9.

West ★★★ FRENCH/PACIFIC NORTHWEST The credo at West is deceptively simple: "True to our region, true to the seasons." That means fresh, organic, locally harvested seafood, game, and produce are transformed into extraordinary creations. The menu, and tasting menu in particular, changes regularly, but first courses might include BC spot prawns with chorizo and spring onions, smoked sablefish chowder, or spring lamb risotto. For a main course, you might find fillet of steelhead trout with pea ravioli, seared Qualicum Bay scallops, or duck breast. A carefully chosen wine list from one of the city's top sommeliers includes a selection of affordable wines by the glass and half-bottle. If you're really into cooking, reserve one of the two "chef tables" adjacent to new Chef Quang Dang's bustling kitchen.

2881 Granville St. Ⓒ **604/738-8938.** www.westrestaurant.com. Reservations recommended. Main courses C$16–C$26 lunch, C$29–C$39 dinner; tasting menus C$58–C$89. AE, MC, V. Mon–Fri 11:30am–2:30pm; Sat and Sun 11am–2:30pm; daily 5:30–11pm. Bus: 10.

EXPENSIVE

La Quercia ★★ ITALIAN This intimate dining room has won plaudits for its Northern Italian fair served with flair by chefs Adam Pegg and Lucais Syme. A simple chalkboard lists what's fresh and flavorful for the day, and diners have the option of a five- or nine-course spread. Depending on the season, you might select from trout carpaccio or fresh anchovies followed by risotto, potato gnocchi with sausage, or grilled cuttlefish. The restaurant has been so welcomed by the neighborhood that the same team has opened a less-formal deli La Ghianda across the street (2083 Alma St.; Ⓒ **604/566-9559;** www.laghianda.ca).

3689 W. 4th Ave. Ⓒ **604/676-1007.** www.laquercia.ca. Reservations required. Main courses C$18–C$30. 5 courses C$43; 9 courses C$59. MC, V. Tues–Sun 5–10pm.

Vij's ★★★ INDIAN Vij's doesn't take reservations, as is apparent by the line outside every night, but patrons huddled under the neon sign don't seem to mind since they're treated to tea and *papadums* (a thin bread made from lentils). Inside, the decor is as warm and subtle as the seasonings, which are all roasted, hand-ground, and used with studied delicacy. The menu changes monthly, though some of the more popular entrees remain constant. Recent offerings included wine-marinated lamb popsicles and BC spot prawns and halibut with black chickpeas in coconut-lemon curry. Vegetarian selections abound, including beans in yellow mustard seed and coconut curry, and Indian lentils with naan and Indian lentils with naan and *raita* (yogurt-mint sauce). The wine and beer list is short but carefully selected. And for teetotalers, Vij's has developed a souped-up version of the traditional Indian chai, the *chaiuccino*. In 2004 Vij opened Rangoli right next door, for lunch and takeout.

1480 W. 11th Ave. Ⓒ **604/736-6664.** www.vijsrestaurant.ca. Reservations not accepted. Main courses C$24–C$28. AE, MC, V. Daily 5:30–10pm. Bus: 10.

MODERATE

Maenam ★★ 🍴 THAI The feeling of freshness pervades in this white-walled, reed-screened eatery on W. 4th Avenue, and the food delivers the same delight. From deceptively spicy green papaya salad to the wild prawn cakes with cucumber relish, dishes ring with simple and carefully selected ingredients. Service is attentive and the room quickly fills with a Kitsilano crowd of young-professionals.

1938 W 4th Ave. ✆ **604/730-5579.** www.maenam.ca. Reservations accepted. Main courses C$14–C$18. AE, MC, V. Tues–Sat noon–2:30pm; daily 5–11pm. Bus: 4 or 7.

Trattoria Italian Kitchen ★ ITALIAN Although it's fairly casual and Kits-friendly, this restaurant is run with the same polished service as downtown dining rooms. You can't make a reservation here, so plan accordingly. The line begins to form at 5:30pm, and by 7pm, you may have to wait an hour or more for a table (you can order a drink while you're waiting). The menu covers excellent pizzas with delicious toppings (housemade sausage with leeks and fingerling potatoes, or roasted squash and gorgonzola); pastas like linguine *vongole* with manila clams, spaghetti carbonara, or the sharable platter of spaghetti and meatballs (the meatballs are made of Kobe beef). Main courses are seasonal and might include seared wild spring salmon or grilled lamb chops. The wine list includes all the major Italian vintages.

1850 W. 4th Ave. ✆ **604/732-1441.** www.trattoriakitchen.ca. Reservations not accepted. Main courses C$13–C$24. AE, MC, V. Mon–Thurs 11:30am–1am; Fri 11:30am–2am; Sat 10:30am–2am; Sun 10:30am–1am. Bus: 4 or 7.

INEXPENSIVE
The Naam Restaurant ★ ☺ VEGETARIAN Back in the '60s, when Kitsilano was Canada's hippie haven, the Naam was tie-dye central. Things have changed since then, but Vancouver's oldest vegetarian and natural-food restaurant still retains a pleasant granola feel, and it's open 24/7. The decor is simple, earnest, and welcoming, and includes well-worn wooden tables and chairs, plants, an assortment of local art, a nice garden patio, and live music every night. The brazenly healthy fare ranges from all-vegetarian burgers, enchiladas, and burritos to tofu teriyaki, Thai noodles, and a variety of pita pizzas. The sesame fries with miso gravy are a Vancouver institution.

2724 W. 4th Ave. ✆ **604/738-7151.** www.thenaam.com. Main courses C$8–C$15. AE, MC, V. Daily 24 hr. Live music every night 7–10pm. Bus: 4 or 22.

Sophie's Cosmic Café ☺ FAMILY STYLE/AMERICAN For a fabulous home-cooked, diner-style breakfast in a laid-back but buzzy atmosphere, come to this Kitsilano landmark. On Saturday and Sunday mornings get here early, or you may have to wait a half-hour or more to get in. You can also have a good, filling lunch or dinner here. Every available space in Sophie's is crammed with toys and knickknacks from the 1950s and 1960s, so, understandably, children are inordinately fond of the place. Crayons and coloring paper are always on hand. The menu is simple and includes pastas, burgers and fries, great milkshakes, and a few classic Mexican and "international" dishes, but it's the breakfast menu that draws the crowds.

2095 W. 4th Ave. ✆ **604/732-6810.** www.sophiescosmiccafe.com. Main courses C$7.50–C$16. MC, V. Mon 8am–2:30pm; Tues–Sun 8am–8pm. Bus: 4 or 7.

The East Side
MODERATE
East is East ★ VEGETARIAN/INTERNATIONAL Filled with rugs, pillows, and low wooden tables, East is East presents a harem of spices for food-lovers. The roti rolls come in a dozen combinations, from Spice Caravan (chickpeas and cauli-flower) to the Silk Road (miso salmon in coconut milk). The Silk Road feast is a

heartier all-you-can-eat option—diners start by selecting two dishes from a raft of vegetarian and meat dish choices. Even if you're just shopping along the Main Street boutiques, stop in for a veritably spicy chai tea (the best in Vancouver). There's a second location in Kitsilano at 3243 W. Broadway (✆ **604/734-5881**) that serves the same menu.

4413 Main St. ✆ **604/879-2020.** www.eastiseast.ca. Reservations recommended on weekends. Main courses C$13–C$19. MC, V. Daily 11am–10pm.

The Locus Café CASUAL/SOUTHWESTERN   Even if you arrive by your lonesome, you'll soon have plenty of friends because the Locus is a cheek-by-jowl kind of place, filled with a friendly, funky crowd of artsy Mount Pleasant types. The big bar is overhung with "swamp-gothic" lacquer trees and surrounded by a tier of stools with booths and tiny tables. The cuisine originated in the American Southwest and picked up an edge along the way, as demonstrated in the pulled chicken sandwich with spicy black bean mayo served on a baguette. Keep an eye out for fish specials, such as grilled halibut with bacon and tomato vinaigrette. If you're in the mood for a burger, try the organic beef patty topped with caramelized onion and edam cheese. Draft beers are pulled from local-favorite breweries, including Phillips in Victoria and North Vancouver's Red Truck.

4121 Main St. ✆ **604/708-4121.** www.locusonmain.com. Reservations accepted. Main courses C$12–C$24. MC, V. Mon–Wed 10am–midnight; Thurs & Fri 10am–1am; Sat 9am–1am; Sun 9am–midnight. Bus: 3.

Organic Lives RAW/VEGETARIAN   You may expect a raw food restaurant to be laid-back, but this east side eatery has the buttoned-down appearance of one of Vancouver's busiest kitchens. That's because the team of chefs turn fresh herbs, vegetables, nuts, and fruits into delectable food creations. Entrées go beyond salads, with raw food options for pasta, sushi, and curries. The zughetti is fascinatingly creamy with a cashew-dill sauce, while the lasagna layers nuts, sun-dried tomatoes, basil pesto, and zucchini. And dessert doesn't let up either: strawberry shortcake and caramel cinnamon pie both tempt fiercely.

1829 Quebec St. ✆ **778/588-7777.** www.organiclives.org. Main courses C$12–C$21. AE, MC, V. Daily 9am–9pm.

EXPLORING VANCOUVER

A city perched on the edge of a raw, uninhabited wilderness, Vancouver offers unrivaled opportunities for exploring the outdoors. But within the city limits, Vancouver is intensely urban, with buzzy sidewalk cafes and busy shopping streets. A forest of glass-fronted high-rises rings the central part of the city, reminding some visitors of New York or Shanghai. But similarities with other places begin to pall as you come to realize that Vancouver is entirely its own creation: a young, self-confident, sparklingly beautiful city like no other place on Earth.

The Top Attractions
DOWNTOWN & THE WEST END
Bill Reid Gallery of Northwest Coast Art ★★   This downtown museum-gallery showcases the work of the great Northwest coast First Nations artist Bill Reid, who died in 1998. Permanent installations include the Raven's Trove: Gold and Silver

Masterworks by Bill Reid; the monumental bronze sculpture Mythic Messengers, Reid's masterful composition of 11 intertwined figures recounting traditional Haida myths; a monumental cedar tribute pole carved by Haida Chief 7idansuu (James Hart) honoring Reid.

639 Hornby St. © **604/682-3455.** www.billreidgallery.ca. Admission C$10 adults, C$7 seniors and students, C$5 children 6–17; C$25 families. Wed–Sun 11am–5pm.

Stanley Park ★★★ ☺   The green jewel of Vancouver, Stanley Park is a 400-hectare (988-acre) rainforest jutting out into the ocean from the edge of the busy West End. Exploring the second-largest urban forest in Canada is one of Vancouver's quintessential experiences. The park, created in 1888, is filled with towering western red cedar and Douglas fir, manicured lawns, flower gardens, placid lagoons, and countless shaded walking trails that meander through it all. The famed **seawall ★★★** runs along the waterside edge of the park, allowing cyclists and pedestrians to experience the magical interface of forest, sea, and sky. One of the most popular free attractions in the park is the **collection of totem poles ★★★** at Brockton Point, most of them carved in the 1980s to replace the original ones that were placed in the park in the 1920s and 1930s. The area around the totem poles features open-air displays on the Coast Salish First Nations and a small gift shop/visitor information center.

The park is home to lots of wildlife, including beavers, coyotes, bald eagles, blue herons, cormorants, trumpeter swans, brant geese, ducks, raccoons, skunks, and gray squirrels imported from New York's Central Park a century ago and now quite at home in the Pacific Northwest. (No, there are no bears.) For directions and maps, brochures, and exhibits on the nature and ecology of Stanley Park, visit the **Lost Lagoon Nature House** (© 604/257-8544; daily 10am–6pm July 1 to Labour Day, weekends only outside this period; free admission). Most Sundays at 9am or 1:30pm, rain or shine, they offer Discovery Walks of the park (pre-registration recommended). Equally nature-focused but with way more wow is the **Vancouver Aquarium ★★** (see below). Next to the former children's farmyard (now closed) is **Stanley Park's Miniature Railway ★** (© 604/257-8531), a diminutive steam locomotive that pulls passenger cars on a circuit through the woods.

Swimmers head to **Third Beach** and **Second Beach** (p. 69), the latter with an outdoor pool beside English Bay. For kids there's a free **Spray Park** near Lumberman's Arch, where they can run and splash through various water-spewing fountains. Perhaps the best way to explore the park is to rent a bike (p. 70) or in-line skates, and set off along the seawall. The wonderful **horse-drawn carriage ride ★★★** operated by **AAA Horse & Carriage Ltd.** (© 604/681-5115; www.stanleypark.com) is one of the most enjoyable ways to tour the park. Carriage tours depart every 20–45 minutes mid-March through October from the Coal Harbour parking lot on Park Drive near the Georgia Street park entrance and the park information booth. The ride lasts an hour and covers portions of the park that many locals have never seen. Rates are C$30 for adults, C$28 for seniors and students, and C$16 for children 3 to 12. Of the three restaurants located in the park, the best is the **Fish House in Stanley Park,** where you can have lunch, afternoon tea, or dinner.

Stanley Park. © **604/257-8400.** vancouver.ca/parks. Free admission; charge for individual attractions. Park does not close. Bus: 19; the Vancouver Trolley Company (© **604/801-5515**) operates an around-the-park shuttle bus mid-June to early Sept: C$10 for adults, C$5 for children 4–11, and C$25 for families. Parking entire day C$10 summer, C$5 winter.

Vancouver Aquarium Marine Science Centre ★★ ☺ One of North America's largest and best, the Vancouver Aquarium houses more than 70,000 marine animals. From platforms above or through underwater viewing windows you can watch the white beluga whales flashing through their pools. (One of the belugas gave birth in June 2008, and another in June 2009.) There are also sea otters, Steller sea lions, and Pacific white-sided dolphins.

845 Avison Way, Stanley Park. ℰ **604/659-FISH** (3474). www.vanaqua.org. Summer admission C$27 adults; C$21 seniors, students, and youths 13–18; C$17 children 4–12; free for children 3 and under. Summer daily 9am–7pm; winter daily 9:30am–5pm. Bus: 19. Parking C$10 per day summer, C$5 winter.

Vancouver Art Gallery ★★ Designed as a courthouse by B.C.'s leading early-20th-century architect Francis Rattenbury (the architect of Victoria's Empress Hotel and the Legislature buildings), and renovated into an art gallery by B.C.'s leading late-20th-century architect Arthur Erickson, the Gallery is an excellent stop to see what sets Canadian and West Coast art apart from the rest of the world. Along with an impressive collection of paintings by B.C. native **Emily Carr ★★★** are examples of a unique Canadian art style created during the 1920s by members of the "Group of Seven," which included painter Lawren Harris, who moved to Vancouver in 1940. The Gallery also hosts rotating exhibits of contemporary sculpture, graphics, photography, and video art from around the world. Watch for a Friday event called FUSE—a melding of live performance, music, and art. DJs and gallery tours keep the infrequent but locally popular evenings going until 1am.

750 Hornby St. ℰ **604/662-4719.** www.vanartgallery.bc.ca. Admission C$20 adults, C$14 seniors, C$13 students, C$7 kids 5–12; C$50 families. Wed–Mon 10am–5pm; Tues 10am–9pm. SkyTrain: Granville. Buses: 4, 5, 6, 7, 10 all stop within 2 blocks.

GASTOWN & CHINATOWN

Dr. Sun Yat-Sen Classical Chinese Garden ★★ This small reproduction of a Classical Chinese scholar's garden truly is a remarkable place, but to get the full effect, it's best to take the guided tour, which is included with admission. Untrained eyes will only see a pretty pond surrounded by bamboo and oddly shaped rocks. The engaging guides, however, can explain this unique urban garden's Taoist yin-yang design principle, in which harmony is achieved through dynamic opposition. To foster opposition (and thus harmony) in the garden, Chinese designers place contrasting elements in juxtaposition: Soft-moving water flows across solid stone; smooth, swaying bamboo grows around gnarled immovable rocks; dark pebbles are placed next to light pebbles in the paving. Moving with the guide, you discover the symbolism of intricate carvings and marvel at the subtle, ever-changing views.

578 Carrall St. ℰ **604/662-3207.** www.vancouverchinesegarden.com. Admission C$12 adults, C$10 seniors, C$9 students, free for children 4 and under; C$25 families. Free guided tour included. May–June 14 and Sept daily 10am–6pm; June 15–Aug daily 9:30am–7pm; Oct–Apr Tues–Sun 10am–4:30pm. Bus: 19 or 22.

THE WEST SIDE

Granville Island ★★★ ☺ Almost a city within a city, Granville Island is a good place to browse away a morning, an afternoon, or a whole day. You can wander through a busy public market jammed with food stalls, shop for crafts, pick up some fresh seafood, enjoy a great dinner, watch the latest theater performance, rent a yacht, stroll along the waterfront, or simply run through the sprinkler on a hot summer day; it's all there and more. If you only have a short period of time, make sure you spend at least part of it in the **Granville Island Public Market ★★★**, one of the best all-around markets in North America.

Once a declining industrial site, Granville Island started transforming in the late 1970s when the government encouraged new, people-friendly developments. Maintaining its original industrial look, the former warehouses and factories now house galleries, artist studios, restaurants, and theaters; the cement plant on the waterfront is the only industrial tenant left. Access to Granville Island is by Aquabus from the West End, Yaletown, or Kitsilano, or by foot, bike, or car across the bridge at Anderson Street (access from W. 2nd Ave.). Avoid driving over on weekends and holidays— you'll spend more time trying to find a parking place than in the galleries. Check the website for upcoming events or stop by the info center, behind the Kids Market.

Located on the south shore of False Creek, under the Granville St. Bridge. For studio and gallery hours and other information about Granville Island, contact the information center at ℂ **604/666-5784.** www.granvilleisland.com. Public market daily 9am–7pm. For information on getting to Granville Island, see "By Miniferry," earlier in this chapter. Bus: 50.

H. R. MacMillan Space Centre ★ ☺   In the same building as the Museum of Vancouver (see below), the space center and observatory has hands-on displays and exhibits that will delight budding astronomy buffs and their parents (or older space buffs and their children). Displays are highly interactive: In the Cosmic Courtyard, you can try designing a spacecraft or maneuvering a lunar robot. Or, punch a button and get a video explanation of the *Apollo 17* manned-satellite engine that stands before you. The exciting **Virtual Voyages Simulator ★★** takes you on a voyage to Mars—it's a thrilling experience for kids and adults. In the GroundStation Canada Theatre, video presentations explore Canada's contributions to the space program and space in general. The Star Theatre shows movies—many of them for kids—on an overhead dome.

1100 Chestnut St. (in Vanier Park). ℂ **604/738-7827.** www.spacecentre.ca. Admission C$15 adults; C$11 seniors, students and children 5–10; children 4 and under free; C$45 families (up to 5, maximum 2 adults). July to early Sept daily 10am–5pm; early Sept–June Mon–Fri 10am–3pm, Sat and Sun 10am–5pm. Closed Dec 25. Bus: 2 or 22.

Museum of Anthropology ★★★ ☺   In 1976, B.C. architect Arthur Erickson created a classic Native post-and-beam-style structure out of poured concrete and glass to house one of the world's finest collections of Northwest coast Native art. A major renovation and re-branding completed in 2010 more than doubled the gallery space and added new luster to this remarkable showplace.

Enter through doors that resemble a huge, carved, bent-cedar box. Artifacts from different coastal communities flank the ramp leading to the Great Hall's **collection of totem poles.** Haida artist Bill Reid's masterpiece, *The Raven and the First Men,* is worth the price of admission all by itself. The huge carving in glowing yellow cedar depicts a Haida creation myth, in which Raven—the trickster—coaxes humanity out into the world from its birthplace in a clamshell. Some of Reid's fabulous jewelry creations in gold and silver are also on display. Behind the museum, overlooking Point Grey, are two **longhouses** built according to the Haida tribal style, resting on the traditional north–south axis. Ten hand-carved totem poles stand in attendance along with contemporary carvings on the longhouse facades.

6393 NW Marine Dr. (at Gate 4). ℂ **604/822-5087.** www.moa.ubc.ca. Admission C$14 adults; C$12 seniors, students and children 6–18; free for children 5 and under; C$7 for all Tues 5–9pm. Spring/summer daily 10am–5pm, Tues 10am–9pm; fall/winter Wed–Sun 10am–5pm, Tues 10am–9pm. Closed Dec 25 and Dec 26. Bus: 4 or 99 (10-min. walk from UBC bus loop).

Museum of Vancouver   Located in the same building as the H. R. MacMillan Space Centre (see above), the Museum of Vancouver is dedicated to the city's history, from its days as a Native settlement and European outpost to its 20th-century maturation into a modern urban center. The exhibits have been remounted and revitalized to make them more interesting to the casual visitor. Of most importance here is the wonderful collection of First Nations art and artifacts. Hilarious, campy fun abounds in the 1950s Room, with its vinyl diner booth and neon signs. Next to this is another fun, and socially intriguing, room devoted to Vancouver's years as a hippie capital, with film clips, commentary, and a replica hippie apartment.

1100 Chestnut St. ✆ **604/736-4431.** www.museumofvancouver.ca. Admission C$12 adults, C$10 seniors, C$8 children 5–17. July and Aug Fri–Wed 10am–5pm, Thurs 10am–8pm; Sept–June Tues, Wed and Fri–Sun 10am–5pm; Thurs 10am–8pm. Bus: 2 or 22, then walk 3 blocks south on Cornwall Ave. Boat: False Creek Ferry to Heritage Harbour. Bus: 2 or 22.

THE EAST SIDE

Science World at TELUS World of Science ★ ☺   This big, blinking geodesic dome was built for Expo '86 on the eastern end of False Creek. Inside, it's a hands-on scientific discovery center where you and your kids can (depending on the current exhibits) light up a plasma ball, walk through a maze, wander through the interior of a camera, create a cyclone, watch a zucchini explode as it's charged with 80,000 volts, stand inside a beaver lodge, play in wrist-deep magnetic liquids, create music with a giant synthesizer, and watch mind-bending three-dimensional slide and laser shows, as well as other optical effects. Throughout the day, special shows, many with nature themes, are presented in the OMNIMAX Theatre—a huge projecting screen equipped with surround sound.

1455 Quebec St. ✆ **604/443-7443.** www.scienceworld.ca. Admission C$21 adults, C$17 seniors and students, C$14 children 4–12, free for children 3 and under; C$57 families (2 adults with up to 4 of their children). OMNIMAX ticket C$5 adults. Sept–June Mon–Fri 10am–5pm, Sat and Sun 10am–6pm; July–Aug daily 10am–6pm; holidays 10am–6pm. SkyTrain: Main St.–Science World.

NORTH VANCOUVER & WEST VANCOUVER

Capilano Suspension Bridge & Park ★   Vancouver's first and oldest tourist trap (built in 1889), this attraction still works—mostly because there's still something inherently thrilling about walking across a narrow, shaky walkway 70m (230 ft.) above a canyon floor, held up by nothing but a pair of tiny (although exceedingly strong) cables. Set in a beautiful 11-hectare (27-acre) park about 15 minutes from downtown, the suspension bridge itself is a 137m-long (450-ft.) cedar-plank and steel-cable footbridge, which sways and bounces gently above the Capilano River. Opened in 2011, **Cliffhanger** connects suspended walkways to get a better view of granite cliffs and the Capilano Canyon. The **Treetops Adventure** attraction features more bridges and walkways, only these are attached to giant tree trunks 30m (100 ft.) above the rainforest floor.

3735 Capilano Rd., North Vancouver. ✆ **604/985-7474.** www.capbridge.com. Admission $30 adults, C$28 seniors, C$24 students, C$19 children 13–16, C$10 children 6–12, free for children 5 and under. May–Sept daily 8:30am–dusk; Oct–Apr daily 9am–5pm or later. Hours change monthly. Closed Dec 25. Bus: 246 or 236 from Lonsdale Quay. There is also a free shuttle from some downtown hotels. Car: Hwy. 99 north across Lions Gate Bridge to exit 14 on Capilano Rd.

Grouse Mountain ★★ ☺   Once a local ski hill, Grouse Mountain has developed into a year-round mountain recreation park. It's fun if you're sports minded or like the outdoors; if not, you might find it disappointing. Located only a 15-minute drive from downtown, the **Skyride gondola ★★** transports you to the mountain's 1,250m (4,101-ft.) summit. (Hikers can take a near vertical trail called the Grouse Grind.) On a clear day, the **view ★★★** from the top is the best around: You can see the city and the entire lower mainland, from far up the Fraser Valley east across the Strait of Georgia to Vancouver Island. Visible from downtown, the new **Eye of the Wind** turbine takes you up a further 57m (187 ft.) to a 360-degree viewing tower atop the windmill. There's an extra admission charge, and the windmill can accommodate up to 36 people in the viewing tower. In the lodge, **Theater in the Sky ★** shows wildlife movies. Outside, in the winter, you can ski and snowboard (26 runs, 13 runs for night skiing/snowboarding; drop-in ski lessons available), go snowshoeing, skate on the highest outdoor rink in Canada, take a brief "sleigh ride" (behind a huge snow-cat), see reindeer, and the kids can play in a special snow park. In warmer weather, you can wander forest trails, take a scenic chair ride, enjoy a lumberjack show or Birds in Motion demonstrations, visit the Refuge for Endangered Wildlife, or ride on the mountain-bike trails. Most of these activities are included in the rather exorbitant price of your Skyride ticket; you have to pay extra for a lift ticket and equipment rentals. For a budget option: make dinner reservations at **The Observatory** restaurant (**℅ 604/980-9311**) and the Skyride plus general admission activities are free.

6400 Nancy Greene Way, North Vancouver. ℅ **604/984-0661.** www.grousemountain.com. Skyride C$40 adults, C$36 seniors, C$24 children 13–18, C$14 children 5–12, free for children 4 and under. Full-day ski-lift tickets C$55 adults, C$45 seniors and children 13–18, C$25 children 5–12. Skyride free with advance Observatory Restaurant reservation. Daily 9am–10pm. Bus: 240 from W Georgia St. and transfer to bus 236, or take bus 232 from Phibbs Exchange. SeaBus: Lonsdale Quay, then transfer to bus 236. Car: Hwy. 99 north across Lions Gate Bridge, take North Vancouver exit to Marine Dr., then up Capilano Rd. for 5km (3 miles). Parking C$3 for 2 hr. in lots below Skyride.

Vancouver's Parks

Park and garden lovers are in heaven in Vancouver. The wet, mild climate is ideal for gardening, and come spring the city blazes with blossoming cherry trees, magnolia or "tulip" trees, rhododendrons, camellias, azaleas, and spring bulbs—and roses in summer. Gardens are everywhere. For general information about Vancouver's parks, call ℅ **604/873-7000,** or try vancouver.ca/parks. For information on **Stanley Park ★★★**, the lord of them all, see p. 64.

In Chinatown, the **Dr. Sun Yat-Sen Classical Chinese Garden ★★** (p. 65) is a small, tranquil oasis in the heart of the city, built by artisans from Suzhou, China; right next to it, accessed via the Chinese Cultural Centre on Pender Street, is the pretty (and free) **Dr. Sun Yat-Sen Park,** with a pond, walkways, and plantings.

On the West Side you'll find the magnificent **UBC Botanical Garden,** one of the largest living botany collections on the West Coast, and the sublime **Nitobe Memorial Garden.** Also on the West Side, **Queen Elizabeth Park**—at Cambie Street and West 33rd Avenue—sits atop a 150m-high (492-ft.) hill (thought to be an extinct volcano) and is the highest urban vantage point south of downtown, offering panoramic views in all directions. Along with the rose garden in Stanley Park, it's Vancouver's most popular location for wedding-photo sessions, with well-manicured gardens and a profusion of colorful flora. There are areas for lawn bowling, tennis, pitch-and-putt golf, disc golf, and picnicking. The **Bloedel Conservatory** (℅ **604/257-8584**) stands next to the park's huge sunken garden, an amazing reclamation of an abandoned rock quarry. A 21.3m-high (70-ft.) domed structure, the conservatory (May–Sept open Mon–Fri 9am–8pm and 10am–9pm weekends; Oct–April daily

10am–5pm) houses a tropical rainforest with more than 100 free-flying tropical birds. Admission to the conservatory is C$5 for adults, with discounts for seniors, children, and families. Take bus no. 15 to reach the park.

Vancouver's 22-hectare (54-acre) **VanDusen Botanical Garden,** 5251 Oak St., at West 37th Avenue (✆ **604/878-9274;** www.vandusengarden.org), located just a few blocks from Queen Elizabeth Park and the Bloedel Conservatory, concentrates on whole ecosystems. From towering trees to little lichens on the smallest of damp stones, the gardeners at VanDusen attempt to re-create the plant life of a number of different environments. Should all this tree gazing finally pall, head for the farthest corner of the garden to the devilishly difficult Elizabethan garden maze. Admission April through September: C$10 adults, C$7.50 seniors and youths 13 to 18, C$5.50 children 3 to 12, and C$24 families. Reduced admission October through March. Open daily 10am to dusk. Take bus no. 17. **Note:** The garden lost hundreds of trees in the December 2006 windstorm that also devastated Stanley Park.

Adjoining the University of British Columbia (UBC) on the city's west side at Point Grey, **Pacific Spirit Regional Park,** called the **Endowment Lands** by longtime Vancouver residents, is the largest green space in Vancouver. Comprising 763 hectares (1,885 acres) of temperate rainforest, marshes, and beaches, the park includes more than 50km (31 miles) of trails ideal for hiking, riding, mountain biking, and beachcombing.

OUTDOOR ACTIVITIES

An excellent resource for outdoor enthusiasts is **Mountain Equipment Co-op,** 130 W. Broadway (✆ **604/872-7858;** www.mec.ca).

BEACHES   Only about 12% of Vancouver's annual rainfall occurs during June, July, and August; 60 days of summer sunshine is not uncommon, although the Pacific never really warms up enough for a comfortable swim. Still, **English Bay Beach ★★,** at the end of Davie Street off Denman Street and Beach Avenue, is a great place to see sunsets. The bathhouse dates to the turn of the 20th century, and a huge playground slide is mounted on a raft just off the beach every summer.

On **Stanley Park's** western rim, **Second Beach ★** is a short stroll north from English Bay Beach. A playground, a snack bar, and an immense heated oceanside **pool ★** (✆ **604/257-8371**), open from Victoria Day weekend (late May) through Labour Day weekend, make this a convenient and fun spot for families. Admission to the pool is C$5.95 for adults, C$4.15 for seniors and youths 13 to 18, and C$2.95 for children 3 to 12. Farther along the seawall, due north of Stanley Park Drive, lies secluded **Third Beach.** Locals tote along grills and coolers to this spot, a popular place for summer-evening barbecues and sunset-watching.

On the West Side, **Kitsilano Beach ★★★,** along Arbutus Street near Cornwall Street, is affectionately called Kits Beach. It's an easy walk from the Maritime Museum and the False Creek ferry dock. If you want to do a saltwater swim but can't handle the cold, head to the huge (135m/443-ft.) heated (25°C/77°F) **Kitsilano Pool ★★.** Admission is the same as for Second Beach Pool, above.

Farther west on the other side of Hastings Mill Park is **Jericho Beach** (west end of Point Grey Rd.). **Locarno Beach,** at the north end of Trimble and Tolmie streets, and **Spanish Banks,** on Northwest Marine Drive, lead to the Point Grey Foreshore that wraps around the northern point of the UBC campus and University Hill. Near

4

UBC is **Wreck Beach** ★★★—Canada's largest nude beach. You get down to Wreck Beach by taking the steep Trails 4 or 6 on the UBC campus that lead down to the water's edge. Wreck Beach is also the city's most pristine and least-developed sandy stretch, bordered on three sides by towering trees.

For information on any of Vancouver's many beaches, call ✆ **604/738-8535** (summer only).

CANOEING & KAYAKING   Both placid, urban False Creek and the incredibly beautiful 30km (19-mile) North Vancouver fjord known as Indian Arm have launching points that can be reached by car or bus. Prices range from about C$40 per 2-hour minimum rental to C$70 per 5-hour day for single kayaks and about C$60 for canoe rentals. Customized tours range from C$75 to C$150 per person. Paddleboards generally run C$19 per hour, or C$29 for 2 hours.

Ecomarine Ocean Kayak Centre, 1668 Duranleau St., Granville Island (✆ **888/425-2925** or 604/689-7575; www.ecomarine.com), has 2-hour, daily, and weekly kayak rentals, as well as courses and organized tours. The company also has an office at the **Jericho Sailing Centre,** 1300 Discovery St., at Jericho Beach (✆ **604/224-4177;** www.jsca.bc.ca). In North Vancouver, **Deep Cove Canoe and Kayak Rentals,** 2156 Banbury Rd. (at the foot of Gallant St.; ✆ **604/929-2268;** www.deepcovekayak.com), is an easy starting point for anyone planning an Indian Arm run. It offers hourly and daily rentals of canoes and kayaks, as well as lessons and customized tours.

Lotus Land Tours, 2005-1251 Cardero St. (✆ **800/528-3531** or 604/684-4922; www.lotuslandtours.com), runs guided kayak tours on Indian Arm that come with hotel pickup, a barbecue salmon lunch, and incredible scenery. The wide, stable kayaks are perfect for first-time paddlers. One-day tours cost C$165 for adults, C$155 seniors, and C$125 for children 5 to 12.

CYCLING & MOUNTAIN BIKING   Cycling in Vancouver is fun, amazingly scenic, and very popular. Cycling maps are available at most bicycle retailers and rental outlets. Some West End hotels offer guests bike storage and rentals. Hourly rentals run around C$8 for a one-speed "Cruiser" to C$16 for a top-of-the-line mountain bike or tandem; C$30 to C$65 for a day, helmets and locks included. Popular shops that rent city and mountain bikes, child trailers, child seats, and in-line skates (protective gear included) include **Spokes Bicycle Rentals,** 1798 W. Georgia St. (✆ **604/688-5141;** www.spokesbicyclerentals.com), at the corner of Denman Street at the entrance to Stanley Park, and **Bayshore Bicycle and Rollerblade Rentals,** 745 Denman St. (✆ **604/688-2453;** www.bayshorebikerentals.ca). **Note:** Be advised that wearing a helmet is mandatory, and one will be included in your bike rental.

The most popular cycling path in the city runs along the **seawall** ★★★ around the perimeter of Stanley Park. Offering magnificent views, this flat, 10km (6¼-mile) pathway attracts year-round bicyclists, in-line skaters, and pedestrians. Another popular route is the **seaside bicycle route,** a 15km (9⅓-mile) ride that begins at English Bay and continues around False Creek to the University of British Columbia. Some of the route follows city streets that are well marked with cycle-path signs.

Serious mountain bikers also have a wealth of world-class options within a short drive from downtown Vancouver. The trails on **Mount Fromme** near **Grouse Mountain** (p. 67) are some of the lower mainland's best. Local mountain bikers love the cross-country ski trails around **Hollyburn Lodge** in **Cypress Provincial Park,** just northeast of Vancouver on the road to Whistler on Hwy. 99. Closer to downtown, both **Pacific Spirit Park** and **Burnaby Mountain** offer excellent beginner and intermediate off-road trails.

FISHING   Five species of salmon, rainbow and Dolly Varden trout, steelhead, and sturgeon abound in the local waters around Vancouver. To fish, anglers over the age of 16 need a **nonresident saltwater or freshwater license.** Licenses are available online (www.fishing.gov.bc.ca) as well as province-wide from more than 450 vendors, including tackle shops, sporting-goods stores, resorts, service stations, marinas, charter-boat operators, and department stores. Freshwater fishing licenses cost C$20 for 1 day and C$36 for 8 days. Saltwater (tidal waters) fishing licenses for nonresidents cost C$7 for 1 day, C$19 for 3 days, and C$31 for 5 days. Fly-fishing in national and provincial parks requires special permits, which you can get at any park site for a nominal fee. Permits are valid at all Canadian parks.

The B.C. *Tidal Waters Sport Fishing Guide* and *B.C. Freshwater Fishing Regulations Synopsis,* and the *B.C. Fishing Directory and Atlas,* available at many tackle shops, are good sources of information. Another good source of general information is the **Fisheries and Oceans Canada** website (www.pac.dfo-mpo.gc.ca).

Bonnie Lee Fishing Charters Ltd., 1676 Duranleau St., Granville Island (✆ **866/933-7447** or 604/290-7447; www.bonnielee.com), is an outstanding outfitter that also sells fishing licenses.

GOLF   With five public 18-hole courses, half a dozen pitch-and-putt courses in the city, and dozens more nearby, golfers are never far from their love. For discounts and short-notice tee times at more than 30 Vancouver-area courses, contact the **A-1 Last Minute Golf Hot Line** (✆ **800/684-6344** or 604/878-1833; www.lastminutegolfbc.com).

A number of excellent public golf courses, maintained by the **Vancouver Board of Parks and Recreation** (✆ **604/280-1818** to book tee times; vancouver.ca/parks), can be found throughout the city. **Langara Golf Course,** 6706 Alberta St., around 49th Avenue and Cambie Street (✆ **604/713-1816;** vancouver.ca/parks/golf/langara), built in 1926 by the Canadian Pacific Railway and recently renovated and redesigned, is one of the most popular golf courses in the province. Depending on the course, summer greens fees range from C$14 to C$43 for an adult, with discounts for seniors, youths, and off-season tee times.

The public **University Golf Club,** 5185 University Blvd. (✆ **604/224-1818;** www.universitygolf.com), is a great 6,300-yard, par-72 course with a clubhouse, pro shop, locker rooms, bar and grill, and sports lounge.

Leading private clubs are situated on the North Shore and in Vancouver. Check with your club at home to see if you have reciprocal visiting memberships with one of the following: **Capilano Golf and Country Club,** 420 Southborough Dr., West Vancouver (✆ **604/922-9331;** www.capilanogolf.com); **Marine Drive Golf Club,** 7425 Yew St. (✆ **604/261-8111;** www.marine-drive.com); **Seymour Golf and Country Club,** 3723 Mt. Seymour Pkwy., North Vancouver (✆ **604/929-2611;** www.seymourgolf.com); **Point Grey Golf and Country Club,** 3350 SW Marine Dr. (✆ **604/261-3108;** www.pointgreygolf.com); and **Shaughnessy Golf and Country Club,** 4300 SW Marine Dr. (✆ **604/266-4141;** www.shaughnessy.org). Greens fees range from C$35 to C$80.

HIKING   Great trails for hikers of all levels run through Vancouver's dramatic environs. You can pick up a local trail guide at any bookstore. Good trail maps are also available from **International Travel Maps and Books,** 12300 Bridgeport Rd.,

4

VANCOUVER | Outdoor Activities

Richmond (✆ 604/273-1400; www.itmb.com), which also stocks guidebooks and topographical maps. The retail store is open Mon to Sat from 9:30am to 5pm or you can order maps online.

If you're looking for a challenge without a long time commitment, hike the aptly named **Grouse Grind ★★** from the bottom of **Grouse Mountain** (p. 67) to the top; then buy a one-way ticket (C$5) down on the Grouse Mountain Skyride gondola.

For a bit more scenery with a bit less effort, take the Grouse Mountain SkyRide up to the **Grouse chalet** and start your hike at an altitude of 1,100m (3,642 ft.). The trail north of **Goat Mountain** is well marked and takes approximately 4–6 hours round-trip, though you may want to build in some extra time to linger on the top of Goat and take in the spectacular 360-degree views of Vancouver, Vancouver Island, and the snowcapped peaks of the Coast Mountains.

ICE-SKATING   The highest ice-skating rink in Canada is located on **Grouse Mountain** (p. 67). In the city, **Robson Square Ice Rink** (✆ 604/646-3557) re-opened for the 2010 Olympics after years of closure. During the winter, daily public skating is free and skate rentals are available for C$3. The **West End Community Centre** (870 Denman St.; ✆ 604/257-8333; www.westendcc.ca) rents skates at its enclosed winter rink. The **Kitsilano Ice Rink** (2690 Larch St.; ✆ 604/257-6983; vancouver.ca/parks) has an ice surface through mid-June. Before the Vancouver Canucks moved out to UBC, the enormous **Burnaby 8 Rinks Ice Sports Centre** (6501 Sprott St., Burnaby; ✆ 604/291-0626; www.icesports.com/burnaby8rinks) was the team's official practice facility. It has eight rinks, is open year-round, and offers lessons and rentals. Call ahead to check hours for public skating at all these rinks.

JOGGING   Local runners traverse the **Stanley Park seawall ★★★** and the park paths around **Lost Lagoon** and **Beaver Lake.** If you're a dawn or dusk runner, take note that this is one of the world's safer city parks. However, if you're alone, don't tempt fate—stick to open and lighted areas. Other prime jogging areas are **Kitsilano Beach, Jericho Beach,** and **Spanish Banks** (see "Beaches," earlier in this chapter); all of them offer flat running paths along the ocean. You can also take the seawall path from English Bay Beach south along **False Creek.** If you feel like doing a little racing, competitions take place throughout the year; ask for information at any runners' outfitters such as **Forerunners,** 3504 W. 4th Ave. (✆ 604/732-4535), or **Running Room,** 679 Denman St. (corner of Georgia; ✆ 604/684-9771). Check www.runningroom.com for information on clinics and events around Vancouver.

SKIING & SNOWBOARDING   World-class skiing lies outside the city at the **Whistler Blackcomb Ski Resort,** 110km (68 miles) north of Vancouver; see chapter 9. However, you don't have to leave the city to get in a few runs. It seldom snows in the city's downtown and central areas, but Vancouverites can ski before work and after dinner at the three ski resorts in the North Shore Mountains. These local mountains played host to the freestyle and snowboard events in the 2010 Winter Games.

Grouse Mountain Resort, 6400 Nancy Greene Way, North Vancouver (✆ 604/984-0661, snow report 604/986-6262; www.grousemountain.com), is about 8km (5 miles) from the Lions Gate Bridge and overlooks the Burrard Inlet and Vancouver skyline (p. 67). Four chairs take you to 26 alpine runs. The resort has night skiing, special events, instruction, and a spectacular view, as well as a terrain park for snowboarders. All skill levels are covered, with three beginner trails, 15 blue trails, and six black-diamond runs. Rental packages and a full range of facilities are available.

Mount Seymour Provincial Park, 1700 Mt. Seymour Rd., North Vancouver (℃ 604/986-2261; www.mountseymour.com), has the area's highest base elevation; it's accessible via four chairs and a tow. In addition to day and night skiing, the facility offers snowboarding, cross-country, and tobogganing, as well as 10km (6⅕ miles) of snowshoeing trails. The resort specializes in teaching first-timers. Camps for children and teenagers, and adult clinics, are available throughout the winter. Shuttle service is available during ski season from various locations on the North Shore, including the Lonsdale Quay SeaBus. **Cypress Bowl,** at the top of Cypress Bowl Rd. (℃ 604/926-5612, snow report 604/419-7669; www.cypressmountain.com), has the area's longest vertical drop (610m/2,010 ft.), challenging ski and snowboard runs, and 19km (11⅕ miles) of track-set cross-country ski trails (including 7.5km/4⅔ miles set aside for night skiing). Snowshoe tours and excellent introductory ski packages are available. *Note:* Cypress was home to the 2010 Winter Olympics freestyle skiing (moguls and aerials), snowboarding (half-pipe and parallel giant slalom), and brand-new skicross events.

SWIMMING The **Vancouver Aquatic Centre,** 1050 Beach Ave., at the foot of Thurlow Street (℃ 604/665-3424), has a heated, 50m (164-ft.) Olympic pool, saunas, whirlpools, weight rooms, diving tanks, locker rooms, showers, child care, and a tot pool. Admission is C$6 for adults, C$3 for children 3 to 12. The new, coed **YWCA Fitness Centre,** 535 Hornby St. (℃ 604/895-5800; www.ywcahealthand fitness.com), in the heart of downtown, has a six-lane, 25m (82-ft.), ozonated (much milder than chlorinated) pool, steam room, whirlpool, conditioning gym, and aerobic studios. A day pass is C$16 for adults. UBC's **Aquatic Centre,** 6121 University Blvd. (℃ 604/822-4522; www.aquatics.ubc.ca), located next door to the Student Union Building and the bus loop, sets aside time for public use. Admission is C$6 for adults, C$5 for youths 13 to 17, and C$4 for seniors and children 3 to 12. See also "Beaches," p. 69.

TENNIS The city maintains more than 180 outdoor hard courts that operate on a first-come, first-served basis from 8am until dusk. There is a 30-minute time limit when all courts are full. Predictably, heavy usage times are evenings and sunny weekends. With the exception of the Beach Avenue courts, which charge a nominal fee in summer, all city courts are free.

Stanley Park has four courts near Lost Lagoon and 17 courts near the Beach Avenue entrance, next to the Fish House Restaurant. During the summer season (May–Sept), six courts are taken over for pay tennis and can be pre-booked by calling ℃ 604/605-8224. **Queen Elizabeth Park's** 17 courts service the central Vancouver area, and **Kitsilano Beach Park's** ★ 10 courts service the beach area between Vanier Park and the UBC campus.

The **UBC Tennis Centre,** 6160 Thunderbird Blvd. (℃ 604/822-2505; www.tennis.ubc.ca), opened a new facility in 2011 and has 12 indoor courts and one outdoor. Indoor courts are C$20 to C$26 per hour, depending on the time.

WHITE-WATER RAFTING A 2½-hour drive from Vancouver, on the wild Nahatlatch River, **Reo Rafting,** 845 Spence Way, Anmore (℃ 800/736-7238 or 604/461-7238; www.reorafting.com), offers some of the best guided white-water trips in the province, at a very reasonable price. One-day packages—including lunch, all your

4

VANCOUVER

Outdoor Activities

gear, and 4 to 5 hours on the river—start at C$129 for adults. Multiday trips and group packages are available, and they can provide transportation from Vancouver.

Only a 1½-hour drive from the city is **Chilliwack River Rafting** (© **800/410-7238;** www.chilliwackriverrafting.com), which offers half-day trips on the Chilliwack River and in the even hairier Chilliwack River Canyon. The cost is C$89 for adults, C$74 children 12 to 18, and C$69 for children under 12.

WILDLIFE-WATCHING Orcas, or killer whales, are the largest mammals to be seen in Vancouver's waters. Three pods (families), numbering about 80 whales, return to this area every year to feed on the salmon that spawn in the Fraser River starting in May and continuing into October. The eldest female leads the group; the head of one pod is thought to have been born in 1911. From April through October, daily excursions offered by **Vancouver Whale Watch,** 12240 2nd Ave., Richmond (© **604/274-9565;** www.vancouverwhalewatch.com), focus on the majestic whales plus Dall's porpoises, sea lions, seals, eagles, herons, and other wildlife. The cost is C$125 per person (slightly lower rates for a semi-covered boat). **Steveston Seabreeze Adventures,** 12551 No. 1 Rd., Richmond (© **604/272-7200;** www.seabreezeadventures.ca), also offers whale-watching tours for about the same price. Both companies offer a shuttle service from downtown Vancouver.

Thousands of migratory birds following the Pacific flyway rest and feed in the Fraser River delta south of Vancouver, especially at the 300-hectare (740-acre) **George C. Reifel Bird Sanctuary,** 5191 Robertson Rd., Westham Island (© **604/946-6980;** www.reifelbirdsanctuary.com), which was created by a former bootlegger and wetland-bird lover. Many other waterfowl species have made this a permanent habitat. More than 268 species have been spotted. The huge, snowy white flocks of snow geese arrive in October and stay in the area until mid-December. (High tide, when the birds are less concealed by the marsh grasses, is the best time to visit.) An observation tower, 7km (4⅓ miles) of paths, free birdseed, and picnic tables make this wetland reserve an ideal outing spot from October to April, when the birds are wintering in abundance. The sanctuary is wheelchair accessible and open daily from 9am to 4pm. Admission is C$5 for adults and C$3 for seniors and children.

To hook up with local Vancouver birders, try the **Vancouver Natural History Society** (© **604/737-3074;** www.naturevancouver.ca). This all-volunteer organization runs birding field trips most weekends; many are free.

During the winter, thousands of bald eagles—in fact, the largest number in North America—line the banks of the **Squamish, Cheakamus,** and **Mamquam** rivers to feed on spawning salmon. To get there by car, take the scenic **Sea-to-Sky Highway** (Hwy. 99) from downtown Vancouver to Squamish and Brackendale; the trip takes about an hour. Alternatively, you can take a **Greyhound** bus from Vancouver's Pacific Central Station, 1150 Station St. (© **800/661-8747;** www.greyhound.ca); trip time is 1¾ hours. Contact the **Squamish Adventure Centre** (© **604/815-4994;** www.squamishchamber.com) for more information.

The annual summer salmon runs attract more than bald eagles. Tourists also flock to coastal streams and rivers to watch the waters turn red with leaping coho and sockeye. The salmon are plentiful at the **Capilano Salmon Hatchery** in North Vancouver and **Goldstream Provincial Park** out on Vancouver Island, and many other fresh waters.

Stanley Park (p. 64) is home to a heron rookery (the birds nesting in Pacific Spirit Park have moved on). Ravens, dozens of species of waterfowl, raccoons, skunks, beavers, gray squirrels (imported from New York's Central Park a century ago), and even coyotes are also full-time residents. The **Stanley Park Ecology Society** (© **604/257-8544**) runs regular nature walks in the park. Call or check their website (www.stanleyparkecology.ca) for more information, or drop by the **Lost Lagoon Nature House** in Stanley Park (p. 64).

VANCOUVER SHOPPING

Vancouver's a fun place to shop because it's international and cosmopolitan but hasn't lost its funky, fun-loving edge. There are stores galore, and most of them are not in malls. Blessed with a climate that seems semitropical in comparison to the rest of Canada, Vancouverites never really developed a taste for indoor malls (though there is one, the Pacific Centre, right downtown). Below are a few thoughts on where to start your shopping expeditions.

Shopping A to Z

ANTIQUES   **Bakers Dozen Antiques,** 3520 Main St. (© **604/879-3348;** www. dodaantiques.com), specializes in antique toys, model ships and boats, folk art, and unusual 19th- and early-20th-century furniture. **Uno Langmann Limited** at 2117 Granville St. (© **604/736-8825;** www.langmann.com.) caters to upscale shoppers and specializes in European and North American paintings, furniture, silver, and objets d'art from the 18th through early 20th centuries.

BOOKS   **Macleod's Books** (455 W. Pender St.; © **604/681-7654**) is the kind of dusty, old-fashioned, used bookstore true booklovers and bibliophiles love to explore, stacked high with reasonably priced books covering every conceivable subject. **International Travel Maps and Books,** 12300 Bridgeport Rd., Richmond (© **604/273-1400;** www.itmb.com), has the best selection of travel books, maps, charts, and globes in town, plus an impressive selection of special-interest British Columbia guides. This is the hiker's best source for detailed topographic charts of the entire province. The only problem is that they've closed their handy downtown store and moved out to Richmond.

   Kidsbooks, 3083 W. Broadway (© **604/738-5335;** a second location is at 3040 Edgemont Blvd., North Vancouver, © **604/986-6190;** www.kidsbooks.ca), features the largest and most interesting selection of children's literature in the city, and also has an amazing collection of puppets, games, and toys, and holds regular readings.

DEPARTMENT STORES   From the establishment of its early trading posts during the 1670s to its modern coast-to-coast department-store chain, **The Bay (Hudson's Bay Company),** 674 Granville St. (© **604/681-6211;** www.hbc.com), has built its reputation on quality goods. You can still buy a Hudson's Bay woolen "point" blanket, but you'll also find Tommy Hilfiger, Polo, DKNY, and more.

   Hills of Kerrisdale, 2125 W. 41st Ave. (© **604/266-9177;** www.hillsof kerrisdale.com), the neighborhood department store in central Vancouver, is a city landmark. Carrying full lines of quality men's, women's, and children's clothes, as well as furnishings and sporting goods, it's a destination for locals because the prices are often lower than those in the downtown core.

   Adjoining Pacific Centre Mall, **Holt Renfrew** (737 Dunsmuir St.; © **604/681-3121;** www.holtrenfrew.com) is a high-end trend-stocker featuring all the hot designers in a department store format.

FASHION Vancouver has the Pacific Northwest's best collection of clothes from Paris, London, Milan, and Rome, in addition to a great assortment of locally made, cutting-edge fashions. It seems that almost every month a new designer or independent boutique opens in Yaletown, Kitsilano, Gastown, or on Main Street. International designer outlets include **Chanel Boutique,** inside Holt Renfrew at 737 Dunsmuir St. (© **604/682-0522**); **Salvatore Ferragamo,** 918 Robson St. (© **604/669-4495**); and **Gianni Versace Boutique,** 757 W. Hastings St. (© **604/683-1131**).

Big-name designs can be found anywhere, but **Dream Apparel,** 311 W. Cordova St. (© **604/683-7326**), is one of the few places to show early collections—clothing and jewelry—of local designers.

Please Mum, 2951 W. Broadway (© **604/732-4574**; www.pleasemum.com), sells attractive Canadian-designed toddler's and children's cotton clothing.

Proudly Canadian, **Roots Canada,** 1001 Robson St. (corner of Burrard St.; © **604/683-4305**; www.roots.com), features sturdy casual clothing, including leather jackets and bags, footwear, outerwear, and athletic wear for the whole family. Specializing in unique retro clothing, **Woo Clothing,** 4366 Main St. (© **604/687-8200**; www.woovintage.com), has a rack-packed store in Mount Pleasant. Expect lots of ranch wear, denim, and a few Hawaiian prints, along with Asian, swing, and rockabilly designs.

True Value Vintage Clothing, 4578 Main St. (© **604/876-2218**), has a collection of funky fashions from the 1930s through the 1990s, including tons of fake furs, leather jackets, denim, soccer jerseys, vintage bathing suits, formal wear, smoking jackets, sweaters, and accessories.

FIRST NATIONS ART & CRAFTS You don't have to purchase a pricey antique to acquire original Coast Salish or Haida work. As the experts at the **Museum of Anthropology** explain, if an item is crafted by any of the indigenous Pacific Northwest artisans, it's a real First Nations piece of art. Galleries will tell you about the artist, and explain how to identify and care for these beautifully carved, worked, and woven pieces. Bold, traditional, and innovative geometric designs, intricate carvings, strong primary colors, and rich wood tones are just a few of the elements you'll find in First Nations crafts. Even if you're not in the market, go gallery-hopping to see works by Haida artists **Bill Reid** (the province's best-known Native artist) and **Richard Davidson,** and by Kwakwaka'wakw artist and photographer **David Neel.**

Coastal Peoples Fine Arts Gallery, 1024 Mainland St. (© **604/685-9298**; www.coastalpeoples.com), showcases an extensive collection of fine First Nations jewelry. The motifs—Bear, Salmon, Whale, Raven, and others—are drawn from local myths and translated into 14-karat or 18-karat gold and sterling silver creations. Inuit sculptures and items made of glass or wood are also worth a look. Custom orders can be filled quickly and shipped worldwide. There is also a Gastown location at 312 Water St. (© **604/684-9222**), and the two are a short Canada Line trip apart.

In a re-creation of a trading post interior, **Hill's Native Art,** 165 Water St. (© **604/685-4249**; www.hillsnativeart.com), established in 1946 and claiming to be North America's largest Northwest coast Native art gallery, sells ceremonial masks; Cowichan sweaters; moccasins; wood sculptures; totem poles; silk-screen prints; soapstone sculptures; and gold, silver, and argillite jewelry.

The **Lattimer Gallery,** 1590 2nd Ave. (© **604/732-4556**; www.lattimergallery.com), showcases museum-quality Pacific Northwest First Nations art, including ceremonial masks, totem poles, limited-edition silk-screen prints, argillite sculptures, and expensive gold and silver jewelry.

FOOD You'll find **salmon** everywhere in Vancouver. Many shops package whole, fresh salmon with ice packs for visitors to take home. Shops also carry delectable smoked salmon in travel-safe, vacuum-packed containers. Some offer decorative cedar gift boxes; most offer overnight air transport. Try other salmon treats such as salmon jerky and Indian candy (chunks of marinated smoked salmon), which are available at public markets such as **Granville Island Public Market** and **Lonsdale Quay Market** in North Vancouver.

The works at **Chocolate Arts,** 1620 W. 3rd Ave. (✆ **604/739-0475;** www. chocolatearts.com), are made with exquisite craftsmanship. Seasonal treats include pumpkin truffles around Halloween or eggnog truffles for Christmas. They even make chocolate toolboxes filled with tiny chocolate tools. Look for the all-chocolate diorama in the window—it changes every month or so.

Murchie's Tea & Coffee, 825 W. Pender St. (✆ **604/669-0783;** www. murchies.com), has been the city's main tea and coffee purveyor for more than a century. You'll find everything from Jamaican Blue Mountain and Kona coffees to Lapsang Souchong and Kemun teas. The knowledgeable staff will help you decide which flavors and blends fit your taste. A fine selection of bone china and crystal serving ware, as well as coffeemakers and teapots, are also on sale.

The South Seas have always been a source of intrigue. The **South China Seas Trading Company,** Granville Island Public Market (✆ **604/681-5402;** www. southchinaseas.ca), re-creates a bit of that wonder, with a remarkable collection of rare spices and hard-to-find sauces. Look for fresh Kaffir lime leaves, Thai basil, young ginger, sweet Thai chile sauce, and occasional exotic produce like mangosteens and rambutans. Pick up recipes and ideas from the knowledgeable staff.

JEWELRY At **Costen Catbalue,** 1832 W. 1st Ave. (✆ **604/734-3259;** www.costen catbalue.com), one-of-a-kind pieces in platinum and gold are made on the premises by the metalsmith and artist team Mary Ann Buis and Andrew Costen. The two artists' styles complement each other; Buis favors contemporary and clean lines, and Costen's designs tend toward a more ornate Renaissance style.

If you've never seen West Coast Native jewelry, it's worth making a trip to **The Raven and the Bear,** 1528 Duranleau St. (✆ **604/669-3990**) on Granville Island. Deeply inscribed with stylized creatures from Northwest mythology, these rings, bangles, and earrings are unforgettable. (See also "First Nations Art & Crafts," above.)

SHOES **John Fluevog Boots & Shoes Ltd,** 837 Granville St. (✆ **604/688-2828;** www.fluevog.com), has a growing international cult following of designers and models clamoring for his under-C$300 urban and funky creations. You'll find outrageous platforms and clogs, Angelic Sole work boots, and a few bizarre experiments for the daring footwear fetishist. A flagship store, where the shoes are designed, is in Gastown at 65 Water St.

SPECIALTY Want money to burn? At Chinese funerals, people burn *joss*—paper replicas of earthly belongings—to help make the afterlife for the deceased more comfortable. **Buddha Supply Centre,** 4158 Main St. (✆ **604/873-8169**), has more than 500 combustible products to choose from, including $1-million notes (drawn on the bank of hell), luxury penthouse condos, and that all-important cellphone.

Beautifully displayed, the large collection of soaps, bath oils, shampoos, and other body products at **Escents,** 1744 Commercial Dr. (✆ **604/255-4505;** www.escents aromatherapy.com), come in a variety of scents, such as the fresh ginger-citrus twist or the relaxing lavender sea. Locally produced and made with minimal packaging, the all-natural, environmentally friendly products come in convenient sizes and prices and can be individually blended to fit your mood. An additional store is at 2579 W. Broadway.

Lush, 1020 Robson St. (© **604/687-5874;** www.lush.ca), has the look of an old-fashioned deli with big wheels of cheese, slabs of sweets, and vats of dips and sauces, but all those displays are really soaps (custom cut from a block), shampoos, skin treatments, massage oils, and bath bombs made from all-natural ingredients.

If you want to bring home a few gifts from the sea, then select from the **Ocean Floor's,** 1522 Duranleau St. (© **604/681-5014**), collection of seashells, ship models, lamps, chimes, coral, shell jewelry, stained glass, and marine brass.

A family business since 1935, the **Umbrella Shop,** 526 W. Pender St. (© **604/669-1707;** factory store at 1106 W. Broadway, © 604/669-9444; www. theumbrellashop.com), carries an amazing assortment of quality umbrellas in every size, shape, and color.

TOYS Probably the only mall in North America dedicated to kids, the **Kids Market,** 1496 Cartwright St. (© **604/689-8447;** www.kidsmarket.ca), on Granville Island, features a Lilliputian entryway; toy, craft, and book stores; play areas; and services for the younger set, including a "fun hairdresser."

Kites on Clouds, The Courtyard, 131 Water St. (© **604/669-5677**), has every type of kite. Prices range from C$10 to C$20 for nylon or Mylar dragon kites to around C$200 for more elaborate ghost clippers and nylon hang-glider kites.

WINE Ten years of restructuring, reblending, and careful tending by French and German master vintners have won the province's vineyards world recognition. When buying B.C. wine, look for the VQA (Vintner Quality Alliance) seal on the label; it's a guarantee that all grapes used are grown in British Columbia and meet European standards for growing and processing.

Summerhill, Cedar Creek, Mission Hill, and **Okanagan Vineyards** are just a few of the more than 50 local estates producing hearty cabernet sauvignons, honey-rich ice wines, and oaky merlots. These wines can be found at any government-owned **BC Liquor Store,** such as the one at 1716 Robson St. (© **604/660-9031**), and at some privately owned wine stores.

If you're looking for a particular B.C. vintage, try **Marquis Wine Cellars,** 1034 Davie St. (© **604/684-0445;** www.marquis-wines.com), first. The owner and staff of this West End wine shop are dedicated to educating their patrons about wines. They conduct evening wine tastings, featuring selections from their special purchases. They also publish monthly newsletters. In addition to carrying a full range of British Columbian wines, the shop also has a large international selection.

The Okanagan Estate Wine Cellar, The Bay, 674 Granville St. (© **604/689-2323**), sells a great selection of British Columbian wines by the bottle and the case.

VANCOUVER AFTER DARK

For the best overview of Vancouver's nightlife, pick up a copy of the weekly *Georgia Straight* (www.straight.com). The Thursday edition of the *Vancouver Sun* contains the tabloid-format weekly entertainment section *Westcoast Life.* The monthly *Vancouver* magazine (www.vanmag.com) is filled with listings and strong views about what's really hot in the city. Or, get a copy of *Xtra! West* (www.xtra.ca), the free gay and lesbian biweekly tabloid, available in shops and restaurants throughout the West End.

The **Alliance for Arts and Culture,** 100-938 Howe St. (© **604/681-3535;** www.allianceforarts.com), is a great information source for all performing arts, literary events, and art films. The office is open Monday through Thursday from 9am to 5pm.

Half-price tickets for same-day shows and events are available at the **Tickets Tonight** (www.ticketstonight.ca) kiosk (daily 10am–6pm) in the **Tourism Vancouver Visitor Centre,** 200 Burrard St. (© **604/684-2787** for recorded events info). The visitor center is open daily from 8:30am to 6pm.

The Performing Arts

Three major theaters in Vancouver regularly host touring performances. The **Orpheum Theatre,** 801 Granville St. (© **604/665-3050;** www.vancouver.ca/theatres), is a 1927 theater that originally hosted the Chicago-based Orpheum vaudeville circuit. The theater now hosts the Vancouver Symphony and pop, rock, and variety shows. The Queen Elizabeth Theatre and the Vancouver Playhouse comprise the **Queen Elizabeth Complex,** 630 Hamilton St., between Georgia and Dunsmuir streets (© **604/665-3050;** www.vancouver.ca/theatres), home to the Vancouver Opera and Ballet British Columbia. The 668-seat Vancouver Playhouse presents chamber-music performances and recitals. Located in a converted turn-of-the-20th-century church, the **Vancouver East Cultural Centre** (the "Cultch" to locals), 1895 Venables St. (© **604/251-1363;** www.thecultch.com), coordinates an impressive program that includes avant-garde theater productions, performances by international musical groups, and children's programs. On the UBC campus, the **Chan Centre for the Performing Arts,** 6265 Crescent Rd. (© **604/822-2697;** www.chancentre.com), showcases the work of the UBC music students and local choirs and hosts various concerts. Designed by local architectural luminary, Bing Thom, the Chan Centre's crystal-clear acoustics are the best in town.

THEATER   An annual summertime Shakespeare series, **Bard on the Beach,** is presented in Vanier Park (© **604/739-0559;** www.bardonthebeach.org). You can also bring a picnic dinner to Stanley Park and watch **Theatre Under the Stars** (see below), which features popular musicals and light comedies.

The **Arts Club Theatre Company** (© **604/687-1644;** www.artsclub.com; tickets C$29–C$74), presents dramas, comedies, and musicals at the 450-seat Granville Island Stage (1585 Johnston St.), with post-performance entertainment in the Backstage Lounge. The Arts Club **Revue Stage** is an intimate, cabaret-style showcase for small productions, improvisation nights, and musical revues. The Art Deco **Stanley Industrial Alliance Stage** (2750 Granville St.) plays host to longer-running plays and musicals. The box office is open 9am to 7pm.

Some students at UBC are actors in training, and their productions at **Frederic Wood Theatre,** 6354 Crescent Rd., Gate 4, University of British Columbia (© **604/822-2678;** www.theatre.ubc.ca; tickets C$22 adults, C$15 seniors, C$10 children), are extremely high caliber.

From mid-July to mid-August, favorite musicals like *Annie, Singin' in the Rain,* and *Bye Bye Birdie* are performed outdoors at **Theatre Under the Stars,** Malkin Bowl, Stanley Park (© **877/840-0457** or 604/734-1917; www.tuts.ca; tickets C$29–C$44 adults, C$27–C$42 children 5–15, by a mixed cast of amateur and professional actors. Bring a blanket (it gets chilly once the sun sets) and a picnic for a relaxing evening.

CLASSICAL MUSIC & OPERA   Western Canada's only professional choral ensemble, **Vancouver Chamber Choir,** 1254 W. 7th Ave. (© **604/738-6822;**

www.vancouverchamberchoir.com), presents main stage performances (tickets C$23–C$47 adults, C$20–C$47 seniors & students) as well as concerts in local churches (C$25–C$28 adults, C$10 rush tickets for students). I've always been impressed with the quality of the stagings and performances at the **Vancouver Opera,** 835 Cambie St. (✆ **604/683-0222;** www.vancouveropera.ca; tickets C$24–C$140). The company produces both concert versions and fully staged operas, often sung by international stars. The season runs October through April, with performances in the Queen Elizabeth Theatre.

At its home in the Orpheum Theatre during the fall, winter, and spring, the **Vancouver Symphony,** 601 Smithe St. (✆ **604/876-3434;** www.vancouversymphony. ca; tickets C$27–C$165; discounts available for seniors and students), under the baton of maestro Bramwell Tovey, presents a variety of year-round concerts. The box office is open from 6pm until showtime.

DANCE For fans of modern dance, the time to be here is early July, when the **Dancing on the Edge Festival** (✆ **604/689-0926;** www.dancingontheedge.org) presents about 30 original pieces over a 10-day period. For more information about other festivals and dance companies around the city, contact the **Dance Centre** at ✆ **604/606-6400** or www.thedancecentre.ca.

Ballet British Columbia, 1101 W. Broadway (✆ **604/732-5003;** www.ballet bc.com; tickets C$48–C$70), strives to present innovative works along with more traditional productions by visiting companies. Performances are usually at the Queen Elizabeth Theatre, at 630 Hamilton St.

Laughter & Music

COMEDY CLUB/IMPROV SHOW Part comedy, part theater, and partly a take-no-prisoners test of an actor's ability to think extemporaneously, **Vancouver TheatreSports League,** Improv Centre, 1502 Duranleau St. (✆ **604/738-7013;** www. vtsl.com; tickets C$11–C$20), involves actors taking suggestions from the audience and spinning them into short skits or full plays, often with hilarious results. Shows are Wednesday at 7:30 and 9pm; Thursday at 7:30 and 9:15pm; Friday and Saturday at 8, 10, and 11:45pm; and Sunday at 7:30pm.

STRICTLY LIVE The Vancouver International Jazz Festival (✆ **604/872-5200;** www.coastaljazz.ca) takes over many venues and outdoor stages around town every June. The festival includes a number of free concerts.

The **Vancouver Folk Music Festival** (✆ **604/602-9798;** www.thefestival. bc.ca) is one of the big ones on the West Coast. It takes place outdoors in July on the beach at Jericho Park.

Live bands play every day of the week at the **Roxy,** 932 Granville St. (✆ **604/331-7999;** www.roxyvan.com; cover C$5–C$13), a raucous, no-holds-barred club, which also features bartenders with Tom Cruise *Cocktail*-style moves. On weekends, the lines are long, the patrons often soused. Dress code: No bags, no backpacks, no track suits, no ripped jeans.

Yale Hotel, 1300 Granville St. (✆ **604/681-9253;** www.theyale.ca; cover Thurs–Sat C$5–C$15), is a century-old tavern on the far south end of Granville, and is Vancouver's one-and-only home of the blues. Shows start most nights at 9pm. On Saturdays, hear an open-stage blues jam from 3 to 7pm.

The Arts Club Backstage Lounge, 1585 Johnston St. (✆ **604/687-1354;** www.thebackstagelounge.com), has a fabulous location under the Granville Bridge, by the water on the edge of False Creek. The crowd is a mix of tourists, theater patrons from that night's performance, and art-school students from neighboring Emily Carr University. Live jazz, rock, or indie bands play most evenings. Daytimes, if the sun's out, the waterfront patio is packed.

Bars, Pubs & Other Watering Holes

City policy has been to concentrate the city's pubs and clubs into two ghettos—er, *entertainment zones*—one along **Granville Street** and the other along **Water and Pender streets** in Gastown. **Yaletown** is a third, more upscale, bar/lounge/club zone. Pubs and clubs can be found in other places, and many are listed below, but if you just want to wander out for a serendipitous pub-crawl, the Granville or Water Street strips are best, with reasonable options also in Kitsilano and along Main Street in Mount Pleasant. Granville Street tends more to Top 40 dance clubs and upscale lounges, while down in Gastown, it's dark cellars spinning hip-hop and house. Yaletown is a fusion of late-night entertainment, dining, and drinking, a place where martinis reign and some of the restaurants turn into cocktail lounges at 11pm.

GASTOWN

The Alibi Room, 157 Alexander St. (at Main St.; ℂ **604/623-3383;** www.alibi.ca), pours a huge selection of craft beers to complement its modern-British-pub-style (yet locally sourced) menu. The room tends toward a revelrous crowd, and the noise amplifies as the night goes on. It's located on the eastern edge of Gastown. A bright, pleasant Irish pub in the dark heart of Gastown, the **Irish Heather,** 210 Carrall St. (ℂ **604/688-9779;** www.irishheather.com), boasts numerous nooks and crannies, some of the best beer in town, and a menu that does a lot with the traditional Emerald Isle spud. The clientele is from all over the map, from artsy types to urban pioneers.

It's the selection of more than 20 bourbons that distinguishes **Peckinpah,** 2 Water St. (ℂ **604/681-5411;** www.peckinpahbbq.com), from other Gastown drink-eat places. The bar snacks are undeniably intriguing yet simple, including corndogs served with "ballpark" mustard.

GRANVILLE STREET

Part of the renewal of Granville Street, the **Lennox Pub,** 800 Granville St. (ℂ **604/408-0881**), fills a big void in the neighborhood; it's a comfortable spot for a drink without having to deal with lines or ordering food. The beer list is extensive, featuring hard-to-find favorites. **The Morrissey,** 1227 Granville St. (ℂ **604/682-0909**), can be crammed elbow-to-elbow with a relaxed crowd that comes for the beer and occasional celebrity rocker sightings. A mix of lounge, restaurant, and club, **Ginger Sixty-Two,** 1219 Granville St. (ℂ **604/688-5494;** www.ginger62.com), is the darling of the fashion-industry trendsetters who love to be spotted here. The room is funky warehouse-chic-meets-adult-rec-room. Comfy crash pads are strategically placed throughout the room, and plenty of pillows prop up those less-than-young in the joints.

YALETOWN LOUNGES

Adjoining glowbal grill, **Afterglow,** 350 Davie St. (ℂ **604/602-0835**), mixes intimate couches and a soft soundtrack (which gets cranked up to deafening decibels as the evening wears on); you can also stay in the low-slung love seats for a long evening's cuddle.

George Ultra Lounge, 1137 Hamilton St. (© **604/628-5555;** www.george lounge.com), is small, loud, crowded, and hedonistic. Look for local glitterati and primo cocktails made by the friendly, showy mixologists who draw their ingredients from the stocked bar.

A SPORTS BAR The city's premier sports bar, **The Shark Club Bar and Grill,** 180 W. Georgia St. (at Beatty St.; © **604/687-4275;** www.sharkclubs.com; cover varies on event nights)—in the Sandman Inn—features lots of wood and brass, TVs everywhere, and on weekend evenings, lots of young women who don't look terribly interested in sports.

BARS WITH VIEWS You're in Vancouver. Odds are you're aware that this is a city renowned for its views. The entire population could make more money living in a dull, flat place like Toronto, but they stay here because of the seductive scenery. As long as that's your raison d'être, you may as well drink in style at one of the places below.

On the water at the foot of Cardero Street, **Cardero's Marine Pub,** 1583 Coal Harbour Quay (© **604/669-7666**), offers a great view of Stanley Park, the harbor, and the North Shore. Overhead heaters take away the chill when the sun goes down. As **Cloud Nine,** 1400 Robson St. (42nd floor of the Empire Landmark Hotel; © **604/687-0511;** cover Fri–Sat after 8pm C$7), a sleek hotel-top lounge, rotates 6 degrees a minute, your vantage point circles from volcanic Mount Baker, the Fraser estuary, and English Bay to Stanley Park, the towers of downtown, the harbor, and East Vancouver. Live entertainment Friday and Saturday nights. **The Dockside Brewing Company,** 1253 Johnson St. (© **604/685-7070;** www.docksidebrewing. com), is located in the Granville Island Hotel and looks out across False Creek to Yaletown and Burnaby Mountain far in the distance. The grub's based on classic seafood dishes (cooked up in a kitchen wrapped by 15.25m/50-foot aquarium), but the beer is among the best in town—brewed-on-the-premises lagers, ales, and por- ters. It's a good idea not to arrive too late: An hour or two after the sun goes down, the mostly 30-something patrons remember that they have homes to go to. Located beneath the flyway of Vancouver International, the **Flying Beaver Bar,** 4760 Inglis Dr., Richmond (© **604/273-0278**), offers nonflyers great views of incoming jets, along with mountains, bush planes, river craft, and truly fine brewpub beer.

BREWPUBS In addition to the brewpubs listed below, don't forget the **Dock- side Brewing Company,** 1253 Johnson St. (© **604/685-7070**), in the Granville Island Hotel, listed under "Bars with Views," above. Winding your way from room to room in **Steamworks Brewing Company,** 375 Water St. (© **604/689-2739;** www.steamworks.com), is almost as much fun as drinking. Upstairs, by the doors, it's a London city pub. Farther in by the staircase, it's a refined old-world club, with wood paneling, leather chairs, and great glass windows overlooking the harbor. Down in the basement, it's a Bavarian drinking hall with long lines of benches, set up parallel to the enormous copper vats. Fortunately, the beer's good. Choose from a half-dozen in-house beers. Every Sunday at **Yaletown Brewing Company,** 1111 Mainland St. (at Helmcken St.; © **604/681-2739;** www.markjamesgroup.com), all pints of brewed-on-the-premises beer are C$4.50, and pizzas are C$8. The excellent beer is complemented by an extremely cozy room, a great summertime patio, and a good appetizer menu.

DANCE CLUBS Generally clubs are open until 2am every day but Sunday, when they close at midnight. In the summer months (mid-June through Labour Day), opening hours are extended to 4am and Granville Street sometimes becomes pedestrian only. **Au Bar,** 674 Seymour St. (© **604/648-2227;** www.aubarnightclub.com; cover C$5–C$8), is packed with beautiful people milling from bar to the table nooks and back again. **The Cellar,** 1006 Granville St. (© **604/605-4350;** www.cellarvan. com; cover C$6–C$12), inhabits that netherworld between dance club, bar, meat market, and personals ads. Dance-club characteristics include a cover charge, small dance floor, and a DJ who mostly spins Top 40. But Cellar patrons are far less interested in groovin' than they are in meeting other Cellar dwellers, a process facilitated by a wall-length message board upon which pickup lines are posted. Located in the heart of Gastown, one of Vancouver's biggest and most legendary rooms (it was formerly Sonar) has been revitalized and reborn as **Fabric Nightclub,** 66 Water St. (© **604/683-6695;** www.fabricvancouver.com; cover C$20). With a 500-plus capacity, couches, a VIP balcony section that overlooks the giant dance floor, plus some of the biggest-name DJs in the world, the club doesn't disappoint. **Shine,** 364 Water St. (© **604/408-4321;** www.shinenightclub.com; cover C$10–C$20), located in a downstairs cellar in Gastown, plays house and hip-hop, with occasional forays into other genres such as reggae.

GAY & LESBIAN BARS The "Gay Village" is in the West End, particularly on Davie and Denman streets. Many clubs feature theme nights and dance parties, drag shows are ever popular, and every year in late July or early August, as Gay Pride nears, the scene goes into overdrive. For information on the current hot spots, pick up a free copy of ***Xtra West!,*** available in most downtown cafes.

Reflecting the graying and—gasp!—mellowing of Vancouver's boomer-age gay crowd, the hottest hangout for gays is the **Fountainhead,** 1025 Davie St. (© **604/687-2222;** www.thefountainheadpub.com), a pub located in the heart of the city's gay ghetto on Davie Street. The Head offers excellent microbrewed draft, good pub munchies, and a pleasant humming atmosphere until the morning's wee hours.

Numbers (1042 Davie St.; © **604/685-4077;** www.numbers.ca) is a multilevel dance club where extroverts hog the dance floor while admirers look on from the bar above. A few doors east, **Celebrities** (1022 Davie St.; © **604/681-6180;** www. celebritiesnightclub.com) welcomes a younger, more party-oriented crowd that flocks to the theme nights.

VICTORIA

by Chris McBeath

O nce a little outpost of the British Empire, Victoria is now wading into the highly internationalized 21st century, and doing it with an appealing vitality that tweaks nostalgia for the past with a thoroughly modern sensibility.

As in Vancouver, you'll be amazed at how nice the people of Victoria are. Of course, you'd be nice, too, if you lived in such a pleasant place surrounded by such stunning physical surroundings. Victoria, with a population of about 325,000, occupies just a tiny corner of an island one-fifth the size of England but far more wild—so wild, in fact, that parts of it still have no roads and the only way to get around is by boat or on foot.

Because of its easy proximity to so much natural beauty, Victoria is waking up to its enormous potential of eco-tourism, cultural heritage, sophisticated dining, and genuinely interesting attractions—at least for the most part. Whale-watching is now a major industry, kayak tours are ever more popular, mountain bikes have taken to competing for road space with the bright-red double-decker tour buses, and "outdoor adventures" are available in just about every form you can think of. Step outside of the Inner Harbour tourist zone and your trip will be even more memorable.

ESSENTIALS
Getting There
BY PLANE
The Victoria International Airport (*©* **250/953-7500;** www.victoria airport.com) is near the Sidney ferry terminal, 22km (14 miles) north of Victoria off the Patricia Bay Highway (Hwy. 17).

Air Canada (*©* **888/247-2262** or 800/661-3936; www.aircanada. com) and **Horizon Air** (*©* **800/547-9308;** www.alaskaair.com) offer direct connections from Seattle, Vancouver, Portland, Calgary, Edmonton, Saskatoon, Winnipeg, and Toronto. Canada's low-cost airline **WestJet** (*©* **888/WEST-JET** [937-8358]; www.westjet.com) offers flights to Victoria from Kelowna, Calgary, Edmonton, and other destinations; WestJet service now extends to a few U.S. cities as well.

Commuter airlines, including floatplanes that land in Victoria's Inner Harbour, provide service to Victoria from Vancouver and destinations within B.C. They include **Harbour Air Sea Planes** (*©* **800/665-0122**

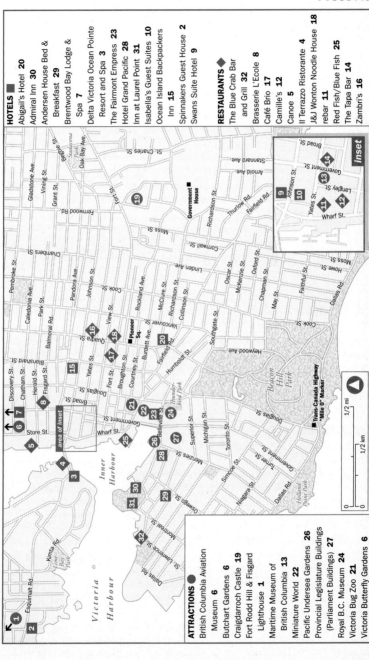

HOTELS ■

Abigail's Hotel **20**
Admiral Inn **30**
Andersen House Bed &
  Breakfast **29**
Brentwood Bay Lodge &
  Spa **7**
Delta Victoria Ocean Pointe
  Resort and Spa **3**
The Fairmont Empress **23**
Hotel Grand Pacific **28**
Inn at Laurel Point **31**
Isabella's Guest Suites **10**
Ocean Island Backpackers
  Inn **15**
Spinnakers Guest House **2**
Swans Suite Hotel **9**

RESTAURANTS ◆

The Blue Crab Bar
  and Grill **32**
Brasserie L'Ecole **8**
Café Brio **17**
Camille's **12**
Canoe **5**
Il Terrazzo Ristorante **4**
J&J Wonton Noodle House **18**
rebar **11**
Red Fish/Blue Fish **25**
The Tapa Bar **14**
Zambri's **16**

ATTRACTIONS ●

British Columbia Aviation
  Museum **6**
Butchart Gardens **6**
Craigdarroch Castle **19**
Fort Rodd Hill & Fisgard
  Lighthouse **1**
Maritime Museum of
  British Columbia **13**
Miniature World **22**
Pacific Undersea Gardens **26**
Provincial Legislature Buildings
  (Parliament Buildings) **27**
Royal B.C. Museum **24**
Victoria Bug Zoo **21**
Victoria Butterfly Gardens **6**

5

VICTORIA | Essentials

85

or 604/274-1277 in Vancouver, or 250/385-9131 in Victoria; www.harbour-air.com); **Pacific Coastal Airlines** (*C* 800/663-2872 or 604/274-8666; www.pacific-coastal.com), and **West Coast Air** (*C* 800/347-2222; www.westcoastair.com). **Kenmore Air** (*C* 800/543-9595; www.kenmoreair.com) and **Helijet Airways** (*C* 800/665-4354; www.helijet.com) offer flights between Seattle, Port Angeles, and Victoria.

GETTING INTO TOWN FROM THE AIRPORT Many car-rental firms have desks at the airport. If you're driving from the airport, take Hwy. 17 south to Victoria; it becomes Douglas Street as you enter downtown.

The **Akal Airporter shuttle bus** (*C* 250/386-2525; www.victoriaairporter.com) has a ticket counter at the airport, and makes the trip downtown in about 45 minutes. Buses leave every half-hour daily from 4:30am to midnight; the fare is C$21 one-way. Drop-offs are made at most hotels, and pickups can be arranged as well. A limited number of hotel courtesy buses also serve the airport. A cab ride into downtown Victoria costs about C$50 plus tip. **Empress/Yellow Cabs** (*C* 250/381-2222; www.empresstaxi.com), and **Blue Bird Cabs** (*C* 250/382-2222; www.taxicab.com), make airport runs.

BY FERRY

Car-carrying **BC Ferries** (*C* 888/223-3779 or 250/386-3431; www.bcferries.com) has three routes from Vancouver to Vancouver Island and Victoria. In the summer, if you're driving, it's a good idea to reserve a space beforehand, especially on long weekends.

BY TRAIN

VIA Rail's *Malahat,* now renamed the Victoria-Courtenay train, is a delightful 2½ hour trip that winds down Vancouver Island's Cowichan River valley through Goldstream Provincial Park to the **E&N Station,** 450 Pandora Ave. (*C* 800/561-8630 in Canada), near the Johnson Street Bridge. This service has been temporarily suspended for track upgrades and car renovations, with the hope that services will resume some time in 2012. For more information, contact **VIA Rail Canada** (*C* 888/842-7245; www.viarail.ca).

BY BUS

Pacific Coach Lines (*C* 800/661-1725 or 604/662-7575; www.pacificcoach.com) provides service between Vancouver and Victoria with daily departures between 5:45am and 7:45pm. Pacific Coach Lines will pick up passengers from the Vancouver cruise-ship terminal and from most downtown hotels. **Greyhound Canada** (*C* 800/661-8147 or 250/385-4411 [in Victoria]; www.greyhound.ca) provides daily service up island between Victoria and Port Hardy with many stops en route.

Visitor Information

Tourism Victoria Visitor Centre, 812 Wharf St. (*C* 800/663-3883 for hotel reservations, or 250/953-2033 for general information; www.tourismvictoria.com), is located on the Inner Harbour, across from the Fairmont Empress hotel. The center is open daily September through April from 9am to 5pm; May and June 8:30am to 6:30pm, and July through August from 9am to 9pm.

For details on the after-dark scene, pick up a copy of *Monday Magazine,* available free in cafes around the city; it's an excellent guide to Victoria's nightlife. The online version (www.mondaymag.com) has detailed entertainment listings.

City Layout

Victoria edged the Inner Harbour in the 1840s and spread outward from there. The areas of most interest to visitors, including **downtown** and **Old Town,** lie along the eastern side of the **Inner Harbour.** (North of the Johnson St. Bridge is the **Upper Harbour,** which is largely industrial but taking on new life as old buildings are redeveloped.) A little farther east, the **Ross Bay** and **Oak Bay** residential areas around Dallas Road and Beach Drive reach the beaches along the open waters of the Strait of Juan de Fuca. Victoria's central landmark is the **Fairmont Empress** hotel on Government Street, right across from the Inner Harbour. If you turn your back to the hotel, downtown and Old Town are on your right, while the **Provincial Legislature Buildings** and the **Royal B.C. Museum** are on your immediate left. Next to them is the dock for the **Seattle–Port Angeles ferries,** and beyond that the residential community of **James Bay,** the city's first neighborhood.

GETTING AROUND
By Public Transportation

BY BUS The Victoria Regional Transit System (B.C. Transit; ✆ **250/382-6161;** www.bctransit.com) operates 40 bus routes through greater Victoria as well as the nearby towns of Sooke and Sidney. Buses run to both the Butchart Gardens and the Vancouver Ferry Terminal at Sidney. Regular service on the main routes runs daily from 6am to just past midnight.

Fares are good throughout the Greater Victoria area. One-way fares are C$2.55 for adults and students and C$1.65 for seniors and children 6 to 11. Transfers are good for travel in one direction only, with no stopovers. A **DayPass,** C$7.75 for adults and students, and C$5.50 for seniors and children 6 to 11, covers unlimited travel throughout the day. You can buy passes at the Tourism Victoria Visitor Centre (see "Visitor Information," above), convenience stores, and ticket outlets throughout Victoria displaying the FAREDEALER sign.

BY FERRY Crossing the Inner, Upper, and Victoria harbors by one of the blue 12-passenger **Victoria Harbour Ferries** (✆ **250/708-0201;** www.victoriaharbour ferry.com) is cheap, fun, and exceptionally expedient from getting from one part of the city to another. May through September, the ferries to the Fairmont Empress, Coast Harbourside Hotel, and Delta Ocean Pointe Resort hotel run about every 15 minutes daily from 9am to 9pm. In March, April, and October, ferry service runs daily 11am to 5pm. November through February, the ferries run only on sunny weekends 11am to 5pm. The cost per hop is C$5 for adults and C$2.50 for children. See "Organized Tours" for other ways to enjoy a ferry ride.

By Car

You can easily explore the downtown area of Victoria on foot. If you're planning out-of-town activities, you can rent a car in town or bring your own on one of the car-passenger ferries from Vancouver, Port Angeles, or Anacortes. Although Victorians complain about traffic density, it is light when compared to other destination cities, largely because the downtown core is so walkable.

RENTALS Car-rental agencies in Victoria include the following: **Avis,** 1001 Douglas St. (✆ **800/879-2847** or 250/386-8468; www.avis.ca; bus no. 5 to Broughton

St.); **Budget,** 757 Douglas St. (© **800/668-9833** or 250/953-5300; www.budget victoria.com); **Hertz,** 2634 Douglas St.(© **800/263-0600** or 385-4440; www.hertz. com); and **National,** 767 Douglas St. (© **800/387-4747** or 250/386-1213; www. nationalvictoria.com). These latter three can be reached on the no. 5 bus to the Convention Centre. Rentals average C$60 per day, but you can often find them for less with various discounts and advance-reservation, Internet specials.

PARKING Metered **street parking** is available downtown, but be sure to feed the meter because rules are strictly enforced. Unmetered parking on side streets is rare. All major downtown hotels have guest parking, usually with a cost involved. Parking lots can be found at **View Street** between Douglas and Blanshard streets, **Johnson Street** off Blanshard Street, **Yates Street** north of Bastion Square, and **The Bay** on Fisgard at Blanshard Street.

DRIVING RULES Some of the best places on Vancouver Island can be reached only via gravel logging roads, on which logging trucks have absolute right of way. If you're on a logging road and see a logging truck coming from either direction, pull over to the side of the road and stop to let it pass.

By Bike

With its numerous bike lanes, paved trails, scenic pedaling routes, cycling festivals, and bike-friendly bylaws, in 2006 Statistics Canada recognized Victoria as the "Cycling Capital of Canada". Helmets are mandatory, and riding on sidewalks is illegal, except where bike paths are indicated. You can rent bikes starting at C$8 per hour and C$35 per day (lock and helmet included) from **Cycle B.C.,** 685 Humboldt St. (© **866/380-2453** or 250/380-2453; www.cyclebc.ca). They also rent out scooters staring at C$16 per hour, and Harley Davidsons at C$58 per hour.

By Taxi

Within the downtown area, you can expect to travel for less than C$10, plus tip. It's best to call for a cab; you won't have much luck if you try to flag one down on the street. Drivers don't always stop, especially when it's raining. Call for a pickup from **Yellow/Empress Cabs** (© **250/381-2222**) or **Blue Bird Cabs** (© **250/382-2222**).

[Fast FACTS] VICTORIA

Business Hours Victoria **banks** are open Monday through Thursday 10am to 3pm and Friday 10am to 6pm. **Stores** are generally open Monday through Saturday 10am to 6pm. Some establishments are open later, as well as on Sundays, in summer. Last call at the city's **bars** and **cocktail lounges** is 2am.

Currency Exchange The best exchange rates in town can be found at banks and by using ATMs. **Royal Bank,** 1079 Douglas St., (© **250/365-4500**) at Fort Street, is in the heart of downtown. Another option is **Calforex Foreign Currency Services,** 606 Humboldt St. (© **250/380-3711**), which is open daily.

Doctor Hotels usually have doctors on call. The **Tillicum Mall Medical Clinic,** 14-3170 Tillicum Rd., at Burnside Street (© **250/381-8112;** bus no. 10 to Tillicum Mall), accepts walk-in patients daily 9am to 9pm.

Hospitals Local hospitals include the **Royal Jubilee Hospital,** 1900 Fort St. (© **250/370-8000,**

emergency 250/370-8212), and the **Victoria General Hospital,** 1 Hospital Way (✆ **250/727-4212,** emergency 250/727-4181). You can get to both hospitals on bus no. 14.

Internet Access In the heart of Old Town, **Stain Internet Café,** 609 Yates St. (✆ **250/382-3352),** is open daily 10am to 2am (C$2.50 per half-hour). Closer to the Legislature, try **James Bay Coffee and Books,** 143 Menzies St. (✆ **250/386-4700),** open daily 7:30am to 10pm (C$1 per 10 min.). Most hotels have Internet access, as does the Victoria Public Library; see below.

Library The **Greater Victoria Public Library** (✆ **250/382-7241;** bus no. 5 to Broughton St.) is at 735 Broughton St., near the corner of Fort and Douglas streets. It offers Wi-Fi access, as well as a dozen terminals.

Luggage Storage & Lockers Coin lockers are available outside the bus station (behind the Fairmont Empress). Take bus no. 5 to the Convention Centre.

Pharmacies Shopper's Drug Mart, 1222 Douglas St. (✆ **250/381-4321;** bus no. 5 to View St.), is open Monday through Friday 7am

to 8pm, Saturday 9am to 7pm, and Sunday 9am to 6pm.

Police Dial ✆ **911.** This is a free call. The **Victoria City Police** can also be reached by calling ✆ **250/995-7654.**

Post Office The **main post office** is at 714 Yates St. (✆ **250/953-1352;** bus no. 5 to Yates St.). There are also postal outlets in **Shopper's Drug Mart** (see "Pharmacies," above) and in other stores displaying the CANADA POST postal outlet sign. Supermarkets and many souvenir and gift shops also sell stamps.

WHERE TO STAY

You'll save big-time if you schedule your holiday from October to May. When the high summer season starts in June, rates tend to skyrocket. Reservations are essential in Victoria June through September. If you arrive without a reservation and have trouble finding a room, **Tourism Victoria** (www.tourismvictoria.com; ✆ 800/663-3883 or 250/953-2033) can make reservations for you at hotels, inns, and B&Bs. It deals only with establishments that pay a fee to list with them; fortunately, most do.

Another good resource is **Canada-West Accommodations Bed & Breakfast Registry,** P.O. Box 86607, North Vancouver, BC V7L 4L2 (www.b-b.com; ✆ 800/561-3223 or 604/990-6730), which specializes in matching guests to the B&Bs that best suit their needs.

The Inner Harbour & Nearby
VERY EXPENSIVE
Delta Victoria Ocean Pointe Resort and Spa ☺   The "OPR," located across the Johnson Street Bridge on the Inner Harbour's north shore, is a big, bright, modern hotel with commanding views of downtown, the Legislature, the Fairmont Empress, and the busy harbor itself. The rooms here are nice and big, and so are the bathrooms. The decor, like the hotel itself, is a blend of contemporary and traditional. All guests have use of the big indoor pool, a good whirlpool, and a fully equipped gym with racquetball and tennis courts. Lots of guests come for the spa, one of the best in Victoria, as is Lure Seafood Restaurant (✆ 250/360-5873), which also boasts the best (and at night, certainly most romantic) dining room views in the city. Kids receive a free welcome kit, and they'll love the pool.

45 Songhees Rd., Victoria, BC V9A 6T3. www.deltavictoria.com. ✆ **800/667-4677** or 250/360-2999. 250 units. C$129–C$399 double; C$439–C$799 suite. Children under 19 stay free in parent's room. Additional adult C$30. AE, DC, MC, V. Underground valet parking C$15. Pets C$35. Bus: 24

to Colville. **Amenities:** Restaurant/lounge; babysitting; concierge; executive-level rooms; health club; Jacuzzi; indoor pool; room service; sauna; spa; 2 lit outdoor tennis courts. *In room:* A/C, TV/ DVD, fridge, hair dryer, Wi-Fi (free).

The Fairmont Empress ★★ ☺ The celebrity-status of the world-renowned Empress makes staying here a memorable experience. To get the most out of your stay, book a room at the Gold level, which comes with larger rooms, a dedicated concierge, breakfast, and evening hors d'oeuvres. The hotel's 256 standard rooms are smallish, offering little in the way of views; those only come with a Deluxe room or the more spacious Signature rooms on the corner. The hotel's fabulous location and first-class amenities—including a kid-friendly indoor pool and luxurious Willow Stream spa— add to the pleasure of staying here. The enormous Empress is firmly traditional in terms of decor. If you don't stay here, you may want to come for the famous afternoon tea (see "Taking Afternoon Tea," p. 96), a relaxing session at the spa, or a cocktail in the wood-paneled Bengal Lounge (which also serves a lunchtime curry buffet).

721 Government St., Victoria, BC V8W 1W5. www.fairmont.com/empress. ⓒ **866/540-4429** or 250/384-8111. 477 units. C$229–C$569 double; C$329–C$769 Gold level double. C$799–C$1500 suite. Children 11 & under stay free in parent's room. Packages available. AE, DC, DISC, MC, V. Underground valet parking C$30. Small pets accepted (C$25). Bus: 5. **Amenities:** 2 restaurants; bar/lounge; tearoom; babysitting; concierge; executive-level rooms; health club; Jacuzzi; indoor lap pool; room service; sauna; spa. *In room:* A/C, TV w/pay movies, fridge, hair dryer, i-Pod dock, Wi-Fi (free).

5 EXPENSIVE

Hotel Grand Pacific ★ On Victoria's bustling Inner Harbour, directly across the street from the Port Angeles–Victoria ferry dock, the Grand Pacific is more luxurious than the Delta Ocean Pointe, and has rooms that are generally more spacious than standard rooms at the Fairmont Empress. Like those other two hotels on the Inner Harbour, the Grand Pacific has its own spa; its health club is better than the others and features a huge ozonated indoor pool. All rooms have balconies and are attractively and comfortably furnished. Suites provide the best views, overlooking the harbor and the Empress. Bathrooms throughout are fairly small but luxuriously appointed.

463 Belleville St., Victoria, BC V8V 1X3. www.hotelgrandpacific.com. ⓒ **800/663-7550** or 250/386-0450. 304 units. C$199–C$389 double; C$249–C$399 suite. Kids 17 years and under stay free in parent's room. Additional person C$30. AE, DC, DISC, MC, V. Self-parking C$15; valet parking C$25. Bus: 30 to Superior and Oswego sts. **Amenities:** 2 restaurants; bar; concierge; health club; Jacuzzi; indoor pool; room service; spa; squash court. *In room:* A/C, TV w/pay movies, fridge, hair dryer, Wi-Fi (free).

Inn at Laurel Point ★★ This art-filled, resort-style hotel occupies a prettily landscaped promontory jutting out into the Inner Harbour, and consists of the original north wing and a newer wing designed by noted Vancouver architect Arthur Erickson. Recent refurbishments have made the latter a real winner, with stylish, contemporary furnishings, Asian artwork, balconies overlooking a Japanese garden, shoji-style sliding doors, and luxurious marble bathrooms with deep soaker tubs and glassed-in showers. In fact, the hotel's overall design reflects the elegant simplicity of Japanese artistic principles—a refreshing change from the chintz and florals found in so many Victoria hotels. Rooms in the north wing come with pocket balconies (every room in the hotel has a water view) and nice bathrooms—but the Erickson Wing is where you want to be. The hotel's **Aura Restaurant** is a trend-setting, dining hot spot.

680 Montreal St., Victoria, BC V8V 1Z8. www.laurelpoint.com. ⓒ **800/663-7667** or 250/386-8721. 200 units. C$199 double; C$309 suite. Additional adult C$25. Children 18 and under stay free in

parent's room. AE, DC, MC, V. Secure parking C$18. Bus: 30 to Montreal and Superior sts. **Amenities:** Restaurant; bar; babysitting; concierge; indoor pool; room service. *In room:* A/C, TV w/pay movies, hair dryer, iPod dock, Wi-Fi (free).

MODERATE

Andersen House Bed & Breakfast ★   The art and furnishings in Andersen House are drawn from the whole of the old British Empire and a good section of the modern world beyond. Each room has a unique style: the sun-drenched Casablanca room on the top floor, for example, boasts Persian rugs, a four-poster queen-size bed, and a boxed window seat. All rooms have private entrances and come with two-person Jacuzzis, books, CD players and CDs, and complimentary Wi-Fi. Rates include a splendid breakfast.

301 Kingston St., Victoria, BC V8V 1V5. www.andersenhouse.com. ⓒ **877/264-9988** or 250/388-4565. 3 units. C$235–C$265 double. Rates include breakfast. MC, V. Free off-street parking. Bus: 30 to Superior and Oswego sts. Children 11 and under not accepted. *In room:* TV/DVD, hair dryer, Jacuzzi, Wi-Fi (free).

Spinnakers Guest House ★ 🍴   This bed-and-breakfast-style guesthouse offers good accommodations at a moderate price. The two separate buildings are owned and operated by the same local entrepreneur who runs Spinnakers Brewpub, and are a 15-minute walk or a 5-minute ferry ride to downtown. The 1884 heritage building on Catherine Street is the more luxurious. Rooms feature queen-size beds, lovely furnishings, in-room Jacuzzis, fireplaces, high ceilings, and lots of natural light. The four Garden Suites units on Mary Street are really self-contained apartments, with separate bedrooms and full kitchens, perfect for longer stays or for families. Guests at both buildings get an in-room breakfast.

308 Catherine St., Victoria, BC V9A 3S8. www.spinnakers.com. ⓒ **877/838-2739** or 250/384-2739. 11 units. C$179–C$279 double. Rates include continental breakfast. AE, DC, MC, V. Free parking. Bus: 24 to Catherine St. *In room:* TV, fireplace (some units), hair dryer, kitchen (some units), Wi-Fi (free).

INEXPENSIVE

Admiral Inn 🍴 ☺   The family-operated Admiral is in a three-story building on the Inner Harbour, near the Port Angeles–bound ferry terminal and close to restaurants and shopping. The combination of clean, comfortable rooms and reasonable rates attracts young couples, families, seniors, and other travelers in search of a harbor view at a moderate price. The rooms are pleasant and comfortably furnished, a bit motel-like, with small bathrooms and balconies or terraces. The more expensive rooms come with a kitchenette, including a small stove. Some suites sleep up to six (on two double beds and a double sofa bed), and all have full kitchens.

257 Belleville St., Victoria, BC V8V 1X1. www.admiral.bc.ca. ⓒ **888/823-6472** or 250/388-6267. 33 units. C$129–C$199 double; C$139–C$229 suite. Additional person C$10. Children 11 and under stay free in parent's room. Rates include continental breakfast. AE, DC, MC, V. Free parking. Bus: 5 to Belleville and Government sts. **Amenities:** Complimentary bikes; free Wi-Fi in lobby. *In room:* A/C, TV, fridge, hair dryer, kitchen/kitchenette (in some units), Wi-Fi (free).

Downtown, Old Town & Nearby
EXPENSIVE

Abigail's Hotel ★★   Tucked into a residential neighborhood just east of downtown, this European-style Tudor boutique inn is a lavish conversion of a 1920s luxury apartment house. If you like small, personalized bed-and-breakfast hotels, you'll enjoy this impeccably maintained property. Each of the 16 rooms in the original building is beautifully furnished with pedestal sinks and goose-down duvets. Some feature soaker tubs and double-sided fireplaces, so you can relax in the tub by the light of the fire. The six Celebration Suites in the Coach House are even more luxurious. There's even a tiny spa. Abigail's is geared to adults; children are discouraged.

906 McClure St., Victoria, BC V8V 3E7. www.abigailshotel.com. © **800/561-6565** or 250/388-5363. 23 units. C$249–C$409 double. Rates include full breakfast. AE, MC, V. Free parking. Bus: 1 to Cook and McClure sts. **Amenities:** Concierge; spa. *In room:* A/C, TV/DVD, fireplace (in some rooms), hair dryer, Jacuzzi (in some rooms), Wi-Fi (free).

Isabella's Guest Suites ★ 👜 Two suites located above Willy's bakery provide affordable, fun, and quite funky accommodations in the heart of the city. The front suite is a large studio with a bed/sitting room that opens into a dining room and full kitchen. Bright colors and cheerful accents, upscale rustic furniture, high ceilings, large windows, and plenty of space make this a great home base for exploring Victoria. The second unit, a one-bedroom suite, overlooks the alley and patio of **Il Terrazzo** restaurant. The living room is painted in bright red, which goes surprisingly well with the wood floors and funky furniture. Both units have king-size beds and are nonsmoking. Breakfast is included and served at the bakery.

537 Johnson St., Victoria, BC V8W 1M2. www.isabellasbb.com. © **250/812-9216.** 2 units. C$165–C$195 double. Rates include continental breakfast. MC, V. Free parking. Bus: 5. *In room:* A/C, TV, hair dryer, kitchen.

Swans Suite Hotel ★★ ☺ One of Victoria's best-loved heritage restorations, just minutes from Bastion Square, Chinatown, and downtown, this charming 1913 heritage building now provides guests with 30 distinctive—and really roomy—suites. Many are split-level, featuring open lofts and huge exposed beams. All come with fully equipped kitchens, dining areas, living rooms, queen-size beds, and original artwork. The two-bedroom suites are like little town houses; they're great for families, accommodating up to six comfortably. The hotel also has one of Canada's largest private art collections. **The Wild Saffron Bistro & Wine Bar** is open daily; and the **Swan's Butterfield Brewpub** is one of the most popular in the city (see p. 111).

506 Pandora St., Victoria, BC V8W 1N6. www.swanshotel.com. © **800/668-7926** or 250/361-3310. 30 units. C$199 studio; C$289–C$359 suite. Children 12 and under stay free in parent's room. Rates include continental breakfast. AE, DC, MC, V. Parking C$9. Bus: 23 or 24 to Pandora Ave. **Amenities:** Restaurant; wine bar; brewpub; baby sitting; room service. *In room:* TV, hair dryer, access to nearby health club, kitchen, Wi-Fi (free).

INEXPENSIVE

Ocean Island Backpackers Inn 🏄 All sorts of travelers make their way to this inexpensive, centrally located hostel (an alternative to the Hostelling International

---

THE OAK BAY "phoenix"

When the iconic **Oak Bay Beach Hotel** (www.oakbaybeachhotel.com) was torn down in 2007, it was not without controversy. The beautiful Tudor-style hotel had been a part of Victoria's heritage since the 1920s, famed as much for its distinctive style and hospitality as for its prestigious guest list. At press time, a completely new $52-million Oak Bay Beach Hotel is set to open in May 2012. Rising above the same Pacific Ocean waterfront as its predecessor, this "phoenix" has blended the charm of the original with an array of 21st century comforts.

network), from families with children to on-the-go seniors and young adults with global wanderlust. The big, comfy lounge/common area always has all kinds of stuff going on, including live music and open-mic evenings. You can buy cheap meals and snacks, use the kitchen, or kick back with a beer or glass of wine. In addition to the dorm rooms, there are 60 private rooms, in various configurations, including some with their own bathrooms. The staff here goes out of its way to help guests make the most of their time in Victoria and on Vancouver Island.

791 Pandora Ave., Victoria, BC V8W 1N9. www.oceanisland.com. ✆ **888/888-4180** or 250/385-1788. 80 units. C$21–C$28 dorm bed; C$28–C$84 private room (some with private bathroom); C$99–C$160 family room. AE, MC, V. Parking C$5. Bus: 70 to Pandora Ave. and Douglas St. **Amenities:** Kitchen; lounge. *In room:* no phone, TV (in some rooms), no phone, Wi-Fi (free).

Outside the Central Area
EXPENSIVE

Brentwood Bay Lodge & Spa ★★★ 🎁   Located on a pristine inlet about 20 minutes north of downtown Victoria, this contemporary timber-and-glass lodge offers the best of everything, including a fabulous spa, boat shuttle to Butchart Gardens, and all manner of eco-adventures, including kayaking, scuba diving, fishing, and boat trips through the surrounding waters. The rooms are beautifully outfitted with hand-crafted furnishings, gas fireplaces, luxurious bathrooms with soaker tubs and body massage showers, balconies, and king-size beds fitted with the highest-quality Italian linens. The six new oceanfront, two-bedroom villas are even more breathtaking. **Sea-Grille** dining room offers fine seasonal menus, and the pub has great pub food as well as live entertainment, from jazz to classical guitar, Wednesday to Friday nights. The hotel has its own marina and is a licensed PADI dive center.

849 Verdier Ave., on Brentwood Bay, Victoria, BC V8M 1C5. www.brentwoodbaylodge.com. ✆ **888/544-2079** or 250/544-2079. 39 units. C$349 double; C$359–C$449 suite; C$989 villa. Rates include continental breakfast. Off-season rates considerably lower. AE, MC, V. Free parking. Take Pat Bay Hwy. north to Keating Crossroads, turn left (west) to Saanich Rd., turn right (south) to Verdier Ave. **Amenities:** Restaurant; pub; cafe; concierge; Jacuzzi; heated outdoor pool; room service; spa. *In room:* A/C, TV/DVD, fireplace, fridge, hair dryer, iPod dock, Wi-Fi (free).

INEXPENSIVE

University of Victoria Housing, Food, and Conference Services 🍴   Available only in the summer when classes aren't in session, staying on campus is a deal to rival hostelling. These are student accommodations, so basic furnishings with single or twin beds; bathrooms, pay phones, and TV lounges on every floor. Linens, towels, and soap are provided. The suites are an extremely good value—each has four bedrooms, a kitchen, a living room, and 1½ bathrooms. For C$5 extra per day, you can make use of the many on-campus athletic facilities. Each of the 28 buildings has a coin laundry. The disadvantage is that the U. Vic. campus is a painfully long way from everywhere—the city center is about a 20-minute drive away.

P.O. Box 1700, Sinclair at Finerty Rd., Victoria, BC V8W 2Y2. www.hfcs.uvic.ca. ✆ **250/721-8395.** 898 units. May–Aug C$46 single; C$56 double; C$150 suite (sleeps 4 people). Rates for single and double rooms include continental breakfast and taxes. MC, V. Parking C$6. Closed Sept–Apr. Bus: 4 or 14 to University of Victoria. **Amenities:** Access to athletic facilities; indoor pool. *In room:* Wi-Fi (free).

WHERE TO EAT

Victoria has jumped on the foodie bandwagon and offers a cornucopia of culinary styles from around the world. Some people erroneously suggest that the dining scene isn't as savvy and sophisticated as Vancouver, but with so much island-grown bounty, many of the area's 700 or so restaurants are exceptionally (and deliciously) creative, and you can be sure to find something for every taste and wallet.

Bear in mind that the touristy restaurants along Wharf Street lean to the mediocre side, catering to folks they know they'll never have to see again. You're better off to head inland (even a block is enough), where the proportion of tourists to locals drops sharply and the quality jumps by leaps and bounds. Victoria is not the kind of late-night, show-off, see-and-be-seen dining city that Vancouver is; restaurants in Victoria tend to close around 10pm. Reservations are strongly recommended for prime sunset seating during summer, especially on Friday and Saturday.

Note: Because Victoria is so compact, most of the restaurants listed in this chapter are in downtown or Old Town and no more than a 10-minute walk from most hotels.

The Inner Harbour
EXPENSIVE
The Blue Crab Bar and Grill ★★★ SEAFOOD   One of Victoria's best bets for seafood and terrific harbor views across the water, the Blue Crab combines excellent fresh ingredients and a fairly uncomplicated preparation. The Crab sources most of its ingredients locally, and it's a member of OceanWise, a group dedicated to sustainable fishing practices. For lunch you can tuck in to Pacific seafood chowder or a grilled arctic char sandwich; at dinner, try the fresh oysters, a Cortes Island clam and mussel pot, fresh halibut with pasta, or the signature hot pot of local seafood prepared with ginger and lemon-grass broth. The award-winning wine list features midrange and top-end vintages, drawn mostly from B.C., Washington, and California.

In the Coast Hotel, 146 Kingston St. ⓒ **250/480-1999.** www.bluecrab.ca. Reservations recommended. Main courses lunch C$10–C$25, dinner C$20–C$35. AE, DC, MC, V. Daily 6:30am–10pm (dinner from 5pm).

MODERATE
Canoe ★ PUB GRUB/PACIFIC NORTHWEST   What was once a Victorian power station is now one of Victoria's loveliest and liveliest brewpub restaurants, with an outdoor patio overlooking the harbor toward the Johnson Street Bridge and an industrial-inspired interior with massive masonry walls and heavy timber crossbeams. Canoe is popular because it has something tasty for every palate, all made with local ingredients whenever possible. The kitchen offers intriguing variations on standard pub fare and bar snacks, including thin-crust pizzas, classic burgers, and their signature pot pie. Head upstairs for finer fare such as premium top sirloin steak, seafood curry, or the day's fresh fish. The beer is excellent; the award-winning wine list is small but select.

450 Swift St. ⓒ **250/361-1940.** www.canoebrewpub.com. Reservations recommended for weekend dinner and Sun brunch. Main courses C$13–C$32; pub fare and bar snacks C$9–C$17; lunch special C$12. AE, MC, V. Sun–Wed 11:30am–11pm; Thurs 11:30am–midnight; Fri–Sat 11:30am–1am.

Downtown & Old Town
EXPENSIVE
Brasserie L'Ecole ★★ FRENCH   In the overheated world of food fashion, it's so refreshing to find simple French bistro fare deftly prepared and served at amazingly reasonable prices. Honesty is what's on offer at this warm, comfortable restaurant. L'Ecole's menu changes daily, depending entirely on what comes in fresh from Victoria's hinterland farms. Preparation is simple, no big reductions or fanciful jus, just

shellfish, local fish, meats with red-wine sauces, and fresh vegetables with vinaigrettes. The wine list is small, but has good wine to match the excellent food.

1715 Government St. © **250/475-6260.** www.lecole.ca. Reservations recommended. Main courses C$22–C$29. AE, MC, V. Tues–Sat 5:30–11pm.

Café Brio ★★ PACIFIC NORTHWEST/ITALIAN This award-winning restaurant is one of Victoria's best and buzziest spots for casual but top-flight dining. The Tuscan-influenced cuisine strongly reflects the seasons, fresh local meats and produce, and Pacific seafood. The menu changes daily, but appetizers always include locally harvested oysters, a wonderful house-made paprika sausage, and a choice of delicious charcuterie, all made on the premises. For entrees, choose from handmade pasta (such as fresh herb-ricotta agnolotti) or roasted or poached wild fish. The wine list is excellent, with an impressive selection of B.C. and international reds and whites. The service is friendly and knowledgeable, and the kitchen stays open as long as guests keep ordering. The entire menu is available in half portions.

944 Fort St. © **250/383-0009.** www.cafe-brio.com. Reservations recommended. Main courses C$16–C$45. AE, MC, V. Daily 5:30–9:30pm.

Camille's ★★★ PACIFIC NORTHWEST The most romantic of Victoria's restaurants, Camille's is also one of the very best. Tucked away in two rooms beneath the old Law Chambers, its decor contrasts white linen with century-old exposed brick, stained-glass lamps, and candlelight. The chef-owner was one of the founders of a Vancouver Island farm cooperative, so true to form, the ever-changing menu is seasonal and packed with locally sourced ingredients, usually found within a 100-mile radius of the restaurant. To sample a bit of everything, try the five-course tasting menu at C$90, or C$120 with wine pairings. The reasonable and extensive wine list comes with liner notes that are amusing and informative.

45 Bastion Sq. © **250/381-3433.** www.camillesrestaurant.com. Reservations recommended. Main courses C$26–C$37. AE, MC, V. Tues–Sun 5:30–10pm.

Il Terrazzo Ristorante ★ ITALIAN The food here is always good and even though some (jaded?) locals deem the place overrated, this atmospheric spot in a converted heritage building off Waddington Alley is always a top contender for Victoria's best Italian restaurant. The northern Italian cooking includes wood-oven-roasted meats, fish, and pizzas, as well as homemade pastas. An emphasis on fresh produce and local seafood sets the tone for the menu, with appetizers such as artichokes stuffed with salmon and crabmeat drizzled with a light lemon-cream sauce, and entrees like salmon crusted with almond and black pepper and baked in the wood-burning oven, or a fabulous rack of lamb. The mood is bustling and upbeat, complete with an atmospheric courtyard furnished with flowers, marble tables, wrought-iron chairs, and heaters. The wine list is enormous, with some 1,200 vintages.

555 Johnson St. (off Waddington Alley). © **250/361-0028.** www.ilterrazzo.com. Reservations recommended. Main courses C$15–C$37. AE, MC, V. Mon–Fri 11:30am–3pm; daily 5–10pm.

MODERATE

Smoken Bones Cookshack ★★★ CAJUN/CREOLE 🍖 It was only a matter of time until this top-ranked eatery found a downtown address in preference to its former, out-of-town strip mall location. It's a great move and thankfully, nothing else has changed. The food here is plentiful, tasty, and prepared with a superlative southern flair, in large part because of the in-house natural wood-smoking techniques that see pork ribs spending hours in the smoker. Southerners themselves have high praise also for the cookshack's spicy Gumbo, fresh-baked cornbread, braised collard greens, and butter-fried cabbage. And you can't get much better than that! Kids portions and sharing plates make it a great find for family dining.

1701 Douglas St. ☎ **250/391-6328.** www.smokenbones.ca. Reservations recommended. Main courses C$12-C$20. MC, V. Sun-Wed 11am-10pm; Thurs 11am-11pm; Fri & Sat 11am-midnight.

The Tapa Bar 🍴 TAPAS   The perfect meal for the commitment-shy, tapas are small and flavorful plates that you combine together to make a meal. Tapas to be sampled in this warm and welcoming spot include fried calamari, hearts of palm, and grilled portobello mushrooms. However, don't pass up on the *gambas al ajillo*— shrimp in a rich broth of garlic.

620 Trounce Alley. ☎ **250/383-0013.** www.tapabar.ca. Tapas plates C$7–C$15. AE, MC, V. Mon–Thurs 11:30am–11pm; Fri–Sat 11:30am–midnight; Sun noon–10pm.

TAKING AFTERNOON tea

Far from a simple cup of hot water with a Lipton tea bag beside it, a proper afternoon tea is both a meal and a ritual.

Any number of places in Victoria serve afternoon tea; some refer to it as high tea. Both come with sandwiches, berries, cookies, and tarts, but high tea usually includes some more substantial savory fare such as a meat-and-vegetable-filled turnover. Though the caloric intake can be hefty, it's really more about the ritual than the potential weight gain. For that reason, you don't want to go to any old teahouse. Note that in summer it's a good idea to book *at least* a week ahead.

If you want, and can afford, the best experience, head to the **Fairmont Empress ★★★**, 721 Government St. (☎ **250/384-8111;** p. 90), where tea is served in the Tea Lobby, a busy and beautifully ornate room at the front of the hotel, for C$49 to C$60. Reservations are essential and a "smart casual" dress code is in effect (no torn jeans, short shorts, or flip-flops).

More affordable, less crowded, and just as historic is tea on the lawn of **Point Ellice House,** 2616 Pleasant St. (☎ **250/380-6506;** www.pointellice house.ca), where the cream of Victoria society used to gather in the early 1900s. Afternoon tea costs C$23 and

includes a half-hour tour of the mansion and gardens, plus the opportunity to play a game of croquet. Phone ahead for reservations and Christmas hours.

If you want your tea in a historic garden setting, head over to **Abkhazi Garden,** 1964 Fairfield Rd. (☎ **250/598-8096;** bus no. 1 from downtown), where tea is served daily in the small, modernist house built by Russian Prince and Princess Abkhazi.

Set in impeccably maintained gardens, "Afternoon Tea at the Gardens" at the **Butchart Gardens Dining Room Restaurant ★★★**, 800 Benvenuto Ave. (☎ **250/652-8222;** www.butchart gardens.com; p. 98), is a memorable experience. You can savor this fine tradition for C$27 per person. Reservations recommended.

What the **White Heather Tea Room ★★**, 1885 Oak Bay Rd. (☎ **250/595-8020**), lacks in old-time atmosphere it makes up for with the sheer quality and value of the tea, and the charm of proprietress and tea mistress Agnes. For those feeling not so peckish, try the Wee Tea at C$14; for those a little hungrier, the Not So Wee Tea at C$18. If you feel like going the whole hog, try the Big Muckle Great Tea for Two at C$42. Call for reservations.

Zambri's ITALIAN   Newly relocated to Victoria's new landmark Atrium Building, this airy, cosmopolitan restaurant is known for its honest and fresh Italian cuisine served in an unpretentious, no-nonsense style. During the day, the place has a lively vibe, in part because it's the latest hot spot for busy execs, and in part because its window stretches the entire length of the restaurant and overlooks the streetscape, so dining here is like eating on a piazza in Italy. The lunch menu includes daily pasta specials and a handful of entrees such as fresh rockfish or salmon. In the evenings, the atmosphere is slightly more formal, with table service and a regularly changing a la carte menu. Menu items veer from penne with sausage and tomato to pasta with chicken liver pâté or local lamb with caponata and polenta.

820 Yates St. © **250/360-1171.** www.zambris.ca. Reservations not accepted. Lunch C$8–C$15; dinner main courses C$15–C$30. MC, V. Daily 11am–2:30pm and 5–10pm.

INEXPENSIVE

J&J Wonton Noodle House 🍴 🏮 CHINESE   This place doesn't go overboard on the atmosphere, but it's perfectly pleasant, and more importantly, you won't find better noodles anywhere in Victoria. The kitchen is glassed in so you can watch the chefs spinning out noodles. Lunch specials—which feature different fresh seafood every day—are good and cheap, so expect a line of locals at the door. If you miss the specials, noodle soups, wontons, and other dishes are also quick, delicious, and inexpensive. Dinner is pricier.

1012 Fort St. © **250/383-0680.** www.jjnoodlehouse.com. Main courses C$11–C$20; lunch specials C$7–C$15. MC, V. Tues–Sat 11am–2pm and 4:30–8:30pm. Bus: 5.

rebar ☺ VEGETARIAN   Even if you're not hungry, it's worth dropping in here for a juice blend—say grapefruit, banana, melon, and pear with bee pollen or blue-green algae for added oomph. If you're hungry, rejoice: rebar is the city's premier purveyor of vegetarian comfort food. Disturbingly wholesome as that may sound, rebar is not only tasty, but also fun, and a great spot to take the kids for brunch or breakfast. The room—in the basement of an 1890s heritage building—is bright and funky, the service is friendly and casual, and the food tends toward the simple and wholesome. The menu features quesadillas, omelets, and crisp salads. Juices are still the crown jewels, with more than 80 blends on the menu.

50 Bastion Sq. © **250/361-9223.** www.rebarmodernfood.com. Main courses C$10–C$18. AE, MC, V. Mon–Thurs 8:30am–9pm; Fri–Sat 8:30am–10pm; Sun 8:30am–3:30pm. Reduced hours in the winter.

Red Fish/Blue Fish 🏮 FISH AND CHIPS   Working out of a repurposed ship's container, these are some of the most innovative take-out fish and chips to be found. Here's where to try wild Pacific halibut, salmon, or cod coated with a light tempura batter, grilled-seared tuna; fish tacos; and mushy edamame, a quirky twist on mushy peas, plus hand-cut potatoes, some slathered in curry. Tables are forbidden on the dock, so the café provides stools for waterside dining, year round.

1006 Wharf St. (on the pier below). © **250/298-6877.** www.redfish-bluefish.com. Main courses C$10–C$17. MC, V. Daily 11:30am–7pm (may close earlier in wet weather).

EXPLORING VICTORIA

Victoria's top draws are its waterfront—the beautiful view created by the Fairmont Empress and the Provincial Legislature Buildings on the Inner Harbour—and its historic Old Town. Two must-see attractions are the Butchart Gardens, about a

20-minute drive from downtown, and the Royal B.C. Museum on the Inner Harbour. So attractive is this small capital city, though, that folks sometimes forget what a beautiful and wild part of the world it's set in. If you have time, step out of town and see some nature: sail out to see killer whales, beachcomb for crabs, kayak along the ocean shorelines, cycle some trails, or hike into the hills for fabulous views and scenery.

Seeing the Sights

THE TOP ATTRACTIONS

British Columbia Aviation Museum ★   Located adjacent to Victoria International Airport, this small hangar is crammed with a score of original, rebuilt, and replica airplanes. The collection ranges from the first Canadian-designed craft ever to fly (a bizarre kitelike contraption) to slightly more modern water bombers and helicopters. Thursdays you can watch the all-volunteer crew in the restoration hangar working to bring these old aircraft back to life. Allow an hour.

1910 Norseman Rd., Sidney. ✆ **250/655-3300.** www.bcam.net. Admission C$8 adults, C$6 seniors, free for children 12 and under. Summer daily 10am–4pm; winter daily 11am–3pm. Bus: Airport.

Butchart Gardens ★★★   After Robert Butchart exhausted the limestone quarry near his Tod Inlet home, about 22km (14 miles) from Victoria, his wife, Jenny, gradually landscaped the deserted eyesore into the resplendent Sunken Garden, opening it for public display in 1904. Over the years, a Rose Garden, Italian Garden, and Japanese Garden were added. Today, these internationally acclaimed gardens—still in the family—display more than a million plants throughout the year.

June through September, musical entertainment is provided free Monday through Saturday evenings, and there are **fireworks displays ★★★** on Saturdays in July and August. A very good lunch, dinner, and afternoon tea are offered in the Dining Room Restaurant in the historic residence; afternoon and high teas are also served in the Italian Garden (reservations recommended). Allow 2 to 3 hours; in peak summer months you'll encounter less congestion in the garden if you come very early or after 3pm. Admission prices vary according to season.

800 Benvenuto Ave., Brentwood Bay. ✆ **866/652-4422** or 250/652-4422; dining reservations 250/652-8222. www.butchartgardens.com. Admission C$18–C$29 adults, C$8–C$15 youths 13–17, C$2–C$3 children 5–12, free for children 4 and under. Daily 9am–sundown (call or visit website for seasonal closing times); visitors can remain in gardens for 1 hr. after gate closes. Bus: 75; C$4.50 round-trip. Take Blanshard St. (Hwy. 17) north toward the ferry terminal in Saanich, then turn left on Keating Crossroads, which leads directly to the gardens—about 20 min. from downtown Victoria; it's impossible to miss if you follow the trail of billboards.

Craigdarroch Castle ★   Located in the highlands above Oak Bay, Robert Dunsmuir's home, built to cement his status and please his socially ambitious wife in the 1880s, is a stunner. The four-story, 39-room Highland-style castle is topped with stone turrets and chimneys, and filled with opulent Victorian splendor: detailed woodwork, Persian carpets, stained-glass windows, paintings, and sculptures. The nonprofit society that runs Craigdarroch does an excellent job showcasing the castle. You're provided with a self-tour booklet; several volunteer docents are happy to provide further information. The castle also hosts many events throughout the year, including theater performances, concerts, and dinner tours. It is not wheelchair accessible. Allow about 45 minutes for castle tour.

1050 Joan Crescent (off Fort St.). © **250/592-5323**. www.craigdarrochcastle.com. Admission C$14 adults, C$13 seniors, students C$9, C$5 children 5–12, free for children 4 and under. June 15 to Labour Day daily 9am–7pm; day after Labour Day to June 14 daily 10am–4:30pm. Closed Dec 25–26 and Jan 1. Bus: 11 to Joan Crescent. Take Fort St. out of downtown, just past Cook, and turn right on Joan Crescent.

Fort Rodd Hill & Fisgard Lighthouse   Perched on an outcrop of volcanic rock, the **Fisgard Lighthouse** has guided ships toward Victoria's sheltered harbor since 1873. The light no longer has a keeper (the beacon has long been automated), but the site itself has been restored to its 1873 appearance. Two floors of exhibits in the light keeper's house recount stories of the lighthouse, its keepers, and the terrible shipwrecks that gave this coastline its ominous moniker "the graveyard of the Pacific."

Adjoining the lighthouse, **Fort Rodd Hill** is a preserved 1890s coastal artillery fort sporting camouflaged searchlights, underground magazines, and its original guns. Audiovisual exhibits bring the fort to life with the voices and faces of the men who served at the outpost. Displays of artifacts, room re-creations, and historic film footage add to the experience. Allow 1 to 2 hours.

603 Fort Rodd Hill Rd. © **250/478-5849**. www.fortroddhill.com. Admission C$4 adults, C$3.50 seniors, C$2 children 6–16, free for children 5 and under, C$10 families. Feb 15–Oct daily 10am–5:30pm; Nov–Feb 14 daily 9am–4:30pm. Head north on Douglas St. until it turns into Hwy. 1. Stay on Hwy. 1 for 5km (3 miles), then take the Colwood exit (exit 10). Follow Hwy. 1A for 2km (1¼ miles), then turn left at the 3rd traffic light onto Ocean Blvd.; follow the signs to the site.

Maritime Museum of British Columbia   Housed in the former provincial courthouse, this museum is dedicated to recalling B.C.'s rich maritime heritage. The displays do a good job of illustrating maritime history, from the early explorers to the grand ocean liners. An impressive collection of ship models and paraphernalia—uniforms, weapons, gear—is complemented by photographs and journals. The museum also shows films. Allow 1 hour.

28 Bastion Sq. © **250/385-4222**. www.mmbc.bc.ca. Admission C$12 adults, C$10 seniors and students, C$5 children 6–11, free for children 5 and under, C$30 families. Sept 16–June 14 daily 9:30am–4:30pm; June 15–Sept 15 daily 9:30am–5pm. Closed Dec 25. Bus: 5 to View St.

Miniature World ☺   It sounds cheesy—hundreds of dolls, miniatures, and scenes from old fairy tales, but Miniature World, inside the Fairmont Empress (the entrance is around the corner), is actually kinda cool, and kids love it. You walk in, and you're plunged into darkness, except for a moon, some planets, and a tiny spaceship flying up to rendezvous with an orbiting mother ship. Farther in are re-creations of battle scenes, a miniature Canadian Pacific Railway running all the way across a miniature Canada, Victorian dollhouses, and a three-ring circus and midway. Better yet, most of these displays do something: The train moves at the punch of a button, and the circus rides whirl around and light up as simulated darkness falls. Allow about 30 minutes to see it all.

649 Humboldt St. © **250/385-9731**. www.miniatureworld.com. Admission C$12 adults, C$11 seniors, C$10 youths, C$8 children 4–12, free for children 3 and under. Summer daily 8:30am–9pm; fall/winter daily 9am–5pm; spring daily 9am–7pm. Closed Dec 25. Bus: 5, 27, 28, or 30.

Pacific Undersea Gardens   Those with some knowledge of Vancouver Island's marine environment will tell you that many of the creatures on display here are not indigenous to these waters, but your kids might enjoy a visit. One of the star attractions is a remarkably photogenic octopus (reputedly the largest in captivity). Injured seals and orphaned seal pups are cared for in holding pens alongside the observatory as part of a provincial marine-mammal rescue program. Allow 1 hour.

490 Belleville St. © **250/382-5717.** www.pacificunderseagardens.com. Admission C$12 adults, C$11 seniors, C$9 youths 12–17, C$6 children 5–11, free for children 4 and under. Sept–Apr daily 10am–4pm; May–June daily 10am–5pm; July–Aug daily 9am–8pm. Bus: 5, 27, 28, or 30.

Provincial Legislature Buildings (Parliament Buildings) ★★ Built between 1893 and 1898 at a cost of nearly C$1 million, the Provincial Legislature Buildings (which some diehard Anglophiles insist on calling "the Parliament buildings") are one of the most noteworthy landmarks on Victoria's Inner Harbour. The 40-minute tour can come across like an eighth-grade civics lesson, but it's worth it to see the fine mosaics, marble, woodwork, and stained glass. The anecdotal asides are fun, too.

501 Belleville St. © **250/387-3046.** www.leg.bc.ca. Free admission. Victoria Day (late May) to Labour Day Mon–Thurs 9am–5pm, Fri–Sun 9am–7pm; Sept to late May Mon–Fri 9am–5pm. Tours offered every 20–30 min. in summer; in winter call ahead for the public tour schedules as times vary due to school-group bookings. Bus: 5, 27, 28, or 30.

Royal B.C. Museum ★★★ ☺ One of North America's best regional museums, the Royal B.C. has a mandate to present the land and the people of coastal British Columbia. The second-floor **Natural History Gallery** showcases the coastal flora, fauna, and geography from the Ice Age to the present; it includes dioramas of a temperate rainforest, a seacoast, and a life-size woolly mastodon. The third-floor **Modern History Gallery** presents the recent past, including historically faithful re-creations of Victoria's downtown and Chinatown. On the same floor, the **First Peoples Gallery** ★★★ is an incredible showpiece of First Nations art and culture with rare artifacts used in day-to-day Native life, a full-size re-creation of a longhouse, and a hauntingly wonderful gallery with totem poles, masks, and artifacts. The museum also has an **IMAX theater** showing an ever-changing variety of large-screen movies. On the way out (or in), be sure to stop by **Thunderbird Park,** beside the museum, where a cedar longhouse houses a workshop where Native carvers work on new totem poles. To see and experience everything takes at least 2 hours.

675 Belleville St. © **888/447-7977** or 250/356-7226. www.royalbcmuseum.bc.ca. Admission C$15 adults; C$9.50 seniors, students, and youths; free for children 5 and under; C$38 families. IMAX C$11 adults, C$9.50 students, C$8.75 seniors and children 6–18, C$5 children 5 and under. Museum daily 9am–5pm (June–Sept Fri–Sat 9am–10pm); IMAX daily 9am–8pm. Closed Dec 25 and Jan 1. Bus: 5, 28, or 30.

Victoria Bug Zoo ☺ In the heart of downtown, enter an amazing world of insects: walking sticks, praying mantises, tarantulas, and scorpions, to name a few. Although all the creepy-crawlies are behind glass, an entomologist is on hand to answer questions and show you how to handle some of the multi-legged creatures, which include a 400-leg millipede that stretches the length of your forearm. Even if you're spider-wary, this is a fascinating place. Kids will want to spend at least an hour here.

631 Courtney St. © **250/384-2847.** www.bugzoo.bc.ca. Admission C$9 adults, C$8 seniors, C$7 students, C$6 children 3–16 free for children 2 and under. Daily 11am–5pm. Any downtown bus.

Victoria Butterfly Gardens ☺ This is a great spot for kids, nature buffs, or anyone who just likes butterflies. An ID chart allows you to identify the hundreds of exotic butterflies fluttering through this lush tropical greenhouse. Species range from the tiny Central American Julia (a brilliant orange butterfly about 3 in. across) to the

Southeast Asian Giant Atlas Moth (mottled brown and red, with a wingspan approaching a foot). You'll also see tropical birds, fish, and exotic plants, including an orchid collection. Allow 1 hour.

1461 Benvenuto Ave. (P.O. Box 190), Brentwood Bay. © **877/722-0272** or 250/652-3822. www. butterflygardens.com. Admission C$15 adults, C$10 seniors and students; C$5 children 5–12; free for children 4 and under. Daily Jan–Mar 10am–4pm; Apr–Sept 10am–7pm; Oct–Dec 10am–6pm. Closed Dec 25. Bus: 75.

PARKS & GARDENS

With the mildest climate in Canada, Victoria's gardens are in bloom year-round. In addition to the world-renowned **Butchart Gardens ★★★** (see above), the **Abkhazi Garden ★**, 1964 Fairfield Rd. (© **250/598-8096;** www.abkhazi.com; entrance: C$10); the free gardens at **Government House,** 1401 Rockland Ave. (© **250/387-2080**); and the gardens at **Hatley Park National Historic Site ★**, Royal Roads University, 200 Sooke Rd., Colwood (© **866/241-0674** or 250/391-2666; www.hatleypark.ca; entrance C$18), several city parks attract strollers and picnickers. The 61-hectare (151-acre), 128-year-old **Beacon Hill Park ★** stretches from Southgate Street to Dallas Road between Douglas and Cook streets. In 1882, the Hudson's Bay Company gave this property to the city. Stands of indigenous Garry oaks (found only on Vancouver, Hornby, and Salt Spring islands) and manicured lawns are interspersed with floral gardens and ponds. Hike up Beacon Hill to get a clear view of the Strait of Georgia, Haro Strait, and Washington's Olympic Mountains. The children's farm, aviary, tennis courts, lawn-bowling green, putting green, cricket pitch, wading pool, and playground make this a wonderful place to spend a few hours with the family. The **Trans-Canada Highway's "Mile 0" marker** stands at the edge of the park on Dallas Road. Just outside downtown, **Mount Douglas Park** has great views of the area, several hiking trails, and—down at the waterline—a picnic/play area with a trail leading to a good walking beach.

Organized Tours

BUS TOURS

Gray Line of Victoria (© **800/663-8390** or 250/388-6539; www.graylinewest. com) conducts a number of tours of Victoria and Butchart Gardens. The 1½-hour "Grand City Tour" costs C$29 for adults and C$18 for children ages 2 to 11. There are daily departures throughout the year, usually at noon and 2pm. For other tours, such as the hop-on/hop-off loop around the city, check the website.

SPECIALTY TOURS

Victoria Harbour Ferries (© **250/708-0201;** www.victoriaharbourferry.com) offers a terrific 45-minute **harbor tour ★** for C$22 adults, C$20 seniors, and C$12 for children under 12. Harbor tours depart from seven stops around the Inner Harbour every 15 or 20 minutes daily 10am to 4pm (longer hours May–Sept). If you wish to stop for food or a stroll, you can get a token good for reboarding at any time during the same day. A 50-minute **Gorge Tour ★** takes you to the gorge opposite the Johnson Street Bridge, where tidal falls reverse with each change of the tide. The price is the same as for the harbor tour; June through September, gorge tours depart from the dock in front of the Fairmont Empress every half-hour 9am to 8:15pm; at other times the tours operate less frequently, depending on the weather. The ferries are 12-person, fully enclosed boats, and every seat is a window seat.

Tallyho Horse Drawn Tours (✆ **866/383-5067** or 250/514-9257; www.tallyho tours.com) has conducted horse-drawn carriage tours in Victoria since 1903. The most romantic tours are the turn-of-the-20th-century, two-person carriage tours, offered by several horse-and-buggy outfits. Competition keeps prices on par with one another from a short-and-sweet 15-minute harbor tour for C$50 to a 90-minute "romance" tour for C$240. All carriage rides start at the corner of Belleville and Menzies streets.

To get a bird's-eye view of Victoria, take a 30-minute tour with **Harbour Air Seaplanes,** 1234 Wharf St. (✆ **800/665-0212** or 250/385-9131; www.harbour-air. com). Rates are C$99 per person. For a romantic evening, try the "Fly and Dine" to Butchart Gardens deal; C$239 per person includes the flight to the gardens, admission, dinner, and a limousine ride back to Victoria.

WALKING TOURS

In addition to several themed, self-guided tour brochures that you'll find at the Tourism Information Centre, these particular tour operators offer background and stories that's hard to beat.

Discover the Past (✆ **250/384-6698;** www.discoverthepast.com) organizes interesting walks year-round. In the summer, **Ghostly Walks** explores Victoria's haunted Old Town, Chinatown, and historic waterfront; tours depart from the front of the Visitor Info Centre nightly at 7:30pm from May through October, Saturdays at 7:30pm from November through February, and Fridays and Saturdays at 7:30pm in March and April. The cost (cash only) is C$15 adults, C$10 seniors and students, C$8 children 6 to 10, and C$30 for families. Check the website for other walks.

The name says it all for **Walkabout Historical Tours** (✆ **250/592-9255;** www. walkabouts.ca). Costumed guides lead tours of the Fairmont Empress, Victoria's Chinatown, Antique Row, and Old Town Victoria, or will help you with your own itinerary. The Empress Tour costs C$10 and begins at 10am daily in the Empress Tea Lobby. Other tours have different prices and starting points.

Travel with Taste (✆ **250/385-1527;** www.travelwithtaste.com) offers an appetizing Urban Culinary Walking Tour around central downtown, during which you can forage your way through hand-crafted chocolates, smoked meats, pâtés, teas, baked treats, and wine. Four-hour tours cost C$89 per person, operate seasonally, and are a must for foodies and for those wanting to get the low-down on the hottest eateries in town. Winery tours can also be arranged.

OUTDOOR ACTIVITIES

BEACHES The most popular beach is Oak Bay's **Willows Beach,** at Beach and Dalhousie roads along the esplanade. The park, playground, and snack bar make it a great place to spend the day building a sand castle. **Gyro Beach Park,** Beach Road on Cadboro Bay, is another good spot for winding down. At the **Ross Bay Beaches,** below Beacon Hill Park, you can stroll or bike along the promenade at the water's edge.

For a taste of the wild and rocky west coast, either hike the oceanside trails in beautiful **East Sooke Regional Park ★★**, or simply head further east to **Botanical Beach ★★★** for its amazing tidal pools and marine life. A terrific day trip for all ages. Take Hwy. 14A west, turn south on Gillespie Road; then take East Sooke Road.

Two inland lakes give you the option of swimming in freshwater. **Elk and Beaver Lake Regional Park,** on Patricia Bay Road, is 11km (6¾ miles) north of downtown

Victoria; to the west is **Thetis Lake,** about 10km (6¼ miles; Hwy. 1 to exit 10 or 1A onto Old Island Hwy. 14, turn right at Six Mile Pub and follow the signs), where locals shed all their clothes but none of their civility.

BIKING   Biking is one of the best ways to get around Victoria. The 13km (8-mile) **Scenic Marine Drive bike path** ★★ begins at Dallas Road and Douglas Street, at the base of Beacon Hill Park. The paved path follows the walkway along the beaches before winding up through the residential district on Beach Drive. It eventually turns left and heads south toward downtown Victoria on Oak Bay Avenue. The **Inner Harbour pedestrian path** has a bike lane for cyclists who want to take a leisurely ride around the entire city seawall. The popular **Galloping Goose Trail** (© 250/478-3344; www.gallopinggoosetrail.com) is part of the Trans-Canada Trail, and runs from Victoria west through Colwood and Sooke all the way up to Leechtown. If you don't want to bike the whole thing, you can park at numerous places along the way, as well as several places where the trail intersects with public transit. Contact **B.C. Transit** (© 250/382-6161; www.bctransit.com) to find out which bus routes take bikes. Bikes and child trailers are available at **Cycle B.C. Rentals,** 686 Humboldt St. (May–Oct; © 250/380-2453; www.cyclebc.ca). Rentals run C$8 per hour and C$35 per day; helmets and locks are included.

BIRDING   The **Victoria Natural History Society** (www.vicnhs.bc.ca) runs regular weekend birding excursions. Their **event line** (© 250/479-2054) lists upcoming outings and gives contact numbers. **Goldstream Provincial Park** and the village of **Malahat**—both off Hwy. 1 about 40 minutes north of Victoria—are filled with dozens of varieties of migratory and local birds, including eagles. **Elk and Beaver Lake Regional Park,** off Hwy. 17, has some rare species such as the rose-breasted grosbeak and Hutton's vireo. Ospreys also nest there. **Cowichan Bay,** off Hwy. 1, is the perfect place to observe ospreys, bald eagles, great egrets, and purple martins.

BOATING, CANOEING & KAYAKING   Ocean River Sports, 1824 Store St. (© 800/909-4233 or 250/381-4233; www.oceanriver.com), can equip you with everything from a single or double kayak or a canoe to life jackets, tents, and dry-storage camping gear. Rental costs for a single kayak range from C$35 for 2 hours to C$55 per day. Multiday and weekly rates are also available. The company also offers numerous **guided tours** ★ of the Gulf Islands and the coast, including overnight excursions. For beginners, try the guided 5½-hour Coastal Kayak Tour of the coast around Victoria or Sooke for C$125.

Rowboats, kayaks, and canoes are also available for hourly or daily rental from **Great Pacific Adventures,** 811 Wharf St. (© 877/733-6722 or 250/386-2277; www.greatpacificadventures.com).

Blackfish Wilderness Expeditions (© 250/216-2389; www.blackfish wilderness.com) offers a number of interesting sailing, camping, and kayak-based tours such as the kayak/boat/hike combo, where you boat to the protected waters of the Discovery Islands, hike one of the islands, and kayak to see the pods of resident killer whales that roam the waters. Day tours start at C$70 per person.

DIVING   The coastline of **Pacific Rim National Park** is known as "the graveyard of the Pacific." Submerged in the water are dozens of 19th- and 20th-century shipwrecks and the marine life that has taken up residence in them. Underwater interpretive trails help identify what you see in the artificial reefs. If you want to take a look for yourself, contact the **Ogden Point Dive Centre,** 199 Dallas Rd. (© 888/701-1177 or 250/380-9119; www.divevictoria.com), which offers a 2-day Race Rocks and

Shipwreck Tour package that starts at C$399 per person, including all equipment and transportation. The **Saanich Inlet,** about a 20-minute drive north of Victoria, is a pristine fjord considered one of the top cold-water diving areas in the world (glass sponges are a rarity found only here). Classes and underwater scuba adventures can be arranged through **Brentwood Bay Lodge & Spa** (p. 93), Canada's only luxury PADI (Professional Association of Diving Instructors) dive resort.

FISHING   Saltwater fishing's the thing out here, but unless you know the area, it's best to take a guide. **Adam's Fishing Charters** (© **250-370-2326;** www.adams fishingcharters.com) is located on the Inner Harbour down below the Visitor Info Centre. Chartering a boat and guide starts at C$95 per hour per boat, with a minimum of 5 hours. Full day charters are around C$800.

To fish, you need a fishing license. Saltwater licenses for nonresidents cost C$7 for 1 day, C$19 for 3 days, and C$31 for 5 days plus a salmon conservation fee of $6. Freshwater licenses for nonresidents cost C$20 for 1 day, and C$36 for 8 days, plus conservation fees that range from C$20 for trout and char to C$60 for sturgeon. Tackle shops sell licenses, have details on current restrictions, and often carry copies of the *B.C. Tidal Waters Sport Fishing Guide* and *B.C. Sport Fishing Regulations Synopsis for Non-Tidal Waters.* Independent anglers should also pick up the *B.C. Fishing Directory and Atlas.* **Robinson's Sporting Goods Ltd.,** 1307 Broad St. (© **888/317-0033** or 250/385-3429), is a reliable source for information, recommendations, lures, licenses, and gear. For the latest fishing hot spots and recommendations on tackle and lures, check out **www.sportfishingbc.com**. You'll find official fishing information at the Fisheries and Oceans Canada website, **www.pac.dfo-mpo.gc.ca**.

GOLFING   Victoria's Scottish heritage doesn't stop at the tartan shops. The greens here are as beautiful as those at St. Andrews. The **Cedar Hill Municipal Golf Course,** 1400 Derby Rd. (© **250/475-7151;** www.golfcedarhill.com), the busiest course in Canada, is an 18-hole, par-67 public course 3km (1¾ miles) from downtown Victoria. It's open on a first-come, first-served basis; daytime weekday greens fees are C$45 and twilight fees (after 3pm) are C$30. Golf clubs can be rented for C$20. The **Cordova Bay Golf Course,** 5333 Cordova Bay Rd. (© **250/658-4444;** www.cordovabaygolf.com), is northeast of the downtown area. Designed by Bill Robinson, the par-71, 18-hole course features 66 sand traps and some tight fairways. Greens fees are C$46 to C$60 depending on day and season; twilight fees range from C$39 to C$59. The **Olympic View Golf Club** (643 Latoria Rd.; © **250/474-3671;** wwwgolfbc.com) is one of the top 35 golf courses in Canada, with two waterfalls and 12 lakes sharing space with the greens.

The star of Vancouver Island golf courses, and the most expensive to play, is **Westin Bear Mountain Golf Resort & Spa,** 1999 Country Club Way (© **888/533-2327** or 250/391-7160 for tee time bookings; www.bearmountain.ca). There's the 18-hole, 6,595m (7,212-yd.), par-72 Mountain course designed by Jack Nicklaus and his son, and the slightly shorter 18-hole, 6,224m (6,807-yd.), par-71 Valley Course. Golf carts (included with fee) and collared shirts (blue jeans not permitted) are mandatory on this upscale, mountaintop course that features breathtaking views and a spectacular 19th hole for recreational betting. Nonmember greens fees, depending on when you reserve and the time you play, range from C$79 (twilight) to C$150.

You can call **A-1 Last Minute Golf Hot Line** at © **800/684-6344** for substantial discounts and short-notice tee times, or check out www.lastminutegolfbc.com.

HIKING **Goldstream Provincial Park** (30 min. west of downtown along Hwy. 1) is a tranquil site for a short hike through towering cedars and past clear, rushing waters.

The hour-long hike up **Mount Work** provides excellent views of the Saanich Peninsula and a good view of Finlayson Arm. The trail head is a 30- to 45-minute drive. Take Hwy. 17 north to Saanich, then take Hwy. 17A (W. Saanich Rd.) to Wallace Drive, turn right on Willis Point Drive, and right again on Ross-Durrance Road, looking for the parking lot on the right. Signs are posted along the way. Equally good, though more of a scramble, is the hour-plus climb up **Mount Finlayson** in Gowland-Tod Provincial Park (take Hwy. 1 west, get off at the Millstream Rd. exit, and follow Millstream Rd. north to the very end).

The very popular **Sooke Potholes** trail wanders up beside a river to an abandoned mountain lodge. Take Hwy. 1A west to Colwood, then Hwy. 14A (Sooke Rd.). At Sooke, turn north on Sooke River Road, and follow it to the park.

For a taste of the wild and rocky west coast, hike the oceanside trails in beautiful **East Sooke Regional Park** ★★. Take Hwy. 14A west, turn south on Gillespie Road, and then take East Sooke Road.

For serious backpacking, go 104km (65 miles) west of Victoria on Hwy. 14A to Port Renfrew and the challenging **West Coast Trail** ★★★ (p. 164), extending 77km (48 miles) from Port Renfrew to Bamfield in a portion of **Pacific Rim National Park** ★★★ (p. 162). The trail was originally a lifesaving trail for shipwrecked sailors. Plan a 7-day trek for the entire route; reservations are required, so call ✆ **604/663-6000.**

For something less strenuous but still scenic, try the **Swan Lake Christmas Hill Nature Sanctuary,** 3873 Swan Lake Rd. (✆ **250/479-0211;** www.swanlake. bc.ca). A floating boardwalk winds its way through this 40-hectare (99-acre) wetland past resident swans; the adjacent Nature House supplies feeding grain on request.

WATERSPORTS The Crystal Pool & Fitness Centre, 2275 Quadra St. (✆ **250/361-0732**), is Victoria's main aquatic facility. The 50m (164-ft.) lap pool; children's pool; diving pool; sauna; whirlpool; and steam, weight, and aerobics rooms are open Monday through Thursday 5:30 to 11pm, Friday 5:30am to 10:30pm, Saturday 6am to 6pm, and Sunday 8:30am to 4pm. Drop-in admission is C$5.50 for adults, C$4.25 for seniors, C$3.75 for students, C$2.75 for children 5 to 12, and free for children 4 and under. Beaver Lake in Elk and Beaver Lake Regional Park (see "Birding," above) has lifeguards on duty and picnicking facilities along the shore.

Surfing has recently taken off on the island. The best surf is along the west coast at **China, French,** and **Mystic beaches** ★. To get there, take Blanshard Street north from downtown, turn left onto Hwy. 1 (Trans-Canada Hwy.), then after about 10km (6¼ miles), take the turnoff onto Hwy. 14A (Sooke Rd.). Follow Hwy. 14A north along the coast. The beaches are well signposted.

Windsurfers skim along outside the Inner Harbour and on Elk Lake when the breezes are right. Though French Beach, off Sooke Road on the way to Sooke Harbour, has no specific facilities, it is a popular local windsurfing spot.

WHALE-WATCHING The waters surrounding the southern tip of Vancouver Island teem with orcas (killer whales), harbor seals, sea lions, harbor and Dall porpoises, and bald eagles. All whale-watching companies offer basically the same tour; the main difference comes in the equipment they use: Some use a 12-person Zodiac, where the jolting ride is almost as exciting as seeing the whales, whereas others take a larger, more leisurely craft. Both offer excellent platforms for seeing whales. In high season (June to Labour Day), most companies offer several trips a day. Always ask if the outfitter is a "responsible whale-watcher"—that is, doesn't go too close to disturb or harass the whales. Expect to pay C$95 to C$115 for a 2- to 3-hour trip. Among the most reputable companies is **Prince of Whales,** 812 Wharf St. (✆ **888/383-4884** or 250/383-4884; www.princeofwhales.com), just below the Visitor Info Centre; and **Orca Spirit Adventures** (✆ **888/672-ORCA** [6722] or 250/383-8411; www. orcaspirit.com), which departs from the Coast Harbourside Hotel dock.

VICTORIA SHOPPING

Victoria has dozens of specialty shops, and because the city is built on a pedestrian scale, you can easily wander from place to place seeking out whatever treasure you're after. The multi-level Bay Centre anchors the city core with mainstream wares, but streets such as **Trounce Alley,** Chinatown's **Fan Tan Alley** (Canada's narrowest commercial street), and funky **LoJo** (Lower Johnson) are far more interesting. Nearly all the listings below are within a short walk of the Fairmont Empress; for those shops located more than 6 blocks from the hotel, bus information is provided. Stores in Victoria are generally open Monday through Saturday from 10am to 6pm; some, but not many, are open on Sundays during the summer. Explorers beware: The brick-paved **Government Street promenade,** from the Inner Harbour 5 blocks north to Yates Street, is a jungle of cheap souvenir shops. There are gems in here, but you'll have to pass T-shirt stores, knickknack emporiums, and countless maple-syrup bottles.

Shopping A to Z

ANTIQUES   Victoria has long had a deserved reputation for antiques—particularly those of British origin. In addition to those listed below, check out **Romanoff & Company Antiques,** 837 Fort St. (✆ **250/480-1543**); and for furniture fans, **Charles Baird Antiques,** 1044A Fort St. (✆ **250/384-8809**).

The farthest from downtown, **Faith Grant's Connoisseur Shop Ltd.,** 1156 Fort St. (✆ **250/383-0121;** www.faithgrantantiques.com; bus: 10 to Fort and Cook sts.), is also the best. The 16 rooms of this 1862 heritage building contain everything from Georgian writing desks to English flatware, not to mention fine ceramics, prints, and paintings. Furniture is especially strong here. Sadly, the place is up for sale and only time will tell if this fabulous find will have to relocate.

Vanity Fair Antiques & Collectibles, 1044 Fort St. (✆ **250/380-7274;** www. vanityfairantiques.com; bus: 10 to Blanshard or Cook St.), is fun to browse, with showcases galore of crystal, glassware, furniture, and lots more.

ART   Soaring white walls and huge arched windows make the **Fran Willis Gallery,** 1619 Store St. (✆ **250/381-3422;** www.franwillis.com; bus: 5 to Douglas and Fisgard), one of Victoria's most beautiful gallery spaces. The collection is strong in contemporary oils, mixed media, and bronzes, almost all by B.C. and Alberta artists.

Winchester Galleries, 796 Humboldt St. (✆ **250/382-7750;** www.winchester galleriesltd.com), a slightly daring gallery, features contemporary oil paintings. Unlike elsewhere in town, few wildlife paintings ever make it to the walls.

BOOKS   All bookstores should look as good as **Munro's Books,** 1108 Government St. (✆ **250/382-2464;** www.munrobooks.com), a mile-high ceiling in a 1909 heritage building, complete with heavy brass lamps and murals on the walls. The store stocks more than 35,000 titles, including an excellent selection about Victoria and books by local authors. The staff is friendly and very good at unearthing obscure titles.

DEPARTMENT STORE & SHOPPING MALL The Bay Centre, between Government and Douglas sts., off Fort and View sts. (*©* **250/952-5690;** www.thebay centre.ca), is named after its anchor store, Hudson's Bay Company (*©* **250/385-1311**). The rest of the complex houses a full shopping mall disguised as a block of heritage buildings.

FASHION **Breeze,** 1150 Government St. (*©* **250/383-8871**), a high-energy store for women, carries a number of trendy lines, such as Mexx, Powerline, and Mac+Jac. Shoes by Nine West and Steve Madden, plus stylish accessories, complete the look.

Still Life, 551 Johnson St. (*©* **250/386-5655**), originally known for its vintage clothes, has updated and moved to a contemporary style that includes fashions from Diesel, Workwear, and Toronto designer Damzels-in-this-Dress.

W. & J. Wilson's Clothiers, 1221 Government St. (*©* **250/383-7177**), Canada's oldest family-run clothing store, has been owned/managed by the Wilsons since 1862. Look for sensible casuals or elegant cashmeres and leathers for men and women, from British, Scottish, and other European designers.

FIRST NATIONS ARTS & CRAFTS Natives from the nearby Cowichan band are famous for their warm, durable sweaters knit with bold motifs from hand-spun raw wool. In addition to these beautiful knits, craftspeople create soft leather moccasins, moose-hide boots, ceremonial masks, sculptures carved from argillite or soapstone, baskets, bearskin rugs, and jewelry. The **Quw'utsun' Cultural Centre** (p. 138) also has a large gift shop where you can watch artisans at work.

Alcheringa Gallery, 665 Fort St. (*©* **250/383-8224;** www.alcheringa-gallery. com), began as a shop handling imports from the Antipodes, but it has evolved into one of Victoria's truly great stores for aboriginal art connoisseurs. All the coastal tribes are represented in Alcheringa's collection, along with pieces from Papua New Guinea. The presentation is museum quality, with prices to match.

Beautiful and expensive First Nations artwork is sold in **Art of Man Gallery,** 721 Government St. (*©* **250/383-3800;** www.artofmangallery.com), located off the Tea Lobby in the Fairmont Empress hotel. You'll find high-quality works by some of the best-known artists in British Columbia.

Hill's Native Art, 1008 Government St. (*©* **250/385-3911;** www.hillsnativeart. com), is the store for established artists from up and down the B.C. coast, which means the quality is high, and so are the prices (although you can find good-quality work here for under C$300). Of course, you don't stay in business for 50 years without pleasing your drop-in customers, so Hill's has its share of dream catchers and other knickknacks.

FOOD & WINE All those old-fashioned English sweets you love but can never find in North America (such as horehound drops and lemon sherbets) are sold at the **English Sweet Shop,** 738 Yates St. (*©* **250/382-3325;** www.englishsweets.com). They also sell English marmalade, lemon curd, jam, chutneys, tea, and biscuits—you get the picture. There's a smaller version, the **British Candy Shoppe,** 2 blocks away at 638 Yates St. (*©* **250/382-2634**).

It's worth coming to **Murchie's,** 1110 Government St. (*©* **250/383-3112;** www. murchies.com), just to suck up the coffee smell or sniff the many specialty teas, including the custom-made blend served at the Fairmont Empress' afternoon tea.

Rogers' Chocolates, 913 Government St. (☎ **250/881-8771**; www.rogers chocolates.com), bills itself as "quite possibly the best chocolates in the world," and with original Tiffany glass, old-fashioned counters, and free samples, this 100-year-old shrine could possibly live up to the claim.

Before setting up shop at **Silk Road Aromatherapy and Tea Company,** 1624 Government St. (☎ **250/704-2688;** www.silkroadtea.com; bus: 5 to Douglas and Fisgard sts.), the two Victoria women who run this store first trained to become tea masters in China and Taiwan. Their Victoria store on the edge of Chinatown sells a wide variety of teas, including premium loose blends and tea paraphernalia such as teapots, mugs, and kettles; they offer a full line of aromatherapy products as well. The latest addition is the spa, which offers a range of treatments at very reasonable prices.

The Wine Barrel, 644 Broughton St. (☎ **250/388-0606;** www.thewinebarrel. com), sells more than 300 B.C. wines and wine accessories. It's known for carrying the largest selection of B.C. ice wines in Victoria.

JEWELRY High-quality, handcrafted Canadian jewelry is sold in **Artina's,** 1002 Government St. (☎ **250/386-7000;** www.artinas.com).

At **Jade Victoria,** 911 Government St. (☎ **250/384-5233**), you'll find jewelry made from British Columbia jade, which is mined in northern Vancouver Island, then crafted in Victoria and China into necklaces, bracelets, and other items.

The Patch, 719 Yates St. (☎ **250/384-7070**), the Island's largest provider of body jewelry, has studs, rings, and other bright baubles for your nose, navel, or nipple, much of it quite creative and reasonably priced.

OUTDOOR CLOTHES & EQUIPMENT **Ocean River Sports,** 1824 Store St. (☎ **250/381-4233;** www.oceanriver.com), is the place to go to arrange a sea kayak tour—they'll be happy to rent you a boat and all the gear. This is also a good spot for outdoor clothing and camping "musts", like solar-heated showers or espresso machines.

Robinson's Outdoor Store, 1307 Broad St. (☎ **250/385-3429;** www.robinsons outdoors.com), also has something for virtually every type of outdoor enthusiast. They also sell fishing licenses.

Walkers Shoes, 1012 Broad St. (☎ **250/381-8608**), specializes in the finest European walking shoes for men and women.

PUBLIC MARKETS Market Square, 560 Johnson St. (☎ **250/386-2441**), was constructed from the original warehouses and shipping offices built in the 1800s. This pleasant and innovative heritage reconstruction features small shops and restaurants surrounding a central courtyard, often the site of live performances in summer.

VICTORIA AFTER DARK

Monday Magazine, a weekly tabloid published on Thursdays, is the place to start. Its listings section provides comprehensive coverage of what's happening in town and is particularly good for the club scene. If you can't find *Monday* in cafes or record shops, visit it online at **www.mondaymag.com**.

For information on theater, concerts, and arts events, contact the **Tourism Victoria Visitor Centre,** 812 Wharf St. (☎ **800/663-3883** or 250/953-2033; www. tourismvictoria.com). You can also buy tickets for Victoria's venues from the Visitor Centre, but only in person.

The Performing Arts

The **Royal Theatre,** 805 Broughton St., and the **McPherson Playhouse,** 3 Centennial Sq., share a common box office (✆ **888/717-6121** or 250/386-6121; www. rmts.bc.ca). The **Royal**—built in the early 1900s and renovated in the 1970s—hosts concerts by the Victoria Symphony and performances by the Pacific Opera Victoria, as well as touring dance and theater companies. The **McPherson**—built in 1914 as the first Pantages Vaudeville Theatre—is home to smaller stage plays and performances by the Victoria Operatic Society.

THEATER Performing in an intimate playhouse that was once a church, the **Belfry Theatre Society ★★**, 1291 Gladstone Ave. (✆ **250/385-6815;** www.belfry.bc.ca; bus no. 22 to Fernwood St.), is an acclaimed theatrical group that stages four productions (usually works by contemporary Canadian playwrights) October through April, and one show in August. Tickets are C$28 to C$38.

The **Intrepid Theatre Company,** 1205 Broad St. (✆ **250/383-2663;** www. intrepidtheatre.com), runs two yearly theater festivals. In spring it's the **Uno Festival of Solo Performance ★★**, a unique event of strictly one-person performances. Come summer, Intrepid puts on the **Victoria Fringe Festival ★★**. Even if you're not a theater fan—*especially* if you're not—don't miss the Fringe. More than 50 performers or small companies from around the world put on amazingly inventive plays. The festival runs from late August to early September.

Theatre Inconnu, 1923 Fernwood Rd. (✆ **250/360-0234;** www.theatreinconnu. com), is Victoria's oldest alternative theater group. The quality is excellent, and tickets are inexpensive. It produces Victoria's annual Shakespearean Festival, which takes place in the historic St. Ann's Academy, at 835 Humboldt St., in July and August.

The **Langham Court Theatre,** 805 Langham Court (✆ **250/384-2142;** www. langhamcourttheatre.bc.ca), performs works produced by the Victoria Theatre Guild, a local amateur society dedicated to presenting a wide range of dramatic and comedic works. From downtown, take bus no. 14 or 11 to Fort and Moss streets.

OPERA The **Pacific Opera Victoria ★★**, 1815 Blanshard St. (✆ **250/385-0222;** www.pov.bc.ca), presents three productions annually from October to April. Performances are normally at the McPherson Playhouse and Royal Theatre. Tickets cost C$30 to C$130. The **Victoria Operatic Society,** 10-744 Fairview Rd. (✆ **250/381-1021;** www.vos.bc.ca), presents Broadway musicals and other popular fare at the McPherson Playhouse. Tickets cost C$20 to C$48.

ORCHESTRAL & CHORAL MUSIC The well-respected Victoria Symphony Orchestra, 610-620 View St. (✆ **250/385-6515;** www.victoriasymphony.bc.ca), kicks off its season on the first Sunday of August with Symphony Splash, a free concert performed on a barge in the Inner Harbour. Regular performances begin in September and last through May. The Orchestra performs at the Royal Theatre or the University Farquhar Auditorium. Tickets average C$60 for most concerts.

DANCE Dance recitals and full-scale performances by local and international dance troupes such as DanceWorks and the Scottish Dance Society are scheduled throughout the year. Call the **Visitor Centre** at ✆ **250/953-2033** to find out who's performing when you're in town.

COMEDY & SPOKEN WORD **Mocambo,** 1028 Blanshard St. (✆ **250/384-4468**), a coffeehouse near the public library, hosts a range of spoken-word events through the week (multimedia fusion demos, philosopher's cafes, argument for the joy of it), then lets loose on Saturdays with improv comedy. There is no cover.

Music & Dance Clubs

MUSIC FESTIVALS   **Folkwest** (www.folkwest.ca) is a free multicultural celebration of song, food, and crafts, from late June to early July on Ship Point.

Every day at noon from early July to late August, **Summer in the Square** (© **250/361-0388**), a popular festival in downtown's Centennial Square, offers free music during weekday lunch hours, and every evening. Each day features a different band and musical style. The festival's showstoppers are the Concerts Under the Stars held each Sunday from 7 to 9:30pm; the series features some 15 local bands over its 6-week run.

The Jazz Society runs a hotline listing jazz events throughout the year. Its raison d'être, however, is **JazzFest International** (© **250/388-4423**; www.jazzvictoria. ca), held from late June to early July. The more progressive of Victoria's two summer jazz fests, this one offers a range of styles from Cuban, salsa, and world beat to fusion and acid jazz. This organization also puts on the excellent **Blues Bash** on Labour Day weekend on an outdoor stage in Victoria's Inner Harbour.

LIVE MUSIC   **Swans Butterfield Brewpub** (see "Bars & Pubs," below) presents a live band every night.

Hermann's Jazz Club, 753 View St. (© **250/388-9166**; www.hermannsjazz. com; cover C$5–C$10), cultivates a community-center feel, which is definitely and defiantly *not* chic. Still, it consistently delivers Victoria's best old-time live jazz and Dixieland with the opportunity to jam. Open Wednesday through Saturday at 8pm, Sunday at 4:30pm.

Lucky Bar, 517 Yates St. (© **250/382-5825**; www.luckybar.ca; cover C$5–C$20), is a long, low, cavernous space with a pleasantly grungy feel to it. The place doesn't get into gear until after 9pm, and features a mix of DJs and live bands.

DANCE CLUBS   Venues for the hip, 20-somethings are constantly morphing from one concept to another. Check with **Tourism Victoria** (p. 86) as to the latest happening places; most open Monday through Saturday until 2am, and Sunday until midnight. Drinks run from C$4 to C$8.

Sugar, 858 Yates St. (© **250/920-9950**; www.sugarnightclub.ca; cover Fri–Sat C$3–C$6), is one club that has weathered the test of time, as has its old-fashioned disco ball. Open Thursday through Saturday only; lineups start at 10pm, so come early. DJs spin mostly hip-hop, house, and Top 40 tunes.

Lounges, Bars & Pubs

LOUNGES   The **Bengal Lounge,** in the Fairmont Empress, 721 Government St. (© **250/384-8111**), is one of the last outposts of the old empire—a Raffles or a Harry's Bar—except the martinis are ice-cold and jazz plays in the background (and on weekends, live in the foreground). Lately it's attracted the young and elegant lounge-lizard crowd.

The Reef, 533 Yates St. (© **250/388-5375**; www.thereefrestaurant.com), is a Caribbean restaurant that transforms into a funky reggae lounge when the sun has faded away. Features include great martinis and good tunes, and a DJ now and again.

BARS & PUBS   **Big Bad John's,** in the Strathcona Hotel, 919 Douglas St. (© **250/383-7137**), is Victoria's first, favorite, and only hillbilly bar. It's a low, dark warren of a place, with a crowd of drunk and happy rowdies.

If it's a nice night, head for **Canoe,** 450 Swift St. (© **250/361-1940;** www.canoebrewpub.com), and its fabulous outdoor patio overlooking the Upper Harbour. The beer is brewed on the premises, and the food is fun and hearty.

Darcy's Wharf Street Pub, 1127 Wharf St. (© **250/380-1322;** www.darcys pub.ca), is a large, bright, harborfront pub featuring a range of fine brews, pool tables, occasional live bands, and a lovely view of the sunset. The crowd is young and lively.

One of the best brewpubs in town, **Spinnakers,** 308 Catherine St. (© **250/386-2739;** www.spinnakers.com; bus: 24 to Songhees Rd.), did it first and did it well. Spinnakers' view of the harbor and Legislature is fabulous. The brewed-on-the-premises ales, lagers, and stouts are uniformly excellent, and the pub grub is always good. An on-site bakery sells various beer breads. The weekends often feature a band. There are also dartboards and pool tables.

The Sticky Wicket, 919 Douglas St. (© **250/383-7137**), is yet another pub in the Strathcona Hotel (see Big Bad John's, above)—but the Wicket is a standout. The beautiful wood interior spent many years in Dublin before being shipped here to Victoria. Elevators can whip you from deepest Dublin up three floors to the outdoor patio balcony, complete with beach volleyball.

Few drinking spots are more intriguing—or more enjoyable—than **Swans Butterfield Brewpub,** in Swans Hotel, 506 Pandora Ave. (© **250/361-3310**). The intrigue comes from the founding owner's vast Pacific Northwest and First Nations art collection. The enjoyment comes from the room itself, on the ground floor of a beautifully converted 1913 feed warehouse across from the Johnson Street Bridge. The beer here is brewed on-site and delicious. There's live entertainment every night.

GAY & LESBIAN BARS   Victoria's entertainment options for the gay and lesbian community are few. A good resource for local contacts can be found online at **www.gayvictoria.ca**.

Hush, 1325 Government St. (© **250/385-0566;** www.hushnightclub.ca), is a straight-friendly space (crowd is about 50/50) featuring top-end touring DJs spinning house, trance, and disco house, as well as live music. The experience is more like a rave. Cover charges range between C$10 to C$25 depending on the entertainment. It's open Wednesday to Sunday.

Paparazzi Night Club, 642 Johnson St. (© **250/388-0505;** www.paparazzi nightclub.com), is Victoria's principal gay and lesbian nightclub. It has a full menu and a lounge that is large enough to host drag shows. Enjoy an offbeat selection of techno, disco, and hip-hop music, or sing a little karaoke—there are thick binders full of songs. Paparazzi is open Monday to Friday 3pm to 2am, and 1pm to 2am on the weekend. There's a C$5 cover charge on Fridays and Saturdays after 9pm.

6

SOUTHERN VANCOUVER ISLAND & THE GULF ISLANDS

by Chris McBeath

S tretching more than 450km (280 miles) from Victoria to the northwest tip of Cape Scott, Vancouver Island is one of the most fascinating destinations in Canada, a mountainous bulwark of deep-green forests, rocky fjords, and wave-battered headlands. For an area so easily accessible by car, the range of wildlife here is surprising: Bald eagles float above the shorelines, seals and sea lions slumber on rocky islets, and porpoises and orca whales cavort in narrow passes between islands.

The British Columbia capital, Victoria, is the ideal place to begin exploring the island; see chapter 5 for complete coverage of the city.

Duncan, the "City of Totem Poles" in the Cowichan Valley north of Victoria, reveals another facet of Vancouver Island culture. This lush green valley is the ancestral home of the Cowichan tribe, famed for its hand-knit sweaters; it also houses some of the island's best wineries and organic farms, making it a gastronomical hub.

Nestled just off the island's east coast lie the Gulf Islands. The fact that they are only reached by a confusing network of ferries just enhances their sense of remoteness and mystery. Part arty, counterculture enclave, part trophy-home exurb, and part old-fashioned farm and orchard territory, the Gulf Islands are full of contradictions and charm. The largest, Salt Spring Island, is a haven for artists who are attracted to its mild climate and pastoral landscapes.

Running down the spine of Vancouver Island is a lofty chain of mountains that functionally divides the island into west and east. In the west, which receives the full brunt of Pacific storms, vast rainforests grow along inaccessible, steep-sided fjords. Paved roads provide access in only a few places, and boat charters, ferries, and floatplanes are the preferred means of transport. Much of this region, including Pacific Rim National Park, is covered in Chapter 7.

The east side of Vancouver Island, and in particular the area from Nanaimo southward, is home to the vast majority of the island's population of 750,000. Protected by the mainland of British Columbia, the climate here is drier and warmer than on the storm-tossed west coast, and agriculture is a major industry. Tourism is also key to the local economy: The southeast portion of Vancouver Island has the warmest median temperatures in all of Canada, and tourists and retirees flood the area in search of rain-free summer days.

While the Gulf Islands and the southern portions of Vancouver Island were long ago colonized by European settlers, the original First Nations peoples are very much a part of cultural and political life in the area. Historically, the Pacific coast of British Columbia was one of the greatest centers of art and culture in Native America, and this past is beautifully preserved in many museums and in several villages. Modern-day First Nations artists are very active, and nearly every town has galleries and workshops filled with their exquisite carvings, paintings, and sculpture.

ESSENTIALS

Getting There

BY PLANE Victoria is the island's major air hub, with jet, commuter-plane, and floatplane service from Vancouver and Seattle. See chapter 5 for details.

Both standard commuter aircraft and floatplanes provide regularly scheduled service to a number of other island communities from both Victoria and Vancouver. All of the southern Gulf Islands, as well as many towns, can be reached by scheduled harbor-to-harbor floatplane service, either from Vancouver International's seaplane terminal or from downtown Vancouver's Coal Harbour terminal. In fact, it's easy to arrange a chartered floatplane for almost any destination along coastal Vancouver Island. Since floatplanes don't require airport facilities, even the most remote fishing camp can be as accessible as a major city.

Commercial airline service is provided by **Air Canada** (© 888/247-2262; www. aircanada.com), **Horizon Air** (© 800/252-7522; www.horizonair.com or www. alaskaair.com), **Pacific Coastal** (© 800/663-2872; www.pacificcoastal.com), and **WestJet** (© 888/937-8538; www.westjet.com).

Commuter seaplane companies that serve Vancouver Island include **Harbour Air Seaplanes** (© 800/665-0212 or 604/274-1277; www.harbour-air.com), **Tofino Air** (© 866/486-3247 for Tofino base, 888/436-7776 for Sechelt base, or 800/665-2359 for Gabriola base; www.tofinoair.ca), and **West Coast Air** (© 800/665-0212 or 604/274-1277; www.westcoastair.com).

BY FERRY BC Ferries (© 888/BCFERRY [223-3779]; www.bcferries.com) operates an extensive year-round network that links Vancouver Island, the Gulf Islands, and the mainland. Major routes include the crossing from Tsawwassen to Swartz Bay and to Nanaimo, and from Horseshoe Bay (northwest of Vancouver) to Nanaimo. In summer, reserve in advance. If you're taking a car, beware: Ticket prices add up quickly.

Washington State Ferries (© 888/808-7977 in Washington, 206/464-6400 in the rest of the U.S., or 250/381-1551 in Canada; www.wsdot.wa.gov/ferries) has daily service between Anacortes, in Washington, to Sidney, on Vancouver Island. One-way fares for a car and driver are around US$75 in high season.

The year-round passenger ferries run by **Victoria Clipper** (✆ **800/888-2535;** www.victoriaclipper.com) depart from Seattle's Pier 69; adult round-trip tickets range from US$134 to US$155 with Internet specials available for advance bookings.

From Port Angeles, Washington, the year-round (except for a 2-week maintenance break in Jan) Black Ball Transport's car ferry **MV *Coho*** (✆ **360/457-4491** in Port Angeles, or 250/386-2202 in Victoria; www.cohoferry.com) offers service to Victoria for US$17 per adult foot passenger, US$61 per vehicle and driver.

BY BUS   One of the easiest ways to get to Vancouver Island destinations is by bus. Conveniently, the bus will start its journey from a city center (such as Vancouver), take you directly to the ferry dock and onto the ferry, and then deposit you in another

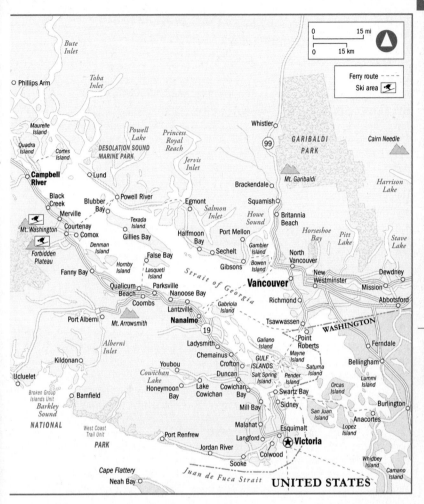

city center (Victoria or Nanaimo). A lot of the hassle of ferry travel is minimized, and the costs are usually lower than other alternatives. (If you're traveling to Vancouver on VIA Rail or Amtrak, bus connections are easy—the bus and train share the same terminal.)

Pacific Coach Lines (✆ 800/661-1725 or 604/662-8074; www.pacificcoach. com) offers bus service via BC Ferries from Vancouver to Victoria. The one-way fare is C$44 for adults, including the ferry crossing. **Greyhound Canada** (✆ 800/661-8747 or 604/482-8747; www.greyhound.ca) provides several daily trips between Vancouver and Nanaimo, the transfer point to Island Bus which continues Greyhound services further north. One-way fare is C$20 non-refundable, C$24 refundable plus ferry crossing of C$14.

Visitor Information

For general information on Vancouver Island, contact **Tourism Vancouver Island,** Ste. 501, 65 Front St., Nanaimo, BC V9R 5H9 (© **250/754-3500;** fax 250/754-3599; www.vancouverisland.travel). Also check out **www.vancouverisland.com**.

Getting Around

While Vancouver Island has an admirable system of public transport, getting to remote sights and destinations is difficult without your own vehicle.

BY FERRY   BC Ferries (© **888/BCFERRY** [223-3779]; www.bcferries.com) routes link Vancouver Island ports to many offshore islands, including the southern Gulf Islands of Denman, Gabriola, Galiano, Hornby, Kuper, Mayne, the Penders, Salt Spring, Saturna, and Thetis. Except for Salt Spring (and that's fairly limited), none of these islands has public transport, so once there, you'll need to hoof it, hitch it, hire a taxi, or arrange for bike rentals. Most innkeepers will pick you up from the ferry if you've reserved in advance.

BY TRAIN   VIA Rail's E&N Railiner, also known as the *Malahat* (© **888/VIA-RAIL** [842-7245] or 250/383-4324; www.viarail.ca), provides a daily round-trip run from Victoria to Courtenay in period passenger cars. The train passes through beautiful landscapes and takes about 4½ hours each way. At press time, service had been temporarily suspended for track upgrades and car renovations, with the intention that it will be reintroduced some time in 2012. Call for further information.

BY BUS   Greyhound Canada (© **800/661-8747;** www.greyhound.ca) runs buses between Victoria and Nanaimo with stops at smaller centers along Hwy. 1 (see "By Car," below).

BY CAR   **The southern half of Vancouver Island is well served by paved highways. The trunk road between Victoria and Nanaimo is **Hwy. 1, the Trans-Canada. This busy route alternates between four-lane expressway and congested two-lane highway, and requires some patience and vigilance, especially during the summer months. North of Nanaimo, the major road is **Hwy. 19,** which is now almost all four-lane expressway The older sections of 19, all closer to the island's east coast, are now labeled 19A. North of Campbell River, a long, unimproved section of Hwy. 19 continues all the way to Port Hardy. Passing lanes are minimal so getting behind a logging truck, or an RV heading north, can be frustratingly slow. **Hwy. 4** is the island's other major road system, which connects Parksville with Port Alberni and on to Ucluelet and Tofino, on the rugged west coast. This paved road is mostly two-lane, and portions of it are not only extremely winding and hilly, weather can change on a bend. Access to gasoline and car services is no problem, even in more remote north Vancouver Island.

Rental cars are readily available. Agencies include **Avis** (© **800/879-2847** in Canada, 800/331-1212 in the U.S.; www.avis.com), **Budget** (© **800/268-8900** in Canada, 800/527-0700 in the U.S.; www.budget.com), and **National** (© **877/222-9058** in Canada and the U.S.; www.nationalcar.com).

THE GULF ISLANDS ★★

The Gulf Islands are a collection of several dozen mountainous islands that sprawl across the Strait of Georgia between the British Columbia mainland and Vancouver Island. While only a handful of the islands is served by regularly scheduled ferries,

Since many B&Bs on the Gulf Islands are geared to adults, families with young children will find cottage resorts and private rentals the best-value (and most child-friendly option). **Gulf Island Vacation Rentals** (1564 Fort St., Victoria, BC, V8S 5J2; www.gulfislandvacationrentals.com; ☎ **866/595-8989** or 250/595-8989) is a clearinghouse of private homes, bed-and-breakfast rooms, and cottages available for rental on the Gulf Islands. Note that for all accommodations, it's mandatory to make reservations well in advance, as the ferry system doesn't exactly make it easy to just drive on to the next town to find a place to stay.

this entire area is popular with boaters, cyclists, kayakers, and sailboat enthusiasts. Lying in the rain shadow of Washington State's Olympic Mountains, the Gulf Islands have the most temperate climate in all of Canada, without the heavy rainfall common in much of coastal British Columbia. In fact, the climate here is officially semi-Mediterranean!

The Gulf Islands are the northern extension of Washington's San Juan Islands, and they share those islands' farming and seafaring past. Agriculture, especially sheep raising, is still a major industry. The past few decades, however, have seen radical changes in traditional island life: The sheer beauty of the land- and seascapes, the balmy climate, and the relaxed lifestyle have brought a major influx of new residents. These islands were a major destination for Vietnam War–era draft evaders, many of whom set up homes, farms, and businesses here. The islands quickly developed a reputation as a countercultural hippie enclave, a reputation they still maintain. As the original radicals become the islands' retirees, urban escapees and younger generations of free spirits have come to grow organic vegetables, cultivate vineyards, explore an artistic urge, and hang out in the coffee shops.

Paralleling this youthful influx is another kind of land rush. Moguls, celebrities, and other wealthy refugees from urban centers have moved to the islands in droves. The quality of facilities has shot up: Many of the islands now boast fine restaurants, elegant inns, and a multitude of craft studios and art galleries. The population influx is having some unexpected consequences. Groundwater is a precious commodity on these arid islands, and some inns will ask guests to monitor their water use. Adding to the problem is that saltwater aquifers underlie parts of the islands: Corrosive salt water doesn't do anyone much good.

Despite the one-direction migration, the Gulf Islands remain a charming destination. The islands are still underdeveloped, and some of the best restaurants and lodgings are tucked away in forests down long roads. There's little in the way of organized activities: no water slides, theme parks, and few major resorts; just incredible scenery, great biking and kayaking, lovely inns, and fine dining.

Gulf Islands National Park Reserve, 2220 Harbour Rd., Sidney (☎ **250/654-4000;** www.pc.gc.ca), protects 34 sq. km (13 sq. miles) of the islands' unique marine ecosystem on 15 islands and more than 50 islets, plus 26 sq. km (10 sq. miles) of marine areas. A large portion of the reserve is on smaller Gulf Islands, such as Prevost, Portland, D'Arcy, and Tumbo, which have no BC Ferries service and can be reached only by kayak, canoe, water taxi, or private boat. The park includes land on Mayne and North and South Pender islands, though it is Saturna—the most remote

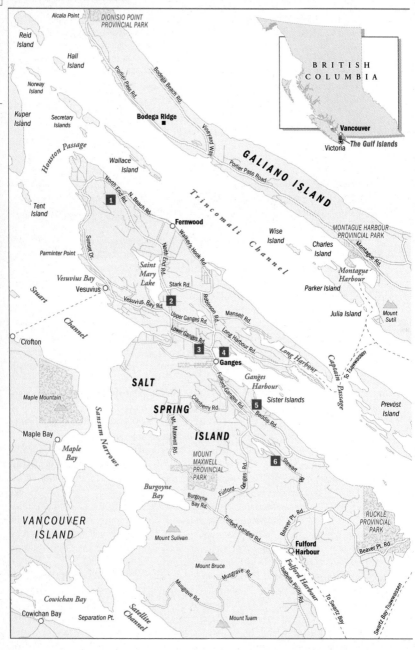

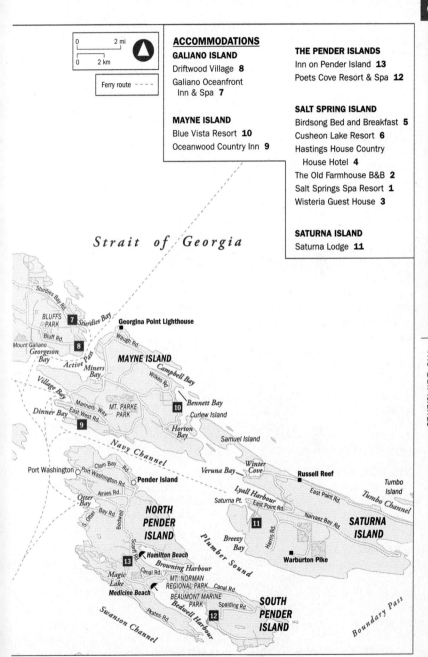

ACCOMMODATIONS

GALIANO ISLAND
Driftwood Village **8**
Galiano Oceanfront
   Inn & Spa **7**

MAYNE ISLAND
Blue Vista Resort **10**
Oceanwood Country Inn **9**

THE PENDER ISLANDS
Inn on Pender Island **13**
Poets Cove Resort & Spa **12**

SALT SPRING ISLAND
Birdsong Bed and Breakfast **5**
Cusheon Lake Resort **6**
Hastings House Country
   House Hotel **4**
The Old Farmhouse B&B **2**
Salt Springs Spa Resort **1**
Wisteria Guest House **3**

SATURNA ISLAND
Saturna Lodge **11**

0   2 mi
0   2 km

Ferry route - - - -

Strait of Georgia

Sturdies Bay Rd.

BLUFFS PARK **7**
Sturdies Bay
Bluff Rd. **8**
Mount Galiano
Georgeson Bay
Waugh Rd.
Georgina Point Lighthouse

Active Pass
Miners Bay
MAYNE ISLAND
Campbell Bay
Wilkes Rd.

Village Bay
Mariners Way
MT. PARKE PARK
East West Rd.
Bennett Bay **10**
Curlew Island
Dinner Bay
9
Horton Bay
Samuel Island

Navy Channel

Port Washington
Clam Bay Rd.
Port Washington Rd.
Pender Island
Amies Rd.
Veruna Bay
Winter Cove
Russell Reef
Tumbo Island

Tumbo Channel

Otter Bay
S. Otter Bay Rd.
Bedwell
NORTH PENDER ISLAND
Scarff Rd.
Lyall Harbour
Saturna Pt.
East Point Rd.
East Point Rd.
Narvaez Bay Rd.
11
SATURNA ISLAND

Hamilton Beach **13**
Magic Lake
Canal Rd.
Medicine Beach
Browning Harbour
MT. NORMAN REGIONAL PARK
Canal Rd.
BEAUMONT MARINE PARK
Spalding Rd.
Plumber Sound
Breezy Bay
Harris Rd.
Warburton Pike

Swanson Channel
Pirates Rd.
Bedwell Harbour
12
SOUTH PENDER ISLAND

Boundary Pass

and undeveloped of the islands served by BC Ferries—that has the most parkland acreage.

Essentials

GETTING THERE

BY FERRY **BC Ferries** (✆ **888/BCFERRY** [223-3779] in North America, or 250/386-3431; www.bcferries.com) operates four different runs to the southern Gulf Islands, from Tsawwassen on the British Columbia mainland, and from Swartz Bay, Crofton, and Nanaimo on Vancouver Island. The system was designed primarily to get commuters to their jobs on the mainland or in Victoria. Getting exactly where you want to be, exactly when you want to be there, is anything but straightforward (and not always possible). Be aware that the ferries are not very large; to ensure that you make the one you want, arrive at least 30 minutes early (45–60 min. on summer weekends). You can make reservations on the routes from Tsawwassen, but not on the other runs.

Ticket pricing is confusing. There are separate fares for drivers, passengers, and vehicles, plus fees for bikes, kayaks, and canoes on most runs. Tickets from Vancouver Island (Chemainus, Crofton, Nanaimo, or Swartz Bay) are calculated as return fares; that is, when you buy a ticket and depart from one of these ports, you don't have to buy an additional ticket if you are returning to the same port. However, all fares via Tsawwassen are one-way: You pay going and coming. To make it more puzzling, outward-bound fares from Tsawwassen are more expensive than the same journey back to the mainland. Sample peak-season fares: a car and two passengers from Swartz Bay to Salt Spring Island, C$43; a single foot passenger, C$11.

BY PLANE A number of commuter airlines offer regular floatplane service from either Vancouver Harbour or Vancouver International Airport. One-way tickets to the islands usually cost C$85 to C$95 per person, not a bad fare when you consider the time and hassle involved in taking a ferry. However, floatplanes are small and seats sell out quickly, so reserve ahead of time. Call **Harbour Air Seaplanes** (✆ **800/665-0212** or 604/274-1277; www.harbour-air.com), or **Seair Seaplanes** (✆ **800/447-3247** or 604/273-8900; www.seairseaplanes.com). **Kenmore Air** (seaplanes; ✆ **866/435-9524;** www.kenmoreair.com) operate flights from Seattle to Victoria, and various Gulf Island and Vancouver Island destinations.

VISITOR INFORMATION

For general information on the Gulf Islands, contact **Tourism Vancouver Island,** Ste. 501, 65 Front St., Nanaimo, BC V9R 5H9 (✆ **250/754-3500;** www.vancouver island.travel). Another good comprehensive resource is **www.gulfislandstourism. com/index.php**.

GETTING AROUND

Most innkeepers will pick up guests at the ferry or floatplane terminals, if given sufficient notice. There's also taxi service on most islands. Most taxis will quote you a fixed price for a journey when you phone to reserve the trip. Be sure to confirm the price when you're picked up.

BY BICYCLE Winding country roads and pretty landscapes make the Gulf Islands a favorite destination for cyclists. Although the islands' road networks aren't exactly large—and roads are quite steep and narrow—it can be great fun to bike the back roads, jump a ferry, and peddle to an outlying pub for lunch. Bikes can be taken

If you're planning to make a circuit of the five southern Gulf Islands, consider starting with Saturna Island. Saturna is far easier to reach by ferry from Swartz Bay on Vancouver Island than it is from its sister Gulf Islands (there's not even scheduled service between Saturna and Salt Spring Island). To get to Saturna from Tsawwassen on the mainland requires a change of ferries, and island hopping will often require criss-crossing over the same routes.

onboard BC Ferries for a small surcharge. Note, though, that the narrow roads fill up in summer, making them more idyllic for cycling other times of the year. Several parks have designated mountain-bike trails. Rentals are available on most islands.

BY KAYAK   The Gulf Islands' lengthy and rugged coastline, plus their proximity to other more remote island groups, make them a good base for kayaking trips. Most of the islands have kayak outfitters; however, not all of them will offer rentals separate from guided tours. If you're an experienced kayaker and just want to rent a kayak, call ahead to inquire. Kayaks and canoes can be taken on the ferries for a small fee.

Salt Spring Island

The largest of the Gulf Islands, Salt Spring is—to the outside world—a bucolic getaway filled with artists, sheep pastures, and cozy B&Bs. While this image is mostly true, Salt Spring is also a busy cultural crossroads: Movie stars, retirees, high-tech telecommuters, and hippie farmers all rub shoulders here. The hilly terrain and deep forests afford equal privacy for all lifestyles, and that's the way the residents like it.

Salt Spring is divided geographically into three distinct lobes, almost as if it were once three separate islands that somehow got pushed together. Most of the population lives in the area around Ganges and Vesuvius; the rugged lower third of the island is the least developed. Although Salt Spring's configuration makes for a lot of coastline, there are very few beaches, as the underlying granite forms headlands that drop straight into the sea.

GETTING THERE   Salt Spring Island is served by three different routes on **BC Ferries** (© **888/BCFERRY** [223-3779]; www.bcferries.com). From Tsawwassen on the mainland, ferries depart two to four times a day for Long Harbour, on the island's northeast coast. If you're on Vancouver Island, you can choose the Crofton–Vesuvius Bay run or the Swartz Bay (Victoria) to Fulford Harbour crossing.

Regular floatplane service operates from Vancouver International Airport and Vancouver's Inner Harbour seaplane terminal to Ganges Harbour. See "Essentials" (p. 113) for contact information.

VISITOR INFORMATION   The Salt Spring Chamber of Commerce operates a visitor center at 121 Lower Ganges Rd., Salt Spring Island, BC V8K 2T1 (© **866/ 216-2936** or 250/537-5252; www.saltspringtourism.com).

GETTING AROUND   If you don't have a car, you will need to rely on a bike or call **Silver Shadow Taxi** (© **250/537-3030**). **Gulf Islands Water Taxi** (© **250/537-2510**; http://members.unet.ca/~watertaxi) offers scheduled speedboat service between Salt Spring, Mayne, and Galiano islands on Saturdays during July and August, plus Pender and Saturna islands on all school days during the rest of the year (the water taxi serves as the "school bus" for island students). There are morning and late afternoon scheduled services for commuters and students; charters are also available. The taxi leaves from Government Dock in Ganges Harbour. Fares are C$15 from any one point to another, or C$25 for a round-trip. Reservations are recommended; bikes are transported free of charge; kayaks are C$5.

EXPLORING THE ISLAND

With a year-round population of 10,500 residents, Salt Spring is served by three ferries, making it by far the easiest of the Gulf Islands to visit. Not coincidentally, Salt Spring also has the most facilities for visitors. The center of island life is **Ganges,** a little village with gas stations, grocery stores, and banks, all overlooking a busy pleasure-boat harbor. You can easily spend an hour to most of a day poking around the art galleries, boutiques, and coffee shops here.

Salt Spring is quite the artists' colony, and many people visit expressly to see the studios of local artists and craftspeople. Stop by the visitor center for the **Studio Tour Map** (or download a copy from www.saltspringstudiotour.com), which pinpoints over 30 island artists—glass blowers, painters, ceramists, weavers, carvers, and sculptors, many of whom are available for visits.

Pegasus Gallery, Mouat's Mall, 1-104 Fulford-Ganges Rd. (© **800/668-6131** or 250/537-2421; www.pegasusgallery.ca), displays a mix of contemporary Canadian painting and sculpture as well as Native carving and basketry. On Fridays from 5 to 9pm, a dozen Ganges galleries remain open late for the **Gallery Walk.** From mid-May to mid-September, **ArtCraft** (© **250/537-0899;** www.artcraftgallery.ca) features the work of more than 250 local artists at Mahon Hall, just north of Ganges at Park Drive and Lower Ganges Road (WinterCraft, the holiday version, is held in Dec).

Not to be missed is **Market in the Park ★** (www.saltspringmarket.com), held April through October, Saturdays from 8am to 4pm, on the waterfront's Centennial Park. The market brings together a lively mix of craftspeople, farmers, musicians, and bakers. It's great fun, and a good chance to shop for local products.

BIKING   Although Salt Spring has the best network of paved roads, it's not the best island for cycling. With ferries unleashing cars throughout the day, there's a lot more traffic here than you'd expect. However, these same ferries—plus the **Gulf Islands Water Taxi** (see "Getting Around," above)—make Salt Spring a convenient base for cyclists. For rentals (starting at C$30 a day), contact **Salt Spring Adventure Co.,** at the Saltspring Marina in Ganges Harbour (© **877/537-2764** or 250/537-2764; www.saltspringadventures.com).

HIKING   **Ruckle Provincial Park** (www.env.gov.bc.ca/bcparks), on the southeast corner of the island, is the largest provincial park in the Gulf Islands; its entrance is 10km (6¼ miles) from the Fulford Harbour ferry terminal on Beaver Point Road. Eight kilometers (5 miles) of trails wind through forests to rocky headlands where the tide-pool exploring is excellent; some trails are designated for mountain bikes. Ruckle Park is also the only public campground on Salt Spring.

KAYAKING   **Island Escapades,** 163 Fulford-Ganges Rd. (© **888/529-2567** or 250/537-2553; www.islandescapades.com), offers a 2-hour introduction to kayaking on the placid waters of Cusheon Lake, for C$55 with guided 3-hour ocean tours for C$70. **Salt Spring Adventure Co.** (see "Biking," above) offers kayak rentals in addition to instruction and guided tours. Rentals start at C$35 for 2 hours to C$55 for a full day. **Sea Otter Kayaking,** 149 Lower Ganges Rd. (© **877/537-5678;**

www.seaotterkayaking.com), offers a number of guided day-trips (C$115 including lunch), sailing-paddling adventures, and multiday expeditions to more remote islands.

WHERE TO STAY

Ruckle Provincial Park, off Beaver Point Road (www.env.gov.bc.ca/bcparks; © **250/391-2300**), has 78 campsites for C$18. Contact Discover Camping (www.discover camping.ca; © **877/559-2115**) for reservations.

Birdsong Bed and Breakfast ★★   This friendly and beautifully furnished B&B offers spectacular harbor views, epic breakfasts, and a relaxed make-yourself-at-home vibe—pretty much exactly what you're looking for in an ideal island getaway. Each of the three large guest rooms is decorated with an artful blend of antique and modern, all with private baths and individual balconies (or patio). Extras include high-end bedding and fireplaces (in two rooms). This expansive property sits amid extensive gardens and 139 sq. m (1,500 sq. ft.) of decks (plus hot tub), so there's always a new view and hidden nook to explore. If you want more room or privacy, there's also a two-bedroom cottage with full kitchen (breakfast is not included with the cottage, but is available for C$20 per person). Birdsong is just 10 minutes south of Ganges. Convenient—but just far enough away to make this superlative B&B seem a world away. Minimum stay requirements may apply.

153 Rourke Rd., Salt Spring Island, BC V8K 2E6. www.birdsongbedandbreakfast.com. © **250/537-4608.** 4 units. C$155–C$175 double; C$185 cottage. Low-season rates available. MC, V. *In room:* TV (upon request), CD player, hair dryer, no phone, Wi-Fi (free).

Cusheon Lake Resort   With its location right on the shores of Cusheon Lake, this family-oriented resort has a holiday-camp feel. The one- and two-bedroom log cabins and A-frame chalets are spotlessly clean and furnished in a no-nonsense style that suits families and people who want a self-catering getaway without an abundance of frills. The kitchen is well stocked with all the essentials, including coffee filters. Beach towels are also part of the deal because there's so much to do in and around the lake: canoeing, swimming, rowing, picnicking, and lawn games. Although there's generally a 2- or 3-night minimum stay, if there's an opening, they'll accept 1-night stands.

171 Natie Lane, Salt Spring Island, BC V8K 2C6. www.cusheonlake.com. © **250/537-9629.** 16 units. Mid-May to mid-Oct C$154–C$232; lower rates in off season. Additional adult C$20. Weekly rates available. MC, V. **Amenities:** Outdoor hot tub; canoes & rowboats; Wi-Fi. (free), *In room:* Fridge, kitchen, no phone.

Hastings House Country House Hotel ★★   Idyllic sophistication has turned this replica of a 16th-century English country mansion (built in the 1930s) into one of the region's top stays. Located within a few minutes walk of Ganges, and set amidst 9-hectares (22-acres) of beautiful gardens, vegetable gardens, an orchard and fabulous harbor views, the whole place exudes a country estate elegance that combines vintage integrity with modern luxury. Many of the original farm buildings have also been converted into superb accommodation. For example, the old barn contains five suites plus a spa. If you prefer new construction, ask for the Hillside Suites. If fine dining is your thing, the restaurant here is superlative (see "Where to Eat").

160 Upper Ganges Rd., Salt Spring Island, BC V8K 2S2. www.hastingshouse.com. © **800/661-9255** or 250/537-2362. 18 units. From C$495 double, including breakfast and afternoon tea. Extra person C$75 per night. Discounts outside of July–Sept. Weekly cottage rental available. 2-day, spa, and gourmet packages available. AE, MC, V. Children 16 and over welcome. **Amenities:** Restaurant; complimentary bikes; golf course nearby; spa. *In room:* TV, CD player, fridge, hair dryer, Wi-Fi (free), robes.

Old Farmhouse B&B ★★   One of the best-loved accommodations in the Gulf Islands, the Old Farmhouse combines top-quality lodgings and great multi-course breakfasts. This Victorian-era homestead was built in 1894 amid 1.2 hectares (3 acres) of meadows and orchards—in fact, the enormous 500-year-old arbutus tree in the front yard may be the world's largest. The bedrooms are in a stylistically harmonious guesthouse adjoining the original farmhouse. Each room has a balcony or patio; the decor incorporates perfect country touches—floral wallpaper, wainscoted walls—without lapsing into Laura Ashley excess. The farm's old chicken house has been transformed into the charming Chateau de Poulet, a cozy one-bedroom suite with a king-size bed. The extensive meadows are perfect for lolling with a book or a game of croquet.

1077 N. End Rd., Salt Spring Island, BC V8K 1L9. www.bbcanada.com/oldfarmhouse. © **250/537-4113.** 3 units. C$200. Rates include full breakfast. MC, V. Closed Oct–May. Call to inquire about children and pets. **Amenities:** Jacuzzi; Wi-Fi (free) *In room:* Hair dryer, no phone.

Salt Springs Spa Resort   Salt Spring's notorious saltwater aquifers are put to good use at this ocean-side spa and chalet resort on the north end of the island. The center offers a variety of traditional Ayurvedic and modern holistic body, beauty, and fitness therapies including facials, massage, aromatherapy, and mineral baths utilizing the spa's salt spring water. Even if you're not into the spa scene, Salt Springs Spa Resort is worth considering for its knotty-pine chalets, which face the busy waters of Trincomali Channel and overlook Wallace Island. Each rustic-looking unit has a full kitchen, wood-burning fireplace, porch with gas grill, and two tubs: a therapeutic tub with jetted mineral water and a soaker tub.

1460 N. Beach Rd., Salt Spring Island, BC V8K 1J4. www.saltspringresort.com. © **800/665-0039** or 250/537-4111. 13 chalets. Late June to Aug C$199–C$299 double; Sept–Oct, Mar to late June, and Dec 21–31 C$135–C$219 double; Nov–Feb except winter holidays C$109–C$199 double. 2- and 3-bedroom suites available. Extra person C$20 per night. 2-night minimum stay in summer. Packages available. AE, MC, V. Free parking. **Amenities:** Free bikes; golf course nearby; badminton court; free rowboats. *In room:* Hair dryer, no phone, Wi-Fi (free).

Wisteria Guest House ★★ 🏠   This rambling inn, tucked off a side street in Ganges, was once a small nursing home. There's little evidence of its institutional past, however, as the new owners have done a sensational job of updating the rooms, adding new features, and injecting lots of color and energy into the operation. In the main guesthouse, there are two sets of rooms that share adjacent bathrooms. These inexpensive rooms are perfect for friends or families traveling together, functioning like a small apartment. The two additional guest rooms, two studios with private entrances, and the standalone cottage all have private bathrooms. All rooms are spacious, beautifully decorated, and absolutely shipshape, and there's a comfortable central lounge and dining area where you'll enjoy a fantastic breakfast—one of the owners was formerly the pastry chef at the New York Westin Hotel.

268 Park Dr., Salt Spring Island, BC V8K 2S1. www.wisteriaguesthouse.com. © **888/537-5899** or 250/537-5899. 9 units. From C$99 guest-room double with shared bathroom; from C$119 guest-room double en suite bathroom; from C$129 studio double with kitchenette or self-contained cottage. Breakfast included in rates. AE, MC, V. Children and pets welcome in cottage and studios. **Amenities:** Common room w/TV, beverage service, fridge, and microwave. *In room:* Hair dryer, no phone, Wi-Fi (free).

WHERE TO EAT

Bruce's Kitchen CANADIAN   Chef-owner Big Bruce loves his trade, which he applies with gusto in this open kitchen. Diners sit at communal tables so that the entire atmosphere takes on the conviviality, aromas, and relationship of a neighbor's kitchen. Dinner revolves around three courses of local food with wine pairings, and menus vary week to week. Items have included roast prime rib with Bruce's Mom's Yorkshire pudding; quiche with Tuscan ham, caramelized onions, local chevre; and vegetarian chili with house-made cornbread. Pot pies are a classic; breads and scones are baked daily. The place is so popular, and so small (it seats only 20 people), that most items are available as take-out. Winter hours, especially January through March, vary. Please call ahead to confirm.

149 Fulford-Ganges Rd. (aka Gasoline Alley). ℂ 250/931-3399. www.bruceskitchen.ca. 3-course table d'hote C$50; take out C$5-C$12. MC, V. Sept–June Mon–Thurs 11am–5pm, Fri–Sat 11:30am–7pm, closed Sunday; July & Aug Mon–Thurs 11am–7pm, Fri–Sat 8am–4pm, Sun 11am–3pm.

Calvin's Bistro ★ CANADIAN If you ask a local where to eat in Ganges, chances are the answer will be Calvin's, a friendly, bustling restaurant with good prices and flavorful food. Ingredients are fresh and local, like the island lamb available in multiple preparations. Wild fish is often available on the broad menu that ranges from a brochette of halibut to Northwest bouillabaisse, a tangy tomato bisque rich with salmon, mussels, clams, and halibut. In good weather, deck seating overlooks the marina. The charmingly energetic Swiss owners will make you feel very welcome—if you want stuffy, formal service, this isn't your restaurant.

133 Lower Ganges Rd. ℂ **250/538-5551.** Reservations recommended. Dinner main courses C$16–C$28. MC, V. Tues–Sat 11:30am–2pm and 5pm to closing.

Hastings House ★★ CONTEMPORARY CANADIAN Easily the most elegant culinary experience on the island, the rose-trellis-covered dining room at Hastings House combines old-world sophistication with the freshest of ingredients. In addition to a la carte choices, there are four-course menus that change daily and incorporate local produce and fish; many of the herbs and vegetables are grown on the grounds. The four-course meal includes an appetizer (perhaps ahi sashimi and prosciutto salad with onion marmalade), a small seafood course (such as gingered scallops with citrus cream), and a choice of four main dishes: Salt Spring lamb is nearly always featured, as is local salmon, Dungeness crab, or other seasonal fish. For the full "genteel" experience, start your evening with cocktails served by the fireplace, and return there for a post-dinner liqueur and coffee.

160 Upper Ganges Rd. ℂ **800/661-9255** or 250/537-2362. www.hastingshouse.com. Reservations required. Prix-fixe 4-course dinner C$85 (C$110 with pairings). AE, MC, V. Mar to Oct 12pm-1pm and 5:30pm-7:30pm. Closed Nov–Feb.

House Piccolo ★ CONTINENTAL Located in a heritage home in Ganges, House Piccolo offers excellent food and a good wine list in moderately formal surroundings. The Finnish origins of the chef are reflected in the northern European accents on the unusual menu, particularly the fish specials that feature the best of the local catch. You might see salmon chowder Finlandia; local black cod drizzled with red wine, honey, and balsamic vinegar reduction; or roasted venison with rowan- and juniper-berry-scented demi glace.

108 Hereford Ave. ℂ **250/537-1844.** www.housepiccolo.com. Reservations recommended. Main courses C$25–C$38. AE, DC, MC, V. Daily 5–9pm.

Moby's Marine Pub PUB This airy pub offers the island's best entertainment (live music most weekends, plus karaoke on Fri evenings) and is a great spot for a burger and a pint of local beer. Located just east of Ganges, the dining room overlooks the harbor; in summer, a lively cocktail scene develops on the sunny waterfront deck. The menu offers the usual pub grub with twists—lamb burgers, local seafood fajitas.

24 Upper Ganges Rd. © **250/537-5559.** Reservations not accepted. Main courses C$8–C$24. MC, V. Sun–Thurs 10am–midnight; Fri–Sat 10am–1am.

Galiano Island

Galiano is an elongated string bean of an island stretched along the Gulf Islands' eastern flank. Though Galiano looks, on the map, like just a long, skinny sand spit, it is in fact the crest of an underground mountain range, with rocky, cliff-faced shorelines and dense forests.

Galiano is the closest Gulf Island to Vancouver, and many of the properties here are second homes of the city's elite. The rural yet genteel feel of the island is perfect for a romantic getaway or a relaxing break from the hassles of urban life. However, don't come to Galiano looking for high-octane nightlife or boutique shopping. There isn't much of a town on the island, just a few shops and galleries at Sturdies Bay. However, there are a number of notable and unique eateries and excellent inns and B&Bs.

GETTING THERE   **BC Ferries** serves Sturdies Bay from both Tsawwassen and Swartz Bay. Floatplanes serve Galiano Island from the docks at Montague Harbour. **Harbour Air Seaplanes** and **Seair Seaplanes** are your best options here. For contact information, see p. 120.

VISITOR INFORMATION   Contact Galiano Island Chamber of Commerce (© **866/539-2233;** www.galianoisland.com). A seasonal information booth sits at the top of the ferry dock ramp.

EXPLORING THE ISLAND

Galiano is perhaps the most physically striking of the Gulf Islands, particularly the mountainous southern shores. Mount Sutil, Mount Galiano, and the exposed cliffs above Georgeson Bay (simply called the Bluffs) rise above sheep-filled meadows, shadowy forests, and fern-lined ravines. **Active Pass,** the narrow strait that separates Galiano from Mayne Island, is another scenic high spot: All the ferry and much of the pleasure-craft traffic between Vancouver and Victoria negotiates this turbulent, cliff-lined passage. Watch the bustle of the boats and ferries from **Bellhouse Provincial Park,** a picnicking area at the end of Jack Road, or head to **Montague Harbour Provincial Park,** a beautiful preserve of beach and forest. Like Salt Spring Island, Galiano is also a center for artists and craftspeople; look for studio signs in your travels. The **Art and Soul Craft Gallery,** 2540 Studies Bay Rd. (© **250/539-2944**), represents many island artists including glassblowers, potters and weavers.

BIKING   The farther north you go on Galiano, the more remote, making this area a favorite among cyclists. While you won't have to worry too much about traffic on the 30km-long (19-mile) paved road that runs up the island's west side, there are enough steep ascents to keep your attention focused. Mountain bikers can follow unmaintained logging roads that skirt the eastern shores. Contact **Galiano Bicycle Rental,** 36 Burrill Rd. (© **250/539-9906;** www.galianoisland.com/galianobicycle), for rentals. A full day's rental is C$35.

HIKING   Several short hikes lead to Active Pass overlooks, including the trail to the top of 330m (1,083-ft.) Mount Galiano and the cliff-edge path in Bluffs Park. Bodega

Ridge is a park about two-thirds of the way up the island, with old-growth forest, wildflowers, and views of the distant Olympic and Cascade mountain ranges.

KAYAKING   Home to otters, seals, and bald eagles, the gentle waters of Montague Harbour are a perfect kayaking destination. In addition to rentals, **Gulf Island Kayaking** (⑦ **250/539-2442;** www.seakayak.ca) at Montague Harbour Marina offers kayak and canoe rentals as well as a variety of guided part- and whole-day trips, including a 3-hour sunset paddle for C$55. If you want to really get away, consider a custom multiday kayaking/camping trip.

WHERE TO STAY

The only campground is at **Montague Harbour Provincial Marine Park** (www. env.gov.bc.ca/bcparks; ⑦ **250/539-2115** for reservations, or 250/391-2300 for information) with 40 sites (15 walk-in and 25 drive-in; a portion of each takes reservations) for C$21. The camp offers beach access, but no showers or flush toilets.

Driftwood Village ☺ 🛉   This venerable choice is perfect as a comfortable retreat for couples or in summer as a laid-back vacation with the kids and pets in tow. The cottages, of differing vintages and styles, are scattered around an 8-hectare (2-acre) garden complete with ponds, flowers, and fruit trees. Most have fireplaces and decks with views onto Sturdies Bay, and all are decorated with a sense of eclectic artfulness that will instantly bring back youthful memories of idealized lakeside holidays.

205 Bluff Rd. E., Galiano Island, BC V0N 1P0. www.driftwoodcottages.com. ⑦ **866/502-5457** or 250/539-5457. 10 units. C$129 studio doubles and 1-bedroom cottages; C$160 1- or 2-bedroom luxury double cottages. Off-season and shoulder-season rates available. Extra person C$20. Rates include ferry pickup. MC, V. Pets accepted for C$10 per night. **Amenities:** Jacuzzi; badminton court. *In room:* TV or TV/DVD, full kitchen, no phone, no Wi-Fi.

Galiano Oceanfront Inn & Spa ★★   A boutique destination spa resort, every room is its own eco-conscious retreat overlooking Active Pass. Each room is invitingly uncluttered, with open-beam ceilings and décor that includes chocolate-brown cork floors and a ledge-rock wood-burning fireplace that conceals a plasma TV/DVD player. At a push of a button, a hidden table emerges from the cherry-wood wall for intimate, in-suite dining. A push of another button reveals a massage table for in-room spa services. The deluxe Villa suites have large terraces, outdoor wood-burning fireplaces, outdoor baths, and outdoor grills in addition to upscale full kitchens. The **eat** restaurant, with notable regional cuisine (see review below), is in a separate, even more stunning building filled with Northwest Native art; Madrona del Mar Spa, a complete beauty and wellness center, shares the waterfront building. The inn is a 5-minute walk from the ferry terminal, and provides electric smart cars for guests to explore the island.

134 Madrona Dr., Galiano Island, BC V0N 1P0. www.galianoinn.com. ⑦ **877/530-3939** or 250/ 539-3388. 20 units. C$249–C$299 double, includes full breakfast; C$425 Villa suite, breakfast not included. MC, V. Free parking. **Amenities:** Restaurant; lounge; golf course nearby; outdoor Jacuzzi; room service; gardens; wine shop. *In room:* TV/DVD, CD player, fridge, hair dryer, minibar, robes, Wi-Fi (free).

WHERE TO EAT

The convivial **Daystar Market Café** (⑦ **250/539-2800**) is just north of Sturdies Bay at the intersection of Georgeson Bay and Porlier Pass roads. Part of an organic- and health-food store, it serves mostly vegetarian meals for lunch and dinner daily. **Montague Café,** at the Montague Harbour Marina (⑦ **250/539-5733**), offers light dining right on the water. **Hummingbird Pub,** 47 Sturdies Bay Rd. (© **250/ 539-5472**), is a friendly, woodsy spot for beer and a burger.

eat ★★ CONTEMPORARY CANADIAN This gorgeous dining room in the Galiano Oceanfront Inn has one of the best views in the Gulf Islands, overlooking the harbor and ferry traffic on Active Pass: A nine-sided post-and-beam room with glass walls lets you take it all in. The small, focused menu, featuring wild salmon, local crab, and island lamb, is enhanced with seasonal fish, shellfish, and produce bought directly from farmers and fishers, who just may deliver their goods to the pier outside the dining room. Much thought goes into the wine list, which is full of unusual choices from local micro-wineries (there are over 25 on the islands). The result is a unique and full expression of Gulf Islands cuisine. In summer months, lunch and dinner are served on the patio, which is flanked by a wood-fired pizza oven.

134 Madrona Dr. © **250/539-3388.** www.galianoinn.com. Reservations suggested. Main courses C$18–C$30. MC, V. Dinner daily from 5:30pm; lunch served July to Labour Day only. Call for hours.

Mayne Island

A medley of rock-lined bays, forested hills, and pastureland, Mayne island was once a center of Gulf Island agriculture, noted for its apple and tomato production. Many of the island's early farmhouses remain, and a rural, lived-in quality is one of Mayne's most endearing features.

GETTING THERE BC Ferries serves Mayne Island with regularly scheduled runs from both Tsawwassen and Swartz Bay. **Harbour Air** and **Seair Seaplanes** all offer floatplane service between Mayne and Vancouver. For contact information, see p. 120.

VISITOR INFORMATION The Mayne Island Community Chamber of Commerce has no bricks-and-mortar headquarters, but volunteers do maintain a resource site (www.mayneislandchamber.ca). Useful maps and event information are usually posted on bulletin boards in the windows of the gas station (which doubles as a video rental place) and grocery store. This is where you can also purchase a copy of *The Mayneliner,* a monthly publication of gossip, happenings, and island issues.

EXPLORING THE ISLAND

Miner's Bay is by default the commercial center of the island, though in most locales this somewhat aimless collection of homes and businesses wouldn't really qualify as a village. It's this understated approach to life that provides Mayne Island with its substantial charm. Don't let the rural patina fool you: Some of the lodgings and restaurants are world-class, and even though organized activities are few, it's hard to be bored on such a lovely island.

Mayne doesn't boast the provincial parks and public lands that the other Gulf Islands do, though there are several beach-access sites that provide opportunities for swimming in warm weather and beachcombing during other times of the year. **Bennett Bay,** on the northeast coast, is the best swimming beach. **Campbell Bay,** just northwest, is another favorite pebble beach. **Dinner Bay Park** is lovely for a picnic.

On a sunny day, the grounds of the **Georgina Point Lighthouse** offer dramatic views. Located on the island's northern tip, this lighthouse juts into Active Pass and overlooks the southern shores of Galiano Island, less than a mile away.

Mayne Island has a delightful history, too, so its heritage gaol is now a community museum, and its clapboard Agricultural Hall the venue for fairs, island stage productions, and entertainment. The island has its fair share of artists; the widely available map of the island lists more than 20 studios that are open to visitors.

BIKING Mayne is one of the best islands for cyclists. The rolling hills provide plenty of challenges, yet the terrain is considerably less mountainous than that of the other islands. For rentals, contact **Mayne Island Kayaking,** below.

HIKING The roads on Mayne are usually quiet enough that they can also serve as paths for hikers. Those looking for more solitude should consider **Mount Parke Regional Park,** off Fernhill Road in the center of the island. The park's best views reward those who take the 1-hour hike to Halliday Viewpoint.

KAYAKING Bennett Bay Kayaking (📞 250/539-0864; www.kayakmayne island.com) at Seal Beach in Miner's Bay, rents kayaks starting at C$35 for 2 hours, or C$70 for a full day. The company will drop off kayaks at any of three launching points on the island (Bennett Bay, Horton Bay, and Piggott Bay), and will even pick up kayaks (and too-weary kayakers) from other destinations.

WHERE TO STAY & EAT

Manna Bakery Café, on Fernhill Road in Miner's Bay's tiny strip mall (📞 **250/539-2323**), is the place to go for a cappuccino and fresh-baked cinnamon roll. Just above the marina in Miner's Bay, the **Springwater Lodge** (📞 **250/539-5521**) is a comfortably ramshackle pub/restaurant with great views and a destination sun-drenched deck; try the fish and chips, and onion rings.

Blue Vista Resort ☺ This venerable resort has had a facelift, and is a favorite for families traveling with kids and pets. On the warm eastern side of Mayne Island—close to beaches, kayaking, and hiking—the comfortable, unfussy cabins are a great value and come with full kitchen, deck, and barbecue; some have a fireplace. You have a choice of studio, one-, and two-bedroom cabins; one-bedroom units have ramps for wheelchair access.

563 Arbutus Dr., Mayne Island, BC V0N 2J0. www.bluevistaresort.com. 📞 **877/535-2424** or 250/539-2463. 9 units. C$99–C$150 double. Extra person C$10. Off-season and weekly rates available. MC, V. Pets accepted with prior approval for C$15 per night. **Amenities:** Ferry pickup. *In room:* TV/DVD, kitchen, no phone.

Oceanwood Country Inn ★★ This waterfront English country inn has a contemporary feel, and is as posh as it gets on Mayne. The living room features a crackling fireplace, full bookshelves, a DVD library, board games, and a nice selection of music. Each guest room is luxuriously comfortable; most are romantic, with deep-soaker bathtubs and private balconies. Many have fireplaces. Continental breakfast includes hot-from-the-oven croissants, homemade granola, and exotic fruit juices. Dining at Oceanwood is a grazing experience through the afternoon, as in tapas and wine on a deck overlooking Navy Channel, and a quality dinner of regional cuisine. This is a gated property, so the deer haven't ravaged the gardens of tulips, irises, and other tasty morsels as they have most Mayne gardens.

630 Dinner Bay Rd., Mayne Island, BC V0N 2J0. www.oceanwood.com. 📞 **250/539-5074.** 12 units. Mid-June to mid-Sept C$159–C$365; mid-Sept to mid-Dec and early Jan to mid-June C$139–C$259. Extra person C$25. Rates include full breakfast and afternoon tea. MC, V. **Amenities:** Restaurant; bar; free bikes; golf course nearby; Jacuzzi; sauna; Wi-Fi (free). *In room:* Hair dryer, no phone.

Wild Fennel Food & Wine REGIONAL Located in the middle of the island at Fernhill Centre, the funky ambiance here, never mind the terrific food, will brighten your day. The drinks list features mostly local ciders, micro-brewed beer, and BC wines. The menu changes weekly according to food availability and freshness, but the crab cakes are a standing favorite, as are the restaurant's shellfish soups. The bison burger's pretty darn good, too. The small deck and garden fill up fast on sunny days.

574 Fernhill Rd., ℂ **250/539-5987.** Reservations accepted. Main courses lunch C$9, dinner C$18. MC, V. Wed–Sat 11:30am–2:30pm & 5:30–9pm.

The Pender Islands

The Penders consist of North and South Pender islands, separated by a very narrow channel that's spanned by a one-lane bridge. North Pender is much more developed, though that's all relative out in the Gulf Islands. It has a rather startling housing development on its southwest side, a 1970s suburb plopped down on an otherwise rural island. Neither of the Penders seems to share the long-standing farming background of the other Gulf Islands, so except where it's developed, forests are thick and all-encompassing. The Penders do have some lovely beaches and public parks with good hiking trails. Toss in a handful of local artists, and you have the recipe for a tranquil island retreat.

GETTING THERE   **BC Ferries** serves Pender Island with regularly scheduled runs from both Tsawwassen and Swartz Bay. The commuter airlines mentioned in previous sections also offer floatplane service to and from Vancouver. For more information, see p. 120.

VISITOR INFORMATION   There is no formal information center on Pender Island, although you can pick up brochures at the mall, **The Driftwood Centre** (4605 Bedwell Harbour Rd., ℂ **250/629-6555**). You can also contact the **Pender Island Chamber of Commerce** (ℂ **866/468-7924;** www.penderislandchamber. com).

EXPLORING THE ISLANDS

Mount Norman Regional Park, which encompasses the northwest corner of South Pender Island, features hiking trails through old-growth forest to wilderness beaches and ridge-top vistas. Access to trails is just across the Pender Island bridge.

The extensive network of roads makes these islands good destinations for cyclists. Bike and scooter rentals are available at **Otter Bay Marina,** 2311 McKinnon Rd. (ℂ **250/629-3579**), where you'll also find **Mouat Point Kayaks** (ℂ **250/629-6939**). If beachcombing or sunning are more your style, try **Hamilton Beach** on the east side of North Pender, or **Medicine Beach** and the beaches along **Beaumont Marine Park,** both of which flank Bedwell Harbour.

WHERE TO STAY & EAT

The dining scene on the Penders is surprisingly diverse, although for a casual meal with lots of conviviality, you can't beat stopping by the Driftwood Centre (which you're likely to do for groceries) and visiting **Pender Island Bakery** (ℂ **250/629-6453;** www.penderislandbakery.com). It's an excellent spot to indulge your sweet tooth, pick up picnic supplies, and enjoy an easy lunch with home-made soups, sandwiches, and salads.

Hope Bay Café ★★ NEW CANADIAN   When the 1903 general store burned down a few years ago at Hope Bay, a tiny community perched above a rocky harbor, a group of island artists and merchants pooled resources to rebuild a new commercial center in this lovely waterfront spot. In the corner with the best views is the Hope Bay Café, a very pleasant, light-filled dining room whose informality veils some very serious and delicious cooking. Although the restaurant changes hands rather frequently, every new owner/chef/entrepreneur seems to keep this delightful eatery a worthwhile venture. While the printed menu is small, and includes dishes such as pan-seared black cod with sweet pea cream or pistachio-crusted halibut, the real attractions are the specials that vary seasonally as local ingredients become available.

4301 Bedwell Harbour Rd. ✆ **250/629-6668.** www.hopebaycafe.com. Main courses C$16–C$26. MC, V. Wed–Fri 11am–3pm and 5–8pm; Sat–Sun 10am–3pm and 5–8pm.

Inn on Pender Island ☺ 🍴   Situated next to Prior Centennial Provincial Park, this modest inn offers a choice of nine motel-style lodge rooms or three studio log cabins, many with ocean views and some with private Jacuzzis. Lodge rooms are clean and spacious; cabins have fireplaces and deck swings. Children and pets are welcome. **Memories at the Inn** is a fully licensed restaurant, and although the decor's a bit plain, it's a popular choice for affordable dining. Menu items include pastas, fish and chips, pork ribs, and chicken. The homemade pizza is exceptionally good.

4709 Canal Rd., N. Pender Island, BC V0N 2M0. www.innonpender.com. ✆ **800/550-0172** or 250/629-3353. 12 units. C$89–C$99 lodge double; C$159 cabin. Children stay free in parent's room (C$10 per night if use of a cot is required). MC, V. Small pets (C$5). **Amenities:** Restaurant; Jacuzzi. *In room:* TV/DVD, fridge, kitchenette (in cabins only), Wi-Fi (free).

Poets Cove Resort and Spa ★★★   This impressive resort is open year round, and offers so much to do that you never have to leave its confines. Accommodations range from 22 modern lodge rooms (all face west to catch glorious sunsets) to deluxe two- and three-bedroom cottages, and spacious, family-oriented villas; most have private hot tubs. Children's programs and a 110-slip marina make Poets Cove popular with families and boaters alike. The bright **Aurora Restaurant** is easily the most sophisticated place to eat on the Penders. Unsurprisingly, the menu features local fish and shellfish, as well as local lamb—a standout. **Syrens Lounge & Bistro** offers casual dining inside or on the enormous deck, with a kid-friendly menu. If you're staying in a cottage or villa, you can order items from the "raw menu" to barbecue yourself. The **Susurrus Spa** is a destination unto itself, with six large treatment rooms, a steam cave, and oceanfront Jacuzzi. Eco tours, kayak and charter boat rentals are on your doorstep, as are two swimming pools (one for adults only).

9801 Spalding Rd., S. Pender Island, BC V0N 2M3. www.poetscove.com. ✆ **888/512-7638** or 250/629-2100. 46 units. C$189–C$299 double lodge room; C$339–C$449 2-bedroom villa; C$419–C$529 3-bedroom villa; C$359–C$519 2-bedroom cottage; C$489–C$699 3-bedroom cottage. Extra person C$25. AE, MC, V. Free parking. **Amenities:** Restaurant; bar; health club; 2 pools; spa; sports equipment rental; tennis court; market w/beer and wine sales; marina. *In room:* TV/DVD, fireplace, fridge, hair dryer, robes, Wi-Fi (free), soaker tubs, balcony or patio.

Saturna Island

The most remote of the southern Gulf Islands served by ferries, Saturna is both pristine and, compared with its neighbors, mostly vacant (pop. 350). Whereas other islands are best described as rural, Saturna is truly wild. It's not surprising that the new Gulf Islands National Park Reserve has its largest presence on Saturna: About half the island is now protected as reserve land.

Served by direct ferries from Swartz Bay and a few indirect sailings from Tsawwassen, Saturna is hard to get to. It's easiest to ferry to Vancouver Island and then back out, or over to Pender Island, which has direct sailings to Saturna. If you are planning

131

to visit all the Gulf Islands, start your journey on Saturna; it's easier to get away from Saturna by ferry than it is to get to it. Self-sufficiency is the name of the game here in terms of getting around; there are no bike rentals or cab services. Any visit to Saturna should include a stop at **Saturna Island Family Estate Winery** (🕐 877/918-**3388** or 250/539-5139), a small, well-established winery in an extremely dramatic setting. Perched between massive cliffs and the sea, the setting is reminiscent of Corsica. The tasting room, open daily 11am to 4:30pm from May to October, is reached by a precipitous single-track road with a 20% grade. The tasting room bistro also offers soups and salads for lunch.

Its remoteness makes Saturna a favorite destination of outdoorsy types. The island boasts nice beaches, including Russell Reef, Veruna Bay, and Shell Beach at **East Point Regional Park.** This park, with its still-active lighthouse, is a good spot to watch for orcas. Hikers can drive to **Mount Warburton Pike ★** and follow the **Brown Ridge Nature Trail.** Views from this craggy cliff-faced peak are astonishing, taking in southern Vancouver Island, the San Juan Islands, and the Olympic Peninsula. Kayakers can explore the rocky islets surrounding **Tumbo Island,** just offshore from Saturna's eastern peninsula. Facilities are few and far between, though in several cases, exemplary. For more information, check out **www.saturnatourism.com**.

WHERE TO STAY & EAT

In addition to lunch at the winery (above); diners can also turn to the deli and cafe at the **Saturna General Store,** 101 Narvaez Bay Rd. (🕐 **250/539-2936**), open Thursday through Saturday in summer, and the **Lighthouse Pub,** at the ferry terminal (🕐 **250/539-5725**), open daily in summer. Be sure to inquire about current dining options when making reservations—and bring a picnic hamper just in case.

Saturna Lodge ★   This well-established resort, which began its life as a 1940s boardinghouse, has been revamped into a very comfortable, upscale bed-and-breakfast. If your idea of an island getaway is seclusion and genteel comfort, this is your lodging. Set amid gardens, with views onto Boot Cove, the lodge has taken on a winery theme—each of the charming guest rooms is named for a wine or grape varietal. The Sauterne Room is the largest suite with soaker tub, private deck, and king-size bed. Families will like the ground-floor rooms with private entrances, where a twin-bed room and a queen room share a large bathroom. The attractive main-floor lounge overlooks the gardens and has a fireplace, small library, and television.

130 Payne Rd., Saturna Island, BC V0N 2Y0. www.saturna.ca. 🕐 **866/539-2254** or 250/539-2254. 6 units. C$119–C$169 double. Extra person C$35. Rates include breakfast. Special packages available. MC, V. No pets. **Amenities:** Guest lounge w/books, videos, and board games; free bikes, Jacuzzi, ferry shuttle. In room: TV/DVD, hair dryer, no phone, robes, Wi-Fi (free).

WEST OF VICTORIA: SOOKE & BEYOND

Sooke: 30km (19 miles) W of Victoria

Following Hwy. 14 west from Victoria, the suburbs eventually thin; by the time you reach Sooke, the vistas open up to the south, where Washington's Olympic Mountains prop up the horizon. There are a number of reasons to explore this part of the island.

Hwy. 14 gives access to beaches and parks with good swimming and recreation, finally leading to Port Renfrew, a rough-and-ready deep-sea fishing village that's also the southern trail head for the famous West Coast Trail (see chapter 7). Day-trippers from Vancouver also come out to visit **Botanical Beach Provincial Park ★,** an area with spectacular tide-pool formations, unique geology, and one of the richest intertidal zones on the entire North American West Coast. About 4km (2½ miles) south of Port Renfrew, Botanical Beach is a ledge of sandstone that juts out into the churning waters of the Strait of Juan de Fuca. Over the millennia, tidal action has carved out pits and pools, in which you'll find sea urchins, clams, periwinkles, giant anemones, chitons, and sea stars. In spring and fall, watch for gray whales in the strait. Check local tide tables to maximize opportunities for wildlife-viewing and tide-pool exploration: A low tide of 1.2m (4 ft.) or less is best. Picnic facilities and toilets are available.

Ambitious backcountry drivers can make a loop journey from Hwy. 14. From Port Renfrew, a good logging road leads up the San Juan River valley, connecting to the southern shores of Cowichan Lake just west of Duncan. You can make this drive in 1 day, or divide the trip up by planning to spend the night camping at Cowichan Lake or at one of Duncan's moderately priced hotels.

VISITOR INFORMATION   Head for the **Sooke Region Museum Visitors and Information Centre** (2070 Phillips Rd., right off Sooke Rd./Hwy. 14; ✆ **866/888-4748** or 250/642-6351). It's open daily 9am to 5pm in July and August, and Tuesday through Sunday the rest of the year. The staff here is exceptionally helpful and will come up with innumerable ideas of what to see and do, from zip-lining to hiking routes.

In & Around Sooke

Before arriving in Sooke, history buffs should take a detour to **Fort Rodd Hill & Fisgard Lighthouse National Historic Site,** 603 Fort Rodd Hill Rd. (✆ **250/478-5849**). Here's where to find the oldest lighthouse on Canada's west coast, now converted into a quaint museum, as well as a park filled with old military installations that kids love to discover. The little town of Sooke is quiet, and although it doesn't offer a lot to divert the visitor, there are a number of recreation areas nearby that warrant a stop. **East Sooke Regional Park** is a beautiful rainforest, with picturesque coves and plenty of well-groomed trails, some of which are wheelchair accessible. **Sooke Potholes Provincial Park** is more intriguing for its curious geologic formation. The Sooke River flows down a series of rock ledges, pooling in waist-deep swimming holes before dropping in waterfalls to another series of pools and waterfalls. In July and August, the normally chilly river water warms up. The trails that link the pools are nice for a casual hike. There are more trails in adjacent **Sooke Mount Provincial Park.** To reach these parks, drive west on Route 14 almost to the town of Sooke; turn right on Sooke River Road. Fifteen kilometers (9⅓ miles) west of Sooke is **French Beach Park,** a sand-and-gravel beach that's one of the best places to watch for gray whales. The park has 69 campsites. For the adventurous of heart, **Adrenaline Zip Adventures** (5128C Sooke Rd.; ✆ **250/642-1933;** www.adrenalinezip.com) have created a series of eco-experiences. These include zipping between the treetops of the rainforest, as well as whale-watching and ocean-kayaking adventures.

WHERE TO STAY & EAT

Best Western Premier-Prestige Oceanfront Resort   As one of only two *Premier* Best Westerns in Canada, this new waterfront resort opened in 2011 as Sooke's first full-service hotel. It is the flagship of the Prestige hotel group. Each guest room floor is themed in contemporary decor: there is a colonial, tropical, and a stylish monochromatic metropolitan floor, as well as an opulent and glitzy penthouse level. Furnishings are sumptuous, and all rooms have water or waterfront views, although a top spot to enjoy the vistas are from the colonnade balcony, or garden gazebo. The folks behind the Ric's Grill steakhouses run the mix restaurant here, as well as a great sushi bar and cafe. The spa, with its range of massage, hydrotherapy and refinement services, completes the line-up for a destination that touches upon the wilder, west coast experience, for those looking for an alternative to downtown Victoria.

6929 West Coast Rd. Sooke, BC V9Z 0V1. www.prestigeinn.com. © **877/737-8443** or 250/642-0805. 122 units. C$209–C$299 double, C$319–C$599 suite, C$599–C$999 one-bedroom suite. Children 16 years and younger stay free in parent's room. Packages available. AE, MC, V. Pets (C$25). **Amenities:** 2 restaurants; lounge; fitness center; hot tub; indoor pool; room service; spa; boat launch; marina (under development). *In room:* A/C, TV w/pay movies, fridge, hair dryer, kitchenette (some), Wi-Fi (free).

Markham House B&B and Honeysuckle Cottage ★★

On the outskirts of Sooke, nestled in the woods, sits this admirably well-executed Tudor-style home on 4 hectares (10 acres) of landscaped grounds. The rooms are outfitted with antiques, featherbeds, and duvets. The cottage has its own kitchenette, wood stove, and hot tub. The main house features an elegant parlor with fireplace, plus a hot tub. Breakfasts are sumptuous and healthy. Outside, you can sit by the trout pond, play bocce, or practice your golf swing on the minifairway and green. Of course, you may also want to head out to the water or explore the region's parks, and your gracious hosts will help you make plans.

1775 Connie Rd., Sooke, BC V9Z 1C8. www.markhamhouse.com. © **888/256-6888** or 250/642-7542. 4 units. July–Sept and mid-Dec to Jan 3 C$120–C$195 double; C$250 cottage. Additional adult C$25. Special packages & off-season discounts available. Rates include full breakfast, turn-down service, and afternoon tea on day of arrival. AE, DC, MC, V. Take Hwy. 14 W. (Sooke Rd.) to Connie Rd. Approx. 25km (16 miles) from Victoria. Pets allowed in cottage. Children 16 and older welcome. **Amenities:** Golf course nearby; Jacuzzi; pool, badminton; croquet; gazebo. *In room:* TV/DVD, fireplace, robes, Wi-Fi (free).

Markus' Wharfside Restaurant ★

PACIFIC NORTHWEST   Owned by a chef and a sommelier, this small restaurant has such a loyal, local following that the menu changes weekly, not only to keep them coming back, but to take advantage of the freshest, most seasonal ingredients available. Whether it's for freshly-caught seafood such as sautéed spot prawns or an oven-roasted chicken, or a flat iron steak grilled to perfection, this is a gem of a find.

1813 Maple Ave., Sooke. © **250/642-3596.** www.markuswharfsiderestaurant.com. Main courses C$14–C$32. MC, V. Tues–Sat 5:30–10pm.

Point-No-Point Resort ★

Located 64km (40 miles) west of Victoria, this lovely resort is the ultimate getaway both for a meal or a stay-over with cozy cabins set right on the ocean. The spectacular setting boasts a wide, rugged beach as your front yard, and 16 hectares (40 acres) of wilderness around you. This resort has been welcoming guests since 1952, so it knows a thing or two about hospitality. All cabins have fireplaces and kitchens; newer ones have hot tubs and decks, and two are wheelchair accessible. If Wi-Fi is important to you, rooms nearer the lodge have a stronger and more reliable signal. Lunch and traditional tea are served daily in a central teahouse overlooking the Juan de Fuca Strait. Dinner is served Wednesday through Sunday.

This long-distance hiking trail links China Beach Park, just past the town of Jordan River, to Botanical Beach Provincial Park, near Port Renfrew, along a stretch of near-wilderness coastline. Similar to the famed West Coast Trail but less extreme, the rugged 47km (29-mile) trail offers scenic beauty, spectacular hiking, wildlife-viewing, and roaring surf in its course along the Pacific coastline of the Strait of Juan de Fuca. Most of the trail is designed for strenuous day or multi-day hiking. Unlike the West Coast Trail, it can be easily broken down into day-long segments between trail heads accessed along Hwy. 14: China Beach, Sombrio Beach, Parkinson Creek, and Botanical Beach. Plan on 3 days to hike the entire length; campsites are regularly spaced along the trail.

Conditions are always changing, so obtain up-to-date information before proceeding by checking the trail-head information shelters. If you're camping, keep a tide chart handy and refer to trail-head postings about points that will be impassable at high tide. Wear proper footwear—the trail gets very muddy—and appropriate clothing, plus rain gear if you're going to camp. And leave a plan of your trip (including which trail you're hiking), with arrival and departure times, with a friend or relative. Also, don't leave a car full of valuables in the trail-head parking lots—break-ins are common.

For information on Juan de Fuca Marine Park, contact **BC Parks** (© **250/ 391-2300;** www.env.gov.bc.ca/bcparks).

Either way, the food is excellent. Reservations are a must; main courses are C$22 to $36.

1505 West Coast Hwy. (Hwy. 14), Sooke, BC V0S 1N0. www.pointnopointresort.com. © **250/646- 2020.** 25 units. C$180–C$270 cabin double. 2- or 3-night minimum stay on weekends and holidays. Off-season rates available. Summer fishing packages available. AE, MC, V. Free parking. 64km (40 miles) west of Victoria. Small pets accepted (C$10 and C$100 refundable dog deposit). No children in cabins with hot tubs. **Amenities:** Restaurant/teahouse *In room:* Kitchen, no phone, Wi-Fi (free).

Sooke Harbour House ★★★ This inn at the foot of a beautiful pebble-and-sand spit, 30km (19 miles) west of Victoria, has earned an international reputation for the warmth of its welcome, the quality of its food and lodging, and the drama of its vistas. Each individually decorated suite boasts a fireplace, bathrobes, antiques, fresh flowers, and views of the water—most have unusual nooks and corners that make them unique. The three top-floor rooms, very spacious suites with 6m (20-ft.) cathedral ceilings and beautiful furnishings, are perfect for romantic getaways. Since the inn owns one of the largest public art collections on Vancouver Island, it is a showcase of multi-dimensional art; the beauty extends to the gardens—with sculptures, herbs and flowers—and its food. The award-winning regional cuisine here has seduced thousands of palates: Haida Gwaii ling cod is served with a lemon thyme potato gnocchi in a shrimp and carrot cream; smoked organic duck breast comes with fresh buffalo milk mozzarella, heirloom tomatoes, hazelnut and arugula pesto, while innovative terrines come in combinations such as Campbell River venison and port poached fig. Edible flowers and herbs, grown in an expansive kitchen garden, are used to perfection. Try the home-made sorbets such as raspberry mint or the blueberry sage. It's these sorts of combinations that have made Sooke House one of the top dining rooms in Canada. Whether you're staying here or not, reservations are a

NORTH OF VICTORIA: goldstream provincial park

North of Victoria, the Island Highway climbs up over the high mountain ridge called the Malahat, shedding the suburbs as it climbs. Goldstream Provincial Park is a tranquil arboreal setting that overflowed with prospectors during the 1860s gold-rush days, hence its name. Today, its natural beauty attracts hikers, campers, and birders who stop to spend a few hours or days in the beautiful temperate rainforest.

Hiking trails take you past abandoned mine shafts and tunnels as well as stands of Douglas fir, lodgepole pine, red cedar, indigenous yew, and arbutus trees. The **Gold Mine Trail** leads to Niagara Creek and the abandoned mine. The **Goldstream Trail** goes to the salmon-spawning areas. Three species of salmon make

annual salmon runs up the Goldstream River during the months of October, November, December, and February. Visitors can easily observe this natural wonder along the riverbanks. Goldstream is also a major attraction for bird-watchers, as numerous bald eagles winter here each year. January is the best month for spotting these majestic creatures.

For information on all provincial parks on the South Island, contact **BC Parks** (© 250/391-2300; www.env.gov.bc.ca/bcparks). Goldstream Park's **Freeman King Visitor Centre** (© 250/478-9414) offers guided walks and talks, plus programs geared toward kids throughout the year. It's open daily from 9:30am to 6pm; parking is free. Take Hwy. 1 about 20 minutes north of Victoria.

must and book early: the wait list can sometimes run up to 3 weeks. A typical four-course dinner costs around C$75 (excluding wine); multi-course extravaganzas, with pairings, can run up to C$180 per person.

1528 Whiffen Spit Rd., Sooke, BC V9Z 0T4. www.sookeharbourhouse.com. © **800/889-9688** or 250/642-3421. 28 units. July–Sept C$379–C$589 double; rates include breakfast. Children 12 and under stay free in parent's room. AE, MC, V. Free parking. Follow Hwy. 14 to Sooke. About 1.6km (1 mile) past the town's 3rd traffic light, turn left onto Whiffen Spit Rd. Pets allowed for C$40 per night. **Amenities:** Restaurant; babysitting; bike rentals; concierge; room service; spa; garden tours; art gallery *In room:* Fridge, hair dryer, Jacuzzi, steam shower, Wi-Fi (free).

17 Mile House PUB   For inexpensive but reliable fare, the 17 Mile House has the most character in the area. Built in the late 1800s, this establishment became a regional hub in the 1920s when it installed the only phone around. Today, you can sup on a nice salad, burger, or one of many pasta, meat, or seafood entrees while admiring the old wood, brick, and tile interior. You might tap out a tune on the pub's 150-year-old piano or settle for a game of billiards; Saturdays feature live music.

5126 Sooke Rd. © **250/642-5942.** www.17milehouse.com. Main courses C$8–C$24. Sun–Thurs 11am–11pm; Fri–Sat 11am–midnight. MC, V. On Sooke Rd. (Hwy. 14) btw. Connie Rd. and Gillespie Rd.

DUNCAN & THE COWICHAN VALLEY

Duncan: 57km (35 miles) N of Victoria

The Cowichan Valley is one of the richest agricultural areas on Vancouver Island. The Cowichan Indians have lived in the valley for millennia, and today the band's reservation spreads immediately to the south of the town of Duncan. European settlers, drawn by the valley's deep soil and warm temperatures, established farms here in the 1870s. Although the orchards and sheep pastures of yore remain, the valley's location also makes it one of the few sites in western British Columbia for vineyards.

For visitors, the town of Duncan may seem a pretty low-key place, but its centrality to excellent recreation and cultural sights makes it a comfortable hub for exploring this part of Vancouver Island. Cowichan Lake is a popular summertime getaway, with swimming beaches and boating. Maple Bay and Cowichan Bay are marina-dominated harbor towns with good pubs and restaurants, plus enchanting views. And don't forget those wineries: Cowichan Valley is home to several good ones, most with tasting rooms.

Essentials

GETTING THERE Duncan is 57km (35 miles) north of Victoria on Hwy. 1. It's also a stop on VIA Rail's **E&N Railiner,** the *Malahat,* which is expected to reopen in 2012 after an extensive upgrade program of both track and train. For information, contact **VIA Rail** (© **888/VIA-RAIL** [842-7245] or 250/383-4324; www.viarail.ca). **Greyhound Canada** © **800/661-8747;** www.greyhound.ca) offers bus transport from Victoria to Duncan. A one-way fare from Victoria to Duncan is C$18.

VISITOR INFORMATION The **Duncan-Cowichan Visitor Information Centre,** 381A Trans-Canada Hwy. (© **250/746-4636**), is open from April 15 to October 15. Online, go to www.city.duncan.bc.ca. For year-round information on the entire valley, contact the Cowichan Tourism Association, 25 Canada Ave., Duncan (© **888/ 303-3337;** www.cowichan.bc.ca).

Exploring the Area
DUNCAN: THE CITY OF TOTEM POLES

Duncan is a welcoming city of 5,300, with a mix of First Nations peoples and descendants of European settlers. Congested Hwy. 1 runs to the east of the old town center, and you'll miss Duncan's old-fashioned charm if you don't get off the main drag (follow signs for Old Town Duncan).

Downtown Duncan still bustles with stationers, dress shops, bakeries, haberdasheries, cafes, candy shops—it's the quintessential small and friendly Canadian town. The main reason to make a detour downtown is to see the city's impressive collection of modern **totem poles.** The First Nations peoples of this region are famed for their carving skills. However, most historic totem poles are now in museums or are rotting in front of abandoned villages, and for a long time few First Nations artists had any reason to keep the old skills and traditions alive. In the 1980s, the mayor of Duncan began an ambitious project of commissioning local First Nations artists to carve new totem poles, which were then erected around the city. Today, with more than 80 totem poles rising above the downtown area, Duncan's public art is one of the world's largest collections of modern totem carving, a wonderful assemblage that represents the continuation of an ancient art form unique to the Northwest coast.

The totem poles are scattered around the city, mostly in the pedestrian-friendly downtown area: Simply follow the yellow shoe-prints on the pavement. You can also take a free guided tour, which starts from in front of the Cowichan Valley Museum, at the E&N Railway station, Station Street and Canada Avenue. The 45-minute tours are given from May to mid-September, Tuesday through Saturday, every hour, on the hour, from 10am to 4pm. Meet at the train station on Canada Avenue. Reserve for groups of five or more by calling the **Duncan Business Improvement Area Society** (② 250/715-1700).

The B.C. Forest Museum Park/BC Discovery Centre ☺ This 41-hectare (101-acre) site explores the history of the logging industry. Over the years, the focus of the exhibits has shifted from an unreflective paean to tree cutting to a more thoughtful examination of sustainable forestry practices, woodland ecosystems, and the role (sometimes surprising) of wood products in our lives. No matter what you may think of logging as a practice, the history of forestry in British Columbia is fascinating, and this museum does a good job of presenting both the high and low points. Kids will love the vintage steam train, which circles the grounds on narrow-gauge rails.

2892 Drinkwater Rd., 2km (1¼ miles) north of Duncan on Hwy. 1 (near Somenos Lake). ② **250/715-1113.** www.bcforestmuseum.com. Admission C$14 adults, C$12 seniors and students 13–18, C$9 children 5–12. Apr to Oct daily 10am–4:30pm. Closed Nov to Mar. Take Hw. 1 past Duncan, watching for the double-span bridge over the Cowichan River. The center is approximately 3km (13/4 miles) past the bridge, off the highway to the right, after the fourth set of traffic lights at Beverley St.

Quw'utsun' Cultural Centre ★ The Cowichan (Quw'utsun') people were the original inhabitants of this valley, and the tribe's cultural history and traditional way of life are the focus of Quw'utsun' Centre, on the southern edge of downtown Duncan ("Quw'utsun'" means "warming your back in the sun"). The parklike enclosure along the Cowichan River contains several modern longhouse structures flanked by totem poles. Join a guided tour of the village, or take a seat in the theater to watch the excellent presentation *The Great Deeds,* a retelling of Cowichan myth and history. At the building devoted to traditional carving, you can talk to carvers as they work, and even take up a chisel yourself. The Cowichan tribes are famous for their bulky sweaters, knit with bold motifs from hand-spun raw wool. The gallery at Quw'utsun' is the best place in the valley to buy these sweaters (expect to pay around C$250), as well as carvings, prints, jewelry, and books. In summer, the **Riverwalk Café** (② **250/746-4370**) serves authentic native cuisine, including a designed-to-share, Salish Afternoon Tea for two (C$22), Thursday through Saturday in July and August. There's also a midday alder-planked salmon barbecue feast with drumming and storytelling. Call ahead for details.

200 Cowichan Way. ② **877/746-8119** or 250/746-8119. www.quwutsun.ca. Admission C$15 adults, C$12 seniors and students 13–17, C$8 children 12 and under and First Nations individuals. Daily Apr–Sept 10am–5pm. Take Hwy. 1 past Duncan, cross the double-span bridge over the Cowichan River & take Cowichan Rd. E. en route to Duncan Mall.

COWICHAN BAY

This small but busy port town edges along the mouth of the Cowichan River. Many visitors come to walk the boardwalks and admire the boats amid the sounds, smells, and sights of a working harborside village, just 7km (4⅓ miles) southeast of Duncan. The **Cowichan Bay Maritime Centre,** 1761 Cowichan Bay Rd. (② **250/746-4955;** www.classicboats.org), tells the story of the clash of Native and European cultures in the Cowichan Valley. It also serves as a workshop for the building of wooden boats. Hours are daily from 9am to dusk between April and October, with admission by donation. Be sure to stop at Arthur Vickers Gallery, 1719 Cowichan Bay Rd., ② **250/748-7650** (his brother, Roy Vickers, has a gallery in Tofino), as well as at **Hilary's Artisan Cheese Company** and **True Grain Bread,** sharing space at 1725 Cowichan Bay Rd. (② **250/746-7664**). This outlet for local farm cheeses and artisanal and organic bread makes a perfect stop for outfitting a picnic. For ice cream, **The Udder Guy's Old Fashioned Ice Cream** (1721 Cowichan Bay Rd., ℂ **250/ 954-5555**) is hard to beat. Ingredients are fresh, and packed with flavor with no artificial additives.

KAYAKING **Cowichan Bay Kayak and Paddlesports,** 1765 Cowichan Bay Rd. (ℂ **888/749-2333** or 250/748-2333; www.cowichanbaykayak.com), offers kayak rentals and guided tours from the docks on Cowichan Bay. A 3-hour paddle around the Cowichan River estuary with a stop at Genoa Bay is C$50. A 2-hour single kayak rental is C$30.

WHALE-WATCHING **Ocean Ecoventures,** 1745 Cowichan Bay Rd. (ℂ **866/ 748-5333** or 250/748-3800; www.oceanecoventures.com), offers year-round, 3- to 4-hour whale-watching trips on 7m (23-ft.) rigid-hull inflatable boats. You're almost guaranteed to see orcas, and chances are good that you'll also see gray whales, harbor and Dall porpoises, sea lions, and bald eagles. Trips are C$109 adults and C$79 children 12 and under.

MAPLE BAY & GENOA BAY

Maple Bay is a lovely harbor town 7km (4⅓ miles) northeast of Duncan. Take Tzouhalem Road east to Maple Bay Road; then head northeast. Although not a major destination, it's worth the short drive just to take in the view—a placid bay of water beneath steep-sloped mountains. Ponder the vista at the **Brigantine Inn ★**, on Beaumont Avenue (ℂ **250/746-5422**), a friendly pub with local brews and a bayside deck. If you're into **diving,** Maple Bay is worth exploring—it's said to have been one of Jacques Cousteau's favorite dive spots.

Genoa Bay is directly south of Maple Bay. This tiny harbor is actually on Cowichan Bay, though the mountainous terrain mandates that overland transport make a circuitous route around Mount Tzouhalem. Again, the point of the journey is the charm of the location. Enjoy a drink or a meal at the **Genoa Bay Cafe** (see "Where to Eat," below), a floating restaurant in the midst of extraordinary visual wonder.

COWICHAN VALLEY VINEYARDS

The warm summers and mild winters of the Cowichan Valley make this one of the few areas in western British Columbia where wine grapes flourish. Pinot noir, pinot gris, Marechal Foch, and Gewürztraminer are popular varietals. The following wineries welcome guests, and most will arrange tours with sufficient notice. For more information, see **www.wineislands.ca**.

Blue Grouse Vineyards and Winery, 4365 Blue Grouse Rd., south of Duncan, off Lakeside Road near Koksilah Road (ℂ **250/743-3834;** www.bluegrousevineyards. com), is open for tastings from 11am to 5pm Wednesday through Sunday from April to September, Wednesday through Saturday October through December, and Saturdays only January through March.

Cherry Point Vineyards, 840 Cherry Point Rd., near Telegraph Road southeast of Cowichan Bay in eastern Cobble Hill (ℂ **250/743-1272;** www.cherrypointvineyards. com), is one of the most prominent Cowichan Valley wineries, with national awards to prove it. The tasting room is open daily from 10am to 5pm; with a bistro open for lunch May through September.

Zanatta Winery and Vineyards, 5039 Marshall Rd., south of Duncan near Glenora (ℂ **250/748-2338;** www.zanatta.ca), is open April through early October, Wednesday through Sunday from noon to 4:30pm. It's open the same hours the rest of October through December, but on weekends only. Its restaurant, Vinoteca, is open Wednesday through Sunday, noon to 3pm, from April through early October, weekends only November to December.

Another twist on the local scene is **Merridale Ciderworks,** 1230 Merridale Rd., Cobble Hill, west of Hwy. 1 (© **800/998-9908** or 250/743-4293; www.merridale cider.com), which produces both apple and pear cider. Tastings are available daily 10:30am to 5:30pm. In addition, meals are available at **La Pommeraie Bistro** Monday through Sunday from 11:30am to 4pm.

COWICHAN LAKE, COWICHAN RIVER & THE BACKCOUNTRY

Cowichan Lake, 28km (17 miles) west of Duncan on Hwy. 18, is a long, narrow lake nestled between mountain slopes. With an area population of about 3,000, the lake is one of the primary summer playgrounds for valley residents. A number of provincial parks provide access to swimming beaches, boat landings, and campsites; **Gordon Provincial Park,** on the lake's south shore, is the most convenient for Duncan-based travelers.

Backcountry explorers can follow the roads along both sides of 30km-long (19-mile) Cowichan Lake to access remote areas of Vancouver Island's wilderness west coast. Well-maintained forestry roads from Cayuse and Honeymoon Bay, on the south side of the lake, lead to **Port Renfrew,** one of the starting points of Pacific Rim National Park's famed West Coast Trail (see "West of Victoria: Sooke & Beyond," earlier in this chapter, as well as chapter 7, "Central Vancouver Island"). From here, paved roads connect to Sooke and Victoria. From the west end of Cowichan Lake, gravel roads lead to **Nitinat Lake,** renowned for its windsurfing, and **Carmanah/ Walbran Provincial Park,** a vast preserve of misty old-growth forests.

The Cowichan River flows east out of Cowichan Lake. The **Cowichan River Trail,** which passes through fern glades and forests, provides excellent access to the beautiful jade-green waters. The 20km (12-mile) hiking trail begins just east of Cowichan Lake (follow signs from Hwy. 18 for Skutz Falls Trailhead) and follows the river to Glenora, southeast of Duncan. The river is popular for steelhead and trout fishing, as well as kayaking. Some canyon rapids are considered too dangerous for passage; ask locally before setting out.

Where to Stay
IN & AROUND DUNCAN

Best Western Cowichan Valley Inn ★ This is Duncan's most comfortable full-service lodging, conveniently located for visiting the B.C. Forest Discovery Centre. Its handsomely furnished guest rooms come with numerous amenities. A wheelchair-accessible room is available. The hotel's restaurant, Choices, is one of the best family restaurants in Duncan, and the hotel's beer-and-wine shop is one of the best places in town to purchase local wines.

6474 Trans-Canada Hwy., Duncan, BC V9L 6C6. www.cowichanvalleyinn.com. © **800/927-6199** or 250/748-2722. 42 units. C$179–C$210 double. Extra person C$10. Senior and AAA discounts available. Children 17 and under stay free in parent's room. AE, DC, DISC, MC, V. Free parking. Located 2km (1¼ miles) north of Duncan. Pets allowed with approval. **Amenities:** Restaurant; pub; exercise room; golf course nearby; outdoor pool; beer-and-wine store; volleyball court. In room: A/C, TV, fridge, hair dryer, Wi-Fi (free).

Fairburn Farm Culinary Retreat & Guesthouse ★ 🎁 If you're a foodie looking for a back-to-the-land vacation, this could well be it. The beautifully preserved farmhouse, with handsome guestrooms and a cottage, lies within 53 working hectares (131 acres) of a working farm (including a buffalo herd) plus forested areas with trails. Staying here doesn't only mean cooking demonstrations and classes, it might also include mushroom-hunting expeditions, bread-making forums, tours of local farms, vineyards, cideries, cheese-making operations, and trips to the Duncan farmers' market—one of the best in B.C.—to buy the freshest and most flavorful ingredients for a learn-to-gourmet-cook "participation"-style dinner. These hands-on affairs are designed to appeal to your inner foodie and are offered to overnight guests on Thursday, Friday, and Saturday evenings. Call ahead to find out what's on the calendar during your stay, as events are timed to the cycles of the seasons and harvest.

3310 Jackson Rd., Duncan, BC V9L 6N7. www.fairburnfarm.bc.ca. © **250/746-4637**. 7 units. June–Sept C$165–C$190 guesthouse double; C$950 cottage per week (does not include breakfast). Lower off-season rates. Rates include breakfast. Extra person C$20. MC, V. Free parking. Closed Oct 15–Nov 15. **Amenities:** Common room. *In room:* No phone, Wi-Fi (free).

IN COWICHAN BAY

Dream Weaver B&B ★ This handsome Victorianesque structure with wraparound porch is newly constructed as a B&B, offering large, stylish units with expansive views across the bay. The location—right above the harbor—couldn't be better. The top-of-the-line room is also top-of-the-house: The very spacious Magnolia Suite encompasses the entire attic floor, complete with dormers and quirky ceiling angles, fireplace, soaker tub, and picture window. Each suite has its own character, and is decorated with rich colors and fabrics—plus a dash of knowing restraint. All rooms have private bathrooms; two rooms have two-person Jacuzzi tubs.

1682 Botwood Lane, Cowichan Bay, BC V0R 1N0. www.dreamweaverbedandbreakfast.com. © **888/748-7689** or 250/748-7688. C$125–C$200 double. Lower off-season rates. Extra person C$25. MC, V. Free parking. *In room:* A/C, TV/DVD, CD player, fireplace, fridge, Wi-Fi (free).

Oceanfront Grand Resort and Marina ★★ This recently renovated hotel sits immediately above the marina in Cowichan Bay, with incredible views of the harbor and the peaks of Salt Spring Island. You have a choice of one- or two-bedroom units, all with oceanfront views, full kitchens, and separate living rooms. While regular rooms are perfectly nice and very large, the premium rooms resemble very swank apartments, with luxury linens, fine furniture, and marble floors. Apart from the lovely guest rooms, the Grand provides top-notch services and amenities. Fitness and pool facilities are comprehensive and beautifully maintained. The resort also offers fine dining, with Vancouver Island's largest Sunday brunch, with a 120-item buffet (C$20 adult, half price for children 10 and under). Best of all, you're just steps from the marina, where you can rent a kayak, charter a sailboat, or have a drink and watch the tides.

1681 Cowichan Bay Rd., Cowichan Bay, BC V0R 1N0. www.thegrandresort.com. © **800/663-7898** or 250/715-1000. 57 units. C$159–C$179 1-bedroom suite; C$219 2-bedroom suite. Extra person C$10. AE, MC, V. Free parking. **Amenities:** Restaurant, bar; complimentary guest computer in lobby; gym; hot tub; indoor pool; sauna; wine and liquor shop. *In room:* TV/DVD player, hair dryer, kitchenette, Wi-Fi (free).

Where to Eat

For a truly charming experience, consider lunching at a Cowichan Valley vineyard (for winery contact information, see above). **Vinoteca**, at Zanatta Winery, offers Italian-style farm lunches April through early October, Wednesday to Sunday noon to 3pm. **The Bistro at Cherry Point Vineyards** serves very tempting salads, sandwiches, and light entrees, and is open daily 11:30am to 3pm May through September. **La Pommeraie Bistro** at Merridale Ciderworks offers very satisfying country cuisine daily 11:30am to 4pm.

IN & AROUND DUNCAN

Bistro 161 ★ BISTRO   A haven for contemporary fine dining, Bistro 161 is in a renovated home, with patio seating in good weather. The husband-and-wife chef-owners come from an international background, and the tempting menu offers a selection of well-prepared dishes from around the world: French cassoulet, East Indian duck biryani, homey stuffed chicken, plus a selection of pasta and local seafood. The wine list features a number of local vintages. The pace can seem leisurely (nearly everything is house-made and cooked to order), but the quality is very high.

161 Kenneth St. ✆ **250/746-6466.** www.bistro161.com. Reservations recommended. Main courses C$17–C$28. MC, V. Mon–Sat 11am–3pm and 5–9pm.

Craig Street Brew Pub ★ BREWPUB   Wine and cider aren't the only delectable liquids to flow in the Cowichan Valley. This attractive brewpub in downtown Duncan serves up house-brewed lagers, ales, and porters, plus a selection of regional guest pours, local wines, and cocktails. The antique back bar adds old-world character, and the wood-beamed interior is cozy (the fireplace adds warmth in winter); in summer there's a rooftop deck. The menu offers pub favorites such as thin-crust pizza, burgers, panini sandwiches, and salads, but with main course specials that will make you push your tankard aside and take notice: pork tenderloin with orange-ginger glaze, or saffron halibut with red pepper aioli.

25 Craig St. ✆ **250/737-BEER** (2337). www.craigstreet.ca. Reservations not accepted. Main courses C$8–C$18. MC, V. Mon–Wed 11am–11pm; Thurs–Sat 11am–midnight; Sun 11am–10pm.

Just Jakes BURGERS/LIGHT DINING   JJ's is affiliated with Craig Street, but is a much more laid-back and funky restaurant that's best described as a cross between a family-friendly, fern-filled bar and a soda fountain. The staff is young and engaging which goes down well with families; the C$4 KidZ menu is terrific value The main menu offers a wide selection of burgers, salads, steaks, and pasta: pleasantly passé food that perfectly mirrors Duncan's attractively slow-paced downtown.

45 Craig St. ✆ **250/746-5622.** www.justjakes.ca. Reservations recommended. Main courses C$6–C$22. AE, MC, V. Mon–Thurs 11am–9pm; Fri–Sat 11am–11pm; Sun 10am–8pm.

IN COWICHAN BAY

Masthead Restaurant ★★ PACIFIC NORTHWEST   Housed in a historic, clapboard building that was once the town's original hotel, the Masthead is one of the top regional, seasonal dining experiences in the Cowichan Valley. Its handsome dining room is perched above the marina and offers wonderful views of the bay (in summer, the deck doubles as an outdoor dining area). Locally caught wild salmon comes with hazelnut risotto, and pan-roasted venison is served with sautéed corn and chanterelle mushrooms. The daily changing three-course table d'hôte menu at C$34 is an excellent value. The dining room sparkles with crystal and candlelight, the mood deepened with black glass tabletops. The wine list is a work of love (with multiple pages of "geek" wines) and the choice of Scotch whisky prodigious.

1705 Cowichan Bay Rd., Cowichan Bay. ✆ **250/748-3714.** www.themastheadrestaurant.com. Reservations recommended. Main courses C$20–C$34. MC, V. Daily from 5pm.

Rock Cod Café SEAFOOD   Rock Cod Café has the best fish and chips in the area, so at peak times this place gets busy. After all, when the fish is pulled straight off the boats and put right into the pan, what would you expect? The chalkboard menu is crammed with whatever else is fresh from local producers. Since the cafe has a liquor license—something most British fish-and-chip shops can't boast—you can turn a humble meal into an afternoon's worth of pleasure.

4–1759 Cowichan Bay Rd., Cowichan Bay. © **250/746-1550.** Reservations recommended in summer. Main courses C$7–C$17. MC, V. Daily 11am–9pm.

IN GENOA BAY

The Genoa Bay Cafe ★ PACIFIC NORTHWEST   Located a 20-minute drive east of Duncan, this unpretentious cafe is well worth the trip. The food is creative, contemporary, and always "home-cooked" tasty; examples include local roast leg of lamb served with mango chutney glaze (the house specialty), and slow-roasted ribs with apple-cranberry barbecue sauce. From the dining room or the deck, you can feast on the dramatic scenery; watch the comings and goings of sailboats and yachts in the adjacent marina; and simply enjoy welcoming and friendly service.

5100 Genoa Bay Rd., Genoa Bay Marina, Genoa Bay. © **250/746-7621.** www.genoabaycafe.com. Reservations recommended. Main courses C$16–C$34. MC, V. Thurs–Sun 11:30am–2:30pm; daily 5:30–10pm.

EN ROUTE TO NANAIMO
Chemainus: The City of Murals

Settled in the 1850s by European farmers, Chemainus quickly became a major timber-milling and -shipment point, due to the town's Horseshoe Bay, the oldest deepwater port on the Canadian West Coast. Prosperity saw the building of handsome homes and a solid commercial district. By the mid–20th century, the sawmills here were among the largest in the world, fed by the seemingly unending supply of wood from Vancouver Island's vast old-growth forests. When the mills closed in 1983, the town slid into decline. Economic prospects for Chemainus seemed dim until someone had the bright idea of hiring an artist to paint a mural depicting the town's history. Tourists took notice, and soon mural painting became the raison d'être of this town of only slightly more than 3,500 residents. Chemainus claims to be Canada's largest permanent outdoor art gallery. Much of downtown is now covered with murals, most dealing with area history and local events.

Stop by the **Chemainus Visitor Info Centre,** 9758 Chemainus Rd. (© **250/246-3944**), open from May to early September, for a walking-tour map of the murals, or go to **www.muraltown.com** for an online map. Across the street from the visitor center in Heritage Park is an informational kiosk where you can join a horse-drawn wagon tour of the murals from Chemainus Tours (© **250/246-5055;** www.chemainustours.com) for C$12 for adults, C$5 for kids. Or simply follow the yellow shoe-prints painted on the sidewalks. Much of the town is quiet and pedestrian-oriented, making it a pleasant place for a stroll and a good spot for lunch. **Old Town Chemainus,** along Willow and Maple streets, is filled with Victorian cottages converted into shops and cafes. The **Chemainus Theatre,** 9737 Chemainus Rd. (© **800/565-7738** or 250/246-9820; www.chemainustheatrefestival.ca), is a late-19th-century opera house that is now a popular dinner theater. The season runs February to December; call ahead to reserve.

WHERE TO STAY & EAT

There aren't lots of choices for fine dining in Chemainus. **Willow Street Café,** 9749 Willow St. (✆ **250/246-2434**), is a hip eatery serving up sandwiches, wraps, and salads; the deck is the best people-watching perch in town; open daily from 9am to 5pm. **Kudo's Japanese Restaurant,** 9875 Maple St. (✆ **250/246-1046**), serves sushi and other Japanese cuisine and is open for lunch and dinner daily.

A Scented Garden Staying here puts you within steps of the oceanfront, Old Town, and Chemainus Theatre. The renovated family home makes a comfortable B&B with a contemporary West Coast atmosphere. Rooms are appointed with country furnishings and decor, and include queen beds. The Island Thyme room features a double Jacuzzi, while the Mountainview room overlooks Mount Brenton. Breakfast is served in a common-area-lounge where there's a shared fridge, coffee, and tea, although the crows-nest viewing loft (accessed via a ladder) is a treat to hang out in, as much for its harbor views as for its lofty privacy. Or grab a sunny spot in the garden which, true to its namesake, is filled with lavender, honeysuckle vines, and other scented flora.

9913 Maple St. Chemainus, BC V0R 1K1. www.ascentedgardenbb.com. ✆ **877/224-9202** or 250/246-6796. 2 units. C$100–C$120 double. MC, V. **Amenities:** Lounge. *In room:* TV/DVD player, fridge, Wi-Fi (free).

Cedar & Yellow Point

South of Nanaimo, a forested peninsula juts out into the waters of the Georgia Strait. The land is rural and mostly undeveloped. The little community of Cedar is as close as the area comes to a town; this wouldn't qualify as much of a destination if it weren't for the fact that one of Vancouver Island's most popular lodges and one of its best restaurants are located here. It's a short drive from Nanaimo, and a detour through the forests and farmland makes for a pleasant break from Hwy. 1.

WHERE TO STAY

Yellow Point Lodge ★★ ♦ Beloved Yellow Point Lodge, a family-oriented resort and activity-focused summer camp established in the 1930s, is located on 73 hectares (180 acres) of forested waterfront, with over 2.5km (1½ miles) of rocky beach and secluded coves. The three-story log-and-stone building has an enormous lobby, a huge fireplace, and a dining room where guests share communal meals, all with wondrous views of the southern Gulf Islands. Inside the lodge are a number of comfortable hotel-like rooms, and scattered around the woods are cabins and cottages in a wide range of styles from rustic "barrack-style" beach cabins that share communal wash houses to more luxurious one-, two-, and three-bedroom cottages with fireplaces. If this unique blend of summer camp and recreation resort appeals to you, reserve well ahead—the lodge is a summer tradition for people of all incomes.

3700 Yellow Point Rd., Ladysmith, BC V9G 1E8. www.yellowpointlodge.com. ✆ **250/245-7422.** 53 units, 27 with private bathroom, most with shower only. C$199–C$225 double, C$175–C$220 cabin, C$138 barrack. Rates include all meals. AE, MC, V. Children must be 14 or older. **Amenities:** Licensed dining room; ferry, bus, train, or airport shuttle available for small fee; free bikes; golf course nearby; Jacuzzi; outdoor saltwater pool; sauna; 2 tennis courts; free canoes and kayaks; volleyball and badminton courts, Wi-Fi (free) *In room:* Fridge (in some cabins), no phone.

WHERE TO EAT

The Crow & Gate ★ ♦♦ PUB This Tudor-style pub on a 4-hectare (10-acre) farm is a friendly haven of English style, with low ceilings, handcrafted beams, and gleaming brass accents complemented by a brick fireplace and leaded-glass windows. The menu offers British standards like ploughman's lunch, steak and kidney pie, cold pork pie, Scotch eggs, and—every Wednesday and Saturday evening—roast beef and Yorkshire pudding. In summer, sit out on the flower-decked patio. Sorry, no minors.

2313 Yellow Point Rd. © **250/722-3731.** www.crowandgate.com. Reservations recommended for dinner. Main courses C$9–C$24. MC, V. Daily 11am–11pm; closes early when not busy and on some holidays (call ahead). Take the old Island Hwy. (Hwy. 19) north past Cassidy, or exit Island Hwy. 1 at Hwy. 19 to Cedar and Harmac. Cross the Nanaimo River, then turn right on Cedar Rd., which leads onto Yellow Point Rd. Continue for 1.6km (1 mile).

The Mahle House ★ PACIFIC NORTHWEST   The Mahle (pronounced "Molly") House is located in a tiny country town, in a salmon-pink heritage home overlooking a park. From this unlikely address (10 minutes south of Nanaimo), it has developed a huge reputation for excellent regional cuisine emphasizing locally grown, mostly organic produce and meats. On the weekly changing menu you might choose free-range chicken breast stuffed with Dungeness crab and served with lemon-grass sauce, or Chinook salmon, scallops, and porcupine prawns with saffron aioli and lemon oil. The award-wining wine list is extensive. The restaurant also offers "adventure" nights, when it's chef's choice: a Wednesday five-course dinner for C$40, a Thursday evening five-course tapas dinner for C$30 per person, and a three-course Sunday "country dinner" for C$35.

2104 Hemer Rd (at Cedar and Hemer rds.) © **250/722-3621.** www.mahlehouse.ca. Reservations recommended. Main courses C$18–C$34. AE, MC, V. Wed–Sun from 5pm. Closed Dec 21–29 and Jan 1–15.

CENTRAL VANCOUVER ISLAND

7

by Chris McBeath

Central Vancouver Island's major population center is Nanaimo, the arrival point for visitors taking ferries from the mainland, or catching a seaplane into its pretty downtown harbor. Once the site of a major 19th-century coal-mining operation, the city has long since moved away from its dependence upon resource extraction; it now sparkles with redevelopment, taking advantage of its scenic location—overlooking a bay full of islands, the choppy waters of Georgia Strait, and the glaciated peaks of the mainland. In 2011, World Health Organization identified a number of "fresh air" cities globally, and Nanaimo was among the most pollution-free on the planet.

A short distance north of Nanaimo, the coastline gives way to the towns of Parksville, Qualicum Beach, Courtenay, and Comox, which are famous for their warm, sandy beaches and numerous golf courses.

In sharp contrast to the serenity of the island's mainland-protected east coast, the wild, raging beauty of the Pacific Ocean on Vancouver Island's west coast entices photographers, hikers, kayakers, and divers to explore Pacific Rim National Park, Long Beach, and the neighboring towns of Ucluelet, Tofino, and Bamfield. Thousands of visitors arrive between March and May to see Pacific gray whales pass close to shore as they migrate north to their summer feeding grounds. More than 200 shipwrecks have occurred off the shores in the past 2 centuries, luring even more travelers to this eerily beautiful underwater world. And the park's world-famous West Coast Trail beckons intrepid backpackers to brave the 5- to 7-day hike over the rugged rescue trail—established after the survivors of a shipwreck in the early 1900s died from exposure because there was no land-access route for the rescuers. ***Note:*** See the "Vancouver Island" map (p. 114) to locate areas covered in this chapter.

ESSENTIALS

Getting There

BY PLANE   See chapter 5 for details on flights to **Victoria,** the main air hub for all of Vancouver Island.

Nanaimo and Comox/Courtenay have regular air service. **Air Canada Jazz** (✆ 888/247-2262; www.aircanada.com) offers service to Vancouver from Nanaimo. **Pacific Coastal Airlines** (✆ 800/663-2872; www.pacific-coastal.com) and Air Canada connector **Central Mountain Air** fly to/from Comox and Vancouver, while **WestJet** (✆ 888/937-8538; www.westjet.com) provides Comox with nonstop service to/from Edmonton and Calgary.

Smaller towns in central Vancouver Island can be reached via floatplane, either from Vancouver International's seaplane terminal or from downtown Vancouver's Coal Harbour terminal.

Commuter seaplane companies include **Harbour Air Seaplanes** (✆ 800/665-0212 or 604/688-1277; www.harbour-air.com), **Tofino Air** (✆ 866/486-3247 for Tofino base, 888/436-7776 for Sechelt base, or 800/665-2359 for Gabriola base; www.tofinoair.ca), and **West Coast Air** (✆ 800/347-2222; www.westcoastair.com).

BY FERRY   BC Ferries (✆ 888/223-3779 or 250/386-3431; www.bcferries.com) links Vancouver Island, the Gulf Islands, and the mainland. Major routes include the crossing from Tsawwassen to Swartz Bay and to Nanaimo, and from Horseshoe Bay (northwest of Vancouver) to Nanaimo. In summer, reserve in advance. Sample fares are included in the regional sections that follow.

BY BUS   One of the easiest ways to get to and from Vancouver Island destinations is by bus. **Greyhound Canada** (✆ 800/661-8747; www.greyhound.ca) provides six daily trips between Vancouver and Nanaimo. Fare is C$18 (non-refundable) and C$21 (refundable) one-way.

Visitor Information

For information on central Vancouver Island, contact **Tourism Vancouver Island,** Ste. 501, 65 Front St., Nanaimo (✆ 250/754-3500; www.helloBC.com/vi or www.vancouverisland.travel). Also check out **www.vancouverisland.com**.

Getting Around

While Vancouver Island has an admirable system of public transport, getting to remote sights and destinations is difficult without your own vehicle.

BY FERRY   BC Ferries (✆ 888/223-3779 or 250/386-3431; www.bcferries.com) routes link Vancouver Island ports to many offshore islands.

BY TRAIN   A scenic way to travel is on **VIA Rail's E&N Railiner,** the *Malahat* (✆ 888/VIA-RAIL [842-7245]; www.viarail.ca), which runs a daily schedule from Victoria to Courtenay. The service was temporarily suspended for track upgrades and car refurbishments. It is planned to resume in summer 2012.

BY BUS   Greyhound Canada (✆ 800/661-8747; www.greyhound.ca) operates regular daily service between Victoria and Tofino-Ucluelet. The 7-hour trip, departing Victoria at 7:30am and arriving in Tofino at 2:30pm, costs C$65 (non refundable) and C$73 (refundable). The bus also stops in Nanaimo and can pick up passengers arriving from Vancouver on the ferry. The **Tofino Bus** (*C* **866/986-3466;** www.tofinobus. com) also offers bus service from Victoria and Vancouver to Tofino-Ucluelet. A one-way ticket from Victoria to Tofino is C$74 and to Ucluelet C$64. The company also runs a shuttle service between the two towns for C$16 each way, which includes Pacific Rim National Park. **Island Link Bus** *C* **250/954-8257;** www.islandlink bus.com) runs a passenger express service between BC Ferries' terminals, and Vancouver, Victoria, and Comox airports to Tofino and Ucluelet.

BY CAR   The southern half of Vancouver Island is well served by paved highways. The trunk road between Victoria and Nanaimo is **Hwy. 1,** the Trans-Canada, which requires some patience, especially during the busy summer months. North of Nanaimo, the major road is **Hwy. 19,** a new four-lane expressway that runs 128km (80 miles) to Campbell River. The older sections of 19, all closer to the island's east coast, are now labeled 19A. The other major paved road system on the island, **Hwy. 4,** connects Parksville with Port Alberni and on to Ucluelet and Tofino, on the rugged west coast. This road is mostly two-lane, and portions of it are extremely winding and hilly.

Rental cars are readily available. Agencies include **Avis** (*C* **800/879-2847** in Canada, 800/331-1212 in the U.S.; www.avis.com), **Budget** (*C* **800/268-8900** in Canada, 800/527-0700 in the U.S.; www.budget.com), and **National** (*C* **877/222-9058** in Canada and the U.S.; www.nationalcar.com).

NANAIMO & GABRIOLA ISLAND

Nanaimo: 113km (70 miles) N of Victoria

For over a century, Vancouver Island's second-largest city (pop. 80,000) was the center of vast coal-mining operations, without much in the way of cultural niceties. In the last 30 years, however, Nanaimo has undergone quite a change. With its redeveloped waterfront, scenic surroundings, good restaurants and lodging, and a location central to many other Vancouver Island destinations, downtown Nanaimo makes a pleasant stop for a few days. It may have been the Cultural Capital of Canada in 2008, but the title is a bit of a stretch. Nanaimo is a fairly sprawling city, complete with suburban strip malls and plenty of traffic, so outside of its waterfront and downtown core, you need to travel a bit to discover its riches—such as the Petroglyph Provincial Park, the beautiful trail system on Newcastle Island, and its hot spots for scuba diving.

Just a 20-minute ferry ride from Nanaimo Harbour is Gabriola Island, though it feels a world away. Gabriola makes a marvelous day trip, providing a little of everything—sandy beaches, galleries, petroglyph sites, tide pools, and a sense of wooded serenity.

Essentials
GETTING THERE
BY PLANE   Regular service between Vancouver and Nanaimo Airport, 24km (15 miles) south of the city, is offered by **Air Canada Jazz** (*C* **888/247-2262;** www. aircanada.com).

Harbour Air Seaplanes (*C* **800/665-0212;** www.harbour-air.com) and **West Coast Air** (*C* **800/347-2222;** www.westcoastair.com) offer floatplane flights from downtown Vancouver to Nanaimo Harbour; West Coast Air also has flights to Nanaimo from Vancouver International Airport's floatplane base. **Orca Airways**

(📞 **888/359-6722;** www.flyorcaair.com) also provides service between Vancouver, Nanaimo, and Victoria.

BY CAR   Nanaimo is 111km (69 miles) from Victoria via Hwy. 1, the Trans-Canada Highway. At Nanaimo, Hwy. 1 crosses the Georgia Strait via the Horseshoe Bay ferry. North of Nanaimo, the main trunk road becomes Hwy. 19. It's 153km (95 miles) from Nanaimo to Campbell River, 206km (128 miles) to Tofino.

BY FERRY   BC Ferries (📞 **888/223-3779** or 250/386-3431; www.bcferries.com) operates two major runs to Nanaimo. The crossing from Horseshoe Bay in West Vancouver to Nanaimo's Departure Bay terminal is one of the busiest in the system; expect delays, especially at rush hour and summer weekends. The Tsawwassen ferry arrives and departs at Nanaimo's Duke Point terminal, 16km (10 miles) south of town off Hwy. 1. Duke Point is not served by public transit and the route is used primarily by trucks and commercial vehicles, but if you're traveling by car, it's a good alternative. Tickets for both ferries are C$15 per passenger and C$58 per car, with slightly lower midweek and low-season prices.

BY TRAIN   Via Rail operates *The Malahat,* a daily service between Victoria and Courtenay with various stops, including Nanaimo. In 2011, the route was temporarily closed for upgrades until summer 2012. For information, contact **VIA Rail (📞 888/ VIA-RAIL** [842-7245]; www.viarail.ca).

BY BUS   Greyhound Canada (📞 **800/661-8747;** www.greyhound.ca) provides seven daily trips between Vancouver and Nanaimo; fares are C$19 (non-refundable) and C$21 (refundable). Although non-Greyhound buses continue both north and south from Nanaimo, Greyhound handles all reservations.

VISITOR INFORMATION
Contact **Tourism Nanaimo,** Beban House, 2290 Bowen Rd., Nanaimo, BC V9T 3K7 (📞 **800/663-7337** or 250/756-0106; www.tourismnanaimo.com). In summer, an **info center** operates out of the Bastion, at Pioneer Waterfront Plaza. Tourism Vancouver Island is also based in Nanaimo (see p. 147).

GETTING AROUND
Nanaimo Regional Transit System (📞 **250/390-4531;** www.rdn.bc.ca) provides public transport in the Nanaimo area. Fares are C$2.25 for adults and C$2 for seniors and youths. For a cab, call **AC Taxi** (📞 **800/753-1231** or 250/753-1231) or **Swiftsure Taxi** (📞 **250/753-8911**).

The **BC Ferries** route to Gabriola Island leaves from behind the Harbour Park Shopping Centre on Front Street (note that this is not the same dock as either the Tsawwassen- or Horseshoe Bay–bound ferries), roughly every hour between 7am and 11pm. In summer, the round-trip fare is C$9 per person, plus C$21 for a car. You can bring your bike free of charge.

Exploring Nanaimo

Nanaimo's steep-faced waterfront has been restructured with tiers of walkways, banks of flowers, marina boardwalks, and floating restaurants. Called **Pioneer Waterfront Plaza,** the area fills on Fridays with the local farmers' market. The **Bastion,** a white fortified tower, rises above the harbor as a relic of the 1850s when it was part of a Hudson's Bay Company trading post. In summer, The Bastion doubles as a tourist information center.

Nanaimo

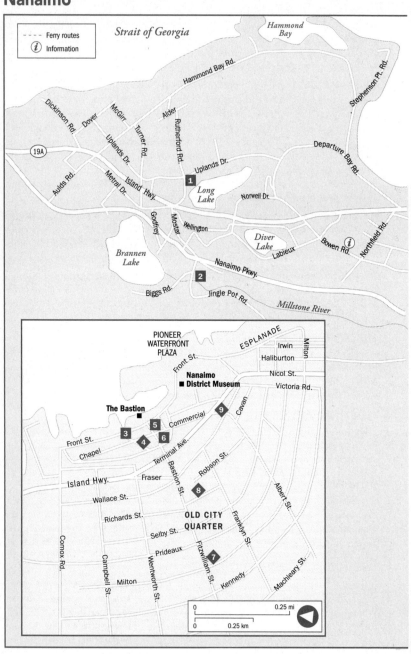

Strait of Georgia

Hammond Bay

- - - Ferry routes
(i) Information

Hammond Bay Rd.

Stephenson Pt. Rd.

Dickinson Rd.

Dover

McGirr

Alder

Turner Rd.

Rutherford Rd.

Departure Bay Rd.

19A

Uplands Dr.

Island Hwy.

Uplands Dr.

Auids Rd.

Metral Dr.

Godfrey

Mostar

Wellington

Long Lake

Norwell Dr.

Diver Lake

Bowen Rd.

(i)

Northfield Rd.

Labieux

Brannen Lake

Nanaimo Pkwy.

Biggs Rd.

Jingle Pot Rd.

Millstone River

PIONEER WATERFRONT PLAZA

Front St.

ESPLANADE

Irwin

Milton

Haliburton

Nicol St.

Nanaimo
■ District Museum

Victoria Rd.

The Bastion ■

Cavan

Commercial

Front St.

Chapel

Terminal Ave.

Island Hwy.

Fraser

Bastion St.

Robson St.

Albert St.

Wallace St.

Richards St.

OLD CITY QUARTER

Franklyn St.

Selby St.

Comox Rd.

Prideaux

Fitzwilliam St.

Kennedy

Machleary St.

Campbell St.

Milton

Wentworth St.

0   0.25 mi

0   0.25 km

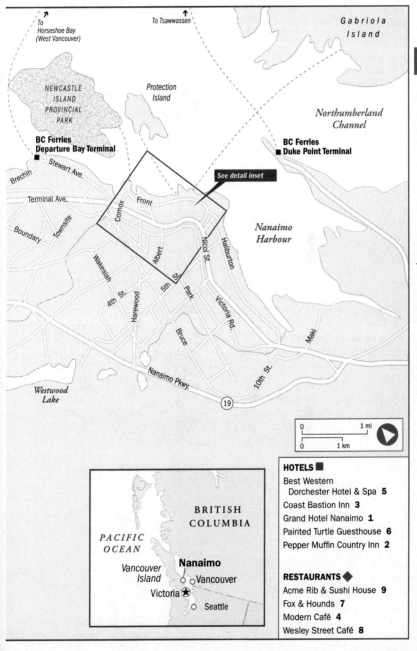

To Horseshoe Bay
(West Vancouver)

To Tsawwassen

Gabriola Island

NEWCASTLE ISLAND PROVINCIAL PARK

Protection Island

Northumberland Channel

BC Ferries
Departure Bay Terminal

Stewart Ave.

Brechin

Terminal Ave.

Boundary

Townsite

Comox

Front

See detail inset

BC Ferries
Duke Point Terminal

Nanaimo Harbour

Wakesiah

Albert

Nicol St.

Haliburton

4th St.

Harewood

5th St.

Park

Victoria Rd.

Maki

Bruce

Nanaimo Pkwy.

10th St.

Westwood Lake

19

0   1 mi
0   1 km

BRITISH COLUMBIA

PACIFIC OCEAN

Vancouver Island

Nanaimo

Vancouver

Victoria

Seattle

HOTELS ■

Best Western
 Dorchester Hotel & Spa **5**
Coast Bastion Inn **3**
Grand Hotel Nanaimo **1**
Painted Turtle Guesthouse **6**
Pepper Muffin Country Inn **2**

RESTAURANTS ◆

Acme Rib & Sushi House **9**
Fox & Hounds **7**
Modern Café **4**
Wesley Street Café **8**

Only in Nanaimo: The World Championship Bathtub Race

From its beginnings in 1967, Nanaimo's signature summer draw has grown into a weeklong series of events that shows off the city's good-natured spirit. In the early days, fewer than half of the original racing vessels—old claw-foot tubs fitted with engines—completed the crossing of 58km (36-mile) Georgia Strait from Nanaimo Harbour to Vancouver's Fisherman's Cove. These days, most contestants race in specially designed tubs that look like single-person speedboats. The race is the climax of late July's **Marine Festival,** which includes a street fair, parade, and traditional "Sacrifice to the Bathtub Gods." For information, go to www.bathtubbing.com.

Nanaimo's busy natural port has ferry links to Vancouver, Horseshoe Bay, and to Tsawwassen to the south, as well as to lovely **Gabriola Island** and to **Newcastle Island,** a car-free provincial park on the harbor's northern flank. Throughout the day, floatplanes buzz in and out of the boat basin, shuttling commuters back and forth to Vancouver and other coastal communities. If you're up for a walk, the **Harbourside Walkway** stretches 4km (2½ miles) from the heart of the city all the way to Departure Bay.

The old downtown, just behind the Bastion and centered on Commercial, Front, and Bastion streets, is a series of pleasant winding streets behind the harbor. **Artisan's Studio,** 70 Bastion St. (© 250/753-6151), is a co-op gallery that displays the work of local artists and craftspeople. **Hill's Native Art,** 76 Bastion St. (© 250/755-7873) is a reputable place for First Nations art.

The **Old City Quarter** is an uptown section of the city center that was severed from the harborfront area when the Island Highway cut through downtown. Now reached from the harbor by walking up the Bastion Street overpass, the 3-block area has been redeveloped into housing, boutiques, and fine restaurants.

Nanaimo District Museum   Nanaimo's regional museum is a worthwhile introduction to the area's past, first as a home for the Snunéymuxw (the name from which Nanaimo derives) people and then as a coal-mining boomtown. The museum relocated to the new and adjacent Vancouver Island Conference Centre in 2008. The expanded exhibit gallery portrays the unique aspects of Nanaimo's location, character, and natural history, featuring the Snunéymuxw First Nation, "colorful" citizens, and the coal mining, industrial, and social development of the community. Be sure to visit the Bastion, the last free-standing, original wooden HBC bastion in North America.

100 Museum Way. © **250/753-1821.** www.nanaimomuseum.ca. Admission C$2 adults, C$1.75 seniors, C75¢ children 6–12. Mid-May to Labour Day daily 10am–5pm; day after Labour Day to mid-May Tues–Sat 10am–5pm.

Ferrying to Newcastle Island

Just outside Nanaimo harbor, **Newcastle Island Marine Provincial Park** (© **250/754-7893;** www.newcastleisland.ca) is an ideal destination for hikers, cyclists, and campers. The island was home to two Salish Indian villages before British settlers discovered coal here in 1849. The Canadian-Pacific Steamship Company purchased the island in 1931, creating a resort with a dance pavilion, teahouse, and floating hotel. The 300-hectare (741-acre) island has now largely returned to its natural state. It now attracts outdoorsy types with its many trails; selected walks range from 2 to 4km (1.3–2.5 miles). The popular Mallard Lake Trail leads through the wooded interior toward a freshwater lake; the Shoreline Trail runs across steep cliffs, onto sand and gravel beaches suitable for swimming, and up to a great eagle-spotting perch. The park maintains 18 campsites, with toilets, wood, fire pits, and water. Rate is C$16.

From April to Canadian Thanksgiving (mid-Oct), **Nanaimo Harbour Ferry** (© **250/729-8738**) offers ferry service to Newcastle Island from the wharf at the peninsula tip of **Maffeo-Sutton Park** (just north of downtown), operating daily between 10am and 9pm in July and August, and until 5pm the rest of the year. The round-trip fare for the 10-minute crossing is C$9 for adults and C$5 for children 12 and younger. Bikes and dogs are free.

Exploring Gabriola Island

Much of Gabriola (pop. 4,500) is reached along North Road and South Road, two country lanes that provide a loop route around the island. A third road, Taylor Bay Road, departs from the ferry dock to access Gabriola's rocky northern reaches. It takes about half an hour to drive from one end of the island to the other. Visitors must be self sufficient; there is no public transit.

The main commercial center is just up the hill from the ferry terminal and is often referred to as **Folklife Village** (© **250/247-9332;** www.gabriolaisland.org), where you'll find a first-rate Visitor Information Center. Stop by **Gabriola Artworks,** 575 North Rd. (© **250/247-7412;** www.gabriolaartworks.com), an excellent gallery of local arts and crafts. **Sandwell Provincial Park** is one of Gabriola's nicest beaches and picnic areas, with paths leading through old-growth forests and to views of the Entrance Island lighthouse.

At the southern end of Gabriola is Silva Bay, a marina resort featuring an excellent restaurant and pub, as well as Canada's only traditional wooden boat-building school—visitors are welcome to view works-in-progress every Friday afternoon. Just south of Silva Bay is **Drumbeg Provincial Park,** which has a good swimming beach.

Gabriola Island and the area around Nanaimo are rich in prehistoric **petroglyph rock carvings.** On the South Road, near the United Church (about 10km/6¼ miles from the ferry terminal), a short path leads to a mix of fantastical creatures and abstract shapes scratched in sandstone. Park in the church lot and follow the signs. *Note:* The Snunéymuxw regard these petroglyphs as sacred and frown on people taking pictures or rubbings of them.

Taylor Bay Road leads to more parks and beaches on the north end of the island. **Gabriola Sands Provincial Park** protects two of the island's best beaches, at Taylor Bay and Pilot Bay. Here's where to find another key island attraction: the Malaspina Galleries, an amazing series of sandstone formations carved by the surf into shapely caves and caverns. Toward the end of the road (now called Berry Point Rd.) is the **Surf Lodge,** 885 Berry Point Rd. (© **250/247-9231;** www.surflodge.com), with a pub and restaurant overlooking the Georgia Strait.

Outdoor Pursuits

BUNGEE JUMPING Wild Play Element Park, 35 Nanaimo River Rd. (© **888/716-7374;** www.wildplayparks.com; follow signs from Nanaimo Lakes exit off Hwy. 1, south of Nanaimo), has North America's first legal bridge jump, which sends you over the Nanaimo River for C$100. For another adrenaline rush at this recreation hot spot (which also includes sky diving, paintball, and a high-elevation swing), consider a ride on the zip-line (C$25), which launches daredevils, attached to a steel cable by a climbing harness, across a wooded canyon at speeds near 100kmph (62 mph). The zip trips are also a part of an aerial obstacle course of plank bridges, swinging logs, scramble nets, and tree ladders.

SCUBA DIVING ★★ While all of the waters off Vancouver Island are known for their superior diving opportunities, The Cousteau Society calls those around Nanaimo "the best temperate water diving in the world, second only to the Red Sea." Nicknamed the "Emerald Sea," its water is clear enough to see the likes of giant Pacific octopi, colorful sea anemones, and herds of marine mammals. Nanaimo has the largest artificial upright reef in the world, made up of a number of sunken vessels, including the HMCS *Saskatchewan* and the HMCS *Cape Breton,* which together form a reef 228m (748 ft.) in length. A third boat, the rescue tug *Rivtow Lion,* lies in shallow water just off Newport Island and is used for training. One of the single best dives in the Northwest is at **Dodds Narrows,** between Vancouver Island and Mudge Island. It boasts outstanding visibility, a high concentration of wildlife, and dramatic rock formations. Other area dives include **Snake Island Wall,** with a drop-off that seems to extend into the abyss.

Nanaimo Dive Outfitters (2205 Northfield Rd.; © **250/756-1863;** www. nanaimodiveoutfitters.ca) offers diving instruction, equipment rentals, and boat charters to most of the top diving spots in the Nanaimo area. Another local outfitter, **Mamro Adventures,** 1–5765 Turner Rd., Ste. 203 (© **250/756-8872;** www.mamro. com), can accommodate six passengers on trips of 1 to 10 days. Popular excursions include Port Hardy, famed for its dense marine-mammal population, and the Gulf Islands, Sunshine Coast, and Georgia Strait.

Where to Stay

IN NANAIMO

Best Western Dorchester Hotel ★ For the price, quality, and excellent downtown location, the Dorchester is hard to top. The hotel stands on the most venerable spot in Nanaimo: the site of the Hudson's Bay Company trading post in the 1850s, and then of the city's old opera house. Reminders of the opera-house days remain: The handsome chandeliers are all original, as are the ornate columns flanking the dining room. Guest rooms are comfortably furnished, though not exactly spacious. Pay a bit extra for a bayside room—the view is fantastic. Check the hotel website for seasonal Internet rates not available elsewhere.

70 Church St., Nanaimo, BC V9R 5H4. www.dorchesternanaimo.com. © **800/661-2449** or 250/ 754-6835. 65 units. C$120–C$175 double. Extra person C$10 per night. Senior, AAA, and Internet discounts, and corporate and off-season rates available. AE, DC, DISC, MC, V. Limited free parking. Pets accommodated for C$20 per night. **Amenities:** Restaurant; lounge. *In room:* A/C, TV with p/movies, hair dryer, Wi-Fi (free).

Coast Bastion Inn & Spa ★ At this modern high-rise hotel at the heart of downtown, every room boasts a waterfront view, and the Harbourside Walkway scene is just seconds away. It's worth the splurge for a superior room, with upgraded amenities and views from two sides. Two wheelchair-accessible rooms are available. The hotel connects to the Port Theatre complex.

11 Bastion St., Nanaimo, BC V9R 6E4. www.coasthotels.com. ℂ **800/663-1144** or 250/753-6601. 178 units. C$140–C$255 double; C$195–C$265 suite. Extra person C$10. Senior and AAA discounts, theater packages, and off-season rates available. AE, DC, DISC, MC, V. Valet parking C$12; self-parking C$7.50. Pets allowed for C$10 per day. **Amenities:** Restaurant; lounge; babysitting; health club; Jacuzzi; room service; sauna; spa. *In room:* A/C, TV w/movies, fridge, hair dryer, iPod dock, Wi-Fi (free).

Grand Hotel Nanaimo ★   The Grand Hotel is the area's most luxurious lodging. Rooms range from 56-sq.-m (603-sq.-ft.) suites with two TVs, a fireplace, kitchenette, and king-size bed to simpler but still very comfortable standard rooms. Deluxe rooms have jetted tubs and fireplaces; many rooms have balconies. There are two wheelchair-accessible units. The public areas are handsome, particularly the lobby with its soaring ceilings and chandelier. The Grand Hotel is about a 10-minute drive northwest of the city center.

4898 Rutherford Rd., Nanaimo, BC V9T 4Z4. www.thegrandhotelnanaimo.ca. ℂ **877/414-7263** or 250/758-3000. 72 units. C$160–C$220 double. Extra person C$15 per day. Low season, senior, and AAA discounts available. AE, MC, V. **Amenities:** Restaurant; lounge; fitness center; exercise room; indoor heated pool; room service. *In room:* A/C, TV, fridge, hair dryer, Wi-Fi (free).

Painted Turtle Guesthouse 🏠   A European-style hostel with a real sense of style, this repurposed vintage hotel is in the very center of downtown. The vibe is fun and filled with youthful energy, though guests here are by no means limited to the young. Travelers of all ages find this a pleasant place to stay, as it has a modern, bright, and airy communal lounge and kitchen alongside a variety of room types, from four-bed dorm rooms to doubles, and two-, three-, and four bedroom options for groups. In true hostel fashion, the bathrooms are down the hall, but they are clean and well furnished. All linens and towels are provided; there's even a concierge desk to help you plan and book local excursions. The entire facility is well-maintained and nicely decorated, and the owners do their best to ensure you have a great stay.

121 Bastion St., Nanaimo, BC V9R 3A2. www.paintedturtle.ca. ℂ **866/309-4432** or 250/753-4432. 20 rooms. C$25 dorm single; C$76–C$90 double. Discounts for Hostelling International members. MC, V. **Amenities:** Great room w/fireplace, games, common area, and library; full self-catering kitchen; storage for bikes, skis, snowboards, luggage. *In room:* No phone, Wi-Fi (free).

Pepper Muffin Country Inn ★ ☺   This country B&B on 2.4 hectares (6 acres) offers a rural getaway just minutes from downtown. A stream plays host to beaver, otter, and trout, and local crags are home to pileated woodpeckers and turkey buzzards. Although newly constructed as an inn, the building was designed with quirky angles and rooflines, and is tastefully furnished with antiques. Each guest room has a private entrance, balcony, and a private en suite bathroom. Bike trails and lakes are accessible nearby.

3718 Jingle Pot Rd., Nanaimo, BC V9R 6X4. www.peppermuffin.com. ℂ **866/956-0473** or 250/756-0473. 3 units. C$129 double. Rates include breakfast. 2-night minimum stay. AE, MC, V. **Amenities:** Outdoor hot tub. *In room:* TV/VCR, hair dryer, Wi-Fi (free).

Where to Eat

In central Nanaimo there are several casual spots worth knowing about. **Tina's Diner,** 187 Commercial St. (ℂ **205/753-5333**), is a classic '50s diner with big eggy breakfasts and sandwiches for lunch. **McClean's Specialty Foods,** 426 Fitzwilliam St. (ℂ **250/754-0100;** www.mcleansfoods.com), offers over 100 varieties of cheese, including many from Vancouver Island, plus other picnic comestibles. **Mon Petit Choux,** 101–120 Commercial St. (ℂ **250/753-6057;** www.monpetitchoux.ca), is a

On the Waterfront

In summer, for a pint of ale and a burger in a marvelous location, take the 10-minute Protection Connection ferry ride to the **Dinghy Dock Floating Marine Pub,** on Protection Island (☏ **250/753-2373**). It's exactly what its name says—a floating pub—and boasts spectacular sunset views of Nanaimo and the Vancouver Island mountains. The ferry leaves on the hour from the Commercial Inlet boat basin, below Pioneer Waterfront Plaza.

You'll get a wonderful view of the harbor from the **Lighthouse Bistro and Pub,** off Harbourside Walkway at 50 Anchor Way (☏ **250/754-3212**). Open daily from 11am to midnight and until 1am in summer (the restaurant closes earlier), this floating pub is adjacent to the city's floatplane base—watch these planes take off just beside your table.

quintessential French bakery with excellent breads and pastries, plus an espresso bar. Light meals are available for breakfast and lunch.

Fox & Hounds PUB FARE   British food is served all day, there's beer on draught and roast dinners every Sunday; the shelves are even stocked with English sodas such as Tango and Ribena. Easily recognized by the bright red phone booth at its entrance, this pub is located just 2 blocks up from the Old City Quarter and is worth the uphill climb. The decor is classic English pub. Servings are generous and tasty. You don't have to be a Brit to appreciate this gem, though there are a fair number of English accents in the crowd.

247 Milton St. ☏ **250/740-1000.** Main courses C$10–C$24. MC, V. Daily noon–10pm.

Modern Cafe ★ CONTEMPORARY CANADIAN   This chic, arty cafe is a good spot to have a quiet meal, or meet friends for late-night dessert and coffee. One menu is devoted to tapas, like almond-crusted baked brie with cranberry apple compote and West Coast fish cakes in creamy chipotle sauce, while another features "hand helds" or sandwiches. Main dishes feature local meats and vegetables—the Veggie Stack, a tower of portobello mushrooms, mashed yams, tomatoes, and won tons, is a nice break from rich meat dishes, as is the house-made vegetarian ravioli. With contemporary art on the redbrick walls, Modern Food's setting exudes a level of casual sophistication unusual for Nanaimo.

221 Commercial St. ☏ **250/754-5022.** www.themoderncafe.ca. Main courses C$14–C$25. MC, V. Sun–Mon 11am–11pm; Thurs–Sat 11am–midnight.

Wesley Street Café ★★ CONTEMPORARY CANADIAN   Nanaimo's premier fine-dining restaurant serves the city's most up-to-date food in a comfortably formal Old Town Quarter dining room. Dining progresses from a casual lunch of gourmet soups and sandwiches to a more sophisticated dinner menu that may offer roast quail with an exotic mushroom stuffing, a herb-crusted albacore tuna with grand fir–infused rhubarb glaze, and a porcini mushroom and roast garlic stuffed chicken. Monday through Thursday, the cafe offers three-course dinners for an unbelievable C$30. The huge wine list features many B.C. selections. Dine inside or, in summer, opt for the flower-covered patio.

321 Wesley St. ☏ **250/753-6057.** www.wesleycafe.com. Reservations required. Main courses C$24–C$32. AE, MC, V. Tues–Sat 11:30am–2pm and 5:30–9pm.

PARKSVILLE & QUALICUM BEACH

37km (23 miles) N of Nanaimo

These twin resort towns near the most popular beaches on Vancouver Island now market themselves as the tourist region of Oceanside. Spending a week here is a family tradition for many residents of British Columbia. With miles of sand and six golf courses, it's the perfect base for a relaxing vacation. Parksville (pop. 10,500) and Qualicum Beach (pop. 7,500) are also good stopping-off points for travelers making the trip to or from Victoria and Tofino.

Essentials

GETTING THERE Greyhound (© 800/661-8747; www.greyhound.ca) offers bus transport from Nanaimo to the Parksville and Qualicum area along the Hwy. 1/Hwy. 19 corridor; one-way fare from Victoria to Parksville is C$35 (non-refundable) and C$40 (refundable). **VIA Rail's** *Malahat* (© 888/VIA-RAIL [842-7245] or 250/383-4324; www.viarail.ca), stops in both towns on its daily trip from Victoria to Courtenay. Renovations have temporarily ceased these services until summer 2012. **KD Air** (© 800/665-4244, 604/688-9957, or 250/752-5884; www.kdair.com) offers several daily flights from Vancouver to the Qualicum Beach Airport for C$250 round-trip. Otherwise, the closest available air service is at Nanaimo or Comox.

VISITOR INFORMATION For information on Qualicum Beach and Parksville, contact the **Oceanside Tourism Association** (© 250/248-6300; www.visit parksvillequalicumbeach.com). For information once you're there, go to the **Qualicum Beach Visitor Information Centre,** 2711 W. Island Hwy., Qualicum Beach (© 250/752-9532; www.qualicum.bc.ca), or the **Parksville Visitor Info Centre,** 1275 E. Island Hwy. (© 250/248-3613; www.parksvillechamber.com).

Exploring the Area

While Qualicum Beach and Parksville share similar beaches and are all but connected by country-club developments and marinas, there are differences. Parksville has several large resorts and beachfront hotels, and is more of a developed strip without much of a town center. In contrast, Qualicum Beach has more of a town center with shopping and cafes—but this part of town is a few miles inland, away from the beach.

In Qualicum Beach, you can access the beach from many points along Hwy. 19A, the old Island Highway. Likewise, in Parksville, the beach is accessible downtown from the old Island Highway, near the junction of Hwy. 4A, and at the adjacent Parksville Community Beach and Playground. However, the best beaches are preserved in **Rathtrevor Beach Provincial Park,** just east of Parksville's town center. The 348-hectare (860-acre) park offers trails, bird-watching sites, and a campground.

Note: If you're looking for miles of broad, white-sand strands lapped by azure water, you might be surprised. The sea is quite shallow here, with a very gentle slope. When the tide goes out, it exposes hundreds of acres of gray-sand flats. When the tide is in, the beach disappears beneath the shallow waters. There are benefits to this: The summer sun bakes the sand while the tide is out, so when the tide comes back in, the shallow water is warmed by the sand, thus making the water agreeable for swimming.

When you're not on the beach, one particularly good place to stop in Qualicum Beach is the **Old School House,** 122 Fern Rd. W. (© **250/752-6133;** www.the oldschoolhouse.org), which now houses galleries, studios, and a gift shop. It also holds frequent Sunday afternoon concerts and jazz gatherings on Tuesday evenings.

There's no better place for a garden stroll than the **Milner Gardens and Woodland,** 2179 W. Highland Hwy. (© **250/752-6153;** www.milnergardens.org), a heritage garden comprising 24 hectares (59 acres) of old-growth, Douglas-fir forest and 4 hectares (10 acres) of planted gardens. The Milner Gardens are part of a 1930s estate, which also includes a historic home where Queen Elizabeth II once stayed. Given to the local university in 1996, the estate was gradually turned into a destination garden by a small army of horticulture students and local volunteers. Plantings include an artist's garden and many unusual rhododendrons, at their most colorful in late spring. Paths thread through the forests, and garden tours are available. Open 10am to 5pm daily from May through Labour Day. The gardens close November through January, and offer variable hours the balance of the off-season months, so call ahead. Admission is C$10 adults, C$6 students 12 and older. Afternoon tea is served in the Milner house, and not included in the entrance fee.

HORNE LAKE CAVES PROVINCIAL PARK

West of Qualicum Beach, **Horne Lake Caves Provincial Park** (© **250/248-7829;** www.hornelake.com) is one of Vancouver Island's best outdoor-adventure destinations. While a lakeside park area makes for terrific camping, swimming, and canoeing, a system of caves on the slopes of the Beaufort Range attract spelunkers, neophyte and experienced, for half- or full-day excursions. Bring at least two sources of light, and, in summer, rent a helmet from the park office. From mid-June to Labour Day, the park offers guided tours, like the family-oriented Riverbend Cave Interpretive Program, as well as rappelling adventures. Some extreme programs have a minimum age of 15 years. The park is located 26km (16 miles) west of Qualicum Beach, off exit 75 from Hwy. 19 or 19A. From here on in, the road is mostly gravel which, when wet weather creates ridges and crevices, can take some careful maneuvering.

Where to Stay

Campsites at **Rathtrevor Beach Provincial Park** (© **800/689-9025** for reservations, or 250/248-9449 in the off season), open year-round, go for C$15 to C$24.

Crown Mansion   In its heyday, this former private home entertained celebrities and royalty. Fully renovated to its original 1930s elegance, the mansion is now a boutique hotel with six large guest rooms. All are superbly furnished with hardwood floors, plush throws and linens, and a hint of Hollywood personality that adds an understated pizzazz. The dining room, where complimentary continental breakfast is served, central lobby, and a library are graced with antiques and magnificent fireplaces. The mansion overlooks The Qualicum Memorial Golf Course and is connected to several walking trails.

292 Crescent Rd. E., Qualicum Beach, BC V9K 0A5. www.crownmansion.com. © **250/752-5776.** 6 units. May–Sept C$155–C$225 double. Additional adult C$20. MC, V. **Amenities:** Lounge. *In room:* TV/DVD player, hair dryer, iPod dock, Wi-Fi (free).

Pacific Shores Resort and Spa ★   Adjacent to the Nature Trust Bird Sanctuary and part of the Englishman River Estuary, the resort is set on a landscaped 5.5 hectares (14 acres). There are 102 two-bedroom suites that become studios or one-bedroom suites on demand by opening up or shutting off connecting doors, thereby creating quite a mix of accommodations. Studio suites are like regular hotel rooms but when configured with extra bedrooms, they offer full kitchens, fireplaces, washers/dryers, and all the home-away-from-home amenities you need. Families love the place in summer for its child-friendly spaces, including an outdoor playground. In off season, the venue becomes a quieter and more romantic retreat. **The Aquaterre Spa** offers a full selection of spa and massage treatments. **The Landing West Coast Grill** offers regional fine dining plus two saltwater aquariums as walls—reportedly, the largest private aquarium in B.C.

1600 Stroulger Rd., Nanoose Bay, BC V9P 9B7. www.pacific-shores.com. © **866/986-2222** or 250/468-7121. 102 units. C$110–C$175 hotel room; C$260–C$345 1–2-bedroom condo; C$500 3-bedroom condo. AE, MC, V. Free parking. **Amenities:** Restaurant; lounge; babysitting; health club; Jacuzzis; picnic and barbecue area; large indoor pool w/"ozonated" water; sauna; complimentary use of kayaks and canoes; outdoor children's play area; convenience store and deli;. *In room:* TV/DVD player, fireplace, fridge, kitchen (multi-bedroom suites), Wi-Fi (free).

Quality Resort Bayside 🍴 Perched right above the sands in central Parksville, this resort offers lots of amenities at moderate prices. Half of the rooms face the beach, and the other half look onto the mountains of Vancouver Island; all are comfortably furnished and have balconies. Bayside Bistro offers afternoon tea as well as West Coast cuisine, with summer seating on the deck. The bar focuses more on pub fare, darts, pool, and satellite sports broadcasts.

240 Dogwood St., Parksville, BC V9P 2H5. www.qualityresortparksville.com. © **800/663-4232** or 250/248-8333. 59 units. July–Sept C$129–C$189 double. Lower rates in off season. Extra person C$15. AE, DC, DISC, MC, V. Free parking. Pets allowed for C$15. **Amenities:** Oceanview restaurant; bar; golf course nearby; health club w/squash courts; Jacuzzi; indoor pool; room service. *In room:* A/C, TV, hair dryer, Wi-Fi (free).

Tigh-Na-Mara Resort Hotel ★★★ ☺ This time-honored log-cabin resort just keeps getting better. Established in the 1940s on a forested waterfront beach, Tigh-Na-Mara has expanded over the years with an ever-widening variety of accommodations choices (all log built), including studio and one-bedroom lodge rooms, plus one- and two-bedroom cottages. All choices have fireplaces, full bathrooms, and a kitchen. The cottages are comfortably lived-in and homey, while the condos are new and lavish, especially those at ocean-side. Families will especially appreciate the lengthy list of supervised child-friendly activities (many of them free); the restaurant in the log-and-stone lodge serves an eclectic version of Northwest cuisine. The impressive **Grotto Spa** ★★ is the largest in the province and offers a mineral pool, body and massage treatments, plus a full line of aesthetic spa services. The spa also offers the spa-client-only **Treetop Tapas and Grill,** where friends and couples wine and dine in bathrobes after their treatments.

1155 Resort Dr., Parksville, BC V9P 2E5. © **800/663-7373** or 250/248-2072. www.tigh-na-mara.com. 192 units. July–Aug C$199–C$329 double. Rates vary throughout the year. Extra person C$10–C$20. 2- to 7- night minimum stays apply in midsummer and on holidays. AE, MC, V. Free parking. Pets allowed in cottages Sept–June, add C$30 per stay. **Amenities:** 2 restaurants; lounge; babysitting; bike rental; children's programs; concierge; fitness center; indoor pool; sauna; spa; unlit tennis court; paddle boats; basketball; children's outdoor playground; table tennis. *In room:* TV w/pay movies, gas or wood-burning fireplace,fridge, kitchen, Wi-Fi (free).

Where to Eat

Beach House Café INTERNATIONAL   Located right at the water's edge, this bistro-style cafe is a local favorite, serving good food without a lot of frills. We're talking soup-and-sandwich lunches and casual, intimate dinners. Some lunch items are repeated at dinner, although in the evening, you'll be treated to house fortes, such as a bouillabaisse loaded with local seafood. Homemade pies, whether savory stead-and-mushroom, or sweet rhubarb-and-strawberry, are a must. It's a tiny place that fills up quickly so if you make reservations, be on time.

2775 W. Island Hwy., Qualicum Beach.© **250/752-9626.** www.thebeachhousecafe.ca. Reservations suggested. Main courses C$10–C$22. MC, V. Daily 11am–2:30pm and 5–10pm.

Kalvas Restaurant SEAFOOD   Inside the rustic-looking log cabin is an intimate, and bustling dining room which many locals choose as their special-occasion restaurant. The specialties are steaks and seafood prepared in traditional supper-club style: sole amandine, New York steak, steamed Dungeness crab served with drawn butter, and nine preparations of Fanny Bay oysters. Ask for the house-made spaetzles.

180 Molliet St., Parksville.© **250/248-6933.** Reservations recommended. Main courses C$12–C$60. MC, V. Daily 5–10pm.

Lefty's Fresh Foods INTERNATIONAL   Originally a vegetarian eatery, Lefty's has added healthy chicken and meat dishes so that its menu has broad appeal. The emphasis is on modern comfort food: salads, sandwiches, burgers, pasta, stir-fries, and focaccia pizzas. In addition to the original Qualicum Beach location, where the line-ups can sometimes try your patience, there's also a Lefty's in Parksville. Both locations are noteworthy for their home-baked desserts.

710 Memorial St., Qualicum Beach, and 101–280 E. Island Hwy., Parksville.© **250/752-7530** (Qualicum) and **250/954-3886** (Parksville). www.leftys.tv. Main courses C$8–C$20. AE, DC, MC, V. Thurs–Sat 8am–10pm (to 9pm off season); Sun–Wed 8am–8pm.

Shady Rest Waterfront Pub & Restaurant CANADIAN   There's been an eatery here since 1924, although today's look neither hints to its heritage nor detracts from the real show—the beachside vistas. Both the restaurant and the pub here have outdoor seating, and both serve the same Qualicum Beach–style comfort food breakfast through dinner. The no-frills items are good and the more ambitious items vary between excellent and adequate. Weekend brunches are winners.

3109 W. Island Hwy., Qualicum Beach.© **250/752-9111.** www.shadyrest.ca. Reservations recommended for dinner. Main courses C$10–C$25. MC, V. Daily 8am–9pm; pub open 11am–1am.

EN ROUTE TO VANCOUVER ISLAND'S WEST COAST

From Parksville, Hwy. 4 cuts due west, climbing up over the mountainous spine of Vancouver Island before dropping into Port Alberni, at the head of the Pacific's Alberni Inlet. From here, you can join the **MV *Frances Barkley*** ★ as it plies the inlet's narrow waters, delivering mail, supplies, and passengers to isolated communities. Bamfield, the southern terminus of the mail-boat run, is one of the two departure points for the West Coast Trail. Mail boats from Port Alberni also negotiate the waters of Barkley Sound and the Broken Group Islands before arriving at Ucluelet, a gentrifying fishing port.

The Drive to Port Alberni

Crossing the island is a remarkable drive full of diversions, whether it's to walk through old-growth forest, picnic beside picturesque rivers, stop off at **Coombs** (look for the goats atop the roof at **The Old Country Market**) or take a tour of the **World**

Parrot Refuge (2116 Alberni Hwy; ℂ **250/248-5194;** www.worldparrotrefuge. org). Nearby, the **North Island Wildlife Recovery Centre,** 1240 Leffler Rd., Errington (ℂ **250/248-8534;** www.niwra.org), takes in injured and orphaned wildlife, with the goal of returning them to the wild. Guided tours of the center are available March through October, and include: many hands-on exhibits; the Eagle Flight cage (Canada's largest), where eagles can be viewed through one-way glass; an extensive public viewing area that houses the non-releasable wildlife; and a nature trail around the center's release pond, showing B.C.'s flora. It's open mid-March through October, daily from 9am to 5pm; admission is C$8 adult, C$3 children. Take a left from Hwy. 4 onto Bellevue Road; turn right onto Ruffels Road and then left onto Leffler Road.

Just 3km (1¾ miles) west of the junction with Hwy. 19, turn south to **Englishman's Falls Provincial Park.** Easy trails lead to both the upper and lower falls. Picnic tables and a basic campground are available. Below the cliffs of 1,818m (5,965-ft.) Mount Arrowsmith, Hwy. 4 passes along the shores of **Cameron Lake.** The western end of the lake is preserved as **MacMillan Provincial Park,** with a magnificent stand of old-growth forest called Cathedral Grove.

Finally, you'll reach **Port Alberni,** a hardworking town of nearly 20,000. The busy port is home to a number of fishing charters and boat-tour companies, as well as the mail boats that offer day trips to Bamfield and Ucluelet. If you need a hotel, the two to consider are the **Coast Hospitality Inn,** 3835 Redford St. (www.hospitalityinn portalberni.com; ℂ **877/723-8111** or 250/723-8111), with doubles from C$139; and the **Best Western Barclay Hotel,** 4277 Stamp Ave. (www.bestwesternbarclay. com; ℂ **800/563-6590** or 250/724-7171), with rooms from C$149 in high season.

MV Frances Barkley ★

A truly unique way to experience the area is with **Lady Rose Marine Services** (ℂ **800/663-7192** Apr–Sept, or 250/723-8313; www.ladyrosemarine.com), which operates MV *Frances Barkley,* a packet freighter that delivers mail, groceries, newspapers, and other supplies to communities along the Alberni Inlet and Barkley Sound. The boat take sightseers to the wild outback of Vancouver Island, for a fascinating glimpse into the daily life of remote fishing and logging communities. You'll likely spot bald eagles, bears, orcas, and porpoises. Kayakers and canoeists en route to the Broken Group Islands take the vessel to a base camp at Sechart, while hikers bound for the West Coast Trail and day trippers catch a ride to Bamfield, a picturesque fishing village, much of which is built on stilts over the water. Year-round, the freighter departs from north Harbour Quay at 8am on Tuesday, Thursday, and Saturday, and returns to Port Alberni around 5pm.

June through September, there are additional 8am sailings on Monday, Wednesday, and Friday to Ucluelet via Sechart near the Broken Group Islands, arriving back in Port Alberni at 7pm (see box on p. 167). From the first Sunday in July to the first Sunday in September, there's an extra 8am Sunday sailing to Bamfield via Sechart.

Round-trip fares are double the one-way fare. One-way fare to Bamfield is C$35. One-way fare to Ucluelet is C$37. You can go to Kildonan for C$26 each way, or to Sechart for C$35. Children 8 to 15 pay half the adult fare. Bring windproof jackets and hats, as the weather can change dramatically during the course of the trip. Reservations are required.

THE WEST COAST TRAIL ★ & PACIFIC RIM NATIONAL PARK ★

The west coast of Vancouver Island is a magnificent area of old-growth forests, stunning fjords (or "sounds" in local parlance), rocky coasts, and sandy beaches. Although **Pacific Rim National Park** (www.pc.gc.ca) was established in 1971, it wasn't until 1993 that the area really exploded into the greater consciousness. That was when thousands of environmentalists from around the world gathered to protest the clear-cutting of old-growth forests in Clayoquot Sound. When footage of the protests ran on the evening news, people who saw the landscape for the first time were moved to come experience it firsthand. Tourism in the area has never looked back.

Three units make up the park. Along the southwest coast is a strip of land that contains the 77km (48-mile) **West Coast Trail,** which runs between Port Renfrew (covered in chapter 6) and Bamfield (see above). The trail is considered one of the world's great hikes: a grueling 5- to 7-day journey—with frequent dangerous river crossings and rocky scrambles—that is not for the inexperienced. **Broken Group Islands** is a wilderness archipelago in the mouth of Barkley Sound, and a popular diving and kayaking spot (p. 167). **Long Beach** fronts onto the Pacific between Ucluelet and Tofino. Long Beach is more than 30km (19 miles) long, broken here and there by rocky headlands and bordered by tremendous groves of cedar and Sitka spruce. Park entry is C$7.80 adults, C$6.80 seniors, C$3.90 youths, and C$20 families.

The town of **Ucluelet** (pronounced "You-*clue*-let," meaning "safe harbor") sits on the southern end of the Long Beach peninsula, on the edge of Barkley Sound. Though it has a winter population of only 1,900, thousands of visitors arrive between March and May to see the Pacific gray whales.

At the far northern tip of the peninsula, **Tofino** (pop. 1,600) borders beautiful Clayoquot Sound. Hikers and beachcombers come to Tofino simply for the scenery. Others use it as a base from which to explore the sound—it's the center of the local eco-tourism business. No small number of travelers arrive here with eating in mind: This remote town is noted for its excellent restaurants.

Essentials

GETTING THERE

BY PLANE Orca Airways (✆ 888/359-6722 or 604/270-6722; www.flyorcaair.com) offers year-round flights between Vancouver International Airport and Tofino. **Tofino Air** (✆ 855/647-7560 or 250/250-4454; www.tofinoair.ca) also operates a schedule between Tofino and Vancouver International Airport and Vancouver Harbour.

BY CAR Tofino, Ucluelet, and Long Beach all lie near the end of Hwy. 4 on the west coast of Vancouver Island. From Nanaimo, take the Island Highway (Hwy. 19) north for 52km (32 miles). Just before the town of Parksville is a turnoff for Hwy. 4, which leads to the mid-island town of Port Alberni (38km/24 miles) and then to the coastal towns of Tofino (135km/84 miles west of Port Alberni) and Ucluelet (103km/64 miles west). The road is paved but very winding after Port Alberni.

BY FERRY A 4½-hour ride aboard the **Lady Rose Marine Services** (✆ 800/663-7192 Apr–Sept, or 250/723-8313; www.ladyrosemarine.com) MV *Frances Barkley* takes you from Port Alberni to Ucluelet. See p. 161 for more information.

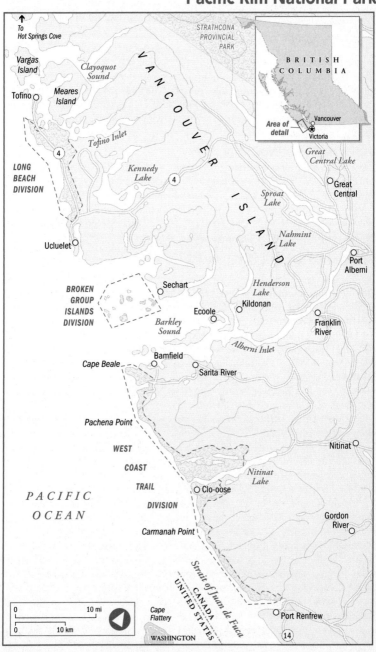

BY BUS   Greyhound Canada (© 800/661-8747; www.greyhound.ca) operates regular daily service between Victoria and Tofino-Ucluelet. The 7-hour trip, departing Victoria at 7:30am and arriving in Tofino at 2:30pm, costs C$65. The bus also stops in Nanaimo and can pick up passengers arriving from Vancouver on the ferry. The **Tofino Bus Company** (© 866/986-3466; www.tofinobus.com) also runs a daily service from Victoria and Vancouver to Tofino-Ucluelet. A one-way ticket from Vancouver (hotel-to-hotel) is C$74 (including ferry crossing); from Victoria is C$68; and from Nanaimo, C$45. **Island Link Bus** (© 250/954-8257; www.islandlinkbus. com) runs a passenger express service between BC Ferries' terminals and Vancouver, Victoria, and Comox airports, to Port Alberni at fares that are comparable to the above.

VISITOR INFORMATION

The **Pacific Rim Visitor Centre,** located just north of the Tofino-Ucluelet junction with Hwy. 4 (© 250/726-4600; www.pacificrimvisitor.ca), is a clearinghouse of information on the west coast of Vancouver Island. It's open all year. From October through March, it's open Tuesday to Saturday 10am to 4pm; through mid-June, it's open the same days but till 5pm. From mid-June through September, it's open daily 9am to 7pm. The center is a good washroom stop.

The Hike of a Lifetime: The West Coast Trail

The rugged West Coast Trail has gained a reputation as one of the world's greatest extreme hiking adventures. Each year, about 9,000 people tackle the entire challenging 77km (48-mile) route, and thousands more hike the very accessible 11km (6¾-mile) **oceanfront stretch** at the northern trail head near Bamfield. Imperative for the full hike are a topographic map and tidal table, stamina for rock climbing as well as hiking, and advanced wilderness-survival and minimum-impact camping knowledge. Go with at least two companions, pack weatherproof gear, and bring 15m (50 ft.) of climbing rope per person. Only 52 people per day are allowed to enter the main trail (26 from Port Renfrew, 26 from Bamfield), and registration with the park office is mandatory. Most people make the hike in 5 to 7 days.

The West Coast Trail travels through temperate coastal rainforest dominated by old-growth spruce, hemlock, and cedar. The shoreline includes everything from sandy beaches to rocky headlands and wide sandstone ledges, as well as caves, arches, tidal pools, and waterfalls. Be prepared to clamber, climb, use rope ladders, scramble netting, and balance upon logs traversing gulleys.

If you hike the trail from May 1 through June 14 or September 16 to September 30, which the park service considers shoulder season, you no longer need reservations. Simply show up at one of the trail **information centers** at Gordon River in the south or Pachena Bay in the north, attend the orientation session, and set off. Reservations are a must if you intend to hike the trail in high season, June 15 through September 15, and should be made as early as possible for the season ahead as spots fill up quickly. Call **Tourism British Columbia** (© 800/435-5622 or 250/387-1642) after April 1 to schedule your entry reservation. In summer, you can also contact the **parks service** (© 250/728-3234 or 250/647-5434; www.pc.gc.ca) for information. There's a C$25 non-refundable booking fee and C$128 trail-use fee. If you want to try your luck, there are six daily first-come, first-served wait-list openings at each trail head information center. The park service says you'll probably wait 1 to 3 days for an opening.

Diving the Graveyard of the Pacific

The waters off the park's West Coast Trail are known throughout the world as "the graveyard of the Pacific." Hundreds of 19th- and 20th-century shipwrecks silently attest to the hazards of sailing without an experienced guide in these unforgiving waters. Underwater interpretive trails narrate the history of the area—rated among the world's best by the Cousteau Society. Follow the links at **www.3routes.com** for an index of diving outfitters that serve Vancouver Island dive sites.

Ucluelet

When fishing was the premier industry on the coast, a constant flow of ships frequented Ucluelet's processing and packing plants. With the boom in eco-tourism, however, the town is scrambling to reinvent itself. It now offers a few fine B&Bs and cabin resorts but has yet to catch up to Tofino. Ucluelet is cheaper though, just as close to Long Beach, and more likely to have vacancies in the high season.

Fishing, kayaking, and whale-watching are the main attractions. For custom fishing charters, contact **Roanne Sea Adventures,** in the boat basin (© 250/726-4494; www.roanne.ca). To combine lodging with your fishing expedition, check out **Island West Resort,** 1990 Bay St. (© 250/726-7515; www.islandwestresort.com), or, for more luxury, Oak Bay Marine Group's **Canadian Princess Resort** (see below).

Subtidal Adventures, 1950 Peninsula Rd., in the West Ucluelet Mall (© 877/444-1134 or 250/726-7336; www.subtidaladventures.com), offers bear- and whale-watching trips, kayaking expeditions, and a sunset cruise into the Broken Group Islands (C$89 adult). **Aquamarine Adventures,** Small Craft Harbour Floathouse 200, near the base of Hemlock Street (© 866/726-7727 or 250/726-7727; www.westcoastwhales.com), operates whale-watching tours (C$89) using 12-seater Sundancers, rigid-hulled inflatable vessels that allow for maximum maneuverability. **Majestic Ocean Kayaking,** 1167 Helen Rd. (© 800/889-7644 or 250/726-2868; www.oceankayaking.com), offers 3-hour kayak trips around Ucluelet harbor (C$67 adults) and more adventurous day- and multi-day trips to the Broken Group Islands (from C$245 adults).

The 3km (1.9-mile) **Wild Pacific Trail** takes you out to the Amphitrite Lighthouse, a prime whale-watching spot, and is reason alone to visit Ucluelet, with its boardwalks, stairs and gravel paths that follow the edge of the forest to bluffs high above the ocean. Another must-do is the **Ucluelet Mini Aquarium** (Waterfront Promenade near Whisky dock). Housed in a converted shipping container, this tiny attraction only opens May through September, and packs a punch into its fascinating, hands-on displays of local marine life; it has big plans to create a more permanent (and year-round) center.

WHERE TO STAY

Ucluelet has a number of newish condo developments with cookie-cutter accommodations, but for something more unique, reserve at one of the following.

Black Rock Resort ★★ Stunningly situated on a rocky promontory above the pounding Pacific, the Black Rock Resort is *the* place to stay in Ucluelet if you're

7

CENTRAL VANCOUVER ISLAND

The West Coast Trail & Pacific Rim National Park

looking for upscale, fashion-forward design. Rooms feature large, beautifully furnished rooms with incredible vistas: From your floor-to-ceiling windows or balcony, watch for whales, or just relax and watch the waves blasting against the rocks. (***Note:*** Lower priced rooms have forest views.) You have a choice of room types: large studio-style hotel rooms or one- and two-bedroom suites, all decorated with somewhat chilly contemporary decor (nothing to distract from the view). All units have gas fireplaces, kitchenettes, and particularly elegant bathrooms, with "rain" showerheads, heated floors, and two-person soaker tubs. The resort's spa, called Drift, offers an extensive range of rejuvenating and restorative treatments. The restaurant, Fetch, offers marvelous regional fine dining (see below).

Marine Drive (P.O. Box 310 596), Ucluelet, BC V0R 3A0. www.blackrockresort.com. ✆ **877/762-5011** or 250/726-4800. 133 units. C$265–$345 double; C$359–C$659 1- and 2-bedroom suite. Lower off-season rates. **Amenities:** Restaurant; lounge; free airport transfers; hot tub; plunge pool; room service; spa. *In room:* TV/DVD player, gas fireplace, kitchenette, iPod dock, Wi-Fi (lodge rooms), balcony.

Canadian Princess Resort   If you're coming to Ucluelet to fish—or even if you're not—the Canadian Princess Resort is an enjoyable and high-spirited place to stay. You can lodge either on land in standard hotel-style rooms or in traditional bunk-roomed cabins onboard the *Canadian Princess,* a former survey ship permanently moored adjacent to the hotel in Ucluelet's central Boat Basin. Hotel accommodations are very comfortable, while the ship cabins are authentically snug, with the toilet and shower down the hall. Also aboard the ship are a fine-dining restaurant and two lounges, all with charming maritime decor. The resort focuses on fishing trips out into the Pacific—each day, cabin cruisers set out on guided fishing trips; gear is provided.

1943 Peninsula Rd., Ucluelet, BC V0R 3A0. www.canadianprincess.com. ✆ **800/663-7090** or 250/726-7771. 76 units. C$89–C$215 double ship stateroom, C$145–C$345 on-shore double. Additional adult C$25. Guided fishing packages available AE, MC, V. Closed mid-Sept to late Feb. **Amenities:** Restaurant; 2 lounges; Wi-Fi (free, hotel only). *In room (hotel):* A/C,TV (in on-shore rooms), hair dryer.

Terrace Beach Resort ★   Owned by actor Jason Priestley, this oceanfront assemblage of cottages, oceanfront cabins, lofts, and suites is set along boardwalks and decks amid magnificent old-growth spruce and firs. The resort feels like an old-time fishing village, huddled before the waves except that all the accommodations are modern and top-notch. Each of the differently styled units is individually decorated, and most have private hot tubs, full kitchens (no ovens, but a gas barbecue on the deck), dining areas, and large four-piece bathrooms. Some of the cabins are truly commodious, with four stories, sleeping up to eight, and room for six in the hot tub!

1002 Peninsula Rd. (Box 96), Ucluelet, BC V0R 3A0. www.terracebeachresort.ca. ✆ **250/726-2901.** 20 units. C$109–C$199 suites; C$199–C$349 lofts; C$349–C$369 cabins. Extra person C$10. Children 12 and under stay free in parent's room. 2-night minimum stay during high season. MC, V. Pets $20 per stay. **Amenities:** Wi-Fi (free). *In room:* TV/VCR, CD player, fireplace, hair dryer, kitchen, Jacuzzi and/or jetted tub, gas barbecue.

WHERE TO EAT

Fine dining is only just beginning to have a presence in Ucluelet, as urban refugees with a flair for cooking try to make a go of coastal living. Overlooking the harbor is **Eagle's Nest Marine Pub,** 140 Bay St. (✆ **250/726-7515**), open Monday to Saturday 10am to midnight and Sunday 10am to 10pm, with traditional pub grub. The **Stewart Room Restaurant** on the Canadian Princess, 1943 Peninsula

BROKEN GROUP islands

Lying off the coast of Ucluelet in Barkley Sound are the Broken Group Islands, an archipelago of about 300 islands and islets that are part of Pacific Rim National Park. Due to the relatively calm waters, abundant wildlife, and dramatic seascapes, these islands are popular destinations for experienced sea kayakers and ocean canoeists. Divers can explore historic shipwrecks as well as reefs teeming with marine life. The underwater dropoffs shelter populations of feather stars, rockfish, and wolf eels that grow as long as 2m (6½ ft.) and sometimes poke their heads out of their caves.

Access to the Broken Group Islands is limited. In Ucluelet, you'll find a number of operators who can arrange a trip, including **Majestic Ocean Kayaking** (see above), with fully guided 4-day trips to the islands beginning at C$1060. You can also pass through the islands on a packet freighter from Port Alberni (see MV *Frances Barkley*, on p. 161).

Sechart is also the site of the **Sechart Whaling Station Lodge,** an operation of **Lady Rose Marine Services** (ⓒ **800/ 663-7192** Apr–Sept, or 250/723-8313; www.ladyrosemarine.com). It primarily serves the needs of kayakers, though it's open to anyone who wants a unique wilderness experience. Rates are C$150 per person or C$235 for two people sharing the same room, including three family-style meals a day. The only ways to get to the lodge are via the MV *Frances Barkley* or a **Water Taxi** (ⓒ **250/720-7358**) from Bamfield, or your own vessel. Kayak rentals are available. For reservations, contact Lady Rose Marine Services (above).

(ⓒ **250/726-7771**), offers seafood and fine dining aboard a 71m (233-ft.) moored ship. And for local flavor—both in character, and food—you can't beat **Ukee Dogs** (1576 Imperial Lane; ⓒ **250/726-2103**), which dishes out tasty chili, meat pies, and cookies from a converted gas station, Monday to Saturday, 8:30am to 3:30pm. It's a good place to pick up take-out.

Fetch ★★ CONTEMPORARY CANADIAN   Not only does this restaurant have an eye-popping view of the surging Pacific and trendsetting decor, but it also has Andrew Springett, former chef at the Wickaninnish Inn. He brings all his skills and magic to this stunning new restaurant. As much as possible, all ingredients are sourced locally, and that's good news, as the waters off Ucluelet are abundant with excellent quality fish and shellfish, and Vancouver Island has myriad small farms and ranches. Springett is a master at combining vibrant flavors and textures, such as parsnips and apples with crispy duck confit, and curried Dungeness crab with mango and fennel. Service is excellent, and every bite is a revelation. If you're in the mood for a drink and a snack, the lounge menu at Float will also provide great pleasure.

Marine Dr. ⓒ **250/726-4800.** www.blackrockresort.com. Reservations required. Main courses C$26–C$30. AE, MC, V. Daily 7:30am–9pm.

Norwoods ★ BISTRO   It has all the stylings of a wine bar, and with its open kitchen, you know that food is taken seriously. Menu items are composed of small plates for sharing and aid experimentation with an eclectic mix of styles, food fusions, and surprising combinations. Look for local salmon ceviche in a chili-and-lime marinade, with shaved fennel and orange salad, and chutney; traditional beef carpaccio; and local albacore tuna with a seaweed and ginger salad. The menu leans to seafood;

larger plates do include duck, lamb, and filet mignon. Most menu items offer wine pairing suggestions.

1714 Peninsula Rd. © **250/726-7001.** www.norwoods.ca. Main courses C$14–C$30. MC, V. Daily 6–11pm.

Wickanninish Restaurant CANADIAN   Not to be confused with the restaurant at the Wickaninnish Inn up the road, this dining room sits right on, and above, one of the prettiest parts of Long Beach. There isn't a better spot to savor the area's expansive sands, either inside from behind huge windows or on a heated oceanfront sun deck. Menu items can be overly ambitious, so stick to the more simple descriptions. Lunches cover excellent soups, sandwiches, crepes, and quiches; dinners include pasta, seafood, and standards such as New York strip steak. This is one of the most romantic spots to view a West Coast sunset.

Wickaninnish Interpretive Centre, Long Beach. © **250/726-7706.** www.wickaninnish.ca. Reservations recommended. Main courses C$19–C$44. AE, MC, V. Daily mid-Mar to mid-Sept. 11:30am–9:30pm. Closed mid-Sept to mid-Mar.

Tofino

Once the center of massive environmental protests that drew the world's attention, Tofino is now a rather schizophrenic town—part eco-tourism outfitters, activists, and serious granolas; part former loggers and fishermen; and part Tla-o-qui-aht and Ahousaht peoples, who live mostly outside the town. Conflict was common in the early years, but recently all parties seem to have learned to get along.

The reason for Tofino's popularity is not hard to fathom. Tofino offers incredible marine vistas at the end of a thin finger of land, battered by the Pacific to the west and lapped by Tofino Sound on the east. The town is notched with tiny bays and inlets, with a multitude of islands, many of them very mountainous, just off the coast. Farther east, the jagged, snowcapped peaks of Strathcona Park fill the horizon.

Tofino is becoming more crowded and subject to a particular brand of gentrification. On the beaches south of town, luxury inns serve the rarified demands of upscale travelers attracted to the area's scenery. There are more fine-dining restaurants and boutiques here than can possibly be justified by the town's size. Dining is as big a draw as sea kayaking for many Tofino visitors.

With all the bustle, it can be difficult at times to find solitude in what's actually still an amazingly beautiful and wild place. Accordingly, more people decide to avoid the crowds and visit Tofino in winter, to watch dramatic storms roll in from the Pacific.

OUTDOOR PURSUITS

FISHING   Sportfishing for salmon, steelhead, rainbow trout, Dolly Varden char, halibut, cod, and snapper is excellent off the west coast of Vancouver Island. **Clayoquot Ventures** (© **888/534-7422** or 250/725-2700; www.tofinofishing.com) organizes fishing charters throughout the Clayoquot Sound area. Deep-sea and both saltwater and freshwater fly-fishing excursions are offered. The company supplies all the gear, a guide, and a boat. Prices start at a minimum of C$115 per hour, with a minimum of 5 hours. **Lance's Sportfishing Adventures** (© **888/725-6125** or 250/725-2569; www.fishtofino.com) combines fishing trips aboard 7.3m (24-ft.) offshore vessels with a visit to Hot Springs—the advantage being that you'll enjoy the springs before the crowds. Rates are C$110 per hour for a 6-hour minimum and include all gear. A nonresident saltwater or freshwater license is available at tackle shops, which also carry *BC Tidal Waters Sport Fishing Guide, BC Sport Fishing Regulations Synopsis for Non-Tidal Waters,* and the *BC Fishing Directory and Atlas.*

HIKING   In and around **Long Beach,** numerous marked trails 1 to 3.5km (.6–2.2 miles) long take you through the thick, temperate rainforest edging the shore. The **Gold Mine Trail** (about 3.5km/2.2 miles long) near Florencia Bay still has a few artifacts from the days when a gold-mining operation flourished here. The partially boardwalked **South Beach Trail** (less than 1.5km/.9 mile long) leads through the moss-draped rainforest onto small, quiet coves like Lismer Beach and South Beach, where you can see abundant life in the rocky tidal pools. The 1km (.6-mile) **Schooner Beach Trail,** just south of Tofino, passes through mature rainforest before dropping onto scenic Schooner Beach, at the northern end of the park's Long Beach. The **Big Cedar Trail,** on Meares Island, is a 3km (1.9-mile) boardwalked path that was built to showcase the old-growth forest. Maintained by the Tla-o-qui-aht band, the trail has a long staircase leading up to the Hanging Garden Tree, which is said to be between 1,000 and 1,500 years old. Many Tofino outfitters offer tours and boat transportation to the trail.

Nearer to town, the paths in the 5-hectare (12-acre) **Tofino Botanical Gardens,** 1084 Pacific Rim Hwy. (© **250/725-1220;** www.tbgf.org), meander past theme gardens and old-growth forest and wind down to Tofino Inlet. Admission is C$10 for adults, C$6 for students, and free for children under 12. Open daily from 9am to dusk.

KAYAKING   Perhaps the quintessential Clayoquot experience, and certainly one of the most fun, is to slip into a kayak and paddle out into the sound. For beginners, half-day tours to Meares Island (usually with the chance to do a little hiking) are an especially good bet. For rentals, lessons, and tours, try **Pacific Kayak,** 606 Campbell St., at Jamie's Whaling Station (© **250/725-3232;** www.pacifickayak.com). The **Tofino Sea-Kayaking Company,** 320 Main St., Tofino (© **800/863-4664** or 250/725-4222; www.tofino-kayaking.com), offers kayaking packages ranging from 4-hour paddles around Meares Island (from C$74 per person) to weeklong paddling and camping expeditions. Instruction by experienced guides makes even your first kayaking experience a comfortable, safe, and enjoyable one.

Guides from the Nuu-chah-nulth First Nation also give tours on oceangoing canoes. **Tla-ook Cultural Adventures** (© **877/942-2663** or 250/725-2656; www.tlaook.com) offers paddle trips aboard stylized dugout canoes, with commentary by First Nations guides to Meares Island (C$65 per person) and other Clayoquot Sound destinations.

SURFING   The big, lashing waves that the Pacific delivers to Long Beach have become popular with surfers. A number of businesses have sprung up to address their needs, including **Pacific Surf School,** 440 Campbell St. (© **888/777-9961** or 250/725-2155; www.pacificsurfschool.com), which offers lessons and camps for beginners, plus rentals and gear sales. A 3-hour group lesson is C$79; private lessons are also available. **Live to Surf Inc.,** 1180 Pacific Rim Hwy. (© **250/725-4464;** www.livetosurf.com), is Tofino's oldest surf shop, since 1984. It also has the largest selection of new and used boards, and offers lessons and advice on local beaches. **Surf Sister** (625 Campbell St., © **877/724-7873** or 250/725-4456; www.surfsister.com) is geared to women, with its mother-daughter camps and yoga surf retreats.

WHALE-WATCHING, NATURE TOURS & BIRDING   A number of outfitters conduct tours through this region inhabited by gray whales, bald eagles, porpoises, bears, orcas, seals, and sea lions. In addition, Hot Springs Cove, accessible only by water, is a natural hot spring 67km (42 miles) north of Tofino. Take a water taxi, sail, canoe, or kayak up to Clayoquot Sound to enjoy swimming in the steaming pools and bracing waterfalls. A number of kayak outfitters and boat charters offer trips to the springs.

March to October, **Jamie's Whaling Station** (606 Campbell St., Tofino; ℭ **800/ 667-9913** or 250/725-3919; and 168 Fraser Lane, Ucluelet www.jamies.com) uses a 20m (66-ft.) power cruiser as well as a fleet of Zodiacs for tours to watch the gray whales. In addition to whale-watching and hot springs expeditions, **Seaside Adventures** (ℭ **888/332-4252** or 250/725-2292; www.seaside-adventures.com) offers bear-watching trips from May through September. Fares for both companies' expeditions generally run between C$80 and C$100 per person for a 2- or 3-hour tour.

March to November, **Remote Passages,** Meares Landing, 71 Wharf St. (ℭ **800/ 666-9833** or 250/725-3330; www.remotepassages.com), runs daily 2½-hour whale-watching tours in Clayoquot Sound on Zodiac boats, costing C$84 for adults and C$69 for children under 12. The company also conducts a 7-hour whale-watching/ hot springs trip at C$110 for adults and C$95 for children under 12. Reservations are recommended.

For bird-watchers, the protected waters of Clayoquot Sound and the beaches of Pacific Rim National Park offer fantastic birding opportunities. **Just Birding** (ℭ **250/725-2520;** www.justbirding.com) offers a range of bird-watching adventures, from walking tours of the beaches to paddle trips to bald eagle habitat to boat tours for offshore pelagic birding. Guided trips begin at C$79 per person.

RAINY-DAY ACTIVITIES: SHOPPING, STORM-WATCHING & MORE

When you'd rather be indoors, snuggle up with a book at the **Wildside Booksellers and Espresso Bar,** 320 Main St. (ℭ **250/745-4222**), or get a massage or salt glow at the **Ancient Cedars Spa** at the Wickaninnish Inn (ℭ **250/725-3100**).

Or, check out the galleries. The **Eagle Aerie Gallery,** 350 Campbell St. (ℭ **250/ 725-3235**), constructed in the style of a First Nations longhouse, features the innovative work of Tsimshian artist Roy Henry Vickers. The **House of Himwitsa,** 300 Main St. (ℭ **250/725-2017;** www.himwitsa.com), is also First Nations owned/ operated. The quality and craftsmanship of the shop's artwork, masks, baskets, totems, gold and silver jewelry, and apparel are excellent. The **Reflecting Spirit Gallery,** 441 Campbell St. (ℭ **250/725-4229**), offers medicine wheels, rocks, and crystals, as well as a great selection of Native art, carvings, wood crafts, and pottery.

Watching the winter storms from big windows has become very popular in Tofino. For a slight twist on this, try the outdoor storm-watching tours offered by the **Ocean's Edge ★** (ℭ **250/726-7099;** www.oceansedge.bc.ca). Owner Bill McIntyre, former chief naturalist of Pacific Rim National Park, can explain how storms work and the best locations to get close to them without getting swept away.

WHERE TO STAY

There are easily 100 or more places to stay in Tofino and the surrounding area; most have brochures and/or listings at the information centers, including at **Tourism Tofino,** 455 Campbell St. (www.tourismtofino.com; ℭ **888/720-3414** or 250/ 725-3414).

Best Western Tin-Wis Resort ☺ The Tla-o-qui-aht First Nations band runs this large, hotel-like lodge on MacKenzie Beach. All rooms are spacious, with oceanfront views. Although the Tin-Wis is less deluxe than some of the neighboring beachfront lodges, it's also a good deal less expensive while offering perfectly comfortable rooms and fine amenities. Options include queen loft units and deluxe king rooms with fireplaces, kitchenettes, and Jacuzzi tubs. Most units have sofa beds, making them a good choice for families. The Calm Waters restaurant features contemporary Pacific Northwest cuisine with a focus on local First Nations ingredients.

1119 Pacific Rim Hwy. (Box 380), Tofino, BC V0R 2Z0. www.tinwis.com. © **800/661-9995** or 250/725-4445. 85 units. C$239–C$299 double. Substantially lower off-season rates. Senior, AAA, and group discounts available. AE, DISC, MC, V. **Amenities:** Restaurant; lounge; well-equipped exercise room; large Jacuzzi; sauna. *In room:* TV, fridge, hair dryer, Wi-Fi (free).

The Clayoquot Wilderness Resort ★★ 🎁

This isolated, upscale resort reinvented modern "glamping" (glamorous camping), featuring luxurious, safari-style tent accommodations that are geared to tender-footed eco-adventurers and seekers of a one-of-a-kind experience. Twenty canvas platform tents, beautifully furnished with Adirondack-style furniture, Oriental rugs, antiques, and other comforts, serve as guest suites, 12 have new luxury en suite bathroom tents. There are also public-area tents: one "lounge" even offers internet access. The heart of the outpost is the ranch-style log cookhouse, with a towering double-sided fieldstone fireplace in the open-kitchen. Located on the Bedwell River, a short boat or plane ride from Tofino, the entire complex is a surrounded by pristine wilderness which the resort maintains through self-sustaining, impressive eco-practices. Packages include all meals as well as your choice of myriad activities, such as horseback riding, bear-watching, sailing, kayaking, and fishing. After a full day's adventure, retreat to the three spa-treatment tents for a massage or a revitalizing soak in a wood-fired hot tub. Most packages also include return airfare from Vancouver.

P.O. Box 130, Tofino, BC V0R 2Z0. www.wildretreat.com. © **888/333-5405** in North America or 250/725-2688. 20 tents. Mid-May to late Sept. 3-day packages from C$4,750 per person double occupancy. Includes all activities, meals, and transport. AE, MC, V. **Amenities:** Restaurant; bar; Jacuzzi; sauna; watersports equipment; Wi-Fi (free). *In room:* No phone.

The Inn at Tough City ★

This is possibly Tofino's nicest small inn and certainly the quirkiest (by the way, Tough City was an early nickname for Tofino). Built from salvaged and recycled material, including 45,000 recycled bricks, it's filled with antiques, stained glass, and bric-a-brac. The rooms are all unique, with cheerful jewel-toned walls and a dollop of thrift-store chic; several feature soaker tubs, fireplaces, or both. Some rooms have balconies. The on-site restaurant, Tough City Sushi, features seafood and the best (and only) sushi in town. It's open for dinner year-round, lunch in summer season only.

350 Main St. (P.O. Box 8), Tofino, BC V0R 2Z0. www.toughcity.com. © **877/725-2021** or 250/725-2021. 8 units. Mid-May to mid-Oct C$189–C$239 double. Shoulder and off-season discounts. Closed Dec–Feb. AE, MC, V. Pets C$10 per night. **Amenities:** Restaurant; lounge. *In room:* TV, hair dryer, Wi-Fi (free).

Long Beach Lodge Resort ★★

Perched just above the waves of Cox Bay, the views from the lodge's magnificent great room take in oodles of surfing enthusiasts and, when the tide is out, vast expanses of sand. This extremely handsome log-and-stone resort—which readers of *Conde Nast Traveler* voted as one of the top three resorts in Canada in 2011—epitomizes West Coast style: comfortably elegant, yet casual enough for a snooze beside the huge granite fireplace. Accommodations include lodge rooms (with less expensive rooms facing the forest, not the Pacific) and free-standing duplex cottages. Surfing enthusiasts usually take the units that edge the sand. All feature fir furniture, slate-floored bathrooms with soaker tubs and separate showers, and loads of rich decor (including original artwork); some rooms have fireplaces and balconies/patios. A Surf Centre Club is set to open in spring 2012.

1441 Pacific Rim Hwy. (Box 897), Tofino, BC V0R 2Z0. www.longbeachlodgeresort.com. ✆ **877/844-7873** or 250/725-2442. 60 units. Late June to Oct 1 C$309–C$409 double, C$499–C$589 cottage. 3-night minimum cottage stay in high season. Lower shoulder and off-season rates; packages available. Rates include continental breakfast buffet. Extra person C$30. AE, MC, V. Pets allowed in some cottages C$50). **Amenities:** Restaurant; exercise room; lodge great room w/fireplace. *In room:* TV/DVD, CD player, fridge, hair dryer.

Middle Beach Lodge ★★

Set among tall hemlocks, with a steep slope down to a private beach, the rustic ambience of Middle Beach makes it less pretentious than some of the area's other resorts. Perhaps it's because much of the complex was built with recycled lumber, so it has a weathered appeal. Assorted accommodations include a "beach house" with standard hotel rooms, two lodges (one family oriented, one adults only) with a mix of suites and guest rooms, and oceanfront cabins, some of which can sleep seven. Although most units have decks, soaker or Jacuzzi tubs, gas fireplaces, CD players, and kitchenettes, phone the lodge to discuss specific room features, as there are many subtle variations. The high-beamed restaurant and lounge overlook the ocean, and both are good spots to enjoy a coffee or something stronger. The dining area is open for breakfast and dinner during high season; opening hours are more sporadic in winter.

400 Mackenzie Beach Rd. (P.O. Box 100), Tofino, BC V0R 2Z0. www.middlebeach.com. ✆ **866/725-2900** or 250/725-2900. 45 rooms, 19 cabins. C$140–C$245 double; C$245–$460 suite & cabin. 2-night minimum stay required. Shoulder and off-season rates available. Rates include complimentary continental breakfast. AE, MC, V. **Amenities:** Restaurant; exercise room, Wi-Fi (free) *In room:* TV/DVD player (suites and cabins only), fridge, kitchenette, no phone.

Red Crow Guest House ★

While the Wickaninnish and other coastal lodges show you the wild, stormy west-facing side of Tofino, the Red Crow displays the kinder, subtler beauty on the peninsula's east side. By the sheltered waters of Jensen Bay (excellent for viewing eagles, seals, and shorebirds), this pleasant Cape Cod–style home sits in 2.8 secluded hectares (7 acres) of old-growth forest. Two rooms are in the lower level of the house (with private entrances), opening out onto a fabulous view of the bay—perhaps best seen from the inn's outdoor hot tub. Rooms here are large and pleasant, with queen- or king-size beds and 1920s-style furnishings. In addition, there's a charming two-bedroom garden cottage with full kitchen. Guests have free use of bikes, and canoes are available for exploring offshore islands.

1064 Pacific Rim Hwy. (Box 37), Tofino, BC V0R 2Z0. www.tofinoredcrow.com. ✆ **250/725-2275.** 2 rooms, 1 cottage. C$195 suite double; cottage $245 double. Shoulder and off-season rates available. Extra person C$30. V only. *In room:* CD player, fridge, hair dryer, no phone, Wi-Fi (free).

Whalers on the Point Guesthouse

This woodsy but modern hostel is one way to save money in an increasingly expensive town. Located downtown, with views of Clayoquot Sound, it offers both shared and private rooms; wheelchair-accessible rooms are available. The hostel offers discounted activities through local outfitters.

81 West St. (Box 296), Tofino, BC V0R 2Z0. www.tofinohostel.com. ✆ **250/725-3443.** 55 beds. May–Sept C$32–C$34 dorm single, C$95–C$100 private double; Oct–Apr C$25–C$30 dorm single, C$55–C$65 private double. Hostelling International member, multiday, and family discounts available. MC, V. **Amenities:** Internet kiosk; kitchen; sauna; Wi-Fi (free); TV room. *In room:* No phone.

The Wickaninnish Inn ★★★   No matter which room you book at this beautiful inn of cedar, stone, and glass, you'll wake to a magnificent view of the untamed Pacific. The Wick, as it's affectionately known, is on a rocky promontory, surrounded by an old-growth spruce and cedar rainforest and the sprawling sands of Chesterman Beach. Perennially ranked as one of the top inns in North America, the Wick succeeds by blurring the distinction between outdoors and indoors through rustic and local art, textile-rich furnishings, architecture, and building materials, not to mention its vast wall of windows. Every room features a private balcony, oceanfront view, fireplace, down duvet, soaker tub and stone-lined shower, and luxurious bath amenities. Adjacent to the original lodge is the Wickaninnish on the beach, with even more luxurious two-level guest suites and a health club. Winter storm-watching packages have become so popular that the inn is nearly as busy in winter as it is in summer. The Pointe Restaurant (see "Where to Eat," below) is one of the top dining rooms in western Canada. The staff can arrange whale-watching, golfing, fishing, and diving packages. Affiliated with Aveda, the inn's Ancient Cedars Spa offers a host of packages and beauty and relaxation treatments.

Osprey Lane at Chesterman Beach, P.O. Box 250, Tofino, BC V0R 2Z0. www.wickinn.com. ℂ **800/333-4604** in North America, or 250/725-3100. 75 units. From C$420–580 double. Special packages available year-round. Reduced shoulder and off-season rates. AE, MC, V. **Amenities:** Restaurant; bar; coffee lounge; babysitting; health club; spa; beach access; shuttle service. *In room:* A/C, TV/DVD player, fireplace, fridge, hair dryer, iPod dock, Wi-Fi, (free).

CAMPING

The 94 campsites on the bluff at **Green Point** are maintained by Pacific Rim National Park (ℂ **250/726-3500**). The grounds are full every day in July and August, and the average wait for a site is 1 to 2 days. Leave your name at the ranger station when you arrive to be placed on the list. You're rewarded for your patience with a magnificent ocean view, pit toilets, fire pits, pumped well water, and free firewood (no showers or hookups). Sites are C$18 to C$24. The campground is closed October to March.

The **Bella Pacifica Resort & Campground,** 3.5km (2 miles) south of Tofino on the Pacific Rim Highway (400 MacKenzie Beach, P.O. Box 413, Tofino, BC V0R 2Z0; www.bellapacifica.com; ℂ **250/725-3400**), is another sought-after campsite. Privately owned, it has 170 private sites nestled amid the trees; 18 are virtually on the beach, including a separate area for motor homes, and all come with picnic tables, hook-ups, and outlets. You'll also find flush toilets, fire pits, firewood, coin-operated hot showers, and laundry facilities. High season rates are C$38 to C$48 per two-person campsite. Reserve at least a month in advance for a summer weekend; open mid-February to mid-November.

WHERE TO EAT

For a cup of java and a snack, **Caffé Vincenté,** 441 Campbell St. (ℂ **250/725-2599**), offers a touch of urban style near the entrance to town, plus two terminals with Internet access. If you're in self-catering mode, head for **The Wildside** (1180 Pacific Rim Hwy.; ℂ **250/725-9453**) where surfers tend to congregate, or the **Breakers** (430 Campbell St.; ℂ **250/725-2558**; www.breakersdeli.com).

The Common Loaf Bake Shop BAKERY/CAFE   Locally famous as the gathering place for granolas and lefty rabble-rousers back when they amassed in Tofino to take their stand against logging practices, the Loaf has since expanded, which just goes to show you can make money selling idealism along with your muffins. Located at the "far" end of town, the Common Loaf does baked goods really well: muffins, cookies, whole-grain breads, and sticky cinnamon buns. It also serves soups, curry, and pizza for lunch.

180 First St. ℂ **250/725-3915.** Reservations not accepted. Main courses C$4–C$14. No credit cards. Summer daily 8am–9pm; winter daily 8am–6pm.

The Pointe Restaurant ★★ PACIFIC NORTHWEST   The famed restaurant at the Wickaninnish Inn hangs over the water's edge at Chesterman Beach, its multi-sided design providing a 240-degree view of the roaring Pacific. It's an incomparable backdrop to an exceptional dining experience that can only be described as pure Pacific Northwest. The menu focuses on farm-fresh, organic Vancouver Island ingredients, such as quail, lamb, and rabbit, and just-caught local seafood including Dungeness crab, spotted prawns, halibut, and salmon. Grilled octopus is served with baby shrimp and pancetta vinaigrette, while chestnut-honey glazed duck breast comes with fresh porcini pasta. Service is top-notch and the wine list consistently wins top awards from *Wine Spectator*. A chef's four-course tasting menu showcases the best of the season.

The Wickaninnish Inn, Osprey Lane at Chesterman Beach. ℂ **800/333-4604** or 250/725-3100. Reservations required. Main courses C$34–C$52; tasting menu C$80; C$150 with pairings. AE, MC, V. Daily 8am–9:30pm.

The Schooner ★ PACIFIC NORTHWEST   This big red barn of a building looks like the sort of place that serves up family-style crab suppers—and so it did until a few years ago. However, after a major menu and decor makeover, the Schooner is now one of Tofino's top fine-dining choices. As you'd expect, local fish and shellfish in hearty yet sophisticated preparations dominate the menu. A signature dish is Halibut Bowden Bay, in which local halibut is stuffed with crab, shrimp, and brie and served with an apple brandy peppercorn sauce. The Thai-inspired Pacific Rim Seafood Hot Pot is another favorite. Breakfasts here are legendary. In good weather, dine on the deck with views across Tofino Inlet to myriad offshore islands.

331 Campbell St. ℂ **250/725-3444.** www.schoonerrestaurant.ca. Reservations suggested. Main courses C$20–C$36. MC, V. Daily 9–11:30am, noon–3pm, and 5–9:30pm.

Shelter ★★ PACIFIC NORTHWEST   You don't come to this landlocked restaurant for the view, but rather for the cooking, which is remarkable in its bright flavors and textures. Shelter, which buys most of its fish and fresh ingredients directly from producers—right off the boat and right off the land—is one of the best of Tofino's new crop of restaurants. Their signature bouillabaisse is stuffed with local fish and shellfish and simmered in a fire-roasted tomato broth; a delicate halibut filet surmounts a bed of spot-prawn risotto. The wine list leans to local award-winning white wines, chosen to highlight the delicate flavors of fish and seafood. A plus is that most are available by the glass.

601 Campbell St. ℂ **250/725-3353.** www.shelterrestaurant.com. Reservations recommended. Main courses C$16–C$34. MC, V. Daily 11am–10pm.

SOBO INTERNATIONAL   This friendly, ambitious restaurant with "fresh food from here and there" got its start as a catering wagon in the Tofino Botanical Gardens, where it was discovered and written up by visiting journalists from the likes of the *New York Times*. It's since moved downtown and during the day, SOBO serves tasty but informal dishes such as smoked seafood chowder, soba noodle salad, and fish tacos. The evening, however, unveils a more formal dinner service with a creative approach: House-made pappardelle noodles are topped with duck ragu, and roast quail comes glazed with chili and honey. There's a deli counter for takeout items like wood oven pizzas, and frozen fish chowder to heat up later.

311 Neill St. (C) **250/725-2341.** www.sobo.ca. Reservations recommended on weekends. Main courses C$9–C$28. MC, V. Daily 11am–9pm.

DENMAN & HORNBY ISLANDS

From Qualicum Beach, follow Hwy. 19A, the "old highway" north, passing forests and viewpoints that look onto Denman and Hornby Islands in the Georgia Strait. Along the way, you'll pass through several small communities, including **Fanny Bay,** Vancouver Island's most renowned oyster farming area; ask for Fanny Bay oysters by name at local restaurants. Just north of Fanny Bay is Buckley Bay, the ferry terminus for Denman and Hornby Islands.

A haven for aging flower children and Vietnam draft dodgers who stayed north of the 49th parallel, there's a distinct bohemian charm here that speaks to 1960s-era creativity. For a laid-back place for a quiet family vacation, these islands are close to perfect. Hornby Island's beaches and provincial parks are another excellent reason to make the journey, with their trails along the bluff, and magnificent sandstone formations. The gentle waters around and between these islands are famed for sea kayaking. For more information on Hornby and Denman Islands, go to www.hornbyisland.com and www.denmanisland.com.

GETTING THERE Local **BC Ferries** (C) 250/386-3431) operate year-round between Buckley Bay and Denman Island; the dozen daily ferry trips take 10 minutes each way, and round-trip tickets cost C$9 per passenger and C$21 per vehicle. To reach Hornby Island, you'll need first to cross to Denman; the ferry to Hornby leaves from Denman's southern shore. The same number of daily ferries make the 10-minute crossing between the two islands, with the same fares as above.

The islands are great for two-wheel exploration. Ferry passengers can bring bikes on the ferry for free; most B&Bs provide bikes for guest use.

Exploring the Islands

Denman Island (pop. 1,200) offers a pleasant mix of beaches, art galleries, and opportunities to picnic and relax. Just up the hill from the ferry landing is the rather quaint **Denman Village.** Here's where to find the island's primary gathering spot, the old-fashioned **Denman Island General Store** (C) 250/335-2293), with a cafe, gasoline, and a liquor store. While you're in the village, check out the **Denman Island Craft Shop** (C) 250/335-0881), which represents over 70 island craftspeople, many of whom open their studios up to summer visitors. Denman also has a number of sandy beaches, including **Bayle Point,** which looks out over Chrome Island Lighthouse, and beautiful **Fillongley Provincial Park.**

Hornby Island (pop. 1,300) is, if possible, even more laid-back, decentralized, and alternative than Denman. The commercial center of the island, the **Hornby Island Co-op** general store (C) 250/335-1121) is on the opposite side of the island from the ferry landing, at the corner of Central and Shields roads, and sells groceries, liquor, deli, and gasoline. Next to the Co-op is **Island Potters** (C) 250/335-1153), which offers both paintings and pottery from area artists. An intriguing addition to Hornby Island is **Carbrea Vineyard and Winery,** 1885 Central Rd. (C) **250/335-3120**), a small, family-owned winery where you can sample estate Pinot gris,

Gewürztraminer, and an unusual fortified blackberry wine. Call to confirm tasting room hours. Gardeners will love **Old Rose Nursery,** 1020 Central Rd. (② **250/335-2602**), a long-established nursery that specializes in heritage and English roses. The display garden, with over 1,000 mature rose plants, is open to the public from late May through July, but it is at its peak in mid- to late June. Phone ahead for hours.

Tribune Bay Provincial Park on Hornby is one of the finest white-sand beaches on the Canadian west coast; during low tides in summer, the sun bakes the sand, which then warms the incoming tides, making the water perfect for swimming. Hornby is also a great destination for birding. The Heliwell Bluffs in **Heliwell Bay Provincial Park** are home to thousands of nesting birds in the high cliffs along the coast; walking trails edge along the cliffs, making this a dramatically scenic hike.

KAYAKING

The calm waters here, flecked with islands and home to abundant sea and bird life, are some of the most renowned for kayaking in all B.C. On Denman, **Denman Hornby Canoes and Kayaks,** 4005 East Rd. (② **250/335-0079;** www.denman paddling.ca), handles rentals for both islands, as well as half- and full-day guided excursions. One of their most popular trips is to Sandy Island, a favorite destination of sea kayakers off the northern tip of Denman Island. Called Tree Island by locals, the island is accessible only by boat or, at low tide, by foot. With a mere 33 hectares (81 acres), the small island is essentially a broad sand spit peppered with trees; in summer, the shallow water gets beautifully warm for swimming.

Where to Stay & Eat

Lodging is limited on these two islands, and comprised largely of campsites and one- and two-bedroom B&Bs that more often than not, are a part of somebody's home. Be sure to have a reservation in place before making the ferry trip. Check www.hornby island.com and www.denmanisland.com for listings.

ON DENMAN ISLAND

There aren't many places to eat on Denman. **Café on the Rock,** in the general store in Denman Village (② **250/335-2999**), is open for three meals daily, and serves light entrees, vegetarian meals, and home-made desserts; it also serves alcohol. The **Kaleidoscope Market,** in Denman Village (② **250/335-0451**), has a deli. The only public campground is at **Fillongley Provincial Park** (www.env.gov.bc.ca/ bcparks), where sites are C$21. For reservations, contact Discover Camping (www. discovercamping.ca; ② **800/689-9025**).

Denman Island Guest House and Hostel This turn-of-the-century farm-house-cum-inn has a laid-back island atmosphere and rustic guest rooms with a shared bathroom. There are both dorm-style hostel rooms and traditional rooms, all filled with funky old furniture and a pleasant Summer of Love atmosphere. On the main floor is a licensed coffeehouse, and there's a hot tub in the back for soaking up the mellow island vibe.

3806 Denman Rd., Denman Island, BC V0R 1T0. ② **250/335-2688.** 5 units. C$24 dorm single; C$50 private double. MC, V. **Amenities:** Coffee shop; bike rentals; hot tub; Wi-Fi. *In room:* No phone.

ON HORNBY ISLAND

The only waterside watering hole on the island is the **Thatch Pub**, 4305 Shingle Spit Rd. (② **250/335-0136**). It sits beside the Hornby Island Resort (see below), and doubles as the only place with ATM access and a liquor store. As for camping, **Tribune Bay Campground,** 5200 Shields Rd. (www.tribunebay.com; ✆ **250/335-2359**), is the largest on Hornby. It has 114 campsites, 18 with hookups, and is adjacent to Tribune Bay Provincial Park, with its sandy beaches, and within walking distance of the Co-op grocery store. Sites are C$35.

Hornby Island Resort Book months in advance if you want to get a spot at this popular waterfront resort, mainly because it's the only show in town and it's located next to the ferry terminal. The rustic cottage rooms are plainly furnished and come with small bathrooms and full kitchen; the campsites are well maintained, fairly private, and separated by roses and honeysuckle plants. Facilities include a playground, hot showers, a laundry, and the licensed Wheelhouse Restaurant that is open daily in summer for lunch and dinner. It closes from early October through mid-May.

4305 Shingle Spit Rd., Hornby Island, BC V0R 1Z0.✆ **250/335-0136.** 2 lodge rooms, 2 cottages, 8 campsites. C$110 double lodge room; C$135 cottages per night (2-night minimum on weekends in May, June, and Sept), or $1,100 per week July to Labour Day; C$35 campsites. Off-season and weekly rates available. MC, V. **Amenities:** Restaurant; pub; tennis court; Wi-Fi; playground; beach volleyball; horseshoe pitch. *In room:* TV, no phone.

Sea Breeze Lodge ★ This well-loved resort offers comfortable waterfront cottages, with a choice of studio, one, or two bedrooms, all with private baths and some with full kitchens and fireplaces. The 5-hectare (12-acre) property is beautifully situated above a secluded stretch of beach. The cottages have been around a while, and have a pleasant, lived-in quality that more than makes up for the slightly faded gentility of the furnishings. The lodge dining room is the best place to eat on the islands, though it is only open seasonally, and because rates are inclusive of all meals, preference is given to guests over non-guests. Either way, reservations are advised as same-day openings are few and far between. Rates drop substantially in the off season, when rooms are sold without any meal plan.

Big Tree 3-2, Hornby Island, BC V0R 1Z0. www.seabreezelodge.com. ✆ **888/516-2321** or 250/335-2321. 16 cottages. C$160–C$180 per adult per day, or C$1,000–C$1,050 per adult per week, including 3 meals daily. Discounted rates for children. Lower off-season rates. MC, V. **Amenities:** Restaurant; hot tub; sauna; grass tennis court; Wi-Fi (free); playground; dock. *In room:* No phone.

COURTENAY & COMOX

62km (39 miles) N of Qualicum Beach

Facing each other across the Courtenay Estuary, Comox (pop. 13,000) and Courtenay (pop. 24,000) are twin towns that provide a bit of urban polish to a region rich in outdoor recreation. Because they're north of the Victoria-to-Tofino circuit that defines much of the tourism on Vancouver Island, these towns are refreshingly untouristy. Comox has a working harbor with a fishing fleet; Courtenay, a lumber-milling center, has an old downtown core where the shops have largely transformed into boutiques, but which still seems homey. Which isn't to say that these towns lack sophistication: You'll find excellent lodging and restaurants, as well as the new and opulent Crown Isle Golf Resort. Depend on the pace of change to quicken even further: The Comox Valley is the one of the fastest-growing regions of Vancouver Island.

Courtenay and Comox are also stepping-off points for adventures in the Beaufort Mountains, just to the west. From Mount Washington Alpine Resort, trails lead into the southeast corner of Strathcona Provincial Park. There are also adventures to be had at sea level: The shallow Courtenay Estuary is home to abundant wildlife, particularly birds and sea mammals, and is a popular destination for sea kayakers.

Essentials

GETTING THERE

BY PLANE **Comox Valley Regional Airport** (© 250/890-0829; www.comoxairport.com), north of Comox, welcomes daily flights from Vancouver, Calgary, and Edmonton. The airport is served by **Pacific Coastal Airlines** (© 800/663-2872; www.pacificcoastal.com); Air Canada via **Central Mountain Air** (© 888/865-8585; www.flycma.com); and **WestJet** (© 888/937-8538; www.westjet.com).

BY FERRY BC Ferries (© 888/BC-FERRY [223-3779] in B.C., www.bcferries.com) crosses from Powell River on the mainland to Little River, just north of Comox. The one-way fare is C$13 per passenger and C$40 per vehicle. Nanaimo's Duke Point and Departure Bay are the closest terminals with connections to the Vancouver area. If you'd like to see the Sunshine Coast on your way to Comox/Courtenay—and stay overnight to make it possible and worthwhile—cross from Horseshoe Bay to Langdale in Gibsons, then drive along Hwy. 101 to Earl's Cove in Sechelt, crossing again to Saltery Bay, finally ferrying from Westview in Powell River to Comox.

BY TRAIN & BUS Courtenay, which is 90 minutes north of Nanaimo on Hwy. 19, is also the terminus for **VIA Rail's** *Malahat* (© 888/VIA-RAIL [842-7245]; www.viarail.ca), which offers daily service from Victoria. The service has ceased temporarily for upgrades and is slated to resume in summer 2012. **Greyhound Canada** (© 800/661-8747; www.greyhound.ca) offers bus transport from Nanaimo to the Comox and Courtenay area along the Hwy. 19 corridor. One-way fare from Victoria to Courtenay is C$44 (non refundable) and C$50 (refundable).

VISITOR INFORMATION

Contact the **Comox Valley Visitor Info Centre,** 2040 Cliffe Ave., Courtenay (© 888/357-4471 or 250/334-3234; www.discovercomoxvalley.com).

Exploring the Area

Hwy. 19A becomes Cliffe Avenue as it enters Courtenay. It then crosses the Courtenay River and continues north toward Campbell River, bypassing the old town centers of both Courtenay and Comox. This is a comparative blessing, as it allows these commercial districts to quietly gentrify without four lanes of traffic shooting past. The new Inland Hwy. 19 bypasses the towns altogether; the Comox Valley Parkway exit will take you from the highway over to Cliffe Avenue.

COURTENAY

Courtenay's town center revolves around Fourth, Fifth, and Sixth streets just west of the Courtenay River. It's a pleasant place for a stroll, with a number of boutiques, art galleries, and housewares shops to browse. It's also the heart of Courtenay's dining and coffee shop culture.

Stop by the **Comox Valley Art Gallery,** 580 Duncan Avenue at Sixth Street (© 250/338-6211), a public contemporary exhibition space for local and regional artists. The gallery shop carries the work of more than 100 artists. The **Artisans Courtyard,** 180B Fifth St. (© 250/338-6564), is a co-op with more than 60 members. Next door is the **Potter's Place,** 180B Fifth St. (© 250/334-4613), which offers the works of 29 potters, ranging from porcelain to raku.

The **Courtenay District Museum & Paleontology Centre,** 207 Fourth St. (℃ **250/334-0686;** www.courtenaymuseum.ca), tells the story of the region's First Nations peoples with a good collection of masks, basketry, and carvings. The museum's highlight is a 12m (39-ft.) cast skeleton of an elasmosaur, a Cretaceous-era marine reptile. (The Comox Valley was once covered by a tropical sea, and the area now yields a wealth of marine fossils.) With four departures daily June through August, the museum leads 3-hour **fossil tours** of its paleontology lab and to a local fossil dig for C$25 adults, C$20 seniors and students, C$15 children 4 to 12, or C$75 per family. Call ahead for reservations; tours also run on Saturdays in April and May. Admission to the museum alone is by donation. Summer hours are Monday to Saturday 10am to 5pm and Sunday noon to 4pm. Winter hours are Tuesday to Saturday 10am to 5pm.

Kitty Coleman Woodland Gardens, 6183 Whittaker Rd. (℃ **250/338-6901;** www.woodlandgardens.ca), just north of Seal Bay Park, is another treasure. These spectacular, half-wild gardens must be seen to be believed, for the 3,000 rhododendrons alone. There are 9.7 hectares (24 acres) to explore, so bring along good rubber-soled shoes; the bark-mulch trails can be slippery. Admission is $8 adults; opening hours are daily, year round, 9am to dusk.

COMOX

The old center of Comox is small, with just a few shops and cafes to tempt travelers. What's definitely worth exploring, however, is the **marina area** in Comox Harbour. Walkways offer views of the boats and the bay; rising above it all are the jagged peaks of Strathcona Park. Another excellent place for a stroll is **Filberg Heritage Lodge and Park,** 61 Filberg Rd. (℃ **250/334-9242** [festival] or 250/339-2715 [lodge]; www.filberg.com). A full 3.6 hectares (9 acres) of lawn and forest, plus a petting zoo, surround a handsome Arts and Crafts–style home. Once a private residence, the lodge is now open for tours from 11am to 5pm on Easter weekend plus weekends in May and September, and daily from 8am to dusk, July to Labour Day.

PARKS & BEACHES

Continue past the marina on Comox Road to **Gooseneck Park,** a local favorite. **Saratoga Beach** and **Miracle Beach Provincial Park** are about a half-hour drive north of Courtenay on Hwy. 19. **Seal Bay Regional Nature Park and Forest,** 24km (15 miles) north of Courtenay off Hwy. 19, is a 714-hectare (1,764-acre) preserve laced with hiking and mountain-biking trails. Hours are from 6:30am to 11pm.

Outdoor Pursuits

KAYAKING With the Courtenay Estuary and Hornby, Tree, and Denman islands an easy paddle away, sea kayaking is very popular. **Comox Valley Kayaks,** 2020 Cliffe Ave., Courtenay (℃ **888/545-5595** or 250/334-2628; www.comoxvalleykayaks. com), offers rentals, lessons, and tours as well as canoe and stand-up paddle boards. Rentals start at C$15 for 1 hour; C$25 for 4 hours.

SKIING **Mount Washington Alpine Resort** ★ (℃ **888/231-1499,** 250/338-1386, or 250/338-1515 for snow report; www.mtwashington.ca or www.tourism mountwashington.com) is a 5-hour drive from Victoria and open year-round (for hiking or skiing, depending on the season). The summit reaches 1,588m (5,210 ft.), and the mountain averages 860 centimeters (339 in.) of snow per year. A 505m (1,657-ft.) vertical drop and 60 groomed runs are served by eight lifts and a beginners' tow. Fifty-five kilometers (34 miles) of Nordic track-set and skating trails connect to Strathcona

Provincial Park. The resort has seen a massive surge in development, and now has accommodations for 4,000 guests and seven restaurants and pubs. Lift rates are C$62 for adults, C$50 for seniors and students, and C$33 for kids 7 to 12. Take the Strathcona Parkway 37km (23 miles) to Mount Washington, or use turnoff 130 from Inland Hwy. 19.

7 Where to Stay

The **Travelodge Courtenay,** 2605 Cliffe Ave. (✆ **800/795-9486** or 250/334-4491; www.travelodgecourtenay.com), offers extras at a relatively modest cost. The motel's clean, unfussy rooms start at C$94 double.

Best Western Westerly Hotel   The Westerly presents a rather off-putting visage: The three-story slant-fronted wall of glass that encases the lobby probably seemed like a stylish idea when the hotel was first built . . . But once you get past the exterior, you'll discover that the guest rooms are spacious and nicely furnished, with a full complement of extras like an indoor pool and health club. Ask for rooms in the back wing, as they are newer and offer balconies, some overlooking the river. Unfortunately, these rooms are also closest to the steel bridge that links Courtenay and Comox, and these rooms can sometimes be noisy. In most ways, however, this central location is a plus, as the Westerly is within easy walking distance of Courtenay's vibrant downtown area, and also near the shopping centers along Cliffe Avenue.

1590 Cliffe Ave., Courtenay, BC V9N 2K4. www.bestwestern.com. ✆ **800/668-7797** or 250/338-7741. 108 units. C$115–C$180 double. Extra person C$20. Off-season and senior rates available. Ski and golf packages available. AE, MC, V. Pets accepted (C$10). **Amenities:** Restaurant; pub; lounge; exercise room; Jacuzzi; indoor pool; limited room service; sauna; liquor store. In room: A/C, TV w/pay movies, hair dryer, Wi-Fi (free).

Crown Isle Resort ★★ 🍴   For the money, these golf resort villas and guest rooms are an incredible deal, and you don't have to be a golfer to make the most of the facilities. The villas overlook the first fairway and are just yards from the spectacular clubhouse. They are truly large and filled with luxury touches: Many have gourmet kitchens, Jacuzzis, fireplaces, VCRs, and balconies. Another building has "Fairway Rooms," which are well-appointed hotel-style rooms with balconies, some with kitchenettes. Guests have access to the state-of-the-art fitness equipment in the resort clubhouse, and, of course, there's the par 72, platinum-rated 18-hole golf course. The main lodge is home to a rather splendid collection of antique and classic cars, as well as **The Silverado Steak House,** the region's destination steak dining room.

399 Clubhouse Dr., Courtenay, BC V9N 9G3. www.crownisle.com. ✆ **888/338-8439** or 250/703-5050. 90 units. From C$159 Fairway Room; from C$259 1- & 2-bedroom villa; lower shoulder and off-season rates. Extra person C$25. Children 17 & under stay free in parent's room. Golf and ski packages available. AE, MC, V. Free parking. **Amenities:** 2 restaurants; pub; golf course; health club; room service. In room: A/C, TV/DVD player, hair dryer, Wi-Fi (free).

Kingfisher Oceanside Resort and Spa ★★   Located 7km (4⅓ miles) south of Courtenay, this long-established resort has modernized with an added bank of beachfront suites and a classy spa. The older motel units are large, nicely furnished rooms with balconies or patios, most with views of the pool and the Strait of Georgia. The newer one-bedroom suites are splendid, each with a full kitchen, two TVs, a fireplace, and a balcony that juts out over the beach; most suites have a two-person whirlpool tub in addition to a full bathroom with heated tile floors. Our favorite is no. 401, on the end of the building, with banks of windows on two sides. The spa offers a wide selection of treatments and body work, including thalassotherapy (water massage) baths and wraps, massage, reiki, and facials. Guests also have access to a steam cave and sauna. **Kingfisher restaurant** is one of the best places to eat in Courtenay (see "Where to Eat").

4330 Island Hwy. S, Courtenay, BC V9N 9R9. www.kingfisherspa.com. © **800/663-7929** or 250/338-1323. 64 units. From C$170 double oceanview room; C$220–C$350 suite. Extra person C$25. Golf, ski, spa packages available. Senior & low season discounts available. AE, DC, DISC, MC, V. Free parking. Pets allowed in some rooms (C$25). **Amenities:** Restaurant; lounge; oceanview fitness room; hot tub; outdoor heated pool; room service; full-service spa; tennis court; shuttle service; canoe & kayak rentals. *In room:* TV/DVD player, fridge, hair dryer, Wi-Fi (free).

Old House Village Hotel and Spa ★★   There's nothing old about this boutique hotel, which exudes West Coast style with its timber frame, locally made furniture, stonework, windows, and natural hues. Spread over two buildings, this complex is anchoring the redevelopment along the shores of the Courtenay River. The studio, one- and two-bedroom suites include a king-size sofa bed. There's also a full kitchen in all suites, replete with modern appliances and a washer/dryer. The two-level Penthouse Suite is more like a mini-townhome with a loft bedroom. It's very romantic and a perfect place for a getaway. The **Oh Spa** has an extensive menu of beauty, rejuvenating, and revitalizing treatments.

1730 Riverside Lane, Courtenay, BC V9N 8C7. www.oldhousevillage.com. © **888/703-0202** or 250/703-0202. 79 suites. C$149–C$289 double. Extra person C$20. Children 15 & under stay free in parent's room. MC, V. Free parking. **Amenities:** Restaurant; bar; exercise room; hot tub; pool; infrared sauna; spa. *In room:* A/C, 2 TVs, fireplace, full kitchen, Wi-Fi (free).

Where to Eat

Atlas Café ★ 🍴 INTERNATIONAL   This cafe serves up affordable, flavorful variations on world cuisine. The globe-trotting menu hops from Asia and the Mediterranean to Mexico and the Pacific Northwest. Happily, many of the dishes are vegetarian. Portions are large, so this is a good destination for a hungry group with different tastes. Although some of the meat dishes passed C$20, the majority of dishes are between C$12 and C$17. The decor is quite sophisticated—the bar is an aquamarine jewel box and the dining room boudoir red. The only downside: The wine list is limited, especially considering B.C.'s burgeoning wine culture.

250 Sixth St., Courtenay. © **250/338-9838.** www.atlascafe.ca. Reservations accepted for parties of 6 or more only. Main courses C$10–C$25. MC, V. Mon 8:30am–3:30pm; Tues–Sat 8:30am–10pm; Sun 8:30am–9pm.

The Black Fin Pub PUB   On the short walk from downtown Comox to the marina, you'll pass this hospitable pub overlooking the harbor. The menu is large and, for a pub, quite interesting; some of the dishes feature Asian flavors. Entrees range from schnitzel to curry chicken, though with waterfront views, you might find local pan-fried oysters, grilled wild salmon, and halibut fish and chips hard to resist. The usual burgers and sandwiches are also in abundance. Sunday brunch is served until 2pm, and there's an afternoon tea on Monday and Thursday.

132 Port Augusta St., Comox. © **250/339-5030.** Reservations accepted for parties of 4 or more in early evening. Main courses C$11–C$28. AE, MC, V. Food service Sun–Thurs 11am–10pm; Fri–Sat 11am–10:30pm. Hours may be extended in summer.

Kingfisher Oceanside Restaurant ★ SEAFOOD/CONTINENTAL   The dining room at this resort brings together waterfront views with high-quality cuisine. In addition to regular items, the menu includes low-fat, low-calorie spa choices such as tandoori-rubbed wild salmon. Pray that you're around for the summertime bimonthly (once a month in winter) Friday-evening seafood buffet, with an incredible selection of local fish and seafood (C$65).

4330 Island Hwy. S., 7km (4½ miles) south of Courtenay. © **250/338-1323.** www.kingfisherspa. com. Reservations advised. Main courses C$20–C$32. AE, DC, DISC, MC, V. Daily 7–10:30am, 11am–2pm, and 5–9pm.

Locals ★★★ PACIFIC NORTHWEST   Local farmers and suppliers make up to 15 deliveries a day to this brilliant restaurant, which is why it's located in an easy-to-access shopping mall. Everything on the ever-changing menu is so fresh you can taste the minerals in the potatoes that were, more than likely, in the ground that morning. Dishes include a bison carpaccio appetizer; marinated boneless chicken leg stuffed with chorizo sausage meat, and a fresh basil risotto with sundried tomato. The farm-to-fork philosophy and eco-aware operating standards are everywhere, including a floor made of recycled tires. Wines from local vineyards are superbly paired. Service is attentive without being disruptive.

364 8th St., Courtenay. © **250/338-6493.** www.localscomoxvalley.com. Reservations recommended. Main courses C$18–C$29. MC, V. Tues–Sun 11am–9pm.

Toscanos ITALIAN   Toscanos is a cheerful restaurant located between downtown Comox and Comox Harbor, with a million-dollar view of the bay and distant Beaufort Mountains. The dining room is rather minimalist, lacking the rustic clutter that passes for decor in many Italian restaurants. The menu is divided between pasta dishes and chicken, veal, and seafood entrees. Desserts include classics tiramisu and profiteroles.

140 Port Augusta, Comox. © **250/890-7575.** www.toscanos.ca. Reservations recommended. Main courses C$14–C$25. MC, V. Mon–Sat 11am–2pm and 5–9pm. Closed on major holidays.

NORTHERN VANCOUVER ISLAND

By Chris McBeath

I n this chapter, we cover the portion of Vancouver Island from the town of Campbell River—the "Salmon-Fishing Capital of the World"—northward. West of Campbell River lies Strathcona Provincial Park, the oldest provincial park in British Columbia and the largest on Vancouver Island.

The waters along the island's northeast coast near Port McNeill are home to both resident and transient orca whales; the latter move annually from Johnstone Strait to the open Pacific. In this vicinity are also two tiny unique communities: the First Nations town of Alert Bay on Cormorant Island, and Telegraph Cove, a historic boardwalk community on pilings above the rocky shore.

The Island Highway's final port of call, Port Hardy is the starting point for the Inside Passage ferry cruise up the northern coast. It carries passengers bound for Prince Rupert, where it meets the ferries to the Queen Charlotte Islands and to Alaska, and links to the Yellowhead Highway and VIA Rail's *Skeena* run (see chapter 10 for complete coverage of these destinations).

Note: See the "Vancouver Island" map (p. 114) to locate areas covered in this chapter.

ESSENTIALS
Getting There

BY PLANE   See chapter 5 for information on Vancouver Island's major air hub, **Victoria.**

The **Campbell River and District Regional Airport,** located south of Campbell River off Jubilee Parkway, has regularly scheduled flights on commuter planes to and from Vancouver on **Pacific Coastal Airlines** (© **800/663-2872;** www.pacific-coastal.com). Pacific Coastal Airlines is the only scheduled air carrier with flights to/from Port Hardy and Victoria/ Vancouver.

BY FERRY   BC Ferries (© 888/BC-FERRY [223-3779] or 250/386-3431; www. bcferries.com) operates a route linking Powell River to Comox, not too far south of Campbell River, but reaching Powell River from other points on the mainland requires taking two other ferries—a daunting and costly prospect if your destination is Campbell River and points north (see p. 178 for details). Nanaimo's Duke Point and Departure Bay are the closest terminals with connections to the Vancouver area. Port Hardy also connects with Prince Rupert via a 15-hour journey that winds through the Inland Passage. Sample fares are included in the regional sections that follow.

BY BUS   Greyhound Canada (© 800/661-8747; www.greyhound.ca) offers three daily trips between Nanaimo and Campbell River (one-way: C$39 refundable; C$34 non-refundable) Only one bus daily goes all the way to Port Hardy (one-way: C$75 refundable; C$60 non-refundable).

Visitor Information

For general information on Vancouver Island, contact **Tourism Vancouver Island,** Ste. 501, 65 Front St., Nanaimo (© **250/754-3500;** www.helloBC.com/vi or www. vancouverisland.travel). Also check out **www.vancouverisland.com**.

Getting Around

While Vancouver Island has an admirable system of public transport, getting to remote sights and destinations is difficult without your own vehicle.

BY FERRY   BC Ferries (© 888/BC-FERRY [223-3779] in B.C., or 250/386-3431; www.bcferries.com) links Vancouver Island ports to many offshore islands, including Quadra, Alert Bay, and Sointula. None of these islands has public transport, so once there you'll need to hoof it, hitch it, hire a taxi, or arrange for bike rentals. Most innkeepers will pick you up if you've reserved in advance.

BY BUS   See "Getting There," above, for information.

BY CAR   North of Nanaimo, the major road on Vancouver Island is **Hwy. 19,** a particular improvement being the new 128km (80-mile) four-lane expressway between Parksville and Campbell River. The older sections of 19, all closer to the island's east coast, are now labeled 19A. North of Campbell River, a long, two-lane section of Hwy. 19 continues all the way to Port Hardy. Access to gasoline is no problem, even in more remote northern areas, but don't head out on a long stretch of unpaved road without filling up.

   Rental cars are readily available. Agencies include **Avis** (© **800/331-1084** in Canada, 800/331-1212 in the U.S.; www.avis.com), **Budget** (© **800/268-8900** in Canada, 800/527-0700 in the U.S.; www.budget.com), and **National** (© **877/222-9058** in Canada and the U.S.; www.nationalcar.com).

CAMPBELL RIVER & QUADRA ISLAND

Campbell River: 45km (28 miles) N of Courtenay; 266km (165 miles) N of Victoria

With its economic roots in forestry, Campbell River (pop. 33,000) gives the impression of a town that works for a living. Look beyond the main drag, however, and you'll

Campbell River

- - - Ferry route
ⓘ Information

0   0.25 mi
0   0.25 km

McDonald Rd.
8

Island Highway
Vanstone Rd.

Tyee
Spit

Perkins Rd.

Campbell
River
Estuary

Public
Boat Ramp

19

BRITISH
COLUMBIA

Campbell
River

Vancouver

Victoria

Strait
of
Georgia

Meredith Rd.

Woodburn Rd.

7

Campbell River

28

19

Willow St.

Tamarac St.

15th Ave.
14th Ave.

Petersen Rd.

16th Ave.

Homewood Rd.

Ironwood St.

Greenwood St.

Fir St.

Dogwood St.

Cedar St.

Alder St.

Spit Road

19A

Island Highway

Discovery Harbour

Quadra Island Ferry

6
ⓘ
■ Discovery Harbour
Shopping Centre

13th Ave.

9th Ave.

8th Ave.

7th Ave.

Government
Dock

Fishing Pier

5
4

Cheviot Rd.

Shetland Rd.

Petersen Rd.

Walworth Rd.

E.R.T. Rd.

Ridge Rd.

Willis Rd.

Dogwood St.

Cedar St.

6th Ave.

5th Ave.

4th Ave.

3rd Ave.

Birch St.

Museum at
■ Campbell River

19A

Thulin St.

3

1

2nd Ave.

Birch St.

Alder St.

McLean St.

Thulin St.

2

HOTELS ■
Anchor Inn & Suites **3**
Best Western Austrian
   Chalet Village **2**
Coast Discovery Inn **5**
Heritage River Inn **7**
Painter's Lodge Holiday &
   Fishing Resort **8**

RESTAURANTS ◆
Dick's Fish & Chips **4**
Fusilli Grill **1**
Harbour Grill **6**
Legends Dining Room **8**

see how urban retirees, in their quest to find reasonable land values, are creating gentrified enclaves here too.

For years, the city has been known as the "Salmon-Fishing Capital of the World." Between Quadra Island and Campbell River, the broad Strait of Georgia squeezes down to a narrow 1.6km-wide (1-mile) channel called Discovery Passage. All of the salmon that enter the Strait of Juan de Fuca near Victoria to spawn in northerly rivers funnel down into this tight churning waterway with 4m (13-ft.) tides. Historically, vast hauls of incredibly large fish have been pulled from these waters; fishing lodges have lined these shores for decades. However, salmon numbers at Campbell River have fallen drastically in recent years, and the days of pulling 60-pound chinooks from the turbulent waters are largely over. Today, you're as likely to take a wildlife-viewing trip on the sound as go fishing for salmon—and if you do fish, there are numerous restrictions.

Salmon or no salmon, there are plenty of other attractions in and around Campbell River. The city has an excellent museum with a world-class collection of Native arti-facts heading the list, and hiking on Quadra Island and in Strathcona Provincial Park appeals to outdoorsy types. Also, the historic Kwakwaka'wakw Cultural Centre has reopened on Quadra Island, which holds a fascinating collection of repatriated First Nations potlatch masks and totems. To reach Quadra Island, take the 10-minute ferry from downtown Campbell River to Quathiaski Cove, on Quadra Island. Trips depart roughly every hour from about 6:30am to 10:30pm (no Sun 7:30am sailing). Round-trip fares are C$8 per adult passenger, C$20 per vehicle; you can bring a bike for free.

Essentials

GETTING THERE   By Plane   The **Campbell River and District Regional Airport,** south of Campbell River off Jubilee Parkway, has regular flights on com-muter planes from Vancouver on Pacific Coastal Airlines (© **800/663-2872;** www. pacific-coastal.com).

By Car   On the four-lane Inland Highway (Hwy. 19), Campbell River is 45km (28 miles) north of Courtenay and 266km (165 miles) north of Victoria. Campbell River is the end of this newly improved stretch of roadway. The old Island Highway, Hwy. 19A, also runs into the center of Campbell River, right along the water as you approach town.

By Bus   Greyhound Canada © **800/661-8747;** www.greyhound.ca) offers bus transport from Victoria to Port Hardy, stopping at Nanaimo, Campbell River, and other towns along the way. One-way fare from Victoria to Campbell River is C$64 refundable; C$51 non-refundable. Nanaimo to Campbell River is C$40 refundable; C$32 non-refundable. (Nanaimo is the closest ferry service to the Vancouver area.)

VISITOR INFORMATION   The **Campbell River Visitor Info Centre,** 1235 Shoppers Row (© **877/286-5705** or 250/830-0411; www.visitorcentre.ca or www. campbellriver.travel), is open daily in July and August, and Monday through Saturday the rest of the year.

Exploring Campbell River

Downtown Campbell River won't win any awards for quaintness. Busy Island High-way whizzes through town, and the commercial district is dominated by strip malls. The surrounding area offers excellent recreation, however, and lodging is relatively inexpensive, so the city makes a good launching pad for exploration.

The Museum at Campbell River ★ ☺   Campbell River's captivating museum is worth seeking out for the carvings and artifacts from local First Nations tribes; the contemporary carved masks are especially fine. Also compelling is the sound-and-light presentation *The Treasures of Siwidi,* which uses traditional masks to retell an ancient Native myth. You can see a replica of a pioneer-era cabin, tools from the early days of logging, and exhibits on the salmon fishing industry. The gift shop is a great place to buy Native art and jewelry.

470 Island Hwy. © **250/287-3103.** www.crmuseum.ca. Admission C$6 adults, C$4 seniors and students, C$15 families, free for children 5 and under. Mid-May to Sept daily 10am–5pm; Oct to mid-May Tues–Sun noon–5pm.

Outdoor Pursuits

DIVING   The decommissioned **HMCS *Columbia*** was sunk in 1996 near the sealife-rich waters of Seymour Narrows off the Quadra Island's west coast. For information on diving to this artificial reef and on other diving sites (with enticing names like Row and Be Damned, Whisky Point, Copper Cliffs, and Steep Island) in the Campbell River area, contact **Beaver Aquatics** (© **250/287-7652;** www.beaveraquatics.ca).

FISHING   The coho salmon in these waters weigh up to 9-kilograms (20 lb.), and even these are dwarfed by the tyee—14-kilogram-plus (31-lb.-plus) chinook (king) salmon. But fishing isn't what it once was in Campbell River. Some salmon runs are now catch-and-release only, and others are open for limited catches; many fishing trips are now billed more as wildlife adventures than hunting-and-gathering expeditions.

To fish here, you need nonresident saltwater and freshwater licenses, available at outdoor-recreation stores throughout Campbell River, including **Painter's Lodge Holiday & Fishing Resort,** 1625 McDonald Rd. (© **800/663-7090** or 250/286-1102; www.painterslodge.com). The staff at the lodge can also provide information on guided boats and fishing rules.

If you'd like to get out onto the waters and fish, be sure to call ahead and talk to an outfitter or the tourist center to find out what fish are running during your visit and if the seasons have opened. Even if you encounter salmon restrictions, which tend to apply to the coho and tyee, there are other fish in the sea, halibut being a favorite.

There are dozens of fishing guides in the Campbell River area, with a range of services that extends from basic to pure extravagance. Expect to pay around C$85 per hour for 4 to 5 hours of fishing with a no-frills outfitter in a 17-ft. open Boston Whaler. A flashier trip, say, a Grady White or Trophy Vessel, can cost more than C$120 per hour. The most famous guides are associated with the Painter's Lodge and its sister property, April Point Lodge on Quadra Island (see "Where to Stay," below). A few smaller fishing-guide operations include **Coastal Wilderness Adventures** (© **866/640-1173** or 250/287-3427; www.coastwild.com); **Coastal Island Fishing Adventures** (© **888/225-9776** or 250/287-3831; www.coastalislandfishing.com); and **CR Fishing Village & RV Park,** 260 Island Hwy. (© **250/287-3630;** www.fishingvillage.bc.ca).

You can also check out the Info Centre's directory of fishing guides by following the links at www.campbellriverchamber.ca. Most hotels in Campbell River also offer fishing/lodging packages; ask when you reserve.

HIKING   For day hikes, drive to Strathcona Provincial Park (below), or explore Quadra Island's Mount Seymour or Morte Lake parks. For a pleasant hike closer to

Campbell River, drive west 6km (3¾ miles) on Hwy. 28 to **Elk Falls Provincial Park.** Easy 1- to 2-hour hikes lead to a fish hatchery and let you explore a stream with beaver ponds. From the park, you can also join the **Canyon View Trail,** a loop hike that follows the banks of the Campbell River.

RAFTING TOURS **Destiny River Adventures,** 1630 North Island Hwy (ⓒ **800/ 923-7238** or 250/287-4800; www.destinyriver.com), offers half-day (C$109) and full day (C$149) excursions May to early August, as well as multiple-night camping trips to Nimpkish River—the largest volume river on Vancouver Island. When the salmon are running by the thousands, there's even an opportunity to snorkel and swim alongside them.

WILDLIFE TOURS Eagle Eye Adventures (ⓒ **877/286-0809** or 250/286-0809; www.eagleeyeadventures.com) offers a range of excursions via Zodiac and floatplane. A popular 4-hour trip takes you up a series of sea rapids, with the chance to see bears, eagles, orcas, and sea lions. Excursions start at C$109 for adults, C$79 for children under 13. Check the company's website for other options. **Painter's Lodge** (see "Fishing," above) also offers wildlife-watching trips.

Camping

The 122 campsites at **Elk Falls Provincial Park** go for C$16 in summer (see also "Hiking," above). **Miracle Beach Provincial Park** has 201 sites, at C$28 for an overnight stay. Contact **Discover Camping** (ⓒ **800/689-9025**) for reservations.

Where to Stay

Anchor Inn & Suites ☺ Each spacious room here has a balcony and ocean view. Best of all, because the inn is on the ocean side of busy Island Highway, you won't have to look over the traffic to see the water. In addition to the standard rooms there are five themed suites that fulfill the most whimsical dreams. Decor runs from exotic Arabian and wild African to an Arctic-inspired room with an igloo-style bed canopy. The Western will appeal to kids, as they have bunk beds hidden in a "jail cell." The restaurant serves all three meals, and in the evening, adds sushi to the tried-and-true regular fare of pasta, chicken, and steak.

261 Island Hwy., Campbell River, BC V9W 2B3. www.anchorinn.ca. ⓒ **800/663-7227** or 250/286-1131. 77 units. C$130 double; C$249–C$289 theme room double. Extra person C$10. Theme, honeymoon, golf, and fishing packages available. AE, MC, V. Free parking. **Amenities:** Restaurant; lounge; exercise room; hot tub; indoor pool. *In room:* TV w/pay movies, fridge, hair dryer, Wi-Fi (free).

Best Western Austrian Chalet Village Overlooking Discovery Passage, this updated (and no smoking) oceanfront hotel offers a choice of regular or housekeeping units (with kitchenettes); some rooms are in loft chalets. The hotel has extras like an exercise room and table tennis, good for families, as is the BBQ courtyard where you can grill up your just-caught catch. Rates include continental breakfast. The staff can arrange whale-watching, fishing, or golfing trips. Across the street, **Heron's Landing Oceanside Hotel** (ⓒ **888/923-2849;** www.heronslandinghotel.com), is an excellent choice if this hotel is full.

462 S. Island Hwy., Campbell River, BC V9W 1A5. www.bwcampbellriver.com. ⓒ **800/667-7207** or 250/923-4231. 60 units. May–Sept from C$140 double, from C$165 kitchenette unit, loft chalet, or minisuite. Lower off-season rates. Extra person C$10. Senior and AAA discounts available. Children 13 and under free. AE, DC, DISC, MC, V. Pets allowed (C$20). **Amenities:** Restaurant and pub

adjacent; exercise room; Jacuzzi; indoor pool; sauna; courtyard w/BBQs; miniature putting green; table tennis. *In room:* TV, fridge, hair dryer, Wi-Fi (free), balcony or patio.

Coast Discovery Inn Part of the sprawling Discovery Harbour Marina and Shopping Centre, the Coast is right in the thick of downtown and offers dramatic views from its upper stories. It's a bit noisy by day, but since nothing much happens in Campbell River after 10pm, the location doesn't affect a quiet night's sleep. The accommodations are spacious and recently updated with furnishings, bedding, and a paint job. Superior rooms offer ocean views, bathrobes, Jacuzzi tubs, and upgraded toiletries. The marina can accommodate 70 yachts as well as smaller pleasure craft, and offers guided fishing tours. The pub features live evening entertainment Thursday through Saturday.

975 Shoppers Row, Campbell River, BC V9W 2C4. www.coasthotels.com. ⓒ **800/663-1144** or 250/287-7155. 90 units. C$145–C$165 double. Extra person C$10. Family plan, senior, and AAA discounts, and corporate rates available. AE, MC, V. Pets accepted C$20 per night. **Amenities:** Restaurant; pub; exercise room; Jacuzzi; room service. *In room:* TV w/pay movies and Nintendo, hair dryer, Wi-Fi (free).

Heritage River Inn 🐟 An extensive upgrade inside and out refreshed the former Rustic Motel to warrant a new name. Located on .8 hectares (2 acres) of parkland beside a heritage river, the motel-style inn is especially pretty in summer when it's all decked out with flowers. It still offers moderately priced rooms with everything you'll need for a comfortable stay (some have full kitchens). There are also three two-bedroom suites and a three-bedroom cabin (all with kitchen). Book well in advance if you want to snag one of the few smoking rooms.

2140 N. Island Hwy., Campbell River, BC V9W 2G7. www.heritageriverinn.com. ⓒ **800/567-2007** or 250/286-6295. 41 units. C$90–C$100 double. Extra person C$10. Kitchen C$10 extra. Rates include continental breakfast. AE, MC, V. Free parking. Pets allowed for C$10 per night. **Amenities:** Jacuzzi; sauna; barbecue. *In room:* A/C, TV, fridge, hair dryer, Wi-Fi (free), microwave.

Painter's Lodge Holiday & Fishing Resort ★★ An international favorite of avid fishermen and celebrities, this resort has welcomed the likes of John Wayne, Bob Hope, and Goldie Hawn. Built in 1924 on an awe-inspiring wooded point overlooking the Discovery Passage, the lodge retains a rustic grandeur, with spacious rooms and suites decorated in natural wood and pastels. Four secluded, self-contained cottages are also available for rent. Wrapped in windows, the lodge's restaurant, **Legends** (see "Where to Eat," below), boasts a view of the Passage from every table. Be sure to visit **April Point Resort & Spa** on Quadra Island (see p. 191); the speedboat trip (10 minutes in each direction) is included in hotel rates and there are bicycle rentals there so you can explore the island. Guided fishing tours are offered.

1625 McDonald Rd., Box 460, Campbell River, BC V9W 5C1. www.painterslodge.com. ⓒ **800/663-7090** or 250/286-1102. 94 units. C$175–C$219 double; C$239–C$299 cottage. Extra person C$20. Off-season discounts available. AE, MC, V. Closed mid Oct–early Apr. **Amenities:** Restaurant; pub; lounge; babysitting; bike and scooter rentals; children's center; health club; 2 Jacuzzis; heated outdoor pool; 2 unlit tennis courts; kayak rentals. *In room:* TV, hair dryer, Wi-Fi (free).

Where to Eat

In addition to the restaurants listed below, try **Koto,** 80 10th Ave. (ⓒ **250/286-1422**), an excellent sushi bar, open Tuesday through Friday from 11am to 2pm and Tuesday through Saturday from 5:30 to 9pm.

Dick's Fish & Chips FISH & CHIPS 🍴 Located beside Discovery Launch near the Quadra Island ferry, Dick's is everything you would wish for in a fish 'n chips shanty. The restaurant floats on a dock brimming with pots of geraniums and overlooking all the boating action; tables inside are cheek by jowl to a bustling kitchen, and traditional favorites are served in newspaper. There's cod, salmon, and halibut alongside fries (potato and yam), onion rings, mushy peas, and home-style coleslaw. Burgers, chicken, wraps, and hot dogs round out the menu. Call ahead for takeout.

1003B Island Hwy., Campbell River. ✆ **250/287-3336.** www.dicksfishandchips.com. Main courses C$7–C$16. MC, V. Daily 11:30am–9pm.

Fusilli Grill ITALIAN A good, casual Italian restaurant located in the suburbs southwest of downtown, Fusilli Grill makes almost all of its own pasta and utilizes local produce, meats, and seafood as much as possible. Lunch features a variety of sandwiches on fresh-baked focaccia. At dinner, there's a choice of pasta, steak, fish, and chicken dishes, plus a few Mexican and Asian options for variety. The takeout menus are a real value: a three-course pasta lunch is C$9.50; dinner is C$11.

4–220 Dogwood St. ✆ **250/830-0090.** www.fusilligrill.bc.ca. Reservations recommended. Main courses C$12–C$28. DC, MC, V. Tues–Fri 11am–4:30pm; Daily 4:30–9:30pm.

Harbour Grill ★ CONTINENTAL/SEAFOOD Don't be put off by its shopping mall locale; this bright and modern restaurant is on the water side, so offers great views of Discovery Passage alongside a traditional menu of mid-20th-century fine dining. Yes, you can actually order a real chateaubriand here, an arm-size roast of beef tenderloin drizzled with béarnaise and topped with asparagus plus other classics like duck with orange sauce and veal Oscar. In summer, fresh seafood receives more contemporary preparations. The wine list features many VQA wines from B.C., as well a good selection from France, Australia, and California.

112–1334 Island Hwy., in the Discovery Harbour Mall. ✆ **250/287-4143.** www.harbourgrill.com. Reservations recommended. Main courses C$25–C$38. AE, DC, MC, V. Daily from 5:30pm.

Legends Dining Room ★ INTERNATIONAL Floor-to-ceiling windows afford a water view to every table, which adds to the panache of this intimate fine-dining room. If you're having dinner here, consider hopping that water taxi for a pre-dinner cocktail at April Point (the boat shuttle is a 10-minute ride each way). Return with salt spray in your hair, ready for a great meal at Legends. Start with the excellent smoked salmon–stuffed mushroom caps. The entrees have regional flair—try the Cuban-style pork chops, marinated in rum and tandoori spices and served with apple and sun-dried cranberry chutney. As you'd expect at a fishing resort, fish and seafood are menu favorites. *Note:* The restaurant often opens at 5am to get fishing enthusiasts off to a good start.

At Painter's Lodge, 1625 McDonald Rd. ✆ **250/286-1102.** Reservations recommended. Main courses C$19–C$37. AE, DC, MC, V. Daily 7am–10pm. Closed mid Oct–early Apr.

Quadra Island

Touring Quadra Island, which sits right across Discovery Channel from Campbell River, is a delight and best done by car, bike, or scooter (rentals are at April Point Resort; see below). The main reason to make the 10-minute ferry crossing is to visit the excellent **Nuyumbalees Cultural Centre ★★**, Wei Wai Road in Cape Mudge Village (✆ **250/285-3733;** www.nuyumbalees.com). It has one of the world's best collections of artifacts, ceremonial masks, and tribal costumes once used by the Cape

Mudge Band in elaborate potlatch ceremonies conducted to celebrate births, deaths, tribal unity, the installment of a new chief, marriages, and other important occasions. Bands and villages spent months, even years, planning feasts and performances, carving totem poles, and amassing literally tons of gifts for their guests. The Canadian government outlawed the potlatch in 1922 as part of an enforced-assimilation policy, then lifted the ban in 1951. During the time potlatches were outlawed, the artifacts in the Kwakiutl Museum were removed to museums and private collections in eastern Canada and England, where they were preserved and cataloged. The collection was repatriated to the Cape Mudge Band beginning in 1979; the current cultural center and museum was built in the early 1990s.

The *Ah-Wa-Qwa-Dzas* (a place to relax and tell stories) is across the street from the cultural center and serves as a venue for salmon barbecues, storytelling, and traditional dance performances. The museum's gift gallery has a good selection of artwork, prints, and carvings of many talented local artists, as well as books and cards, jewelry, and clothing. Behind the museum is **K'Ik'Ik G'Illas,** or "The House of Eagles," a longhouse-like structure used to teach carving, dancing, and other traditional ways of life. Ask at the museum to tour the building, which has two carved house posts and an especially impressive totem pole in addition to colorful carvings and wall murals. In the lobby of the museum, you can make petroglyph rubbings from fiberglass castings of ancient stone carvings. Across from the museum is a park where a series of petroglyphs document a few of the island's ancient legends.

The cultural center is open Tuesday to Saturday from 10am to 5pm from May through September. Admission is C$10 for adults, C$5 for children under 11, and C$5 for seniors. Family admission is C$25.

WHERE TO STAY & EAT

April Point Resort & Spa ★ Secluded April Point Lodge, world famous for its saltwater fishing charters, has magnificent views of the Discovery Passage. The sister resort to Painter's Lodge, just across the channel, there's free boat-taxi service between the two properties for registered guests, which makes it easy to go from Campbell River for drinks or dinner, or to use the pool, tennis courts, and Jacuzzis at Painter's Lodge. Accommodations range from deluxe suites with Jacuzzi tubs to comfortable 1- to 4-bedroom "woodsy cabins", all of which have ocean views and decks. The Aveda Concept Spa provides luxury pampering in a Japanese-style structure overlooking the water, and the restaurant is a go-to destination for sushi and fresh, northwest cuisine. Facilities include helicopter access and seaplane service to Vancouver, as well as a marina and a multi-room guest house for groups.

900 April Point Rd., Quadra Island (P.O. Box 248), Campbell River, BC V9W 4Z9. www.aprilpoint. com. ✆ **800/663-7090** or 250/285-2222. 56 units. C$169–C$209 lodge; C$209–C$355 cabin or guesthouse. Extra person C$20. AE, MC, V. Closed mid-Oct to early Apr. **Amenities:** Restaurant; sushi bar; lounge; babysitting; bike and scooter rentals; spa; kayak rentals. *In room:* TV, hair dryer, Wi-Fi (free).

Tsa-Kwa-Luten Lodge Owned by the Laichwiltach Cape Mudge Band, this modern luxury resort is designed to resemble a Native Big House. Overlooking the Discovery Passage, it offers lodge suites, waterfront cabins, and two four-bedroom guest houses, as well as an excellent (primarily) seafood restaurant. All rooms have an ocean view and either a balcony or patio; contemporary decor balances the earth-tone floors, bedspreads, and walls, and are a backdrop to Native art. Many units have fireplaces; the cabins contain full kitchens. There are also 13 RV sites with full hookups. The staff can arrange fishing trips and heli-fishing charters.

1 Lighthouse Rd., Box 460, Quathiaski Cove, Quadra Island, BC V0P 1N0. www.capemudgeresort.
bc.ca. © **800/665-7745** or 250/598-3366. 35 units. C$105–C$145 double; C$180–C$379 cottage
and guesthouse; C$40 oceanside RV site. Additional adult C$20. Lower shoulder-season rates.
Meal plans available. AE, DC, MC, V. Free parking. Children 11 and under stay free in parent's
room. Small pets accepted in RV sites. Closed mid-Oct to mid-Apr. **Amenities:** Restaurant;
lounge; bike rentals; exercise room; Jacuzzi; sauna; lit tennis courts nearby. *In room:* Hair dryer,
Wi-Fi (free).

STRATHCONA PROVINCIAL PARK ★★

38km (24 miles) W of Campbell River

British Columbia's oldest provincial park, and the largest on Vancouver Island at 250,000 hectares (617,763 acres), **Strathcona Park** is located west of Campbell River and Courtenay. Mountain peaks, many glaciated or mantled with snow, dominate the park, and lakes and alpine meadows dot the landscape. Roosevelt elk, Vancouver Island marmot and wolf, and black-tailed deer have evolved into distinct species, due to Vancouver Island's separation from the mainland. **Buttle Lake** provides good fishing for cutthroat and rainbow trout and Dolly Varden.

Summers in Strathcona are usually pleasantly warm; evenings can be cool. Winters are fairly mild except at higher elevations, where heavy snowfall is common. Snow remains year-round on the mountain peaks and may linger into July at higher elevations. Rain can be expected at any time of year.

Essentials

GETTING THERE   Campbell River and Courtenay are the primary access points for the park. Hwy. 28 passes through the northern section of the park and provides access to Buttle Lake, 48km (30 miles) west of Campbell River. There are two access routes to the Forbidden Plateau area from Courtenay. To reach Paradise Meadows from Courtenay and Hwy. 19, follow signs to Mount Washington Resort via the Strathcona Parkway. Twenty-five kilometers (16 miles) up the parkway, you'll come to the resort's Nordic Lodge road on the left. Turn onto this road and go another 1.6km (1 mile) to the Paradise Meadows parking lot. To reach Forbidden Plateau, follow the signs on the Forbidden Plateau road from Hwy. 19 and Courtenay. It's 19km (12 miles) to the former Forbidden Plateau ski area (now closed) and the trail head.

VISITOR INFORMATION   Contact the **BC Parks District Manager,** Box 1479, Parksville (© **250/337-2400** or 250/474-1336; www.env.gov.bc.ca/bcparks).

Seeing the Highlights

The Buttle Lake area (off Hwy. 28) and the Forbidden Plateau area (accessed through Courtenay) both have something to offer visitors. Just outside the park boundaries, **Strathcona Park Lodge** (see "Where to Stay," below) offers lodging, dining, and a variety of activities. The rest of the park is largely undeveloped and requires hiking or backpacking into the alpine wilderness to see and enjoy much of its scenic splendor.

A paved road joins **Hwy. 28** (the Gold River Hwy.) near the outlet of **Buttle Lake** and winds its way southward, hugging the shoreline. Along this scenic road are numerous cataracts and creeks that rush and tumble into the lake.

Some of the more prominent peaks include Mount McBride, Marble Peak, Mount Phillips, and Mount Myra. **Elkhorn Mountain,** at 2,192m (7,192 ft.), is the second-highest mountain in the park. Elkhorn, along with Mount Flannigan and Kings Peak, can be seen from Hwy. 28. The highest point on Vancouver Island at 2,200m (7,218 ft.), the **Golden Hinde** stands almost in the center of the park to the west of Buttle Lake.

A second area of the park, **Forbidden Plateau,** is accessed by gravel road from Courtenay. Those who hike into the plateau are rewarded with an area of subalpine beauty and views that extend from the surrounding glaciers and mountains to farmlands and forest.

The 440m (1,444-ft.) **Della Falls,** one of the 10 highest waterfalls in the world (and the highest in Canada), is located in the southern section of the park, and is reached by a rugged multiday hike (see "Hiking," below).

Hiking

FROM THE BUTTLE LAKE AREA   The 3km (2-mile) Upper Myra Falls Trail starts just past the Westmin mine operation. This 2-hour hike leads through old-growth forests and past waterfalls. The 6.5km (4-mile) Marble Meadows Trail starts at Phillips Creek Marine Campsite on Buttle Lake. It features alpine meadows and limestone formations; allow 6 hours round-trip. The 900m (2,953-ft.) Lady Falls Trail, which begins at the Hwy. 28 viewing platform, takes about 20 minutes and leads to a picturesque waterfall.

FROM THE PARADISE MEADOWS TRAIL HEAD (MOUNT WASHINGTON)
The 2km (1.2-mile) Paradise Meadows Loop Trail is an easy walk through subalpine meadows, taking about 45 minutes. The 14km (8.7 mile) Helen McKenzie–Kwai Lake–Croteau Lake Loop Trail takes 6 hours and offers access to beautiful lakes and mountain vistas. There's designated camping at Kwai Lake. From Lake Helen McKenzie, the trail follows forested slopes over rougher terrain before rising to a rolling subalpine area to Circlet Lake, which offers designated camping. Allow 4 hours.

FROM FORBIDDEN PLATEAU   The 5km (3-mile), 2-hour **Mount Becher Summit Trail** starts at the former ski lodge and goes up one of the runs to the trail head near the T-bar. It provides excellent views of the valley and the Strait of Georgia.

OTHER TRAILS IN STRATHCONA PARK   The **Della Falls Trail** is 32km (20 miles) round-trip. It starts at the west end of Great Central Lake (btw. Port Alberni and Tofino on Hwy. 4) and follows the old railway grade up the Drinkwater Valley. You must take a boat across the lake to get to the trail head. At **Great Central Lake RV Resort & Marina,** 11000 Great Central Lake Rd. (📞 **250/723-2657;** www.great centrallake.ca), you can take a high-speed water taxi or rent a motorboat or canoe. The whole trip will take 3 to 6 days. The trail passes historic railroad logging sites and accesses Love Lake and Della Lake. Some unbridged river crossings can be hazardous.

Camping

Buttle Lake, with 85 sites, and **Ralph River,** with 76 sites, are both located on Buttle Lake, accessible via Hwy. 28 (the Gold River Hwy.) west of Campbell River. Sites go for C$16. The campgrounds have water, toilets, and firewood (www.discover camping.ca; 📞 **800/689-9025**).

Where to Stay

Strathcona Park Lodge & Outdoor Education Centre ★★ This rustic lodge, north of Strathcona Park along upper Campbell Lake, has something to offer everyone who loves the outdoors—from families to Golden Agers. The Lodge is somewhere between Outward Bound and Club Med, with numerous all-inclusive packages which include activities such as climbing and rappelling, canoeing, fishing, kayaking, orienteering, and swimming, to name a few. The lodge is also a lovely place to just hang out and is a good base for exploring the park; guides can be hired by the hour. All accommodations are sparely yet comfortably furnished. Some chalet units have shared bathrooms; all other rooms have private bathrooms. The lakefront cabins with kitchens are the most charming, though you must reserve well in advance. From mid-March through mid-November, the Whale Room serves three buffet-style meals daily, with guests sitting at long communal tables, while the Canoe Club Café offers more traditional restaurant-style meals.

40km (25 miles) west of Campbell River on Hwy. 28. Mailing address: Box 2160, Campbell River, BC V9W 5C5. www.strathcona.bc.ca. © **250/286-3122.** 39 units. From C$40–C$88 chalet double with shared bathroom; from C$139–C$160 double with private bathroom; C$175–C$440 cabin. 2- or 3-night minimum stays in cabins. Adventure packages and off-season discounts available. MC, V. **Amenities:** Restaurant; babysitting; children's programs; exercise room; sauna; canoe and kayak rentals. *In room:* No phone.

WEST TO GOLD RIVER & NOOTKA SOUND

Hwy. 28 continues past Strathcona Park another 9km (5⅔ miles) to **Gold River** (pop. 2,049), a logging port and mill town just to the east of the Muchalet Inlet, and the only major northwestern island community accessible by paved road. The wild coastline around the **Nootka Sound,** to the west of Gold River, was the site of the first European settlement in the northwest, founded by British Captain James Cook in 1778. The tiny coastal communities, logging camps, and fishing ports here are almost completely isolated from roads, and rely on the **MV *Uchuck III*,** a converted World War II minesweeper, for public transport and movement of goods. Passengers are welcome to travel aboard MV *Uchuck III* as it goes between Gold River, Nootka Sound, and Kyuquot Sound.

Late September through early May, the Tahsis Inlet day trip leaves on Tuesdays at 9am, traveling into Nootka Sound and up the Tahsis Inlet between Vancouver and Nootka islands to the village of Tahsis. The 9-hour round-trip costs C$65 for adults, C$60 for seniors, and C$30 for children 6 to 12.

From early June to mid-September, the MV *Uchuck III* runs a day trip on Saturdays from Gold River to Friendly Cove, or Yuquot, the ancestral home of the Mowachaht people. The return trip runs 6 to 7½ hours and costs C$75 for adults, C$70 for seniors, and C$40 for kids.

On Thursdays year-round, the boat departs for Kyuquot Sound, to the north. This 2-day trip goes up the Tahsis and Esperanza inlets to the open sea and eventually the village of Kyuquot, where passengers stay overnight before returning the following day. The cost, which includes lodging, is C$695 for two. A similar trip departs Mondays for Zeballos, a former gold-mining town and good wildlife-viewing spot just a way from Tahsis. This trip costs C$475 for two, including lodging.

For more information on other trips (including a twice yearly repositioning trip btw. Gold River and Victoria at C$475), or to make reservations, contact **Nootka Sound Service Ltd.** (🕿 **250/283-2515** or 250/283-2325; www.mvuchuck.com). The MV *Uchuck III* will also take kayakers to various destinations on its routes; inquire for details.

If you need accommodations in Gold River, contact the **Tourist Info Centre** (🕿 **250/283-2202;** www.goldriver.ca) or try the **Ridgeview Motor Inn,** 395 Donner Ct. (🕿 **800/989-3393** or 250/283-2277; www.ridgeview-inn.com), where doubles range from C$99 to C$135 in high summer season.

TELEGRAPH COVE, PORT MCNEILL, ALERT BAY & PORT HARDY

Port McNeill: 198km (123 miles) N of Campbell River

It's a winding 198km (123-mile) drive through forested mountains along the Island Highway (Hwy. 19) from Campbell River to **Port McNeill,** on northern Vancouver Island. But the majestic scenery, crystal-clear lakes, and unique wilderness along the way make it worthwhile.

The highway rejoins the coast along **Johnstone Strait,** home to a number of orca (killer whale) pods, which migrate annually from the Queen Charlotte Strait south to these salmon-rich waters. Whale-watching trips out of Port McNeill and Telegraph Cove are the principal recreational activities; this is one of the most noted whale-watching areas in British Columbia.

Also worth a visit is the island community of **Alert Bay,** a traditional First Nations townsite filled with totem poles and carvings. The museum houses a famous collection of ceremonial masks and other artifacts.

The Island Highway's terminus, **Port Hardy,** is 52km (32 miles) north of Port McNeill. Although it's a remote community of only 5,470, Port Hardy is the starting point for two adventures along the rugged Pacific coast: the Inside Passage ferry cruise (see chapter 10) to Prince Rupert and the Discovery Coast ferry cruise to Bella Bella, with road access to the B.C. interior (see chapter 10).

Essentials

GETTING THERE There are three principal ways to get to Vancouver Island's northernmost towns and islands: by car, bus, and plane. You can also reach Port Hardy from the north via the Inside Passage ferry from Prince Rupert (see chapter 10).

By Plane Pacific Coastal Airlines (🕿 **800/663-2872;** www.pacific-coastal.com) flies daily from Vancouver to Port Hardy Airport.

By Car Telegraph Cove is 198km (123 miles) north of Campbell River along the Island Highway (Hwy. 19). Port McNeill is another 9km (5⅔ miles) north. Port Hardy is 238km (148 miles) north of Campbell River.

By Bus Greyhound Canada 🕿 **800/661-8747;** www.greyhound.ca) offers bus transport from Victoria and Nanaimo to Port Hardy and other towns in northern Vancouver Island. One-way fare from Nanaimo to Port Hardy is C$78 refundable;

C$70 non-refundable. The one-way fare from Victoria to Port Hardy is C$99 refundable; C$89 non-refundable.

VISITOR INFORMATION The **Port McNeill Visitor Info Centre,** 1594 Beach Dr. (© **250/956-3131;** www.portmcneill.net), is open year-round on weekdays and daily in summer from 10am to 6pm. The **Alert Bay Visitor Info Centre,** 116 Fir St. (© **250/974-5024;** www.alertbay.ca), is open in summer daily from 9am to 6pm, and the rest of the year Monday through Friday from 9am to 5pm. The **Port Hardy Visitor Info Centre,** 7250 Market St. (© **250/949-7622;** www.ph-chamber. bc.ca), is open June through September daily from 8:30am to 7pm, and October through May Monday through Friday from 8:30am to 5pm. These folks also provide an **accommodations' reservations service** for Port Hardy and Prince Rupert (for those going to Prince Rupert with BC Ferries).

Telegraph Cove

Telegraph Cove (pop. 20—on a good day), 22km (14 driving miles) southeast of Port McNeill—by way of the Island Highway and then a stretch of paved road—is one of the few remaining elevated-boardwalk villages on Vancouver Island. The historic community got its start in 1912 as a one-room telegraph station that marked the end of a cable, strung tree to tree, all the way from Victoria. When messages were received, the operator hopped into a boat and rowed to the community of Alert Bay, on Cormorant Island, to deliver the news. Many of the original buildings still stand, perched on stilts above the water; one houses a great restaurant-pub; another is home-base for a mini-museum, as well as whale-watching and kayaking operators.

Although virtually deserted in winter, Telegraph Cove bustles in summer. On one side of the cove lies the comfortably rustic **Telegraph Cove Resort,** with its historic boardwalk homes available as holiday rentals (see below). Opposite lies **Telegraph Cove Marina & RV Park** (www.telegraphcove.ca; © **877/835-2683** or 250/928-3161) with motel-like accommodations and an RV park offering a birds-eye view of the busy boat basin.

WHALE-WATCHING & OTHER OUTDOOR PURSUITS

Telegraph Cove is right on the Johnstone Strait, a narrow passage that serves as the summer home to hundreds of orcas as well as dolphins, porpoises, and seals. Bald eagles also patrol the waterway, and more unusual birds pass through the area, an important stop on the Pacific Flyway.

Seventeen kilometers (11 miles) south of Telegraph Cove, the **Robson Bight Ecological Reserve** ★★ provides fascinating whale-watching. Orcas regularly beach themselves in the shallow waters of the pebbly "rubbing beaches" to remove the barnacles from their tummies. Boat tours are not allowed to enter the reserve itself, but you can watch from nearby areas. **Stubbs Island Whale-Watching,** at the end of the Telegraph Cove boardwalk (© **800/665-3066** or 250/928-3185; www.stubbs-island.com), offers tours from May through early October in boats equipped with hydrophones, so you can hear the whales' underwater communication. In high season, these 3½-hour cruises cost from C$94 for adults.

From May to mid-October, **Tide Rip Tours,** 28 Boardwalk (© **888/643-9319** or 250/339-5320; www.tiderip.com), offers daylong boat excursions to watch grizzly bears for C$288. Other wildlife-viewing trips are available.

For kayaking tours, contact **Telegraph Cove Sea Kayaking** (© **888/756-0099** or 250/756-0094; www.tckayaks.com), which offers guided day trips out onto

Telegraph Cove (C$175 per person) or Johnstone Strait (C$325 per person), where you might kayak with orcas. Kayak rentals are also available, as are multi-day kayak-camping trips for more adventurous souls.

WHERE TO STAY & EAT

Although both of the following establishments have mailing addresses in Port McNeill, they are located in or near Telegraph Cove.

Hidden Cove Lodge   Built years before a road reached this isolated harbor, Hidden Cove was meant to be approached by boat, and it still saves its best face for those who arrive this way. The handsome lodge, with a cathedral-ceilinged great room, is nestled beside a secluded cove. The guest rooms are clean and simply decorated, all with private bathrooms. Three self-contained cabins have efficiency kitchens and decks. Hidden Cove's easygoing, unaffected atmosphere belies the fact that it attracts the rich and famous. The restaurant, open to non-guests by reservation only, serves quality international dishes. Whale-watching, birding, heli-fishing, kayaking, and hiking tours can be arranged.

Lewis Point, 1 Hidden Cove Rd., Box 258, Port McNeill, BC V0N 2R0. www.hiddencovelodge.com. ℰ/fax **250/956-3916.** 8 lodge rooms, 3 cottages. C$170 lodge double, includes breakfast; C$199 1-bedroom cottage; C$299 2-bedroom cottage. Extra person C$25. 2-night minimum stay. Off-season rates available. MC, V. Free parking and moorage for boaters. Take the Island Hwy. (Hwy. 19) to turnoff for Telegraph Cove/Beaver Cove; turn right and follow signs. The lodge is 6.5km (4 miles) from Telegraph Cove. **Amenities:** Restaurant; hot tub; golf course nearby. *In room:* No phone.

Telegraph Cove Resorts   Most of the accommodations here are refurbished homes from the 1920s and 1930s, and include everything from small rooms in a former fishermen's boardinghouse on the boardwalk to shoreside three-bedroom homes that sleep up to nine. All have bathrooms and kitchens, but no phones or TVs. Wi-Fi is 'iffy' at best. There are also hotel-style rooms (no kitchens) at the Wastell Manor, a large home built in 1912. Although none of the historic properties are fancy, they are clean and make for a unique experience—it really is like staying in a historic logging camp. Amenities include the Old Saltery Pub and the Killer Whale Café. Both are good, which is fortunate because they really are the only shows in town. In addition, 120 campsites are a short walk from the village, among the trees. Open May through mid-October, the campground provides hot showers, laundry, toilets, fire pits, and water.

Box 1, Telegraph Cove, BC V0N 3J0. www.telegraphcoveresort.com. ℰ **800/200-HOOK** (4665) or 250/928-3131. 24 units. June–Sept C$115–C$305 cabin/suite; tent sites C$25–C$30. Lower rates May & early Oct. Extra person C$10. Packages available. MC, V. Closed mid-Oct to Apr. Pets allowed in some cabins for C$5 per night. **Amenities:** Restaurant; pub; kayak rentals. *In room:* No phone.

Port McNeill & Alert Bay

Port McNeill (pop. 3,000) is a logging and mill town—not particularly quaint—that serves as an access point for whale-watching and other wildlife tours, numerous outdoor-recreation opportunities, and the ferry to Alert Bay, a fascinating destination for anyone interested in First Nations culture.

BC Ferries (ℰ **888/223-3779;** www.bcferries.com) runs daily service between Port McNeill and Alert Bay. The crossing takes about 45 minutes; peak fares are C$10 per passenger, C$24 per vehicle. If you're going to Alert Bay mostly to visit the

U'mista Cultural Centre, you can easily leave your vehicle at Port McNeill. It's about a 20-minute, easy walk from the ferry dock to the center.

EXPLORING ALERT BAY

Alert Bay (pop. 1,000) has been a Kwakwaka'wakw (Kwagiulth) village for thousands of years so, in spite of Scottish immigration, its rich First Nations heritage is one of the best preserved, visible in its architecture, world-renowned collection of totem carvings, wall murals, and artifacts. Evidence of those early immigrants is, however, still very much a part of the community, as in the **Anglican Church** on Front Street. The cedar building was erected in 1881; its stained-glass window designs reflect a fusion of Kwakwaka'wakw and Scottish motifs. It's open in summer Monday through Saturday from 8am to 5pm.

Walk a mile from the ferry terminal along Front Street to the island's two most interesting attractions: a 53m (174-ft.) **totem pole**—the world's highest—stands next to the **Big House,** the tribal community center. The cedar totem pole features 22 figures of bears, orcas, and ravens. The Big House is usually closed to the public, but visitors are welcome to enter the grounds to get a closer look at the building, which is covered with traditional painted figures. In July and August, the **T'sasala Cultural Group** (© 250/974-5475; www.tsasala.org) presents dance performances in the Big House, usually at 1pm, usually Wednesday through Saturday. The cost is C$15 for adults and C$6 for children under 12. A few yards down the road from the Big House is the **U'Mista Cultural Centre ★★**, Front Street (© 250/974-5403;** www.umista.org), which displays a magnificent array of carved masks, cedar baskets, copper jewelry, and other potlatch artifacts. The potlatch was traditionally a highly important ceremony for the Kwagiulth: While dancers and singers performed in elaborate masks and robes, villagers would engage in ritual gift-giving, exchanging ceremonial objects, totems, shields, and other hand-carved artifacts created especially for the ritual. However, in the 1880s, the Canadian government outlawed the ceremony as part of an effort to "civilize" the Kwagiulth, and, in 1921, its officers confiscated the entirety of the band's potlatch treasures and regalia, disbursing them to museums in eastern Canada and private collectors.

By the 1970s and 1980s, pressures from Native groups and changes in government perspectives resulted in the partial repatriation of potlatch ceremonial artifacts to the Kwagiulth, who established the U'Mista Cultural Centre to exhibit this wondrous collection. Admission is C$8 for adults, C$7 for seniors and students, and C$1 for children 12 and under. The museum is open in summer daily from 9am to 5:30pm, and in winter Monday through Friday from 9am to 5pm. Call for spring and fall hours.

WHALE-WATCHING & OTHER OUTDOOR PURSUITS

Orcas, dolphins, and eagles all gather along Johnstone Strait to snack on fish that converge at this narrows between Vancouver Island and a series of tightly clustered islands.

From Port McNeill, **Mackay Whale Watching Ltd.,** 1514 The Wharf (© 877/663-6722 or 250/956-9865; www.whaletime.com), offers daily tours to Johnstone Strait on a 17m (56-ft.) passenger cruiser with hydrophone. A 4- to 5-hour trip costs C$105.

Seasmoke Tours/Sea Orca Expeditions (Government Dock, Alert Bay; © 800/668-6722 in B.C., or 250/974-5225; www.seaorca.com) offers 5- to 8-hour whale-watching sailing trips from Alert Bay from June to September. You can also arrange to be picked up from the **Alder Bay Resort** on Vancouver Island (© **250/956-4117;** www.alderbayresort.com), convenient if you don't want to make the ferry crossing to Alert Bay. Excursions aboard a 13m (43-ft.), hydrophone-equipped sailboat include tea and scones. Five-hour tours cost C$180. Seasmoke also offers tour/lodging packages at two bungalows on Alert Bay.

WHERE TO STAY & EAT

If you can't get into the recommended Telegraph Cove–area resorts and don't want to continue on to Port Hardy or Campbell River, try Port McNeill's **Dalewood Inn,** 1703 Broughton Blvd. (© **877/956-3304**), which rents rooms for C$105 in high season and offers on-premises restaurants and pubs. Just across the road is the new **Black Bear Resort,** 1812 Campbell Way (www.blackbearresort.net; © **866/956-4900** or 250/956-4900), which has rooms starting at C$120 double, which includes complimentary continental breakfast.

Alert Bay Camping & Trailer Park, Alder Road, Alert Bay (© **250/974-5213**), has a great view of the Johnstone Strait and nature trails that fan out from the 23 sites. Rates are C$14 to C$18. Full hookups, flush toilets, hot showers, a free boat launch, and boat tours make this a great deal.

In Alert Bay, the 1918 **Old Customs House Restaurant,** 19 Fir St. (© **250/974-2282;** www.bedbreakfasthome.com/alert-bay), has a menu of burgers, pasta, and fish and chips; it's open for three meals daily. There are also three bed-and-breakfast rooms upstairs, going for C$65 to C$95 double.

Nimpkish Hotel ★ This vintage waterfront hotel in Alert Bay has undergone a top-to-bottom makeover to emerge as the most comfortable and gracious place to stay for miles around. Many of the rooms have wonderful water views and balconies; all are furnished with the kind of low-key elegance that you don't expect on a remote island. The pub, with its large deck that extends over the water, is a perfect spot for a sundowner drink.

318 Fir St., Alert Bay, BC V0N 1A0. www.nimpkishhotel.com. © **888/646-7547** or 250/974-5716. 9 units. C$100–C$185 double. Rates include continental breakfast. Low-season rates available. MC, V. **Amenities:** Pub; sunroom. *In room:* TV, fireplace, fridge, Wi-Fi (free).

Port Hardy

Port Hardy is the final stop on the Island Highway. This sizable community is slowly moving away from a resource-based economy: Fishing, forestry, and mining have waned—though not disappeared—and the town is gradually developing an economy based on tourism.

A principal reason to venture here is the ferry to **Prince Rupert**—in fact, the ferry is a mainstay of the local tourism industry. The night before the 15-hour Inside Passage ferry runs, the town is booked up and reservations are needed at most restaurants. Port Hardy is also the departure point for the Discovery Coast ferry cruise (see chapter 10).

Many visitors come for the fishing. Halibut is plentiful, and the runs of salmon in local rivers continue to be strong. Eco-adventurers also come for the diving, hiking, and coastal kayaking. While you're here, check out the **Port Hardy Museum,** 7110 Market St. (© **250/949-8143**), that holds relics from early Danish settlers, plus a collection of stone tools from about 8,000 B.C. found just east of town. Admission is by donation. The gift shop is one of the few places in town where you can find local carving and artwork. Hours are from mid-May to mid-October Tuesday through

Saturday from 11:30am to 5:30pm, and from mid-October to mid-May Wednesday through Saturday from noon to 5pm.

OUTDOOR PURSUITS

DIVING   Water clarity and tidal action have made this one of the best diving locations in the world. There are more than two dozen outfitters in the area, some of which will provide fully equipped dive boats. A good resource is **North Island Diving and Kayaking,** 8625 Shipley St. (© **250/949-7392;** www.odysseykayaking. com). For more information on diving in the region, follow the links at www.3routes. com.

FISHING   From Port Hardy, you can arrange day charter trips with local outfitters. **Catala Charters and Lodge** (© **800/515-5511** or 250/949-7560; www.catala charters.net) offers guided 4-hour fishing trips for up to four people for C$500. **Codfather Charters** (© **250/949-6696;** www.codfathercharters.com) offers year-round multiday fishing charters and accommodations in a waterfront lodge.

To simply rent a boat, contact **Hardy Bay Boat Rental,** Quarterdeck Marina at 6555 Hardy Bay Rd. (© **250/949-7048** or 250/949-0155; www.hardybayfishing. com). Rates start at C$25 per hour or C$200 per day depending on your choice of boat.

Port Hardy is the stepping-off point for trips to remote **fishing camps,** many with long pedigrees and well-to-do clientele. One of the only camps directly accessed from Port Hardy is **Duval Point Lodge** (© **250/949-6667;** www.duvalpointlodge.com), which offers multiday packages from its base camp about 8km (5 miles) north of town (accessed by boat). Guests receive a short training session; groups are then given their own boat and pointed to the channel. From here on, you keep your own schedule and run expeditions as you see fit. Guests stay in two, two-story floating lodges, each with four bedrooms, a mix of private and shared bathrooms, and a full kitchen. The outfitter provides rod and reel, bait, boat, cleaning area, and freezers. Guests do their own cooking. Guides are available, though part of the fun here is the satisfaction of running your own boat and interacting with other guests. The lodge also has two land-based log cabins, each with three bedrooms. Anyone who comes in their own boat can stay in these cabins; rates start at C$570 for 4 midweek nights. Boat/lodging packages start at C$970 for 4 nights/5 days of fishing and accommodations. The lodge is closed October through May. Duval Point is not for those looking for five-star comforts and pampering. But if you want access to excellent fishing and adventure with congenial hospitality, it's a great value.

KAYAKING   **North Island Diving and Kayaking,** 8625 Shipley St. (© **250/949-7392;** www.odysseykayaking.com), offers day-long guided paddles to islands in the protected waters of Beaver Harbour near Port Hardy starting at C$99, as well as longer, customized trips. Rates include lunch and transportation. Kayak rentals are also available.

Mothership Adventures (© **888/833-8887** or 250/202-3229; www.mothership adventures.com) cruises out of Port McNeil, and is one of the neatest ways to paddle these northern waters and inlets. Home base is a beautifully restored heritage vessel, MV *Columbia III,* which travels from bay to inlet, dropping off kayakers mid-route for guided explorations, before picking them up for at the end of the day for an on-board evening of relaxation and home-cooked food. All-inclusive 4- and 7-day trips start at C$1500, and run June through September.

Hiking Cape Scott

Cape Scott Provincial Park is a 21,870-hectare (54,042-acre) coastal wilderness at the northwest tip of Vancouver Island. It is true wilderness, with little development other than trails. But for visitors looking to experience primal forests and miles of wild beaches, the park is a magical destination. The trail head for all park trails, in the extreme southeast corner of the park, is reached by a 67km (42-mile) part-paved, part-gravel road from Port Hardy. From there, follow signs for Winter Harbour or Holberg, and follow signs for the park from Holberg.

The park is characterized by 64km (40 miles) of spectacular ocean frontage, including about 23km (14 miles) of wide, sandy beaches, running from Nissen Bight in the north to San Josef Bay in the south and interspersed with rocky promontories and headlands. **Nels Bight,** midway between the eastern boundary of the park near Nissen Bight and the Cape Scott Lighthouse, is a 3km-long (1¾-mile), white-sand beach; it's considered the most impressive of the nine beaches in the park. **Hansen Lagoon** is a stopping place for Canada geese and a variety of waterfowl traveling the Pacific Flyway. Deer, elk, black bear, otter, cougars, and wolves are in evidence in the forested and open uplands, and seals and sea lions inhabit offshore islands.

The easiest and most popular hike in the park is the 2.5km (1.6-mile) one-way from the trail head to **San Josef Bay.** The trail leads through forest along the San Josef River, reaching the beach in about 45 minutes. Once at the beach, you can explore the ruins of the Henry Ohlsen home and post office, a relic of the Danish settlements of the early 1900s. The first section of beach is wide and white, flanked by rocky cliffs, and makes a great spot for a picnic. San Josef Bay is also a good place to explore by kayak; surfers ride the high waves here as well.

For long-distance hikers, the highlight of the park is the 24km (15-mile) one-way trail out to the **Cape Scott Lighthouse** at the very northern tip of Vancouver Island. Most hikers manage it in 3 days, with 2 nights spent at Nels Bight campground—which means you won't be carrying your gear on the final leg to Cape Scott. Nels Bight is a spectacular coastline of sand and rocky beaches, and is a popular place to camp; fresh water is available.

There is no best time to visit the park, although midsummer is generally preferred, as the trails are less muddy. Facilities in the park are minimal. Be sure to wear waterproof boots, and if you're spending the night, be prepared for sudden changes of weather any time of year. For more information, contact **BC Parks District Manager** (© **250/956-2260;** www.env.gov.bc.ca/bcparks).

WHERE TO STAY & EAT

Port Hardy has several well-worn hotel complexes. The lodgings recommended below are significantly more attractive than most of the alternatives, so reserve well in advance, especially on days when the ferries run. Likewise, most restaurants in Port Hardy are very basic. The hotel restaurant suggested below isn't fancy, but it's better than the alternatives.

The **Wildwoods Campsite,** Forestry Road (www.wildwoodscampsite.com; © **250/949-6753**), is off the road to the ferry terminal. The 60 sites offer fire pits, hot showers, toilets, beach access, and moorage for C$15 to C$20. Tenters will like the wooded sites at **Quatse River Campground,** 5050 Hardy Rd. (www.quatse campground.com; © **250/949-2395**), with 62 sites at C$20 to C$25. It sits across the way from a salmon hatchery center that's quite a jewel to find in such a small community.

Eco Escapes Cabins ★   Perched high on a hill, nearly everything about these getaway cabins has the health of the planet in mind. Design elements include salvaged timber, environmentally friendly paint and products, low flush toilets, eco-bat (insulation made from repurposed pop bottles), local river rock on bathroom floors, rugs and blinds of renewable bamboo, solar power, recycled water, and other earth-friendly programs. Each studio unit (save one) is small but not at all cramped, even though there's a queen bed, kitchen with tiny eating table and a lounge area. Decor is tasteful, rustic, and cozy. They're located about a 4-minute drive north to the ferry. Rates include a continental breakfast basket that is left at your door each morning. Wi-Fi is available by request and depending on your cabin location.

6305 Jensen Cove Rd., Port Hardy, BC V0N 2P0. www.ecoscapecabins.com ⓒ **250/949-8524.** 6 units. May–Sept C$80–C$185; Oct–Apr C$80–C$100. *In room:* Kitchen, no phone, limited Wi-Fi (free).

Glen Lyon Inn   This attractive hotel and restaurant development sits right above the Hardy Bay marina, above the mouth of the Glen Lyon River. All rooms have views of the harbor, the to-ing and fro-ing of boat traffic, and the wooded hills beyond. Rooms are recently renovated; most have balconies, fridge, and microwave, while suites have fireplaces, two-person jetted tubs, and stereos. The Harbourview Restaurant and **Malone's pub** are probably the tops for dining in Port Hardy.

6435 Hardy Bay Rd., Port Hardy, BC V0N 2P0. www.glenlyoninn.com. ⓒ **877/949-7115** or 250/949-7115. C$110–C$160 double; C$145–C$195 suite. Extra person C$10. AE, DC, MC, V. **Amenities:** Restaurant; pub; exercise room; marina. *In room:* A/C, TV, fridge and microwave (most rooms), hair dryer, Wi-Fi (free).

Oceanview B&B   Perched on a bluff overlooking Port Hardy Bay, Oceanview is a comfortably furnished, spotless modern home. A large room with two queen-size beds and a bathroom overlooks the cul-de-sac and gardens; the other spacious units offer views of the bay. Free coffee, tea, and hot cocoa are served in the evening. The hostess offers a friendly welcome and advice on local travel.

7735 Cedar Place, Box 1837, Port Hardy, BC V0N 2P0. www.island.net/~oceanvue. ⓒ/fax **250/949-8302.** 3 units, 2 with shared bathroom. C$100–C$130 double. Extra person C$15. Rates include continental breakfast. No credit cards. Children must be 12 or older. *In room:* TV, hair dryer, no phone, Wi-Fi (free).

THE SUNSHINE COAST & WHISTLER

By Chloë Ernst

One of British Columbia's most scenic drives and the province's most celebrated year-round recreation center are both just north of Vancouver, making great destinations for a weekend away or a short road trip. The Sunshine Coast Highway is the name given to Hwy. 101 as it skirts the islands, fjords, and peninsulas of the mainland's Strait of Georgia coast. The scenery is spectacular, and the fishing, First Nations, and logging communities along the route offer friendly hospitality. No small part of the charm of this drive is the ferry rides: To reach road's end at Lund, you'll need to take two ferries, both offering jaw-dropping vistas of glaciered peaks floating above deep-blue waters. To make this route into a full loop trip, catch a third ferry from Powell River across the Strait of Georgia to Comox, and begin your exploration of Vancouver Island (see chapters 5, 6, 7, and 8).

The road to Whistler is equally spectacular, as it follows fjordlike Howe Sound, flanked by cliffs and towering peaks. But there's more to do here than gawk at the landscape: Whistler is Canada's premier skiing destination in winter (it hosted the ski events for the 2010 Winter Olympics) and buzzes with golf, hiking, mountain biking, and white-water rafting in summer. Accommodations, dining, and recreational facilities are first-class, and the well-planned lodging developments have yet to overwhelm the natural beauty of the valley.

THE SUNSHINE COAST

Powell River: 172km (107 miles) N of Vancouver

It's a travel writer's truism that the "getting there" part of a trip is half the fun. In the case of the Sunshine Coast—that strip of wildly scenic waterfront real estate north of Vancouver, along the mainland Strait of Georgia coast—the "getting there" is practically the entire reason for making the journey. But what a journey!

Backed up against the high peaks of the glaciated Coastal Mountain range, overlooking the tempestuous waters of the Strait of Georgia and on to the rolling mountains of Vancouver Island, this maritime-intensive trip involves two ferry rides and a lovely meandering drive between slumbering fishing villages. It eventually terminates at Lund, the end of the road for the Pacific Coast's Hwy. 101.

Powell River is the only town of any size along this route. Long a major lumber-milling center, Powell River is beginning to focus on tourism as a supplement to its resource-based economy. Diving in the sea-life-rich waters of the Georgia Strait is a particularly popular activity along the Sunshine Coast.

Essentials

GETTING THERE

BY CAR & FERRY   Getting to Powell River and the Sunshine Coast requires taking a couple of ferries. From West Vancouver's Horseshoe Bay **BC Ferries** (© 888/ **BC-FERRY** [223-3779] or 250/386-3431; www.bcferries.com) terminal, ferries embark for Langdale, a 40-minute crossing. Driving north along Hwy. 101, the road hugs the coast along the Sechelt Peninsula, terminating 81km (50 miles) later at Earls Cove, where another ferry departs for a 50-minute crossing to Saltery Bay. The fare for each ferry is C$13 per passenger, C$44 to C$45 per car. From Saltery Bay, Powell River is another 31km (19 miles). Lund and the terminus of Hwy. 101 are another 28km (17 miles).

You can also cross to Comox/Courtenay, on central Vancouver Island, from Powell River. This popular 75-minute crossing makes for a scenic loop tour of British Columbia's rugged coast and islands. The fare is C$13 per passenger, C$41 per vehicle. (See chapter 7 for coverage of Comox and Courtenay.)

BY BUS   **Malaspina Coach Lines** (© 877/227-8287; www.malaspinacoach. com) offers service from Vancouver to Powell River via Hwy. 101 and the Sechelt Peninsula.

BY PLANE   **Pacific Coastal Airlines** (© 800/663-2872 or 604/273-8666; www.pacificcoastal.com) flies from Vancouver to Powell River.

VISITOR INFORMATION   Contact the **Powell River Visitor Centre,** 4871 Joyce Ave. (© 877/817-8669 or 604/485-4701; www.discoverpowellriver.com).

Exploring the Area

Although Powell River is only 172km (107 miles) north of Vancouver, it feels light-years removed from the urban sprawl. It's probably because of the ferries: Commuting from the Sunshine Coast—the name given to the rocky, mountain-edged coastline that lies in the rain shadow of Vancouver Island—wouldn't make sense if you worked in Vancouver's financial district.

Hwy. 101 is a very scenic route, with soaring peaks topping 2,500m (8,202-ft.) to the east and the swelling blue waters of the Strait of Georgia to the west. The first town north of the Horseshoe Bay–Langdale Ferry is **Gibsons** (pop. 4,182), a bucolic seaside community that served as the setting for the 1980s TV series *The Beachcombers.* Much of the action took place in **Molly's Reach Restaurant,** 647 School Rd. (© 604/886-9710; www.mollysreach.ca), which has evolved from a film set of a restaurant into a real eatery with fine home-style cooking. Wander along the Gibsons Seawalk, which leads from the Government Wharf to Gibsons Marina, and watch fishing boats unload their catch. **Roberts Creek Provincial Park,** 14km (8⅔ miles) west of town, has a great tide-pool area that's perfect for picnicking.

Twenty-two kilometers (13⅔ miles) north of Gibsons is **Sechelt** (pop. 8,454), an arty little town on a sandy finger of land—all that connects the Sechelt Peninsula to mainland British Columbia. The town is a delightful clutter of galleries and cafes. The **Sechelt First Nation** is headquartered here; the imposing House of Hewhiwus contains a cultural center, the Tems Swiya Museum (② **604/885-6012**), and gift shop. A couple of miles north of Sechelt is **Porpoise Bay Provincial Park,** with a nice beach, quiet campground, and riverside trail.

Continue north along Hwy. 101, past the turning to Madiera Park and Pender Harbour, and admire views of Vancouver Island. Drive past the Earls Cove ferry terminal to **Skookumchuk Narrows Provincial Park.** All of the seawater that lies behind 40km-long (25-mile) Sechelt Peninsula—which includes three major ocean inlets—churns back and forth through this passage in an amazing display of tidal fury. It's about an hour's walk to the park's viewing area. Tides are so fierce, causing boiling whirlpools and eddies, that they actually roar.

Powell River (pop. 12,957) is dominated by one of the world's largest pulp and paper mills. That said, the town sits on a lovely location, and if you're feeling adventurous, it's a major center for diving and kayaking.

The old portion of town is called the **Townsite,** a company town that grew up alongside the original lumber mill near the harbor. A designated National Historic District, it contains more than 30 commercial buildings and about 400 residential buildings, all in late Victorian style. Ask at the visitor center for the heritage walking-tour brochure. The **Powell River Historical Museum,** 4798 Marine Ave. (② **604/485-2222;** www.powellrivermuseum.ca), has one of the largest archives of historical photos in the province, along with artifacts from the native Sechelt. It's open year-round Monday through Friday from 9am to 4:30pm, plus the same hours on weekends from June to Labour Day. Admission is C$2 adult.

From Powell River, many travelers take the ferry over to Comox/Courtenay on Vancouver Island and continue the loop back south. However, Powell River isn't the end of the road. That honor goes to tiny **Lund,** 28km (17 miles) north on Hwy. 101. The main reason to make the trip is to say you did it, and to pop into the century-old Lund Hotel for a drink or a meal.

Outdoor Pursuits

CANOEING & KAYAKING   The Sunshine Coast, with its fjord-notched coastline, myriad islands, and protected waters, makes for excellent kayaking. The **Desolation Sound** area, north of Lund, is especially popular. The **Powell Forest Canoe Route,** a 4- to 8-day backcountry paddle, links eight lakes in a 57km (35-mile) circuit. **Powell River Sea Kayaks** (② **866/617-4444** or 604/483-2160; www.bcseakayak.com) has its office 30km (19 miles) north of Powell River on Okeover Inlet, and offers rentals and tours to adjacent Desolation Sound.

DIVING   The center for diving along the Sunshine Coast, Powell River boasts visibility of over 30m (98 ft.) in winter, lots of sea life, and varied terrain. Area dive spots include five shipwrecks and several boats sunk as artificial reefs. **Alpha Dive and Kayak,** 7074 Westminster St. (② **604/485-6939;** www.divepowellriver.com), is one of the area's leading outfitters, with a shop in Powell River and diving operations in Okeover Inlet and Desolation Sound Marine Park.

Where to Stay & Eat

IN SECHELT

Four Winds B&B ★   It's hard to imagine a more compelling site: a thrust of bare rock stretching out into the Strait of Georgia, backed up against a grove of fir and spruce. This modern home is lined with picture windows, all the better to capture the astonishing view of islands and sea, frequently visited by whales, herons, and seals. One guest room and two suites are beautifully decorated and have a hot tub or Jacuzzi; the second-floor suite has a balcony. Most notably, one of the owners is a licensed massage therapist, and will schedule sessions utilizing craniosacral therapy, and neuromuscular and hot-stone techniques.

5482 Hill Rd., Sechelt, BC V0N 3A8. www.fourwindsbeachhouse.com. ℂ **800/543-2989,** 604/885-3144, or 604/740-1905. Fax 604/885-3182. 3 units. C$139–C$219 double. Rates include full breakfast. MC, V. **Amenities:** Golf course nearby; hot tub; Jacuzzi; spa treatments. *In room:* A/C, TV/DVD/VCR, fridge, hair dryer, Wi-Fi (free).

IN HALFMOON BAY

Rockwater Secret Cove Resort ★★   "Glamping" isn't exactly an attractive word, but it's been invented to describe the pleasures of "glamour camping," which attain a very high level at Rockwater Secret Cove Resort. Canvas wall tents stand on platforms above a thrust of rock jutting out into the sea. Forget memories of dusty scouting trips: The Tenthouse Suites have the amenities of a luxury hotel room—king-size beds with fine linens, hydrotherapy tubs for two, propane fireplaces, rainforest showers, heated slate floors, and private verandas overlooking the Straight of Georgia. In season, the resort also offers massage treatments in the "spa without walls"—private outdoor platforms with spacious views. If tents aren't your thing, the resort also offers more conventional lodging, a choice of cabins and lodge rooms and suites, all beautifully furnished. The resort also offers a wide selection of recreational opportunities, from yoga to mountain biking to naturalist-led hikes.

5356 Ole's Cove Rd., Halfmoon Bay, BC V0N 1Y2. www.rockwatersecretcoveresort.com. ℂ **877/296-4593** or 604/885-7038. Fax 604/885-7036. 15 tenthouse suites, 14 rooms and suites, 11 cabins. Tenthouse suites C$226–C$469 double (low–high season rates); rooms and suites C$139–C$289 double; cabins C$154–C$269 double. Extra person C$25. AE, MC, V. **Amenities:** Restaurant; lounge; heated outdoor pool; recreation room; spa treatment facilities; barbecue .pit; dock; sun decks. *In room:* TV (rooms, suites, cabins), fridge, hair dryer, Wi-Fi (free), robes.

IN MADEIRA PARK

Painted Boat Resort Spa & Marina ★   This beautifully located timeshare development offers families or friends traveling together the opportunity to rent elegantly furnished two-bedroom suites right on the rocky coast of Malaspina Strait. The entire complex is newly built, and interiors are right out of a design magazine, with full kitchens, granite countertops, stainless steel appliances, stone fireplaces, two bathrooms, and abundant windows and French doors leading out onto decks and patios where gorgeous waterfront vistas await. All very nice, but it's the abundant facilities at Painted Boat that really make it stand out. The marina offers kayak tours and rentals, the fitness facilities are top-notch, and in summer there's an infinity pool. For relaxation and pampering, the resort offers a spa with treatments rooms and an outdoor spa garden. Best of all, **The Restaurant at Painted Boat ★★** (ℂ **604/883-3000**) is the best place to eat for miles around, with a menu rich with local fish and seafood.

12849 Lagoon Rd., Madeira Park, BC V0N 2H0. www.paintedboat.com. *866/902-3955* or 604/883-2456. Fax 604/883-2122. From C$240 for up to four people. Extra person 6 and older C$35. **Amenities:** Restaurant; lounge; health club; Jacuzzi; seasonal infinity pool; spa; kayak rentals. *In room:* TV/DVD, full fireplace, kitchen, Wi-Fi (free), gas grill, deck or patio.

IN POWELL RIVER

Beach Gardens Resort ★ Long popular with divers and kayakers, the Beach Gardens—just south of Powell River—has 48 new rooms, all with incredible views overlooking Malaspina Strait. Several banks of perfectly comfortable older rooms, also with views and some with full kitchens, rent at a discount. Amenities include a marina, dive store, pub, and beer-and-wine store.

7074 Westminster St., Powell River, BC V8A 1C5. www.beachgardens.com. *800/663-7070* or 604/485-6267. Fax 604/485-2343. 77 units. C$99–C$145 double. Children 15 and under free. AE, MC, V. Free parking. Pets allowed. **Amenities:** Waterfront restaurant; liquor store; marina w/fishing and diving charters; dive supply store; kayak, bike, and dive rentals; moorage. *In room:* A/C, TV, hair dryer, free Wi-Fi (only in newer rooms), private deck overlooking Malaspina Strait.

Desolation Sound Resort ★★ About 40 minutes north of Powell River on Okeover Inlet near Lund is Desolation Sound Resort, which offers luxury and a wilderness experience rolled into one. Accommodations are in extremely attractive chalets perched on high pilings above a steeply sloping shoreline. These log structures, built by local craftspeople, come in various configurations and sleep up to eight. Spaces are fully modern and beautifully maintained, with cedar interiors, full kitchens, hardwood floors, and tasteful decor—some units have private hot tubs, and all have decks (with gas grills) overlooking the water. Chartered boating, kayaking, or diving trips can be arranged; guests are free to use resort canoes and kayaks.

2694 Dawson Rd., Okeover Inlet, Powell River, BC V8A 4Z3. www.desolationresort.com. *800/399-3592* or 604/483-3592. Fax 604/483-7942. 13 units. July–Sept C$149–C$289 double, C$229–C$424 chalet; May–June C$129–C$259 double, C$259–C$399 chalet; Mar–Apr, Oct C$109–C$199 double, C$199–C$314 chalet; closed Nov–Feb. Extra person C$25 per night. Discounts for stays over 3 nights. Packages available. AE, MC, V. Pets allowed in off season for additional charge. **Amenities:** Free use of kayaks and canoes; powerboat rentals and charter cruises can be arranged. *In room:* Kitchen, no phone.

WHISTLER: NORTH AMERICA'S PREMIER SKI RESORT ★

120km (75 miles) N of Vancouver

The premier ski resort in North America, according to *Outside, Skiing,* and *Condé Nast Traveler* magazines, the **Whistler Blackcomb** complex boasts more vertical feet, more lifts, and more ski terrain than any other ski resort in North America. And it isn't all just downhill skiing: There's also backcountry, cross-country, snowboarding, snowmobiling, heli-skiing, tubing, and sleigh riding. In summer, there's mountain biking, rafting, hiking, golfing, wildlife watching, and horseback riding. And then there's **Whistler** itself, a full-service resort town with a year-round population of 10,000 plus 125 hotels and lodgings.

The towns north of Whistler, **Pemberton** and **Mount Currie,** are refreshment stops for cyclists and hikers and gateways to the icy alpine waters of **Birkenhead Lake Provincial Park** and the majestic **Cayoosh Valley,** which winds through the glacier-topped mountains to the Cariboo town of Lillooet.

The area got the ultimate seal of approval from the International Olympic Committee when Whistler landed the opportunity to stage many of the alpine events for the 2010 Winter Games. So come test yourself on the same slopes that Olympic champions have skied on.

Essentials

GETTING THERE

BY CAR Whistler is about a 2-hour drive from Vancouver along Hwy. 99, also called the **Sea-to-Sky Highway ★**. The drive is spectacular, winding along the edge of Howe Sound before climbing up through the mountains.

Large parking lots along Fitzsimmons Creek, between Whistler Village and Upper Village, provide day parking for skiers. A full day costs C$9 in winter, C$14 in summer. Most hotels charge a minimum fee of C$20 for overnight parking.

BY BUS **Perimeter Whistler Express,** 8695 Barnard St., Vancouver (✆ 888/717-6606 or 604/717-6600; www.perimeterbus.com), operates door-to-door bus service from Vancouver International Airport and downtown Vancouver hotels to Squamish and the Whistler Bus Loop, as well as most Whistler hotels and properties. Buses depart five times daily in the summer and nine times in winter. The trip typically takes 2½ to 3 hours; roundtrip fares to Whistler Village are C$118 for adults and C$60 for children 2 to 12. By law, children under 1.22 meters (4 feet) require a car seat that parents must provide. Reservations are required year-round. **Greyhound,** Pacific Central Station, 1150 Station St., Vancouver (✆ 800/661-8747 or 604/683-8133 in Vancouver, or 604/932-5031in Whistler; www.greyhound.ca), operates service from the Vancouver Bus Depot to the Whistler bus loop as well as the Creekside bus depot at 2029 London Lane. The trip takes about 2½ hours; one-way fares are C$29 for adults and C$21 for children ages 2 to 11. **Pacific Coach Lines** (✆ 800/661-1725 or 604/662-7575; www.pacificcoach.com) operates one-way and return bus service from Vancouver International Airport and Vancouver hotels to Whistler area hotels for C$45 to C$70 each way. **Snowbus** (✆ 888/794-5511; www.snowbus.ca) offers service to/from Whistler and Vancouver area suburbs (Richmond, Burnaby, North Vancouver) and other neighborhood locations in addition to downtown Vancouver and the airport. There are hosts and free movies during the journey. Also available is a SnowCard (free, but must be picked up in advance), which offers discounts on Snowbus transportation. One-way fare between Vancouver and Whistler is C$35. Snowbus operates daily, though only during ski season.

BY TRAIN From May through September, **Rocky Mountaineer** (✆ 877/460-3200 or 604/606-7245; www.rockymountaineer.com) offers Thursday to Monday service between North Vancouver and Whistler on the **Whistler Mountaineer ★★★**. The refurbished trains with vintage dome observation cars depart North Vancouver at about 8am (transportation from most hotels to the station is provided) and arrive at 11:30am in Whistler; departure time from Whistler is 3pm, arriving back in North Vancouver at 7pm. Breakfast is served on the way up, and a light meal on the return. Standard adult round-trip "Classic" fare is C$235 for adults, C$165 for children 2 to 11.

VISITOR INFORMATION

The **Whistler Visitor Centre,** easy to find on the Village Bus Loop at 4230 Gateway Dr., Whistler, BC V0N 1B4 (✆ 877/991-9988 or 604/935-3357; www.whistler.com), is open daily 8am to 10pm, although sometimes closes at 8pm during the slower

Whistler Village

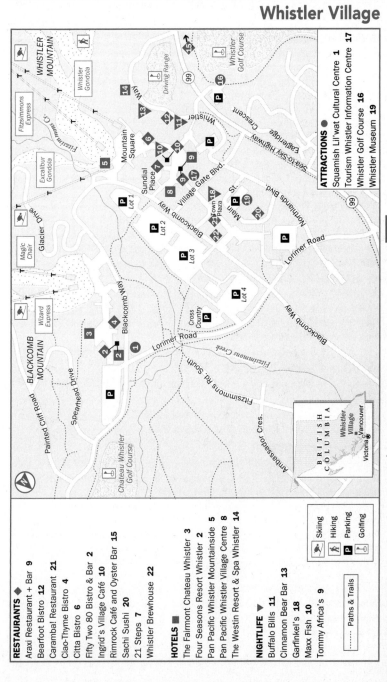

RESTAURANTS ◆
Araxi Restaurant + Bar **9**
Bearfoot Bistro **12**
Carambal Restaurant **21**
Ciao-Thyme Bistro **4**
Citta Bistro **6**
Fifty Two 80 Bistro & Bar **2**
Ingrid's Village Café **10**
Rimrock Café and Oyster Bar **15**
Sachi Sushi **20**
21 Steps **7**
Whistler Brewhouse **22**

HOTELS ■
The Fairmont Chateau Whistler **3**
Four Seasons Resort Whistler **2**
Pan Pacific Whistler Mountainside **5**
Pan Pacific Whistler Village Centre **8**
The Westin Resort & Spa Whistler **14**

NIGHTLIFE ▼
Buffalo Bills **11**
Cinnamon Bear Bar **13**
Garfinkel's **18**
Maxx Fish **10**
Tommy Africa's **9**

ATTRACTIONS ●
Squamish Lil'wat Cultural Centre **1**
Tourism Whistler Information Centre **17**
Whistler Golf Course **16**
Whistler Museum **19**

Skiing 🎿
Hiking 🥾
Parking **P**
Golfing ⛳

------ Paths & Trails

WHISTLER MOUNTAIN
BLACKCOMB MOUNTAIN

BRITISH COLUMBIA
Whistler Village
Vancouver
Victoria

spring and fall seasons. For pre-trip planning and bookings, contact **Tourism Whistler** (☏ **800/WHISTLER** [800/944-7853] or 604/932-0606; www.whistler.com).

GETTING AROUND

Be sure to pick up a map when you get to Whistler and study it—the curving streets are made for pedestrians but defy easy negotiation by drivers, particularly in the winter darkness. **Whistler Village** is at the base of the ski runs at Whistler Peak. The **Upper Village,** at the base of Blackcomb ski runs, is just across Fitzsimmons Creek from Whistler Village. As development continues, the distinction between these two "villages" is disappearing, though Whistler Village is the center for most restaurants, shopping, and the youthful nightlife scene. The Upper Village, centered on the Four Seasons and Fairmont Chateau Whistler hotels, is quieter and more upscale. However, both villages are compact, and signed trails and paths link together shops, lodgings, and restaurants in the central resort area. The walk between the two village resort areas takes about 10 minutes.

Many smaller inns, B&Bs, restaurants, and services are located outside the nucleus of Whistler Village and Upper Village. **Creekside** is a large development south (downhill) from Whistler Village (there are lifts onto Whistler Mountain from Creekside—in fact, this was the original lift base for the resort), while the shores of **Alta Lake** are ringed with residential areas and golf courses.

BY BUS   The year-round Whistler and Valley Express (WAVE) **public bus system** (☏ **604/932-4020;** www.bctransit.com) offers 10 routes in the Whistler area. Buses have both bike and ski racks. Most routes cross paths at the Gondola Transit Exchange off Blackcomb Way, near the base of the Whistler Mountain lifts. Other than riding the free village shuttle, which runs between the lifts and local hotels, a one-way transit fare costs C$2.50 for adults and C$2 for seniors and students.

BY TAXI   Whistler Taxi (☏ **800/203-5322** or 604/932-3333) operates round-the-clock. Taxi tours and airport transport are also offered by **LimoJet Gold** (☏ **604/273-1331**).

BY CAR   Rental cars are available from **Avis** in the Cascade Lodge, 4315 Northlands Blvd. (☏ **800/230-4898** or 604/932-1236).

SPECIAL EVENTS

Downhill ski competitions are held December to May, including the **TELUS Winter Classic** (Jan), and the **TELUS World Ski & Snowboard Festival** (Apr). In August, mountain bikers compete in **Crankworx.**

Early September ushers in the **Jazz on the Mountain** (www.whistlerjazzfest.com), featuring live performances in the village squares and the surrounding clubs. **Cornucopia** (www.whistlercornucopia.com) is Whistler's premier wine-and-food festival. Held in November, the opening gala showcases top wineries from the Pacific region plus lots of food events and tastings from local chefs.

Hitting the Slopes

WHISTLER BLACKCOMB RESORT   The namesake mountains of **Whistler Blackcomb Resort,** 4545 Blackcomb Way, Whistler, BC V0N 1B4 (☏ **800/766-0449** in North America, 604/687-7507 snow report in Vancouver, or 604/932-4211 snow report in Whistler; www.whistlerblackcomb.com), are jointly operated by Intrawest, so your pass gives access to both ski areas. You can book nearly all accommodations and activities in Whistler from their website.

FROM peak to peak

Intrawest, the corporation behind Whistler Blackcomb Resort, built the record-defying gondola that links together the peaks of Whistler (elev. 2,182m/7,159 ft.) and Blackcomb (elev. 2,284m/7,493 ft.) mountains. The **Peak 2 Peak Gondola** has the longest free-span lift in the world at 3km (1¾ miles) and a total length of 4.4km (2¾ miles). The Peak 2 Peak Gondola is also the highest detachable lift in the world, at 436m (1,427 ft.) above the valley floor. The gondola includes 28 cars carrying up to 28 passengers each,

with cars leaving approximately every minute. The cars take 11 minutes to span the valley, traveling from peak to peak. Clearly, the gondola offers skiers greater flexibility for skiing the highest runs of both mountains and offers summer visitors one of the most attention-grabbing gondola rides in the world. From late June through mid-October, a day ticket to the gondola is C$45 adult, C$38 seniors and youths 13 to 18, and C$21 children 7 to 12.

From its base in Whistler Village, **Whistler Mountain** has 1,530m (5,020 ft.) of vertical and over 100 marked runs that are serviced by a total of 19 lifts. From its base in Upper Village, **Blackcomb Mountain** has 1,609m (5,279 ft.) of vertical and over 100 marked runs that are served by a total of 17 lifts. The PEAK 2 PEAK gondola, the longest in the world, connects the two mountains. Both mountains also have bowls and glade skiing, with Blackcomb offering glacier skiing well into July. Together, the two mountains comprise the largest ski resort in North America, offering over 3,307 skiable hectares (8,171 acres).

During winter, lift tickets for 2 days of skiing on both mountains range from C$132 to C$192 for adults, C$112 to C$163 for seniors and teens 13 to 18, and C$66 to C$96 for children 7 to 12. Lifts are open 8:30am to 3:30pm or 4pm (only to 3pm from season opening to late Jan). Whistler Blackcomb offers ski lessons and guides for all levels and interests. Phone **Guest Relations** at © **800/766-0449** for details. Ski, snowboard, and boot rentals are available from the resort, and can be booked online. In addition, dozens of independent shops provide equipment rentals. **Affinity Sports** (www.affinityrentals.com) has multiple locations in the Whistler area, with online reservations available. **Summit Ski** (© **866/608-6225** or 604/932-6225; www.summitsport.com) has hotel locations including the Delta Whistler Village Suites and Hilton Whistler Resort and rents high-performance and regular skis and snowboards.

BACKCOUNTRY SKIING The **Spearhead Traverse,** which starts at Whistler and finishes at Blackcomb, is a well-marked backcountry route that has become extremely popular. **Garibaldi Provincial Park** (© 604/898-3678) maintains marked backcountry trails at **Diamond Head, Singing Pass,** and **Garibaldi Lake.** These are ungroomed and unpatrolled trails, and you have to be self-reliant—you should be at least an intermediate skier, bring appropriate clothing and avalanche gear, and know how to use it. There are several access points along Hwy. 99 between Squamish and Whistler.

CROSS-COUNTRY SKIING The 32km (20 miles) of easy-to-very-difficult marked trails at Lost Lake start at the Lorimer Road bridge over Fitzsimmons Creek, just west of Upper Village. Passes are C$20 per day. The Lost Lake trails link to the

Nicklaus North Golf Course, with cross-country ski trails leading through the undulating golf course grounds along the shores of Green Lake. **Cross Country Connection** (✆ **604/905-0071**; www.crosscountryconnection.bc.ca) is located in the park, offering Nordic ski rentals and lessons. The website also has a downloadable map of the park trails. The 40-km (25-mile) **Valley Trail System** in the village becomes a well-marked cross-country ski trail during winter. **Whistler Olympic Park** in the **Callaghan Valley** (✆ **877/764-2455** or 604-964-0060; www.whistlerolympicpark. com) was developed for the cross-country, biathlon, Nordic combined, and ski jumping events for the Vancouver 2010 Olympic and Paralympic Winter Games. Located about 12km (7½ miles) southwest of Whistler, these two areas combine to offer more than 90km (56 miles) of cross-country ski trails as well as routes for snowshoeing. A cross-country day pass is C$20 adults; lessons and tours are also available.

HELI-SKIING & BOARDING   Forget lift lines and crowds. Ride a helicopter to the crest of a Coast Range peak and experience the ultimate in powder skiing. If you're a confident intermediate-to-advanced skier in good shape, consider joining a heli-ski trip. **Whistler Heli-Skiing** (✆ **888/HELISKI** [435-4754] or 604/905-3337; www.whistlerheliskiing.com) offers a three-run day, with 1,400 to 2,300m (4,593–7,546 ft.) of vertical helicopter lift, which costs C$815 per person. **Coast Range Heli-Skiing** (✆ **800/701-8744** or 604/894-1144; www.coastrangeheli skiing.com) offers a four-run day, with about 1,829 to 3,658m (6,000–12,000 ft.) of vertical helicopter lift, which costs C$960 per person. Both trips include a guide and lunch.

SNOWCAT SKIING & BOARDING   Lifts and choppers aren't the only way up a mountain. **Powder Mountain Catskiing** (✆ **877/PWDRFIX** [793-7347] or 604/|932-0169; www.powdermountaincatskiing.com) uses snowcats to climb up into a private skiing area south of Whistler where skiers and boarders will find 1,740 skiable hectares (4,300 acres) on two mountains. The price, C$499 per person, pays for a full day of skiing, usually 6 to 10 runs down 2,100 to 3,000 vertical meters (6,890–9,942 ft.) of untracked powder, plus transport to/from Whistler, lunch, snacks, and guides.

Other Winter Pursuits

DOG SLEDDING   Explore the old growth forests of the Callaghan Valley on a dog sled run with **Canadian Snowmobile Adventures Ltd.** (Carleton Lodge, 4290 Mountain Sq.; ✆ **604/938-1616**; www.canadiansnowmobile.com). Operating from mid-December through March, 3-hour dog-sled tours cost C$175 per person based on two adults per sled.

ICE CLIMBING   Climb a frozen waterfall with **Coast Mountain Guides** (✆ **604/932-7711**; www.coastmountainguides.com). Guides provide all equipment; beginners welcome. Climbs start at C$177 per person, based on a three-person group.

SLEIGH RIDING   For an old-fashioned horse-drawn sleigh ride, contact **Blackcomb Horsedrawn Sleigh Rides** (✆ **604/932-7631**; www.blackcombsleighrides. com). Giant Percheron horses lead the way, and comfortable sleighs with padded seats and cozy blankets keep you warm. A number of tours are available, starting with basic half-hour rides for C$55 for adults, and C$35 for children 3 to 12. Longer rides and dinner sleigh-ride combos are also available. Tours depart from base 2 on Blackcomb Mountain.

SNOWMOBILING The year-round ATV/snowmobile tours offered by **Canadian Snowmobile Adventures Ltd.,** Carleton Lodge (© **604/938-1616;** www.canadian snowmobile.com), are a unique way to take to the Whistler Mountain trails. A 3-hour Mountain Safari on Blackcomb Mountain costs C$159 for a single rider and C$125 per person riding double. For a longer (4 hour) and heartier backcountry option, ride to a remote cabin on Sproatt Mountain and tuck into a Canadian-style breakfast for C$199 for a single driver and C$169 each for two sharing a snowmobile.

SNOWSHOEING Snowshoeing makes a great family outing; kids really enjoy the experience of walking on snow. Most ski rental outfits also offer snowshoe rentals, so you won't have to look far to find a pair. If you want to just rent the snowshoes and find your own way around, rentals are typically C$20 per day. One of the best is **Lost Lake Cross Country Connection** (© **604/905-0071;** www.crosscountryconnection.ca).

Warm-Weather Pursuits

BIKING Whistler is world famous for its mountain biking. While many gonzo riders come from around the world to test themselves on the many technical trails, others come to enjoy the gentler pleasures of simply biking through the forest.

Some of the best mountain-bike trails in the village are in **Whistler Mountain Bike Park** (© **866/218-9690** or 604/904-8134; www.whistlerbike.com), which offers more than 200km (124 miles) of lift-serviced trails and mountain pathways with more than 1,507m (4,944 ft.) of vertical drop. The park is divided between the Fitzsimmons and Garbanzo zones, serviced by four lifts; the trail system is labeled from green circle to blue square to black diamond and double black diamond. High season per-day lift tickets and park admission are C$55 adults, C$49 seniors and youths 13 to 18, and C$30 children 7 to 12. There's also the **Air Dome,** a 780-sq.-m (8,396-sq.-ft.) covered indoor mountain bike training facility with a huge foam pit, ramps, and a quarter pipe and half pipe. A 3-hour pass is C$17. If you're not ready for daredevil riding on the mountain, the 40km (25-mile) paved **Valley Trail** is a pedestrian/bicycle route linking parks, neighborhoods, and playgrounds around Whistler Village. For other biking trails, check out the comprehensive Whistler biking website at www.whistlermountainbike.com.

In summer, nearly every ski shop switches gears and offers bike rentals. You'll have absolutely no problem finding a bike to rent in Whistler Village. If you want to call ahead and reserve a bike, try **Whistler Bike Co.,** 4205 Village Square (© **604/938-9511;** www.bikeco.ca). Prices range from C$40 per day for a commuting-style bike to C$65 to C$125 per day for a high-end mountain bike.

CANOEING & KAYAKING The 3-hour River of Golden Dreams Kayak & Canoe Tour is a great way to get acquainted with an exhilarating stretch of slow-moving glacial water that runs between Green Lake and Alta Lake behind the village of Whistler. Book through the **Whistler Visitor Centre** (© **877/991-9988**). Unguided packages run C$49 per person and include transportation and gear.

GOLF Robert Trent Jones, Jr.'s **Fairmont Chateau Whistler Golf Club,** at the base of Blackcomb Mountain (© **877/938-2092,** or pro shop 604/938-2095), is an 18-hole, par-72 course. The 6,067m (6,635-yd.), par-72 signature course was selected in 1993 as Canada's best new golf course by *Golf Digest* magazine. Greens fees are C$109 to C$159 in high season. A multiple-award-winning golf course, **Nicklaus North** at Whistler (© **800/386-9898** or 604/938-9898; www.nicklaus north.com) is a 5-minute drive north of the village on the shores of Green Lake. The

6,365m (6,961-yd.), par-71 course's mountain views are spectacular. Greens fees are C$39 to C$149. The 6,105m (6,676-yd.) **Whistler Golf Club** (© **800/376-1777** or 604/932-3280; www.whistlergolf.com), designed by Arnold Palmer, features nine lakes, two creeks, and magnificent vistas. In addition to the 18-hole, par-71 course, the club offers a driving range, putting green, and pitching area. Greens fees are C$59 to C$129.

HIKING There are numerous easy hiking trails in and around Whistler. (Just remember—never hike alone, and bring plenty of water with you.) You can take ski lifts up to Whistler and Blackcomb mountains' trails during summer, but you have a number of other choices as well. The **Lost Lake Trail** starts at the northern end of the Day Skier Parking Lot at Blackcomb. The 32km (20 miles) of marked trails that wind around creeks, beaver dams, blueberry patches, and lush cedar groves are ideal for biking, cross-country skiing, or just strolling and picnicking.

The **Valley Trail System** is a well-marked paved trail connecting parts of Whistler. The trail starts on the west side of Hwy. 99 adjacent to the Whistler Golf Course and winds through quiet residential areas, as well as golf courses and parks. Garibaldi Provincial Park's **Singing Pass Trail** is a 4-hour hike of moderate difficulty. The fun way to experience this trail is to take the Whistler Mountain gondola to the top and walk down the well-marked path that ends in the village.

The Whistler Village Gondola (Whistler Base) and Wizard Express–Solar Coaster Express (Blackcomb Base) are open in summer and provide access to the Peak 2 Peak Gondola (see above) as well as miles of alpine hiking trails, including the Peak Interpretive Walk; guided hikes are available.

Nairn Falls Provincial Park is about 32km (20 miles) north of Whistler on Hwy. 99. It features a 1.6km-long (1-mile) trail leading you to a stupendous view of the icy-cold Green River as it plunges 60m (197 ft.) over a rocky cliff into a narrow gorge on its way downstream. On Hwy. 99 north of Mount Currie, **Joffre Lakes Provincial Park** is an intermediate-level hike leading past several brilliant-blue glacial lakes up to the very foot of a glacier. At the north end of Green Lake, the **Ancient Cedars** area of Cougar Mountain is an awe-inspiring grove of towering cedars and Douglas firs. Some of the trees are over 1,000 years old and measure 3m (9¾ ft.) in diameter.

HORSEBACK RIDING **Adventure Ranch** near Pemberton (© **604/894-5200;** www.adventureranch.net) leads 2-hour horseback tours for C$69 from its Lillooet River–side ranch, 30 minutes from Whistler.

JET BOATING **Whistler Jet Boating** (© **604/905-9455;** www.whistlerjet boating.com) takes guests up the Lillooet River from near Pemberton. The tour surges past large rapids, spectacular glacier peaks, and traditional Native fishing camps. Deer, bear, osprey, and spawning salmon are frequently seen. This 3-hour-long trip is C$109; kids 5 to 15 get a C$10 discount.

RAFTING **Wedge Rafting** (Carleton Lodge, Whistler Village; © **888/932-5899** or 604/932-7171; www.wedgerafting.com) offers rafting runs on the Green River, Elaho and Squamish Rivers, and Cheakamus River. The best for first-timers, the Green River trip lasts about 2½ hours, with return transport from Whistler to the wilderness launch area. Tours cost C$89, with up to six daily departures. The tour down the Elaho and Squamish rivers takes about 8 hours, includes snacks and a barbecue lunch, and costs C$165. Discounts are available for children 10 to 16; however, they must weigh at least 41kg (90 lb.).

Whistler: North America's Premier Ski Resort

THE SUNSHINE COAST & WHISTLER

ZIP-LINING One of Whistler's most popular year-round thrills is the steel zip-line rides offered by **Ziptrek Ecotours** (☎ **866/935-0001** or 604/935-0001; www.ziptrek. com). Zip-lining involves gliding along a suspended steel cable using a pulley and climbing harness at speeds up to 80kmph (50 mph). Guided tours include the Bear Tour that links five zip-lines that range in length from 61 to 335m (200–1,100 ft.), spanning the 13⅓ hectares (33 acres) in the valley between Whistler and Blackcomb Mountains, an area of untouched coastal temperate rainforest. Among the five ziplines of the adrenaline-pumping Eagle tour, the monster runs 610m (2,000ft.) and drops 20 stories to end in Whistler Village itself. Tickets are C$109 (Bear Tour) and $129 (Eagle Tour) adults, C$89 and C$109, respectively, for seniors and youths 6 to 14. For those not up to zip-lining, Ziptrek also offers **TreeTrek,** a network of suspended boardwalks, aerial stairways, and bridges at heights of over 61m (200 ft.) in the tree canopy. Tickets are C$39 adults and C$29 seniors and youth 14 and under.

Exploring the Town

SEEING THE SIGHTS The **Squamish Lil'wat Cultural Centre** (☎ **866/441-7522;** www.slcc.ca) is an architecturally stunning showcase of soaring glass and stone, designed to celebrate the joint history and living cultures of the Squamish and Lil'wat First Nations. The facility includes both indoor and outdoor space, anchored by the monumental Great Hall with traditional artifacts and 67m (220-ft.) glass plank walls revealing stunning mountain and forest views. The center also features a gallery of Squamish and Lil'wat sacred cultural treasures and icons, plus a shop for First Nations art. Outdoors is a Squamish longhouse, which was the traditional dwelling of the Squamish people, and a replica Lil'wat "ístken" or "Pit House," which was the traditional dwelling of the Lil'wat people. The center is open daily 9:30 or 10am to 5pm, and admission is C$18 adult, C$14 seniors and students, C$11 youths 13 to 18, and C$8 kids 6 to 12.

To learn more about Whistler's heritage, flora, and fauna, visit the **Whistler Museum,** 4333 Main St., off Northlands Boulevard (☎ **604/932-2019;** www. whistlermuseum.com). The museum is open daily 10am to 4pm. Admission is C$7 for adults, C$5 seniors and students, C$4 youths 7 to 18, and free for children 6 and under.

Gallery Row in the Hilton Whistler Resort consists of four galleries including the **Whistler Village Art Gallery** (☎ **604/938-3001**) and the **Black Tusk Gallery** (☎ **604/905-5540**). These and the **Adele Campbell Gallery** (☎ **604/938-0887**) all feature collections of fine art, sculpture, and glass.

SHOPPING Whistler Village, and the area surrounding the Blackcomb Mountain lift, brim with clothing, jewelry, craft, specialty, gift, and equipment shops open daily 10am to 6pm. You'll have absolutely no problem finding interesting places to shop in Whistler—both quality and prices are high.

SPAS Nearly all the large and medium-size hotels now feature spas, and a number of independent spas line the streets of Whistler Village. The **Vida Wellness Spa** at the Fairmont Chateau Whistler Resort (☎ **604/938-2086**) is considered one of the best in Whistler and has two couples rooms. It offers massage therapy, aromatherapy, skin care, body wraps, and steam baths. Another noteworthy hotel spa is the Westin Resort's **Avello Spa,** 400–4090 Whistler Way (☎ **877/935-7111** or 604/935-3444; www.whistlerspa.com), which offers a host of spa services as well as holistic and hydrotherapy treatments. **The Spa at Four Seasons Resort** (☎ **604/935-3400**) has 14 treatment rooms, a Vichy shower, yoga and fitness classes, and a vast assortment of luxurious treatments from mineral scrubs to wildflower baths. Using Finnish hydrotherapy techniques, **Scandinave Spa** (8010 Mons Rd.; © **604/935-2424;** www.scandinave.com) will certainly soothe tired muscles. Outdoor baths are set in a coniferous forest. There's a cedar sauna, steam room, hot pool, and cold waterfall. Bath-only access costs C$58, with add-on Swedish, hot stone, and deep tissue massages available. The therapists at **Whistler Physiotherapy** (© **604/932-4001** or 604/938-9001; www.whistlerphysio.com) have a lot of experience with the typical ski, board, and hiking injuries. There are two Whistler locations: 339–4370 Lorimer Rd., at Marketplace, and 202–2011 Innsbruck Dr., next to Boston Pizza in Creekside.

Where to Stay

For a first-time visitor, figuring out lodging at Whistler can be rather intimidating. One of the easiest ways to book rooms, buy ski passes, and plan activities is to visit the official Whistler Blackcomb Resort website at **www.whistlerblackcomb.com**. Most hotels and condo developments are represented at this one-stop shopping and information site. Lodgings in Whistler are very high quality, and the price of rooms is equally high. The hotels listed below offer superlative rooms with lots of extras. However, the smaller inns offer great value and excellent accommodations, often with services and options that can, for many travelers, make them a more attractive option than the larger hotels. At these smaller, owner-operated inns, rates typically include features that are sometimes available for an extra fee at hotels. These inns are located outside of the central villages and usually offer a quieter lodging experience than the hotels in Whistler Village.

In addition to the hotels and inns below, Whistler is absolutely loaded with condo developments. To reserve one of these units—which can range from studios, to one- to five-bedroom fully furnished condos, to town houses and chalets, with prices from around C$175 to C$1,500 and up a night—many travelers find the easiest thing to do is simply decide on a price point and call one of the central booking agencies. **Whistler Accommodation Reservations** (www.whistler.com; © **800/944-7853**) can book a wide range of rooms, suites, and vacation rentals in the Whistler area and provide a customized package with lift tickets and transportation. **Whistler Superior Properties** (www.whistlersuperior.com; © **877/535-8282** or 604/932-3510); **Whistler Accommodations** (www.whistleraccommodation.com; © **866/905-4607** or 604/905-4607) focuses on condos and hotels in the Upper Village.

One other excellent booking service is **Allura Direct** (www.alluradirect.com; © **866/4-ALLURA** [425-5872] or 604/707-6700), through which owners of rental properties in Whistler rent directly to the public (and you escape the 2% local hotel tax, though 12% provincial HST is still levied). The website has an excellent search engine, and offers lots of information and photos of numerous properties located throughout Whistler. Though owners are screened—we encountered no problems and got a fabulous deal on a one-bedroom condo—quality can vary, so we recommend you do your homework and book only with those owners who accept credit cards.

Reservations for peak winter periods should be made by September at the latest.

IN THE VILLAGE & UPPER VILLAGE

Fairmont Chateau Whistler ★★★   The Fairmont re-creates the look of a feudal castle at the foot of Blackcomb Mountain, but with every modern comfort added. Massive wooden beams support an airy peaked roof in the lobby, while in the hillside Mallard Lounge, double-sided stone fireplaces cast a cozy glow on the couches and leather armchairs. Rooms and suites are very comfortable and beautifully furnished, and feature duvets, bathrobes, and soaker tubs (some offer stunning views of the slopes). Fairmont Gold service guests can have breakfast or relax après-ski in a private lounge with the feel of a Victorian library, and the rooms have fireplaces. All guests can use the heated outdoor pool and Jacuzzis, which look out over the base of the ski hill. The hotel's **Vida Wellness Spa** ★ is among the best in town. The Fairmont pays attention to the needs of skiers, with a recreation concierge, ski storage next to the slopes, and ski valets to help make pre- and après-ski as easy and pleasant as possible.

4599 Chateau Blvd., Whistler, BC V0N 1B4. www.fairmont.com/whistler. © **800/606-8244** or 604/938-8000. Fax 604/938-2291. 550 units. Spring–fall C$239–C$329 double, C$319–C$1399 suite; winter C$359–C$799 double, C$439–C$1,459 suite; holidays C$359–C$799 double, C$439–C$3,159 suite. AE, MC, V. Underground valet parking C$35. Pets are welcome. **Amenities:** 4 restaurants; bar; babysitting; children's programs; concierge; executive-level rooms; health club; 18-hole golf course; Jacuzzi; heated indoor/outdoor pool; room service; sauna; outstanding spa facility; 2 tennis courts; secure ski and bike storage; rooms for those w/limited mobility. *In room:* A/C, TV w/pay movies and video games, fridge, hair dryer, Wi-Fi (paid).

Four Seasons Resort Whistler ★★★

The Four Seasons Resort Whistler is a très chic, très elegant monument to refinement. Easily the most refined and elegant of Whistler's hotels, the Four Seasons is monumental in scale—the expansive stone, glass, and timber lobby is like a modern-day hunting lodge—while maintaining the atmosphere of a very intimate and sophisticated boutique hotel—a rare achievement. All rooms have a balcony, fireplace, and very large, amenity-filled bathrooms with soaker tubs. The standard room is a very spacious 48 sq. m (517 sq. ft.), and superior and deluxe level rooms are truly large. A separate wing of the hotel contains expansive private residences with two to four bedrooms. With 14 treatment rooms, the exquisite **Spa at the Four Seasons Resort** ★ is one of Whistler's largest, and a heated outdoor pool and three whirlpool baths fill half the hotel courtyard.

4591 Blackcomb Way, Whistler, BC V0N 1B4. www.fourseasons.com/whistler. © **888/935-2460** or 604/935-3400. Fax 604/935-3455. 273 units and 37 residences. Spring, summer & fall C$305–C$465 double, C$525 suite; winter C$405–C$650 double, from C$720 suite. AE, DC, DISC, MC, V. Underground valet parking C$33. **Amenities:** Restaurant; lounge; concierge; executive-level rooms; health club; Jacuzzis; heated outdoor pool; room service; superlative spa; ski and bike storage; rooms for those w/limited mobility. *In room:* A/C, TV/DVD/CD player, hair dryer, minibar, Wi-Fi (free).

Pan Pacific Whistler Mountainside ★★

The Pan Pacific's slightly older and more family-oriented Mountainside all-suite property has a lot going for it, with top-notch furnishings, kitchenettes, and loads of amenities. Comfortable as the rooms are, however, the true advantage to the Pan Pacific Mountainside is its location at the foot of the Whistler Mountain gondola. Not only can you ski right to your hotel, but thanks to a large heated outdoor pool and Jacuzzi deck, you can sit at the end of the day sipping a glass of wine, gazing up at the snowy slopes, and marvel at the ameliorative effects of warm water on aching muscles. With sofa beds and fold-down Murphy beds, the studio suites are fine for couples, while the one- and two-bedroom suites allow more space for larger groups or families with kids.

4320 Sundial Crescent, Whistler, BC V0N 1B4. www.panpacific.com. © **888/905-9995** or 604/905-2999. Fax 604/905-2995. 121 units. Spring–fall C$139–C$229 studio, C$189–C$359 suite; winter C$199–C$769 studio, C$249–C$1,169 suite. AE, MC, V. Underground valet parking C$25. **Amenities:** Restaurant; pub; concierge; fitness center w/whirlpool and steam room; Jacuzzi; heated outdoor pool; room service; ski, bike, and golf bag storage; rooms for those w/limited mobility. *In room:* A/C, TV, DVD player, CD player, fridge, hair dryer, kitchen, Wi-Fi (free).

Pan Pacific Whistler Village Centre ★★★ The Pan Pacific chain has two handsome properties in Whistler, both just steps off Blackcomb Way in Whistler Village. The suites in the Village Centre are more like apartments than hotel rooms; it's also more couples-oriented than its family-friendly sister property. All one-, two-, and three-bedroom suites have a balcony, fireplace, flatscreen TV, full kitchen with granite counters, soaker tub, bathrobes, handsome furniture, and floor-to-ceiling windows to let in the amazing mountain vistas. The penthouse suites are truly magnificent, with cathedral ceilings, massive stone fireplaces, multiple balconies, and loads of room. The Village Centre has a fitness center with sauna, massage therapy and spa treatment rooms, a lap pool, and two hot tubs. Rates include a full breakfast buffet.

4299 Blackcomb Way, Whistler, BC V0N 1B4. www.panpacific.com. *C* **888/966-5575** or 604/966-5500. Fax 604/966-5501. 83 units. Spring, summer, and fall C$159–C$269 1-bedroom; winter C$219–C$849 1-bedroom. AE, MC, V. Underground valet parking C$25. **Amenities:** Restaurant; pub; concierge; fitness center; Jacuzzi; heated outdoor pool; room service; sauna; ski, bike, and golf bag storage; ski rentals; rooms for those w/limited mobility. *In room:* A/C, TV w/pay movie channels, fridge, hair dryer, kitchen, Wi-Fi (free).

The Westin Resort and Spa Whistler ★★★ Talk about location: The all-suite Westin Resort snapped up the best piece of property in town and squeezed itself onto the mountainside at the bottom of the Whistler gondola. It's central to all the restaurants and nightspots in Whistler Village, yet slightly apart from the crowds. The two-towered hotel is built in the style of an enormous mountain chalet with cedar timbers and lots of local granite and basalt finishings. All 419 suites received an update in 2009 and offer full kitchens, soaker tubs, slate-lined showers, and an elegant and restful decor. The beds, Westin's signature Heavenly Beds, are indeed divine. The hotel's **Avello Spa ★** is extremely well-appointed for après-ski pampering and the indoor/outdoor pool, hot tubs, steam baths, and sauna will warm up ski-weary limbs.

4090 Whistler Way, Whistler, BC V0N 1B4. www.westinwhistler.com. *C* **888/634-5577** or 604/905-5000. Fax 604/905-5640. 419 units. C$160–C$900 junior suite; C$210–C$1,100 1-bedroom suite. Children 17 and under stay free in parent's room. AE, MC, V. Parking C$32. **Amenities:** Restaurant; bar; babysitting; concierge; health club; indoor and outdoor Jacuzzi; indoor-outdoor pool; room service; sauna; spa. *In room:* A/C, TV w/pay movies, hair dryer, kitchenette, Wi-Fi (paid).

OUTSIDE THE VILLAGE

Alpine Chalet Whistler ★★ This cozy alpine-style lodge sits in a quiet location near Alta Lake and the Whistler Golf Club, and focuses on health and wellness with yoga classes and nutrition programs. The entire inn is designed to provide luxurious lodgings, privacy, and a welcoming sense of camaraderie in the comfortable, fireplace-dominated guest lounge. There are two room types: standard lodge rooms are comfortable and will suit the needs of most skiers and travelers; signature rooms are larger and feature fireplaces, vaulted ceilings, fine linens, bathrobes, and other upscale amenities you'd expect at a classy hotel. Some rooms have balconies or terraces.

3012 Alpine Crescent, Whistler, BC V0N 1B3. www.alpinechaletwhistler.ca. *C* **800/736-9967** or 604/935-3003. Fax 604/935-3008. 8 units. C$230–C$480 double. Rates include full breakfast. MC, V. Free parking. **Amenities:** Guest lounge; 8-person hot tub; steam room; yoga room. *In room:* A/C, TV/DVD, hair dryer, MP3 docking station, Wi-Fi (free), heated floor.

Cedar Springs Bed & Breakfast Lodge ★ ☺ The no-children policy at many Whistler inns can be a real challenge for families, but the Cedar Springs provides an excellent solution. One suite has two queen-size and two twin beds—just the ticket for large families. What's more, the lodge is just next door to a park, biking paths, and a sports center with swimming pool. Cedar Springs also offers excellent accommodations for couples and solo travelers. The large honeymoon suite boasts a fireplace and balcony. Most rooms feature handmade pine furniture; all have bathrooms with heated tile floors. A sauna and hot tub on the sun deck overlooking the gardens add to the pampering after a day of play. Lodge owners Jackie and Joern offer lots of extras such as complimentary shuttle service to ski lifts, heated ski gear storage, bike rentals, and free Wi-Fi.

8106 Camino Dr., Whistler, BC V0N 1B8. www.whistlerbb.com. ⓒ **800/727-7547** or 604/938-8007. Fax 604/938-8023. 8 units. Winter C$85–C$135 single, C$109–C$279 double; spring, summer, and fall C$69–C$79 single, C$95–C$175 double. Rates include full breakfast. AE, MC, V. Free parking; 2-minute walk to public transport. Take Hwy. 99 north toward Pemberton 4km (2½ miles) past Whistler Village. Turn left onto Alpine Way, go a block to Rainbow Dr., and turn left; go a block to Camino Dr. and turn left. The lodge is a block down at the corner of Camino and Cedar Springs Rd. **Amenities:** Bike rentals; Jacuzzi; sauna; guest lounge w/TV/VCR/DVD; secure ski and heated gear storage. *In room:* Hair dryer, no phone, Wi-Fi (free).

Chalet Luise B&B Inn ★★

This homey inn is just outside of Whistler Village, so park the car and walk to dining, shopping, and recreation. Chalet Luise is a very charming small inn with just the right Bavarian touch to create a festive, holiday-card atmosphere. The guest rooms are bright and cheerful, and come with pine furniture and high-quality linens; some have fireplaces and balconies. At the back is a gazebo with hot tub; the large guest lounge has a TV, fireplace, and a self-service coffee bar with a microwave for guest use. There are a number of decks, all lovingly festooned with flowerpots in summer. All rooms have private bathrooms. Breakfast is a buffet of fresh baked goods plus a hot main course.

7461 Ambassador Crescent, Whistler, BC V0N 1B7. www.chaletluise.com. ⓒ **800/665-1998** or 604/932-4187. Fax 604/938-1531. 8 units. Summer C$89–C$179; winter C$125–C$269 double. Rates include full breakfast. MC, V. Free parking. **Amenities:** Hot tub; sauna; ski and bike storage; guest lounge. *In room:* Hair dryer, Wi-Fi (free).

Durlacher Hof Pension Inn ★★ 🛏

This lovely inn boasts both an authentic Austrian feel and a sociable atmosphere. Both are the result of the exceptional care and service shown by owners Peter and Erika Durlacher. Guests are greeted by name at the entryway, provided with slippers, and then given a tour of the three-story chalet-style property. The rooms vary in size from comfortable to quite spacious and come with goose-down duvets and fine linens, private bathrooms (some with jetted tubs) with deluxe toiletries, and incredible mountain views from private balconies. Better still is the downstairs lounge, with a welcoming fireplace and complimentary après-ski appetizers baked by Erika; likewise, breakfasts are substantial and lovingly prepared. Peter and Erica are fonts of knowledge about local restaurants and recreation; they will happily arrange tours and outings.

7055 Nesters Rd., Whistler, BC V0N 1B7. www.durlacherhof.com. ⓒ **877/932-1924** or 604/932-1924. Fax 604/938-1980. 8 units. C$139–C$279 double. Extra person C$35. Rates include full breakfast and afternoon tea. MC, V. Free parking. Take Hwy. 99 about 1km (⅔ mile) north of Whistler Village to Nester's Rd. Turn left and the inn is immediately on the right. **Amenities:** Sauna; shared guest fridges; ski and bike storage; 1 room for those w/limited mobility. *In room:* Hair dryer, no phone, Wi-Fi (free).

Edgewater Lodge 🛏

This lodge has probably the most unique location of any lodging in Whistler. It sits on a jut of land that thrusts into Green Lake, a quiet 3km (1¾ miles) north of Whistler Village. From each room, there are gum-swallowing vistas across the lake to Wedge Mountain and the ski slopes on Whistler and

Blackcomb. The intimate lodge offers personal and professional service. Rooms sleep three to five people and all have sofa beds in the sitting room. All share a large lobby guest area with couches and a huge fireplace. The Edgewater is also noteworthy for its fine Northwest cuisine dining room.

The lodge is very convenient to all-season recreation—in summer, you can fish and boat in Green Lake, or test your drive on the adjacent Nicklaus North Golf Course. Come winter, in addition to downhill skiing, ice-skating and cross-country skiing are right out the front door—the valley's major Nordic ski trail runs right by the property.

8020 Alpine Way, Whistler, BC V0N 1B8. www.edgewater-lodge.com. © **888/870-9065** or 604/ 932-0688. Fax 604/932-0686. 12 units. High season C$199–C$339 double; low season from C$155– C$185 double. AE, MC, V. Free parking. **Amenities:** Restaurant; lounge; Jacuzzi. *In room:* TV, hair dryer, Wi-Fi (free).

Hostelling International Whistler 🔧   One of the few inexpensive spots in Whistler, this brand-new purpose-built hostel served as part of the athletes' village during the 2010 Winter Olympics before opening to the public as a hostel. A reliable bus route (about a 30-min ride) connects the hostel to the ski slopes. There is an on-site cafe, lounge with a fireplace, common kitchen, TV lounge and game room, and storage for bikes, boards, and skis. In the summer, guests have use of a barbecue and outdoor patio. As with all hostels, most rooms and facilities are shared, but several private rooms with ensuite bathrooms (including showers) and TVs are available. Book by September at the latest for the winter ski season.

1035 Legacy Way, Whistler, BC V0N 1B1. www.hihostels.ca. © **866/762-4122** or 604/962-0025. 180 beds (in 14 private rooms & 4-bed dorms). C$85–C$145 private room (IYHA members), C$95– C$155 private room (nonmembers); C$31–C$36 shared room (members), C$35–C$40 shared room (nonmembers). Two-year adult membership C$35. MC, V. Free parking. Drive North along Hwy. 99 & turn right on Cheakamus Lake Rd. at Function Junction (first traffic light in Whistler), cross the bridge & continue on to Legacy Way. **Amenities:** Guest lounge; kitchen; ski storage; W-Fi (free).

Inn at Clifftop Lane ★★   This large home, built as a B&B, sits above the Whistler Village on a quiet side street just south of Whistler Creekside, and offers large and beautifully furnished rooms. The inn strikes that perfect balance between the hominess of a B&B and the formality of a small boutique hotel. Each of the guest rooms is spacious, with an easy chair and living area, plus a bathroom with a jetted tub and bathrobes. The home is filled with books and decorated with antiques and folk art collected during the owners' travels, lending a cheerful élan to the breakfast rooms and guest lounge. Outdoors, steps lead through the forest to a hot tub and a private deck. This is a great choice for travelers seeking understated comfort and elegance with friendly, professional service.

2828 Clifftop Lane, Whistler, BC V0N 1B2. www.innatclifftop.com. © **888/281-2929** or 604/938- 1229. Fax 604/938-9880. 5 units. Summer from C$125–C$145; winter from C$149–C$185. Ski packages available. Rates include full breakfast. AE, MC, V. Free parking. **Amenities:** Lounge; hot tub; ski storage; library. *In room:* TV w/DVD, hair dryer, Wi-Fi (free), robes, jetted tub.

Nita Lake Lodge ★★   Close to the restaurants and lifts at Whistler Creekside, Nita Lake Lodge has a woodsy feel without giving up a note of luxury. From the deep soaker tubs with adjacent rain showers in the spa-style bathrooms to fireplaces and covered balconies, the overall feel is pure coziness, snuggled up with finery. An on-site spa offers Ayurvedic treatments that tie in with restaurant dining options and yoga programs. Aura Restaurant is a burgeoning dining spot with chef Tim Cuff at the helm. The **Whistler Mountaineer** (p. 208) ends its Sea-to-Sky run at the station next door.

2131 Lake Placid Rd., Whistler, BC V0N 1B2. www.nitalakelodge.com. (𝒞 **888/755-6482** or 604/
966-5700. 77 units. C$229–$599 studio. C$269–C$649 1-bedroom. AE, MC, V. Valet parking C$30;
self-parking C$20. **Amenities:** Restaurants; bar; cafe: concierge; health club; Jacuzzi; room service;
sauna; spa; bikes; fishing rods. *In room:* A/C, TV, DVD, hair dryer, kitchenette, MP3 docking station,
Wi-Fi (free).

Where to Eat

Whistler overflows with dining choices, with cuisines ranging from Japanese to
Pacific Northwest. You'll have no trouble finding high-quality, reasonably priced food.
Ingrid's Village Café, just off the Village Square at 4305 Village Stroll (𝒞 **604/932-
7000**), is a locals' favorite for simple, homelike food, for both quality and price. A
large bowl of Ingrid's soup costs just C$4.50, while a veggie burger comes in at C$7.
It's open daily 7am to 6pm.

  Citta Bistro, in the Whistler Village Square (𝒞 **604/932-4177**), has a great
heated patio and serves thin-crust pizzas such as the Whistler, topped with Italian
ham, portabella mushrooms, and grilled peppers, as well as gourmet burgers such as
the Rancher, topped with balsamic onions, mozzarella, and barbecue sauce. Main
courses are C$12 to C$17; it's open daily 11am to 1am. The **Whistler Brewhouse,**
4355 Blackcomb Way (𝒞 **604/905-2739**), is a great spot for a microbrew ale, a
plate of wood-fired pizza or rotisserie chicken (C$16–C$37), and a seat on the patio;
open daily 11:30am to midnight, until 1am on weekends. **Sachi Sushi,** 4359 Main
St. (𝒞 **604/935-5649**), is the best of Whistler's many sushi restaurants—the udon
noodles and hot pots are excellent as well. Sushi rolls cost from C$8 to C$17; open
daily at 5pm, and Tuesday to Friday 12 to 2:30pm.

Araxi Restaurant & Bar ★★★ CONTEMPORARY CANADIAN   Frequently
awarded for its wine list, as well as voted best restaurant in Whistler, this is one of the
resort's top places to dine. Outside, the heated patio overlooks the village square, while
inside, the artwork, antiques, and terra-cotta tiles provide a subtle Mediterranean
ambience that serves as a theater for the presentation of extraordinary food. Diners
have a choice of a la carte items or a four-course tasting menu, which changes
monthly, for C$58. The kitchen makes the most of local ingredients such as house-
smoked trout, Pemberton cheese and lamb, and Howe Sound oysters. Executive Chef
James Walt has a deft hand, producing dishes that are inventive yet tradition-based
and full of flavor: steelhead trout is served with a squid risotto, the smoked pork rack
chop comes with salsa verde, and Agassiz hazelnuts accompany homemade ricotta
gnocchi. Don't hesitate to ask for a suggestion when contemplating the nearly encyclopedic wine list—the wine staff here is exceedingly friendly and knowledgeable.
4222 Village Sq. (𝒞 **604/932-4540.** www.araxi.com. Main courses C$20–C$38. AE, MC, V. Daily
11am–3pm and 5–10pm.

Bearfoot Bistro ★★★ PACIFIC NORTHWEST   One of the very best in Whistler, Barefoot Bistro has created an enormous following for its regional, seasonal
cuisine. The emphasis is on innovation, new flavors, and unusual preparations—in
short, this is a cutting-edge restaurant for serious gastronomes. In the dining room,
choose either three or five courses from the admirably broad menu, with selections
such as duck cassoulet, lamb with yellow chanterelles, and Arctic char with preserved
lemon and quinoa. There's nothing ordinary about the food, or the wine list, which
has earned awards from *Wine Spectator* magazine. The frozen-walled Belvedere ice
room is the setting for vodka tastings (C$36). A number of specialty tasting menus

are also available. Appetizers and more casual meals are available in the fireside room and the cozy Champagne Bar.

4121 Village Green. © **604/932-3433.** www.bearfootbistro.com. Reservations required on weekends. Tasting menus C$39–C$159. AE, DISC, MC, V. Daily 5–10pm.

Caramba! Restaurant MEDITERRANEAN   The room is bright and filled with the pleasant buzz of nattering diners. The kitchen is open, and the smells wafting out hint tantalizingly of fennel, artichoke, and pasta. Caramba! is casual dining, but its Mediterranean-influenced menu offers fresh ingredients, prepared with a great deal of pizzazz. Try the pasta, free-range chicken from the wood-fired rotisserie, or whole trout. Better still, if you're feeling especially good about your dining companions, order a pizza or two; a plate of grilled calamari; some hot spinach, cheese, and artichoke-and-shallot dips; and perhaps some sautéed chicken livers.

12–4314 Main St., Town Plaza. © **604/938-1879.** www.caramba-restaurante.com. Main courses C$13–C$39. AE, MC, V. Daily in summer 11:30am–10:30pm. In winter, Mon–Thurs 5–10pm, Fri–Sun 11:30am–10pm.

Ciao-Thyme Bistro and Fitz Pub ★ CASUAL/PACIFIC NORTHWEST 👜
This popular spot in the Upper Village is a favorite with locals and a dream come true for visitors who want to eat well on a limited budget. The space is small, and the lines can be long (reserve if you're coming for dinner), but the fresh, delicious food is worth the wait. The bistro is a great spot for breakfast (until 3pm), lunch, or dinner (the only meal they serve in the winter), with a simple menu that extends from free-range egg omelets to hearty soups (like the rich seafood chowder) and delicious sandwiches (try the pulled pork). The kids' menu features standards like grilled cheese sandwiches and pasta. Dinner options are a tad more upscale, with lobster tail risotto and roasted elk with barley. The menu is the same in both the bistro and the pub next door.

2-4573 Chateau Blvd., Upper Village. © **604/932-7051.** www.ciaothymebistro.com. Main courses C$13–C$26. AE, DC, MC, V. Spring–fall daily 8am–4pm & 6–10pm (closed Mon & Tues in May); winter daily 6–10pm.

Fifty Two 80 Bistro & Bar ★ SEAFOOD/CANADIAN   The suave lounge at the upscale Four Seasons Resort Whistler celebrates "fire and ice"—fire from the stone fireplace and dramatic backlit onyx panels and ice from the display of fresh fish and shellfish that greets diners. The design may be high-concept, but the food is more easygoing and hearty. For appetizers, the Pacific Northwest chowder, brimming with local seafood, is a great choice. Fish tacos, prime Canadian steaks, and fresh fish entrees round out the menu. There are a good selection of après ski pub snacks, from salmon sliders to lobster potato skins.

4591 Blackcomb Way (in the Four Seasons Whistler Resort). © **604/935-3400.** Reservations recommended. Main courses C$18–C$46. AE, DC, DISC, MC, V. Daily noon–midnight.

Rimrock Cafe and Oyster Bar ★★ SEAFOOD   Upstairs in a long, narrow room with a high ceiling and a massive stone fireplace at one end, Rimrock is very much like a Viking mead hall of old. It's not the atmosphere, however, that causes people to hop in a cab and make the C$5 journey out from Whistler Village. What draws folks in is the food. The first order of business should be a plate of oysters. Chef Rolf Gunther serves them up half a dozen ways, from raw with champagne to Rasputin with vodka and caviar. For my money, though, the signature Rimrock oyster is still the best: broiled with béchamel sauce and smoked salmon. Other appetizers are seared scallops or spinach salad with smoked duck. Main dishes are focused on seafood and game. Look for lobster and scallops with toasted almond butter and crispy leeks or pan-fried venison with porcini gnocchi. The accompanying wine list has a number of fine vintages from B.C., California, New Zealand, and Australia.

2117 Whistler Rd. (© **877/932-5589** or 604/932-5565. www.rimrockwhistler.com. Three-course menu C$49–C$68; main courses C$39–C$54. AE, MC, V. Daily 6–9:30pm.

21 Steps INTERNATIONAL/TAPAS   The steps in question lead up to a second-floor dining room overlooking the central plaza of Whistler Village—a great vantage point for enjoying well-priced, made-from-scratch food while you people-watch. The menu is divided into a selection of small and large plates, though servings are generous—a couple of small plates should appease the standard appetite. The cooking borrows a little from Asia, a little from Italy, but everything is prepared with gusto. My favorite is garlic chile prawns, scattered with scallions, peanuts, and crispy wontons. Combine that small plate with bite-size bacon-wrapped slices of filet mignon, served with horseradish aioli, and you've got a fine meal. On the third floor is a smaller, more intimate space called the Attic that serves as a lounge.

4433 Sundial Place (Whistler Village Square). (© **604/966-2121.** www.21steps.ca. Main courses C$15–C$30. AE, MC, V. Daily 5:30pm–midnight.

Whistler After Dark

For a town of just 10,000, Whistler has a more-than-respectable nightlife scene. You'll find concert listings in the *Pique,* a free local paper available at cafes and food stores. **Tommy Africa's,** 4216 Gateway Dr. (© **604/932-6090**), and the dark and cavernous **Maxx Fish,** in Whistler Village Square below the Amsterdam Cafe (© **604/932-1904**), cater to the 19- to 22-year-old crowd; you'll find lots of beat and not much light. The crowd at **Garfinkel's,** at the entrance to Village North (© **604/932-2323**), is similar, though the cutoff age can reach a little higher. The **Cinnamon Bear Bar** in the Hilton (© **604/966-5060**) and **Buffalo Bills,** across from the Whistler Gondola (© **604/932-6613**), cater to a more mature crowd. Bills has a pool table, a video ski machine, and a smallish dance floor. For a taste of everything, try the four- or five-bar **Whistler Club Crawl** (© **604/722-2633**; www.whistlerclubcrawl.com), which is a guided tour running on Thursday and Saturday nights. The C$50 per person cost includes dinner, five drinks, and cover charges.

NORTHERN BRITISH COLUMBIA

By Chloë Ernst

When you're talking about the "north" in Canada, you have to be careful. Although the following destinations are certainly northerly—at least a day's very long drive from Vancouver, or by a 15-hour ferry trip from Vancouver Island—most of the towns and sights are geographically in British Columbia's midsection. But by the time you reach Prince George or Prince Rupert, you'll feel the palpable sense of being in the north: The days are long in summer and short in winter, and the spruce forestlands have a primordial character. First Nations peoples make up a larger percentage of the population here than in more southerly areas, and Native communities and heritage sites are common.

One of the most dramatic ways to reach northern British Columbia is by ferry. The BC Ferries Inside Passage route operates between Port Hardy, on Vancouver Island, and Prince Rupert, on the mainland; this full-day ferry run passes through mystical land- and seascapes, with excellent wildlife-viewing opportunities. From Prince Rupert—a fishing town with an excellent First Nations arts museum—you can catch another ferry to Haida Gwaii, formerly known as the Queen Charlotte Islands, which lie truly on the backside of beyond. Part of these islands, the name of which means 'islands of the people' in the Haida language, is preserved as Gwaii Haanas National Park Reserve, a refuge of rare flora and fauna, and the ancient homeland of the Haida people.

Inland from Prince Rupert, the Yellowhead Highway (Hwy. 16) follows the mighty Skeena and Bulkley rivers past First Nations villages and isolated ranches, finally reaching Prince George, the largest city in northern British Columbia. Prince George is also a transportation gateway. Whether you're coming west from Edmonton, east from Prince Rupert, north from Vancouver, or south from Alaska, you'll pass through this city at the junction of the Fraser and Nechako rivers.

From Hwy. 16, there are two options for travelers who wish to explore realms even farther north. The famed 2,232km (1,387-mile) Alaska Highway—the only overland route to the 49th state—begins at Dawson Creek, BC, and officially ends in Delta Junction, AK. The first 974km (605 miles) of the route wind across northern British Columbia, through black-spruce forest and over the Continental Divide. The Alaska Highway exercises an irresistible attraction to die-hard road-trippers, many of them retirees with RVs. Another route north, the Stewart-Cassiar Highway, also labeled Hwy. 37, leaves the Yellowhead Highway west of the Hazeltons, cutting behind the towering Coast Mountains to eventually join the Alaska Highway in the Yukon.

Frigid weather and short days make winter travel difficult in northern British Columbia; rather, explore this beautiful wilderness landscape under the glow of the summer's midnight sun.

THE INSIDE PASSAGE ★ & DISCOVERY COAST

The ferry cruise along British Columbia's Inside Passage combines the best scenic elements of Norway's rocky fjords, Chile's Patagonian range, and Nova Scotia's wild coastline. While many people experience the Inside Passage as part of an expensive Alaska cruise, you can see the same scenery for far less money on a BC ferry. **BC Ferries** (© **888/BC-FERRY** [223-3779] or 250/386-3431; www.bcferries.com) operates the **Inside Passage ferry** between Port Hardy (see chapter 8) and Prince Rupert (on the mainland, see below), with occasional stops at the small island communities of Bella Bella and Klemtu. These mid-route stopovers became so popular that, in 1996, the company added the **Discovery Coast ferry** to its schedule. Dedicated to serving remote coastal villages, the ferry weaves through islands to the Discovery Coast communities of Bella Coola, Ocean Falls, Denny Island (Shearwater), Bella Bella, and Klemtu. The BC Ferries system also connects Prince Rupert to remote **Haida Gwaii**, the ancestral home of the Haida people (see later in this chapter).

For information on the region, go to the **Northern BC Tourism Association** website at www.hellobc.com/nbc. You can also contact the **Prince Rupert Visitor Centre** at 100 1st Ave W., Prince Rupert, BC V8J 1A8 (© **800/667-1994** or 250/624-5637; www.visitprincerupert.com); or the **Prince George Visitor Centre,** 1300 First Ave. (© **800/668-7646** or 250/562-3700; www.tourismpg.com), as starting points for your enquiries.

The Inside Passage ★★

Fifteen hours may seem like a long time to be on a boat. But you'll never get bored as the **Inside Passage ferry** noses its way through an incredibly scenic series of channels and calm inlets, flanked by green, forested islands. Whales, porpoises, salmon, bald eagles, and sea lions line the route past the mostly uninhabited coastline. This 507km (315-mile) BC Ferries run between Port Hardy and Prince Rupert follows the same route as expensive Alaska-bound cruise ships, but at a fraction of the cost. Two boats service the route: the MV **Northern Adventure** ★, with luxurious-feeling cabins and a glassed-in viewing gallery, and the MV **Northern Expedition.** The ferry from Port Hardy initially crosses a couple hours' worth of open sea through Smith Sound—where waters can be rough—before ducking behind Calvert Island. Except for a brief patch of open sea in the Milbanke Sound north of Bella Bella, the rest of the trip follows a narrow, protected channel between the mainland and a series of islands.

The actual Inside Passage begins north of Bella Bella, where the ferry slips along the shorelines of mountainous Princess Royal and Pitt islands. The channel between the islands and the mainland is very narrow—often less than a mile wide. The scenery is extraordinarily dramatic: Black cliffs drop thousands of feet directly into the channel, notched with hanging glacial valleys and fringed with forests. Powerful waterfalls shoot from dizzying heights into the sea. Eagles float along thermal drafts, and porpoises cavort in the ferry's wake. Even in poor conditions (the weather is very unpredictable here), this is an amazing trip.

Mid-May through September, either the 117m (384-ft.) *Northern Adventure* ferry or 150m (492-ft.) *Northern Expedition* cross every other day, leaving Port Hardy (or, heading southbound, from Prince Rupert) at 7:30am and arriving in Prince Rupert (or, Port Hardy) at 10:30pm. In midsummer, with the north's long days, the trip is made almost entirely in daylight. Both ferries carry more than 600 passengers and crew, as well as more than 100 vehicles. You can wander around the decks, choosing from indoor lounges with wide windows and an ever-changing view, or outside deck seating. On board you'll find a cafeteria, restaurant, snack bar, playroom, and gift shop. Midsummer one-way, peak-season fares between Prince Rupert and Port Hardy are C$180 per adult car passenger or walk-on, C$410 for a normal-size vehicle. A car with two passengers totals C$770; fuel surcharges are sometimes added. Reservations are mandatory. The ship's cabins rent for between C$90 and C$120 for day use. Ferry service to/from Prince Rupert and Port Hardy continues at least once weekly the rest of the year, with somewhat lower fares; service, however, runs overnight, not during the day, as in summer. See the BC Ferries website for dates and prices. In summer, the ferry leaves both Prince Rupert and Port Hardy at 7:30am, so under normal circumstances, you'll arrive at your destination at 10:30pm—thus you probably won't need a cabin to sleep in. You should, however, make lodging reservations at your destination in advance; by the time the ship docks and you wait to drive your car off, it can be close to midnight.

At Prince Rupert, you can also catch an **Alaska Marine Highway ferry** (© **800/ 642-0066;** www.dot.state.ak.us/amhs), which stops here on its run between Bellingham, Washington, and Skagway, Alaska. Passenger fare from Prince Rupert to Skagway is US$171 per adult; a car and two adult passengers starts at US$716. The trip from Prince Rupert to Skagway can range anywhere from 35 to 50 or more hours, depending on the number of stops.

The Discovery Coast Passage

Also departing from Port Hardy, the Discovery Coast's **MV *Queen of Chilliwack*** (which is slated to be replaced in the near future) connects small, mostly First Nations communities along the fjords and islands of the northern coast, including Bella Bella, Shearwater, Ocean Falls, and Klemtu. The most popular part of this run is the summer-only service to Bella Coola, which links to Hwy. 20, a paved and gravel road that's a day's drive from Williams Lake, in central British Columbia's Fraser Valley (see "Williams Lake" in chapter 11). There are three variations on the route.

In summer, a direct ferry runs northbound on Thursday to Bella Coola. On Tuesday the route is a circular run with stops in Bella Bella and Shearwater before the ferry docks in Bella Coola and returns to Port Hardy. The Saturday circuit goes to the above ports as well as Klemtu and Ocean Falls before returning via Bella Coola (there's a map on the BC Ferries website to help you make sense of the different routings). The Tuesday departure requires a night on the boat; the Thursday trip is completed within the day; and the Saturday departure requires 2 nights aboard. In high season, fares between Port Hardy and Bella Coola are C$180 per adult passenger and C$355 for a car. Note that there is no reason to take a car to any of these destinations except for Bella Coola, as there is otherwise no road system to drive on.

For sleeping, you might snag one of the extra-wide reclining seats. Otherwise, BC Ferries recommends bringing a tent or cot, which you can set up on the leeward side of the boat. You can rent pillows and blankets; lockers and showers are available. Pets are allowed on board, but must remain in vehicles on the car deck; owners can descend to those decks to tend to their pets' needs.

PRINCE RUPERT

491km (305 miles) N of Port Hardy; 756km (470 miles) W of Prince George

British Columbia's most northerly coastal city, Prince Rupert (pop. 13,000) is a city in transition. For years a major fishing and timber port, it is now turning to tourism to bolster its economy. Although scarcely a fancy place, Prince Rupert has much to offer travelers. Eco-tourism has taken off, sport fishing is excellent in local rivers and in the protected waters of Chatham Sound, and the town is a convenient hub for exploring yet more distant sights of the Pacific Northwest. From here, ferries go north to Alaska, west to Haida Gwaii, and south to Vancouver Island and Bellingham, Washington.

Prince Rupert exudes a hardworking, good-natured vigor, and the population is a well-integrated mix of First Nations and European-heritage Canadians. You'll experience the palpable sense of being on the northern edge of the world, which gives the city—situated on a series of rock ledges above the broad expanse of the Pacific—a sense of purpose and vitality.

Essentials

GETTING THERE   By Ferry   For information on BC Ferries service from Port Hardy and Alaska Marine Highway service between southeast Alaska and Washington, see "The Inside Passage," above. For information on BC Ferries service to Haida Gwaii, see later in this chapter.

By Train   A **VIA Rail** (© **888/VIA-RAIL** [842-7245]; www.viarail.ca) train, the *Skeena*, operates between Prince Rupert and Prince George 3 days weekly. One-way fares start at C$73 and the train follows the same route as the Yellowhead Highway along the scenic Skeena River valley. At Prince George, travelers can continue to Jasper, with connections to the main VIA Rail line between Vancouver and Toronto.

By Plane   Air Canada (© **888/247-2262;** www.aircanada.ca) provides service between Vancouver and Prince Rupert. **Hawkair** (© **800/487-1216;** www.hawkair. ca) also offers daily service from Vancouver.

Both these airlines fly into Prince Rupert's Digby Island airport, which is indeed on an island. Upon collecting their luggage, arriving passengers board a bus that meets every scheduled flight and transports all passengers to the ferry terminal. Once there, the entire bus boards the ferry and crosses to Prince Rupert. The bus deposits the passengers at the Highliner Plaza Hotel (815 1st Ave. W.). Taxis are available. The bus/ferry fare from the airport to Prince Rupert is included in your airline ticket so there's no fee assessed for the service while you're traveling. The entire voyage takes roughly 35 minutes. While this process may sound complex, in fact it's as simple as collecting your luggage and getting on the bus. The driver takes care of the rest. To catch a flight from Digby Island, the process works in reverse. Meet the airport bus at the Highliner Plaza Hotel. Once loaded, it proceeds across the ferry to the airport. Call the airport bus at © **250/622-2222** to find out when the bus leaves for your flight.

By Car   Prince Rupert is the terminus of the Yellowhead Highway, Canada's most northerly transcontinental roadway. Between Prince Rupert and Prince George, the route is 722km (449 miles) of extraordinary scenery. For car rentals, call **National** (*C* **800/CAR-RENT** [227-7368] or 250/624-5318; www.nationalcar.com). If you are planning on renting a car while in Prince Rupert, reserve well in advance, as the cars get snapped up fast, especially on days when trains or ferries arrive.

By Bus   Greyhound Canada (*C* **800/661-8747** or 250/624-5090; www. greyhound.ca) serves Prince Rupert and Prince George with two buses daily each way in summer. The one-way fare is about C$130, with discounts available for advanced or online purchase.

VISITOR INFORMATION   The **Prince Rupert Visitor Centre,** 100 First Ave. West (*C* **800/667-1994** in Canada, or 250/624-5637; www.tourismprincerupert. com), is in the prominent longhouse-style Museum of Northern BC (see below), about 2km (1¼ miles) from Hwy. 16. The center is open daily June through September (or when the last cruise ship visits) and Tuesday through Saturday year-round.

Exploring the Area

Prince Rupert gets more than 17 hours of sunlight a day in summer. And despite its far-north location, this coastal city enjoys a mild climate most of the year. Mountain biking, cross-country skiing, fishing, kayaking, hiking, and camping are just a few of the region's popular activities.

Northern British Columbia's rich First Nations (Native Canadian) heritage has been preserved in Prince Rupert's museums and archaeological sites. But you don't need to visit a museum to get a sense of the community's history. Relics of the city's early days are apparent in its old storefronts, miners' shacks, and churches. Built on a series of rocky escarpments, the city rises ledge by ledge, starting at the harbor with the train station and the **Kwinitsa Railway Museum** (*C* **250/627-1915** or 250/ 627-3207). This area is overlooked by the old commercial center, with several blocks of turn-of-the-20th-century storefronts still busy with commerce.

The bustling **Cow Bay** district on the north waterfront, with galleries, seafood restaurants, and gift shops, is Prince Rupert's major center for tourist activity. Just south of Atlin Terminal is Prince Rupert's cruise-ship dock, which serves a number of cruise lines. The downtown area is overlooked by the historic residential area, which is dominated by massive stone churches.

Museum of Northern British Columbia ★   This museum displays artifacts of the Tsimshian, Nisga'a, Tlingit, and Haida First Nations, who have inhabited this coast for more than 10,000 years. There are also artifacts and photographs from Prince Rupert's 19th-century European settlement. In summer, the museum sponsors a number of special programs, including heritage and totem walking tours of Prince Rupert. The gift shop is one of the best places in town to buy Native art. The carving shed, sponsored by the museum, has closed. But ask at the museum to see if there may be an artisan group renting the space.

100 First Ave. West *C* **250/624-3207.** Fax 250/627-8009. www.museumofnorthernbc.com. Admission C$5 adults, C$2 students, C$1 children 6–11, C$10 families. Summer Mon–Sat 9am–8pm, Sun 9am–5pm; winter Mon–Sat 9am–5pm.

North Pacific Cannery National Historic Site ★★   Salmon canning was one of the region's original industries, back when the salmon run up the Skeena River was one of the greatest in North America. The province's oldest remaining salmon

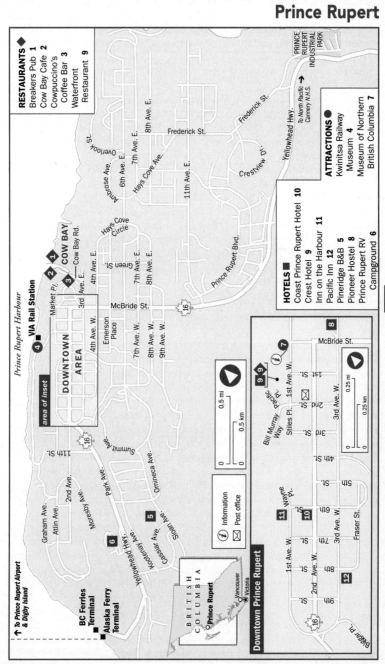

cannery, the village was built on the waterfront of Inverness Passage in 1889 and was home to hundreds of First Nations, Japanese, Chinese, and European workers and their families. Every summer, fishing fleets dropped off their catches at the cannery, where the salmon was packed and shipped out to world markets. This company-owned community reached its apex from 1910 to 1950, when the workforce numbered 400 and the community grew to about 1,200; the cannery has been closed since 1968.

Now a National Historic Site, the North Pacific Cannery complex includes the cannery building, various administration buildings and residences, the company store, a hotel, and a dining hall—a total of over 25 structures linked by a long boardwalk (the land is so steep here that most of the houses were built on wharves). Workers were segregated by race: the Chinese, Japanese, and First Nations workers had their own micro-neighborhoods along the boardwalk, all overseen by the European bosses. Guided tours of the cannery complex, offered on the hour, provide a very interesting glimpse into a forgotten way of life.

The **boardinghouse** now operates as historically authentic lodging, the **Bunkhouse Hostel,** which is rustic but clean and cheerful with small rooms and squeaky floors—a very unique experience. Doubles cost from C$45 for one bed or C$65 for two. The **Mess Hall Café** is open during museum hours.

20km (12 miles) south of Prince Rupert in Port Edward. Mailing address: Box 1104, Port Edward, BC V0V 1G0. ℰ **250/628-3538.** www.northpacificcannery.ca. Admission C$12 adults, C$6 students 5–18, free for children 4 and under, and C$25 families. July and Aug daily 9:30am–5pm (Thurs till 8pm); May, June, and Sept Tues–Sun 9:30am–5pm. Closed Oct–Apr. Take the Port Edward turnoff on Hwy. 16 and drive 5km (3 miles) past Port Edward on Skeena Dr.

Archaeological, Wildlife & Adventure Tours

Prince Rupert is at the center of an amazingly scenic area, but unless you have your own boat, you'll find it hard to get around. A good option is to sign on with a local tour operator. One of the most unusual excursions is the **Pike Island Natural and Historical Discovery Tour,** given by Tsimshian guides. Tiny Pike Island, called Laxspa'aws by the Tsimshian, is 9km (5⅔ miles) from Prince Rupert in Venn Passage, and is at the center of a rich archaeological area that was once one of the most densely populated regions in pre-Contact Native America. The island has three village sites that were abandoned 18 to 20 centuries ago. Although none have been excavated, guides point out the house depressions in the forest floor and discuss the midden deposits, the shellfish and bone piles that were essentially the garbage pits of these prehistoric people. The 3.5-hour tours are offered from May to Labour Day on a varying schedule; they cost C$57 adults, C$44 children 5 to 12, and children 4 and under free. The trails on the island are not difficult, but are not wheelchair accessible. The Pike Island tours are offered by **Seashore Charters** (ℰ **800/667-4393** or 250/624-5645; www.seashorecharters.com), which has an office at Atlin Terminal. Seashore Charters offer a variety of other tours, including whale- and grizzly-watching.

One of Prince Rupert's most unique adventures takes you to Canada's only wildlife preserve dedicated to the grizzly bear. Access to the **Khutzeymateen Grizzly Bear Preserve,** northwest of Prince Rupert, is highly restricted, and a very limited number of outfitters can offer trips to this pristine wilderness, home to abundant numbers of *Ursus horribilis.* There's no other access to the preserve, and humans are forbidden to actually land. Although **Prince Rupert Adventure Tours** (ℰ **800/201-8377** or 250/627-9166; www.adventuretours.net) is not one of the outfitters that are allowed into the Khutzeymateen preserve itself, this outfitter does offer affordable day trips to the inlet near the wilderness area. Of course the grizzlies don't recognize boundaries, so the chances of viewing bears, as well as other wildlife such as eagles, seals, and mountain goats, is excellent, as they come down to the shoreline to gorge on sedge grass. A 6-hour trip, including a sack lunch, is offered May through July and costs C$195 for adults. **Seashore Charters** (✆ **800/667-4393** or 250/624-5645; www. seashorecharters.com) also offers full-day tours to the inlet for C$149 adults, C$112 children 5 to 12, and children 4 and under free.

For a historical self-guided walking tour of the city, contact the **Museum of Northern BC** (✆ **250/624-3207**), which sells walking-tour booklets for C$2. If a cruise ship is docked, there will likely be guided tours. Check with the visitor center.

Other Outdoor Pursuits

FISHING   Prince Rupert is famed for its excellent sportfishing. There are dozens of charter operators based in town. The **Prince Rupert Visitor Centre,** in the same building as the Museum of Northern BC, (✆ **800/667-1994** in Canada, or 250/ 624-5637; www.visitprincerupert.com), can steer you to the one that best serves your needs.

Fishing charters can range in length from a half-day to a weeklong trip, and range in facilities from rough-and-ready boats to luxury cruisers. Expect a guided trip to cost from C$500 per person per day. Long-established companies include **Frohlich's Fish Guiding** (✆ **250/627-8443;** www.fishprincerupert.com) and **Predator Fishing Charters** (✆ **250/627-1993**).

HIKING   Far West Sports, 125 First Ave W. (✆ **250/624-2568**), is one of the best sources of information about hiking and mountain-biking trails. The area experiences annual as well as seasonal changes in trail conditions, and some hiking and backcountry ski areas are too challenging for beginners. There are a number of good hiking options right in Prince Rupert. One trail follows Hays Creek from McBride Street down to the harbor. Just 6.4km (4 miles) east on Hwy. 16 is a trail head for three more wilderness hikes. The 4km (2.5-mile) loop **Butze Rapids Trail** winds through wetlands to Grassy Bay and to Butze Rapids, a series of tidal cataracts. The sometimes-steep trail to the **Tall Trees** grove of old-growth cedars and to the viewpoint on **Mount Oldfield** requires more stamina. Check with the visitor center for more information.

KAYAKING & CANOEING   The waters surrounding Prince Rupert are tricky, and rough tidal swells and strong currents are common. **Skeena Kayaking** (✆ **250/624-5246;** www.skeenakayaking.ca) offers kayak trips along the Skeena River. A 4-hour ocean kayak rental is C$50 at the harborside location.

Where to Stay

The **Pioneer Hostel,** 167 Third Ave. E. (www.pioneerhostel.com; ✆ **888/794-9998** or 250/624-2334), is in a historic rooming house within easy walking distance of both downtown and Cow Bay. Pioneer Hostel is well-run and clean and is perhaps one of the smartest-looking in the province with its summer flower baskets. Accommodations run from C$22 to C$80 a person.

A mile from the ferry terminal, **Prince Rupert RV Campground,** 1750 Park Ave. (www.princerupertrv.com; ✆ **250/627-1000**), has 77 full-hookup and 10 unserviced sites, plus open areas for tent camping. Facilities include laundry, showers, toilets, playground, phones, and free Wi-Fi. Reserve in advance in summer. Rates range from C$21 for tenters to C$35 for RVs.

Coast Prince Rupert Hotel Right downtown, the six-story Coast offers views of the harbor and mountains from just about every spacious room. Rooms are well maintained and feature standard business travel furnishings. A 2011 renovation gave the rooms a stylish upgrade. Breakfast and lunch is available daily at Charlie's, just off the lobby, while dinner, drinks, and entertainment are served at the sports bar Johnny B's. There's dancing at the basement club The Underground.

118 Sixth St., Prince Rupert, BC V8J 3L7. www.coasthotels.com. © **800/716-6199** or 250/624-6711. Fax 250/624-3288. 93 units. From C$139 double. Extra person C$15. Family plan, corporate, and off-season rates, and senior and AAA discounts available. AE, DC, DISC, MC, V. **Amenities:** Restaurant; lounge; night club; guest passes to full-service health club; room service; beer-and-wine store. *In room:* A/C, TV, fridge (on request), hair dryer, Wi-Fi (free).

Crest Hotel ★ The Crest offers the best views in town, good dining, and beautifully furnished, though not expansive, rooms. Situated on the bluff's edge overlooking Tuck Inlet, Metlakatla Pass, and the harbor, this is one of the finest hotels in northern British Columbia. The rooms feature quality furniture, feather duvets, and a relaxed stylishness. Standard rooms come with either two doubles or one queen-size bed; suites feature king-size beds. The top-floor suites have the added luxury of loft ceilings, and the harborside rooms feature down duvets. The wood-paneled lobby and common rooms are opulent, and it's hard to imagine more impressive views anywhere than from the jutting outdoor hot tub and the well-equipped fitness room. The staff will happily set you up with fishing charters and wildlife-viewing trips. The Waterfront Restaurant is the best in town (see "Where to Eat," below), and Charley's Lounge, with a heated deck, has the city's best year-round view from a bar stool.

222 First Ave. W., Prince Rupert, BC V8J 1A8. www.cresthotel.bc.ca. © **800/663-8150** or 250/624-6771. Fax 250/627-7666. 102 units. C$144–C$199 double; C$239–C$309 suite. AE, DISC, MC, V. Free parking. Small pets allowed for C$25. **Amenities:** Restaurant; coffee shop; bar; exercise room; Jacuzzi; room service; sauna. *In room:* TV, fridge (on request) hair dryer, Wi-Fi (free).

Inn on the Harbour 🛏 A true water's edge lodging, the Inn on the Harbour is perched above the waterfront and boasts rooms with quiet, ocean views. The soft colors are well-suited to travelers seeking a restful stay. Four rooms have luxe Euro-style bathrooms with heated floors and soaker tubs. Rooms on the water side have binoculars. The property is non-smoking and has barrier-free rooms available.

720 First Ave. W., Prince Rupert, BC V8J 3V6. www.innontheharbour.com. © **800/663-8155** or 250/624-9107. Fax 250/627-8232. 49 units. June–Sept C$149–C$165 double. Oct–May C$129–C$145 double. Rates include continental breakfast. Senior discounts available. AE, MC, V. *In room:* TV, fridge, hairdryer. Wi-Fi (free).

Pacific Inn This motor lodge is a reasonable value for its large, basic rooms in a convenient location, midway between downtown and the ferry docks. The owners take pride in the place, but it's still a bit rough around the edges. It's good for crashing late night after arriving on the ferry. The front desk will arrange local tours and activities.

909 Third Ave. W., Prince Rupert, BC V8J 1M9. www.pacificinn.bc.ca. © **888/663-1999** or 250/627-1711. Fax 250/627-4212. 77 units. C$100–C$175 double. Rates include continental breakfast. Off-season rates and senior discounts available. AE, MC, V. Pets allowed for C$10. **Amenities:** Restaurant. *In room:* TV, fridge (on request), hair dryer, Wi-Fi (free).

Pineridge B&B ★★ 🍴 This very attractive B&B sits above the town, between downtown and the ferry terminals, and offers the largest and most sophisticated rooms in Prince Rupert. The uncluttered bedrooms are furnished with quality art (the owners previously had a gallery in town) and feature soothing colors, handsome pine furniture, and nice touches such as bathrobes and down duvets. Guests share a large sitting room with a TV (there are none in the rooms), fridge, couches, a library, phone, and games. The traditional European breakfast is a highlight of the stay. The entire house is tastefully decorated with clean-lined, modern furnishings and local art and crafts. The friendly hosts will help you plan activities and arrange charters.

1714 Sloan Ave., Prince Rupert, BC V8J 3Z9. www.pineridge.bc.ca. © **888/733-6733** or 250/627-4419. Fax 250/624-2366. 3 units. C$99 double (taxes included). Rates include full breakfast. MC, V. Closed Oct–Mar. Follow signs to ferry terminal, turn left (or from ferry turn right) onto Smithers St., go 2 blocks, and turn right onto Sloan Ave. Not suitable for children. *In room:* Hair dryer, phone (on request), Wi-Fi (free).

Where to Eat

Cowpuccino's Coffee Bar, 25 Cow Bay Rd. (© **250/627-1395**), is a friendly, slightly funky coffee shop with good homemade muffins at breakfast and desserts in the evening. **Java dot Cup,** 516 Third Ave West (© **250/622-2822**), serves good coffee and also operates as an Internet cafe.

Breakers Pub ★ PUB   Breakers is a popular pub with a harbor view and well-prepared bar food, like club and steak sandwiches. The offerings range from salads and wraps to pasta, pizza, and grilled local fish. This is a hopping social spot, with a game room and dance floor; the young and prosperous of Prince Rupert gather here to get happy with a microbrew or two.

117 George Hills Way (on the Cow Bay Wharf). © **250/624-5990.** www.breakerspub.ca. Reservations not needed. Main courses C$8–C$24. AE, MC, V. Mon–Thurs 11:30am–11pm; Fri–Sat 11:30am–1am; Sun noon–midnight.

Cow Bay Café ★ PACIFIC NORTHWEST   This homey place is like a little Vancouver neighborhood cafe plunked down on the edge of a dock. The casual, slightly hippie atmosphere feels refreshing so far north, and is nicely matched by the menu, which features lots of vegetarian options. Choices include salads, pastas, soups, and sandwiches; at night, fresh fish is prepared with zest. Order dessert when you order the rest of your meal, because popular items often sell out by the end of the evening.

205 Cow Bay Rd. © **250/627-1212.** Reservations recommended. Main courses C$11–C$29. AE, MC, V. Tues noon–2:30pm; Wed–Sat noon–2:30pm and 6–8:30pm.

Waterfront Restaurant ★★ PACIFIC NORTHWEST   Easily Prince Rupert's most sophisticated restaurant, the Waterfront is flanked by banks of windows that overlook the busy harbor. The white-linen-and-crystal elegance of the dining room is matched by the inventiveness of the cuisine. Understandably, much of the menu is devoted to local seafood; Fisherman's Chowder features cream and thyme broth spiked with salmon, halibut, and shrimp. Pan-fried halibut cheeks are topped with three-mustard and caper berry sauce. "Casual plates" feature smaller portions, salads, and tempting appetizers such as seared sea scallops with mango salsa. The wine list features a number of impressive B.C. vintages.

In the Crest Hotel, 222 First Ave. W. © **250/624-6771.** www.cresthotel.bc.ca. Reservations suggested. Main courses C$11–C$40. AE, DISC, MC, V. Mon–Fri 6:30am–10pm; Sat and Sun 7am–10pm.

HAIDA GWAII

The misty and mysterious islands of Haida Gwaii were the muse for 19th-century painter Emily Carr, who documented her impressions of the towering totem poles and longhouses at the abandoned village of Ninstints, on Anthony Island. The islands still lure artists, writers, and photographers wishing to experience their haunting beauty.

Haida Gwaii—officially renamed from the Queen Charlotte Islands in 2009—is the homeland of the Haida people. Sometimes referred to as the Vikings of the Pacific, the Haida were mighty seafarers, and during raiding forays, ranged as far south along the Pacific Coast as Oregon. The Haida were also excellent artists, carvers of both totems and argillite, a slatelike rock that they transformed into tiny totemic sculptures and pendants. The Haida today make up about half of the islands' population of 6,000.

Haida Gwaii has a reputation as the "Canadian Galapagos," as these islands—ranging between 51 and 136km (32–85 miles) from the mainland—have evolved their own endemic species and subspecies of flora and fauna. The Haida Nation designated a region of the island a Haida Heritage Site in 1985 and the Canadian government later preserved the southern portion of Moresby Island as **Gwaii Haanas National Park Reserve and Haida Heritage Site ★★**. UNESCO named SGang Gwaay a World Heritage Site in 1981. In 2010, a marine conservation area has been added to the protected region, continuing the shared stewardship of the area.

The islands are primordial and beautiful, but visiting them requires some planning. In fact, if you're reading this in Prince Rupert and thinking about a spur-of-the-moment trip to the islands, you may want to call ahead to check availability. Lodging is limited, and reservations are necessary in high season. The most interesting areas—the abandoned Haida villages—are accessible only by boat or plane, and Gwaii Haanas limits the number of people who can access the archaeological sites each day. There are only 125km (78 miles) of paved roads, and none of them even come close to the park or the islands' wild western coastline. In short, simply showing up on Haida Gwaii is not a good idea. The best way to visit is by arranging, in advance, to join a guide or outfitter on a kayaking, flightseeing, sailing, or boating excursion.

That said, there are day-trip options into the park as well as lots to do and see around the other islands of Haida Gwaii, be it taking a totem tour, visiting the excellent heritage museum, or fishing for crabs on North Beach.

Essentials

GETTING THERE   By Ferry   BC Ferries (© **888/BC-FERRY** [223-3779] in B.C., or 250/386-3431; www.bcferries.com) crosses between Prince Rupert and Skidegate, on northerly Graham Island. The 6½- to 7-hour Hecate Strait crossing can be quite rough; take precautions if you're prone to seasickness. Ferries run daily in summer; call ahead to reserve. The one-way high-season tickets are C$41 for a passenger and C$147 for most passenger vehicles.

By Plane   Air Canada (© **888/247-2262;** www.aircanada.ca) provides daily flights from Vancouver to Sandspit Airport on northern Moresby Island. **Pacific Coastal Airlines** (© **800/663-2872** or 604/273-8666; www.pacific-coastal.com) provides daily service from Vancouver's South Terminal to Masset during the summer and service Sundays to Fridays during the shoulder and winter season. **North Pacific Seaplanes** (© **800/689-4234** or 250/627-1341; www.northpacificseaplanes.com), based in Prince Rupert, offers daily floatplane service to Masset.

VISITOR INFORMATION   The **Queen Charlotte Visitor Centre,** 3220 Wharf St., Queen Charlotte (© **250/559-8316;** www.qcinfo.ca), is generally open daily May through September. The info center offers a booking and reservation service, as well as a board to connect with other travelers to share charters into the park.

GETTING AROUND   In Haida Gwaii, the island-to-island **Skidegate–Alliford Bay ferry** operates 12 daily sailings between the main islands. The return fare is C$8.75 or C$20 per vehicle. With so few roads on the islands, it's fair to ask if it even makes sense to take a car on a short trip. **Budget** (© **800/577-3228** or 250/637-5688; www.budget.com) has a bureau at the Sandspit airport; **Rustic Car Rentals** (© **250/559-4641**) has an office in Queen Charlotte City. Some lodgings also offer car rentals. If renting a vehicle, do not drive on North Beach, or any of the other beaches on the island. Unless you have four-wheel-drive stay off the sand. Locals can likely tell you a story or two about cars being stranded and lost to the rising tide.

Exploring the Islands

Most visitors come to Haida Gwaii to view its abundant and unusual wildlife, and to visit the ancient Haida villages. In both cases, you'll need to either have your own boat or arrange for a guide to get you from the islands' small settlements to the even more remote areas. The islands provide superlative wilderness adventures—camping, hiking, diving, sailing, kayaking, and fishing—although due to their isolation and sometimes extreme weather, you'll need to plan ahead before setting out.

Graham Island is the northern and more populous of the two major islands. **Queen Charlotte City** is a fishing and logging town with a population of about 1,000, sitting above the scenic waters of Beaverskin Bay. Charlotte, as the village is most often dubbed, has the majority of lodgings and facilities for travelers.

Skidegate Village (pronounced "*Skid*-a-gut"), just east of the Skidegate ferry terminal, is home to the **Haida Heritage Centre at K'aay Llnagaay** (© **250/559-4643;** www.haidaheritagecentre.com), which includes the Haida Gwaii Museum, which houses the world's largest collection of argillite carvings, made from the slate-like stone found only in Haida Gwaii. The expansive waterfront facility encompasses 149 sq. m (16,000 sq. ft.) and displays historic totem poles, contemporary and historic Haida art, and extensive photo archives. Admission is C$15 for adults, C$10 students 13 to 18, and C$5 for children 6 to 12. The museum is open daily June to August 10am to 6pm, and Tuesday to Saturday 10am to 5pm from September to May (closed Dec 25–Jan 5). As well, the heritage center has the information and orientation center for **Gwaii Haanas National Park Reserve** (see below).

Along the highway in Skidegate is the office of the **Haida Gwaii Watchmen,** the Native guardians of the islands' Haida villages and heritage sites. Ask at the office for information on visiting these sites.

Heading north from Skidegate on Hwy. 16, **Tlell** is an old agricultural community and now somewhat of an artists' colony; watch for signs pointing to studios. The lone road passes the logging town of Port Clements, the home of the legendary Golden Spruce. The Haida revered the rare, glowing-yellow sitka spruce tree as sacred, but in 1997 an unemployed logger cut it down in protest of industrial logging.

The highway ends at **Masset,** one of the island's largest towns with a population pushing 1,000. **Old Massett,** just north of Masset, is a good place to shop for carvings and jewelry and in recent years has raised a number of totems in front of public buildings. These make a perfect impromptu driving or walking tour. Just north of the

Masset town center, trails lead through the **Delkatla Wildlife Sanctuary,** one of the first southerly landfalls on the Pacific Flyway.

From Masset, continue north and then east on Tow Hill Road to **Naikoon Provincial Park,** where whales can be spotted from the beaches and peregrine falcons fly overhead. The **Agate Beach Campground** (no reservations taken) is a popular place to camp (C$16).

On southern **Moresby Island,** the principal center of population is **Sandspit** (pop. 460). In summer, Parks Canada operates an information center for visitors headed to the wilderness **Gwaii Haanas National Park Reserve, National Marine Conservation Area Reserve, and Haida Heritage Site ★**. The long name indicates the cooperative management that preserves the full ecosystem and heritage of Gwaii Haanas. There are no roads or shore facilities, and access is by boat or floatplane only. Although there are many amazing sights in this part of Haida Gwaii, you'll need to be committed to the journey to get here: The distances are great and the costs high. A few day-trip options do make the area far more accessible, however, and if you're a dedicated wildlife watcher, it may be worth it to see the rare fauna and flora.

Perhaps the most famous site in the park is **SGang Gwaay,** or **Ninstints,** on Anthony Island, an ancient Native village revered as sacred ground by the modern-day Haida. Centuries-old totem poles and longhouses proudly stand in testimony to the culture's 10,000-year heritage. Other frequented villages and sites in the park include Skedans on Louise Island and Hot Spring Island.

Only a limited number of people are allowed to enter Gwaii Haanas per day, and these are apportioned between those on organized tours and those traveling independently. You must make a reservation and register your trip with park authorities, and also attend a mandatory orientation session before entering the park. To make a reservation contact Gwaii Haanas directly: **Gwaii Haanas National Park Reserve,** Box 37, Queen Charlotte City, BC V0T 1S0 (𝒞 **877/559-8818** or 250/559-8818; www.pc.gc.ca/gwaiihaanas). Entry to the park is C$20 per day. The **Haida Gwaii Watchmen** (𝒞 **250/559-8225**) manage access to SGang Gwaay and other ancient villages in the park, and watchmen members who are stationed on the islands will explain the history and cultural significance of the sites you may visit. For travel information, contact **Queen Charlotte Visitor Centre** (𝒞 **250/559-8316**; www.qcinfo.ca).

Tours & Excursions to Gwaii Haanas National Park Reserve

By far the easiest and most convenient way of visiting Gwaii Haanas is by joining a guided tour. Outfitters must be registered with park officials; the list of authorized tour operators is the best place to start shopping for expeditions into the park. Note that the park entry fee of C$20 per day may or may not be included in the cost of tour packages, so ask when booking. Day trips into Gwaii Haanas are the shortest option for getting a sense of the Haida culture, logging history, and natural diversity in the islands. Most trips head to Skedans, an ancient village site where totems that Emily Carr painted slowly decay, or Hot Spring Island. **Moresby Explorers** (𝒞 **800/806-7633** or 250/637-2215 www.moresbyexplorers.com) runs an excellent operation with guided boat tours to Skedans and Hot Spring Island, plus dive tours. **Queen Charlotte Adventures** has tour and kayak itineraries from 1 to 9 or more days (𝒞 **800/668-4288**; www.queencharlotteadventures.com). Expect to pay C$200–C$250 per person, per day.

Many outfitters, such as **Butterfly Tours Great Expeditions** (℡ 604/740-7018; www.butterflytours.bc.ca), offer kayaking packages that suit every age and experience level; Butterfly's 8-day tours to SGang Gwaay cost C$2,280, plus they offer mother-ship cruises and stays in a remote guesthouse. Longtime sea-kayak outfitter **Ecosummer Expeditions** (℡ 800/465-8884 or 250/674-0102; www.ecosummer.com) offers 8-day kayaking trips to Gwaii Haanas, with prices starting at C$2,295. **Pacific Rim Paddling Company** (℡ 888/384-6103 or 604/815-8843; www.pacificrimpaddling.com) also has 8-day kayak trips to the park, for C$2,495.

Sailing into Gwaii Haanas is another popular option, and most sailboat operators also have kayaks aboard for guests' use. **Bluewater Adventures** (℡ 888/877-1770 or 604/980-3800; www.bluewateradventures.ca) offers 8- to 9-day tours starting at C$4,400. **Ocean Light II Adventures** (℡ 604/328-5339; www.oceanlight2.bc.ca) offers 7-day Haida Gwaii sailings on a 21.6m (71-ft.) boat for C$3,100.

Inland Air Charters (℡ 888/624-2577 or 250/559-4222; www.inlandair.bc.ca) offers sightseeing seaplane flights to Skedans, Hot Spring Island, and SGang Gwaay on Anthony Island. The latter trip includes a landing at Rose Bay and a 20-minute boat ride to the ancient village, plus a guided tour. You need to charter the entire plane, at a cost of C$2,625, but the cost can be divided by up to six passengers; check the website, as weight restrictions may apply.

FISHING

Langara Fishing Adventures (℡ 800/668-7544 or 604/232-5532; www.langara.com) offers fishing packages with accommodations at two of the most exclusive lodges in western Canada. Geared toward those who want to be pampered, the outfitter picks up guests at Vancouver Airport and delivers them to Langara Island, just north of Graham Island. There are two lodges: the slightly more rustic Langara Fishing Lodge and the utterly upscale and opulent Langara Island Lodge. At both, rooms are luxurious, and the dining room serves expertly prepared Pacific Northwest dishes. Packages include air transport from Vancouver, lodging, meals, boats, tackle, weather gear, and freezing or canning of your catch. Guided fishing trips cost extra, as do whale-watching and heli-touring. Also available are fishing trips to even more remote fishing lodges in Haida Gwaii. At Langara Fishing Lodge, rates start at C$4,095 for a 4-day trip; at Langara Island Lodge, 4 days cost from C$4,895. Packages are offered April to October.

For something more low-key, **Naden Lodge,** 1496 Delkatla St., Masset (℡ 800/771-8933 or 250/626-3322; www.nadenlodge.bc.ca), offers B&B accommodations and guided fishing trips from a lovely location right above Masset's boat basin. Numerous charter operators can be found in Masset, Queen Charlotte, and Skidegate. Contact the **Queen Charlotte Visitor Centre** (℡ 250/559-8316; www.qcinfo.ca) for suggestions.

Where to Stay & Eat

Food on these remote islands is pretty perfunctory, but the Haida Gwaii dining scene is growing beyond the islands' half-dozen Chinese food restaurants. Stop in at the **Mile Zero Pub,** Collison Avenue at Main Street, Masset (℡ 250/626-3210), for a pint and a fish tale or two. The menu spans roast beef, chicken, burgers, wraps, and sandwiches.

Also in Masset, **Hidden Island RV Resort** at 1440 Tow Hill Rd. has fish and chips that are near legendary (℡ 250/626-5286; www.hidden-island-resort.ca). Just up the road, the **Trout House** (9102 Tow Hill Rd.; no phone; www.trouthouse.ca) offers the finest dining on the island, but is hard to catch open. On your way to Tow Hill and North Beach, be sure to also drop by **Moon Over Naikoon** near North Beach. This off-the-grid bakery is said to take reservations for its cinnamon buns. For the islands' friendliest service, drop by **The Orange Roof** at 373 Beach Rd. in Sandspit. Under its namesake roof find fresh salads, hot pizzas, and a late-night crowd that rolls in from day boat trips in Gwaii Haanas (☎ **250/637-5619**). It's open Wednesday to Sunday.

Dorothy & Mike's Guest House

The atmosphere here is serene: A large deck overlooks the Skidegate Inlet, while gardens surround the house. The warm, cozy guest rooms are filled with local art and antiques; one suite comes with a full kitchen, and all three have private entrances. All guests have access to a common area with an entertainment center and reading library. The inn is within walking distance of the ocean, restaurants, and shopping.

3127 Second Ave. (Box 595), Queen Charlotte City, BC V0T 1S0. www.qcislands.net/doromike. ☎ **250/559-8439.** Fax 250/559-8439. 9 units, 2 with shared bathroom. May–Sept C$79 double with shared bathroom, C$90–C$245 double with private bathroom. Rates include breakfast. Off-season rates available. No credit cards. Drive 3.5km (2 miles) away from the Skidegate ferry terminal on Second Ave. *In room:* TV.

Premier Creek Lodging

Great for the budget-conscious, this heritage lodge dates back to 1910. Many rooms have great views over gardens to Bearskin Bay. There's a range of accommodations, from small, single units with shared bathrooms to suites with kitchens—all have a glowing, rustic charm. There's also a full-fledged hostel in a separate building (C$25).

3101 Third Ave. (Box 268), Queen Charlotte City, BC V0T 1S0. www.qcislands.net/premier. ☎ **888/322-3388** or 250/559-8415. Fax 250/559-8198. 12 units. 8 in hostel. C$40–C$95 double. AE, MC, V. **Amenities:** Bike rentals, fridge; microwave. *In room:* TV, kitchen (some units only), Wi-Fi (free).

Sea Raven Motel

The largest lodging in the Queen Charlottes, the Sea Raven is an unflashy motel with many room types, ranging from simple single units to deluxe accommodations with decks; many have ocean views. A few units sport kitchenettes. The rooms are simply furnished. The charm is a bit lacking here, but the motel is in a convenient location suited to early morning ferry departures or late arrivals.

3301 Oceanview Dr. (Box 519), Queen Charlotte City, BC V0T 1S0. www.searaven.com. ☎ **800/665-9606** or 250/559-4423. Fax 250/559-8617. 39 units. C$79–C$119 double. AE, MC, V. Limited street parking available. Pets allowed for C$10. **Amenities:** Restaurant. *In room:* TV, kitchenette (7 rooms only), Wi-Fi (free).

Spruce Point Lodging

This rustic, woodsy inn, overlooking the Hecate Strait, features rooms with private entrances as well as excellent views. Each unit has a fridge and a choice of either private shower or tub. Some rooms have full kitchen facilities, and all have complimentary tea and coffee service. Your friendly hosts can arrange kayaking packages to the surrounding islands.

609 Sixth Ave., Queen Charlotte City, BC V0T 1S0. www.qcislands.net/sprpoint. ☎ **250/559-8234.** 7 units. C$85 double. MC, V. Drive about 15 min. west on the main road away from the Skidegate ferry terminal, then turn left at Sam & Shirley's Grocery (the corner store). *In room:* TV, fridge.

THE YELLOWHEAD HIGHWAY: FROM PRINCE RUPERT TO PRINCE GEORGE

It's a long 722km (449 miles) from Prince Rupert to Prince George. Even though it's possible to make the journey in 1 long day, it's more pleasant to take it slowly and stop at some of the cultural sights along the way. The route initially follows the glacier-carved Skeena River valley inland, through the industrial city of **Terrace** and to the **Hazeltons,** twin towns with a lovely river setting and excellent First Nations cultural center. **Smithers,** cradled in a rich agricultural valley, is a growing skiing destination, and the most pleasant place along the route to spend a night. Between Burns Lake and Fort Fraser is a series of long, thin lakes, famed for trout and rustic fishing resorts.

Essentials

GETTING THERE   By Car   Terrace is 143km (89 miles) east of Prince Rupert on the Yellowhead Highway (Hwy. 16). From Terrace to Prince George, it's another 575km (357 miles).

By Train   VIA Rail (© **888/VIA-RAIL** [842-7245]; www.viarail.ca) operates three-times-weekly service between Prince George and Prince Rupert, with stops including Smithers, New Hazelton, and Terrace. The train follows the same route as the Yellowhead Highway.

By Bus   Greyhound Canada (© **800/661-8747** or 250/635-3680; www.greyhound.ca) travels between Prince Rupert and Prince George. One-way fare from Prince Rupert to Terrace is about C$28.

VISITOR INFORMATION   Kermodei Tourism, 4511 Keith Ave. (© **877/635-4944** or 250/635-4944; www.visitterrace.com), offers extensive information on the area.

Terrace

The Yellowhead Highway (Hwy. 16) follows the lush Skeena River valley from Prince Rupert, on the coast of the Inside Passage, to the province's interior. It's the gateway to the land-based return route from the Inside Passage ferry cruise. The long, winding valley is home to a diverse community of fishers, loggers, and aluminum and paper-mill workers in Terrace, and is the ancestral home of the Gitxsan, Haisla, Tsimshian, and Nisga'a First Nations. If you want to understand glacial geology, this drive will provide instant illumination. It's easy to picture the steep-sided valley choked with a bulldozer of ice, grinding the walls into sheer cliffs. Streams drop thousands of feet in a series of waterfalls. There are many small picnic areas along this route; plan on stopping beside the Skeena to admire the astonishing view.

　　Terrace is an industrial town of about 11,000 and has only just begun to develop itself for tourism. Stop by the store at the **House of Sim-oi-Ghets,** 5km (3 miles) west of Terrace on Hwy. 16 (© **250/638-1629;** www.kitsumkalum.bc.ca/hos.html), a cedar longhouse owned by the Kitsumkalum tribal band of the Tsimshian Nation. It offers jewelry, carvings, bead and leather work, and moccasins.

WHERE TO STAY & EAT

Best Western Terrace Inn   Overlooking the surrounding mountains, this hotel's well-appointed rooms feature little touches not normally found in the backcountry. A few deluxe accommodations sport Jacuzzi tubs. Tours to the Nisga'a lava beds are available upon request.

4553 Greig Ave., Terrace, BC V8G 1M7. www.bestwestern.com/ca/terraceinn. © **800/488-1898** or 250/635-0083. Fax 250/635-0092. 68 units. From C$123 double. Group, corporate, senior, and weekend discounts available. Rates include breakfast. AE, MC, V. Free parking. **Amenities:** Restaurant; bar; lounge; well-equipped exercise room. *In room:* A/C, TV, fridge, hair dryer, microwave, Wi-Fi (free).

Coast Inn of the West   This comfortable hotel in downtown Terrace offers pleasant, basic rooms in the heart of the town for an excellent value. Facilities include a nightclub open Thursday to Saturday. A daily continental breakfast buffet is on offer for guests. The new **Coast Grill** is a family-style restaurant that's open for breakfast, lunch, and dinner.

4620 Lakelse Ave., Terrace, BC V8G 1R1. www.coasthotels.com. © **800/716-6199** or 250/638-8141. Fax 250/638-8999. 58 units. From C$99 double. Senior and AAA rates available. AE, DC, DISC, MC, V. Pets C$20. **Amenities:** Restaurant; bar; room service. *In room:* A/C, TV, hair dryer, Wi-Fi (free).

North of Terrace & Nisga'a Memorial Lava Beds Provincial Park

Sixty kilometers (37 miles) northwest of town, the **Khutzeymateen Grizzly Bear Sanctuary** is the province's first official preserve of its kind. You must be part of an authorized group or accompanied by a ranger to observe these amazing creatures (see "Archaeological, Wildlife & Adventure Tours," earlier in this chapter), and most depart from Prince Rupert.

North America's rarest subspecies of black bear, the **kermodei,** also makes its home in the valley. The kermodei is unique, a nonalbino black bear born with white fur. Its teddy-bear face and round ears are endearing, but the kermodei is even larger than the impressive Queen Charlotte Islands/Haida Gwaii black bear.

Also north of Terrace, at the **Nisga'a Provincial Park** (officially named Anhluut'ukwsim Laxmihl Angwinga'asanskwhl Nisga'a), vegetation has only recently begun to reappear on the lava plain created by a volcanic eruption and subsequent lava flow in 1750 or so, which consumed this area and nearly all of its inhabitants.

The route to the park's near-lunar landscape begins in Terrace at the intersection of the Yellowhead Highway (Hwy. 16) and Kalum Lake Drive (Nisga'a Hwy.). Follow the paved highway north along the Kalum River past Kitsumkalum Lake. Just past Rosswood is **Lava Lake** (where the park boundary begins). While there are a number of short interpretive trails to volcanic curiosities along the parkway, the primary hiking trail is the 3km (1.9-mile) **Volcanic Cone Trail,** which leads through old-growth forest to a volcanic crater. To protect the site, it is required that you hire a local guide; reservations are mandatory. There are scheduled 4-hour guided hikes at 10am on weekends mid-May to mid-June and daily from mid-June through Labour Day; the cost is C$40 adults. Call Northwest Escapes to join a scheduled tour (© **250/638-8490**). Hikes depart from the **Nisga'a Park Visitor Centre** (www.env.gov.bc.ca/bcparks).

Continuing on Nisga'a Highway, the road picks its way across the lava flow. As you approach the Nass River, the road forks: To the left is the visitor center and to the right is the town of **New Aiyansh,** the valley's largest Nisga'a village, with basic facilities for travelers. The entire trip is 100km (62 miles); allow at least 1½ hours each way. High-quality auto-tour maps (C$3) detail the sites along the route, and are available at local museums and visitor centers.

The Nass River valley is the homeland of the Nisga'a indigenous peoples. In 1998, the Nisga'a and the Canadian federal government concluded an agreement that gives the Nisga'a full title to about 2,000 sq. km (772 sq. miles) of land, a cash settlement, and powers of self-government. The newly built **Nisga'a Museum** (810 Highway Drive, Laxgalts'ap; ✆ **250/633-3050;** www.nisgaamuseum.ca) displays artifacts ranging from objects from the Nisga'a ancestors' daily life to spiritual items used by shamans. The museum is about 45km (28 miles) west of New Aiyansh.

Maps show an unpaved road linking New Aiyansh with Hwy. 37 to the east. Called the Cranberry Connector by locals, it's a heavily rutted and pot-holed logging road that is perfectly passable but very slow going. If your destination is Stewart or Dease Lake, then it's worth inching your way across this shortcut (it will take about 1½ hr. to make the 62km/39-mile journey to Cranberry Junction on Hwy. 37). If you are heading back toward the Hazeltons, however, you're better off returning to Terrace and driving at highway speed up Hwy. 16. The Terrace ski hill, Shames Mountain, has closed, although a community group was seeking to run the mountain at presstime.

The Stewart-Cassair Highway: North to Alaska

Ninety kilometers (56 miles) east of Terrace (and 43km/27 miles west of New Hazelton) is the junction at Kitwanga of Hwy. 16 and the Stewart-Cassiar Highway (also labeled as Hwy. 37), one of two roads leading to the far north of British Columbia, eventually joining the famed Alaska Highway in the Yukon. This route is not as popular as the Alaska Highway, which begins farther east in Dawson Creek, though the scenery is more spectacular and the road conditions about the same. The route is now mostly paved, though there are a few gravel sections. Thus, expect delays due to road construction. To put it mildly, the winters up here are hard on the roads. It's a total of 720km (447 miles) between the Yellowhead Highway and the junction of the Alaska Highway near Watson Lake, in the Yukon.

Even if you don't want to drive all the way to the Yukon or Alaska, you should consider a side trip to the twin communities of **Stewart,** B.C., and **Hyder,** Alaska, 160km (99 miles) north on the Stewart-Cassiar Highway to Meziadin Junction, then 60km (37 miles) west on Hwy. 37A. What a drive! These two, boundary-straddling villages lie at the head of the Portland Canal, a very long and narrow fjord—in fact the world's fourth longest. The setting—the two ports huddle below high-flying peaks and massive glaciers—is alone worth the drive.

From Meziadin Junction, Hwy. 37A immediately arches up to cross the mighty glacier-choked Coast Mountains, before plunging precipitously down to sea level at Stewart. You'll want to stop at the Bear Glacier Rest Area, where massive **Bear Glacier**—glowing an eerie, aqua blue—descends into Strohn Lake, frequently bobbing with icebergs. Watch for mountain goats and bears along this stretch of road.

Stewart (pop. 500) is Canada's most northerly ice-free port, and subsists on logging, mining, and tourism. The tidy little town contrasts vividly with Hyder (pop. 87 in 2010), Stewart's grubby Alaskan cousin: One feels like it's an outpost of an empire, the other feels like it's the end of the road. From mid-July to early September the grizzly and black bear viewing at **Fish Creek** in **Tongass National Forest** near Hyder is astounding—from a raised viewing platform you'll watch grizzlies fishing for salmon in the creek below. Dawn and dusk offer the best bear-spotting chances; the facility is open 6am to 10pm and a day-pass costs $5. Further along Granduc/Salmon Glacier Road, you come to a viewpoint over the massive **Salmon Glacier.**

Facilities in Stewart are basic but serviceable; for good, central accommodation check-in at the the the **King Edward Hotel and Motel,** in Stewart, on Fifth Avenue (www.kingedwardhotel.com; ✆ **800/663-3126** in B.C., or 250/636-2244), which has double rooms for C$99 to C$119. Better still are the delightful, heritage properties of **Ripley Creek Inn** (www.ripleycreekinn.com; ✆ **250/636-2344**). Clean, comfortable rooms are available for C$55 to C$125.

The Hazeltons

The Skeena and Bulkley rivers join at the Hazeltons (pop. approx. 1,400). Straddling two river canyons and set below the rugged Rocher de Boule mountains, the Hazeltons are actually three separate towns: **Hazelton** itself, **South Hazelton,** and **New Hazelton,** all located along an 8km (5-mile) stretch. The junction of these two mighty rivers was home to the Gitxsan and Wet'suwet'en peoples, for whom the rivers provided both transport and a wealth of salmon. In the 1860s a village formed along the river and was the upriver terminus for riverboat traffic on the Skeena from 1886 to 1913. Thus Hazelton became a commercial hub for miners, ranchers, and other frontier settlers farther inland.

The old town center of Hazelton, though small, still has the feel of a pioneer settlement. And you can get a sense of the Gitxsan culture by visiting **'Ksan Historical Village ★★**, off Hwy. 62 (✆ **877/842-5518** or 250/842-5544; www.ksan.org), a re-creation of a traditional village. Some of the vividly painted longhouses serve as studios, where you can watch artists carve masks and hammer silver jewelry. If possible, plan your visit to coincide with a performance by the **'Ksan Performing Arts Group,** a troupe of singers and dancers who entertain visitors with music, masks, costumes, and pageantry. The shop here is a great source for Native art and gifts, and the Wilp Lax Gibuu, or the House of Eating, is a good place to try Native cooking. There's a C$2 admission for entrance to a small museum and the grounds themselves. To see the interior of the longhouses, you'll need to join a guided tour, which costs C$10 for adults, C$8.50 for seniors and students. If you take the tour, you don't have to pay the grounds fee. 'Ksan is open from April through September daily from 9am to 5pm. The rest of the year, only the museum and shop are open, Monday through Friday from 9:30am to 4:30pm.

Crossing the **Hagwilget Suspension Bridge** over the Buckley River delivers some amazing views of the canyon and surrounding mountains. You'll find the bridge as you follow Churchill Road as it branches north toward Hazelton from the highway.

There aren't many lodging choices, but the **28 Inn,** 4545 Yellowhead Hwy. 16, New Hazelton (www.28inn.com; ✆ **877/842-2828** or 250/842-6006), with a dining room and pub, if bland-looking, is clearly the best, with rooms going for C$75 double. All rooms have two double beds. **The Historic BC Café** is on the heritage main street at 1630 Omineca St., Old Hazelton (✆ **250/842-5775**), and serves diner-style food for breakfast, lunch, and dinner. **Rob's Restaurant** is closer to the Yellowhead Highway at 3379 Fielding St. (✆ **250/842-6654**) in New Hazelton. The mix of steak and ribs has a few twists in between, like mushroom gnocchi or a coconut green curry. The **'Ksan Historical Village** (see above) and **Seeley Lake Provincial Park,** 10km (6 miles) west of New Hazelton (✆ **800/689-9025** for reservations), have campgrounds. For advance information on the area, call the **New**

Hazelton Visitor Centre (📞 **250/842-6071** in summer, 250/842-6571 Oct–May). The summer-only **visitor center** is at the junction of highways 16 and 62 (Main St.).

Smithers & the Bulkley Valley

Smithers (pop. 5,600) is located in a stunningly beautiful valley that truly resembles the northern Alps. Flanked on three sides by vast ranges of glaciated peaks, it is cut through by the fast-flowing Bulkley River. The heart of Smithers occupies the old commercial strip on **Main Street,** which is perpendicular to the current fast-food and motel haven that is Hwy. 16. This attractive area is lined with Bavarian-theme storefronts that offer outdoor gear, gifts, and local crafts. But what Smithers really has to offer is found in its gorgeous mountain backdrop. With 2,589m (8,494-ft.) **Hudson Bay Mountain** rising directly behind the town, snowcapped ranges ringing the valley, and the area's fast-flowing rivers and streams, you'll feel the urge to get outdoors. And you can do just that on the snowy slopes of **Hudson Bay Mountain ski resort** (23km/14 miles southwest of town; 📞 **877/898-4754** or 250/847-2550; www.hudsonbaymountain.com). Open late November to mid-April, the ski hill has one chair and two T-bar lifts, along with about 30 groomed trails and a terrain park. Lift tickets are C$50 for adults, C$39 for seniors and youths 13 to 18, and C$28 for children 6 to 12. Facilities include a rental and repair shop, store, cafeteria, and pub.

Driftwood Canyon Provincial Park, 10km (6 miles) northeast of Smithers, preserves fossil-bearing formations laid down 50 million years ago. Considered one of the world's richest fossil beds, the park has interpretive trails leading through a section of exposed creek bed, which was carved by an ice-age glacier. To get here, drive 3km (1¾ miles) east of Smithers and turn east on Old Babine Lake Road.

Regional information can be obtained from the **Smithers Visitor Centre,** 1411 Court St. (📞 **800/542-6673** or 250/847-5072; www.tourismsmithers.com).

OUTDOOR PURSUITS

FISHING   The Bulkley River has excellent fishing for steelhead, chinook, and coho salmon, though restrictions apply. The best fishing areas on the Bulkley are from the confluence of the Morice River south of Smithers to the town of Telkwa.

HIKING   The 13km (8-mile) **Perimeter Trail** is a good place to jog; especially along the Bulkley River in Riverside Park. Two excellent hikes are on **Hudson Bay Mountain.** Three kilometers (1¾ miles) west of Smithers, take Kathlyn Lake Road 10km (6¼ miles) to the trail head. It's an easy .8km (.5-mile) stroll to view the impressive **Twin Falls.** From the same trail head, climb up to Glacier Gulch to get close to the toe of **Kathlyn Glacier.** This strenuous hike is just under 6.4km (4 miles) one-way, but allow at least 3 hours to make the climb.

Follow Hudson Bay Mountain Road west out of Smithers for 10km (6¼ miles) to **Smithers Community Forest,** with an extensive trail system. The easy 4km (2.5-mile) Interpretive Nature Trail makes a loop through the forest. For more rugged hiking, **Babine Mountains Provincial Park** protects 32,400 hectares (80,062 acres) of subalpine meadows, lakes, and craggy peaks. This roadless area is accessible only on foot, but many sights are within the range of day hikers, cross-country skiers, and cyclists. The **Silver King Trail** passes through subalpine forest before reaching an alpine meadow that explodes with wildflowers in July. To reach the Babine Mountains, go 3km (1¾ miles) east of Smithers and take Old Babine Lake Road, 7km (4⅓ miles) north of Driftwood Canyon Provincial Park.

WHERE TO STAY

The well-maintained **Aspen Inn,** 4268 Hwy. 16 (www.aspeninnsmithers.com; ℂ **800/ 663-7676** or 250/847-4551), offers an on-site restaurant and large rooms from C$109. **Riverside Park Municipal Campsite,** 3843 19th Ave. (ℂ **250/847- 1600**), has 40 sites starting at C$19 with dry toilets, fire pits, and water.

Hudson Bay Lodge The largest and most comfortable hotel in Smithers, this is a popular stop for the tour-bus crowds making their way to and from the Prince Rupert ferries. The crowds notwithstanding, the facilities here are high quality. The lodge has a sleekly styled restaurant on the premises, the wood-and-stone **Zoer's Restaurant,** which serves breakfast, lunch, and dinner.

3251 Hwy. 16 E. (Box 3636), Smithers, BC V0J 2N0. www.hudsonbaylodge.com. ℂ **800/663-5040** or 250/847-4581. Fax 250/847-4878. 96 units. From C$99 double. AE, MC, V. **Amenities:** Restaurant; pub w/dining service; fitness room; gift shop; liquor store. *In room:* A/C, TV w/pay movies, hair dryer, Wi-Fi (free).

Stork Nest Inn 🖋 The Stork Nest does more than most Smithers lodgings to look Bavarian, with gables, flowers, and a corbeled roofline. Though the cozy rooms aren't the largest in the province, they are very clean, pleasant, and nicely furnished. The inn's breakfast room is flooded with morning light and the scent of strong coffee. A honeymoon suite features a Jacuzzi, and wheelchair-accessible rooms are available.

1485 Main St. (Box 2049), Smithers, BC V0J 2N0. www.storknestinn.com. ℂ **250/847-3831.** Fax 250/847-3852. 23 units. C$95–C$100 double. Rates include full breakfast. AE, MC, V. Free parking. **Amenities:** Sauna; rooms for those w/limited mobility. *In room:* A/C, TV, fridge, hair dryer (on request), Wi-Fi (free).

WHERE TO EAT

An old native longhouse has been relocated to the **Riverhouse Restaurant and Lounge** (4268 Hwy. 16; ℂ **250/847-4672**), alongside the Aspen Inn, and now serves as a private dining area. Rescued logger saws and thick trunk tables set the scene for hearty, pub-fare dishes served with care. Think pasta with artichoke, shrimp, and scallops, or pork tenderloin marinated in red wine and coffee. Main courses run C$10 to C$31. It's open daily from 6am to 10pm or later. The **Alpenhorn Pub and Bistro,** 1261 Main St. (ℂ **250/847-5366**), is a pleasant, sports-bar type of pub with gourmet burgers, pastas, sandwiches, and ribs (mains C$9–C$30). Enjoy the large outdoor patio in summer. It's open daily from 11am to 10pm for food, and later for drinks.

The Lakes District

Between Smithers and Prince George lies a vast basin filled with glacier-gouged lakes, dense forests, and rolling mountains. There are over 300 lakes, whose combined shorelines add up to more than 4,800km (2,983 miles). Not surprisingly, sportfishing is the main draw here, and rustic fishing lodges are scattered along the lakeshores.

But this isn't an easy place to plan a casual visit. Many of the lodges are fly-in or boat-in, and offer only weeklong fishing packages. Most are very rustic indeed. If this is what you're looking for, contact the Burns Lake Visitor Centre (see below), which can connect you with the lodge or outfitter that suits your needs.

If you have a day to spare and want to explore the region, there's a paved loop starting in Burns Lake that explores the shores of four of the lakes. Take Hwy. 35 south

NORTHERN BRITISH COLUMBIA | The Yellowhead Highway

from Burns Lake, past Tchesinkut Lake to Northside on François Lake. From here, take the free half-hour ferry across François Lake and continue south to Ootsa Lake. Here, the road turns west, eventually meeting back with Hwy. 16 just west of Houston (from where it heads east back to Burns Lake). The journey from Burns Lake to Houston on this route is about 170km (106 miles).

Burns Lake is nominally the center of the Lakes District, and if you end up here needing a place to stay, try the **Burns Lake Motor Inn,** on Hwy. 16 W. (© 800/663-2968 or 250/692-7545), which has typical highway-side rooms and amenities. For information on the region, contact the **Burns Lake Visitor Centre,** 540 Hwy. 16 (© 250/692-3700; www.lakesdistrict.com), open in July and August daily and year-round at varying times; call for hours. An impressive mountain biking park is built on crown land on Boer Mountain.

At Vanderhoof, 130km (81 miles) east of Burns Lake, take Hwy. 27 north 55km (34 miles) to **Fort St. James National Historic Site ★** (© 250/996-7191; www.pc.gc.ca/stjames), one of the most interesting historic sites in northern British Columbia. Fort St. James was the earliest non-Native settlement in the province, a fur-trading fort established in 1806. In summer, costumed docents act out the roles of traders, craftsmen, and explorers. The park is open daily mid-May through September from 9am to 5pm. Summer admission is C$7.80 for adults, C$6.55 for seniors, C$3.90 for youths 6 to 16, and C$20 for families. Audio-guided tours are available.

PRINCE GEORGE

377km (234 miles) W of Jasper, Alberta; 722km (449 miles) E of Prince Rupert

The largest city in northern British Columbia, Prince George (pop. 75,000) makes a natural base for exploring the sights and recreational opportunities of the province's north-central region, which is filled with forested mountains, lakes, and mighty rivers.

There has been settlement at the junction of the Fraser and Nechako rivers for millennia; the two river systems were as much a transportation corridor for the early First Nations people as for the European settlers who came later. A trading post was established in 1807 by Simon Fraser; the Grand Trunk Pacific Railway, which passed through here in 1914, put Prince George on the map.

What makes the city's economic heart beat is lumber—and lots of it. Prince George is at the center of vast softwood forests, and three major mills here turn trees into pulp, and pulp into paper. The economic boom that these mills introduced has brought a relative degree of sophistication to the lumber town—there's a civic art gallery, good restaurants, and the University of Northern British Columbia.

Essentials

GETTING THERE   By Plane   Air Canada (© 888/247-2262; www.aircanada.ca) provides daily service to Prince George to/from Vancouver. **WestJet** (© 888/937-8538; www.westjet.com) also serves Prince George, offering economical flights to the rest of Canada.

By Train   The *Skeena* run on **VIA Rail** (© 888/VIA-RAIL [842-7245]; www.viarail.ca), which operates between Prince Rupert and Jasper, stops overnight in Prince George. Connections to the main VIA Vancouver–Toronto line are available at Jasper. Although the Rocky Mountaineer's Fraser Discovery Route excursion train passes through Prince George, it doesn't stop here.

By Bus **Greyhound Canada** (© 800/661-8747 or 250/564-5454; www.greyhound.ca) serves Prince George with three daily buses from Vancouver. Fares begin at C$89. Greyhound also offers daily buses between Prince Rupert and Jasper along the Yellowhead Highway.

By Car Prince George is about a third of the way across the province on the east–west Yellowhead Highway (Hwy. 16). South from Prince George, Hwy. 97 drops through the Cariboo District on its way to Kelowna (720km/447 miles) and Vancouver (788km/490 miles via Hwy. 1). From Prince George, you can also follow Hwy. 97 north to join the Alaska Highway at Dawson Creek (400km/249 miles).

VISITOR INFORMATION Contact the **Prince George Visitor Centre,** 1300 First Ave. (© 800/668-7646 or 250/562-3700; www.tourismpg.com). It's open daily from 8am to 8pm in summer, closed Sundays in winter.

GETTING AROUND The local bus system is operated by **Prince George Transit** (© 250/563-0011). For a cab, call **Emerald Taxi** (© 250/563-3333) or **Prince George Taxi** (© 250/564-4444).

Car-rental agencies include **Budget** (© 800/268-8900 in Canada, 800/527-0700 in the U.S.; www.budget.com), and **National** (© 800/CAR-RENT [227-7368] in Canada and the U.S.; www.nationalcar.com).

Exploring the Area

Downtown Prince George is located on a spur of land at the confluence of the Fraser and Nechako rivers. The old commercial district at first seems a bit forlorn, but a stroll around the city center—concentrated along Third Avenue and George Street—reveals a down-and-dirty charm that's reminiscent of towns in the Yukon or Northwest Territories. And the prevalence of tattoo parlors, pawnshops, and old-fashioned coffee shops enhances the impression of a rough-and-ready frontier community.

The **Two Rivers Gallery** (© 888/221-1155 or 250/614-7800; www.tworiversart gallery.com) occupies a stylish space in the Civic Centre Plaza, at Patricia Boulevard and Dominion Street. This architecturally innovative, C$5-million structure showcases the work of local and regional artists. There's also a sculpture garden, gift shop, and cafe. Hours are Monday through Wednesday, Friday, and Saturday from 10am to 5pm, Thursday 10am to 9pm, and Sunday from noon to 5pm. Admission is C$7.50 for adults, C$6 for seniors and students, C$3 for children 5 to 12, and C$15 for families. After viewing the gallery, cross Patricia Boulevard and wander the trails in **Connaught Hill Park.** From the top of the hill are good views of the Fraser River and downtown.

The **Prince George Railway and Forestry Museum** (850 River Rd.; © 250/563-7351 www.pgrfm.bc.ca) tells the story of the region's industries. There are dozens of engines, train cars, and cabooses at the site near the present-day rail yard. Admission is adults C$6, seniors C$5, and children 3 to 12 C$3. It's open daily during summer.

There are more than 150 parks within the city limits, many of them linked by the Heritage River Trails system. The best is 24-hectare (59-acre) **Fort George Park,** on the site of the original fur-trading post. On the grounds are a First Nations burial ground, a miniature railway, a one-room schoolhouse, and the **Exploration Place** (© 250/562-1612; www.theexplorationplace.com), a kid-focused science and nature museum. Adults will enjoy the history gallery, which details the customs of the region's Native Carrier people, and moves on to tell the story of the fur-trading and logging past. There are also numerous interactive science exhibits. Admission is C$9.95 for adults, C$7.95 for seniors and students, C$6.95 for children 2 to 12, or C$23 per family. It's open daily 9am to 5pm. The park is on the Fraser River end of 20th Avenue; from downtown, take Queensway Street south, then turn east on 20th Avenue.

The **Heritage River Trails** take you on an 11km (6.8-mile) circuit covering the historic sights of town. The loop starts at Fort George Park, goes along the Fraser River, passes through Cottonwood Island Park and along the Nechako River to the Cameron Street bridge, and leads through town and back to Fort George Park.

Heading 113km (70 mile) east of Prince George on Highway 16, find a grove of tree giants known as the **Ancient Forest.** The trees are similar in size to those in coastal rainforests—only these are located far inland in a dry climate that's hot in summer and very cold in winter. The parking area is marked and a short walk tours through the largest of the trees.

Where to Stay

If you're looking for a bed-and-breakfast, try the **Prince George B&B Hot Line** (✆ **877/562-2626** or 250/562-2222; www.princegeorgebnb.com).

Coast Inn of the North ★ One of the best properties of British Columbia's Coast hotel chain is right in the thick of things in downtown Prince George. The guest rooms are nicely furnished; the corner suites are large, with king-size beds, a balcony, and lots of light and space (some suites have Jacuzzis). The lobby is simply lavish and there are shops and services at street-level. Among the numerous facilities is an indoor pool. Small pets are allowed in the guest rooms.

770 Brunswick St., Prince George, BC V2L 2C2. www.coasthotels.com. ✆ **800/716-6199** or 250/563-0121. Fax 250/563-1948. 155 units. C$130–C$175 double. Extra person C$10. Family plan, corporate, and off-season rates, and senior and AAA discounts available. AE, MC, V. Free parking with engine heater plug-ins. Pets C$10. **Amenities:** 3 restaurants; exercise room; Jacuzzis; indoor pool; room service; saunas. *In room:* A/C, TV, fridge, hair dryer, Wi-Fi (free).

Four Points by Sheraton Prince George ★★ The sleek new Four Points has lots going for it in addition to its relative youth. The rooms are large and very nicely furnished with vibrant textiles, and the hotel is located just west of the old downtown area. The staff goes out of its way to make you feel welcome, and the pool and exercise room are particularly tip-top. If you're here on business, the suites offer lots of room and amenities for road warriors.

1790 Hwy. 97 S., Prince George, BC V2L 5L3. www.starwoodhotels.com/fourpoints. ✆ **800/368-7764** or 250/564-7100. Fax 250/564-7199. 74 units. From C$110 double; from C$140 suite. AE, MC, V. Free parking. **Amenities:** Restaurant; exercise room; room service. *In room:* A/C, TV, fridge, hair dryer, Wi-Fi (free).

Goldcap Travelodge 🗲 If you're looking for value, it's hard to beat the large, clean, unfussy rooms at the Travelodge, right downtown. Kitchen units with microwaves and fridges are available for a small extra fee. An on-site family restaurant is open for three meals daily.

1458 Seventh Ave., Prince George, BC V2L 3P3. www.travelodgeprincegeorge.com. ✆ **800/663-8239** or 250/563-0666. Fax 250/563-5775. 77 units. C$90–C$125 double. Kitchens available for C$10. Off-season rates and senior discounts available. Rate includes continental breakfast. AE, MC, V. Free parking. Pets accepted. **Amenities:** Restaurant; sauna. *In room:* A/C, TV, fridge, microwave, Wi-Fi (free).

The Manor 🛏️   From its beginnings as the Chee Duck Tong Society, this cinder-block building in downtown Prince George has a new life as a budget hostel. Convenient to the VIA Rail station, the hostel offers simple but clean rooms and an exceedingly friendly host. Beds have comfy duvets and the dorms have in-room heating. There's a great variety of accommodations, with dorms, private rooms, deluxe rooms, and apartment-style suites available.

197 Quebec Street, Prince George BC V2L 1W1. www.princegeorgehostel.com. ℂ **250/960-7727.** 23 units. C$30 dorm bed. C$50–C$80 double. MC, V. **Amenities:** Kitchen; TV lounge; airport shuttle; phone. *In room:* Wi-Fi (free).

Ramada Hotel (Downtown Prince George) ★   The grandest of hotels in Prince George, the Ramada offers a variety of top-notch rooms—from standard to presidential—right in the center of the city. The Tower Suites, with a selection of large business and specialty suites that offer free breakfast and high-end toiletries, were refurbished in 2011. Some units have Jacuzzis; all have heated bathroom floors.

444 George St., Prince George, BC V2L 1R6. www.ramadaprincegeorge.com. ℂ **800/830-8833** or 250/563-0055. Fax 250/563-6042. 193 units. C$135–C$175 double. Extra person C$15. Senior discounts available. AE, DC, DISC, MC, V. Free secure, covered parking. Valet parking available. **Amenities:** Restaurant; bar; exercise room; Jacuzzi; large indoor pool; room service; rooms for those w/limited mobility. *In room:* A/C, TV w/pay movies, Wi-Fi (free).

Where to Eat

10

Cimo Mediterranean Grill, 601 Victoria St. (ℂ **250/564-7975**), is a good spot for hand-made pasta.

North 54 ★ CONTEMPORARY CANADIAN   This bustling dining room serves pasta, seafood, and local meats in innovative, Mediterranean-influenced preparations that seem refreshing in northern B.C. The appetizers are tempting, and a couple of these—perhaps bruschetta topped with shrimp, scallops, and tomatoes, and a Caprese filo pizza—could make a meal. But don't miss out on pasta dishes such as seared beef, shallots, and truffle oil with tagliolini. The steaks are just fine, but a real standout for meat eaters is grilled duck breast with a date-orange glaze. Then again, the entree salads might be a better fit after a few days of travel in the carnivorous north.

1493 3rd Ave. ℂ **250/564-5400.** www.north54restaurant.com. Reservations suggested. Main courses C$15–C$45. MC, V. Mon–Fri 11:30am–2pm. Daily 5–9pm.

Ric's Grill STEAKHOUSE   This chic dining room serves an expanded steak and chop menu that mixes old-fashioned meat and potatoes with imaginative New Canadian cuisine. Ric's also features an impressive selection of fish and shellfish dishes, plus pasta, chicken, and salads. It's a stylish and friendly spot for dinner, although has scant options for vegetarians.

547 George St. ℂ **250/614-9096.** Reservations suggested. Main courses C$17–C$37. AE, MC, V. Sun–Tues 4:30–10pm; Wed–Thurs 11:30am–10pm; Fri 11:30am–11pm; Sat 4:30–11pm.

White Goose Bistro BISTRO   A friendly restaurant in downtown Prince George draped in rich mustard and burgundy tones, the White Goose bistro puts a slight twist on classic North American dishes. Take the ostrich burger, for example, that's topped with roasted red pepper, or the house salad with figs, pecans, and goat cheese. Lunch here is one of the best bargains in the province. Picks such as cornmeal-buttered sole, roasted duck leg, or lobster ravioli are all priced at under C$15.

1205 3rd Ave. ℂ **250/561-1002.** www.whitegoosebistro.ca. Main courses C$18–C$38. MC, V. Mon–Fri 11am–2pm and 5–9pm; Sat 5–9pm; closed Sunday.

THE ALASKA HIGHWAY

Constructed as a military freight road during World War II to link Alaska to the Lower 48, the Alaska Highway—also known as the Alcan Highway, and Hwy. 97 in British Columbia—has become something of a pilgrimage route for recent retirees.

Strictly speaking, the Alaska Highway starts at Mile 0 marker in **Dawson Creek,** on the eastern edge of British Columbia, and travels north and west for 2,232km (1,387 miles) to **Delta Junction,** in Alaska, passing through the Yukon along the way. The **Richardson Highway** (Alaska Rte. 4) covers the additional 154.5km (96 miles) from Delta Junction to **Fairbanks.**

Popular wisdom states that if you drive straight out, it takes 3 days between Dawson Creek and Fairbanks. However, this is a very *long* winding road, and RV traffic is heavy. If you try to keep yourself to a 3-day schedule, you'll have a miserable time.

What to Expect

Summer is the only opportunity to repair the road, so construction crews really go to it; you can count on lengthy delays and some very rugged, rutted detours. Visitor centers along the way get notifications of daily construction schedules and conditions, so stop for updates, or follow the links to "Road Conditions" from the website **www.themilepost.com.** You can also call (📞) **867/456-7623** for 24-hour Yukon highway information and (📞) **800/550-4997** for British Columbia highways.

Although there's gas at most of the communities that appear on the road map, most close up early in the evening, and gas prices can be substantially higher than in, say, Edmonton or Calgary. You'll find 24-hour gas stations and plenty of motel rooms in the towns of Dawson City, Fort St. John, Fort Nelson, Watson Lake, and Whitehorse.

Try to be patient when driving the Alaska Highway. In high season, the entire route, from Edmonton to Fairbanks, is one long caravan of RVs. Many people have their car in tow, a boat on the roof, and several bicycles chained to the spare tire. Thus encumbered, they lumber up the highway; loath (or unable) to pass one another. These convoys of RVs stretch on forever, the slowest of the party setting the pace for all.

Driving the Alaska Highway

This overview of the Alaska Highway is not meant to serve as a detailed guide for drivers. For that, you should purchase the annual *Alaska Milepost* (www.themilepost.com), which offers exhaustive, mile-by-mile coverage of the trip (and of other road trips into the Arctic of Alaska and Canada).

The route begins (or ends) at **Dawson Creek,** in British Columbia. Depending on where you join the journey, Dawson Creek is a long 590km (367-mile) drive from Edmonton or a comparatively short 406km (252 miles) from Prince George on Hwy. 97. Dawson Creek is a natural place to break up the journey, with ample tourist facilities. If you want to call ahead to ensure a room, try the spotless **Pomeroy Inn and Suites** (540 Hwy. 2; (📞) **866/782-3577** or 250/782-3700; www.pomeroyinnandsuites.com) for an excellent, if pricey, stay.

From Dawson Creek, the Alaska Highway soon crosses the Peace River and passes through **Fort St. John,** in the heart of British Columbia's far-north ranch country and a booming oil and gas region. The highway continues north, parallel to the Rockies. First the ranches thin, and then the forests thin. Moose are often seen from the road.

From Fort St. John to **Fort Nelson,** you'll find gas stations and cafes every 65 to 80km (40–50 miles), though lodging options are pretty dubious. Fort Nelson is thick with motels and gas stations; because it's hours from any other major service center, this is a good place to spend the night. Try the **Woodlands Inn,** 3995 4711 50th Ave. S. (✆ **866/966-3466** or 250/774-6669 774-3911; www.woodlandsinn.ca).

At Fort Nelson, the Alaska Highway turns west and heads into the Northern Rockies; from here, too, graveled **Liard Highway** (B.C. Hwy. 77; Northern Territories Hwy. 7) continues north to Fort Liard and Fort Simpson, the gateway to **Nahanni National Park,** a very worthy but preparation-demanding side trip.

From Fort Nelson, the Alaska Highway through the Rockies is narrow and winding—and likely to be under construction. Once over the Continental Divide, the Alaska Highway follows tributaries of the Liard River through **Stone Mountain** and **Muncho Lake** provincial parks. Rustic lodges are scattered along the way. The lovely log **Northern Rockies Lodge ★**, at Muncho Lake (www.northern-rockies-lodge. com; ✆ **800/663-5269** or 250/776-3481), has lakeside lodge rooms, log cabins, and campsites.

At the town of **Liard River,** stop and stretch your legs or go for a soak in the two deep-forest soaking pools at **Liard River Hot Springs.** The boardwalk out into the mineral-water marsh is pleasant even if you don't have time for a dip. As you get closer to **Watson Lake** in the Yukon, you'll notice that mom-and-pop gas stations along the road will advertise that they have cheaper gas than at Watson Lake. Believe them, and fill up: Watson Lake is an unappealing town whose extortionately priced gas is probably its only memorable feature. The truth in advertising award goes to **A Nice Motel** (www.anicemotel.com; ✆ **867/536-7222**), a very nicely furnished lodging that's easy to miss behind the local Petro Canada gas station at 609 Frank Trail, where you sign in for the motel. Don't worry—the rooms are easily the best in Watson Lake.

The long road between Watson Lake and **Whitehorse** travels through forests and rolling hills to Teslin and Atlin lakes, where the landscape becomes more mountainous and the gray clouds of the Gulf of Alaska's weather systems hang menacingly on the horizon. Whitehorse is the largest town along the route of the Alaska Highway, and unless you're in a great hurry, plan to spend at least a day here.

Hope for good weather as you leave Whitehorse; the trip past **Kluane National Park** is one the most beautiful parts of the entire route. Tucked into the southwestern corner of the Yukon, a 2-hour drive from Whitehorse, these 21,980 sq. km (8,487 sq. miles) of glaciers, marshes, mountains, and sand dunes are unsettled and virtually untouched—and designated as a **UNESCO World Heritage Site.** Bordering on Alaska in the west, Kluane contains **Mount Logan** and **Mount St. Elias,** respectively the second- and third-highest peaks in North America. (Denali is the highest.)

Because Kluane is largely undeveloped, casual exploration is limited to a few day-hiking trails and aerial sightseeing trips. The vast expanse of ice and rock in the heart of the wilderness is well beyond striking range of the average outdoor enthusiast. The area's white-water rapids are world-class but, likewise, not for the uninitiated. For more information on recreation in Kluane, see the website at **www.pc.gc. ca/kluane**.

After Kluane, the Alaska Highway edges by Kluane Lake before passing Beaver Creek and crossing over into Alaska. From the border to Fairbanks is another 472km (292 miles).

THE CARIBOO COUNTRY & THE THOMPSON RIVER VALLEY

By Chloë Ernst

S outh of Prince George along Hwy. 97 and beyond into British Columbia's interior, the Canadian Wild West hasn't changed much in the past century. This is Cariboo Country, a vast landscape that changes from alpine meadows and thick forests to rolling prairies and arid canyons before it encounters the gigantic glacial peaks of the Coast Mountains. The Cariboo's history is synonymous with the word *gold*.

From Vancouver, the Sea-to-Sky Highway (Hwy. 99) passes through Whistler and the Cayoosh Valley, eventually descending into the town of Lillooet, which was Mile 0 of the Old Cariboo Road during the gold-rush days of the 1860s. Prospectors and settlers made their way north up what's now called the Cariboo Gold Rush Trail (Hwy. 99 and Hwy. 97).

Hwy. 97 follows the gold-rush trail through the towns of 70 Mile House, 100 Mile House, 108 Mile House, and 150 Mile House. The towns were named for the mile-marking roadhouses visited by prospectors and settlers headed north to the gold fields.

The gold-rich town of Barkerville sprang up in the 1860s after a British prospector named Billy Barker struck it rich on Williams Creek. Completely restored, the town brings the rough gold-rush days to life. The streets are only 5.5m (18 ft.) wide, thanks to a drunken surveyor. Nowadays, you can try your hand at panning for the shiny gold flakes and nuggets that still lie deep within Williams Creek.

Gold isn't the only thing that attracts thousands of visitors to this area. Cross-country skiers and snowmobilers take to the creek-side paths in winter; canoeists head a few miles north of Barkerville to the 116km (72-mile) circular Bowron Lake canoe route.

From Williams Lake, back-roads enthusiasts can also drive Hwy. 20 west to the Pacific coastal community of Bella Coola, which in the early days of European exploration was one of the most important First Nations communities on the coast. From Bella Coola, you can catch the Discovery Coast ferry to Port Hardy on the northern tip of Vancouver Island (see chapter 8).

Due east, on the opposite side of Cariboo Country, the Thompson River valley's arid lowlands attract fishers and houseboaters to the shores of the lower Thompson River and the Shuswap Lakes. Heading north from this dry terrain, you'll reach a majestic 540,000-hectare (1.3-million-acre) forested mountain wilderness and waterfalls formed by glaciers and volcanoes—Wells Gray Provincial Park.

CARIBOO COUNTRY ESSENTIALS

Getting There

Whether you travel by train or by car, the trip from Whistler to Cariboo Country is a visually exhilarating experience.

BY CAR   Barely shorter, slower, but also the most scenic, the route from Vancouver along Hwy. 99 (the Sea-to-Sky Hwy.) passes Whistler and Lillooet, continuing to Hwy. 97 and turning north to 100 Mile House. From Vancouver to Quesnel, it's 640km (398 miles) by Highway 99. If you want to bypass the dramatic but slow Hwy. 99 and head straight up to the central Cariboo district, you can take the Hwy. 1 expressway east from Vancouver, then continue following Hwy. 1 through the Fraser Canyon and join Hwy. 97 at Cache Creek.

BY TRAIN   For decades, **BC Rail** operated the *Cariboo Prospector,* which linked Vancouver to Prince George with stops in other towns in the Cariboo Country. In 2002, however, BC Rail discontinued passenger service along this route. **Rocky Mountaineer Vacations** (© 877/460-3200 or 604/606-7245), which operates the very successful excursion train service between Vancouver and Banff and Jasper in the Canadian Rockies, in 2006 began service along this route. The Vancouver to Kamloops leg of these Rocky Mountain journeys follows the Fraser Canyon route. For information, go to **www.rockymountaineer.com**. A second routing departs from North Vancouver, heads to Whistler, and has an overnight stop in Quesnel before continuing on to Jasper, where the train will link with other Rocky Mountaineer Vacations trains and offer a circle route back to Vancouver.

BY BUS   Greyhound Canada (© 800/661-8747; www.greyhound.ca) travels from Vancouver through the Cariboo to Prince George via highways 1 and 97, passing through Kamloops, 100 Mile House, Williams Lake, and Quesnel. Note that these routes do not pass through Lillooet, which has no bus service.

BY PLANE   Central Mountain Air (© 888/865-8585; www.flycma.com) offers daily service between Quesnel and Vancouver. It also offers daily flights between Williams Lake and Vancouver. **Pacific Coastal Air** (© 800/663-2872 or 604/273-8666; www.pacific-coastal.com) links Vancouver to Anahim Lake, Bella Coola, and Williams Lake.

Visitor Information

Contact the **Cariboo Chilcotin Coast Tourism Association,** 204-350 Barnard St., Williams Lake, BC V2G 4T9 (© 800/663-5885 or 250/392-2226; www.land withoutlimits.com).

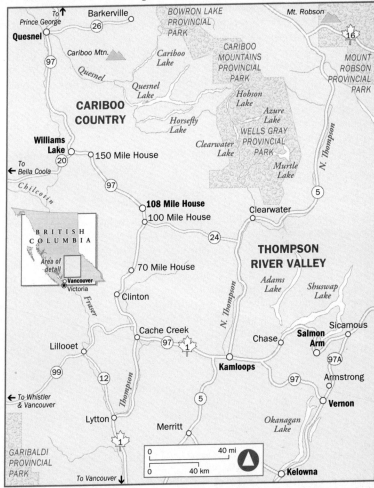

EN ROUTE TO 100 MILE HOUSE

There's nothing subtle about the physical setting of **Lillooet** (pop. 2,324). To the west, the soaring glaciated peaks of the Coast Mountains dominate the sky. To the east rise the steep desert walls of the Fountain Ridge, stained with rusty red and ocher. Cleaving the two mountain ranges is the massive and roaring Fraser River. From the peaks of the Coast Range to the riverbed is a drop of about 2,500m (8,202 ft.)—all of this making for an incredibly dramatic backdrop to the town.

In 1858, a trail was cut from the Fraser Valley goldfields in the south to the town of Lillooet, later established as Mile 0 of the 1860s **Cariboo Gold Rush Trail.** At the big bend on Main Street, a cairn marks MILE 0 of the original Cariboo Wagon Road.

From Lillooet, Hwy. 99 heads north along the Fraser River Canyon, affording many dramatic vistas before turning east to its junction with Hwy. 97. Thirty kilometers (19 miles) north on Hwy. 97 is **Clinton,** the self-avowed "guest-ranch capital of British Columbia." This is certainly handsome ranch country, with broad cattle- and horse-filled valleys rolling between dry mountain walls.

Hat Creek Ranch Now a provincial heritage site, Hat Creek Ranch was built in 1861 and served as a stagecoach inn for miners. This open-air museum of frontier life has more than 20 period buildings, including a blacksmith shop, barn, and stable. There's also a good exhibit on the culture of the region's First Nations Shuswap tribe. In summer, concessionaires operate horse-drawn wagon and horseback rides, plus a ranch-house restaurant. Regular visitor services and guided tours are offered only from May to the end of September.

At junction of Hwy. 99 and Hwy. 97. ℭ **800/782-0922** or 250/457-9722. www.hatcreekranch.com. Admission C$12 adults, C$11 seniors, C$8 children 6–12, C$25 families. May–Sept 30 daily 9am–5pm (July–Aug until 6pm).

Where to Stay

Big Bar Guest Ranch ☺ A longtime favorite for horse-focused family vacations, the Big Bar is a comfortable destination with lots of recreational and lodging options. Summer activities include riding and pack trips, or you can canoe, fish, pan for gold, bike, and go for hayrides. In winter, the ranch remains open for cross-country skiing, snowshoeing, snowmobiling, and ice fishing. The centerpiece of the property is the hand-hewn log Harrison House, built in the early 1900s, which now serves as guest lounge, with a huge stone fireplace, and game area with pool and foosball tables. The Big Bar is the quintessential old-fashioned guest ranch—not a New Age lifestyle resort—where lots of attention is spent on the quality of the horses and the wranglers. Guests will enjoy the family-style meals after a hearty day of horseback riding or hiking. In addition to 10 comfortable, no-fuss lodge rooms in the main lodge, there are 4 quite comfortable one-bedroom log cabins, each with a sleeping loft and fold-out couch, sleeping up to eight, with full kitchens and fireplaces. In addition, other lodging options include tepees, a six-bedroom lodge, and campsites. If you're looking for an Old West adventure, not just an opportunity to dress up in a Stetson and denim, then this might be the guest ranch for you.

54km (34 miles) northwest of Clinton off Hwy. 97. Mailing address: P.O. Box 927, Jesmond, BC V0K 1K0. www.bigbarranch.com. ℭ **877/655-2333** or 250/459-2333. Fax 250/459-2400. 18 units, 4 cabins. C$143 double occupancy in inn; C$250 double occupancy in cabin, 3 night minimum; C$60 per tipi (up to 4 people). Extra adult in cabin C$50 per person. C$30 child over 7 in lodge rooms. C$25 campground site for 2 tents or 1 RV. Three meals: adults C$60, children under 15 C$45. MC, V. **Amenities:** Dining room; fireside lounge; trail rides; fishing pond. *In room:* No phone.

Cariboo Lodge Resort ★ There's been a log lodge on this site for well over a century—the original was built to serve frontier trappers and miners. Times have changed, and so has the Cariboo Lodge. This modern log lodge and motel offers stylish, fully modern guest rooms plus an Old West pub (complete with stuffed animal heads) and restaurant; the resort makes a perfect base for exploring central British Columbia. The proprietors will organize horseback rides, rafting and mountain-biking tours, and cross-country ski trips. Rooms are large and nicely furnished—without the Old West clutter you'd normally expect in such a place. The family suite with fenced-in courtyard and three beds is an excellent deal for C$104.

1414 Cariboo Hwy., Box 459, Clinton, BC V0K 1K0. www.cariboolodgeclintonbc.com. © **877/459-7992** or 250/459-7992. 20 units. From C$84 double. Extra person C$5. AE, MC, V. **Amenities:** Restaurant; pub; liquor store. *In room:* A/C, TV, fridge, Wi-Fi (free).

Echo Valley Ranch and Spa ★ 🎁   East meets West at this remarkable resort, which is both amazingly sumptuous and rather mannered. Occupying a scenic plateau with views over the Fraser River valley, Echo Valley Ranch combines features of a traditional guest ranch—horseback riding and hiking—with Thai and European spa facilities. Guest rooms are in two central lodges—three-story log buildings straight out of *House Beautiful*—or in individual cabins. Even more astonishing is the Baan Thai building, a massive four-story log structure that's half American West, half Thai palace, which contains VIP lodging, conference rooms, and Thai spa treatment space. Guest rooms are very comfortable, and meals are served family-style in the main lodge. Recreation opportunities include horseback riding, hiking, rafting, mountain biking, pack trips, and gold panning. Spa facilities include an indoor pool and Jacuzzi, plus a full selection of therapeutic, aesthetic, and hydrotherapy treatments featuring standard therapies plus Thai stretching and massage. This isn't your typical guest ranch, but if you're looking for upscale spa facilities plus horseback riding, this is the place for you. Check the website for 3- to 14-day spa and recreation packages. The ranch is a member of Small Luxury Hotels of the World.

50km (31 miles) northeast of Clinton. Mailing address: P.O. Box 16, Jesmond, BC V0K 1K0. www.evranch.com. © **800/253-8831** or 604/988-3230. Fax 250/459-0086. 20 units. July–Aug packages start from C$370 per person based on double occupancy, 2-day minimum stay; low-season rates from C$190. Nightly stays sometimes available; contact ranch 2 weeks before proposed arrival dates. Rates include all meals and access to all ranch facilities; horseback riding and guided activities are extra. Packages available. MC, V. Special kids weeks (July, August, Easter, and Christmas); otherwise children 13 and older only. **Amenities:** Restaurant; lounge; exercise room; games room; Jacuzzi; indoor pool; sauna; spa. *In room:* Fridge, hair dryer, robes, Wi-Fi (free).

100 MILE HOUSE & THE SOUTH CARIBOO DISTRICT

100 Mile House: 178km (111 miles) N of Lillooet; 330km (205 miles) S of Prince George

Named for the roadhouse inn that marked the 100th mile north of Lillooet in the days of the Cariboo gold rush, 100 Mile House (pop. about 2,000) is an attractive ranching community at the heart of a vast recreational paradise. There are thousands of lakes in the valleys that ring the town, making canoeing, fishing, and boating popular activities. In winter, the gently rolling landscape, combined with heavy snowfalls, make 100 Mile House a major cross-country ski destination.

Thirteen kilometers (8 miles) north is 108 Mile House, another frontier-era community now famed for its golf course and **108 Mile House Heritage Site** (www.historical.bc.ca). This collection of ranch buildings includes an enormous log barn built to stable 200 Clydesdales, the horsepower that drove the stagecoaches.

For information on this region, contact the **South Cariboo Visitor Centre,** 155 Airport Rd., 100 Mile House (© **877/511-5353** or 250/395-5353; www.southcaribootourism.ca).

Fishing & Watersports

100 Mile House is a pleasant enough little town, but it's the outdoor recreation in the surrounding South Cariboo Lakes District that brings most people here. There are

dozens of lakes, nearly all with rustic fishing resorts as well as provincial parks offering campgrounds and public boat launches. Be sure to pick up the *Cariboo-Chilcotin Fishing Guide* at the visitor center. For tackle, licenses, and advice, head to **Donex Pharmacy,** 145 S. Birch St. (© 250/395-4004).

One lake-filled area lies southeast of 100 Mile House along Hwy. 24, which connects Hwy. 97 with Hwy. 5 at Little Fort, on the Thompson River. This scenic drive climbs up along a high plateau between the watersheds of the Fraser and Thompson rivers. The road leads to so many excellent fishing lakes that it's often referred to as the "Fishing Highway."

On Sheridan Lake, **Loon Bay Resort,** 40km (25 miles) southeast of 100 Mile House (© **250/593-4431;** www.loonbayresort.com), rents tackle, canoes, and motorboats; and maintains cabins (from C$75–C$120 double) and campsites (C$25–C$31).

Perhaps the most beautiful of all these lakes is **Lac des Roches,** 64km (40 miles) east of 100 Mile House. The handsome **Lac Des Roches Resort** (www.lacdes roches.com; © 250/593-4141) offers boat rentals, campsites (C$15), and lakeside cabins (from C$89 double). The Italian restaurant at the resort is one of the finest spots in the area to dine. It's even worthwhile to drop by for a cappuccino (served with chocolates and cookies) and a look at the collection of antique grappa bottles.

Northeast of 100 Mile House is another lake-filled valley. **Canim Lake** is the most developed, with good swimming beaches. The venerable **Ponderosa Resort** (© **250/397-2243;** www.ponderosaresort.com) offers boat rentals, guided fishing, and horseback riding. Motel-style rooms are C$105, cabins are C$115 to C$130, and campsites are around C$28 to C$40.

If you're looking for a wilderness canoeing experience, **Moose Valley Provincial Park** preserves a series of small glacial lakes that are linked by short portage trails. The most popular route begins at Marks Lake and links with 11 other lakes, making for a leisurely 2-day loop paddle. For more information, contact **BC Parks** (www.env. gov.bc.ca/bcparks).

Other Outdoor Pursuits

CROSS-COUNTRY SKIING In February, the town hosts the **Cariboo Marathon,** a 50km (31-mile) Nordic skiing race that draws 150 to 200 contestants. There's an extensive public trail system with more than 150km (93 miles) of groomed trails in the area, with some parts lit at night. Visit **www.100milenordics.com** for trail details and events. Many resorts and guest ranches also have groomed trails.

GOLF The region's finest course is undoubtedly at **108 Golf Resort,** in 108 Mile House (© **800/667-5233** or 250/791-5211; www.108golfresort.com). The 18-hole championship course has two lakes, undulating fairways, and fast putting greens. The resort offers a driving range, a pro shop, and lessons.

Where to Stay & Eat

While the **Firehouse Diner** (231 Birch Ave. S.; © **778/482-5511;** www.firehouse diner.ca) has a fairly typical menu at first glance, many dishes are completely homemade from family recipes. Comfort foods dominate, be it the mozzarella-topped meatloaf, spaghetti and meatballs, or house-smoked beef brisket. Mains ranges from C$9 to C$20.

Hills Health & Guest Ranch This spa and guest ranch offers a full complement of beauty and health treatments as well as activities such as horseback riding, mountain biking, hayrides, downhill skiing on the ranch's own ski area, and cross-country skiing on 167km (more than 100 miles) of private trails. Popular activities include breakfast horseback rides, yoga classes, and lake canoeing. The spa has a variety of offerings, including massage, facials, and reflexology. Also popular are 6- to 30-day weight-loss and physical therapy programs guided by professional nutritionists and therapists. Within the vast spa building are hydrotherapy pools, an aerobics gym, dry saunas, and 18 treatment rooms. The guest rooms are rather basic, featuring ranch-style natural pine decor; also available are three-bedroom chalets with kitchens. The lodge restaurant serves a unique blend of cowboy favorites and spa cuisine, specializing in fondue and hot-rock cooking. All programs, therapies, and activities can be customized to form your own personalized package vacation.

Hwy. 97; Box 26, 108 Mile Ranch, BC V0K 2Z0. www.spabc.com. © **800/668-2233** or 250/791-5225. Fax 250/791-6384. 45 units. From C$55–C$65 per person for bed-and-breakfast; 3-bedroom chalets C$159–C$209. All-inclusive packages available. AE, DISC, MC, V. **Amenities:** 2 restaurants; lounge; bike rentals; exercise room; nearby golf course; Jacuzzi; indoor pool; 2 outdoor ice-skating rinks; full-service spa; ski rentals. *In room:* A/C, TV, Wi-Fi (free).

108 Golf Resort ★ This motel-style resort centers on its fantastic golf course, although even if you're not a duffer, there's a lot to like here. Other activities here include horseback riding, mountain biking, and canoeing. In winter, the golf course is transformed into a vast undulating cross-country center. Guest rooms are large, all with balconies that overlook either the golf course or a small lake. Golf, cross-country-skiing, and horseback-riding packages are available.

13km (8 miles) north of 100 Mile House, 4816 Telqua Dr., Box 2, 108 Mile Ranch, BC V0K 2Z0. www.108golfresort.com. © **800/667-5233** or 250/791-5211. Fax 250/791-6537. 40 units and campsites. C$90–C$130 double. Extra person C$10. Rate includes continental breakfast. Packages available. AE, MC, V. **Amenities:** Bike rentals; Jacuzzi; outdoor pool; sauna; tennis; canoe rentals; stables. *In room:* A/C, TV, fridge, hair dryer, kitchenette (some rooms), microwave, Wi-Fi (free).

Ramada Limited ♨ The area's newest hotel, the Ramada has large, well-furnished rooms in a variety of configurations and styles. In addition to standard hotel rooms there are king-size-bed suites with Jacuzzi tubs, fireplaces, and balconies. Eight suites have kitchenettes. Small pets are allowed in some of the guest rooms. All in all, it's a good value for a quality room in a walkable location.

917 Alder Ave. (Hwy. 97), 100 Mile House, BC V0K 2E0. www.ramada.com. © **877/395-2777** or 250/395-2777. Fax 250/395-2037. 36 units. From C$105 double; from C$165 suite. Rates include continental breakfast. AE, MC, V. Pets C$10. *In room:* A/C, TV, fridge, hair dryer, microwave, Wi-Fi (free).

WILLIAMS LAKE

90km (56 miles) N of 100 Mile House; 539km (334 miles) N of Vancouver

Unabashedly a ranch town, Williams Lake (pop. about 11,000) is known across the West for its large, hell's-a-poppin' rodeo, the **Williams Lake Stampede,** held the first weekend of July. It's also the gateway to the Chilcotin, the coastal mountainous area to the west. As the trade center for a large agricultural area, the lakeside town bustles with activity.

The downtown area is west of the Hwy. 97 strip, centered on Oliver Street. The **Cariboo Friendship Society Native Arts and Crafts Shop,** 99 S. Third Ave. (© **250/398-6831;** www.cariboofriendshipsociety.ca), sells the work of local Native artists. The building that houses the shop was constructed to resemble a Shuswap

The **Williams Lake Stampede** is one of Canada's top rodeos, and is the only British Columbia rodeo on the Canadian Professional Rodeo Association circuit. Begun in the 1920s, the Stampede has grown into a 4-day festival held over the July 1 long weekend. Rodeo cowboys from across Canada and the western United States gather here to compete for prizes in excess of C$11,000 for each professional event.

What makes the Stampede so popular is that in addition to the usual rodeo events—barrel racing, bareback and saddle bronc riding, calf roping, bull riding—there are a number of unusual competitions that provide lots of laughs and action. The Ranch Challenge pits real working cowboys from area ranches in a pouch-passing pony express race, a hilarious wild cow-milking contest, and a cattle-penning contest. There are also chariot races with two-horse teams and a chuck-wagon race with four-horse teams. In a variation on British sheep-dog trials, the Top Dog Competition pits a cowboy and his ranch dog against three unruly cows. The dog puts the cows through a course of barrels, then into a pen; the fastest dog wins.

Other Old West events, such as barn dances, a parade, midway rides, and grandstand entertainment, add to the fun. Because the Stampede is very popular, accommodations go fast—make plans well ahead.

For more information, contact the Williams Lake Stampede, P.O. Box 4076, Williams Lake, BC V2G 2V2 (© **800-71-RODEO** [717-6336] or 250/398-8388; www.williamslakestampede.com). All reserved seats cost C$19; general seating is C$17 adults and C$12 seniors and children under 12.

pit-house dwelling. The old train depot has been in part converted into **Station House Gallery,** 1 MacKenzie Ave. N. at Oliver Street (© **250/392-6113;** www.stationhousegallery.com), with local arts and crafts.

The **Museum of the Cariboo Chilcotin,** 113 N. Fourth Ave. (© **250/392-7404;** www.cowboy-museum.com), is the only museum in B.C. to focus on ranching and rodeo, honoring both the cowboys of the past and those of the present. The museum is home to the B.C. Cowboy Hall of Fame and also features an exhibit on ranching women, Native arrowheads, and a replica blacksmith shop. It's open Monday through Saturday from 10am to 4pm from June through August, and 11am to 4pm Tuesday through Saturday the rest of the year. Admission is C$2 adult.

For information, contact the **Williams Lake Visitor Centre,** 1660 S. Broadway (© **250/392-5025;** www.williamslakechamber.com).

Outdoor Pursuits

Red Shreds Bike and Board Shop, 95 S. First Ave. (© **250/398-7873;** www.redshreds.com), offers a bounty of information on local hiking, mountain biking, and kayaking; bike and kayak rentals; and a number of specialty trail maps.

WHITE-WATER RAFTING The Chilko-Chilcotin-Fraser river system that runs from the Coast Mountains east is a major rafting destination, though not for the faint of heart or the unguided novice. Inquire at the **visitor center** or **Red Shreds** (see above) for information, tours, and rentals.

Where to Stay

Coast Fraser Inn The Fraser Inn overlooks Williams Lake from its hillside perch north of town along Hwy. 97. Large and modern, it offers a level of facilities not usually found in small ranch towns. Most rooms have great views.

285 Donald Rd., Williams Lake, BC V2G 4K4. www.coasthotels.com. © **800/716-6199** or 250/398-7055. Fax 250/398-8269. 79 units. From C$119 double. Extra person C$10. Rate includes breakfast buffet. AE, MC, V. Pets accepted. **Amenities:** Restaurant; exercise room; Jacuzzi; room service; sauna; beer-and-wine store. *In room:* A/C, TV, fridge, hair dryer, Wi-Fi (free).

Drummond Lodge This motel just east of downtown has a lovely location right above the lake and is adjacent to public parkland. Standard rooms are clean and well-furnished while larger suitelike rooms have kitchenettes and balconies overlooking the extensive gardens.

1405 Hwy. 97 S., Williams Lake, BC V2G 2W3. www.drummondlodge.com. © **800/667-4555** or 250/392-5334. Fax 250/392-1117. 24 units. C$80–C$130. MC, V. Pets C$7. **Amenities:** Gardens. *In room:* A/C, TV, Wi-Fi (free).

Sandman Inn and Suites Just 2 blocks from downtown Williams Lake, the Sandman has a newer wing of large one-bedroom suites, plus an older wing with regular hotel units. You'll find the place clean, friendly, and close to everything you'll want to do in Williams Lake. A 24-hour Denny's restaurant shares the premises.

664 Oliver St., Williams Lake, BC V2G 1M6. www.sandman.ca. © **800/726-3626** or 250/392-6557. Fax 250/392-6242. 111 units. C$105–C$179 double. Senior discounts offered. AE, MC, V. Small pets allowed for C$10 per day. **Amenities:** Restaurant; indoor pool; sauna. *In room:* A/C, TV, hair dryer, Wi-Fi (free).

Where to Eat

Gecko Tree CAFE 🍴 This funky breakfast and lunch cafe in downtown Williams Lake makes great coffee to complement the freshly baked sticky buns. It's warm and homey, with a bit of local quirk. Try the Ravenous Redneck sandwich, which layers chicken, bacon, sausage, and cheese with vegetables on homemade bread, or the custom-made quesadillas.

54 MacKenzie Ave. N. (at Oliver St.), Williams Lake. © **250/398-8983.** Main courses C$7–C$15. AE, MC, V. Tues–Fri 7:30am–4pm, Sat 9am–4pm.

WEST ON HWY. 20 TO BELLA COOLA

450km (280 miles) W of Williams Lake

Hwy. 20 cuts through a rugged land of lakes and mountains on its way to Bella Coola, a First Nations village on a Pacific inlet. This journey takes the adventurous driver from Williams Lake and the desert canyons of the Fraser River to glaciated peaks and finally to the shores of a narrow ocean fjord. It's an amazingly scenic trip, but be ready for lots of gravel roads and steep grades. There aren't a lot of facilities along the way, so start out with a full tank of gas. You can easily make this trip in a day, especially in summer, but leave plenty of time to stop and explore.

After climbing up out of the Fraser Canyon, Hwy. 20 winds along the **Chilcotin Plateau,** miles of spacious grasslands that are home to some of the largest ranches in North America. At Hanceville, the route drops onto the **Chilcotin River,** famed for its white-water rafting and kayaking. The **Chilcotin Lodge,** in Riske Creek (© **250/659-5646;** www.chilcotinlodge.com), is a popular place to stop for a home-style meal and exudes a true historic ranch feel. You can camp right on the river at **Bull Canyon Provincial Park,** with 20 sites at C$16 apiece. The park is 7km (4⅓ miles) west of Alexis Creek, 121km (75 miles) west of Williams Lake.

As Hwy. 20 presses closer to the Coast Mountains, the landscape is increasingly dotted with lakes and marshes. At the wee community of **Tatla Lake,** the pavement ends and the gravel begins. **Anahim Lake,** 320km (199 miles) west of Williams Lake and one of the largest settlements on the Chilcotin Plateau (pop. 145), is noted for its fishing and outdoor recreation. The **Escott Bay Resort** (© **888/380-8802** or 250/742-3233; www.escottbay.com) offers cabins starting at C$80 and campsites for C$20. The general store in Anahim Lake is over a century old, and its coffeepot is always on. The enormous glaciated peak that dominates the southern skyline is **Mount Waddington,** which at 4,019m (13,186 ft.) is the highest point in the Coast Mountains.

As you begin the final ascent up to 1,524m (5,000-ft.) **Heckman Pass,** note the **Rainbow Range,** 2,000m-plus (6,562-ft.-plus) peaks that are brilliantly colored by purple, red, and yellow mineralization, although it's a multi-day hike or short flight to get a glimpse of the most spectacular coloring.

Thirty kilometers (19 miles) from Anahim Lake, Hwy. 20 crests Heckman Pass, and then begins **"The Hill."** Bella Coola residents had long dreamed of a road connection to the rest of the province, and a succession of provincial governments promised to build one from the Chilcotin Plateau down to the Pacific. When years went by and nothing happened—civil engineers doubted that a safe road could be made down the steep western face of the Coast Mountains—the locals took matters in their own hands. In 1953, two men in bulldozers set out, one from Heckman Pass, the other from the end of the road at the base of the Coast Mountains. In just 3 months, the two bulldozers kissed blades at the middle of the mountain, and Hwy. 20 was born. You'll feel your heart in your mouth on a number of occasions as you cork-screw your way down the road. The most notorious portion is 10km (6¼ miles) of gravel switchbacks, with gradients up to 18%, over which the road drops more than a kilometer (⅗ mile).

This part of Hwy. 20 passes through **Tweedsmuir Provincial Park,** British Columbia's second-largest park at nearly 1 million hectares (2.5 million acres). This vast wilderness park of soaring mountains, interlocking lakes, and abundant wildlife is accessible by long-distance hiking trails, floatplane, and canoe. For information, contact **BC Parks** (www.env.gov.bc.ca/bcparks).

The town at the end of the road, **Bella Coola** (pop. 1,900), is a disorganized little burg strung along a green glacier-carved valley. Ancestral home to the Bella Coola tribe, Bella Coola once held a Hudson's Bay Company trading fort, then became a fishing center for Norwegian settlers. The waterfront is a busy place in summer, with fishing and pleasure boats coming and going.

Besides the lure of the end of the road, the main reason to drive to Bella Coola is to catch the **BC Ferries Discovery Coast** service (see chapter 8). This summer-only ferry connects Bella Coola with other even more isolated coastal communities. The ferry terminates at Port Hardy, on Vancouver Island, making this an increasingly popular loop trip. The journey lasts 12 to 14 hours. In high season, fares between Port Hardy and Bella Coola are C$180 per adult passenger and C$355 for a car.

Where to Stay & Eat

There are campsites with showers, laundry, a beach, and boat launch at **Bailey Bridge** (℃ 250/982-2342; www.baileybridge.ca). See also the Bella Coola Valley Motel, below.

Bella Coola Valley Inn This is the closest lodging to the ferry terminal, and the inn offers standard motel-style units. Extras include a popular restaurant, with unexpected dishes like sushi and Korean barbecue ribs.

441 MacKenzie St., Box 183, Bella Coola, BC V0T 1C0. www.bellacoolavalleyinn.com. ℃ **888/799-5316** or 250/799-5316. Fax 250/799-5610. 20 units. C$115 double. Extra person C$10. AE, MC, V. **Amenities:** Restaurant; pub; airport and ferry shuttle service; sauna. *In room:* A/C, TV, fridge, Wi-Fi (free).

Bella Coola Valley Motel Located right in the middle of downtown, this motel occupies the site of the old Hudson's Bay Company trading post on the waterfront. Guest rooms are spacious, and all include basic kitchens. RV and tent sites go for C$15.

1224 Clayton St., Box 188, Bella Coola, BC V0T 1C0. www.bellacoolamotel.com. ℃/fax **250/799-5323.** 10 units. C$90–C$110 double. Extra person C$10. AE, MC, V. Free parking. Pets conditionally accepted with deposit. **Amenities:** Free airport shuttle *In room:* TV, kitchen, Wi-Fi (free).

QUESNEL

120km (75 miles) N of Williams Lake; 664km (413 miles) N of Vancouver; 122km (76 miles) S of Prince George

Like most other towns in the Cariboo District, Quesnel (pop. 9,900) was founded during the gold-rush years. Now mostly a logging center, Quesnel serves as gateway to the ghost town of Barkerville and to the canoe paddler's paradise, the Bowron Lake canoe circuit. It also serves as the overnight stop on Rocky Mountaineer Vacations train tour line between Whistler and Jasper.

Quesnel is located on a jut of land at the confluence of the Fraser and Quesnel rivers. The small downtown is almost completely surrounded by these rivers. **Ceal Tingley Park,** on the Fraser side, is a pleasant place for a stroll, and it's one of the few spots where you can get right down to the huge and powerful Fraser. Directly across the street is a Hudson's Bay Company trading post built in 1882; it currently houses **Cariboo Keepsakes** (℃ **250/991-0419**)—a gift shop selling work by local artisans.

The main commercial strip is **Reid Street,** a block east of Hwy. 97. A walk along Reid Street reveals the kinds of old-fashioned shops and services that have been gobbled up by behemoths like Wal-Mart in the United States.

Over on the Quesnel River side of downtown is **LeBourdais Park,** which contains the visitor center and the **Quesnel and District Museum and Archives,** 705 Carson Ave. (℃ **250/992-9580**; www.quesnelmuseum.ca), which tells the story of the gold rush and has good exhibits on the Chinese who worked in the camps. It's open daily May to early September; the rest of the year, Wednesday through Saturday only.

A rodeo, river-raft races, and amusement rides attract thousands to Quesnel during the second week of July for **Billy Barker Days** (℃ **250/992-8716**; www.billy barkerdays.ca). For general information, contact the **Quesnel Visitor Centre,** in LeBourdais Park, 703 Carson Ave. (℃ **250/992-8716**; www.northcariboo.com).

Where to Stay

Ten Mile Lake Provincial Park, 12km (7½ miles) north of Quesnel off Hwy. 97 (✆ 800/689-9025), has 108 campsites from C$16. Open May through September, the park has flush toilets and showers.

Best Western Tower Inn Right in the middle of downtown, though off the busy main thoroughfare, the Tower Inn offers clean, crisp guest rooms. Begbie's Bar and Bistro is a popular eatery and hangout.

500 Reid St., Quesnel, BC V2J 2M9. www.bwtowerinn.ca. ✆ **800/663-2009** or 250/992-2201. Fax 250/ 992-5201. 63 units. C$100–C$149 double. Extra person C$5. AE, MC, V. **Amenities:** Restaurant; bar; exercise room; room service. *In room:* A/C, TV w/pay movies, fridge, hair dryer, Wi-Fi (free).

Ramada Limited ☺ This well-equipped hotel is in the center of Quesnel, and while that's not promising a lot, it's more interesting than staying at a freeway exit. Next door is the city government and civic center, with a fitness center and skating rink. For the price, the rooms are nicely furnished, and there's a pool area for the kids.

383 St. Laurent Ave., Quesnel, BC V2J 2E1. www.ramada.ca. ✆ **800/663-1581** or 250/992-5575. Fax 250/995-2254. 46 units. C$80–C$100 double. Rates include continental breakfast. Pets C$10. AE, MC, V. **Amenities:** Indoor pool; Jacuzzi. *In room:* A/C, TV, fridge, hair dryer, Wi-Fi (free).

Where to Eat

For a casual lunch, visit the flower-trimmed patio at **Granville's Coffee** (383 Reid St.; ✆ **250/992-3667**). The restaurant's kitschy feel is rounded out by a range of comfort foods, from macaroni and cheese to pies and apple crisp. It's open daily.

Mr. Mike's Steakhouse & Bar CANADIAN Mr. Mike's is probably the hippest place in Quesnel, with their own brand of microbrewed beers and a cocktail menu that would make a Yaletown club in Vancouver proud. The dining room serves up eclectic fare that focuses on steaks, but includes grilled salmon and boutique burgers. A few Mexican- and Thai-influenced dishes also make their way onto the menu.

450 Reid St. ✆ **250/992-7742**. www.mrmikes.ca. Reservations recommended. Main courses C$8–C$32. AE, MC, V. Daily 11am–11pm. Until midnight Thurs–Sat.

River Rock Pub and Steakhouse PUB This pub overlooks the Moffat Bridge and the Fraser River, with an outdoor deck to frame the view. The menu is broad, ranging from burgers to steaks to East Indian specialties. Families are welcome, and you're sure to find something that will appeal to everyone.

290 Hoy St. ✆ **250/991-0100**. www.riverrockpub.com. Reservations not needed. Main courses C$10–C$35. MC, V. Sun–Thurs 11am–midnight; Fri & Sat 11am–1am.

EAST TO BARKERVILLE ★ & BOWRON LAKE ★

Barkerville: 86km (53 miles) E of Quesnel

Barkerville is one of the premier tourist destinations in interior British Columbia, as well as one of the most intact ghost towns in Canada. However, what lures paddlers and campers to the Cariboo Mountains today isn't a flash of gold, but the splash of water at the Bowron Lake Provincial Park. Within the park, a chain of six major—and a number of smaller—interconnecting lakes attract canoeists and kayakers who paddle and portage around the entire 116km (72-mile) circuit.

Follow the signs in Quesnel to Hwy. 26 E. The 86km (53-mile) drive to Barkerville takes you deep into the forests of the Cariboo Mountains, where moose and deer are often spotted from the road. The paved highway ends at Barkerville. Bowron Lake is another 26km (16 miles) northeast on a gravel road.

Exploring Barkerville: An Old West Ghost Town

The 1860 Cariboo gold rush was the reason thousands of miners made their way north from the played-out Fraser River gold deposits to Williams Creek, east of Quesnel. **Barkerville ★** was founded on its shore after Billy Barker discovered one of the region's richest gold deposits in 1862. The town sprang up practically overnight; that year, it was reputedly the largest city west of Chicago and north of San Francisco. Many of the claims continued to produce well into the 1930s, but Barkerville's population moved on, leaving behind an intact ghost town that was designated a historic park in the 1950s.

The original 1870 **Anglican church** and 125 other buildings have been lovingly reconstructed or restored. The **Richland courthouse** stages trials from the town's past. From May to Labour Day, "townspeople" dress in period costumes. Visitors can pan for gold, dine in the Chinatown section, or take a stagecoach ride. In winter, the town becomes a haven for **cross-country skiers.** During the holidays, Barkerville hosts a special **Victorian Christmas** celebration.

Admission to the town is C$15 adults, C$14 seniors, C$9.50 teens 13 to 18, C$4.75 children 6 to 12, and C$36 families. Barkerville is open year-round, daily from dawn to dusk, with interpretive activities from mid-May through September. For information, contact **Barkerville Historic Town,** Box 19, Barkerville, BC V0K 1B0 (✆ **888/994-3332** or 250/994-3332; www.barkerville.ca).

WHERE TO STAY & EAT

There are three campgrounds that are part of the historic town. Lowhee, Forest Rose, and Government Hill campgrounds (✆ **866/994-3297** or 250/994-3297; www.barkervillecampgrounds.ca) are open year-round. Sites go for C$23. **Government Hill Campground** is the closest to the park entrance but only has pit toilets. **Lowhee,** 2km (1 mile) from the historic town, has showers, flush toilets, pumped well water, and a sani-station.

The Wells Hotel Established in 1933, the 13 historic rooms at this restored hotel near Barkerville are filled with lovely antique furnishings. The hotel offers amenities that you'll truly appreciate after a day of hiking, canoeing, skiing, or gold-panning: fine dining, a frothy cappuccino, and a soothing hot tub. Guest rooms are tastefully refurbished and decorated with antiques and local artwork. Some units have private bathrooms and/or fireplaces. Continental breakfast is included in all rates.

Pooley St. (Box 39), Wells, BC V0K 2R0. www.wellshotel.com. ✆ **800/860-2299** in Canada, or 250/994-3427. Fax 250/994-3494. 13 units. From C$95 double. Lower winter rates. Rates include breakfast. MC, V. **Amenities:** Restaurant; lounge; pub; bike rental; Jacuzzi. *In room:* Wi-Fi (free).

Paddling Bowron Lake: A Canoeist's Paradise

Twenty-six kilometers (16 miles) northeast of Barkerville over an unpaved road, there's access to a circle of lakes that attracts canoeists and kayakers from around the world. The 149,207-hectare (368,690-acre) **Bowron Lake Provincial Park** is a majestic paddler's paradise set against a backdrop of glacial peaks.

The 7-day circular route is 116km (72 miles) of unbroken wilderness. It begins at Kibbee Creek and Kibbee Lake, flows into Indianpoint Lake, Isaac Lake, and the Isaac River, and continues to McLeary, Lanezi, Sandy, and Unna lakes before entering the final stretch: Babcock Lake, Skoi Lake, the Spectacle Lakes, Swan Lake, and finally Bowron Lake. The long, narrow lakes afford visitors a close look at both shores. You'll catch sight of moose, mountain goats, beavers, black bears, and grizzly bears. Be prepared to portage for a total of 10.8km (6⅔ miles) between some of the creeks that connect the lakes. The longest single portage is 3km (1¾ miles). You must pack everything in and out of the wilderness camps.

The number of canoes and people allowed to enter the park per day is restricted in summer. Permit bookings are handled by **Discover Camping** (© **800/689-9025;** www.discovercamping.ca). Fees for a full circuit are C$60 per person per one-person canoe/kayak, or C$120 per two-person canoe/kayak. There's a reservation fee of C$18. The canoe circuit is open May 15 to Sept 30.

You don't have to make the entire journey to enjoy this incredible setting. Open May through September, the **campground** at the park's entrance is a relaxing spot to camp, fish, boat, take day-long paddles, or take in the abundant flora and fauna.

WHERE TO STAY

Bowron Lake Lodge & Resorts   This rustic resort provides all the creature comforts you could ask for in a wilderness setting. Guests can choose from comfortable motel rooms, cabins (with no hot water and you must bring your own bedding), or campsites. There are 5km (3.1 miles) of trails, 650m (2,133 ft.) of private beach, and an airstrip. Views across the lake and onto the forested craggy peaks are extremely dramatic.

Bowron Lake, 672 Walkem St., Quesnel, BC V2J 2J7. www.bowronlakelodge.com. © **800/519-3399** or 250/992-2733. 16 units, 50 campsites. C$40–C$80 double; C$28 campsite. MC, V. Closed Nov–Apr. **Amenities:** Restaurant; lounge; bike, canoe, and motorboat rentals. *In room:* No phone.

THE THOMPSON RIVER VALLEY

Kamloops: 345km (214 miles) NE of Vancouver; 218km (135 miles) W of Revelstoke

From its juncture with the Fraser River at Lytton, the Thompson River cuts north, then east through an arid countryside grazed by cattle. **Kamloops,** a major trade center for this agricultural region, is increasingly a retirement center for refugees from the mists of the Pacific coast. In the South Thompson River valley, the **Shuswap Lakes** are popular with houseboaters. It's easy to rent a houseboat in **Salmon Arm** and navigate the 1,000km (621 miles) of waterways, landing at campsites and beaches along the way.

Rising up from the dry terrain of Kamloops, heading north along Hwy. 5, the road enters the cool forests of the High Country. High above the town of **Clearwater** is the pristine wilderness of **Wells Gray Provincial Park.**

Kamloops & Vicinity

At the confluence of the north and south forks of the Thompson River, Kamloops (pop. 87,000) is the province's fifth-largest city. The forest-products industry is the city's primary economic force, although Kamloops is also a major service center for ranchers and farmers. For travelers, Kamloops makes a handy stopover between other destinations, and it's developing its own charm and culinary scene. Its greatest attraction is the all-season Sun Peaks Resort, in the mountains north of the city.

ESSENTIALS

GETTING THERE   You can fly into Kamloops on **Air Canada** (© 888/247-2262; www.flyjazz.ca), which operates daily 50-minute flights from Vancouver, and rent a car at the airport from **Budget** (© 800/268-8900 in Canada, 800/527-0700 in the U.S.; www.budget.com), or **National** (© 877/222-9058 or 250/376-4911; www.nationalcar.com).

Kamloops is a junction point for many provincial roads, including the Trans-Canada Highway and the Coquihalla (Hwy. 5), the fastest route to/from Vancouver.

There are six daily **Greyhound Canada** (© 800/661-8747; www.greyhound.ca) buses from Vancouver; the fare is C$60. **VIA Rail** (© 888/VIA-RAIL [842-7245]; www.viarail.ca) passes through on the main transnational route. Kamloops is also the overnight stop for **Rocky Mountaineer** (© 877/460-3200; www.rocky mountaineer.com) luxury train trips from Vancouver to Jasper and Banff. For more information on this train, see p. 27.

VISITOR INFORMATION   Contact the **Kamloops Visitor Info Centre,** 1290 W. Trans-Canada Hwy., at exit 368 (© 800/662-1994 or 250/374-3377; www. tourismkamloops.com).

EXPLORING THE AREA

Kamloops is a sprawling city in a wide river valley flanked by high desert mountains. A major service center for agricultural industries, Kamloops has a gentrifying heritage district, lush city parks, and a surprisingly active nightlife. The downtown core, centered around **Victoria Street,** is a pleasant, tree-lined area. North of downtown along the Thompson is **Riverfront Park,** a lovely expanse of green in an otherwise arid landscape.

Kamloops Art Gallery   This is the only public art museum in the Thompson region and the largest in the province's interior, with a collection of about 2,500 works by mostly local and Canadian artists. The gallery also mounts changing exhibits of international works.

465 Victoria St. © **250/377-2400.** www.kag.bc.ca. Admission C$5 adults and senior couples, C$3 seniors and students, C$10 families; free admission on Thurs. Mon–Sat 10am–5pm (Thurs until 9pm).

Secwepemc Museum & Heritage Park ★   The Secwepemc (pronounced "*She*-whep-m," anglicized as Shuswap) people have lived along the Thompson River for thousands of years. This 4.8-hectare (12-acre) heritage park contains an actual

---

The Salmon Run & Other Special Events

One of nature's most amazing phenomena, the **Adams River Salmon Run** ★, takes place in late October. Salmon return every year but there's a surge every 4 years when 1.5 to 2 million sockeye salmon struggle upstream to spawn in the Adams River. Trails provide riverside-viewing, with trained staff ready to interpret the spectacle. From Kamloops, take the Trans-Canada Highway (Hwy. 1) to Squilax, 10km (6¼ miles) east of Chase. Follow the signs north to Roderick Haig-Brown Provincial Park. The next expected surge of sockeye is in 2014.

In January, the **Reino Keski-Salmi Loppet** (www.skilarchhills.ca) attracts cross-country skiers from across North America to the Larch Hills Cross-Country Ski Hill, east of Kamloops in Salmon Arm.

archaeological site which was inhabited 2,400 to 1,200 years ago, plus reconstructions of traditional villages from five different eras. Also featured are displays of native plants and their traditional uses and a replica of a salmon-netting station.

355 Yellowhead Hwy. (℃) **250/828-9749.** www.secwepemc.org/museum. Admission C$12 adults, C$7 children 7–17 and seniors. June 1 to Labour Day weekend daily 8:30am–4:30pm; Labour Day through May Mon–Fri 8am–4pm.

OUTDOOR PURSUITS

Sun Peaks Resort ★, on Tod Mountain Road, Heffley Creek (www.sunpeaksresort. com; (℃) **800/807-3257** or 250/578-5474, 250/578-7232 for snow report), is a major all-season resort and mountain community with some of the most complete sports and recreation facilities in British Columbia. Of course, in winter the focus is on downhill skiing. Sun Peaks offers great powder skiing on three different mountains, with 1,488 hectares (3,678 acres) of skiable terrain, making it Canada's third-largest ski area. The total vertical drop is 882m (2,894 ft.), with 122 runs serviced by three high-speed quad chairs, two quad chairlifts, one triple chair, and five other lifts. Snowboarders have the run of a 3.6 hectare (9-acre) terrain park with handrails, cars, a fun box, hips, quarter pipes, transfers, and fat gaps that were designed by Ecosign Mountain Planners and some of Canada's top amateur riders. Lift tickets are C$74 for adults, C$59 seniors and youths 13 to 18, and C$37 for children 6 to 12. Nordic skiers have more than 30km (19 miles) of groomed cross-country trails, and 14km (9 miles) of backcountry runs. The resort also offers dog sledding, snowshoeing, and snowmobile trails.

In summer, the lifts continue to operate, providing mountain bikers and hikers access to the high country. Sun Peak's bike park offers 29 trails, dropping 595m (1,952 ft.) through varied terrain. The lifts run daily late June through Labour Day. A day pass to the bike park and lifts costs C$39 adults, C$33 seniors and youths 13 to 18, and C$23 children 6 to 12. For hikers, a ride on the lifts up to alpine trails costs C$18 adults, C$15 seniors and youths 13 to 18, and C$12 children 6 to 12.

The Sun Peaks Resort Golf Course is another top summer draw. At 1,200m (3,937 ft.) above sea level, this 18-hole, Graham Cooke–designed course offers spectacular alpine vistas that are sure to challenge your concentration. And while golfers enjoy the course, other members of the family have the option of horseback riding, canoeing, stand-up paddle boarding, or hiking, all of which can be easily arranged with the resort's Guest Services. The resort offers a wide variety of lodging options including nine hotels, a selection of condos, B&Bs, and one- to four-bedroom town homes and chalets. With a choice of over 20 dining and nightlife options, Sun Peaks offers a more lively social and gastronomic scene that most midsize Canadian cities.

GOLF **Aberdeen Hills Golf Links,** 1185 Links Way ((℃) **250/828-1149** or 250/ 828-1143; www.aberdeenhills.com), is an 18-hole course with panoramic views. **The Dunes,** 652 Dunes Dr. ((℃) **888/881-4653** or 250/579-3300; www.golfthedunes. com), is a Graham Cooke–designed 18-hole championship course. **Kamloops Golf & Country Club,** 2960 Tranquille Rd. ((℃) **250/376-8020;** www.kamloopsgolfclub. com), is an 18-hole course redesigned in 2010. **Pineridge Golf Course,** 4725 E. Trans-Canada Hwy. ((℃) **250/573-4333;** www.pineridgegolf.bc.ca), is an 18-hole course designed to be "the best short course ever built."

Rivershore Estates and Golf Links ★ (330 Rivershore Dr.; (℃) **250/573-4622;** www.rivershoregolflinks.com) is an award-winning Robert Trent Jones, Sr., design and has been host to the Canadian National Championships. For family-friendly golf, **McArthur Island Golf Centre** ((℃) **250/554-3211**) offers a 9-hole course, driving range, miniature golf, pro shop, and restaurant.

WHERE TO STAY

In addition to the following downtown lodgings, you'll find a phalanx of easy-in, easy-out motels at Hwy. 1, exit 368, south and west of the city center.

Plaza Heritage Hotel ★ The Plaza began its life as *the* downtown hotel in Kamloops. A gutting renovation of this 1920s luxury lodging allowed it to once again reclaim that title. In 2011 another revamp of the property restyled the rooms with a more business-like decor. Still, the glorious lobby and heritage elevator boast a sense of grandeur. Luxury touches include hardwood floors, fine furniture, and spacious bathrooms. There are a number of room types and bed configurations—ask the reservation clerk to specify a room that will best serve your needs. The lobby restaurant offers fine dining, while the lounge is a comfortable spot for a friendly brew.

405 Victoria St., Kamloops, BC V2C 2A9. www.plazaheritagehotel.com. ℂ **877/977-5292** or 250/377-8075. Fax 250/377-8076. 67 units. From C$119–C$259 double. Rates include full breakfast. AE, MC, V. **Amenities:** Restaurant; coffee shop; lounge; beer-and-wine store. *In room:* A/C, TV, hair dryer, Wi-Fi (free).

Scott's Inn–Downtown ✦ A standard motel with clean, comfortable rooms and many extra features, Scott's is located in a quiet residential neighborhood within easy walking distance of downtown. Some units have kitchenettes. Save some money here without taking a cut in quality. There's a huge rooftop patio with barbecues for guests to use. The on-site restaurant serves breakfasts to charge you up for the rest of the day.

551 11th Ave., Kamloops, BC V2C 3Y1. www.scottsinn.com. ℂ **800/665-3343** or 250/372-8221. Fax 250/372-9444. 51 units. C$79–C$99 double. C$99–C$129 double with 2 beds. Kitchen C$10 extra. Extra person C$10. Rates include continental breakfast. Group, senior, corporate, and off-season discounts available. AE, MC, V. Pets C$10. **Amenities:** Restaurant; Jacuzzi; indoor pool. *In room:* A/C, TV w/movie channels, Wi-Fi (free).

WHERE TO EAT

Try **Scott's Inn Restaurant** (see above) for hearty, homemade options at budget prices. The eggs benedict is particularly tasty, as are the thick milkshakes. For late night drinks and appetizers visit the humming **Felix on Fourth** (260 Fourth Ave.; ℂ **250/434-4766;** www.felixonfourth.com) or sip the craft brews at the **Noble Pig** (650 Victoria St.; ℂ **778/471-5999;** www.thenoblepig.ca).

Brownstone Restaurant ★★ NEW CANADIAN With the most up-to-date cuisine in Kamloops, the Brownstone also offers period elegance and gracious service in downtown's historic Canadian Imperial Bank of Commerce building, built in 1904. The food is very refined yet full flavored, with a choice of small plates or full dinner service. Duck crepes with brandied hoisin and beef tenderloin with tamarind and a cumin curry are examples of the blend of spicey traditions and innovation that fuels the kitchen. In addition to the gracious dining room, in summer there's dining on a lovely outdoor patio. Catch a well-priced 3-course menu daily from 5 to 6:30pm for C$29.

118 Victoria St. ℂ **250/851-9939.** www.brownstone-restaurant.com. Reservations recommended. Main courses C$23–C$34. MC, V. Mon–Fri 11am–2pm; daily 5–10pm.

Ric's Mediterranean Grill ★ GRILL Part of a western Canadian chain, Ric's is always a solid choice for satisfying fine dining, and there's no better place to make your acquaintance than here, one of the first locations. Out in Kamloops, nobody cares if you mix cuisines, so you'll find a wide-ranging menu—among the tapas, selections such as the bruschetta with prawns and feta cheese; and from the dinner menu,

From Kamloops, the South Thompson River valley extends east to the Shuswap Lakes, a series of waterways that is an extremely popular summer destination for family houseboating parties. With more than 1,000km (621 miles) of shoreline, these long, interconnected lakes provide good fishing, water-skiing, and other boating fun.

The best way to see the lakes is to rent a houseboat; after all, Shuswap is the "Houseboating Capital of Canada." Houseboats come equipped with staterooms, bathrooms, and kitchens. All you need to bring is your bedding and food. Reserve well in advance; by late spring, all boats are usually rented for the high season, July and August. Low-season rates are up to half off the prices below.

Among a fleet of more than 100 vessels, **Twin Anchors Houseboat Vacations** (www.twinanchors.com; © **800/663-4026**) offers five types of boats, ranging from picks for couples and small families to those that can sleep 24 people. All boats have a hot tub, fireplace, barbecue, and waterslide. A week on a two-stateroom CruiseCraft II that sleeps 15 costs C$5,400 per week. Rentals are available in 3-, 4-, and 7-day increments.

Bluewater Houseboats (www.blue waterhouseboats.ca; © **800/663-4024** or 250/836-2255) has a mix of higher-end and older-model boats. As such, it has some good deals for those wanting something simpler. A week on the 8-berth Sport cruiser runs C$1,795.

The main commercial center for the Shuswap Lakes is **Salmon Arm** (pop. 16,000), 108km (67 miles) east of Kamloops on Hwy. 1. Right on the downtown lakefront is the **Prestige Harbourfront Resort & Convention Centre ★★**. A towering castellated structure, the Harbourfront Resort has very stylish and comfortable guest rooms, and public areas are suitably grand. In high season, rates begin at C$200.

chicken with a mushroom marsala sauce, Portuguese short ribs, or halibut with a pistachio crust. The decor matches the food; Ric's is a handsome place with warm wood furnishings and dramatic black and gold accents.

227 Victoria St. © **250/372-7771**. www.ricsgrill.com. Main courses C$16–C$30. AE, MC, V. Mon–Thurs 11am–9:30pm; Fri 11am–10pm; Sat 4–10pm; Sun 4–9:30pm.

The Upper Thompson River Valley

From Kamloops, the North Thompson River flows north into increasingly rugged terrain. The little town of **Clearwater** is the gateway to **Wells Gray Provincial Park,** the mountain wilderness park of choice for purist hikers, waterfall chasers, and outdoor adventurers as the nearby Canadian Rockies become increasingly crowded.

Although **Greyhound** offers bus service daily between Vancouver and Clearwater, you'll need a car to explore the best areas of the High Country. Clearwater is 127km (79 miles) north of Kamloops on Hwy. 5.

The **Clearwater Visitor Centre,** 425 E. Yellowhead Hwy. 5 (© **250/674-2646;** www.clearwaterbcchamber.com), is at Hwy. 5 and Wells Gray Park Road. It's open daily, except closed on Sundays from Thanksgiving (mid-October) to mid-April.

EXPLORING WELLS GRAY PROVINCIAL PARK

Wells Gray Provincial Park (www.env.gov.bc.ca/bcparks) is British Columbia's third-largest park, encompassing more than 540,000 hectares (1.3 million acres) of mountains, rivers, lakes, volcanic formations, glaciers, forests, and alpine meadows. Wildlife abounds, including mule deer, moose, bears, beaver, timber wolves, mink, and golden eagles.

Wells Gray has something to offer everyone: birding and wildlife-viewing, hiking, boating, canoeing, and kayaking. Guide operations offer horseback riding, canoeing, rafting, fishing, and hiking. The history enthusiast can learn about the early home-steaders, trappers, and prospectors, or about the natural forces that produced Wells Gray's many volcanoes, mineral springs, and glaciers.

Most of Wells Gray is remote wilderness that can be viewed only after a vigorous hike or canoe excursion. In the southern quarter of the park, however, a road runs 34km (21 miles) from the park entrance to Clearwater Lake, providing access to many of the park's features as well as its campgrounds and many of its trail heads.

More than twice as tall as Niagara Falls, the park's **Helmcken Falls** plummets 141m (463 ft.) and is an awesome sight easily reached by paved road. The trails are wheelchair accessible. Dawson Falls are shallower, but wider and equally impressive. If you so choose, you could spend a day visiting only waterfalls in the park.

Boating, canoeing, kayaking, and fishing are popular pastimes on **Clearwater, Azure, and Mahood lakes. Murtle Lake** is closed to motorboats. The wilderness camp-grounds along these lakes make perfect destinations for overnight canoe or fishing trips.

Multiday hiking destinations include the area around Ray Farm Homestead, Rays Mineral Spring, and the thickly forested **Murtle River Trail** that leads to **Majerus Falls, Horseshoe Falls,** and **Pyramid Mountain,** a volcanic upgrowth that was shaped when it erupted beneath miles of glacial ice that covered the park millions of years ago.

GUIDED TOURS & EXCURSIONS

Area accommodations make it easy to get out and explore the wilderness. **Trophy Mountain Buffalo Ranch, Helmcken Falls Lodge** (see "Where to Stay," below), and the **Wells Gray Guest Ranch,** Wells Gray Road (© **866/467-4346** or 250/674-2792; www.wellsgrayranch.com), offer or can arrange a wide variety of rec-reational options, including a mix of horseback riding, canoeing, rafting, wildlife watching, and hiking trips in summer, and dog sledding, cross-country snowshoeing, snowmobiling, and ice fishing in winter.

Interior Whitewater Expeditions (© **800/661-7238** in Canada, or 250/674-3727; www.interiorwhitewater.bc.ca) offers half- to 5-day rafting and kayaking trips. Consider a 3-hour white-water screamer on the Clearwater River for C$99, or a more leisurely 3-hour float down the North Thompson for C$78.

Wells Gray Adventures (© **888/SKI-TREK** [754-8735] or 250/587-6444; www.skihike.com) offers backcountry hut-to-hut hiking, wilderness canoeing, snow-shoeing, and cross-country ski trips. Ian Eakins and Tay Briggs run this family-owned company that maintains three chalets nestled deep in the park. Each sleeps up to 12 and is equipped with a kitchen, bedding, sauna, and propane lighting and heat. It's the best of both worlds: You can experience untrammeled wilderness and great rural hospitality. Two of the nicest people you could hope to have as guides, Ian and Tay are extremely knowledgeable about the wildlife and history of the park. They offer guided or self-catered hiking and cross-country ski packages as well as guided 3- and 6-day canoe trips that are custom-designed for families. Guided summer hikes are roughly C$130 to C$145 per person per day; guided winter cross-country ski and snowshoeing trips are roughly C$180 to C$190 per person per day.

WHERE TO STAY

Most campers head to Wells Gray Provincial Park's **Mahood Lake, Clearwater Lake, Pyramid,** and **Murtle Lake campgrounds** ★ (www.discovercamping.ca; ✆ **800/689-9025**), which offer fire pits, firewood, pumped well water, pit toilets, and boat launches. Each of the more than 130 vehicle-accessible sites goes for C$16 per night; check the sign outside the Clearwater visitor center to make sure the grounds aren't full before driving all the way up to the park.

Dutch Lake Motel and Campground ☺   The nicest lodging in the town of Clearwater itself, mostly for the access guests enjoy to a private beach on the motel's namesake: Dutch Lake. The setting is quiet and away from the highway. All guest rooms have balconies or patios; some have kitchenettes. Canoe rentals can be arranged.

333 Roy Rd. (R.R. 2, Box 5116), Clearwater, BC V0E 1N0. www.dutchlakemotel.com. ✆ **877/674-3325** or 250/674-3325. Fax 250/674-2916. 27 units. From C$90 double; campsites C$28–C$30. Lower off-season rates. AE, MC, V. **Amenities:** Restaurant; beach. *In room:* A/C, TV, fridge, hair dryer, Internet (free).

Helmcken Falls Lodge ★   Established in the 1920s as a humble trappers' camp, this venerable property has grown into a handsome complex of buildings that includes a 1940s hand-hewn log lodge, which is now home to Wells Gray's best dining room. Accommodations are in a variety of structures, including two log buildings each with four hotel-style rooms, plus a two-story chalet building, and the original trapper's log cabin with two rustic guest rooms. Helmcken Falls Lodge is noted for its recreational activities. The lodge maintains its own horse herd and offers a variety of guided rides in the park, from 1 hour to overnight. Naturalist-led half- and full-day hikes and canoeing trips through the park are another specialty. Cross-country ski rentals are available in winter. The friendly staff can arrange other recreational opportunities with area outfitters; families are welcome. The lodge also overlooks a 9-hole golf course. Call ahead for dinner reservations in the atmospheric log dining room, with delicious home-cooked meals (open for breakfast and dinner; packed lunches available).

Wells Gray Park Rd., Box 239, Clearwater, BC V0E 1N0. www.helmckenfalls.com. ✆ **250/674-3657.** Fax 250/674-2971. 21 units. C$168–C$199 high-season double. Lower off-season rates. Rafting and kayaking packages available. AE, MC, V. Located 35km (22 miles) north of Clearwater. **Amenities:** Licensed restaurant; horseback riding. *In room:* No phone.

Nakiska Ranch ★★   Gorgeous log cabins, grazing cattle on acres of meadows, and Wells Gray's majestic forests and mountains surround the main lodge of this working ranch. The six log one-bedroom cabins are the original log ranch buildings from the turn of the 20th century, but beautifully renovated and updated with full kitchens, spacious bathrooms, and lovely furnishings straight out of the pages of *House Beautiful.* Each of the cabins has a private patio with gas barbecue; three have fireplaces. In addition, there are lodge rooms that are cozy but basic with two twin beds and private bathrooms. A light-filled family suite has an antique bathtub and lots of sitting areas. The lodge features a TV lounge with movie library; phones and fax machine are also available. Families are welcome. Your hosts will arrange horseback rides and other recreation. Open year-round.

Trout Creek Rd. (off Wells Gray Park Rd.), Clearwater, BC V0E 1N0. www.nakiskaranch.bc.ca. ✆ **800/704-4841** or 250/674-3655. Fax 250/674-3387. 9 units. C$110–C$200 double. MC, V. Drive up Wells Gray Park Rd. for 30km (19 miles); it will take about 20 min. Turn right at the ranch sign onto Trout Creek Rd. The park entrance is a 10-min. drive from the ranch. Small pets accepted. **Amenities:** Lounge. *In room:* Fridge, hair dryer, kitchen (cabins only), no phone.

Trophy Mountain Buffalo Ranch and Campground You can't miss the small buffalo herd grazing in a pasture as you drive up the Wells Gray Park Road. Beyond this pastoral setting stand a log lodge, campsites, and camping cabins. The lodge came into existence nearly a century ago out in Blue River. The abandoned structure was taken apart log by hand-hewn log and reassembled in its present location. The lodge restaurant is fully licensed, and the lodge rooms are clean and made especially cozy by fabulous quilts; all rooms have private bathrooms. The rustic bunkhouses, tent sites, and RV sites are extremely well kept. Dishwashing sinks are set up on the deck of the shower house, where hot water flows liberally. Hiking and horseback-riding trails surround the ranch, and guided rides run to the cliffs overlooking the Clearwater River valley and to the base of a secluded waterfall (C$65 for a 3-hr. trip). This friendly, unfussy guest ranch is just the spot if you're looking for clean and simple accommodations with lots of Old West atmosphere. It's open May through October and December through March (depending on snow conditions).

R.R. 1 (P.O. Box 1768), Clearwater, BC V0E 1N0. www.buffaloranch.ca. ℭ **250/674-3095.** Fax 250/ 674-3131. 7 units, 15 campsites, 2 bunkhouses. C$95–C$110 double; C$19–C$23 campsite; C$35 bunkhouse. MC, V. Drive up Wells Gray Park Rd. for 20km (12 miles); it will take about 15 min. Turn left at the ranch sign. **Amenities:** Licensed restaurant; horseback riding. *In room:* No phone.

WHERE TO EAT

The **Blue Loon Grill,** 449 Yellowhead Hwy. E. (ℭ **250/674-3455**), has good home-style cooking; it's open daily for breakfast, lunch, and dinner. A large patio out back occasionally serves as a stage for live, local entertainers. **Trophy Mountain** (ℭ **250/674-3095**) has a good selection of barbecue and burgers—it's open for breakfast, lunch, and dinner during summer. **Helmcken Falls Lodge** (ℭ **250/674-3657**), described above, and the Black Horse Saloon at the **Wells Gray Guest Ranch,** Wells Gray Road (ℭ **250/674-2792**), offer dinners close to the park; reservations are required. The friendly **Kettle Cafe,** 73 Old N. Thompson Hwy. (ℭ **250/674-3727**), in Clearwater, offers salads, espresso drinks, and fresh-baked snacks.

THE OKANAGAN VALLEY

by Chris McBeath

Just south of the High Country on Hwy. 97, the arid Okanagan Valley, with its long chain of crystal-blue lakes, is the ideal destination for freshwater-sports enthusiasts, golfers, skiers, and wine lovers. Ranches and small towns have flourished here for more than a century; the region's fruit orchards and vineyards will make you feel as if you've been transported to the Spanish countryside. Summer visitors get the pick of the crop—at insider prices—from the many fruit stands that line Hwy. 97. Be sure to stop for a pint of cherries, a box of peaches, homemade jams, and other goodies.

When an Okanagan-region chardonnay won gold medals in 1994 at international competitions held in London and Paris, it was considered the luck of an upstart winery. But when several other Okanagan vintages picked up a number of international medals in 2000, and continued that trend ever since, the valley started to become a oenophile's destination. Most visitors are Canadian, and the valley isn't yet a major tour-bus destination. Get here before they do.

Many retirees have chosen the Okanagan Valley as their home for its relatively mild winters and dry, desert-like summers. It's also a favorite destination for younger visitors, drawn by its four-season outdoor activities, including superb powder skiing at Big White and Sun Peaks mountains, as well as boating, water-skiing, sportfishing, and windsurfing on 128km-long (80-mile) Okanagan Lake. To enjoy the full diversity of the region, plan to cover its length between Osoyoos and Vernon (heading towards Kamloops) with a visit to Naramata Benchlands, near Penticton, en route. Kelowna is the valley's central hub, and the area's largest city.

ESSENTIALS

Getting There

BY CAR The 387km (240-mile) drive from Vancouver via the Trans-Canada Highway (Hwy. 1) and Hwy. 3 rambles through rich delta farmlands and the forested mountains of Manning Provincial Park and the Similkameen River region before descending into the Okanagan Valley's antelope-brush and sagebrush desert. For a more direct route to Kelowna, take the Coquihalla Highway (Hwy. 5), which eliminates more than an hour's driving time. The 203km (126-mile) mountain route runs from Hope through Merritt over the Coquihalla Pass into Kamloops.

BY BUS   Greyhound Canada (© **800/661-8747;** www.greyhound.ca) runs daily buses from Vancouver to Penticton and Kelowna, with service continuing on to Banff and Calgary. The one-way fare to Penticton is C$67.

BY PLANE   Air Canada Jazz (© **888/247-2262;** www.aircanada.ca) and **West-Jet** (© **888/937-8538;** www.westjet.com) offer frequent daily commuter flights from Calgary and Vancouver to Penticton and Kelowna. **Horizon Air** (© **800/547-9308;** www.alaskaair.com), a division of Alaska Air, provides service to and from Seattle and Kelowna.

Visitor Information

Contact the **Thompson Okanagan Tourism Association,** 2280 Leckie Rd., Kelowna (© **800/567-2275** or 250/860-5999; www.totabc.org), which is open daily from 8am to 4:30pm. For information about the Okanagan wineries, contact **Penticton & Wine Country Chamber of Commerce,** 553 Railway St., Penticton (© **800/663-5052** or 250/493-4055; www.tourismpenticton.com). The friendly staff at its Wine Country Visitor Centre can help you with itineraries, restaurants, activities, and lodging. It also has an excellent wine shop, filled with the best B.C. wines and regional cheeses.

TOURING THE WINERIES

British Columbia has a long history of producing wines, ranging from fantastic to truly bad. In 1859, Father Pandosy planted apple trees and vineyards and produced sacramental wines for the valley's mission and first European settlement. Many of the original buildings, including a tiny chapel, are open to the public. Other monastery wineries cropped up, but none worried about the quality of their bottlings. After all, the Canadian government had a reputation for subsidizing domestic industries, such as book publishing and cleric wineries, to promote entrepreneurial growth.

In the 1980s, the government threatened to pull its support of the industry unless it could produce an internationally competitive product. The vintners listened. Rootstock was imported from France and Germany, and European-trained master vintners were hired to oversee the development of the vines and the winemaking process. The climate and soil conditions turned out to be some of the best in the world for winemaking, and today, British Columbia wines are winning international gold medals. Competitively priced, in the range of C$10 to C$50, they represent some great bargains in well-balanced chardonnays, pinot blancs, and Gewürztraminers; full-bodied merlots, pinot noirs, and cabernets; and dessert ice wines that surpass the best muscat d'or.

The valley's more than 100 vineyards and wineries conduct free tours and tastings throughout the year. Pick up a tour map at most wineries and information centers, or visit www.okanagan.com/maps/wine_map.htm. The **Okanagan Wine Festival** (© **250/861-6654;** www.thewinefestivals.com) stages seasonal celebrations of wine and food at area vineyards and restaurants, the largest of which is held in early October.

Contact local visitor centers for information, as new wineries continue to open and established ones reinvent themselves with new and ever more sophisticated facilities.

Vineyard restaurants are particularly in the vanguard, and many tasting rooms now offer food in addition to wine, and some offer lodgings.

OSOYOOS

Just across the border from Washington State on Hwy. 97, **Osoyoos** (pop. 5,200) is a small agricultural town on Osoyoos Lake that's making a rapid transition to being a wine country resort destination in its own right. The steep and narrow mountain slopes that encase the entire Okanagan region are particularly high here, making this the driest and hottest area in all of Canada. All that heat makes great conditions for irrigated fruit crops, wineries, and sun worshipers seeking summer beachfront. Osoyoos Lake has miles of sandy beaches and the warmest lake water in Canada.

A dizzying profusion of boating and water recreation awaits on Osoyoos Lake. To rent jet-boats, power boats, Sea-doos, ski boats, pedal boats, aqua bikes, and pontoon boats, walk along the marinas on Hwy. 3, where you'll find a number of rental services. If you're really not into the jet-boat scene, Osoyoos has one unique feature to interest you. The land in the Okanagan Valley between Osoyoos and Penticton's Skaha Lake is considered the northernmost extension of the Sonoran desert that begins in Mexico. These "pocket deserts"—as the thin strip of arid steppes are called locally—are highly endangered ecosystems, as a century's worth of irrigation has served to put almost all the desert into cultivation.

One area of the Osoyoos desert is preserved at the **Osoyoos Desert Center** (© 877/899-0897 or 250/495-2470; www.desert.org). This interpretive center features nature trails through antelope brush grasslands that are home to many endangered and threatened species such as the burrowing owl, the spadefoot toad, the northern rattler, and the pallid bat. The center is open mid-May to mid-September Wednesday through Monday 9:30am to 4:30pm, with hour-long tours at 10am, noon, and 2pm. The center is also open late April to mid-May and mid-September to early October, but with self-guided tours only. Admission is C$7 adult, C$6 seniors and students, C$5 children 6 to 12, and C$16 for a family. The Desert Center is about 2 miles north of Osoyoos on Hwy. 97, at 146th Street.

Nk'Mip Desert Cultural Centre, 100 Rancher Creek (© 888/495-8555 or 250/495-7901; www.nkmipdesert.com), is another exceptional venture. Created as part of the First Nations development (www.nkmip.com) that includes Spirit Ridge Resort (see below), the center focuses on sharing the aboriginal story as well as desert preservation, with interpretive trails, rappelling adventures, and interactive and static displays, including a reconstructed desert village. The center is open mid-March to the end of October, 9:30am to 4:30pm and to nightfall in July and August. Admission is C$12 adult, C$11 seniors and students; C$8 children 5 to 7, and C$35 for a family.

Nk'Mip Cellars, 1400 Rancher Creek Rd. (© 250/495-2985; www.nkmipcellars. com), is a top Osoyoos-area winery, located at the Spirit Ridge Resort (see below). North America's first First Nations–owned and –operated winery, Nk'Mip Cellars (pronounced *In*-ka-meep) produces a full range of wines; particularly excellent are the pinot blanc, syrah, and a meritage blend. The tasting room is open daily 9am to 5pm.

Contact the **Osoyoos Visitor Info Centre** at 9912 Hwy. 3 (© 888/676-9667 or 250/495-5070; www.destinationosoyoos.com).

Where to Stay & Eat

Spirit Ridge Vineyard Resort & Spa ★★★   This luxury-level lodging overlooks Lake Osoyoos, the steep-sloped Okanagan Valley, and miles of vineyards. Opened in 2007, Spirit Ridge brings a Santa Fe look to the Sonoran desert landscape both architecturally and in its comfortable, interior furnishings and features. Lodgings are in one-bedroom suites, or one- or two-bedroom villas, each with full kitchen, dining and living room (with fireplace), and balcony. The resort offers a full-service spa plus the **Passatempo Restaurant,** with "wine country comfort food." Guests have private access to a rooftop BBQ deck and the beaches on Osoyoos Lake. The 9-hole **Sonora Dunes Golf Course** (🕾 **250/495-4653;** www.sonoradunes. com), **Nk'Mip Cellars Winery** (🕾 **250/495-2985;** www.nkmipcellars.com), and **Nk'Mip Desert Cultural Centre** (🕾 **250/495-7901**) are adjacent.

1200 Rancher Creek Rd., Osoyoos, BC V0H 1V6. www.spiritridge.ca. 🕾 **877/313-9463** or 250/495-5445. 226 units. C$139–C$349 1-bedroom suite; C$175–C$349 1-bedroom villa; C$199–C$429 2-bedroom villa; C$199–C$429 3-bedroom suite. AE, MC, V. Free parking. **Amenities:** Restaurant; lounge; fitness center; golf course; hot tubs; outdoor pools w/water slide; spa; deli/market; rooftop deck; cultural center; winery; beach access. *In room:* A/C, TV/DVD, hair dryer, full kitchen and dining room, Wi-Fi (free).

Watermark Beach Resort ★   A new style of sophistication has arrived in downtown Osoyoos with this gorgeous new vacation complex, made up of oceanfront villas, studio, one- and two-bedroom suites. The contemporary style of its architecture, which has a ton of windows to take full advantage of the water-views, extends to upscale furnishings, linens, and an overall upscale experience without being too over the top. This is a beach-activity resort, after all. In high season, June through September, reservations go by the week, or month, which means a family can really get rooted into all the activities, of which there are a number, including waterslides, a yoga/pilates studio, and a wake-boarding school. The wine bar and bistro are excellent for fresh, local fare and wines. Besides lunch and dinner, it serves small-plates, tapas-style, in the afternoon.

15 Park Pl., Osoyoos, BC V0H 1V0. www.watermarkbeachresort.com. 🕾 **888/755-3480** or 250/495-5500. Studio & 1-bedroom suite C$1,200/week; 2-bedroom & some villas C$2,100–C$2,800/week. AE, MC, V. Free parking. Pets C$25. **Amenities:** Restaurant; lounge; fitness center; hot tub; outdoor pool w/water slide; spa. *In room:* A/C, TV/DVD, hair dryer, kitchen, Wi-Fi (free).

OLIVER

52km (32 miles) S of Penticton

Scarcely a tourist town, Oliver (pop. 4,300) is the center of the Okanagan fruit-growing orchards and exists to serve the needs of local farmers, orchardists, and winemakers.

Many of the long-established wineries that put the region's name on the wine-producing map are in the Oliver area. This includes the high-producing slopes called the "Golden Mile," situated west of Oliver along Road 8. **Festival of the Grape** (🕾 **250/498-6321;** www.sochamber.ca) occurs in the first weekend of October, and is part of the larger Okanagan Wine Festival.

Notable Oliver-area wineries that welcome visitors include **Burrowing Owl Winery ★**, halfway between Osoyoos and Oliver at 100 Black Sage Rd. (🕾 **877/498-0620** or 250/498-6202; www.burrowingowlwine.ca), which makes exceptional wines; its award-winning merlot is one of B.C.'s best. Their **Sonora Room** dining room is an equally excellent vineyard restaurant (closed in late fall), and the 10-bedroom **Guest House at Burrowing Owl** is a top boutique lodging (see below).

Gehringer Brothers Estate Winery, Road 8 between Osoyoos and Oliver (*C* **250/498-3537**), offers German-style wines, including Riesling, pinot gris, pinot noir, and pinot blanc, plus a notable ice wine. Try the crisp Ehrenfelser white wine, which carries intense flavors of apricot and almond. The tasting room is open June through mid-October daily; call for off-season hours.

Near Oliver, **Tinhorn Creek Vineyards,** Road 7 (*C* **888/846-4676;** www. tinhorn.com), is one of the top Okanagan wineries. Specialties include Gewürztraminer, pinot gris, chardonnay, pinot noir, cabernet franc, merlot, and ice wine. **Hester Creek Estate Winery,** off Road 8 at 13163 326 Ave. (*C* **250/498-4435;** www. hestercreek.com), is a charming Mediterranean-style winery, complete with six B&B villa-suites, an open demonstration kitchen for "dine-with-the-chef" cooking classes, as well as an intimate new restaurant, Terrafina. Hester Creek has the only Trebbiano vines in the valley.

The town of **Okanagan Falls** is 20km (12 miles) north of Oliver along Hwy. 97. Adjacent to a wilderness area and bird sanctuary overlooking Vaseaux Lake, **Blue Mountain Vineyards & Cellars,** 2385 Allendale Rd. (*C* **250/497-8244;** www. bluemountainwinery.com), operates a wine shop and tasting room by appointment only. **Blasted Church Vineyards ★**, 378 Parsons Rd. (*C* **250/497-1125;** www. blastedchurch.com), has impossible-to-miss wine labels, and delicious and affordable wines. One of my favorites.

For more information on the region, contact the **South Okanagan Visitor Info Centre,** 36205 93rd St. (*C* **250/498-6321;** www.sochamber.ca).

Where to Stay & Eat

Guest House at Burrowing Owl ★★   The top-echelon Burrowing Owl Winery offers 10 spectacular guest rooms in the midst of a vineyard as well as one, self-contained two-bedroom suite, complete with elevator. This boutique inn has large and airy rooms, filled with light, fine art, native stone, and gracious good taste. Most rooms have king-size beds (two have two doubles), and all have balconies overlooking the grape vines and the nearby desert hills. Relax by the 25m (82-ft.) outdoor pool and patio, and definitely have dinner at the **Sonora Room ★**, the winery's excellent New Canadian restaurant.

100 Black Sage Rd. (R.R. 1, Comp 20, Site 52), Oliver, BC V0N 1T0. www.borrowingowlwine.ca. *C* **877/498-0620** or 250/498-0620. 11 units. July 1 to mid-Oct C$350. 2-night minimum stay in high season. Lower off-season rates. AE, MC, V. Free parking. Closed mid-Dec–to mid-Feb **Amenities:** Restaurant; guest lounge; hot tub; outdoor pool; wine shop and tasting bar. *In room:* A/C, TV, fridge, Wi-Fi (free).

PENTICTON

80km (50 miles) N of Oliver; 60km (37 miles) S of Kelowna; 396km (246 miles) W of Vancouver via the Coquihalla Hwy.

One of the belles of the Okanagan, Penticton (pop. 41,500) is a lovely midsize city with two entirely different lakefronts. Above the town is the toe-end of vast Okanagan Lake; to the south are the upper beaches of Lake Skaha. It's a lovely setting, and a peach of a place for a recreation-dominated holiday. "Peach" has additional significance here, as Penticton is also the center for apple, peach, cherry, and grape production. But there's a lot more to Penticton than agriculture: Facilities range from hostels to world-class resorts, and the restaurants are among the best in this part of British Columbia. The **Penticton & Wine Country Chamber of Commerce** is at 553 Railway St. (© **800/663-5052** or 250/493-4055; www.tourismpenticton.com). It also houses the British Columbia Wine Information Centre and an excellent wine shop with all sorts of local vintages. It's open daily 9am to 6pm.

Exploring the Town

It's hard to beat Penticton's location. With Okanagan Lake lapping at the northern edge of town, Lake Skaha's beaches forming the town's southern boundary, and the Okanagan River cutting between the two, Penticton has the feel of a real oasis. Hemmed in by lakes and desert valley walls, Penticton is pleasantly compact and in summer fairly hums with activity. As elsewhere in the Okanagan Valley, watersports are the main preoccupation, but Penticton also has an air of gentility that suggests there's a little more going on than just jet-skiing.

The old commercial center is along **Main Street** toward the north end of town; there's also a lot of activity along **Lakeshore Drive,** the boulevard that parallels the beachfront of Okanagan Lake. Lined with hotels and restaurants on one side, clogged with sun worshipers on the other, Lakeshore Drive is a very busy place in summer.

Right on the lakefront is the **SS *Sicamous*** (© **250/492-0403**; www.sssicamous. com), a stern-wheeler that plied the waters of Okanagan Lake from 1914 to 1935. Now preserved as a museum, it's beached in the sand, and currently houses a scale model of the historic Kettle Valley Railway. Generally speaking, it's open in summer daily from 9am to 9pm, the rest of the year Monday through Friday from 9am to 4pm. Hours may vary according to community events and festivals.

Even if you're not into sunbathing, a saunter along the **beachfront promenade** is called for. Beach volleyball, sand castles, and a drinks kiosk in the shape of a giant peach are just the beginning of what you'll encounter along this long, broad strand: It's prime people-watching territory. At the eastern end of the beachfront is the **Penticton Art Gallery,** 199 Marina Way (© **250/493-2928**), a showcase for local artists. Admission is C$2. The gift shop is a good spot to pick up a souvenir.

The beach along Skaha Lake is usually more laid-back than the Okanagan lakefront. The relatively more secluded nature of this beach, plus a large water park for the kids, makes it a good destination for families. **Skaha Lake Marina** (© **250/492-7368**) is at the east edge of the beach.

Touring the Wineries

The two main wine-producing areas near Penticton are along the west lake slopes near Summerland, and north along the east slopes of Okanagan Lake near the community of Naramata, one of the first wine-growing regions in British Columbia.

To begin your explorations, follow Upper Bench Road from Penticton, which turns into Naramata Road and leads to **Naramata,** 14km (8¾ miles) north. **La Frenz Winery,** 740 Naramata Rd. (© **250/492-6690**; www.lafrenzwinery.com), makes excellent small-lot bottlings of semillon, viognier, and merlot. **Red Rooster Winery** (891 Naramata Rd; © **250/492-2424**; www.redrooster.com) is another excellent stop, both for its reserve malbecs and Gewürztraminers, and for the art gallery.

Poplar Grove Winery ★, 1060 Poplar Grove Rd. (© **250/493-9463**; www. poplargrove.ca), produces a top-notch claret-style wine; try the cabernet franc if it's available—it's a wonderful wine that sells out every year. Poplar Grove is building a new winery and tasting room on the Naramata Bench; call ahead for hours and opening dates.

Hillside Estate, 1350 Naramata Rd. (✆ **250/493-6274;** www.hillsideestate. com), is open daily (call ahead in midwinter). From Easter weekend until the Okanagan Wine Festival in October, it operates the **Barrel Room Bistro,** a patio restaurant at the winery, open for lunch daily. It opens for dinner on weekends starting May 1, and opens nightly for dinners in mid-June.

Lake Breeze Vineyards, 930 Sammet Rd. (✆ **250/496-5659;** www.lakebreeze. ca), opens its tasting room weekends in April and daily from May 1 through October from 10am to 5pm. Its restaurant, **The Patio,** is open for lunch from May 1 to early October.

Serendipity Winery, 990 Debeck Rd. (✆ **250/496-5299;** www.serendipity winery.com), is one of the newest vineyards on the Benchlands; it started winning awards before it had opened to the public in mid-2011, so if you're wanting to get the scoop on the hottest up-and-coming vintages, stop by here.

North of Penticton along Hwy. 97 near Summerville is the other wine-producing area. **Sumac Ridge Estate Winery,** 17403 Hwy. 97 (✆ **250/494-0451;** www. sumacridge.com), offers tastings daily; the Burgundy-style wines are excellent. Be sure to also try their sparkling wines, which include both traditional and red (Shiraz-based) bubblies. Besides operating a shop and tasting room open daily year-round, the winery runs the fine **Cellar Door Bistro.**

Located 43km (27 miles) north of Penticton, the **Hainle Vineyards Estate Winery,** 5355 Trepanier Bench Rd. (✆ **250/767-2525;** www.hainle.com), was the first Okanagan winery to produce ice wine. The wine shop is open mid-April through October, and weekdays only the rest of the year, for tasting.

If you're a serious taster (and swallower) who prefers not to drink and drive, **OK Wine Shuttle** (www.okwineshuttle.ca) is a hop-on/hop-off service with two routes: the Golden Mile around Oliver, and the Naramata Benchlands near Penticton. Shuttles run every 30 minutes, mid-May to mid-October, with pick-up points in Osoyoos, Penticton, and various wineries. The cost is $35 (cash only). One free publication that might add to your oenophilic experience: *BC Food & Wine Trails* (www. winetrails.ca).

The Kettle Valley Steam Railway

The Kettle Valley Railway, which was completed in 1914 to link coastal communities to the burgeoning mining camps in Kettle River valley, became one of the Okanagan Valley's top draws after much of it was converted into a rails-to-trails pathway for hikers and mountain bikers called the Kettle Valley Rail Trail. Unfortunately, the forest fires of 2003 burned a number of the historic wooden trestles that bridged the route through steep Myra Canyon, closing it for 4 years. The trestles have been rebuilt, and in 2008 this part of the route reopened to hikers and bikers (see "Biking," below).

One section of the Kettle Valley Railway, however, is in use by original steam trains. The **Kettle Valley Railway Society,** 18404 Bathville Rd., Summerland (✆ **877/ 494-8424** in B.C., or 250/494-8422; www.kettlevalleyrail.org), offers a 2-hour journey on a 10km (6¼-mile) section of the original track west of Summerland, 16km (10 miles) north of Penticton. The first Thursday in July to Labour Day, the train runs Thursday through Monday at 10:30am and 1:30pm, departing from the Prairie Valley Station off Bathville Road; from mid-May to early July and from Labour Day to mid-October, the train runs at the same times Saturday through Monday only. In addition, on most Saturdays there's an afternoon train that involves a "train robbery" and bar-becue. Check the website for other additional runs throughout the year. Fares are C$22 for adults, C$20 for seniors, C$17 for students, and C$13 for children 3 to 12.

Outdoor Pursuits

BIKING The best Okanagan Valley off-road bike trail is the Kettle Valley Rail Trail (www.kettlevalleyrail.ca). The tracks and ties have been removed, making way for some incredibly scenic biking. The most picturesque and challenging section of the route is from Naramata, north of Penticton along the east side of Okanagan Lake. The rails-to-trails route climbs up steep switchbacks to Chute Lake and then across 17 trestles (recently rebuilt after burning in a forest fire) as it traverses Myra Canyon. The entire mountain bike route from Naramata to Westbridge in the Kettle River Valley is 175km (109 miles) and can take from 3 to 5 days. For more information on cycling the route, contact the visitor center above, or the **Bike Barn,** 300 W. West-minster (© **250/492-4140**), which offers lots of friendly advice. **Penticton Bicy-cle Rental,** 533 Main St. (© **250/493-0686;** www.freedombikeshop.com), has rentals at C$25 per half-day; C$40 per day. Check **www.spiritof2010trail.ca** for suggested bike routes.

BOATING & WATERSPORTS The Okanagan Valley's numerous local marinas offer full-service boat rentals. One of the most convenient is **Pier Water Sports** (© **250/493-8864;** www.pierwatersports.com) which, as its name suggests, pro-vides for all manner of water activities, including parasailing, jetski rentals, a wake-board school, and waterskiing. It also has an outlet in Peachland.

A popular activity is renting a rubber raft from **Coyote Cruises** (215 Riverside Dr., © **205/492-2115;** www.coyotecruises.ca), in the blue building along the river at Riverside Drive, then floating from Okanagan Lake down to Skaha Lake, which takes about 2 hours. On a hot day, you'll be joined by hundreds of other people in rafts, inner tubes, and rubber dinghies; the water fight of your life is almost guaran-teed. A tube rental and bus return is C$10 adult, C$11 student, C$9 children 5 to 10 years of age. Note that this is a cash-only deal—there's an ATM on site.

SKIING Cross-country and powder skiing are the Okanagan Valley's main winter attractions. Intermediate and expert downhill skiers frequent the **Apex Resort,** Green Mountain Road, Penticton (© **877/877-APEX** [2739], or 250/292-8222, or 250/487-4848, for snow report; www.apexresort.com), with 56 runs and 52km (32 miles) of cross-country ski trails. Day passes are C$63 adults, C$52 seniors and ages 13 to 18, and C$39 kids 12 and under. Facilities include an ice rink, snow golf, a tube park, snow-showing, sleigh rides, casino nights, and racing competitions.

Where to Stay

There are three major lodging areas: the northern lakefront on Okanagan Lake, the southern lakefront on Lake Skaha, and the Main Street strip that connects the two. Penticton has a lot of older motels, many of which have seen years of hard use.

Naramata Heritage Inn & Spa ★★ Tucked away in the tiny community of Naramata, about a 30-minute drive from Penticton, this lovely 1908 building has served as a hotel, private residence, and girls' school before undergoing extensive and loving renovation as a classic wine-country inn. It offers very charming rooms (note that some are authentically small), restored to glow with period finery but with mod-ern luxury—the linens are top-notch and the bathroom's heated tile floors are a nice touch on a cool morning. In addition to en suite bathrooms with showers, rooms also have a claw-foot tub in the bedroom for soaking and relaxing. The inn also offers an Aveda concept spa for upscale pampering, plus the best dining in the area. There are few places in the Okanagan as unique as this.

3625 First St., Naramata, BC V0H 1N0 (19km/12 miles north of Penticton on the east side of Okanagan Lake). www.naramatainn.com. ✆ **866/617-1188** or 250/496-6808. 12 units. High season C$220–C$399 double. Rates include continental breakfast. Lower off-season rates. AE, MC, V. Closed November & January. **Amenities:** Restaurant (see "Where to Eat," below); wine bar; limited room service; spa; Wi-Fi (free), free use of mountain bikes. *In room:* A/C, hair dryer.

Penticton Lakeside Resort Hotel & Casino   Set on the water's edge, this resort has its own stretch of sandy Lake Okanagan beachfront, where guests can sunbathe or stroll along the adjacent pier. The deluxe suites feature Jacuzzis, and the lakeside rooms are highly recommended for their view. All rooms and suites are smartly furnished with quality furniture; all rooms have balconies (some suites have two-person Jacuzzi tubs). The menus at the Hooded Merganser Restaurant and the Barking Parrot Bar & Bufflehead Tapas Room & Patio feature locally grown ingredients. Other facilities include an extensive pool and health club facility, and a casino.

21 W. Lakeshore Dr., Penticton, BC V2A 7M5. www.pentictonlakesideresort.com. ✆ **800/663-9400** or 250/493-8221. 203 units. C$220–C$275 double. Lower off-season rates. AE, DC, DISC, MC, V. Free parking. When you arrive in town, follow the signs to Main St. Lakeshore Dr. is at the north end of Main St. Pets accepted with C$20 fee. **Amenities:** Restaurant; lounge; babysitting; children's center; casino, concierge; health club; Jacuzzi; indoor pool; room service; sauna; tennis courts; watersports equipment rental; volleyball court. *In room:* A/C, TV w/pay movies, hair dryer, Wi-Fi (free).

Ramada Inn & Suites ★   Although it isn't particularly near either lakefront, this relatively new hotel is a good and dependable choice if you have no patience with older and well-worn lodgings that may have a better location. That said, the Ramada is adjacent to the Penticton Golf and Country Club. Rooms are large and comfortably furnished with good dining options and a courtyard garden. The suites have options like stone-fronted fireplaces, Jacuzzi tubs, and full kitchens.

1050 Eckhardt Ave. W., Penticton, BC V2A 2C3. www.pentictonramada.com. ✆ **800/665-4966** or 250/492-8926. 125 units. C$119–C$229 double; C$175–C$289 suite. Additional person C$20. AE, DC, MC, V. Free parking. Pets accepted with C$15 fee. **Amenities:** Restaurant; pub and lounge; fitness center; hot tub; outdoor heated pool; room service; gas barbecues; playground. *In room:* A/C, TV, fridge, Wi-Fi (free), voice mail.

Waterfront Inn 🏄   This older, standard-issue motel is nothing to write home about except that is right across from a park with beach access to Lake Skaha. The rooms are clean and basic, but if you're here for the lakefront action, you'll enjoy the fact that you won't have to cross four lanes of traffic to get to the water. This makes it a winning choice for young families. If budget's a concern, opt for a one-bedroom kitchen suite so you have the option to eat in.

3688 Parkview St., Penticton, BC V2A 6H1. www.waterfrontinn.net. ✆ **800/563-6006** or 250/492-8228. 21 units. High season C$99–C$150 double. Kitchen C$15 extra. AE, MC, V. Closed mid-Oct to Apr. **Amenities:** BBQ, splash pool; sauna; playground. *In room:* A/C, TV, fridge, microwave, Wi-Fi (free).

Where to Eat

The Penticton restaurant scene is, at last, picking up steam and historical favorites are having to work harder to maintain local loyalty. Restaurants such as **La Casa Ouzeria,** 1090 Main St. (✆ **250/492-9144;** www.lacasaouzeria.com); **Salty's Seafood**

Beach House, 1000 Lakeshore Dr. (℡ **250/493-5001;** www.saltysbeachhouse. com); and **Saigon,** 314 Main St. (℡ **250/493-8998**), with its mix of Thai and Vietnamese cuisine, are appealing to a more sophisticated palate. In addition, a number of Penticton-area vineyards now have restaurants; in fact, in good weather, these winery dining rooms are extremely charming places to eat, as most dining is alfresco (there are no bad views in the valley). Of the wineries noted above, Sumac Ridge's **Cellar Door Bistro** (℡ **250/494-0451**) is open daily May to mid-October. Hillside Estate operates the **Barrel Room Bistro,** 1350 Naramata Rd. (℡ **250/493-6274;** www. hillsideestate.com), which is open for lunch daily from Easter weekend through early October, and open for dinner on weekends starting May 1, and nightly for dinners in mid-June. Lake Breeze Vineyards operates **The Patio,** 930 Sammet Rd. (℡ **250/496-5659;** www.lakebreeze.ca), open for lunch from May 1 to early October.

Cobblestone Restaurant ★ PACIFIC NORTHWEST   Found in the beautifully restored Naramata Inn, this fine-dining restaurant combines its 1908 heritage with a savvy, modern make-over. It serves some of the most sophisticated food in the Okanagan Valley in five-course tasting menus; selections using only the freshest, local ingredients, many from its own garden. Wine pairings are available for each of the menus at C$60. Expect refined choices such as seared deep sea scallop and kurobuta pork belly confit with parsnip ravioli, and double-smoked bacon-wrapped quail breast with matsutake mushrooms. At lunch, expect soup, salads, and delicious hearth breads.

3625 First St., Naramata (19km/12 miles north of Penticton on the east side of Okanagan Lake). ℡ **250/496-5001.** www.naramatainn.com. Reservations required. 5-course menu C$75. MC, V. Apr–Oct daily 11:30am–10pm. Call for winter hours.

Granny Bogners CONTINENTAL   Granny Bogners, in a shake-sided heritage home in a quiet residential area, has been a top choice for locals looking for a special-occasion meal. The menu is packed with traditional (perhaps slightly old-fashioned) choices such as chicken *cordon bleu,* filet mignon with béarnaise sauce, grilled salmon, and a number vegetarian options such as vegetable curry with organic quinoa salad. In terms of value-for-money, prices seem to include a premium for such a lovely setting, whether that's for white linens and crystal inside or the garden patio in summer.

302 W. Eckhardt Ave. ℡ **250/493-2711.** www.bogners.ca. Reservations required. Main courses C$25–C$45. AE, MC, V. Wed–Sat 5:30–9:30pm.

Theo's Restaurant ★ GREEK   When a restaurant's been in business for over 30 years, and still gets accolades, it must be doing something right. Authenticity is the name of the game, from its spanakopita, moussaka, and kalamarakia (friend squid), to hot-stuffed grape leaves, slow-cooked lamb, and broiled tiger prawns. The platters for two (C$48) are good value, featuring small portions of several Greek dishes such as beef souvlaki; a fish platter is also offered.

250 Main St. Penticton ℡ **250/492-4019.** www.eatsquid.com. Reservations advised. Main courses C$14–C$25. MC, V. Mon–Sat 11am–10:30pm; Sun 4–10pm.

Villa Rossa Ristorante ★ ITALIAN   Although a couple of competitors are vying for top billing, Villa Rossa continues to be one of the top Penticton options for traditional Italian cuisine. It has an attractive patio shaded by grapevines, just the spot on a warm evening. The menu is varied, with classic dishes such as *osso buco,* chicken Marsala, various veal specialties, and pasta, joining Canadian fare such as steaks and salmon. Good wine list, too.

795 W. Westminster Ave. ✆ **250/490-9595.** www.thevillarosa.com. Reservations suggested. Main courses C$17–C$38. AE, MC, V. Mon–Thurs 11am–10pm; Fri & Sat 11am–11pm; Sun 4pm–10pm.

Zia's Stonehouse Restaurant ★ CONTINENTAL   Located north of Penticton in Summerland, this restaurant is set inside a historic stone home that was built a century ago by an Italian immigrant. Although the menu focuses on Mediterranean preparations of local meats and produce, there are also gestures toward Asian and American cuisine as well. With its dedication to the memory of Italian aunts and their home-style cooking, Zia's often earns local area awards for its romance, atmosphere, and food. In addition to many imported wines, it offers more than 75 local vintages.

14015 Rosedale Ave., Summerland. ✆ **250/494-1105.** www.ziasstonehouse.com. Reservations required. Main courses C$13–C$30. AE, MC, V. Daily 11:30am–2:30pm and 5:30–10pm.

KELOWNA

395km (245 miles) E of Vancouver

Kelowna (pop. 106,700) is the largest city in the Okanagan, and one of the fastest-growing areas in Canada. You won't have to spend much time here to understand why: The city sits astride 128km-long (80-mile) Okanagan Lake at the center of a vast fruit-, wine-, and vegetable-growing area, with lots of sun and a resort lifestyle. This is about as close to California as it gets in Canada. Kelowna is especially popular with retirees, who stream here to escape the Pacific pall of Vancouver and the winter cold of Alberta. Predictably, watersports and golf are the main leisure activities, and it's hard to imagine a better outdoor-oriented family-vacation spot.

With plenty of marinas and a beautiful beachfront park that flanks downtown, you'll have no problem finding a place to get wet. In fact, Kelowna's only problem is its popularity. The greater Kelowna area now has a population of 162,000. Traffic is very heavy, particularly along Hwy. 97 as it inches right through the heart of the city.

Essentials

GETTING THERE   The Kelowna airport is north of the city on Hwy. 97. **Air Canada Jazz** (✆ **888/247-8747;** www.aircanada.com) offers regular flights from Calgary and Vancouver. **Horizon Air** (✆ **800/547-9308;** www.alaskaair.com) offers service from Seattle. **WestJet** (✆ **888/937-8538;** www.westjet.com) operates flights from Vancouver, Victoria, Calgary, and Edmonton.

Greyhound Canada (✆ **800/661-8747;** www.greyhound.ca) travels between Vancouver and Kelowna daily. The adult fare is C$67 non-refundable; C$75 refundable. Three buses per day continue on to Calgary. The now toll-free Coquihalla Highway (Hwy. 5) links Kelowna and the Okanagan to the Vancouver area. The 395km (245-mile) drive from Vancouver takes 4 hours. From Kelowna to Calgary, it's 623km (387 miles) over slower roads.

VISITOR INFORMATION   The **Kelowna Visitor Info Centre** is at 544 Harvey Ave. (✆ **800/663-4345** or 250/861-1515; www.tourismkelowna.com). **Tourism Westside,** 2372 Dobbin Rd. (Hwy 97), West Kelowna (✆ **866/768-3378;** www.tourismwestside.com), promotes the growing number of activities, trails, and attractions in the District of West Kelowna.

GETTING AROUND   The local bus service is operated by **Kelowna Regional Transit System** (✆ **250/860-8121**). A one-zone fare is C$2. For a taxi, call **Checkmate Cabs** (✆ **250/861-1111**) or **Kelowna Cabs** (✆ 250/762-4444).

Exploring the City

Greater Kelowna is a big, sprawling place that has engulfed both sides of Okanagan Lake, but the sights of most interest are contained in a relatively small area. And that's good, because traffic in Kelowna can be vexing. Beware of the heavily traveled **Harvey Street** and the **Okanagan Lake Bridge;** the latter has been rebuilt but traffic jams are still the norm.

Downtown is a pleasant retail area that retains a number of older buildings that now house shops, galleries, and cafes. The main commercial strip is **Bernard Street.** The showpiece of Kelowna is lovely **City Park,** which flanks downtown and the bridge's east side and has over half a mile of wide, sandy beach. At the north edge is a marina where you can rent boats and recreational equipment, or learn to water-ski and parasail.

Continue north through the busy marina to **Waterfront Park,** with an island band shell and promenades along the lakefront and lagoons. The **Grand Okanagan Lakefront Resort** towers above the park, and it's worth a stop to step inside the opulent lobby, or to enjoy a drink beside the pool.

The **Rotary Centre for the Arts,** 421 Cawston Ave. (© 250/717-5304; www.rotarycentreforthearts.com), is a multipurpose venue with a 330-seat performing arts theater, plus two art galleries and a number of open studios for artists and craftspeople. It's a fun place to wander, watching artists at work, and you may find a gift to buy or a piece to add to your collection. The center also contains a lunchtime cafe with soup and sandwiches.

Away from the downtown core but still within the city environs, you'll find delightful diversions that include **Elysium Gardens,** 2834 Belgo Rd. (© 250/491-1386; www.elysiumgardennursery.com), a 1.6 hectare (4-acre) oasis of perennial garden overlooking the pastoral landscapes and mountains beyond; **Carmelis Goat Cheese Artisan,** 170 Timberline Rd. (© 250/764-9033; www.carmelisgoatcheese.com), which is worth the steep drive along the lakeshore mountainside for the views, let alone the cheese; and **Geert Maas Sculpture Gardens,** 250 Reynolds Rd. (© 250/860-7012; www.geertmaas.org), which features one of the largest collections of bronze sculptures in Canada. While you're roaming the countryside, be sure to drop by the **Okanagan Lavender & Herb Farm,** 4380 Takla Rd. (© 250/764-7795; www.okanaganlavender.com), for a wander through its purple fields and gift shop, as well as a visit to nearby **Arlo's Honey Farm,** 4329 Bedford Ln. (© 250/764-2883; www.arloshoneyfarm.com). It sells a number of bee-products and has a fascinating bee-wall and bee-hive education center.

B.C. Orchard Industry Museum This museum, housed in an old apple-packing plant, tells the story of the region's apple-and-soft-fruit industry, with archival photos, equipment, and a hands-on discovery corner. Sharing space with the Orchard Museum is the **Wine Museum** (© 250/868-0441), with a few exhibits on the history of Okanagan wine production. The shop sells a good selection of regional vintages. 1304 Ellis St. © 778/478-0347. www.kelownamuseums.ca. Admission by donation. Mon–Sat 10am–5pm.

Kelowna Art Gallery Kelowna's 1,394-sq.-m (15,005-sq.-ft.) regional gallery hosts nearly 20 shows per year of work by regional, national, and international artists. The permanent collection is a good body of works by primarily British Columbian artists. The shop is a great place for unique handcrafted gifts. 1315 Water St. © 250/762-2226. www.kelownaartgallery.com. C$5 adults, C$4 seniors and students, C$10 families. Tues–Sat 10am–5pm (Thurs to 9pm); Sun 1–4pm.

Kelowna

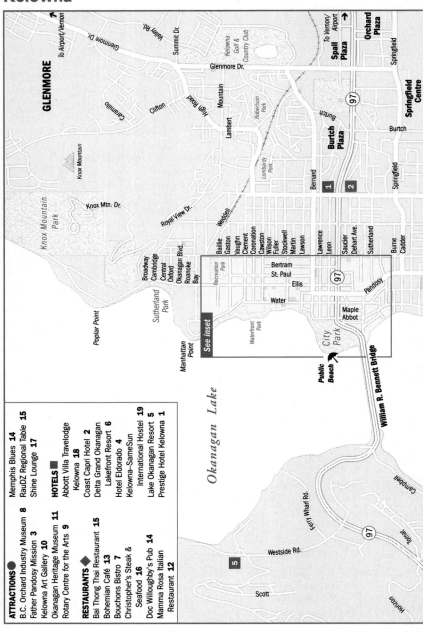

ATTRACTIONS ●
B.C. Orchard Industry Museum **8**
Father Pandosy Mission **3**
Kelowna Art Gallery **10**
Okanagan Heritage Museum **11**
Rotary Centre for the Arts **9**

RESTAURANTS ◆
Bai Thong Thai Restaurant **15**
Bohemian Café **13**
Bouchons Bistro **7**
Christopher's Steak &
  Seafood **16**
Doc Willoughby's Pub **14**
Mamma Rosa Italian
  Restaurant **12**

Memphis Blues **14**
RaudZ Regional Table **15**
Shine Lounge **17**

HOTELS ■
Abbott Villa Travelodge
  Kelowna **18**
Coast Capri Hotel **2**
Delta Grand Okanagan
  Lakefront Resort **6**
Hotel Eldorado **4**
Kelowna–SameSun
  International Hostel **19**
Lake Okanagan Resort **5**
Prestige Hotel Kelowna **1**

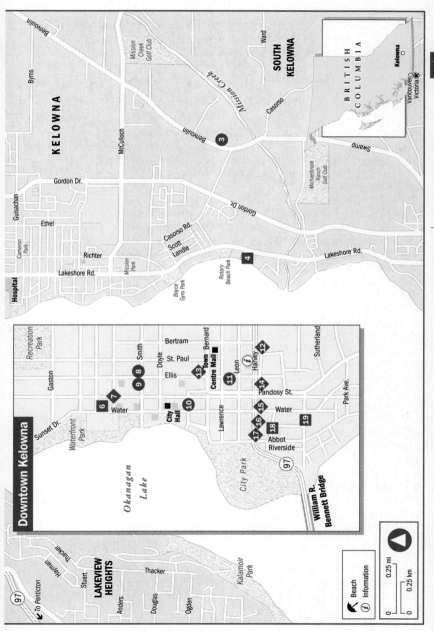

Downtown Kelowna

KELOWNA

SOUTH KELOWNA

Mission Creek Golf Club

Mission Creek

Benvoulin

Byms

Benvoulin

Ward

Casorso

3

BRITISH COLUMBIA

Kelowna

Vancouver

Victoria

Swamp

Michaelbrook Ranch Golf Club

Gordon Dr.

McCulloch

Guisachan

Ethel

Richter

Cameron Park

Hospital

Lakeshore Rd.

Mission Park

Casorso Rd.

Scott

Landle

Boyce Gyro Park

Rotary Beach Park

4

Gordon Dr.

Lakeshore Rd.

Recreation Park

Smith

Bertram

Doyle

St. Paul

Ellis

Town Bernard

Centre Mall

13

Leon

11

12

Harvey

Gaston

9 8

7

6

Water

City Hall

10

Pandosy St.

14

15

Water

Lawrence

16

17 18

Abbot

Riverside

19

Sutherland

Park Ave.

Waterfront Park

Sunset Dr.

Okanagan Lake

City Park

97

William R. Bennett Bridge

LAKEVIEW HEIGHTS

Thacker

Hayman

Stuart

Thacker

Anders

Douglas

Ogden

Kalamoir Park

97

To Penticton

Beach

Information

0   0.25 mi

0   0.25 km

Okanagan Heritage Museum This ambitious museum touches on the history of life in the Okanagan Valley. Starting out with local fossils, exhibits move through the prehistoric culture of the Native Okanagans and on to the lives of the farmers and ranchers. Eclectic only begins to describe the collection—radios, dolls, books—but everything is well curated, and you're sure to find something of interest. For military buffs, the **Okanagan Heritage Museum** group also includes a regional military museum at 1424 Ellis St. (© **250/763-9292**). 470 Queensway Ave. © **250/763-2417.** www.kelownamuseums.ca. Admission by donation. Mon–Sat 10am–5pm.

Touring the Wineries

Just north of city center, **Calona Wines,** 1125 Richter St., Kelowna (© **888/246-4472** or 250/762-3332; www.calonavineyards.ca), offers tastings in western Canada's oldest and largest (since 1932) winery. Many antique winemaking machines are on display, alongside the state-of-the-art equipment the winery now uses.

North of Kelowna is **Gray Monk Estate Winery,** 1055 Camp Rd., Okanagan Centre (© **800/663-4205** or 250/766-3168; www.graymonk.com). Noted for its pinot noirs, Gray Monk has a patio lounge and gives winery tours daily. The tasting room is open daily year-round. The winery's **Grapevine Restaurant** offers serious Continental cuisine in its lake-view dining room, which is open for lunch daily from Easter weekend through October; nightly dinner service begins on May 1.

South of Kelowna on the east side of the lake is **Cedar Creek Estate Winery,** 5445 Lakeshore Rd. (© **250/764-8866;** www.cedarcreek.bc.ca). Cedar Creek produces notable pinot noir, chardonnay, and meritage blends. **The Terrace Restaurant** is open for lunch daily. **Summerhill Pyramid Winery,** 4870 Chute Lake Rd. (© **800/667-8000** or 250/764-8000; www.summerhill.bc.ca), also lies south of downtown. Its extraordinary pyramid has been crafted with such precision that its alignment rivals that of the Great Pyramid of Egypt, and is where kegs of wine are stored. From mid-May to mid- October, pyramid tours are scheduled throughout the day, in between which there is a tasting bar and the **Sunset Organic Bistro** to enjoy. Summerhill's Robert Bateman labeled wines make for a true Canadiana purchase; Robert Bateman being Canada's foremost wildlife artist.

Across Okanagan Lake from Kelowna is Westbank, home to **Mission Hill Wines,** 1730 Mission Hill Rd. (© **250/768-7611;** www.missionhillwinery.com), one of the most architecturally eye-catching wineries in the Okanagan, and a showcase for sculptural works and in summer, Shakespearean revues and concerts. The tasting room is open daily, except for major winter holidays; check the website for tours.

Another delicious experience is the **Quail's Gate Estate,** 3303 Boucherie Rd., Westbank (© **800/420-9463** or 250/769-4451; www.quailsgate.com), famous for its ice wines, chenin blanc, and rich merlot. The **Old Vines Patio Restaurant ★**, with marvelous views of vineyards and the lake, is open daily for lunch and dinner, save for a staff holiday the first 2 weeks in January.

Organized Tours & Excursions

If you want to visit the wineries and leave the driving to someone else, contact **Okanagan Wine Country Tours** (© **866/689-9463** or 250/868-9463; www.okwinetours.com), which offers packages ranging from a 3-hour Afternoon Delight for C$85 to the Daytripper for C$155.

Discover **Okanagan Tours** (© **800/797-6335** or 250/762-1161) also offers wine tours starting from C$79, as well as other packaged activities including golf, powder skiing, mountain bike trips, and fishing charters.

Outdoor Pursuits

BIKING   The Kettle Valley Railway's **Myra Canyon** route near Kelowna has reopened (many of the trestles burned during the Okanagan wildfires in 2003). Although the route is often accessed from Naramata (p. 279), bikers in Kelowna can reach the east side of the route by following Hwy. 33 south from Kelowna. Inquire at **Sports Rent,** 2936 Pandosy St. (© **250/861-5699;** www.sportsrentkelowna.com), for other mountain biking routes in the area, including bike parks at Apex Mountain Resort and Silver Star Mountain Resort. Tourism Westside (www.tourismwest.com) puts out a brochure, *Westside Trail Guide,* that explores many mountain, provincial, and regional park trails. It is also available in print and online.

GOLF   The Okanagan's warm climate is good for more than just growing grapes and apricots. Golf is one of the region's top draws, boasting some 50 golf courses for all levels of play; for information, contact www.totabc.com/trellis/golf. The greens fees throughout the Okanagan Valley range from C$65 to C$175 and are a good value not only because of the beautiful locations, but also for the quality of service at each club.

   Harvest Golf Club, 2725 K.L.O. Rd. (© **800/257-8577** or 250/862-3103), is one of the finest courses in the Okanagan, a championship course in an orchard setting. The **Okanagan Golf Club ★**, off Hwy. 97 near the airport (© **800/446-5322** or 250/765-5955), has two 18-hole courses, the Jack Nicklaus–designed Bear Course and the Les Furber–designed Quail Course.

HIKING   The closest trails to Kelowna are in **Knox Mountain Park,** immediately north of the city. From downtown, follow Ellis Street to its terminus, where there's a parking area and trail head. The most popular trail climbs up the cactus-clad mountainside to the summit, from which you'll enjoy magnificent views of the lake and orchards. Visit www.tourismwestside.com to download the *Westside Trail Guide.*

SKIING & SNOWBOARDING   One of British Columbia's largest ski areas and one of North America's snowboarding capitals, **Big White Ski Resort ★**, 5315 Big White Road, Kelowna (© **250/765-3101,** 250/765-SNOW [7669] for snow report, or 800/663-2772 for accommodation reservations; www.bigwhite.com), is famed for its hip-deep champagne powder snow. The resort spreads over a broad mountain, featuring long, wide runs. Skiers here cruise open bowls and tree-lined glades. There's an annual average of 7.5m (25 ft.) of fluffy powder, so it's no wonder the resort's 118 named runs are so popular. There are 16 lifts, capable of carrying 28,000 skiers per hour. For snowboarders, there is a 150m-long (492-ft.) super pipe with 5.1m (17-ft.) transitional walls and a 120m (394-ft.) standard half pipe. The resort also offers more than 25km (16 miles) of groomed cross-country ski trails, a recreational racing program, and night skiing. Adult lift tickets are C$75. Big White is 55km (34 miles) southeast of Kelowna off Hwy. 33.

   Only a 15-minute drive from Westbank, **Crystal Mountain Resorts Ltd.** (© **250/ 768-5189,** or 250/768-3753 for snow report; www.crystalresort.com) has a range of ski programs for all types of skiers, specializing in clinics for children, women, and seniors. The resort's 20 runs are 80% intermediate-to-novice grade and are serviced by one double chair and two T-bars. The runs are equipped for day and night skiing. There's also a half pipe for snowboarders. It's a popular community mountain; lift tickets start at C$46 adults and C$38 children.

WATERSPORTS   The marina just north of City Park has a great many outfitters that can rent you a boat, jet ski, windsurfing board, or paddle boat. If you want to call ahead, try **Dockside Marine Centre,** 770 Finns Rd. (© **800/663-4737** or

250/765-3995; www.docksidemarine.com), which offers a wide range of boats and watercraft. To try parasailing, call **Okanagan Parasail**, 1310 Water St., at the Grand Okanagan Resort (☏ **250/868-4838**) which offers flights for C$72 single, C$58 as a double—usually a great option for kids.

Where to Stay

Abbott Villa Travelodge Kelowna ✦   For the money, this is one of the best places to stay in Kelowna, as it has one of the best locations downtown—right across from the City Park beaches and within a short walk of shopping, restaurants, theater, and entertainment. The standard-issue motel units are clean and well maintained; the one- and two-bedroom suites have kitchens.

1627 Abbott St., Kelowna, BC V1Y 1A9. www.travelodge.com. ☏ **800/663-2000** or 250/763-7771. 52 units. High season C$195–C$255 double; suites C$329. AE, MC, V. Free parking. Pets C$20. **Amenities:** Restaurant; Jacuzzi; heated outdoor pool; sauna. *In room:* A/C, TV, fridge, Wi-Fi (free).

Coast Capri Hotel   Somewhat apart from the beaches and downtown area, and surrounded by various strip malls, the Coast Capri offers large, smartly furbished rooms, most with balconies and quality hotel amenities. The **Vintage Dining Room** is a great old-fashioned steakhouse—probably the best place in town for an elegant dinner of prime rib or steak, while the more casual **Poolside Grill** features live jazz at the weekends. The adjoining **Beyond Wrapture Spa** (☏ **250/448-8899**) has made its mark by providing innovative vinotherapy treatments from local grape products.

1171 Harvey Ave., Kelowna, BC V1Y 6E8. www.coasthotels.com. ☏ **800/663-1144** or 250/860-6060. 185 units. High season C$195–C$225 double. Pets C$20. AE, MC, V. Free parking. Pets C$20. **Amenities:** 2 restaurants; bar; free airport shuttle; business center; exercise room; Jacuzzi; heated outdoor pool. *In room:* A/C, TV, Wi-Fi (free).

Delta Grand Okanagan Lakefront Resort & Conference Centre ★★★ ☺
Sitting on 10 hectares (25 acres) of beach and parkland, this upscale resort is an easy walk to downtown restaurants and the arts district. The spacious rooms come with opulent furniture and upholstery, plus knockout views from every window. Suites offer Jacuzzi tubs and separate showers; the deluxe condos provide full kitchens— good for families—and the Grand Club rooms, occupying the top two floors of the resort, include secured access and a private lounge (with complimentary breakfast). Two-bedroom units come with full kitchen, fireplace, three TVs, and washer and dryer. The apartment-style Royal Private Villas are especially sumptuous, with access to a private infinity pool. The restaurant and lounge tend to get very busy; they over-look the resort's private marina, as well as the sheltered waterway where kids can troll the waters in pint-sized motorized swans and boats. The state-of-the-art fitness room and spa offers a variety of wellness and aesthetic treatments.

1310 Water St., Kelowna, BC V1Y 9P3. www.deltahotels.com. ☏ **800/465-4651** or 250/763-4500. 390 units. High season C$259–C$399 double; C$389–C$1,639 suites, condos, or luxury villas. Extra person C$20. Off-season discounts available. AE, DC, MC, V. **Amenities:** 3 restaurants; pub; lounge; concierge; health club w/spa; indoor and outdoor pool; room service; watersports equip-ment rentals; casino. *In room:* A/C, TV w/pay movies, hair dryer, minibar, Wi-Fi (free).

Hotel Eldorado ★★   If you like historic inns, this is a charmer, set right on the water with its own marina. With a history dating back to 1926, the entire place has been fully restored and is now decorated with a unique mix of antiques; a wing with 30 new guest rooms and six luxury suites was added in 2005. All rooms are individu-ally decorated, and there's a wide mix of floor plans and layouts. The third-floor guest rooms with views of the lake are the largest and quietest. Some rooms also feature lakeside balconies. On the premises are a boardwalk cafe, lounge, spa, a pool that feels very Art Deco, and a dining room. The staff can arrange boat moorage, boat rentals, and water-skiing lessons.

500 Cook Rd. (at Lakeshore Rd.), Kelowna, BC V1W 3G9. www.eldoradokelowna.com. ℰ **866/608-7500** or 250/763-7500. 55 units. C$179–C$449 double. Lower off-season rates available. AE, DC, MC, V. From downtown, follow Pandosy Rd. south 1.5km (1 mile). Turn right on Cook Rd. **Amenities:** Fine-dining restaurant; bar; boardwalk cafe; fitness center; Jacuzzi; indoor pool; spa services; steam room; marina. *In room:* A/C, TV, hair dryer, Wi-Fi (free).

Kelowna-SameSun International Hostel   If you're on a budget, this centrally located backpackers' lodge is just the ticket. Newly built, it has most of the amenities of a hotel, except many of the guest rooms are dorm style. The huge communal kitchen, the common area filled with couches, and the vast back patio and barbecue area are where everyone hangs out; the bedrooms are clean and comfortable. The private rooms have en suite bathrooms and cable TV. Extras include free continental breakfast and parking. You'll be close to the beach as well as downtown eats and nightlife. There's a new generation of hip, upscale hostels out there, and this is one of the best.

245 Harvey Ave., Kelowna, BC V1Y 6C2. www.samesun.com. ℰ **877/972-6378** or 250/763-9814. 88 beds. C$30 dorm single; $85 private double. MC, V. Free parking. **Amenities:** Wi-Fi (paid); kitchen; TV lounge; hot tub, BBQ area, laundry, patio. *In room:* A/C, no phone.

Lake Okanagan Resort ★   The long, winding road that leads to this secluded hideaway is a sports-car driver's dream come true. And there are many more activities to keep guests occupied once they arrive at this woodsy resort with its country club/summer camp atmosphere. Located on 122 hectares (301 acres) of Okanagan Lake's hilly western shore, it offers multiple-bedroom units for couples, groups, and families. All are very comfortable and well equipped and, since the resort is built on a hill, all rooms have terrific views.

2751 Westside Rd., Kelowna, BC V1Z 3T1. www.lakeokanagan.com. ℰ **800/663-3273** or 250/769-3511. 135 units. C$179–C$329 studio suite; C$299–C$329 1-bedroom suite. Off-season discounts and packages available. AE, MC, V. Free parking. Drive 18km (11 miles) up Westside Rd. **Amenities:** 2 restaurants; 2 bars; summer children's camp; concierge; par-3 golf course; health club; Jacuzzis; 3 outdoor pools; spa; tennis courts; watersports equipment rentals. *In room:* A/C, TV, hair dryer, kitchen, Wi-Fi (free).

Prestige Hotel Kelowna   One of the closest hotels to the City Park beaches, the Prestige Hotel is a cornerstone of downtown Kelowna. Rooms are nicely furnished, large, and comfortable, with glass-fronted balconies; suites come with canopy beds, robes, DVDs, and double Jacuzzis; several have themes, such as the medieval or Egyptian suites. The hotel is part of a Kelowna-based chain of quality properties throughout the Interior and into the Rockies, plus a new resort in Sooke (see p 133).

1675 Abbott St., Kelowna, BC V1Y 8S3. www.prestigeinn.com. ℰ **87/PRESTIGE** (877/737-8443) or 250/860-7900. 67 units. High season C$199–C$229 double; C$269–C$699 suite. Off-season rates and packages available. AE, MC, V. **Amenities:** Restaurant; bar; concierge; exercise room; Jacuzzi; indoor pool; room service. *In room:* A/C, TV w/pay movies, fridge, hair dryer, Wi-Fi (free).

CAMPING

Okanagan Lake Provincial Park (ℰ **250/494-6500**), 11km (7 miles) north of Summerland and 44km (27 miles) south of Kelowna on Hwy. 97, has 168 campsites nestled amid 10,000 imported trees. Sites go for C$30. Facilities include free hot showers, flush toilets, a sani-station, and a boat launch.

Closer to Kelowna is **Bear Creek Provincial Park** (📞 **250/494-6500**), 9km (5⅔ miles) north of Hwy. 97 on Westside Road, about 3km (1¾ miles) west of the Okanagan Lake Floating Bridge. The park has 117 sites for C$30 each.

Where to Eat

For the kind of hearty cooking that fulfills gastronomic stereotypes, try **Mamma Rosa Italian Restaurant,** 561 Lawrence Ave. (📞 **250/763-4114;** www.mamma rosa.ca), a third-generation Italian family restaurant that serves up affordable house-made pastas and very good pizzas. **Bohemian Restaurant,** 363 Bernard Ave. (📞 **250/ 862-3517**), offers tasty and hearty fare, from enormous muffins to soups, sand-wiches, Asian rice bowls, and bigger plates. Sunday brunch is always packed to the rafters.

A number of Kelowna-area vineyards offer dining; check out **Sunset Organic Bistro** at Summerhill (see above); and the **Old Vines Patio Restaurant ★**, at Quail's Gate Estate, 3303 Boucherie Rd., West Kelowna (📞 **250/769-4451;** www. quailsgate.com). Both are open year-round.

Bai Thong Thai Restaurant ★ THAI   Bai Thong has an encyclopedic menu of house specialties, making this the best Thai restaurant in the Okanagan. Almost all dishes can be made vegetarian. Choose from red, green, or yellow curries, or from signature dishes like *goong pad num prick pao,* stir-fried shrimp with fresh vegetables in fiery Thai sauce.

1530 Water St. 📞 **250/763-8638.** Reservations not needed. Main courses C$12–C$18. MC, V. Mon–Fri 11:30am–2:30pm and 5–9:30pm; Sat–Sun 5–9:30pm.

Bouchons Bistro ★ FRENCH   This Gallic transplant offers classic French bis-tro fare just a few blocks from the Okanagan lakefront. The dining room, with ocher walls, stained-glass panels, and handwritten menus, actually feels Parisian. The menu doesn't stray far from classic French cuisine, though dishes are prepared with the freshest and best of local products—the level of cooking at Bouchons will make you appreciate French cuisine once again. Cassoulet is a house specialty, and you can't go wrong with duck confit glazed with honey and spices. A recent game-meat-focused menu offered wonderful wild fowl consommé with foie gras wontons. There's also a five-course table d'hôte for C$40. The wine list is half French, half Okanagan vin-tages. In summer, there's alfresco dining in the garden-like patio.

1180 Sunset Dr. 📞 **250/763-6595.** www.bouchonsbistro.com. Reservations suggested. Main courses C$20–C$36. MC, V. Daily 5:30–10pm.

Christopher's Steak & Seafood STEAKHOUSE   Christopher's is a local favorite for drinks and steaks in a dark, fern bar–like dining room. The decor and menu haven't changed much since the early years of the Reagan administration, but that's a plus if you're looking for Alberta beef served up in simple abundance. Few places still serve up a 24oz Ribeye, and the Chateaubriand (for two) is perfection. Pasta, chicken, and seafood are also offered. The seafood platter is exceptional with crab, lobster, tiger prawns, scallops, mussels, and salmon and/or halibut.

242 Lawrence Ave. 📞 **250/861-3464.** www.christophersrestaurant.ca. Reservations recommended. Main courses C$15–C$45. AE, DC, MC, V. Sun–Thurs 4:30–10pm; Fri–Sat 4:30–11pm.

Doc Willoughby's Pub CANADIAN   For a scene that's casual but on the edge of trendy, with a publike atmosphere but with better food, try Doc Willoughby's, in the heart of downtown. The building was once a pioneer drugstore (note the hammered-tin ceiling), but the interior has been done up in a strikingly contemporary design. This is a good spot for lunch, as the entire front of the restaurant opens to the street; you can watch the to-ing and fro-ing of tourists as you choose from salads, burgers, and sandwiches. At dinner, the eclectic menu offers lots of fish, chicken, and pasta dishes.

353 Bernard Ave. ⓒ **250/868-8288.** www.docwilloughby.com. Reservations not needed. Main courses C$13–C$30. AE, MC, V. Mon–Thurs 11:30am–11pm; Fri–Sat 11:30am–midnight; Sun 4:30–10pm.

Memphis Blues BARBEQUE/GRILL   Although part of a small western Canadian chain, this restaurant feels family-run. It is Kelowna's only authentic barbeque venue, and often wins awards such as best meal for the money, best ribs, best BBQ, and best place to dine alone. Meat is smoked over hardwood for hours on end at low temperatures, resulting in messy-to-eat, ever-so-succulent pulled pork, ribs, and beef brisket. The 1950s diner atmosphere simply adds to the fun.

289 Bernard St. ⓒ **250/868-3699.** www.memphisbluesBBQ.com. Reservations not needed. Main courses C$12–C$25. MC, V. Daily 11am–10:30pm.

RauDZ Regional Table ★★ CONTEMPORARY CANADIAN   This is the hottest of dining spots in Kelowna, and the second solo venture of chef/owner Rod Butters, who has worked at some of western Canada's top restaurants. The cooking focuses on organic, sustainable, fresh, relatively unfussy regional cuisine. Their pictures decorate the walls so you get a real sense of where your food is coming from. Start with a salmon "BLT" with crispy pancetta and fig-anise toasts and move on to duck meatloaf served with garlic-oil-roasted beets and turnips, or oat-crusted arctic char, with maple butter and potato, spinach, and bacon sauté. Service is top-notch; the wine list celebrates the vintages of the Okanagan Valley.

1560 Water St. ⓒ **250/868-8805.** www.raudz.com. Reservations recommended. Main courses C$14–C$30. AE, MC, V. Daily 5–10pm.

Shine Lounge ★ TAPAS   This attractive, modern restaurant is an offshoot of the successful western Canadian Ric's Grill chain, and combines the buzz of an urbane cocktail lounge with a large and wide-ranging international tapas menu. There's something here to please every appetite and taste. Highlights include an orange-and-ginger-glazed duck breast salad, a selection of sashimi, oysters on the half shell, sliders, flatbread pizza, crisp crab and shrimp sushi with pineapple and asparagus, satay—the list of delicious options is endless. The dining room is dark and sleek, with moody lighting, a perfect match for the varied and sophisticated food; in summer, there's an outdoor patio half a story above the street.

1585 Abbott St. ⓒ **250/763-9463.** Reservations recommended. Tapas C$7–C$17. AE, MC, V. Tues–Sat 6–11pm.

VERNON

Vernon (pop. 36,000) is the oldest community in the Okanagan Valley, offering a charming downtown core with murals and heritage facades, and a breathtaking countryside of mountains, ranchlands, and lakes. For those wishing to escape the bustle a few miles south, Vernon and its neighboring hamlets of Armstrong (famous for its cheese), Lumby, and Enderby are year-round holiday destinations for golf, water sports, fishing, mountain biking, and skiing. **Silver Star Mountain Ski Resort** (ⓒ **800/663-4431;** www.skisilverstar.com) 25km (15½ miles) north east of Vernon, offers some of the world's best powder snow for Nordic and downhill skiing. Drive 12km (7½m) north of Vernon, and you'll come to one of the area's most beloved attractions: **Historic O'Keefe Ranch,** 9380 Hwy 97N (© **250/542-7868;** www.okeefe ranch.ca), a late 1800s ranch with historic buildings, old time crafters, and a general store.

The surrounding landscapes are home to wineries such as **Ex Nihilo Vineyards,** 1525 Camp Rd. (© **250/766-5522;** www.exhihilovineyards.com), noted for its Rolling Stone endorsed ice-wines—yes, *those* Rolling Stones; **Gray Monk,** 1055 Camp Rd. (© **250/766-3168;** www.graymonk.com), with its excellent Grapevine Restaurant that's open March to October; and **Edge of the Earth Vineyards,** 4758 Gulch Rd. (© **250/546-2164**), a tiny producer of hand-crafted vegan wines.

More significant is the arrival of two developments. The first was **Predator Ridge** (© **888/578-6688** or 250/543-3436; www.predatorridge.com), an international-caliber golf community. Then came **Sparkling Hill Resort** (see "Where to Stay & Eat"), a first-of-its-kind in North America, European-style wellness center. Although these two projects have given Vernon an international profile, the crowds haven't yet arrived. Enjoy it while you can. Visit www.tourismvernon.com for more information.

Where to Stay & Eat

Sparkling Hill Resort ★★★   Because it is owned by *the* Swarovski family, this sleek European-style resort incorporates more than 3 million crystals into its design: as chandeliers, as fireplaces, in the spa, and in many architectural features. Glass is equally apparent because here, it's all about the lake and mountain views. Guest rooms are spacious with all the modern luxuries you would expect—except for an in-suite coffee maker. These refreshments are available in the spa lounge. And oh, what a spa. It scooped the 2011 *Senses Wellness Award* for Best Mountain Spa Resort within months of opening and little wonder. In addition to regular spa services come seven aromatherapy saunas and steam rooms at varying temperatures and special effects. North America's first Cold Sauna (−110 degrees) is the star. Overnight rates include continental buffet breakfast with lots of cheeses and meats. For the balance of the day, you can expect West Coast cuisine with a full slate of Okanagan wines.

888 Sparkling Pl., Vernon, BC V1H 2K7. www.sparklinghill.com. © **877/275-1556** or 250/275-1610. 152 units. C$225–C$425; penthouse suites from C$500. AE, MC, V. Free parking. **Amenities:** Restaurant; lounge; fitness center; golf course; hot tubs; indoor/outdoor pools; saunas; spa; steam rooms. *In room:* A/C, TV w/pay movies; hair dryer; Wi-Fi (free).

SOUTHEASTERN BRITISH COLUMBIA & THE KOOTENAY VALLEY

By Chloë Ernst

With the high-flying Rockies to the east and the rugged Purcell and Selkirk mountain ranges to the west, southeastern British Columbia has as much beauty and recreation to offer as anywhere else in the province. If you're looking to avoid the crowds at Banff and Jasper national parks on the Alberta side of the Rockies, try one of the smaller parks covered in this chapter.

Trenched by the mighty Kootenay and Columbia rivers, this region has a long history of mining, river transport, and ranching. More recently, the ranches have given way to golf courses, but development out in this rural area of British Columbia is still low-key. And while the ultimate dining experiences here are fewer and farther between, it also means that prices are lower across-the-board—and you won't have to compete with tour-bus hordes while you hike the trails.

In pre-Contact Native America and the early years of western exploration, the Kootenay Valley was a major transportation corridor. Due to a curious accident of geology, the headwaters of the vast Columbia River—which flows north from Columbia Lake for about 275km (171 miles) before bending south and flowing to the Pacific at Astoria, Oregon—are separated from the south-flowing Kootenay River by a low, 2km-wide (1¼-mile) berm of land called Canal Flats. The Kootenay River then zigzags down into the United States before flowing back north into Canada to join the Columbia at Castlegar, British Columbia.

Because a short portage was all that separated these two powerful rivers, Canal Flats was an important crossroads when canoes and riverboats were the primary means of transport. The fact that an easily breached ridge was all that separated two major rivers caught the imagination of an early entrepreneur, William Adolph Baillie-Grohman. In the 1880s, he conceived a plan to breach Canal Flats and divert much of the Kootenay's flow into the Columbia. Unsurprisingly, he ran into opposition from people living and working on the Columbia, and had to settle for building a canal and lock system between the two rivers. Only two ships ever passed through the canal, and today this curiosity is preserved as Canal Flats Provincial Park, 86km (53 miles) north of Cranbrook, with picnic tables, a beach, and a boat launch on Columbia Lake.

REVELSTOKE

410km (255 miles) W of Calgary; 565km (351 miles) NE of Vancouver

Located on the Columbia River at the foot of Mount Revelstoke National Park, Revelstoke sits in a narrow fir-cloaked valley between the Selkirk and the Monashee mountains. It's a spectacular, big-as-all-outdoors setting, and unsurprisingly, Revelstoke makes the most of the outdoor-recreation opportunities on its doorstep. Winter is high season here, as the city is a major center for powder skiing and boarding, heli-skiing, and snowmobiling. Summer activities include rafting, hiking, and horseback riding. The town was established in the 1880s, when the Canadian Pacific Railway pushed through. Much of the handsome downtown core was built then; most restaurants and hotels are housed in century-old buildings. Revelstoke is a charming and beautiful destination, and for years it's been surprisingly unheralded. But with the further development of the new destination ski resort just south of town, Revelstoke is suddenly poised for the big times.

Essentials

GETTING THERE   Revelstoke is 200km (124 miles) from Kelowna on Hwy. 1. It's 565km (351 miles) northeast of Vancouver and 410km (255 miles) west of Calgary. **Greyhound Canada** (✆ **800/661-8747** or 250/837-5874; www.greyhound.ca) operates four buses daily from Vancouver, costing C$93. From Revelstoke to Calgary costs C$60 one-way. Fares increase on weekends.

The winter **Revelstoke Connection** (✆ **888/569-1969;** www.revelstoke connection.com) runs from Kelowna to Revelstoke four times daily. Reservations required 48 hours ahead. Adult return fare costs C$150 (taxes included).

VISITOR INFORMATION   Contact the **Revelstoke Visitor Information Centre,** 204 Campbell St. (✆ **800/487-1493;** www.revelstokecc.bc.ca).

Exploring the Town

Downtown Revelstoke (pop. 8,500) sits on a shelf of land above the confluence of the Columbia and Illecillewaet rivers. Founded in the 1880s, the town center retains a number of original storefronts and is pleasant to explore. You'll see plenty of coffeehouses, galleries, and some standout architectural jewels, like the domed **Revelstoke Courthouse,** 1123 Second St. W. Near Victoria Road and Campbell Avenue, **Grizzly Plaza** is lined with redbrick storefronts. It's the site of the Saturday farmers' market, as well as free live music from late June to late August, nightly from 6:30pm and 9:30pm.

Named for the triple-peaked mountain that dominates the skyline above Revelstoke, **Mt. Begbie Brewery,** 521 First St. W. (✆ **250/837-2756;** www.mt-begbie. com), offers tours of the micro-brewery and samples of its award-winning craft beer. Call to confirm the schedule, although tours generally run Friday and Saturday afternoons in summer and winter ski seasons.

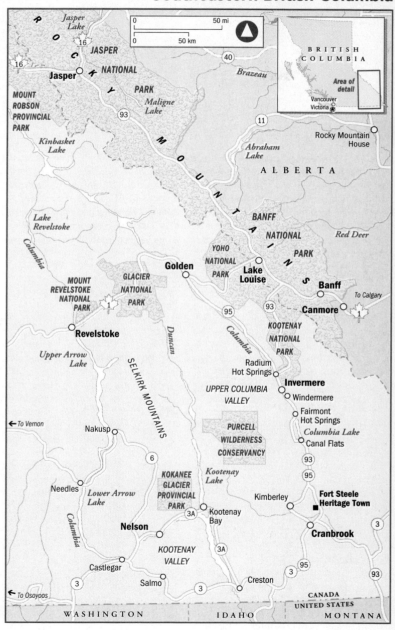

Revelstoke Museum & Archives   Located in the town's original customs and post office, this small museum contains memorabilia from Revelstoke's pioneer mining and railroading days. Upstairs is the community art gallery, with works by local and regional artists.

315 W. First St. *(C)* **250/837-3067.** www.revelstokemuseum.ca. Admission C$5 adults, C$4 seniors and teens, C$12 families, children 12 and under free. Mon–Fri 10am–5pm; Sat 11am–5pm.

Revelstoke Nickelodeon Museum   You won't be shushed in this museum. Hour-long tours include demonstrations of player pianos, phonographs, jukeboxes, and barrel organs—highlighting the marriage of mechanics and music.

111 W. First St. *(C)* **250/837-5250.** www.revelstokenickelodeon.com. Admission C$11 adults, C$5 children 6–16, children 5 and under free, and C$27 families. May–Sept daily 10am–6pm; Oct–April Tues–Sat 11am–4pm.

Revelstoke Railway Museum   It's the railroad that really put Revelstoke on the map, and this noteworthy museum—built to resemble an original Canadian Pacific Railway shop—tells the story of western Canadian rail history. Its collection of antique rolling stock includes a beautifully restored CPR steam engine from the 1940s. Other exhibits focus on the building of the first transcontinental line across Canada and the communications systems that kept the trains running safely.

719 Track St. W., across from downtown on Victoria Rd. *(C)* **250/837-6060.** www.railwaymuseum.com. Admission C$10 adults, C$8 seniors, C$5 children 8–16, C$2 children 4–7, free for children 3 and under, and C$22 families. July–Aug daily 9am–6pm; May–June and Sept–Oct daily 9am–5pm; Nov–April Thurs–Sun 11am–4pm.

Touring the Dams

The Columbia River has the steepest descent of any large river in North America, and in terms of volume, is the continent's fourth-largest river, making it irresistible to hydroelectric dam builders. Two of the many electricity-generating dams on the river are near Revelstoke, although only the closer Revelstoke Dam is open for tours. **Revelstoke Dam,** 6km (3¾ miles) north of Revelstoke on Hwy. 23, is 470m (1,542 ft.) across and 175m (574 ft.) high. Self-guided tours of the renovated visitor center (*(C)* **250/814-6697;** www.bchydro.com) explain how hydroelectricity is produced, how the dams impact the local ecosystem, and the First Nations history of the area. An elevator shoots to the top of the dam, where you'll get a feeling for the immensity of this structure. The visitor center is open mid-May to mid-Oct from 10am to 5pm. Admission C$6 adults, C$5 seniors and youth.

A 145km (90-mile) drive up Hwy. 23 along the shores of Revelstoke Lake takes you to **Mica Dam,** the first large dam on the Columbia—and large it is, much larger than Revelstoke Dam. More than 792m (2,598 ft.) across and 200m (656 ft.) high, Mica Dam forms Kinbasket Lake, which stretches for more than 160km (99 miles) and contains 14.8 trillion cubic meters (523 trillion cubic ft.) of water. There is no longer a visitor center at the dam, which limits the trip to being a scenic drive.

Outdoor Pursuits

Revelstoke is surrounded by rugged mountains with extremely heavy snowfalls (almost 18m/59 ft. annually in the Selkirk Mountains). The town is particularly known as a center for heli-skiing, a sport that employs helicopters to deposit expert skiers high on mountain ridges, far from lifts and ski areas.

BIKING   The mountains around Revelstoke are etched with old logging roads that have been converted into mountain-bike trails; ask at the visitor center for a map.

GOLF   **Revelstoke Golf Club** (© **250/837-4276**) is an 18-hole, par-72 championship course established in 1924, with narrow fairways lined with mammoth conifers and small lakes. The club—one of the oldest in British Columbia—has a driving range, clubhouse with lounge and restaurant, and pro shop. Greens fees are C$58 for 18 holes.

SKIING   **Revelstoke Mountain Resort** (6km/3¾ miles southeast of Revelstoke; © **866/922-8754** or 250/814-0087; www.revelstokemountainresort.com) is a new billion-dollar four-season resort that includes 5 lifts, 56 ski runs, and housing units. The resort is home to the longest lift-serviced vertical in North America, with 1,713 vertical meters (5,620 vertical ft.) of skiing. An eight-person gondola and high-speed quads access the five bowls, terrain park, natural and man-made glades, and vast backcountry terrain that counts above a whopping 202,343 hectares (500,000 acres). Located in the legendary Monashee and Selkirk Mountains along the Columbia River, the resort also differentiates itself by providing downhill, cat skiing, and heli-skiing all from the same base. Lift tickets are C$74 adults, C$57 seniors and children ages 13 to 18, and C$26 children 6 to 12. For cat skiing, the resort offers day packages with unlimited vertical. The C$400 cost includes lunch and après ski.

Based out of the resort, the long-established **Selkirk Tangiers Heli-Skiing** (© **800/663-7080;** www.selkirk-tangiers.com) offers helicopter-assisted skiing and snowboarding trips to more than 200 approved areas in the Monashee and Selkirk mountains, with some runs topping 2,200m (7,218 ft.) in vertical drop. A 3-day package, with access to 10,000 vertical meters (32,808 vertical ft.) of powder, accommodations, and meals, starts at C$2,960. Revelstoke is also one of the home bases of **CMH Heli-Skiing** (© **800/661-0252;** www.cmhski.com), a longtime purveyor of helicopter skiing to remote slopes and glaciers in the Monashee and Selkirk mountains. CMH offers 4-, 5-, 7- and 10-day trips to 10 locations; prices for trips in the Revelstoke area begin at C$4,250 for 5 days, double occupancy, including lodging and food.

SNOWMOBILING   A detailed brochure of snowmobiling trails is available from the visitor center; contact **Great Canadian Snowmobile Tours** (© **877/837-9594** or 250/837-9594; www.snowmobilerevelstoke.com) at Glacier House Resort for guided trips.

WHITE-WATER RAFTING   **Apex Raft Company** (© **888/232-6666** or 250/837-6376; www.apexrafting.com) offers excursions down the Illecillewaet River's Albert Canyon. The trip provides thrills, but nothing too extreme. In summer, daily 3- to 4-hour trips cost C$85 for adults and C$69 for kids 16 and under.

Where to Stay

Martha Creek Provincial Park, just north of Revelstoke on Hwy. 23, sits on Lake Revelstoke and has 21 vehicle-accessible campsites that go for C$21 each on a first-come, first-served basis.

Accommodations are also available at Revelstoke Mountain Resort, just southeast of Revelstoke. The **Nelsen Lodge** offers 209 condo suites at the base of the lifts. The high-end modern style lodgings include full kitchen, fireplace, and washer and dryer. Rates are from C$349 double in the winter and summer high seasons. Near to the Trans-Canada Highway in Revelstoke, the **Sandman Inn** offers more standard hotel rooms from C$119. You can make reservations for both through the Sandman reservations line (www.sandmanhotels.ca; ℭ **800/726-3626** or 250/837-5271).

Courthouse Inn Bed and Breakfast ★   This inn is newly built but designed to fit in architecturally with its historic neighbors close to downtown. The comfortable guest rooms, with hardwood floors, quality furniture, and private baths, are decorated according to themes that reflect history (the Marie Antoinette room is the largest, with a four-poster king bed, while the Court room overlooks the domed Revelstoke Courthouse) or local sights and recreation. Guests share a living room with a fireplace and complimentary coffee, tea, and hot chocolate. Breakfast is served from a menu, with specialties like a seafood or vegetable Korean-style pancake. The hosts are particularly friendly, offering a level of professional service you'd expect at a hotel.

312 Kootenay St., Revelstoke, BC V0E 2S0. www.courthouseinnrevelstoke.com. ℭ **877/837-3369** or 250/837-3369. 10 units. C$120–C$199 double. Rates include full breakfast. MC, V. **Amenities:** Complimentary passes to pool and health club; Wi-Fi (free). *In room:* A/C, hair dryer, no phone, Wi-Fi (free).

Glacier House Resort   Just 5 minutes north from Revelstoke, across the Columbia River in a meadow overlooking the Monashee and Selkirk mountains, is this quiet alpine resort with outstanding amenities and a recreational focus. There are cozy, simply decorated rooms in the spacious lodge building, plus 10 free-standing log chalets that can sleep from 2 to 12 people. Each chalet has a fireplace and deck, and some have TVs, hot tubs, and kitchenettes. In addition to a spa, indoor pool, and sauna, Glacier House also has a restaurant and bar; plus it operates an outfitting company to provide guided hiking, biking, and snowmobiling trips. This is a great destination for a family that wants a backcountry-style vacation without roughing it.

1870 Glacier Lane (Box 250), Revelstoke, BC V0E 2S0. www.glacierhouse.com. ℭ **877/837-9594** or 250/837-9594. Fax 250/837-9592. 27 units. High season C$120–C$160 lodge room; C$160–C$275 chalet. Low season C$90–C$120 lodge room; C$130–C$250 chalet. MC, V. **Amenities:** Restaurant; pub w/pool tables; fitness center; Jacuzzi; indoor pool; sauna; sports equipment rentals. *In room:* TV (in all lodge rooms and larger chalets), fireplace, hair dryer, Wi-Fi (free).

The Hillcrest Hotel, A Coast Resort ★★   On the eastern edge of Revelstoke, this new hotel does its best to look like a grand mountain lodge, complete with turrets, balconies, log beams, stone walls, and a vast lobby dominated by a river-rock fireplace. The Hillcrest has the most complete facilities in Revelstoke, and its rooms are large and superbly comfortable—many offer mountain views, and suites come with Jacuzzis. The only downside is that you'll need to drive to get to downtown Revelstoke.

3km (1¾ miles) east of Revelstoke on Hwy. 1 (Box 1979), Revelstoke, BC V0E 2S0. www.hillcrest hotel.com. ℭ **250/837-3322.** Fax 250/837-3340. 75 units. C$159–C$219 double; C$239–C$349 suite. AE, MC, V. **Amenities:** Restaurant; lounge; exercise room; Jacuzzis; sauna; spa and massage therapy. *In room:* A/C, TV, hair dryer, Wi-Fi (free).

Minto Manor B&B ★   If you enjoy historic homes and gracious B&Bs, the Minto should be your Revelstoke destination. This elegant 1905 Edwardian mansion is full of character and history, offering three spacious guest rooms with private bathrooms, antiques, and an ersatz Victorian decor. Guests share a TV lounge, sitting room, and a music room with two pianos. The house has numerous stained-glass windows and wraparound porches, evoking a cultured feel.

815 MacKenzie Ave. (P.O. Box 3089), Revelstoke, BC V0E 2S0. www.mintomanor.com. ☎ **877/833-9337** or 250/837-9337. Fax 250/837-9327. 3 units. C$95 single, C$105–C$145 double. AE, MC, V. **Amenities:** TV room; complimentary passes to Railway Museum and aquatic center. *In room:* No phone, Wi-Fi (free).

Mulvehill Creek Wilderness Inn and Bed & Breakfast ★★★ 🍴 One of

the best small lodgings in all of British Columbia for its hidden lakeside location, this inn sits in a clearing in the forest, just steps from Arrow Lake and a magnificent 90m (295-ft.) waterfall that generates electricity. The cedar shake–sided lodge has three queen rooms, one king room, and two units with twin beds, plus two fireplace suites (one with Jacuzzi and private deck). All rooms are bright with natural light and decorated with pine furniture and original folk art. The lounge is lined with bookcases; grab a novel and curl up by the fireplace. From the deck, look onto the organic garden, which supplies much of the produce served here, or watch for wildlife. Your hosts will happily arrange cross-country skiing, snowshoeing, horseback-riding, biking, and fishing excursions. A couple of days at Mulvehill may well be the highlight of your trip to British Columbia, and if you're feeling romantic, there's even a wedding chapel. Children 16 and older only.

4200 Hwy. 23 S. (19km/12 miles south of Revelstoke), P.O. Box 1220, Revelstoke, BC V0E 2S0. www.mulvehillcreek.com. ☎ **877/837-8649** or 250/837-8649. 8 units. C$145–C$185 double; C$245 suite. Rates include Swiss-style breakfast. AE, MC, V. Children 16 and older only. **Amenities:** Jacuzzi; heated outdoor saltwater pool; free snowshoes and canoes; hiking trails; picnic areas; sun decks. *In room:* Hair dryer, no phone.

Regent Hotel ★ The finest lodging in downtown Revelstoke, the Regent is a

refurbished heritage hotel facing historic Grizzly Plaza. The bedrooms are of varying sizes (some compact, some large) individually decorated with restrained good taste; some have private Jacuzzis. The One Twelve Restaurant offers fine dining (see "Where to Eat," below).

112 First St. E., Revelstoke, BC V0E 2S0. www.regentinn.com. ☎ **888/245-5523** or 250/837-2107. Fax 250/837-9669. 45 units. C$139–C$199 double. AE, MC, V. Pets accepted in limited rooms for C$15. **Amenities:** Restaurant; lounge; pub; free aquatic center passes; fitness center; outdoor hot tub; sauna. *In room:* A/C, TV, hair dryer, Wi-Fi (free).

SameSun Revelstoke Hostel Located on the edge of downtown, the hostel is

in a spacious older home with oak floors and French doors. There's a large TV area, plus an outdoor patio and shared barbecue.

400 Second St. W., Revelstoke, BC V0E 2S0. www.samesun.com. ☎ **877/972-6378** or 250/837-4050. Fax 250/837-6410. 90 beds. C$25 per person bunk; C$55 per person private room. MC, V. **Amenities:** Computer and Internet access; kitchen; TV lounge. *In room:* No phone.

Where to Eat

For a relaxed drink in a handsome bar, order from the 20 wines by the glass or cheese and charcuterie platters at **Benoît's** (107 Second St. E.; ☎ **250/837-6606;** www.benoitswinebar.com). Without losing its vibe as a friendly ski-bum hangout, **The Village Idiot,** 306 Mackenzie Ave. (☎ **250/837-6240**), serves good and mildly creative pub fare.

One Twelve Restaurant WESTERN CANADIAN This handsome restaurant is one of Revelstoke's best fine-dining options, with a good selection of steaks, seafood (about half the menu options), and Continental cuisine. Seared scallops are topped with lime caramel, and mustard-crusted rack of lamb is a house favorite.

Good service, an intriguing wine list, woodsy but elegant decor, and a fireplace all enhance the experience.

In the Regent Hotel, 112 First St. E. (C) **250/837-2107.** www.regenthotel.ca. Reservations suggested. Main courses C$14–C$42. AE, MC, V. Daily 5:30–9:30pm.

Woolsey Creek Bistro ★ NEW CANADIAN   The menu at this pleasant and informal restaurant blends French accents with North American favorites. Choose from a broad selection of salads and appetizers—you could easily make a meal of the sharing plates, such as the dragon boat bruschetta, tuna tartar, or venison carpaccio. Main courses also emphasize regional and organic produce, meats, and fish; wild B.C. salmon comes with honey-roasted yams, and the ravioli is stuffed with beef and local mushrooms. Desserts are all made in-house. The knotty pine interior is divided into a bar and dining room, though the distinction disappears when the cafe is busy, which is often.

604 Second St. W. (C) **250/837-5500.** www.woolseycreekbistro.ca. Reservations recommended. Main courses C$15–C$26. MC, V. Daily 5–10pm.

MOUNT REVELSTOKE NATIONAL PARK

Just west of Glacier National Park is Mount Revelstoke National Park, a glacier-clad collection of craggy peaks in the **Selkirk Range.** Comprising only 260 sq. km (100 sq. miles), Mount Revelstoke can't produce the kind of awe that its larger neighbor, Glacier National Park, can in good weather; it does, however, offer easier access to the high country and alpine meadows. The park is flanked on the south by Hwy. 1, the Trans-Canada Highway. It has no services or campgrounds, but all tourist services are available in the neighboring town of Revelstoke (see above).

For information, contact **Mount Revelstoke National Park** ((C) **250/837-7500;** www.pc.gc.ca/revelstoke). Entry per day to the park costs C$7.80 for adults, C$6.80 for seniors, C$3.90 for children 6 to 16, and C$20 per family.

Exploring the Park

The most popular activity in the park is the drive up the slopes of **Mount Revelstoke,** for great views of the Columbia River and the peaks of Glacier Park. To reach Mount Revelstoke, take the paved Meadows in the Sky Parkway north from the Trans-Canada Highway (470m [1,542ft.] elevation). Follow the switchbacks for 26km (16 miles) to Balsam Lake (1,500m [4,921ft.] elevation). The parkway is closed to trailers and motor coaches, as it is a very narrow but paved mountain road with 16 steep switchbacks.

At **Balsam Lake,** at the Meadows in the Sky area, free shuttles operated by the parks department make the final ascent up to the top of Mount Revelstoke, but only after the road is clear of snow, usually from early July to late September. If the shuttle isn't running, you have a choice of a 1km (⅔ mile) hike to the alpine trails, or several easy hiking trails around Balsam Lake that lead past rushing brooks through wild-flower meadows. From the lake, the **Eagle Knoll Trail** takes under an hour. At the summit are longer trails, including the 6km (3.7-mile) trail out to **Eva Lake,** or short steep climbs to a historic **Firetower** or parapet viewpoints.

If you don't make the trip up to the Meadows in the Sky area, you can enjoy a short walk in the park from along Hwy. 1. The **Skunk Cabbage Trail** winds through a

Mount Revelstoke & Glacier National Parks

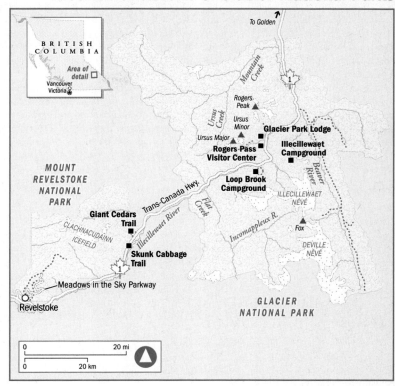

marsh that explodes with bright yellow and odoriferous flowers in early summer. Another popular hike is the **Giant Cedars Trail,** a short boardwalk out into a grove of old-growth cedars that are more than 1,000 years old.

GLACIER NATIONAL PARK

Rogers Pass is 72km (45 miles) E of Revelstoke; 80km (50 miles) W of Golden

Located amid the highest peaks of the Selkirk Mountains, Canada's Glacier National Park amply lives up to its name. More than 400 glaciers repose here, with 10% of the park's 1,350 sq. km (521 sq. miles) lying under permanent snowpack. The reason that this high country is so covered with ice is the same reason that this is one of the more unpopulated places to visit in the mountain West: It snows and rains a lot here.

For information, contact **Glacier National Park** (© **250/837-7500;** www. pc.gc.ca/glacier). A newly opened visitor center with topographical models is at Rogers Pass. There's no charge if you pass through the park on Hwy. 1 without stopping, but if you do stop to hike or picnic, the entry fee is C$7.80 for adults, C$6.80 for seniors, C$3.90 for children 6 to 16, and C$20 per family.

Exploring the Park

The primary attractions in the park are viewpoints onto craggy peaks and hiking trails leading to wildflower meadows and old-growth groves; heavy snow and rainfall lend a near-rainforest feel to the hikes. Spring hikers and cross-country skiers should beware of avalanche conditions, a serious problem in areas with high snowfall and steep slopes. Call the park information number (📞 **250/837-7500**) for weather updates.

Glacier Park is crossed by the Trans-Canada Highway and the Canadian Pacific Railway tracks. Each has had to build snowsheds to protect its transportation system from the effects of heavy snows and avalanches. **Park headquarters** are just east of 1,330m (4,364-ft.) Rogers Pass; stop here to watch videos and see the displays on natural and human history in the park. New exhibits focus on the role of the railroads in opening up this rugged area of Canada. You can sign up for ranger-led interpretive hikes here as well.

Hiking

Several easy trails leave from the park's Rogers Pass visitor center. The wheelchair-accessible **Abandoned Rails Trail** follows a rails-to-trails section of the old CPR track for a 1-hour round-trip journey along a gentle grade through a wildflower-studded basin. The **Balu Pass Trail** is a more strenuous 10km (6-mile) return hike to the base of the glaciers on 2,705m (8,875-ft.) Ursus Major.

The other important trail head is at **Illecillewaet Campground,** west of Rogers Pass along Hwy. 1. Several major trails head up into the peaks from here, including the **Asulkan Valley Trail,** which follows a stream up a narrow valley to a hikers' hut. These trails require more exertion than the trails at Rogers Pass, and will take most of a day to complete.

Farther down the Illecillewaet Valley are two other popular routes. **Loop Brook Trail** is a less than 1-hour saunter through a riparian wetland. The .5km (.3-mile) **Rock Garden Trail** climbs up a valley wall of moss-and-lichen-covered boulders. Stop at the **Hemlock Grove Picnic Area** and follow the boardwalk through the old-growth hemlock forest.

The longest hike in the park is the 42km (26-mile) one-way **Beaver Valley Trail,** which follows the Beaver River on the eastern edge of the park. This trail takes 3 days, one-way, to complete. If you plan on backcountry camping, you'll need to register at the visitor center and purchase a C$9.80 wilderness pass.

Where to Stay

Illecillewaet and **Loop Brook** campgrounds are just west of Rogers Pass off Hwy. 1 and along the Illecillewaet River. Both operate on a first-come, first-served basis. Facilities include flush toilets, kitchen shelters, firewood, and drinking water. Illecillewaet offers guided hikes and fireside programs as well. Rates at both campgrounds are C$22 per night.

Glacier Park Lodge   This large complex is just below Rogers Pass, where Hwy. 1 edges over the Selkirk Range in Glacier National Park. The setting is spectacular: The glaciered faces of towering peaks crowd around a broad cirque blanketed with wildflowers and boulders, at the center of which sits this handsome lodge. Around the lodge, the national park's hiking and cross-country ski trails lead out into the wilderness (the hotel will prepare a picnic lunch for you on request). Guest rooms are

Glacier National Park

SOUTHEASTERN BRITISH COLUMBIA & THE KOOTENAY VALLEY

comfortable and nicely furnished with extra-long beds; three of the suites are large enough to accommodate families.

Rogers Pass, BC V0E 2S0. www.glacierparklodge.ca. © **888/567-4477** or 250/837-2126. Fax 250/837-2130. 50 units. C$99–C$139 double. Children 11 & under stay free with parent. Extra person C$10. AE, DISC, MC, V. Pets C$10. **Amenities:** 2 restaurants; bar; Jacuzzi; heated outdoor pool; room service; sauna. *In room:* TV, Wi-Fi (free).

GOLDEN

139km (86 miles) W of Banff; 710km (441 miles) E of Vancouver

For more than a century, Golden (pop. 4,500) has been known primarily as a transport hub, first as a division point on the transcontinental Canadian Pacific Railway, next as the upstream steamboat terminus on the Columbia River, and then as a junction of two of Canada's busiest highway systems.

Nowadays, Golden is known for its outdoor recreation. The town sits in a breathtaking location in the trenchlike Columbia River valley, between the massive Rocky Mountains and the soaring Purcell Range, within a 90-minute drive of five major national parks. The fact that Golden is near—and not in—the parks is largely the reason for the area's busy feel. Outfitters that offer rafting, heli-skiing, heli-hiking, and other recreation that isn't allowed in the national parks (for conservation reasons) choose to make Golden their base. And with park towns such as nearby Banff trying to limit further development, businesses and outfitters that want a Rocky Mountain hub find Golden a convenient and congenial center. Other than along a short stretch of 9th Avenue North, Golden won't win any awards for quaint charm. It's basically a functional little town with lots of motel rooms in a magnificent location.

Note that Golden and the other communities in this part of the Columbia Valley are in the Mountain Time zone, an hour earlier than the rest of British Columbia.

Essentials

GETTING THERE Golden is at the junction of Hwy. 1 (the Trans-Canada Hwy.) and Hwy. 95. The closest airport is in Calgary. **Greyhound Canada** (© **800/661-8747** or 250/344-2917; www.greyhound.ca) links Golden to Vancouver, Banff, and Calgary, and to Cranbrook to the south. The one-way fare from Golden to Vancouver is C$120; to Calgary, it's C$46.

VISITOR INFORMATION Contact the **Golden Visitor Information Centre,** 500 10th Ave. N. (© **800/622-4653** or 250/344-7125; www.tourismgolden.com).

GETTING AROUND If you need a rental car while in Golden, contact **National,** 915 11th Ave. (© **250/344-9899;** www.nationalcar.com).

Exploring the Area

You could spend several days in the Golden area without realizing that the town has an older downtown core. It's a block west of busy 10th Avenue, on **Main Street.** There's a handful of shops and cafes—a pleasant break from the commercial sprawl along highways 1 and 95.

The **Golden and District Museum,** 1302 11th Ave. (© **250/344-5169;** www.goldenbcmuseum.com), tells the story of Golden's rail history. It also has an old log schoolhouse and blacksmith's shop. Open 10am to 5pm daily in summer, Tues to Sat in winter. Admission is C$5 adults, C$3 senior, C$2 children, and C$10 family.

Outdoor Pursuits

FISHING   The Columbia River runs through town and offers fair fishing for rainbow trout and kokanee salmon. There's better fishing in the **Kinbasket Lake** section of the river, which begins north of Golden.

GOLF   Golden Golf & Country Club (✆ 866/727-7222 or 250/344-2700; www.golfgolden.com) is an 18-hole championship course along the Columbia River. Bill Newis designed the front 9 holes; Les Furber took care of the back 9. The clubhouse includes a pro shop with equipment rentals. Greens fees are C$60 to C$70.

HELI-HIKING   Although based in Banff, **CMH Heli-Hiking** (✆ 800/661-0252 or 403/762-7100; www.cmhski.com) offers a variety of helicopter-assisted hiking packages in the Bugaboo and the Bobbie Burns sub-ranges west of Golden. Two-, 3-, 4-, or 6-day heli-hiking trips involve staying at remote high-country lodges accessible only by long hikes or by helicopter. Prices run C$2,565 for a 3-day trip; rates include lodging, food, and helicopter transport.

Mid-June through September, **Purcell Helicopter Skiing** (✆ 877/435-4754 or 250/344-5410; www.purcellhelicopterskiing.com) offers heli-hiking day trips in the Purcell Mountains west of Golden. Guided day hikes go for C$360 to C$540, including lunch. Sightseeing tours start at C$110 per person. All trips are based on four-passenger minimums.

HELI-SKIING   Banff-based **CMH Heli-Skiing** (see "Heli-Hiking," above) has eight high-country lodges in the mountain ranges near Golden. Prices vary greatly depending on the lodge and time of year, but range from C$5,789 to C$11,850 all-inclusive for a week. Rates include lodging, food, helicopter transport, use of specialized powder skis, and ground transport from the nearest large airport.

If you prefer more of a DIY approach to heli-skiing, **Purcell Helicopter Skiing** (see "Heli-Hiking," above) offers day trips to peaks in the Selkirk and Purcell ranges. Three-run (C$749) and five-run (C$895) packages are available, and include the helicopter ride, lunch, a guide, and instruction; you'll provide your own skis and lodging.

HORSEBACK RIDING   Located at Kicking Horse Mountain Resort, **Flying W Trail Rides** (✆ 250/344-0495; www.flyingwtrailrides.com) offers 1-hour (C$34), 2-hour (C$60), and 3-hour (C$80) trail rides.

SKIING   Kicking Horse Mountain Resort (✆ 866/754-5425; www.kicking horseresort.com) has transformed the winter scene in Golden. Located 14km (8¾ miles) west of Golden, it features a 1,260m-long (4,134-ft.) vertical drop, a gondola lift that takes skiers up above elevations of 2,450m (8,038 ft.), and the Eagle's Eye, the highest-elevation restaurant in Canada. It has five lifts, more than 120 runs, and over 1,133 hectares (2,800 acres) of skiable terrain. Lift tickets are C$75 a day. Several lodging options are now available at the resort, including three lodges, condos, three-bedroom town houses, and resort homes. You can also spend a night at the Eagle's Eye Suites and wake up at the crest of the Selkirk Mountains (at C$2,195 per couple, the views won't be the only unforgettable memory of this overnight stay).

WHITE-WATER RAFTING   The **Kicking Horse River,** which enters the Columbia at Golden, is one of the most exciting white-water runs in Canada, with constant Class III and Class IV rapids as it tumbles down from the Continental Divide through Yoho. A trip down the Kicking Horse will be a highlight of your vacation in the Rockies. Rafting trips are usually offered from mid-May to mid-September.

EXPLORING THE COLUMBIA RIVER
wetlands

South (upstream) from Golden are the Columbia River Wetlands, a 180km-long (112-mile) Wildlife Management Area that supports an incredible diversity of wildlife. More than 270 bird species have been seen in this stretch of river, marsh, and lake. The largest wetlands west of Manitoba, the Columbia River Wetlands are also a major breeding ground for the bald eagle, osprey, and great blue heron. Moose, elk, mink, and beaver make their homes here as well.

Bird-viewing areas include the small Reflection Lake sanctuary south of Golden on Highway 95.

Alpine Rafting (© 888/599-5299 or 250/344-6778; www.alpinerafting.com) offers the daylong Kicking Horse Challenge trip for C$149, including a barbecue steak lunch. A gentler, family-friendly 2-hour introduction to white water goes for C$59 for adults and C$30 for children 12 and under.

Glacier Raft Company (© 877/344-7238 or 250/344-6521; www.glacierraft.com) offers a variety of options. The easygoing scenic float day trip goes to the gentle upper valley of the Kicking Horse; it's for those who want an introduction to rafting or who don't want the thrills of white water. Cost is C$65 for adults and C$40 for kids 12 and under. Two separate day trips explore the white-water sections of the Kicking Horse and cost C$109 to C$149. All day trips include a steak barbecue lunch.

Wet 'n' Wild Adventures (© 800/668-9119 or 250/344-6546; www.wetnwild.bc.ca) offers Kicking Horse trips from Banff, Lake Louise, and Golden. The standard day trip is C$99, including lunch. If you just want to shoot the rapids of the lower canyon, a half-day trip is available for C$69. For beginners, a morning introduction to white water is C$60 for adults and C$40 for children 11 and under, including lunch.

WILDLIFE VIEWING   Visitors can get up close and personal with gray wolves at **Northern Lights Wildlife Wolf Centre,** 1745 Short Rd. (© 877/377-WOLF [9653] or 250/344-6798; www.northernlightswildlife.com). The center offers interpretive talks about wolves and their role in a healthy natural ecosystem. The wolves of Northern Lights, which live in a .5-hectare (1¼-acre) enclosure, have all been adopted from various facilities. Born and bred in captivity, these wolves are not candidates for release into the wild. Admission to the center, which includes a 20-minute introduction to the wolves, is C$12 adults, C$9 seniors and children ages 12 to 16, C$6 children ages 4 to 11, and C$35 for families. For an additional fee, the wolves are also available for custom photographic sessions and nature hikes. In July and August, the center is open daily 9am to 7pm; May, June, and September, it's open daily 10am to 6pm. The rest of the year, it's open daily noon to 5pm.

Where to Stay

Alpine Meadows Lodge ★   This family-owned lodge enjoys a great location—high above Golden, looking across onto the face of the Rockies, yet only 10 minutes to skiing, golf, and tourist services. The lodge, which was constructed from timber felled on the property, has a central three-story great room, flanked by wraparound balconies and open staircases. A huge stone fireplace dominates the living area. The guest rooms are light-filled and airy, with simple, unfussy decor; all of them have Jacuzzi tubs in the bathrooms. In addition, a four-bedroom, two-bathroom chalet with full kitchen is also available for rent. Outdoor recreation is literally right out the door, with paths from the lodge leading to hiking trails in neighboring federal forestland. The staff is very helpful and will make it easy for you to get out into the wilderness or onto the fairways.

717 Elk Rd., Golden, BC V0A 1H0. www.alpinemeadowslodge.com. ⓒ **888/700-4477** or 250/344-5863. Fax 250/344-5853. 10 units, 1 chalet. C$99–C$129 double; C$350–C$425 chalet, with minimum stay requirements. Rates include breakfast. Golf, skiing, rafting, and flightseeing packages available. MC, V. **Amenities:** Jacuzzi; lounge (offers TV and Internet access). *In room:* A/C, hairdryer, no phone, Wi-Fi (free).

Dreamcatcher Hostel 🏠
An open-concept communal area on the main floor, and cozy dorms with down duvets upstairs, make this hostel an exceptional choice for budget travelers. Rustic elements are featured throughout the hostel, from the central stone hearth to the knobbly log bunk beds. The two family suites can sleep five to six people and, like the private rooms, have en-suite bathrooms. All facilities are spacious and impeccably clean.

528 9th Ave. N., Golden, BC V0A 1H0. www.dreamcatcherhostel.com. ⓒ **877/439-1090** or 250/439-1090. 7 units. C$30 dorms. C$77–C$85 private rooms. MC, V. **Amenities:** Lounge; kitchen; garden with barbecue. *In room:* Wi-Fi (free).

Golden Rim Motor Inn ☺
Of the dozens of older motels in Golden, this is best for families, as the indoor pool has a waterslide. Standing above the precipitous Kicking Horse River valley, 1.7km (1 mile) east of Golden, the Golden Rim boasts sweeping views of the Rockies and the Columbia Valley. It offers standard queen-size-bed motel rooms, with some kitchen and Jacuzzi units available.

1416 Golden View Rd., Golden, BC V0A 1H1. www.goldenrim.ca. ⓒ **877/311-2216** or 250/344-2216. Fax 250/344-6673. 81 units. C$79–C$125 double. AE, MC, V. **Amenities:** Restaurant; bar; Jacuzzi; indoor pool w/water slide; sauna. *In room:* A/C, TV, hair dryer, Wi-Fi (free).

Hillside Lodge & Chalets
This stylish, European-style lodge with five standalone chalets sits on 24 forested hectares (59 acres) above the quiet Blaeberry River, 16km (10 miles) north of Golden. Guests stay in comfortable lodge rooms or delightful one- or two-bedroom chalets, the latter with wood stoves, kitchenettes, decks, and handcrafted furniture. All accommodations are recently built, so you'll find everything completely shipshape.

1740 Seward Frontage Rd., Golden, BC V0A 1H0. www.hillsidechalets.com. ⓒ **250/344-7281.** Fax 250/344-7281. 14 units. C$138–C$148 lodge double, includes full German-style breakfast; C$135–C$160 1-bedroom chalet (breakfast not included); C$215 summer cabin; C$230–C$260 2-bedroom chalet (breakfast not included). MC, V. **Amenities:** Dining room (guests only); lounge w/TV. In winter only: exercise room;Jacuzzi; sauna. *In room:* Fridge, hair dryer, no phone.

Kapristo Lodge
Homey, lodge-style Kapristo is an excellent choice for the recreation-oriented vacationer. It sits high above the Columbia Valley, with sweeping views of the Purcell Mountains from the large flagstone-and-planking patio. Guest rooms are comfortably furnished with down quilts and handsome furniture. Some rooms have pullout couches and can sleep up to six. What sets this apart from other lodges around Golden is its friendly informality and its owner's efforts to ensure that guests have a good time, whether rafting a river, riding horseback, or sunning on the deck.

1297 Campbell Rd., Golden, BC V0A 1H7. www.kapristolodge.com. ✆ **866/767-9630** or 250/344-6048. Fax 250/344-6755. 3 units. C$120–C$200 double. Extra person C$35. Rates include breakfast. MC, V. **Amenities:** Dining room (guests only); Jacuzzi; sauna. *In room:* No phone.

Prestige Mountainside Resort Golden ★

Easily the swankest place to stay in Golden itself, the Prestige Inn is recently built and well-appointed, with excellent facilities and a good family restaurant. Guest rooms are spacious, each with two phones and lots of extras. There are a variety of room types, including kitchenettes, themed suites, and large rooms in the Premier Wing that feature common foyers.

1049 Trans-Canada Hwy., Golden, BC V0A 1H0. www.prestigeinn.com. ✆ **877/737-8443** or 250/344-7990. Fax 250/344-7902. 90 units. C$109–C$179 double; C$179–C$399 suite. AE, DISC, MC, V. **Amenities:** Restaurant; bar; concierge; exercise room; Jacuzzi; indoor pool; room service. *In room:* A/C, TV w/pay movies, hair dryer, kitchenette, Wi-Fi (free).

Vagabond Lodge ★★

Kicking Horse Mountain Resort offers a beautiful selection of lodging options, but one of the best is this handsome, small boutique-style hotel. The log-built Vagabond Lodge has beautifully appointed public areas, including a lobby filled with overstuffed chairs and couches, a hand-split log bar and dining area, and a central, pine-spindled staircase, all warmed by an enormous stone fireplace. The guest rooms are large and furnished with woodsy good taste, with such features as feather-rest mattresses and duvets, heated bathroom floors, and balconies (in six rooms). Breakfast is included in rates. The owners are very friendly and will do their best to ensure that you have a great stay. Highly recommended.

1581 Cache Close, Kicking Horse Mountain Resort, Golden, BC V0A 1H0. www.vagabondlodge.ca. ✆ **866/944-2622** or 250/344-2622. Fax 250/344-2668. 10 units. C$155–C$285 double. Rates include breakfast (and lunch during ski season). MC, V. **Amenities:** No-host bar; concierge; hot tub; TV room; secure heated ski storage w/boot dryer; coffee and tea service. *In room:* Hair dryer, no phone, Wi-Fi (free), robes.

Where to Eat

For a quick lunch downtown, climb to the second floor of **Bacchus Books** (409 9th Ave. N.; ✆ **250/344-5600**) where a small cafe serves vegetarian soups, sandwiches, and pastries. To feel like a local, visit the **Big Bend Café** (528 9th Ave. N.; ✆ **250/ 344-6111**) where you will fetch your own cups of bottomless coffee. Specials have a Mexican bent, complemented by more than three dozen kinds of hot sauce available.

Cedar House ★ PACIFIC NORTHWEST

Perched high above the Columbia Valley south of Golden, Cedar House has one of the best views in the region. The log lodge is divided into cozy dining areas and is flanked by decks, all the better to take in the vista. The exciting menu features seasonal specials and local meats and vegetables, all cooked in an open kitchen. Alberta beef with leek and potato gratin and sherry jus, and grilled pork tenderloin marinated in mint and apple cider are simple but worth savoring.

735 Hefti Rd., 10 min. south of Golden on Hwy. 95. ✆ **250/344-4679.** www.cedarhousecafe.com. Reservations recommended. Main courses C$26–C$37. MC, V. Wed–Sun 5–10pm.

Corks Restaurant CONTEMPORARY CANADIAN

The best choice for dining at the Kicking Horse Mountain Resort base is this friendly small restaurant (with a great patio in summer) in the Copper Horse Lodge. Though the dining room features crystal, linen, and candlelight, Corks is more of a casual bistro with a small, though varied menu. You could do far worse than settle for a pizza, with toppings like smoked beef, arugula, goat cheese, or scallops, though that means you'd miss out on the excellent main courses such as the daily pasta creations or chicken with a tahini honey glaze. The wine list has an intriguing selection of New World wines.

2 Cache Close, in the Copper Horse Lodge, Kicking Horse Mountain Resort. (℗) **250/344-6201.** www.copperhorselodge.com. Reservations recommended. Main courses C$19–C$32. MC, V. Daily 4–10pm.

Eagle's Eye Restaurant ★★ NEW CANADIAN   Canada's highest-elevation restaurant, the Eagle's Eye towers above the new Kicking Horse Resort. Diners take the ski gondola 1,200m (3,937 ft.) up to 2,347m (7,700 ft.) above sea level to reach this dining room with a 360-degree view of the nearby Rocky, Selkirk, and Purcell mountain ranges. With a panorama like this, the food needn't be good; it's excellent, however, with an emphasis on Alberta lamb and beef, British Columbia salmon and oysters, and seasonal specials like halibut with double-smoked bacon.

Kicking Horse Resort, west of Golden on Kicking Horse Trail. (℗) **250/439-5425.** www.kicking horseresort.com. Reservations required. Main courses C$28–C$44. AE, MC, V. Summer and winter daily 11am–3pm, Fri–Sat 5–8pm. Closed mid-Oct to mid-Dec and mid-Apr to mid-May. Call to confirm spring opening and fall closing dates.

Eleven 22 Grill & Liquids INTERNATIONAL   This intimate restaurant shows Golden's more youthful and alternative side. A converted house, Eleven 22 offers a number of small plates, pasta and risotto specialties, and a daily changing cannelloni selection. One favorite is *nasi goring,* Indonesian-style fried rice. You can also order up-to-date Canadian main courses such as a pork chop with a sage-apple sauce or roast duck breast with maple glaze, all concocted with local organic ingredients. For the quality and size of servings, prices are very reasonable.

1122 10th Ave. S. (℗) **250/344-2443.** www.eleven22.ca. Main courses C$11–C$24. MC, V. Daily 5–10pm.

Kicking Horse Grill INTERNATIONAL   Housed in a historic log cabin near downtown, this bustling restaurant is a culinary League of Nations: The menu changes every season to reflect not only fresh ingredients, but also the international travels of the owners. Start with leek soup with lychees or a watermelon salad; then move on to Vietnamese tiger shrimp or Dutch meatballs. If you're happy to remain gastronomically in Golden, there's a selection of steaks and chops (including an excellent pork chop with apple, pear, and cilantro marmalade finished with Belgian chocolate flakes). The dining room is a puzzling mix of white linen and Wild West.

1105 Ninth St. (℗) **250/344-2330.** www.thekickinghorsegrill.ca. Reservations recommended. Main courses C$19–C$29. AE, MC, V. Daily 5–9pm.

Whitetooth Mountain Bistro ★ CONTEMPORARY CANADIAN   This downtown Golden bistro is both casual and rather chic, with a friendly vibe that's as welcoming to families as it is to couples on a date. Considering the quality of the cooking, the Whitetooth is also a good value. Your evening meal might be as simple and homey as buffalo meatloaf or mac-and-cheese, or you can order full-on gourmet, such as grilled veal with a tomato-caper chutney. Whitetooth is a great spot for breakfast, because you can wake up to a choice of familiar fried classics or a healthy bowl of yogurt and homemade granola.

427 9th Ave N. (℗) **250/344-5120.** www.whitetoothbistro.com. Reservations not accepted. Main courses C$12–C$28. MC, V. Daily 9am–10pm.

THE KOOTENAY VALLEY: CRANBROOK & NELSON

Cranbrook: 80km (50 miles) N of the U.S.-Canada border

Cranbrook

The largest city in southeastern British Columbia, Cranbrook (pop. 19,000) exists mostly as a trade center for loggers and agriculturists. The town itself has few tourist sights, but Cranbrook is central to a number of historic and recreational areas and offers ample numbers of hotel rooms. Its setting is spectacularly dramatic: a broad forested valley that looks onto the sky-piercing Canadian Rockies and back side of the U.S. Glacier National Park.

ESSENTIALS

GETTING THERE   Cranbrook is near the junction of the north–south Hwy. 93/95 corridor and the east–west Hwy. 3. **Greyhound Canada** (© 800/661-8747; www.greyhound.ca) operates buses that travel on both of these road systems. One-way service from Cranbrook to Golden costs C$38. **Air Canada** (© 888/247-2262; www.aircanada.ca) operates flights from Vancouver to the Cranbrook Airport.

VISITOR INFORMATION   The **Cranbrook Visitor Info Centre** is at 2279 Cranbrook St. N. (© 800/222-6174 or 250/426-5914; www.cranbrookchamber.com).

EXPLORING THE AREA

It's worth getting off the grim Hwy. 95 strip to visit the pleasant downtown area around Baker Street. As you stroll the broad, tree-lined streets, you'll see a number of heritage brick storefronts and commercial buildings. Especially impressive is the grand, turreted 1909 **Imperial Bank** building at Baker and Eighth streets.

Canadian Museum of Rail Travel ★   Cranbrook was established as a rail division point, so it's fitting that the town is home to this fascinating museum that preserves a number of historic rail cars, including several "cars of state" designed for royalty. The Royal Alexandra Hall is a 279-sq.-m (3,003-sq.-ft.) oak-paneled dining room salvaged from Winnipeg's Royal Alexandra Hotel, a CPR hotel torn down in 1971. The ornate moldings, panels, and furniture were carefully numbered and stored for nearly 30 years before being reconstructed here. Other highlights include a complete set of cars built in 1929 for the Canadian Pacific Railway's Trans-Canada Limited run. Rather like a traveling luxury hotel, the restored cars gleam with brass and inlaid walnut and mahogany. In summer, the Royal Alexandra Hall offers tea service.

57 Van Horne St. S. © **250/489-3918.** www.trainsdeluxe.com. Admission for all tours (may vary according to which tours are taken) C$21 adults, C$18 seniors, C$11 students, C$5 children 5 and under. Mid-May to mid-Oct daily 9:45am–6pm; mid-Oct to mid-May Tues–Sat 10am–5pm. Tours start at 11am and are given on the half-hour.

Fort Steele Heritage Town ★ ☺   During the 1864 gold rush, a cable ferry stretched across a narrow section of the Kootenay River, enabling prospectors to safely cross the turbulent waters. A small settlement sprang up, and after another mining boom—this time for silver, lead, and zinc—Fort Steele had more than 4,000 inhabitants. But when the railroad pushed through, it bypassed Fort Steele in favor of Cranbrook. Within 5 years, all but 150 of the citizens had left. In the 1960s, the crumbling ghost town was declared a heritage site. Today, about 60 restored and reconstructed buildings grace the townsite, including a hotel, churches, saloons, and a courthouse and jail. In summer, actors give demonstrations of period skills and occupations. There are also rides on a steam train, horse-drawn wagon, and a variety show at the Wild Horse Theatre. The International Hotel Restaurant serves Victorian fare.

16km (10 miles) northeast of Cranbrook on Hwy. 93/95. © **250/426-7352.** www.fortsteele.bc.ca. Admission to grounds May to mid-Oct C$5, free children 5 and under. Rides and entertainment extra. May–June and Labour Day to mid-Oct daily 9:30am–5pm; July to Labour Day daily 9:30am–6:30pm; mid-Oct to April 10am–4pm. Evening entertainment and restaurant July to Labour Day Tues–Sun.

OUTDOOR PURSUITS

FISHING   More than eight area rivers, including the Elk River, St. Mary River, and Kootenay, are often rated among Canada's top fishing destinations. Trophy fish are taken all season long. For lake fishing, Moyie Lake, 20km (12 miles) south of Cranbrook, has a good stock of kokanee, ling cod, and rainbow trout.

GOLF   The **St. Eugene Mission Golf Resort** (© 877/417-3133; www.steugene. ca) is an 18-hole, Les Furber–designed course with a links section. *Golf Digest* has rated the St. Eugene Mission course as one of the top three new courses in Canada. High-season greens fees are C$55 to C$85. The **Cranbrook Golf Club,** 2700 Second St. S. (© 888/211-8855 or 250/426-6462; www.golfcranbrook.com), is a long-established 18-hole course with greens fees starting at C$49. The **Mission Hills Golf Course** (© 250/489-3009; www.golfingmissionhills.com) has three 9-hole layouts with a par-3 rating, plus a clubhouse and restaurant. The course has added a full-length, all-grass practice facility, plus a 3-hole practice loop. Greens fees are C$20.

SKIING   Ninety-three kilometers (58 miles) east of Cranbrook, on the western face of the Rockies, is one of the best skiing and snowboarding areas in British Columbia. **Fernie Alpine Resort,** Fernie Ski Hill Road, Fernie (© 877/333-2339; 250/423-4655; www.skifernie.com), is a relatively unheralded resort that's popular with in-the-know snowboarders. Average snowfall is about 9m (29 ft.), with a vertical drop of 1,082m (3,550 ft.). There are 140 trails in five alpine bowls, with a total of more than 1,012 hectares (2,500 acres) of skiable terrain served by two high-speed quads, three quads, two triples, and three surface lifts with the capacity to handle 14,916 skiers per hour (but it's never *that* busy). Adult lift tickets are C$76 to C$80. Amenities include lodging (© 800/258-SNOW [7669] for reservations), restaurants, rentals, and instruction. The resort, lodges, and lifts remain open in summer, with hiking, mountain biking, and horseback riding the main activities.

Twenty minutes west of Cranbrook is the **Kimberley Alpine Resort** (© 800/258-7669 or 250/427-4881; www.skikimberley.com), a family-friendly ski resort with over 60% of its 80 runs rated beginning and intermediate. The slopes offer a vertical rise of 751m (2,464 ft.) with 728 hectares (1,800 acres) of skiable terrain serviced by five lifts, including a high-speed quad. There are a number of ski-in, ski-out accommodations.

WHERE TO STAY

Fort Steele Resort & RV Park, 16km (10 miles) north of Cranbrook on Hwy. 95 (www.fortsteele.com; © 250/489-4268), has over 50 tent sites and 120 serviced for RVs costing from C$26 to C$44. It offers pull-throughs, a tenting area, hot showers, a playground, a ball field, and a solar-heated outdoor swimming pool.

Cedar Heights B&B   This contemporary home is situated in a residential area just minutes from downtown Cranbrook. The rooms are beautifully furnished and have private entrances. Two comfortable lounges contain a fireplace, wet bar, fridge, coffee and tea service, and games. From the spacious deck or hot tub, take in the view of the magnificent Rockies.

1200 13th St., Cranbrook, BC V1C 5V8. www.bbcanada.com/cedarheights. ✆ **800/497-6014** or 250/426-0505. Fax 250/426-0045. 3 units. C$90–C$95 single; C$100–C$110 double. Extra person C$30. Rates include full breakfast. MC, V. Children must be 12 or older. **Amenities:** Jacuzzi; computer with Internet; free calls to North America. *In room:* A/C, TV/DVD, hair dryer, Wi-Fi (free).

Prestige Rocky Mountain Resort & Convention Centre ★★   By far the poshest place to stay in Cranbrook itself, the first-class Prestige resort features very large and stylish rooms with lots of extras; some rooms have kitchenettes. The premiere experience is a night in a suite aboard the John Huber Express—a rail car renovated into two king-bed suites with en-suite, heated-floor bathrooms. There's breakfast, lunch, and dinner at Ric's Lounge and Grill. Other perks include a spa offering aromatherapy and massage.

209 Van Horne St. S., Cranbrook, BC V1C 6R9. www.prestigeinn.com. ✆ **877/737-8443** or 250/417-0444. Fax 250/417-0400. 109 units. C$159–C$249 double; from C$189–C$249 suite. Extra person C$10. Off-season rates and golf/ski packages available. AE, MC, V. **Amenities:** Restaurant; bar; full health club (fee); Jacuzzi; indoor pool; room service; spa. *In room:* A/C, TV w/pay movies, fridge, hair dryer, kitchenette (in some), Wi-Fi (free).

St. Eugene Mission Resort ★★   This extraordinary resort is at once both the newest and one of the oldest places to stay in the Cranbrook area. The resort hotel, along with a noted golf course, spa, casino, and First Nations cultural center, is on the grounds of a former residential school built in the early 20th century for the education and acculturation of First Nations children from the Ktunaxa, Okanagan, Shuswap, and Blackfoot Nations. The original mission school structure was renovated and now houses a number of unique guest accommodations; a brand-new adjacent lodge also features rooms and suites. The mission's historic barn is now the golf clubhouse and, in 2004, a health club was added. With financial backing from the Ktunaxa Nation—who run an interpretive center at the resort—and the federal government, the transformation of the old mission has been accomplished with great attention to historic detail. Rooms are simply but elegantly appointed, and the views are magnificent, with miles of open links and pine forest and the Rockies rising to fill the sky.

7777 Mission Rd., Cranbrook, BC VIC 7E5. www.steugene.ca. ✆ **866/292-2020** or 250/420-2000. Fax 250/420-2001. 125 units. C$142–C$180 double; C$260–C$380 suite. Extra person C$20. Golf and ski packages available. Off-season rates available. AE, MC, V. Pets C$25 **Amenities:** Restaurant; lounge; golf course; health club; outdoor pool; sauna; steam room; casino. *In room:* A/C, TV w/movie channels, hair dryer, Wi-Fi (free), robes.

WHERE TO EAT

For a home-style breakfast or lunch, stop in at **The Cottage Restaurant** (13 9th Ave. S.; ✆ **250/426-6516**) where diner-style specialties collide with a country decor.

Allegra Mediterranean Cuisine ★★ MEDITERRANEAN   The chef-owner of this excellent restaurant is from the Italy-fronting cantons of Switzerland, but the menu here spans the sunny foods of the entire Mediterranean basin. Certainly Italian foods make their appearance—with marvelous pasta dishes such as fig and prosciutto-stuffed ravioli—but the flavors of southern France, Spain, North Africa, and beyond are also featured. Smoked duck with a blueberry-fig relish, lobster champagne pasta, and Moroccan-spiced veal are rich facets of an imaginative menu. The dining room is warm and simple, even spartan, but you're here to savor the food, after all.

1225B Cranbrook St. N. (C) **250/426-8812.** www.allegrarestaurant.com. Reservations suggested. Main courses C$14–C$27. MC, V. Wed–Sun 5–9pm.

Heidi's Restaurant ★ CONTINENTAL The menu at this pleasantly refined restaurant, with redbrick walls and potted plants, is dominated by the cuisines of Germany and Italy, with a dash of Argentina. Appetizers range from empanadas with cumin beef to classic escargots. Entrees include steaks from local beef, schnitzels, pastas, fresh fish, and specialties like bison short ribs and seared duck breast served with black-currant sauce, spaetzle, and red cabbage.

821C Baker St. (C) **250/426-7922.** www.heidis.ca. Reservations recommended. Main courses C$9–C$31. AE, MC, V. Mon–Fri 11am–2:30pm; daily 5–9pm (Sun until 8pm).

Nelson ★★

66km (41 miles) N of the U.S.-Canada border

Nelson (pop. 9,250) is quite possibly the most pleasant and attractive town in the British Columbian interior. The late-19th-century commercial district is still intact, with an eclectic mix of old-fashioned businesses, coffeehouses, and fancy boutiques and galleries. Nelson also offers high-quality B&Bs, hotels, and restaurants, and the setting—along a shelf of land above the West Arm of Kootenay Lake—is splendid.

Nelson was born as a silver-mining town in the 1880s, and its veins proved productive and profitable. By 1900, Nelson was the third-largest city in the province, with an architecturally impressive core of Victorian and Queen Anne–style homes. Today, the gracious town center, coupled with convenient access to recreation in nearby lakes, mountains, and streams, has added to Nelson's newfound luster as an arts capital. Nelson claims to have more artists and craftspeople per capita than any other city in Canada. It certainly has an appealingly youthful, comfortably countercultural feel, and makes a great place to spend a day or two.

ESSENTIALS

GETTING THERE Nelson is 66km (41 miles) north of the U.S.-Canada border, 242km (150 miles) north of Spokane, Washington, and 657km (408 miles) east of Vancouver. **Greyhound Canada** ((C) **800/661-8747;** www.greyhound.ca) operates daily service from Vancouver for C$122 one-way.

VISITOR INFORMATION Contact the **Nelson Visitor Info Centre,** 225 Hall St. ((C) **250/352-3433;** www.discovernelson.com).

EXPLORING THE AREA

Nelson's main attractions are, in order, the city itself and what's just beyond. As an introduction to the town's wonderful Victorian architecture, stop by the visitor center for brochures on driving and walking tours of Nelson's significant heritage buildings.

Not to be missed are the château-style **City Hall** (now Touchstones Nelson museum; see below), 502 Vernon St.; and **Nelson Court House,** designed by F. M. Rattenbury, famed for his designs for the B.C. Parliament Buildings and the Empress Hotel, both of which continue to dominate Victoria. Note the three-story, turreted storefront at the corner of Baker and Ward streets, and the **Mara-Barnard building,**

421–431 Baker St., once the Royal Bank of Canada building, with elaborate brick-work and bay windows.

The story of Nelson's human history is told at the **Touchstones Nelson—Museum of Art and History,** 502 Vernon St. (© **250/352-9813;** www.nelson museum.ca), which has a number of exhibits on the Native Ktunaxa and from the silver-mining days when Nelson was one of the richest towns in Canada. Two galler-ies are devoted to changing art exhibits. Summer hours are Monday through Saturday from 10am to 5pm (Thurs till 8pm), and Sunday 10am to 4pm. The museum is closed Monday and Tuesday mid-Sept to mid-May. Admission is C$8 for adults, C$6 for seniors and students, C$4 children 7 to 18, and C$22 families.

Nelson has a number of beautiful parks. **Gyro Park,** at the east end of Vernon Street, features formal gardens, an outdoor pool, and panoramic views of Kootenay Lake and the Selkirk Mountains. **Lakeside Park,** which flanks Kootenay Lake near the base of the Nelson Bridge, offers swimming beaches, tennis courts, and a playground.

You can explore Nelson's lakefront on foot on the **Waterfront Pathway,** which winds along the shore from near the Prestige Resort to Lakeside Park. Or, in summer, hop on the restored **streetcar no. 23,** which runs from Lakeside Park to Hall Street, along the waterfront. At the turn of the 20th century, Nelson had a streetcar system and was the smallest city in Canada to boast such public transport. The system fell out of use in the 1940s, but a stretch of the track remains intact. The streetcar runs on weekends only from Easter weekend to mid-June. It operates daily from mid-June to Labour Day, after which it resumes weekend-only operations until mid-October. Tickets are C$3 for adults, C$2 for seniors and students, and C$8 families.

OUTDOOR PURSUITS

FISHING   Fishing is legendary in 150m-deep (492-ft.) Kootenay Lake, which stretches more than 104km (65 miles) long. For guided trips and advice, contact **Split Shot Charters** (© **877/368-FISH** [3474]; www.split-shot.com).

GOLF   **Granite Pointe Golf Club,** 1123 Richards St. W. (© **250/352-5913;** www.granitepointe.ca), is a hilly 18-hole, par-72 course with fantastic views of Koo-tenay Lake. Greens fees are C$59; rentals, a clubhouse with dining, and a driving range are available.

HIKING   Accessible right in town is a 9km (5.6-mile) rails-to-trails system on the old Burlington Northern line that follows the southern edge of the town along the flanks of Toad Mountain. You can join the path at a number of places; from down-town, follow Cedar Street south to find one entry point. There are some trails and the lakefront of **West Arm Provincial Park** to explore to the east of Nelson, but the closest wilderness hiking is at **Kokanee Glacier Provincial Park,** 21km (13 miles) northeast of Nelson on Hwy. 3A, then 16km (10 miles) north on a gravel road.

KAYAKING   For rentals or a guided 3-hour tour (C$80), contact **Kootenay Kayak Co.,** 639 Baker St. (© **877/229-4959** or 250/505-4549; www.kootenaykayak.com). Full-day paddles and longer excursions also available.

MOUNTAIN BIKING   The visitor center has a free map of old logging roads and rail lines that are available for biking. The Burlington Northern rails-to-trails system (see "Hiking," above) is also open to mountain bikers. For rentals and trail conditions, contact **Gerick Cycle & Sports,** 702 Baker St. (© **877/437-4251;** www.gericks. com).

SKIING Sixteen kilometers (10 miles) south of Nelson off Hwy. 6 is the **Whitewater Ski Resort** (© **800/666-9420** or 250/354-4944; www.skiwhitewater.com), with some of British Columbia's best snow conditions. The ski area is in a natural snow-catching bowl below an escarpment of 2,398m (7,867-ft.) peaks. The average snowfall is 12m (39 ft.), and that snow falls as pure powder. The mountain consists of groomed runs, open bowls, glades, chutes, and tree skiing; 87% of the runs are rated intermediate, advanced, or extreme. There are four lifts; the vertical drop is 623m (2,044 ft.). Lift tickets cost C$63. Facilities include a day lodge with rentals, dining, and drinks. The Nordic Centre has 13km (8 miles) of groomed cross-country ski trails.

If you're looking for backcountry skiing, the **Baldface Lodge** (© **250/352-0006;** www.baldface.net) is your ticket. A short helicopter ride takes you from Nelson to the backcountry lodge, where there are exquisite dining and accommodations, plus snowcat access to 12,950 hectares (32,000 acres) of powder snow terrain. The rates for 3- and 4-day packages vary through the season (see the website for precise costs), but count on spending around C$900 per day for a lodge room in peak season, including unlimited guided snowcat skiing, all meals, transportation, and lodging. In summer, the lodge is open July to October for hiking and mountain biking.

WHERE TO STAY

Best Western Baker Street Inn The Baker Street Inn stands at the end of the historic downtown area, within easy walking distance of both shopping and dining. A recent renovation has given the rooms earth-tone modern textiles, adding a freshness to the very clean and comfortable ambiance.

153 Baker St., Nelson, BC V1L 4H1. www.bwbakerstreetinn.com. © **888/255-3525** or 250/352-3525. Fax 250/352-2995. 70 units. C$149–C$259 double. Extra person C$10. AE, DISC, MC, V. Pets C$15. **Amenities:** Restaurant; lounge; exercise room; Jacuzzi; room service. *In room:* A/C, TV, fridge, hair dryer, microwave, MP3 docking station, Wi-Fi (free).

Cloudside Inn ★ This spacious B&B is perched on a hill just a block off Baker Street, with views of the lake and Kootenay Peak. The handsome painted lady–style Victorian has six rooms with a mix of private and shared bathrooms, plus a garden, patio, and deck. The third floor is a two-bedroom, self-contained apartment. Rates include full breakfast. The proprietors here offer the very epitome of friendly English-style B&B hospitality.

408 Victoria St., Nelson, BC V1L 4K5. www.cloudside.ca. © **800/596-2337** or 250/352-3226. 7 units. C$89–C$209 double; C$169–C$209 apt. Extra person C$15. Golf, spa, romance, and ski packages available. MC, V. Free off-street parking. **Amenities:** Lounge w/TV and Internet access; front and rear sun decks. *In room:* No phone, Wi-Fi (free).

Dancing Bear Inn 🐾 The Dancing Bear is a first-rate hostel right in the thick of things downtown. The atmosphere and furnishings are more like what you'd expect to find in a B&B—a grimy backpackers'flophouse this is definitely not. The furniture is locally made from pine, beds are made up with down duvets, and paintings by area artists grace the walls. This is not your everyday hostel, and even if you're not into the hostelling scene, you'll find it a great place to meet people.

171 Baker St., Nelson, BC V1L 4H1. www.dancingbearinn.com. © **877/352-7573** or 250/352-7573. Fax 250/352-9818. 43 beds. C$23–C$25 dorm bed; C$46–C$60 private unit. Family and group rates, seasonal packages, and discounts for Hostelling International members available. MC, V. Limited free off-street parking. **Amenities:** Computer w/Internet access; Wi-Fi (free); kitchen; common room w/TV/DVD. *In room:* No phone.

Hume Hotel   This beautifully preserved 1898 hotel has been renovated to accommodate modern ideas of comfort while maintaining its vintage charm. For an antique hotel, the rooms are good-size, environmentally friendly, and smartly furnished. You'll want to visit the Hume Hotel even if you're not staying here, just to check out the wonderful bars, nightclub, and lobby area.

422 Vernon St., Nelson, BC V1L 4E5. www.humehotel.com. © **877/568-0888** or 250/352-5331. Fax 250/352-5214. 43 units. C$99–C$149 double. Extra person C$10. Rates include breakfast. Golf and ski packages available. AE, DISC, MC, V. Pets C$10. **Amenities:** 2 restaurants; 2 bars; day spa; liquor store. *In room:* TV, Wi-Fi (free).

New Grand Hotel   Originally built in 1913, the Art Deco New Grand Hotel has been lovingly restored and updated as a hip and happening hotel and nightspot for the young at heart. The renovated rooms wear their age gracefully, without attempting to match a period style. The decor is comfortably eclectic, with hardwood floors, Oriental rugs, contemporary art, and mid-century reproduction furniture. The result is simple, charming, and clutter free. If you're looking for inexpensive rooms, a number of double and triple rooms are available hostel-style, with shared bathrooms and a kitchen area. The hotel's Uptown Sportsbar is a popular bar and grill, while Louie's Steakhouse offers excellent prime beef and martinis.

616 Vernon St., Nelson, BC V1L 4G1. www.newgrandhotel.ca. © **888/722-2258** or 250/352-7211. Fax 250/352-2445. 34 units. C$42–C$47 single; C$69–C$103 double and family rooms. Extra person C$10. AE, MC, V. Pets C$10. **Amenities:** Restaurant; bar; cafe; room service; motorcycle wash. *In room:* A/C, TV, Wi-Fi (free).

Prestige Lakeside Resort & Convention Centre ★   Down on the lake-shore, the Prestige is Nelson's full-service resort, offering spacious, beautiful rooms with all the services you'd expect at a luxury hotel. All units have balconies, and a number of theme rooms (including African and Hamptons ones) will spice up a special occasion. Some rooms have kitchenettes. The Prestige chain has opened another lakeshore lodging, in many ways an adjunct to this large hotel. The Prestige Inn, 1301 Front St., is a smaller boutique hotel with upscale, European-style rooms. Facilities, such as the restaurant and pool, are shared with the sister property; rates are parallel. To contact the Prestige Inn directly, call © 250/352-3595.

701 Lakeside Dr., Nelson, BC V1L 6G3. www.prestigeinn.com. © **877/737-8443** or 250/352-7222. Fax 250/352-3966. 101 units. C$140–C$240 double; C$270–C$650 themed room or suite. Extra person C$20. Off-season rates available. AE, DC, DISC, MC, V. **Amenities:** Restaurant; bar; coffee bar; concierge; exercise room; Jacuzzi; indoor pool; room service; spa; marina. *In room:* A/C, TV w/pay movies, fridge, hair dryer, kitchenette (in some rooms), microwave, Wi-Fi (free).

WHERE TO EAT

The restaurants at the **New Grand Hotel, Prestige Lakeside Resort** and the **Hume Hotel** (see "Where to Stay," above) are good, and a wander down **Baker Street** will reveal dozens of cafes, coffeehouses, and inexpensive ethnic restaurants. The **Full Circle Cafe,** 402 Baker St. (© **250/354-4458**), serves home-style, diner favorites with flavorful twists, and is open for breakfast and lunch daily. Don't miss the **Dominion Café,** 334 Baker St. (© **250/352-1904**), an old diner offering sandwiches, light entrees, baked goods (some are raw food and vegan), and a friendly, relaxed atmosphere. The slickly modern **John Ward Coffee,** 503 Baker St. (© **250/352-0095**), is central to downtown.

All Seasons Café ★★★ NORTHWEST   The All Seasons is reason enough to visit Nelson. Located in a handsome heritage home a block off busy Baker Street, it isn't easy to find, but if you want to eat at British Columbia's best restaurant east of Vancouver, then persevere. Menus, which change seasonally, feature local produce and meats. To start, try the outstanding "pan-kissed" king scallops with apricot puree and a fennel salad. Main courses include a number of vegetarian and fish options, plus meaty creations such as blackened chicken duck breast with preserved lemon aioli and wine-marinated grilled striploin. The wine list has many Okanagan Valley selections, and the service is friendly and professional.

620 Herridge Lane. ⓒ **250/352-0101.** www.allseasonscafe.com. Reservations required. Main courses C$22–C$32. AE, MC, V. Daily 5–10pm.

Bibo ITALIAN   Bibo is a small but atmospheric restaurant and watering hole with a look that's half Old West and half Old World. But the food is straightforward comfort-style European, with house-made pasta and gnocchi, an Italian-style meatloaf with poached egg, and a daily soup served with baguette. An entire menu is devoted to charcuterie and cheeses—with its focus on great cheese, Bibo also serves a killer Swiss cheese fondue.

518 Hall St. ⓒ **250/352-2744.** www.culinafamily.ca/bibo-nelson. Reservations suggested. Main courses C$16–C$28. MC, V. Daily 5–10pm.

THE UPPER COLUMBIA VALLEY: A GOLFING & RECREATIONAL PARADISE

Between Radium Hot Springs and Canal Flats, the Columbia Valley is broad and green, flanked by the towering peaks of the Rockies to the east and the Purcell Mountains to the west. Nestled in the valley are two lovely lakes, Windermere Lake and Columbia Lake, the latter considered the birthplace of the Columbia River. It's a stunningly dramatic landscape, and the entire valley is undergoing extensive development as an upscale resort area, mostly in the form of golf courses and country-club communities. Along what's dubbed the **Columbia Valley Golf Trail** (www. columbiavalleygolftrail.com), you'll find no fewer than nine 18-hole and six 9-hole courses within 40km (25 miles) of each other, and other outdoor recreational activities—skiing, mountain biking, hiking, and rafting—have also developed as a major focus (the following golf courses are dependably open from May–Sept). The main towns in this part of the Columbia Valley are Invermere and Windermere; though they are on opposite sides of Lake Windermere, they're less than 4km (2½ miles) apart over the water.

Panorama Mountain Village & Greywolf Golf Course

Panorama, 20km (12 miles) west of Invermere on Panorama Road (ⓒ **800/663-2929** or 250/342-6941; www.panoramaresort.com), is a major four-seasons resort and residential community. Besides golf and skiing, the recreation-oriented resort offers a host of other activities, including horseback riding, kayaking, ATV touring, tennis, hiking, and mountain biking.

The **Panorama Ski Resort** boasts one of the highest vertical drops in Canada, at 1,219m (3,999 ft.). There are over 120 named runs in 1,152 hectares (2,847 acres) of skiable terrain, with nine lifts including a gondola and two high-speed quads. Fifty-five percent of the runs are intermediate or advanced, and a further 25% are rated expert. Adult day lift tickets are C$73. The resort is also home to the Panorama Snow School and the Greywolf Nordic Ski Centre, with 20km (12 miles) of groomed trails.

The resort also offers heli-skiing packages in the Purcell Mountains behind the resort. A day-trip with three helicopter-assisted descents, including breakfast and lunch, is $734 per person.

In summer, the lifts open to mountain bikers, who find a real challenge in both the single-track trails with natural obstacles and the expert terrain with man-made stunts. The trails aren't for first-timers: 86% are rated intermediate to expert.

Greywolf Golf Course at Panorama (© **888/473-9965** or 250/341-4100; www.greywolfgolf.com) is considered one of B.C.'s top courses, and when it opened in 1999 Greywolf was named best new course of the year in Canada. The 6,529m (7,140-yd.) course has bent grass greens and fairways, and spectacular mountain vistas from every hole. Water comes into play on 14 of 18 holes. The "Cliffhanger" is the signature 6th hole—it requires a drive across a steep-sided gorge. Greens fees are C$99 to C$149 for 18 holes, depending on season.

Panorama offers many lodging options ranging from traditional hotel rooms, hostel accommodations, condominiums, and town houses to private home rentals. Double room rates and studios range from about C$80 to C$200; for information and reservations call © **866/601-7383.** The resort has 10 restaurants, cafes, and bars in the village, with two more choices on the slopes.

Fairmont Hot Springs Resort

People have been visiting the hot water springs at Fairmont for millennia, but the early First Nations people who came here to cure their aches and pains wouldn't recognize it now. The springs are now the center of **Fairmont Hot Springs Resort,** 18km (11 miles) south of Windermere on Hwy. 93/95 (© **800/663-4979** or 250/345-6000; www.fairmonthotsprings.com). Fairmont is a four-season resort, with two famed golf courses, a number of large country-club developments, and a winter ski area, but for many families the big draw is the hot springs. The mineral water here is rich in calcium, but contains no sulfur, the odiferous agent that fouls the air at most hot springs resorts.

The main attraction at the resort is the 297-sq.-m (3,200-sq.-ft.) lap pool filled with hot mineral water, plus a diving pool and several soaker pools. Amazingly, all the water in the pools is drained nightly and refilled with fresh water. At Fairmont, more than 5.7 million liters (1.5 million gal.) of 102°F (39°C) water flow out of the mountain and through the pools per day. Single entry to the pool complex is C$10 adults, C$9 seniors and youths (13–17), and C$8 for children (4–12). Pools reserved for hotel guests are also available as well as massage, hydrotherapy, and other spa services.

Accommodations at Fairmont Hot Springs Resort are in the rambling 144-room lodge or family-style heritage cabins. In addition to the public complex, guest-only hot springs span an outdoor pool and indoor soaker tubs. Hotel amenities include a restaurant, lounge, spa, and fitness facilities. All rooms have cozy robes. Summer high-season rates range from C$99 for a no-view economy room to C$344 for the honeymoon suite. There are also two RV parks at the resort. Fairmont boasts two 18-hole courses and a 9-hole course. **Mountainside Golf Course,** just below the hot springs off Fairway Drive (© **250/345-6514**), is a par-72 course. Mountainside's most famous hole is its 549m (600-yd.) 4th hole. **Riverside Golf Course,** off Riverview Road (© **250/345-6346**), is a championship 18-hole course, with a driving range, full practice area, pro shop, and lessons available. The Riverside is unique in that it spans the Columbia River, and uses the mighty river as a natural water hazard. The Riverside course is 5,950m (6,507 yd.) in length and was named Canada's golf course of the year in 1998. Greens fees for both courses range from C$49 to C$79 for 18 holes. The par 3, 9-hole **Creekside Golf Course** (© **250/345-6660**) is great for learners and families, with rates ranging from C$17 to C$19 and C$49 for families.

Fairmont Hot Springs Ski Resort offers a snowboard park, triple chair lift, and 12 runs for a full day of skiing enjoyment. Fairmont is not as large a ski area as others in the Columbia Valley—it has a vertical drop of 305m (1,000 ft.)—but it's a good place for families or beginners. Adult day lift tickets are C$39.

More Golf Resorts

The Radium Resort, 8100 Golf Course Rd., Radium Hot Springs (© **800/667-6444** or 250/347-9311; www.radiumresort.com), is a year-round destination with a resort community and ample recreational activities, but the focus is on its two golf courses. The **Resort Course** (© **250/347-6266**) is the oldest is the Columbia Valley, built in 1957. This par-69 course offers incredible vistas and some equally dramatic elevation changes that present challenges to golfers used to flatter courses. Greens fees range from C$32 to C$59. The newer **Springs Course** (© **250/347-6200**), designed by Les Furber, follows the rugged natural contours of the land and is often ranked among the top courses in Canada. This par-72 course features four tee boxes per hole to allow for play from 4,721 to 6,188m (5,163–6,767 yd.). Greens fees are C$49 to C$110. The resort offers accommodations in standard hotel-style rooms or in condos, starting at C$129 for a double in high season (summer).

Eagle Ranch Golf Resort, 9581 Eagle Ranch Trail, Invermere (© **877/877-3889** or 250/342-0562; www.eagleranchresort.com), is located on the bluffs above Lake Windermere and the Columbia Wetlands, and the layout weaves in natural features such as deep ravines and hoodoos. This 18-hole, 6,077m (6,646-yd.), par-72 championship golf course is both scenic and very challenging. Greens fees range from C$85 to C$130. The clubhouse restaurant, Saliken, is a destination in its own right. **Copper Point Golf Course,** 651 Hwy. 93/95, Invermere (© **877/418-4653** or 250/341-3392; www.copperpointgolf.com), offers two courses for a total of 36 holes of golf. The original par-70 **Copper Point Course,** with a length of 6,224m (6,807 yd.), lets the natural terrain of the Rockies do the work, as the layout follows the rise and fall of the foothills, with several dramatic elevation changes built into the course. Greens fees are C$55 to C$133. The new-in-2008 **Ridge at Copper Point Course** is, as you might guess, on a series of bluffs above the original course. The rugged terrain is a major factor in the play at this innovative par-62 Masters-style course. With 4,638m (5,072 yd.), the course is faster to play than most area courses yet still very demanding. Greens fees are C$35 to C$75.

PLANNING YOUR TRIP TO BRITISH COLUMBIA

B ritish Columbia is one of the most popular tourist destinations in a country that is itself one of the world's favorite vacation getaways. Safe, civilized, and with very well organized tourism infrastructures that juxtapose urban sophistication with pristine wilderness, piecing together a trip through this beautiful province is simple.

Before setting out, there are a few points to consider. Due to its northerly location, Canada presents four distinct seasons: You'll have a very different experience if you travel in western Canada in summer than in winter. While summer in the north is glorious, there are ample reasons to travel outside of the peak July through September tourist season: Prices are lower and crowds much thinner, for starters. Spring delivers balmy temperatures and breath-taking gardens. Fall promises warm days, crisp nights and glorious autumnal colors. As for winter, if you're a skier, then you'll find that B.C. boasts some of the top ski resorts in the world.

Which brings up another consideration. The urban attractions of B.C. are very compelling, and plenty of travelers come here largely to enjoy the dazzling culture and dining in cities such as Vancouver and Victoria.

Because this is a land of truly astonishing land- and seascapes, even if you are an urban kind of person, you should plan to get outdoors and experience the region's spectacular nature. Outfitters and resorts make it easy to explore the wilderness, whether on a kayak, from a zipline, in snowshoes, or atop a horse.

That's what's so truly remarkable about Canada, and because of its coastal locale, British Columbia in particular. Its cities and towns are the very model of civilized culture, but at the city limits, the wilderness begins. As you plan your trip, be sure to make time to experience both sides of this diverse province.

GETTING THERE

By Plane

Western Canada is linked with the United States, Europe, Australia, and Asia by frequent nonstop flights. Calgary (YYC) and Vancouver (YRV) are the major air hubs; regional airlines connect to smaller centers.

Air Canada (✆ **888/247-2262;** www.aircanada.ca), Canada's dominant airline, has by far the most flights between the United States and Canada, and also offers service to the U.K. out of Calgary and Vancouver. Air Canada also has a number of partner airlines, such as **Air Canada Jazz,** that fly to secondary cities. Flights on these airlines can be booked from the main Air Canada website.

Most major U.S. carriers also fly daily between cities in Canada and the States—these include **American Airlines** (✆ 800/433-7300; www.aa.com), **Delta** (✆ **800/ 221-1212**; www.delta.com), **Northwest** (✆ 800/447-4747; www.nwa.com), **United** (✆ 800/241-6522; www.united.com), and **US Airways** (✆ 800/428-4322; www.usairways.com).

International airlines with nonstop service to Vancouver include **British Airways** (✆ 800/247-9297 in the U.S. and Canada, 0845/773-3377 in the U.K.; www.ba.com), **KLM** (✆ 800/447-7747 in the U.S. and Canada for KLM partner Northwest Airlines), **Lufthansa** (✆ 800/581-6400 in Canada, 800/563-5954 in the U.S., or 0803/803-803 in Germany; www.lufthansa.com), and **SAS** (✆ 800/221-2350 in the U.S. or Canada; www.scandinavian.net). Asian airlines that fly into Vancouver include **China Airlines** (✆ 800/227-5118 or 604/682-6777 in Vancouver; www.china-airlines.com), **Cathay Pacific** (✆ 800/233-2742; www.cathay-usa.com), **Japan Air Lines** (✆ 800/525-3663; www.jal.com), and **Korean Air** (✆ 800/438-5000; www.koreanair.com). Additionally, **Air Canada** offers international flights from Mexico, most cities in northern Europe, and many centers in Asia. Canada's **Air Transat** (✆ 866/847-1112; www.airtransat.com) offers still more options from Europe and Latin America. From the southern hemisphere, both **Qantas** (✆ 800/227-4500 in the U.S. and Canada; www.qantas.com) and **Air New Zealand** (✆ 800/663-5494; www.airnewzealand.ca), offer flights into Vancouver.

Another option is to fly into Seattle, Washington. Airfares are frequently less expensive to Seattle, and the difference in distance to destinations such as the Okanagan Valley and Vancouver Island is negligible (driving from Seattle to Vancouver, for instance, takes about 2½ hr.). Seattle's **Sea-Tac Airport** has nonstop flights from London, Copenhagen, Frankfurt, Seoul, Tokyo, and Hong Kong, among other cities.

By Car

Because Canada and the U.S. share the longest open border on earth, it makes sense that many U.S.-based travelers will consider taking their own car to Canada as a road-trip destination. There are scores of border crossings between Canada and the U.S. (The U.S. freeway system enters at 13 different locations.) However, not all border crossings keep the same hours, and many are closed at night. Before you set off to cross the border at a remote location, ascertain if it will be open when you arrive there.

In addition to having the proper ID to cross into Canada, drivers may also be asked to provide proof of car insurance and show the car registration. If you're driving a rental car, you may be asked to show the rental agreement. It's always a good idea to

Getting There

PLANNING YOUR TRIP TO BRITISH COLUMBIA

clean your car of perishable foodstuff before crossing the border; fruit, vegetables, and meat products may be confiscated and may lead to a full search of the car. Remember that firearms are allowed into Canada only in special circumstances; handguns are almost completely outlawed.

Once in Canada, you'll find that roads are generally in good condition. There are two major highway routes that cross Canada east to west. **Hwy. 1,** which is mostly four lanes, travels from Victoria on the Pacific to St. John's in Newfoundland, a total of 8,000km (4,971 miles)—with some ferries along the way. The **Yellowhead Highway (Hwy. 16)** links Winnipeg to Prince Rupert in B.C. along a more northerly route.

RENTAL CARS   Canada has scores of rental-car companies, including **Hertz** (© 800/654-3001; www.hertz.com), **Avis** (© 800/331-1084; www.avis.com), **Dollar** (© 800/800-3665; www.dollar.com), **Thrifty** (© 800/847-4389; www.thrifty.com), **Budget** (© 800/527-0700 in the U.S., or 800/268-8900 in Canada; www.budget.com), **Enterprise** (© 800/261-7331; www.enterprise.com), and **National Car Rental** (© 877/222-9058; www.nationalcar.com). Nevertheless, rental vehicles tend to get tight during the tourist season, from around mid-May through August; reserve a car early on in your planning process.

Members of the **American Automobile Association (AAA)** should remember to take their membership cards since the **Canadian Automobile Association (CAA; © 800/222-4357;** www.caa.ca) extends privileges to them in Canada.

By Train

Amtrak (© 800/USA-RAIL [872-7245]; www.amtrak.com) can get you into Canada at a few border points, where you can connect up with Canada's **VIA Rail** (© 888/VIA-RAIL [842-7245]; www.viarail.ca) system. On the West Coast, the *Cascades* runs from Eugene, Oregon, to Vancouver, British Columbia, with stops in Portland and Seattle. Amtrak-operated buses may also connect segments of these routes.

Amtrak and VIA Rail both offer a North American Railpass, which gives you 30 days of unlimited economy-class travel in the U.S. and Canada. The Railpass doesn't include meals but you can buy meals on the train or carry your own food.

The problem with traveling on VIA Rail, particularly in western Canada, is that the train runs only 3 days a week. If you want to link your visit between destinations in Alberta and B.C. with a train journey, you may be out of luck unless your schedule is very flexible. Also, if sightseeing, and not just transport, is part of your vacation agenda, then you may also find that your train journey takes place overnight. Because of the way the train is scheduled in many parts of rural Canada, there's just one schedule per train, so the leg crossing into British Columbia via the Canadian Rockies, for instance, will always be overnight, no matter which train you take.

By Bus

Greyhound (© 800/661-8747 in Canada, www.greyhound.ca; in the U.S. © 800/231-2222, www.greyhound.com) operates the major intercity bus system in Canada. In recent years, several of the Greyhound routes between the U.S. and Canada have been terminated. The only international route still in operation in the West is the crossing between Seattle and Vancouver.

International visitors intending to travel across Canada (and/or the U.S.) should consider the **Greyhound North American Discovery Pass.** The pass, which offers unlimited travel and stopovers in the U.S. and Canada, can be obtained from foreign travel agents or through www.discoverypass.com.

By Boat

Ocean ferries operate from Seattle, Anacortes, and Port Angeles, Washington, to Victoria, British Columbia. For details, see the relevant chapters.

GETTING AROUND

B.C. in particular has an admirable public transportation system, making the prospect of seeing most of the sites covered by this guide by linking buses, trains, and ferries a very pleasant one. However, having your own wheels will increase your options, especially if venturing beyond city limits.

By Plane

It's actually cheaper now to fly between major Canadian cities than take the bus or train, as deregulation has resulted in a number of excellent airlines that offer no-frills but perfectly comfortable air travel. These airlines rely on the Internet to create savings in booking flights and other information gathering, so you'll want Internet access to get the best deals. **WestJet** (② **888/937-8538;** www.westjet.com) offers the largest service area, with flights spanning the country from Victoria to St. John's.

In addition to Air Canada flights between major western Canadian cities, the regional **Air Canada Jazz** (② **888/247-2262;** www.flyjazz.ca) flies to smaller centers. Regularly scheduled floatplane service links Victoria and Vancouver harbors, and many island communities in the Strait of Georgia; see those chapters for more information.

By Car

Canadian highways are well maintained, and most are open year-round. For instance, Hwy. 1, which links Vancouver to Calgary, and the Coquihalla Hwy., that cuts through B.C.'s interior, are both open all winter long. Sometimes, snowplow activity or exceptionally icy conditions can cause delays. Note that even though Canada is a major oil producer, various taxes make gasoline generally more expensive than in the U.S., albeit still more affordable than European prices.

DRIVING RULES Wearing seat belts is compulsory for all passengers. Children under 5 must be in child restraints in the back seat. Booster seats are also recommended for children under 145cm (4ft. 9in). Motorcyclists must wear helmets. In British Columbia, it's legal to turn right at a red light after you've come to a full stop. Pedestrians have the right of way. The speed limit on express routes (limited-access highways) ranges from 100-110kmph (62 to 68 mph). Drivers must carry proof of insurance at all times.

By Train

Until last year, VIA Rail's passenger train, the Malahat, ran between Victoria and Courtenay; services were suspended for track and car upgrades, and hopes are high they will resume some time in 2012. Until then, travel is via **Greyhound** and **Tofino Bus** (② **866/986-3466**). Another marvelous B.C. route is the **Skeena,** which links Prince Rupert on the Pacific with Jasper, in the Canadian Rockies. For information on both, contact **VIA Rail** (② **888/VIA-RAIL** [842-7245]; www.viarail.ca).

By Bus

Compared to its U.S. counterpart, **Greyhound Canada** (© 800/661-8747; www.greyhound.ca) offers far superior service and coverage. Not only are the buses newer and cleaner, and the bus stations better kept, but Greyhound Canada is often the only option for land transport in many parts of Canada, including between a number of B.C. communities. On Vancouver Island, private carriers also offer services, particularly on the run between Victoria and Tofino.

By Boat

BC Ferries (© 888/223-3779 or 250/386-3431; www.bcferries.com) operates an extensive car and passenger ferry network along the British Columbia coast. These ferries link the B.C. mainland to Vancouver Island, and also provide service to dozens of smaller island communities. Also notable is the Inland Passage route, which links Port Hardy on the northern tip of Vancouver Island with Prince Rupert, just south of the Alaska Panhandle. This service can be joined with other public transport options to make a really great loop around B.C.

[FastFACTS] BRITISH COLUMBIA

Area Codes   The telephone area code for most of British Columbia, and all of Vancouver Island, including Victoria, is **250.** For Vancouver and the greater Vancouver area, including Squamish and Whistler, it's **604.**

Car Rental   See "Getting There By Car", above.

Cellphones   See "Mobile Phones," below.

Crime   See "Safety," later in this section.

Customs   You'll pass through **Canadian Customs** (© 800/461-9999 in Canada or 204/983-3500) upon arrival and **U.S. Customs** (© 360/332-5771), if you are traveling through the U.S., on your departure.

If you're driving from Seattle, you're most likely to enter British Columbia at the Peace Arch crossing (open 24 hr.; often, there's a 30-min. or longer wait) in Blaine, Washington. You'll go through Customs when you cross the border into Canada and will need to show your passport.

Arriving by air, you'll go through Customs at the airport once you clear passport control. (Even if you don't have anything to declare, Customs officials randomly select a few passengers and search their luggage.)

Visitors arriving by **train, ferry,** or **cruise ship** from the U.S. pass through U.S. Customs before boarding, and Canadian Customs upon arrival.

Disabled Travelers   Accessibility is the norm in British Columbia and, other than a handful of heritage buildings that make ramps and/or elevators a virtual impossibility, you'll find city crosswalks with beeping alerts to guide visually impaired pedestrians as well as hotels, parks, beaches, walkways, and sidewalks well equipped with wheelchair-friendly ramps, as well as most public transit vehicles lift-equipped. For further information about accessible public transportation in the Vancouver region, contact **Translink** (© 604/953-3333;** www.translink.ca). The **Victoria Regional Transit System** (© 250/382-6161) has a downloadable *Guide to Accessible Transit Services* on its website, **www.transitbc.com**, which includes information on which bus routes are equipped with lifts and/or low floors.

British Columbia

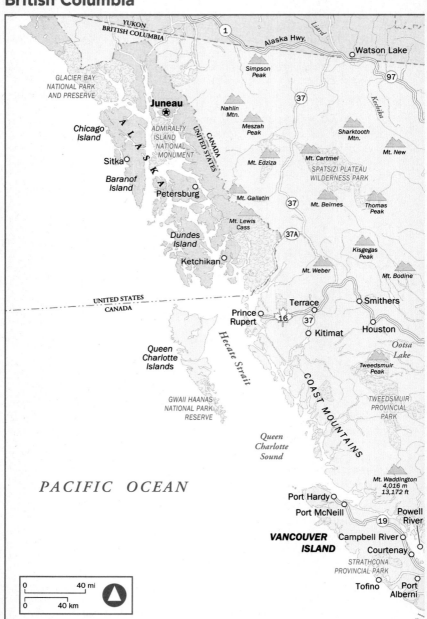

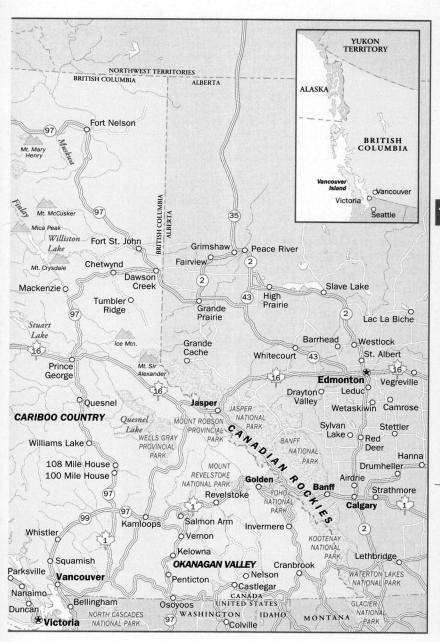

The most notable spot in Victoria that isn't readily wheelchair accessible is the promenade along the water's edge in the Inner Harbour.

The government of Canada hosts a comprehensive Persons with Disabilities website (**www.accesstotravel.gc.ca**) with resources for travelers with disabilities. In addition to information on public transit in cities across Canada, the site also lists accessible camp-sites, parks, coach lines, and a number of links to other services and associations of inter-est to travelers with disabilities. If you can't find what you need online, call ℂ **800/926-9105.**

Also check out the quarterly magazine *Emerging Horizons* (www.emerginghorizons. com), available by subscription ($17 per year in the U.S.; $22 per year outside the U.S.). The "Accessible Travel" link at **Mobility-Advisor.com** (www.mobility-advisor.com) offers a variety of travel resources to disabled persons.

British travelers should contact **Holiday Care** (ℂ **0845/124-9971** in the U.K.; www. tourismforall.org.uk) to access a wide range of travel information and resources for elderly people and individuals with disabilities.

Doctors   For a list of doctors and hospitals in Vancouver, see "Fast Facts Vancouver" on p. 47; for doctors and hospitals in Victoria, see "Fast Facts Victoria" on p. 88.

Drinking Laws   The legal drinking age in British Columbia is 19. Spirits are sold only in government liquor stores, but beer and wine can be purchased from specially licensed, privately owned stores and pubs. Most LCBC (Liquor Control of British Columbia) stores are open Monday through Saturday from 10am to 6pm, but some are open until 11pm.

Driving Rules   See "Getting Around," above.

Electricity   As in the U.S., electric current is 110 to 120 volts AC (60 cycles), compared to 220 to 240 volts AC (50 cycles) in most of Europe, Australia, and New Zealand. Down-ward converters that change 220 to 240 volts to 110 to 120 volts are difficult to find in North America, so bring one with you.

Embassies & Consulates   In Vancouver, the **U.S. Consulate** is at 1075 W. Pender St. (ℂ **604/685-4311**). The **British Consulate** is at 800-1111 Melville St. (ℂ **604/683-4421**). The **Australian Consulate** is at 2050-1075 W. Georgia St. (ℂ **604/684-1177**). Check the Yellow Pages for other countries' consulates.

Emergencies   Dial ℂ **911** for fire, police, ambulance, and poison control. This is a free call.

Family Travel   British Columbia has many child-friendly and family-oriented free activi-ties, both in the wilderness as well as in Vancouver and Victoria, two of the most child-friendly cosmopolitan cities in the world. Where else would you find a market especially for kids? Recommended family travel websites include **Family Travel Forum** (www.family travelforum.com), a comprehensive site that offers customized trip planning; **Family Travel Network** (www.familytravelnetwork.com), an online magazine providing travel tips; and **Travelwithyourkids.com**, a comprehensive site written by parents, for parents, offering sound advice for long-distance and international travel with children. To locate accommo-dations, restaurants, and attractions that are particularly kid-friendly, look for the "Kids" icon throughout this guide.

Gasoline (Petrol)   Gasoline is sold by the liter, not by the gallon. (3.8 L equals 1 U.S. gal.), and by law, must be purchased in advance. Gas prices in British Columbia fluctuate, as they do everywhere else in the world; as of press time, 1 liter cost about C$1.40. Taxes are included in the printed price.

Health   **Hospitals** and **emergency numbers** are listed in the "Fast Facts" sections for Vancouver (p. 47) and Victoria (p. 88).

If you become ill while traveling in Canada, you may have to pay all medical costs upfront and be reimbursed later since plans such as Medicare and Medicaid (in the U.S.)

do not provide coverage for medical costs outside the U.S. Before leaving home, find out what medical services your health insurance covers. To protect yourself, consider buying medical travel insurance (see "Insurance," below.

If you suffer from a chronic illness, consult your doctor before your departure. Pack **prescription medications** in your carry-on luggage and carry them in their original containers, with pharmacy labels—otherwise they won't make it through airport security. Carry the generic name of prescription medicines, in case a local Canadian pharmacist is unfamiliar with the brand name.

For conditions like epilepsy, diabetes, or heart problems, wear a **MedicAlert Identification Tag** (✆ **888/633-4298;** www.medicalert.org), which will immediately alert doctors to your condition and give them access to your records through MedicAlert's 24-hour hotline.

Holidays   For a list of holidays in Canada, see "Calendar of Events," in chapter 2.

Hospitals   Every region in British Columbia has either a major hospital and/or a comprehensive clinic. For a list of doctors and hospitals in Vancouver, see "Fast Facts Vancouver" (p 47); for doctors and hospitals in Victoria, see "Fast Facts Victoria" (p 88).

Insurance   For international travel, most U.S. health plans (including Medicare and Medicaid) do not provide coverage, and the ones that do often require you to pay for services upfront and reimburse you only after you return home.

If you require additional medical insurance, try **MEDEX Assistance** (✆ **800/527-0218;** www.medexassist.com) or **Travel Assistance International** (✆ **800/821-2828;** www. travelassistance.com); for general information on services, call **Europ Assistance USA,** formerly known as Worldwide Assistance Services, Inc., at ✆ **800/777-8710** (www.europ assistance-usa.com).

Travelers from the U.K. should carry their European Health Insurance Card (EHIC), which replaced the E111 form as proof of entitlement to free/reduced cost medical treatment abroad (✆ **0845/605-0707;** www.ehic.org.uk). Note, however, that the EHIC covers only "necessary medical treatment," and for repatriation costs, lost money, baggage, or cancellation, travel insurance from a reputable company should always be sought (www.travel insuranceweb.com).

Travel Insurance   You can get insurance estimates from various providers through **InsureMyTrip.com**. Enter your trip cost and dates, your age, and other information, for prices from more than a dozen companies.

U.K. citizens and their families who make more than one trip abroad per year may find an annual travel insurance policy works out cheaper. Check **www.moneysupermarket. com**, which compares prices across a wide range of providers for single- and multi-trip policies.

Most big travel agents offer their own insurance and will probably try to sell you their package when you book a holiday. Think before you sign. **Britain's Consumers' Association** recommends that you insist on seeing the policy and reading the fine print before buying travel insurance. **The Association of British Insurers** (✆ **020/7600-3333;** www. abi.org.uk) gives advice by phone and publishes *Holiday Insurance*, a free guide to policy provisions and prices. You might also shop around for better deals: Try **Columbus Direct** (✆ **0870/033-9988;** www.columbusdirect.net).

Trip-cancellation insurance will help retrieve your money if you have to back out of a trip or depart early, or if your travel supplier goes bankrupt. Trip cancellation traditionally covers such events as sickness, natural disasters, and State Department advisories. The latest news in trip-cancellation insurance is the availability of **expanded hurricane coverage** and the **"any-reason"** cancellation coverage—which costs more but covers cancellations made for any reason. You won't get back 100% of your prepaid trip cost, but you'll be refunded a substantial portion. **TravelSafe** (✆ **800/523-8020;** www.travelsafe.com) offers both types of coverage. **Expedia** also offers any-reason cancellation coverage for its air-hotel packages. For details, contact one of the following recommended insurers: **Access America** (℡ 800/284-8300; www.accessamerica.com); **Travel Guard International** (℡ 800/826-4919; www.travelguard.com); **Travel Insured International** (℡ 800/243-3174; www.travelinsured.com); and **Travelex Insurance Services** (℡ 800/228-9792; www. travelex-insurance.com).

Auto insurance is compulsory in British Columbia. Basic coverage consists of "no-fault" accident and C$200,000 third-party legal liability coverage. If you plan to drive in Canada, check with your insurance company to make sure that your policy meets this requirement. Always carry your insurance card, your vehicle registration, and your driver's license in case you get pulled over or have an accident. AAA also offers low-cost travel and auto insurance for its members. If you are a member and don't have adequate insurance, take advantage of this benefit. British Columbia's affiliate is BCAA (℡ 800/222-4357 or 604/293-2222).

Note: If you rent a car in British Columbia and plan to take it across the border into the U.S., let your rental company know in advance.

For information on traveler's insurance, trip cancellation insurance, and medical insurance while traveling, please visit www.frommers.com/planning.

Internet & WiFi   Unless you're in a particularly remote area of British Columbia, Wi-Fi and Internet access is generally available. It gets a bit iffy in any mountainous area and in the wilds on Vancouver Island. Almost all hotels in Vancouver and Victoria provide some kind of computer access to guests traveling without their own laptops. In some cases, it's a free public computer in the lobby; in other, more high-end hotels, there may be a charge to use computers in the hotel's business center. To find cybercafes in Vancouver and Victoria, check **www.cybercaptive.com** and **www.cybercafe.com**. For those people traveling with their own computer, almost all hotels, resorts, airports, cafes, and retailers have gone to **Wi-Fi** (wireless fidelity), offering free high-speed Wi-Fi access or charging a fee for 24-hour usage. In the service information for every hotel in this guide, we note whether the hotel offers free Wi-Fi or high-speed Internet access; if not, rates generally average C$15 for 24 hr. Almost invariably, it is large upscale hotels and resorts (such as Westin and the Four Seasons) that charge guests for Internet or Wi-Fi use, though customer dissatisfaction is rapidly edging out this policy.

To locate public Wi-Fi "hotspots," go to **www.jiwire.com**; its Hotspot Finder holds the world's largest directory of public wireless hotspots.

Legal Aid   While driving, if you are pulled over for a minor infraction (such as speeding), never attempt to pay the fine directly to a police officer; this could be construed as attempted bribery, a much more serious crime. Pay fines by mail, or directly into the hands of the clerk of the court. If accused of a more serious offense, say and do nothing before consulting a lawyer. In Canada, as in the U.S., the burden is on the Crown to prove a person's guilt beyond a reasonable doubt, and everyone has the right to remain silent, whether he or she is suspected of a crime or actually arrested. Once arrested, a person can make one telephone call to a party of his or her choice. The international visitor should call his or her embassy or consulate.

LGBT Travelers   Canada is one of the most gay-tolerant travel destinations in the world. Witness the fact that gay marriage is legal in Canada and that the entire nation has nondiscrimination protection for gays and lesbians. While not every rural village is ready for the circuit party set, most gay travelers will encounter little adversity.

Vancouver has the largest gay community in Western Canada, primarily in the **West End** and **Commercial Drive**. Resources include Vancouver's official tourism website, www. tourismvancouver.com; the **Vancouver Pride Society website** (www.vancouverpride.ca); The **Gay Lesbian Transgendered Bisexual Community Centre,** 2–1170 Bute St.

(© **604/684-5307**; www.qmunity.ca); and the biweekly gay and lesbian tabloid, *Xtra! West*, available at cafes, bars, and businesses throughout the West End. The gay and lesbian scene in **Victoria** is small but active. Explore the Pride link under "Plan Your Trip" at www.tourismvictoria.com.

A good clearinghouse for information on **gay Canada** is the website www.gaycanada.com, which features news and links to gay-owned or -friendly accommodations and businesses across Canada.

In addition to these listings, please visit www.Frommers.com for other specialized travel resources.

Mail   At press time, letters and postcards up to 30 grams cost C$1.03 to mail to the U.S. and C$1.75 for overseas airmail service; C59¢ within Canada. You can buy stamps and mail parcels at many Shoppers Drug Mart outlets and the main post office (for locations, see "Post Office," in "Fast Facts: Vancouver," p. 48, and "Fast Facts: Victoria," p. 89) or at any of the postal outlets inside drugstores and convenience stores. Look for a POSTAL SERVICES sign. For more information, visit www.canadapost.ca.

Mobile Phones   Canada is part of the **GSM** (Global System for Mobile Communications), a big, seamless network that makes for easy cross-border cellphone use. GSM phones function with a removable plastic SIM card, encoded with your phone number and account information. If your cellphone is on a GSM system, and you have a world-capable multiband phone such as many Sony Ericsson, Motorola, or Samsung models, you can make and receive calls across Canada. Just call your wireless operator and ask for "international roaming" to be activated on your account. (Many U.S. cellphones are already equipped with this capability and need no further modification to operate in Canada.)

You can **rent a cellphone** at a **Touristinfo Centre** at **Vancouver International Airport** (Touristinfo Centres are found in both the domestic and international terminals), or in the city at the **Vancouver Touristinfo Centre,** 200 Burrard St. (© **604/683-2000**), for a minimum charge (approx. C$50). For current rates and more information, contact the phone provider, **Cita Communications** (© **604/671-4655**; www.cita.info).

Money & Costs   Canadian monetary units are dollars and cents, with dollar notes issued in different colors. The standard denominations are C$5, C$10, C$20, C$50, and C$100. The "loonie" (so named because of the loon on one side) is the C$1 coin that replaced the C$1 bill. A C$2 coin, called the "toonie" because it's worth two loonies, replaced the C$2 bill. *Note:* If you're driving, it's a good idea to have a pocketful of toonies and loonies for parking meters. Almost all stores and restaurants accept American currency, and most will exchange amounts in excess of your dinner check or purchase. However, these establishments are allowed to set their own exchange percentages and generally offer the worst rates of all.

Frommer's lists exact prices in the local currency. The currency conversions provided were correct at press time. However, rates fluctuate, so before departing consult a currency exchange website such as **www.oanda.com/currency/converter** to check up-to-the-minute rates.

THE VALUE OF THE CANADIAN DOLLAR VS. OTHER POPULAR CURRENCIES

C$	US$	UK£	Euro (€)	Aus$	NZ$
1	$1	£0.65	€0.79	A$1.15	NZ$1.41

WHAT THINGS COST IN VANCOUVER & VICTORIA	C$
Transfer to/from airport (transit/taxi)	4.00/40.00
Double room, moderate	200.00–300.00
Three-course dinner for one without wine, moderate	40.00–50.00
Glass of wine	7.00–10.00
Double latte	3.75
Cup of coffee	1.75

In 2011, the Canadian dollar grew considerably stronger, and at press time was virtually at par with the U.S. dollar. The Canadian dollar also gained strength against the British pound, the euro, and the Australian and New Zealand dollars. To offset this change, and because of the recession, hotels and restaurants have generally reduced their prices or kept them the same as last year. Prices in Vancouver are generally a bit higher than in Victoria; and both cities are about 25% more than in the rural areas.

From mid-September to April, prices for hotel rooms in both cities generally drop by at least 20%, and sometimes as much as 50%; the exception to this is Whistler, where winter is the high season and prices rise accordingly. The prices listed in "What Things Cost," above, are approximate.

It's always advisable to bring money in a variety of forms on a vacation: A mix of cash and credit cards is most convenient for most travelers today. You can exchange currency or withdraw Canadian dollars from an ATM upon arrival. ATMs offer the best exchange rates and 24-hour access. Avoid exchanging money at commercial exchange bureaus and hotels, which often have the highest transaction fees.

Traveler's Checks   Traveler's checks in Canadian funds are universally accepted by banks (which charge a fee to cash them), larger stores, and hotels. If your traveler's checks are in a non-Canadian currency, you can exchange them for Canadian currency at any major bank.

ATMs   The easiest and best way to get cash in British Columbia is from an ATM. The Cirrus (✆ **800/424-7787;** www.mastercard.com) and PLUS (✆ **800/843-7587;** www.visa.com) networks span the globe; look at the back of your bank card to see which network you're on, then call or check online for ATM locations at your destination. Be sure you know your personal identification number (PIN) before you leave home, and be sure to find out your daily withdrawal limit before you depart. Many banks impose a fee every time a card is used at a different bank's ATM, and that fee can be higher for international transactions than for domestic ones. On top of this, the bank from which you withdraw cash may charge its own fee.

The 24-hour PLUS and Cirrus ATM systems are widely available throughout British Columbia. The systems convert Canadian withdrawals to your account's currency within 24 hours. Cirrus network cards work at ATMs at BMO Bank of Montreal (✆ **800/555-3000**), CIBC (✆ **800/465-2422**), HSBC (✆ **888/310-4722**), RBC Royal Bank (✆ **800/769-2511**), TD Canada Trust (✆ **866/567-8888**), and at all other ATMs that display the Cirrus logo.

Credit & Debit Cards   Major U.S. credit cards are widely accepted in British Columbia, especially American Express, MasterCard, and Visa. British debit cards like Barclay's Visa are also accepted. Diners Club, Carte Blanche, Discover, JCB, and EnRoute are taken by some establishments, but not as many. The amount spent in Canadian dollars will automatically be converted by your issuing company to your currency when you're billed—generally at rates that are better than you'd receive for cash at a currency exchange. However, the bank will probably add a 3% "adjustment fee" to the converted purchase price. You can also obtain a PIN for your credit card and use it in some ATMs. You usually pay interest from the date of withdrawal and often pay a higher service fee than when using a regular ATM card.

For help with currency conversions, tip calculations, and more, download Frommer's convenient Travel Tools app for your mobile device. Go to www.frommers.com/go/mobile and click on the Travel Tools icon.

Newspapers & Magazines *The Province* is British Columbia's only daily tabloid that is distributed throughout the province. The daily *Vancouver Sun* is also widely available although outside of Metro Vancouver the tendency is to carry the community's local publication.

Packing The proximity of mountains nudging up against the Pacific Ocean translates into mild temperatures and frequent rainfalls. Everyone here dresses West Coast casual, which means except for in some very posh restaurants, ties are unnecessary and fancy cocktail dresses might feel over-the-top. Pack for easy layers with a fleece, umbrella, and a good pair of walking shoes stashed into your luggage. For more helpful information on packing for your trip, download our convenient Travel Tools app for your mobile device. Go to www.frommers.com/go/mobile and click on the Travel Tools icon.

Passports Every international air traveler entering Canada is required to show a passport. **Note:** U.S. and Canadian citizens entering the U.S. at land and sea ports of entry from within the western hemisphere must now present a passport or other documents such as a passport card, compliant with the Western Hemisphere Travel Initiative (WHTI; see www.getyouhome.gov for details; the Canada Border Services Agency website, www.cbsa-asfc.gc.ca, is also helpful).

Australia Australian Passport Information Service (📞 **131-232,** or visit www.passports.gov.au).

Ireland Passport Office, Setanta Centre, Molesworth Street, Dublin 2 (📞 **01/671-1633;** www.foreignaffairs.gov.ie).

New Zealand Passports Office, Department of Internal Affairs, 47 Boulcott Street, Wellington, 6011 (📞 **0800/225-050** in New Zealand or 04/474-8100; www.passports.govt.nz).

United Kingdom Visit your nearest passport office, major post office, or travel agency, or contact the **Identity and Passport Service (IPS),** 89 Eccleston Square, London, SW1V 1PN (📞 **0300/222-0000;** www.ips.gov.uk).

United States To find your regional passport office, check the U.S. State Department website (www.travel.state.gov/passport) or call the National Passport Information Center (📞 877/487-2778) for automated information.

Petrol See "Gasoline," above.

Police Dial 📞 **911** for fire, police, ambulance, and poison control. This is a free call. For non-emergencies, see "Fast Facts Vancouver," p. 48; and "Fast Facts Victoria," p. 89.

Safety Canada is one of the least violent countries on Earth. Using common sense, most travelers should experience few if any threatening situations during a trip to British Columbia. Just be aware that in urban centers, there's always a greater chance for petty theft so keep your valuables out of sight, or in a hotel safe.

The weather and wildlife are probably a greater threat to the average traveler than violence from other human beings. If driving in winter, be sure to carry traction devices such as tire chains in your vehicle, plus plenty of warm clothes and a sleeping bag.

Wildlife is really only dangerous if you put yourself into their habitat in the wrong place at the wrong time. For example, elk can often seem tame, particularly those that live near human civilization. However, during calving season, mother elk can mistake your doting attention as an imminent attack on her newborn. Hiking trails are often closed to hikers during calving season, so be sure to obey all trail postings.

Moose are more dangerous, as they are truly massive and when surprised are apt to charge first and ask questions later. Give a moose plenty of room, and resist the temptation to feed them snacks. Chances are they will come looking for more.

Bears are the most dangerous wilderness denizens to humans. B.C. has its fair share of grizzly bears, one of the largest carnivores in North America, as well as black bears, a smaller, less fearsome cousin. Grizzly bears tend to keep their distance from humans, preferring mountain meadows to human garbage dumps. However, black bears can coexist much more readily with humans, and in some ways pose a more persistent threat. Never come between a bear and its cub, or its food source. Never hike alone in the back woods, and if camping keep food items well away from tents.

Senior Travel   In most of Canada, people age 65 and older qualify for reduced admission to theaters, museums, and other attractions, as well as discounted fares on public transportation. On occasion, even those as young as 55 years old can get these perks. It is less common to receive discounts on lodging, though it does happen, so it is worth asking when you make your lodging reservations.

Members of **AARP,** 601 E St. NW, Washington, DC 20049 (✆ **888/687-2277;** www. aarp.org), get discounts on hotels, airfares, and car rentals. Anyone 50 or older can join.

Discount transit passes for persons over 65 (with proof of age) may be purchased at shops in British Columbia that display a FareDealer sign (Safeway, 7-Eleven, and most newsstands). To locate a **FareDealer vendor,** contact BC Transit (✆ **604/521-0400;** www. transitbc.com).

Smoking   Smoking is prohibited in all public areas, including restaurants, bars, and clubs. Many hotels are now entirely smoke-free. In September 2010 a ban was also instituted on smoking in public parks, including Stanley Park, and beaches.

Student Travel   The southwestern corner of BC is definitely student-oriented territory, and you'll find inexpensive youth hostels run by **Hostelling International** in Vancouver, Victoria, Whistler, and Tofino. These hostels make traveling in BC affordable and fun. For membership information, check the **Hostelling International** websites at **www.hiusa.org** and **www.hihostels.ca**.

Vancouver's University of British Columbia (UBC), Burnaby's Simon Fraser University, the University of Victoria, as well as university campuses in Prince George, Nanaimo, and Kelowna translate into a lot of free and inexpensive, and discounted (with student ID) entertainment options for students, both day and night. In Vancouver, pick up a copy of entertainment weekly *Georgia Straight* to find out what's happening; in Victoria, it's *Monday Magazine*.

Taxes   Hotel rooms, restaurant meals, and most consumer goods are subject to a contentious 12% harmonized federal and provincial sales tax (HST) on most goods and services. It was so unpopular that it was scrapped last year in a referendum, with the promise that the original two-tier tax be reinstated (which would still be 12% on many items). At press time, however, the 12% HST was still in effect. Motor fuels, books, and children's clothing are taxed at 5%. For specific questions, contact the **BC Consumer Taxation Branch** (✆ **604/660-0858;** www.sbr.gov.bc.ca/rev.htm). *Note:* There is no tax rebate program for visitors.

Telephones   Phones in British Columbia are identical to phones in the U.S. The country code is the same as the U.S. code (1). Local calls normally cost C25¢. Many hotels charge C$1 or more per local call and much more for long-distance calls, although more hotels are providing free local service. You can save considerably by using a calling card or your cellphone. You can buy **prepaid phone cards** in various denominations at grocery and convenience stores.

Time Zone British Columbia is in the Pacific time zone, as are Seattle, Portland, San Francisco, and Los Angeles. Pacific Standard Time is 3 hours behind Eastern Standard Time, and 8 hours behind Greenwich Mean Time.

Daylight saving time is in effect from the second Sunday in March to the first Sunday in November.

Tipping Tipping etiquette is the same as in the United States: in hotels, tip bellhops at least C$1 per bag (C$2–C$3 if you have a lot of luggage) and tip the chamber staff C$1 to C$2 per day (more if you've left a big mess for him or her to clean up). Tip the doorman or concierge only if he or she has provided you with some specific service (for example, calling a cab for you or obtaining difficult-to-get theater tickets). Tip the valet-parking attendant C$1 every time you get your car.

In restaurants, bars, and nightclubs, tip service staff and bartenders 15% to 20% of the check, tip checkroom attendants C$1 per garment, and tip valet-parking attendants C$1 per vehicle. As for other service personnel, tip cab drivers 15% of the fare; tip skycaps at airports at least C$1 per bag (C$2–C$3 if you have a lot of luggage); and tip hairdressers and barbers 15% to 20%.

For help with tip calculations, currency conversions, and more, download our convenient Travel Tools app for your mobile device. Go to www.frommers.com/go/mobile and click on the Travel Tools icon.

Toilets You won't find public toilets or "restrooms" on the streets, or at least not any you would want to use, but they can be found in hotel lobbies, bars, restaurants, department stores, railway and bus stations, and service stations. Large hotels and fast-food restaurants are often the best bet for clean facilities.

VAT See "Taxes" above.

Visas Like Canada, Australia and New Zealand are members of the British Commonwealth and therefore need no special visas to travel between their respective countries, only a valid passport. U.S. citizens need only a passport to enter Canada. Visit www.cic.gc.ca/english/visit/visas.asp for a complete list of those countries that require a visa to enter or transit Canada.

Visitor Information For information about travel and accommodations throughout the province, contact **Tourism British Columbia** (300-1803 Douglas St., Victoria, BC V8T 5C3; ✆ **800/HELLO-BC** [435-5622] or 250/356-6363; www.hellobc.com). For destination-specific tourist office locations, see "Visitor Information," in the relevant chapters.

Wi-Fi See "Internet & Wi-Fi" earlier in this section.

AIRLINE WEBSITES

Air Canada
www.aircanada.com

Air France
www.airfrance.com

Air New Zealand
www.airnewzealand.com

Alaska Airlines/Horizon Air
www.alaskaair.com

American Airlines
www.aa.com

British Airways
www.british-airways.com

Delta Air Lines
www.delta.com

Frontier Airlines
www.frontierairlines.com

Hawaiian Airlines
www.hawaiianair.com

Japan Airlines
www.jal.co.jp

JetBlue Airways
www.jetblue.com

Lufthansa
www.lufthansa.com

Qantas Airways
www.qantas.com

Southwest Airlines
www.southwest.com

Spirit Airlines
www.spiritair.com

United Airlines
www.united.com

Virgin America
www.virginamerica.com

Virgin Atlantic Airways
www.virgin-atlantic.com

WestJet
www.westjet.com

Index